COMMENTARY
ON THE
NEW LECTIONARY

COMMENTARY
ON THE
NEW LECTIONARY

by

Gerard S. Sloyan

PAULIST PRESS
New York/Paramus/Toronto

Library of Congress
Catalog Card Number: 75-22781

ISBN: 0-8091-1895-5

Published by Paulist Press
Editorial Office: 1865 Broadway, N.Y., N.Y. 10023
Business Office: 400 Sette Drive, Paramus, N.J. 07652

Printed and bound in the
United States of America

CONTENTS

INTRODUCTION

These comments on the Bible readings for the three-year cycle of the Roman Lectionary, inaugurated on the First Sunday of Advent, November 30, 1969, are intended to help the clergy and others who engage in promoting weekly divine worship. Without a basic knowledge of the selections from the biblical books it will be impossible to preach well, to read publicly, or to select musical and other themes for celebration. There may be times when the exegetical comments will tell individual readers more than they wish to know. In this situation, however, a fullness seems preferable to sketchiness of treatment.

The author does not go on the assumption that the historical and linguistic data provided are necessary to derive some spiritual sense from the biblical passages. There is available in first place the evident religious meaning of most of the readings. Often the liturgy or order of service will suggest another meaning than that of the sacred writers by the selection of passages for particular feasts and seasons or the juxtaposition of the readings. The author has frequently indicated, in writing elsewhere on liturgical preaching, his conviction that critical exegesis should appear in the pulpit rarely if at all. The fruits of such study, however, must constantly be made available to the hearer.

There are almost no "helps for preaching" in the pages that follow, other than those that derive from the texts themselves. Only occasionally has the author indulged in a comment on the liturgical season. He has not hesitated to assume in his readership a general knowledge of the liturgy of the West with its Latin version(s) of the Bible and its service books, both those dating to the reforms of Trent (in use until recently) and the current *Ordo Missae* (1967) deriving from the Second Council of the Vatican.

The new Lectionary of the Roman Church follows the Vulgate in its verse enumeration, often beginning or breaking off in the middle of a verse. The designations "a," "b," and "c" which indicate these partial verses have not been retained, in part because the author has confined his commentary to whole verses. More basically, the verse numbering in the Hebrew and Greek texts at times differs from the Vulgate, while *The New American Bible* (1970) on which this commentary is based will occasionally engage in a verse numbering of its own in the Old Testament part. This is an important caution to users of the Authorized (King James) or Revised Standard Version in particular but also the New English Bible and Jerusalem Bible. They are asked to look at adjacent verses if a citation seems incorrect.

Over the past few years several major Lutheran bodies have opted for required lectionary preaching, using the Roman selections as their basing-point. The Episcopal Church and two Presbyterian Churches in conjunction with the United Church of Christ have likewise devised two different lectionaries for optional use. The Commission on Worship of the Consultation on Church Union has composed still another, adopted by the United Methodist and Christian (Disciples) Churches, which is a conflation of all the previous ones. The numbered designation of ordinary "Sundays of the year" is unfamiliar to others than Roman Catholics and still quite new to them, hence the inclusion here in parentheses of the "Sundays after Pentecost" (subtract one for "Sundays after Trinity").

The Episcopal Church lectionary uses the pseudepigraphical books but the others do not, partly on a canon principle but also because of the general unavailability of these books in pulpit Bibles. The COCU lectionary supplies them (pp. 4f.) for any who might wish to use them in substition. It is estimated that the coincidence of readings, although not readings in their entirety, between the Roman and any non-Roman lectionary runs around 70%. That fact emboldens the author to propose this volume as useful to other Christians than those of his own communion.

On the assumption that large numbers of priests of the Roman Church have access to the *Jerome Biblical Commentary* (Prentice-Hall, 1968), the author cites it only rarely. Undesignated authors are most frequently from *Peake's Commentary on the Bible* (Nelson, 1962) and occasionally the *One Volume Commentary on Holy Scripture* (Abingdon, 1970). *Harper's New Testament Commentaries* (J.N. Sanders on John excepted) are of frequent occurrence, as are the *Doubleday Anchor Bible* volumes. Numerous insights are drawn from individual books and articles (the latter usually not cited, to avoid complexity), with frequent contributions of the author's which he can attribute to no other hand.

The transliteration of Hebrew and Greek phrases has a twofold purpose: to assist onetime students of those tongues to engage in Bible study by using them again, and to let them judge how well the various translators of the Bible have acquitted themselves. The familiar device of arguing against versions for their shortcomings is thus avoided. More important than either reason, however, is the fact that the Bible is a literature and no literature has a proper existence except in the language in which it was composed. It is suggested, therefore, to those who have neither Greek nor Hebrew that they try not to become impatient with the words and phrases in parentheses, resenting them as pedantry; rather, that they attempt to pronounce them and even to study them out a bit so as to come that much closer to the sacred text.

These exegetical comments were first produced on a periodical basis for the Liturgical Conference, Washington, D.C., on the board of which the author serves. He could never have produced them but for the patient editing of its staff at the national office. To them and to the editor of *Homily Service* in particular, Virginia Sloyan, he expresses his gratitude.

Thanks are likewise expressed to Fortress Press, Philadelphia, for permission to reproduce passages from the author's *Jesus on Trial* (1973) and to the Confraternity of Christian Doctrine which owns copyright to *The New American Bible* (1970).

TABLE OF SUNDAYS, FEASTS, AND SEASONS 1975-1980

Year	Cycle	Baptism of the Lord	Sundays after Epiphany	First Sunday of Lent	Easter	Ascension	Pentecost	Sundays after Pentecost²	Trinity	Corpus Christi	Sunday of the Year after Corpus Christi Is³	First Sunday of Advent
1975	A	Jan. 12	5	Feb. 16	Mar. 30	May 8	May 18	28	May 25	June 1	10	Nov. 30
1976	B	Jan. 11	8	Mar. 7	Apr. 18	May 27	June 6	25	June 13	June 20	13	Nov. 28
1977	C¹	Jan. 9	7	Feb. 27	Apr. 10	May 19	May 29	26	June 5	June 12	12	Nov. 27
1978	A	Jan. 15	4	Feb. 12	Mar. 26	May 4	May 14	29	May 21	May 28	9	Dec. 3
1979	B	Jan. 14	7	Mar. 4	Apr. 15	May 24	June 3	26	June 10	June 17	12	Dec. 2
1980	C	Jan. 13	6	Feb. 24	Apr. 6	May 15	May 26	27	June 1	June 18	11	Nov. 30

¹Year evenly divisible by three.

²Number supplied for the preponderance of non-Roman churches which do not use "Sundays of the Year."

³Our new Roman calendar always has 33 Sundays of the year (plus Christ the King as 34th) and computes them backwards to Corpus Christi.

Note: Epiphany (formerly January 6) and Corpus Christi (formerly Thursday after Trinity) always occur on Sunday in the adaptation of the Roman calendar which appears above. Feasts which can replace Sundays in the U.S. are: Christmas (December 25),* SS. Peter and Paul (June 29), Transfiguration (August 6), Assumption of B.V.M. (August 15),* All Saints (November 1).*

*Holy Days of Obligation in the U.S., as are Immaculate Conception of the B.V.M. (December 8) Solemnity of Mary, Mother of God (January 1), and Ascension (Thursday after sixth Sunday of Easter).

YEAR A

ADVENT SEASON

FIRST SUNDAY OF ADVENT (A)

Isaiah 2:1-5. This justly famous oracle contains ideas of a universal peace in the future made familiar by writings of the postexilic period. Since its content is found also in Mi 4:1-3, however, it probably is not to be denied to the 8th c. Later Isaian poetry has a similar vision of peace (e.g., 9:2-6; 11:1-9). While the streaming of the Gentiles to the mountain of the LORD creates the suspicion of later authorship (cf. 56:7), the preexilic Ps 2:10f. expects homage to be paid to him by the rulers of the earth. Ps 72:8-11, 15-17 celebrates his rule from sea to sea, with all kings paying him homage and all nations serving him.

From Zion, the highest mountain (v. 2), the peoples of the earth are to be instructed (v. 3). Judgment among the nations is to come from there; the terms of peace are to be dictated (v. 4) from Jerusalem. The nations shall have peace because they will follow the LORD's instruction. In disputed cases he is to be the arbiter. But they will turn their weapons into implements for the peaceful arts and, in perhaps the best known rendition of v. 4f., they "ain' gonna study war no mo'."

Verse 5 appears in a fuller version in Mi 4:5.

Romans 13:11-14. The whole tenor of chs. 12 and 13 is eschatological, starting with the warning to the Romans that they should not be conformed to this eon (12:2) but transformed by the "renewal of your mind" to the realities of the age to come. In this passage the present epoch is characterized as darkness, sleep, night—the time (*kairos*) or hour (*hōra*, 11) of excesses through drink, lust, and envious quarreling (v. 13). "Salvation"—not personal salvation so much as the dawning of the eschatological day—is drawing closer. The Christian is to live honorably, that is, perform none of the shameful deeds proper to the old eon. He must put on not merely the figurative "armor of light" (v. 12) but the "Lord Jesus Christ" as well. The verb is *enduein*, found also in Col 3:12 ("clothe yourselves with heartfelt mercy, with kindness, humility, meekness, and patience") and in Gal 3:27 in a baptismal context ("All of you who have been baptized into Christ have clothed yourselves with him.") No quarter is to be given to the demands of the flesh (*tēs sarkos*, v. 14), which is not the sex passion particularly but all the unruly desires characteristic of the present, unredeemed age.

3

Matthew 24:37-44. Belloc parapharased the first three verses of today's reading thus:

> They married and gave in marriage,
> They danced at the County Ball,
> And some of them kept a carriage.
> AND THE FLOOD DESTROYED THEM ALL.

These brief pictures from Q of sudden and unexpected change, the world "corrupt and full of lawlessness" swept away by the rising waters (cf. Gn 6:11) and the workaday peasantry reduced to half by catastrophe, are succeeded by a warning to be on guard for the end. "Your Lord is coming" (*ho Kyrios hymōn erchetai*, v. 42) on a day "you cannot know." The thief who obviously does not give the householder notice is an image of the Son of Man who will come without warning.

The Q parallel of vv. 37-41 is Lk 17:26f., 30, 34f. The small differences are that Lk speaks of the Son of Man as "revealed" (*apokalyptetai*, v. 30) rather than of his "coming" (*parousia*, v. 39) and has two men in one bed rather than in a field. Mt has a linking verse not found in Lk, "Stay awake, therefore! You cannot know the day your Lord is coming" (42), taken from the parable of the gatekeeper in Mk 13:35, while Mt's vv. 43f. are paralleled by Lk 12:39f. There again there are slight differences: Mt's characteristic "in the same way" (*dia touto*, v. 44); "in what watch of the night" (*poią phylakę*, v. 43, rendered simply "when" by NAB) for Lk's "at what hour" (*poią hōrą*, 12:39) specifying an exact moment; and different words for "allow" and "house."

The story is used as a vehicle to warn of the general need for watchfulness. Since the coming of the Son of Man was to be a joyous and not a disastrous event for Christians, the application of the parable to readiness for Jesus' return is puzzling. The Gospel of Thomas has two *logia* about a night burglar (21*b*; 103) but neither makes a comparison with the coming of the Son of Man. Jesus' reported use of the flood story (Mt 24:37ff.; Lk 17:26f.) and the destruction of Sodom (Lk 17:28-32) to warn his contemporaries of impending disaster probably accounts for the primitive church's similar use of this parable in connection with his coming: Be prepared for the oncoming catastrophe. The story of the thief by night (cf. 1 Thes 5:2, 4; 2 Pt 3:10) was applied by the church to its own altered situation which was characterized by the delay of the *parousia*.

SECOND SUNDAY OF ADVENT (A)

Isaiah 11:1-10. By common consent, this oracle is thought to occur in a division of the first part of the prophetic collection ("The Book of Judgment," chs. 1-39) which is made up of the opening twelve chapters. NAB further subdivides these chapters into an "Indictment of Israel and Judah" (1-5) and "Immanuel Prophecies" (7-12). Today's pericope sketches the ideal Davidic king, a shoot (*hoter*) from the stump (*gᵉza'*) of David's father Jesse, a bud (*neṣᵉr*) blossoming from his roots (*shorashim*). This future king shall have an outpouring of the divine spirit (*ruaḥ*, connoting power) which is sixfold, listed in three pairs. The first two convey the notion of comprehension or insight, the second two the will to act, and the last two docility or openness. The echo of "fear of the LORD" (*yirᵉath YHWH*, v. 2) found in v. 3 resulted in the listing of a seventh gift of spirit in the LXX and Vulgate, yielding the familiar, concluding "piety and fear of the LORD." The characteristics of a judicious king are spelled out in vv. 3*b*-5: the eschewing of non-evidence such as appearance and hearsay, courageous speech and action against the wicked, and justice and fidelity worn as close to him as belt and waistband. Psalm 72:1-4 paints a similar picture of a just monarch who defends the afflicted, the poor, and the oppressed.

Verses 6-9 are well known for their description of the myth of the return to a trouble-free Eden, Eliade's *in illo tempore*. The tranquil pose of predator and prey, reconciled opposites, is what is of importance here. The "little child to lead them" (v. 6) and the "baby by the cobra's den" (v. 8) are signs of the non-violent character of all nature, the child and baby here bearing no relation to the earlier figures of shoot and bud. It was the Christian identity of Jesus as the just sovereign of the prophecy, coupled with the infancy narrative of Lk, which situated this Isaian menagerie in medieval literature, Handel's *Messiah*, and the modern Christmas card. Nothing in the poetry of vv. 6-10 requires that the "little child" be identified with the offspring of Jesse of vv. 1-5. "Knowledge of the LORD" is the inundating balm of a future earth which shall have a peaceful Zion as its central peak.

Verse 10 constitutes one brief oracle, vv. 11-16 another, both on the theme of the future restoration of Israel. It is to be recalled that Isaiah was summoned to the work of prophecy in the last year of King Uzziah (6:1; 742 B.C.), whose reign was the final gasp of Israel's early splendor (both kingdoms). From Ahaz it was a downhill progression of defeats at the hands of Assyrians, Babylonians, and Greeks. "On that day" of v. 10 refers to the future age when the Gentiles shall seek out the royal dwelling place of Jesse's scion. He shall be a signal or banner to the Gentiles (*nes ammim*, v. 10). This is the name chosen for the small village near Haifa in Galilee where a community of Dutch Christians gives witness by its presence, in reparation, to the fact of the Nazi holocaust. It is without proselytizing intent, hoping to say something to fellow Gentiles by simply being there.

Romans 15:4-9. These remarks on perfect harmony in the community (v. 5) end with praise for God's purpose in Christ with regard to Jews and Gentiles (vv. 8f.) Their immediate context, however, is the discussion in all of ch. 14 and 15:1-3 of the "strong" and "weak" in faith, i.e., the robust and delicate of conscience, who are roughly the same as William James's tough-minded and tender-minded. They have been thought to be the Jewish and Gentile Christians respectively but this categorization is over-facile. The Christian should no more have as the sole canon of his choices pleasing himself than did Christ in dying, but rather, like him, the mutual building up of spirit (vv. 2f.)

The praise of the Hebrew scriptures contained in v. 4, which 2 Tim echoes in 3:15ff., makes those writings a series of lessons on hope through present endurance. The stress here falls on patience and encouragement (v. 5), unity of heart and voice (v. 6) in the one spirit of Christ. 1 Timothy 4:4 takes the thought of Romans, especially 4:14-17, in another direction when it praises all creation as good rather than all scripture as instructive. Mutual acceptance in the Roman community is stressed in Rom (vv. 7-9) but now insofar as it is made up of Jews and Gentiles rather than the strong and the weak. The two pairings are interrelated in that eating closely in house churches might require sensitivity to dietary scruples on the part of some Christian Jews by others and even by Gentiles. Paul nowhere says that since Christ accepted all and became the servant of all (vv. 7f) to the point of death, abstention from foods prohibited under the law might at times be incumbent on Gentiles, but such might be his principle. The scruple against meat offered to idols may have a place here. There were also the abstainers from wine, whom Paul presumably was against dismissing contemptuously as proto-gnostics.

Jesus was the servant of the Jews (lit., of "circumcision," *diakonon . . . peritomēs*, v. 8) because God's fidelity to his own promises required it; of the Gentiles because his mercy suggested it (v. 9). The supporting quotation is from Ps 18:50. If Jesus had no trouble dying for the circumcised as such, believers in him could certainly endure living close to his scrupulous fellow-Jews. The same was true of Jewish proximity to the totally non-observant Gentiles.

Paul is evidently acutely conscious of the cheek-to-jowl situation of his Jewish friends (16:3, 6) and kinsfolk (7, 11) and his beloved Gentiles (16:1-15 *passim*). He either suspects that they may be finding it hard getting on at close range or has positive word to that effect.

Matthew 3:1-12. The commentary on the parallel accounts of John's preaching should be consulted, Mk 1:1-8 (p. 165) and Lk 3:1-6 and 10-18 (pp. 274, 275f.) Jn, too, who goes in another direction, is also of interest (1:6-8, 19-28; cf. pp. 167f.) All are concerned to relate John to Jesus but Mt especially so (cf. 3:13ff.; 11:17-19; 14:1f.; 17:9-13.) Mt does not date the events by the governor and priests in office as Lk does (3:1f.), contenting himself with "in those days" (v. 1). He calls John *ho baptistēs* while Mk uses the participle *baptizōn*, a detail which leads some translations to render the two "Baptist" and "Baptizer" respectively. Mt's "desert (*erēmos*, v. 1) of Judea" is simply "the desert" in Mk and Lk, which the latter expands to "the entire region of the Jordan" (3:3).

John comes proclaiming (*kēryssōn*, v. 1) the close proximity of God's reign. The exact meaning of *ēggiken* is disputed, namely whether it means "draws near" or "has arrived," but despite the certainties expressed by some scholars there are no conclusive arguments for either. (Cf. Werner Kelber, *The Kingdom in Mark*, 1973, pp. 7ff., who rejects word-study in favor of context to determine a realized or futurist meaning). John demands a sense of urgency in response to the impending appearance of God's dominion. He requires an about-face in the thinking of his hearers (their *nous* is to be turned *meta*, "backwards"; *metanoeite* corresponds to the Heb. verb *shubh*, in its accommodated sense "repent" but, more basically, "turn about"). Is 40:3, which Mk quotes in altered form, reads in the Hebrew text: "A voice cries out: In the desert prepare the way of the LORD! Make straight in the wasteland a highway for our God!" Mt refers the quotation to "him," John (v. 3), whereas Mk and Lk apply it to his preaching activity; Mt will put the same charge, "Reform your lives, etc." on Jesus' lips (4:17) while the others do not. Mk, it may be remembered, conflates Is 40:3 with Mal 3:1, omitting mention of the latter's name. The LXX translation of the Isaian verse suited Mt's purpose of messianic fulfillment better than the Hebrew. Even so, he seems to be understanding the LXX's *Kyrios* as Jesus, the one whose way and path must be made straight, rather than Israel's LORD.

The description of John's rough dress (v. 4; cf. Mk 1:6) is patterned on the sketch of Elijah found in 2 Kgs 1:8. Grasshoppers were both edible and eaten; the wild honey was not that of bees but sweet gum from plants. The description of the Jerusalem and Judean crowds confessing their sins and asking for immersion in the river Jordan (vv. 5f.) follows Mk 1:5 closely, while vv. 7-10 are a Q passage (Lk 3:7-9) not duplicated in Mk. In v. 7 Mt narrows the recipients of John's blistering charge to "many of the Pharisees and Sadducees." Their presenting themselves for baptism is noteworthy because unusual. Lk may find it incredible. More likely he wished to broaden the scope of the petitioners, for he speaks of the "crowds" that came to be baptized by John (3:7). Mt and Lk both give the same explanation for the request for baptism by those of ill will. It is a precautionary measure to escape the eschatological wrath. Deeds are what matter (Mt 3:8). Birth from Abraham's stock is of no avail in itself (v. 9). The fire that will consume fruitless trees (v. 10; repeated in a parabolic statement, 7:19) is the final conflagration of judgment (cf. Mal 3:19 for the figure of stubble consumed in a blaze.)

Verses 11f. are closer to the Q of Lk 3:16ff. than Mk's shorter 1:7f. Jesus is "stronger" than John, according to the latter (v. 7; so, too, in Lk), in his imminent baptism "with holy spirit and fire" (Mk, "holy spirit" only). When Mk in a later parable makes a thief the binder of "a strong man" (*ischyros*) in order to plunder his house, Mt (12:29) and Lk (8:21f. with notable differences in phrasing) follow him. John's subjugation to Jesus as sandal-bearer, i.e., disciple or willing slave, and his subordination as a preacher of repentance who brings no gift of spirit or separating power of fire, is a constant in the NT. Not only do these motifs reflect early rivalries between the disciples of the two but they convey the Christian conviction that John announces the imminence of the final epoch while Jesus achieves its inaugural.

THIRD SUNDAY OF ADVENT (A)

Isaiah 35:1-6, 10. The previous chapter has featured the doom of Edom, the sword filled with blood and the land of Edom greasy with fat. In contrast with this wasted land, which is the doing of the LORD in his wrath, there is painted a picture of his salvation. This will be accomplished in terms of the total transformation of nature. When God comes to vindicate his people he will overcome the handicaps of the blind and deaf, the lame and mute—the classes disadvantaged with respect to participation in the temple worship of Israel. If the judgment of God on them has been assumed unfavorable until now, it will in the future be wildly favorable as they burst into dancing and song.

The chronically dry southern and eastern desert will be richly irrigated. All of this leads up to a picture of the high and holy way on which a ransomed people will return to Mt. Zion singing.

The modern state of Israel is a secular state like the United States but it does not hesitate to use the Bible freely for its national purposes. Thus, young agricultural workers in *kibbutzim* are frequently pictured on posters reaping harvests of grain on reclaimed desert land, and at times Is 35:6b-7a will be inscribed beneath.

The "highway" (*maslul*, v. 8) and "holy way" (*derek ha qodesh*) is the LORD's own way, the path for those he has redeemed. Only they shall pass over it, not fools or the unclean; nor are wild beasts to be a threat upon it. In joy and delight shall the ransomed proceed along it to the holy mountain.

James 5:7-10. This reading echoes the previous one, with its metaphor of growth from the soil as a result of moisture. Its theme is patience while the Christian community awaits the presence (*parousia*, vv. 7, 8) of its Lord. The prophets waited patiently, suffering hardship (v. 10). So must Christians (*adelphoi*, lit., "brothers"). Grumbling in the community which can only lead to adverse judgment (*hina mē krithēte*, v. 9) is ill-advised since the judge himself (*ho kritēs*), God or Christ acting for God, stands at the gate poised for judgment.

The urgency that marks this passage argues for an early date of composition. Like all of Jas, it is open to the interpretation that it was a Jewish original revised by Christian hands (eschatological readiness; the model in suffering provided by the prophets and Job; the paraenetic tone throughout).

Matthew 11:2-11. The Q parallel to this material is Lk 7:18-28. The similarities are very close except for some duplication and brief expansion by Lk (vv. 20f.) after Mt's v. 3.

The "works of Christ" (v. 2), surely a church phrase, sums up the miracles of healing, control of nature, and exorcism that have been related in chs 8-10. Q conceives them in messianic terms, hence speaks of Jesus as "He who is to come" (*ho erchomenos*, v. 3; not a known Jewish title) by applying Is 61:1 in a general way to him—the Nazareth synagogue text of Lk 4:18. The Trito-Isaiah's set of deeds to be performed by the one on whom the LORD's spirit rests is only partially reproduced here. Missing are mention of captives, prisoners, and a year of favor from the LORD. The risen dead appear in Is 26:19; the deaf and blind in 29:18; 35:5; the lame one who will leap like a stag in 35:6.

Verse 6 is a macarism or beatitude supplementary to those listed in ch. 5. It praises people who are not put off by Jesus' right to the title "He who is to come" (the same as the anointed one of Is 61:1). Jesus will later say that John "came to you preaching a way [i.e., path] of justice" (*dikaiosynēs*, Mt 21:32). Here he warns John's disciples to walk on that way and not be thrown by obstructions on it such as his fulfillment of signs of the last age. Jesus' phrase here is *hos ean mē skandalisthȩ en emoi.* Later he will say to Peter, when he finds him to be a *satan* or adversary, *skandalon ei emou*: "You are a stone to make me stumble" (more familiarly, "rock of offense to me"). There is a reference to disciples of Jesus who falter when some persecution involving his message occurs (13:21) and another to a group scandalized by him, namely his townsfolk and relatives (13:57). It must not be that way with the well-prepared disciples of John.

The son of Zechariah does not sway in the wind like the sedge-grass along the banks of the Jordan (v. 7). Neither is he recognizable as royalty or part of a prince's retinue (v. 8), a possible reference to Davidic messianism. He is a spokesman for God (*prophētēs*, v. 9) and more; he is the messenger of preparation for the LORD spoken of by Malachi (3:1). Later Mt will identify John with Elijah (17:12f.) as Mk does in the parallel place (9:12f.) While Lk applies the Malachi passage to the Baptizer (7:27), he never puts him in the role of a modern Elijah. (See his silence at 16:16, where Mt 11:14 makes the identification.) This role he reserves for Jesus. In context, Malachi's divine messenger will be a purifier of temple sacrifice (3:1, 3) through his testimony and judgment on a variety of sins against society. In modern parlance, he will bring a "class action."

Verse 11 applies the verb *egēgertai* to John ("there has not been raised up"), a mode of speech confined to the prophets and the risen Christ. He prepares for God's reign in that despite his human greatness—he is exceeded by no mortal—the new epoch that follows is populated by a progeny in which the least believer outruns him. Conzelmann is well known for his use of Lk 16:16 as the verse which signals the onset of "the midpoint of time," Jesus' era, for that evangelist. The case can be made against Conzelmann that while Lk omits Mt 11:12f. from the Q before him because he does not wish to separate the eons of salvation history at this point in his narrative, waiting for 16:16, Mt retains the watershed of history just as effectively.

The puzzling *logion* that is verse 12 is probably a reference to military uprisings calculated to bring on God's reign in Israel, and is related to "the prophets and the law until John" only in the sense of contemporaneousness of epoch. With his preaching he brought on a right understanding of the new age.

FOURTH SUNDAY OF ADVENT (A)

Isaiah 7:10-14. Quaking with fear at the threat of invasion by the Arameans under Rezin and the northern kingdom led by Pekah (7:2), King Ahaz (735-15) is counseled by Isaiah to take heart (vv. 4ff.) The prophet is inspired by the LORD (v. 3) to quote an oracle to the king, the gist of which is that both Aram and Ephraim will have collapsed within sixty-five years—if Ahaz's trust in the LORD is firm (vv. 7ff.) He had previously refused an alliance with them (cf. 2 Kgs

16:5) which brought them to the brink of besieging him and all Judah. This incident takes place near a reservoir "on the highway of the fuller's field" (v. 3). Isaiah has brought along his little son whom he has named Shear-jashub ("a remnant shall return" or "a remnant shall turn back" [to God]). He must mean to say something to the king by having the lad so named accompany him.

The oracle of today's pericope was probably delivered shortly after the encounter. The king's pious response (v. 12) refusing Isaiah's proferred sign (v. 11), which is met by the prophet's instantaneous anger (v. 13), indicates that Ahaz has already decided to go the collaborationist route with Assyria against his northern neighbors (cf. 2 Kgs 16:7ff.) He hopes to stave off the threat of that major power and Isaiah suspects that he has already so decided. In the event, the timetable of Assyrian conquest was that Damascus (Aram) fell in 732 and Samaria (Israel or Ephraim) in 721. The conquering Sennacherib arrived at Judah—then mysteriously withdrew—in 701. But at the time of the "sign of Immanuel" none of this had taken place.

Isaiah's confidence in the power of YHWH is such that he puts no limit on the '*oth* the king may ask (v. 11). The truth in Ahaz's response may be that, since he has already decided what he intends to do, he would be tempting the LORD by naming a sign at this late date.

The exact significance of the sign escapes us because we do not know the identity of the young woman (*ha 'almah*, v. 14). The word is wrongly rendered "virgin" by NAB, whose translators succumbed either to the influence of the LXX (which has *parthenos*) or to pious pressure by external authority. As the footnote points out, *'almah* might have described a virgin bride. There is no reason to suppose, however, that Ahaz was unmarried at the time, hence his future wife Abi a virgin (*bethulah*), as part of the hypothesis that their son Hezekiah was the "Immanuel" of the prophecy (cf. 2 Kgs 18:1f.) The identity of the child of the sign as Hezekiah is probably erroneous, in any case. A careful reading of ch. 8 leads, rather, to the conclusion that Isaiah's own next child by his wife "the prophetess" (8:3)—we have no reason to assume that he took a second, virgin wife—is the "Immanuel" of the sign, in reality if not by name. The son Maher-shalal-hash-baz ("Quick spoils, speedy plunder," in a brief sketch of the expected Assyrian action), has his name recorded in an attested document (8:1, 16, 20) before his conception. Isaiah and the children the LORD has given him are the signs and portents which make the claim "With us is God" (*Immanuel*) a reality. The waters of Shiloah that flow gently (8:6), a quiet pool in Jerusalem, city of the LORD, are rejected through the decision of Ahaz. Therefore the waters of the Euphrates shall flood Judah, "the full width of your land, Immanuel" (8:8).

Identifying the child who is the sign of today's reading is by no means essential to comprehending its impact. It has been theorized above that the son of the young woman is not someone in the royal line. Any impending birth will do, however, since the force of the sign lies in what may be expected in the realm of political events by the time the boy reaches puberty (the meaning of "rejects the bad and chooses the good," 7:15, 16). The significance of a diet of "curds and honey" in his early years is uncertain. While it was rich fare to the desert nomad, it has also been interpreted as an austerity diet. If the latter, then a time of adversity rather than prosperity is indicated. John Bright opts for a nurturing of the child on the food of the gods (found in a variety of Oriental myths) so that he may better choose the right. Yet Bright adds the query: "through a period of distress?"

Romans 1:1-7. Like most of Paul's introductions, this one underscores his divine calling (v. 1) as a slave (*doulos*) of Christ Jesus (cf. Phil 1:1) and an apostle (vv. 1, 5) set apart (*aphōrismenos*) to preach the gospel (vv. 3f.) His greetings here are more extended than in most letters. Since he is not acquainted with "all in Rome" (v. 7) he may simply be using his opening remarks as the occasion for an impersonal—but priceless—development of christology. The "gospel of God" (v. 1) is Paul's work and challenge. Its content is Jesus Christ (vv. 3-6), a man of David's line (v. 3) made (in the sense "designated," *horisthentos*) son of God and our Lord (v. 4). "Son of God in power" is set against Davidic descent, "according to the flesh" (*kata sarka*) being contrasted with "according to the spirit of holiness" (*kata pneuma hagiōsynēs*). This distinction is one between Jesus' Jewish humanity and his special divine calling. He was constituted son of God by (*ex*) his resurrection from the dead. From that point on he was Christ and Lord. A human principle, *sarx*, and a divine principle, *pneuma*, are joined in him.

The greeting in v. 7 is the familiar one of grace and peace, which has the advantage of being meaningful to both Jewish and Graeco-Roman worlds. The gift is invoked by Paul as coming from his familiar dyad, God and Jesus Christ.

Matthew 1:18-24. Lk's birth story is about the conception of a child by a virgin through holy spirit coming on her and power of the Most High overshadowing her (1:35). Mt knows of this tradition but tells rather of how a pious betrothed man scruples to consummate marriage with his fiancée when he discovers her pregnant but not by him. Joseph is called by the angel "son of David," meaning that the child is to have Davidic sonship. (The modern difficulty of Mary's being the sole human begetter of Jesus does not exist for Mt; Jesus' "house" and "family" come through the paternal line.) Joseph is instructed by an angel in a dream not unlike that of the patriarch Joseph in his youth, whose name he bears. Here the divine agency of conception is, as in Lk: *ek pneumatos . . . hagiou* (1:20). Mary's son will save his Jewish people from their sins; hence for Mt the Immanuel prophecy is fulfilled in him. In a profound sense the adult career of Mary's son will mean, "God is with us." The oracle in its LXX form (*parthenos*, "virgin") is peculiarly suited to Mt's *pesher* mentality, viz., the targumic accommodation of texts to a contemporary purpose.

Mt seems to display in his narrative a knowledge of disputes about Jesus' legitimacy. His dream-story has as its chief purpose the setting at rest of the mind of Joseph the legally just man (*dikaios = ṣaddik*, v. 19). The conception of the child is God's doing, hence Joseph need have no scruples. The latter can bestow sonship of David on the child by accepting Mary as his wife. This he does (*kai parelaben tēn gynaika autou*, v. 24). Her virgin motherhood of Jesus means here what it does in the Immanuel oracle and is similar to the motherhoods of Sarah, Rebekah, and Hannah accomplished by divine intervention, namely, that by God's special action Jesus is the elect first-born. Church tradition later took it to mean that and more, namely physical virginity. Since Mt is operating in biblical categories he cannot be demonstrated with certainty to have had this marvel in mind (though it may well be true in addition, as later interpretation took it to be). He concentrates on another marvel, that of divine election.

Whatever the lectionary's reasons for eliminating v. 25 (delicacy over sex? fear of its raising problems in the hearer's minds?), it should not be omitted. It reaffirms that Joseph is not only not the child's father but that the providential plan is given full scope. It says nothing about the subsequent sex life of the couple. Most importantly, it is a summary statement rounding off the pericope with the birth and naming of the child (cf. v. 21), whose name conveys the saving action of YHWH.

CHRISTMAS SEASON

CHRISTMAS MASS AT MIDNIGHT (A)

Isaiah 9:1-6. This oracle sets a great light (v. 1) in contrast to the gloom and darkness which it puts to flight (8:23c). The people's rejoicing—likened to that of merrymaking harvesters or spoilers in war—results from YHWH's release of his people from the burden of oppression (yoke, pole, rod, v. 3) and the boot and cloak of battle (v. 4). Assyria has invaded "the land of Zebulun and the land of Naphthali" (733-32) but the fall of Samaria (722-21) is nowhere mentioned. Albrecht Alt has proposed as candidates for "the seaward road, the land west of the Jordan, and the District of the Gentiles" the three provinces of Dor, Gilead, and Megiddo into which the conquering Assyrians under Tiglath-Pileser III divided the humiliated northern kingdom. In any case, that tragic scene of oppression will yield to one in which a Davidic offspring is enthroned, to whom the four titles of v. 5 are to be attributed. His rule will be peaceful. Judgment and justice will mark it, "both now and forever." Israel's LORD, not any cleverness on the part of the people, will achieve this.

In brief, the passage is a dynastic oracle not unlike those of 2 Sm 7 and 23:1-7 and royal psalms like 2, 21, 89, and 110.

Titus 2:11-14. The section immediately preceding this one has offered counsel to various classes of persons: older men, older women, younger men, and slaves. Verse 11 underlines the fact that God's grace in Jesus Christ has been made manifest to all, even slaves. This age may be an evil one but there is no reason why Christians should not live prudent, just, and temperate lives (*sōphronōs kai dikaiōs kai eusebōs zēsōmen*, v. 12). Only fortitude is lacking from these cardinal virtues. Our blessed hope is the "appearing (*epiphaneian*) of the glory of the great God and of our Savior Jesus Christ" (v. 13). It is not so much the epiphany of Christ that is spoken of as the epiphany of grace (v. 11). God's word has been revealed and it has come to hearers through preaching (*en kērygmati*, 1:3; cf. 3:4). God's grace trains us (v. 12) in the ways of faith, i.e., educates the uninstructed. (Cf. 1 Clement 59:3, which says in a prayer, "through Jesus Christ your beloved child have you taught us, made us holy, and brought us to honor.") In Ti 2:12 we are educated out of godless and worldly ways into those of saving grace.

Christ is called savior (*sōtēr*, v. 13) but he is not called the great God. At the level of christological development represented by the pastoral epistles (1 and 2 Tim; Ti), soteriological functions are transferred from God to Christ. A clear distinction and subordination, however, is maintained. He sacrificed himself in order to cleanse and redeem us and make us a "people of his own" (cf. Dt 14:2; 1 Pet 2:9f.) Verse 13 contains a Hellenistic soteriological statement; "eager (*zēlōtēs*) to do what is right" is equally Hellenistic. Between them is sandwiched a title of the people of Israel from the LXX, in the easy harmony that characterized early Christian cultic language.

The excesses of the Saturnalia are the probable reason for the first inclusion of this reading in the liturgy of Rome.

Luke 2:1-14. Lk's chief concern is to certify the Davidic origins of Jesus. The historical tradition to the effect that Jesus comes from Nazareth in Galilee is evidently available to him. He also wishes to set the birth and the career of Jesus in a wider setting than the Jewish one of his first chapter. There was a census held around A.D. 6 when Quirinius was legate to Syria and Coponius prefect of Judaea. While it is possible to hold, from fragmentary evidence, that Quirinius served in Judaea earlier, or that an earlier census preceded the one we know about, it is wiser to say that Lk's interest is in theological symbolism, not accuracy of details. He wishes to set the event in the context of the Roman empire, making Jesus a Jewish king but one whose reign (1:32f.) will be without political consequences. He establishes Jesus' Davidic Messiahship through Joseph's lineage while at the same time maintaining that God is the child's father.

Joseph "goes up" (*anebē*) to Jerusalem, traveling south from Galilee. Zion, the holy mountain, caused pilgrims to "go up" regardless of the direction from which they came. He goes to enroll in the company of his "betrothed" (*emneusteumenē*, v. 5); a weak manuscript tradition has added "wife" (*gynaiki*), no doubt to allay fears. Question has been raised of the historical likelihood of an imperial census that would send people to their town of ancestry. Lk's historical concern is not at issue, however, whereas his symbolic interest is very much to the fore. Jesus must be born in David's city and the evangelist has the problem of getting the Galilean couple there.

Mary comes to term in Bethlehem (v. 6) and bears her first-born (*prōtotokon*). The term says nothing about subsequent offspring, apologetics quite apart. A first-born (Heb. *bᵉkor*) is that child or beast to come forth first from the womb (cf. Gen 25:25; Ex 22:28f.; Num 18:15ff.) Elsewhere in the NT Jesus is the "first-born of many brothers" (Rom 8:29), "of all creatures" (Col 1:15), "of the dead"

(Col 1:18). Israel is the LORD's first-born (Ex 4:22; cf. Jer 31:9). Benjaminites bear names like Becher (Gen 46:21), Bichri (2 Sam 20:1), Becorath (1 Sam 9:1), in the sense of "beloved." "My beloved (*agapētos*) son" of Mk 1:11 is thought by many to be a rendering of an original *bekor*, derived from the OT texts above.

The "manger" (*phatnē*) of v. 7 has created the Christmas scene, ox and ass being contributed by Is 1:3 (which also has a manger). Luke gives as the reason for these unusual circumstances a crowded caravansery (*katalyma*), a word which will likewise describe the guest room of the last supper. There can be little doubt that he has in mind the contrast between the hospitable shepherds (a despised class in Talmudic writings because of their non-observance) and the inhospitable populace.

Shepherds receive Jesus, once their fear is dispelled by angelic message (vv. 9f.) Bathed in light, they receive a gospel or tidings of greay joy (*chara*) proper to the end-time. The infant in a manger constitutes a sign for them (v. 12). Mt does not use the shepherd-manger motif and so has the astrologers enter the "house" (2:11) where the child was.

The heavenly "host" (*stratia=sebhaoth*) sings a song in two members: to God in highest heaven, glory; to men on their home earth, peace. The gift of heavenly peace is given to men of *eudokia*, that is, on whom God's favor rests. The word is in the genitive and describes the favored condition of humankind which is God's gift to them.

MASS DURING THE DAY (A)

Isaiah 52:7-10. "Your God is King!" is the announcement of the herald of "glad tidings" (*besorah*, the word that underlies the NT *euaggelion*). Peace, salvation—all these things will come to holy Zion in the restoration of Israel from exile. Watchmen will hail the people's triumphant return (v. 8), a ruined Jerusalem will burst into song (v. 9). God has done a work of power in the sight of the nations (v. 10), the literal salvation of his people. The Christian liturgy employs these verses in a transferred sense to describe the birth of Jesus, while in Rom (10:15) Paul will quote v. 7a to describe the work of proclaiming salvation in Christ in which he is engaged.

Hebrews 1:1-6. This work of Hellenist Christian piety (cf. 13:22) and theology views Christ as God's son who is at the same time his wisdom (*hokmah*), "through whom he first created the universe" (v. 2). As God's reflection (*apaugasma*, v. 3; better, "radiance") and the representation (*charaktēr*) of his being, he sustains all by his utterance of power (*to rhēma tēs dynameōs*). These opening phrases may have had their primitive existence as a Jewish hymn to God's wisdom. The writer gives his paean a historical cast by speaking of Christ as enthroned on high once he has "cleansed us from our sins" (v. 3). The thrust of the biblical texts (v. 5, 2 Sam 7:14, Ps 2:7; v. 6, Dt 32: 43*a*; v. 7, Ps 104:4, etc.) is to establish the superiority of Christ to the angels. They are ministers and adorers, he is a son. Undoubtedly the background to these remarks, which may have introduced a Christian sermon, is a certain polemic within the Christian community or with those outside on the mediatorial office of Christ. The author places him high above angelic creatures and insinuates a preexistence of this son with God as his wisdom and his word. The development is not unlike that of the Johannine prologue.

John 1:1-18 (longer); 1:1-5, 9-14 (shorter). The riches of this pericope have inspired volumes. They are not readily captured in a few lines. A preexistent Jewish hymn to wisdom is hinted at by the verse form opted for by NAB (following Brown in *The Anchor Bible*). Even this hymn shows signs of editing, e.g., at v. 14 where the word becomes flesh, a glory dwelling in our midst, as it were the glory of an only son coming from a father (*hōs monogenous para patros*). Clearly the author of the gospel as we have it has taken a Hellenist Jewish or gnostic poem—the two are not mutually exclusive —or even a poem from a circle of the followers of John, and given it a reading in time about Jesus rather than a timeless one. The word's becoming flesh in the midst of humanity (v. 14) is the chief departure from any pattern of gnostic or angelic speculation. There is also inserted a lively disclaimer of the importance of John (vv. 6-8, 15) which is continued from v. 19 onward, when the gospel begins to be fully "historical" in its fashion.

Four figurative modes of speech about divinity are used to describe the relation of God to the man Jesus: in his human existence Jesus is as if word, life, light, and son with respect to God. God can be or have none of these in a strict sense. All are "as if" (*hōs*, v. 14). A dynamic quality in God—viewed variously as speech, life, illumination, and parenthood—is that which is bodied forth when Jesus lives a man among man. That word is God (*theios*, v. 1). Jn does not say, either here or in his gospel for which the introductory eighteen verses are programmatic, that Jesus is God. Jesus is word, light, life, son (all "of God," understood) in human existence.

The manifestation of God in Jesus outruns anything experienced heretofore, says Jn. With Moses came the law, a genuine gift. Through Jesus Christ came *hē charis kai hē alētheia*, the *hesed* w*e* *emeth* of the Jewish covenant but now "enduring love" in eminent degree. Divine "favor" and "dependability" have reached new heights in God's manifestation in Christ.

The notion of preexistence is clear in this hymn but it is God's preexistence as word to this man, indeed to all creation. The author searches for images to convey the divine riches which lately have come tumbling out—*kai charin anti charitos* (v. 16), "love following upon love" or "grace answering to grace." "Ever at the father's side" (*eis ton kolpon tou patros*, v. 18)—God having no chest any more than he is a parent—is Jn's last try at intimacy of relation. As a child snuggles in a father's arms so is Jesus to God, who is the revealer to him of intimate secrets.

See commentary on Jn 1:6-8 below, p. 167.

FIRST SUNDAY AFTER CHRISTMAS (A)
Holy Family

Sirach 3:3-7, 14-17. These verses are a commentary on Ex 20:12: "Honor your father and your mother, that you may have long life in the land which the LORD, your God, is giving you." Doing honor to one's father is said to be a means of atoning for sins (vv. 3, 14), revering one's mother a way of storing up riches (v. 4). Failure to keep this commandment is the equivalent of blasphemy (v. 16). The reward promised for filial piety is the same here as in Exodus, namely a long and prosperous life (v. 6). Service to one's parents is a proof of obedience to the LORD and of a respectful fear of him. When old age or signs of senility overtake one's father, he is not to be chided by those who happen to have retained their youth and vigor (v. 13). Kindness toward a parent in adversity will always redound to the credit of a son or daughter (v. 15).

The answer to one's prayers or being gladdened by children (v. 5) is not so certain a matter as Sirach seems to think it except in the global sense that respect for parents is bound to bring blessings to a household, especially in the next generation.

Colossians 3:12-21. The admonition here given is couched in direct address, a change from the preceding observations in the third person about the "new man" undistinguished by particularities of nationality, religion, or social state. *Because* you are God's chosen ones (*oun*, "therefore") the Colossians are told, clothe yourselves with virtue. The community is addressed (v. 12) as if it were God's special possession (cf. Dt. 4:37; 7:7; Ps 33:12) in terms like those of 1 Pet 2:9. It has been chosen, therefore it should respond with the love (v. 14) which binds all the other virtues together. The "kindness" of v. 12 is *chrēstotes*, a reminder that Suetonius in his *Lives of the Twelve*

Caesars, under Claudius (A.D. 41-54), reports on Jesus as Chrestus, a Latinized form of the adjective *chrēstos* (kind, loving), and evidently the way the unfamiliar term *christos* reached him. The five virtues listed in v. 12 should characterize the dealings of Christians with their fellowmen. Forbearance and forgiveness are equally important (v. 13), while love is the perfect bond (*syndesmos*, v. 14).

Christ's work in the Christian is peace (cf. Jn 14:27; Eph 2:14) and thankfulness (v. 15). Expression of the latter, in response to the gospel preached (*ho logos tou Christou*), should take the form of joyful songs, a Greek word which gives us the English, "ode." Everything is to be done gratefully (*en tēi chariti*, v. 16) in Jesus' name, but the work of thanksgiving takes precedence over all (v. 17).

The general norms of Christian life are followed by specific ones for the family circle. The injunction to wives to be submissive to their husbands (*hypotassesthe*) can be found in Plutarch's *Conjugalia praecepta* and other writings of the time. This is an understanding characteristic of the prevailing social order, which now is to be fulfilled "in the Lord" (v. 18). Love is enjoined on husbands (v. 19) and obedience on children (v. 20). Fathers must not provoke children to anger by picking at them (*mē erethizete*, v. 21) lest discouragement follow.

Except for the important, subsequent social changes which have rendered submissiveness in one direction archaic, the proposals sound like a perfect pattern for domestic peace.

Matthew 2:13-15, 19-23. The dream motif of 1:20 and 2:12 is found again in 2:13 and 2:19. Herod was "searching for the child to destroy him" (v. 13) much as the Pharaoh of old had given a murderous command regarding the males born to the Hebrew women (cf. Ex 1:16, 22). Matthew's account of Jesus' infancy is a midrashic one similar to Philo's *Life of Moses*. It is at the same time in the *pesher* tradition: compromised solutions of biblical texts in aid of a particular interpretation. Verses from Isaiah (cf. Mt 1:23) and Micah (cf. 2:6) have received such treatment. So, now, will citations from Hosea (cf. 2:15) and Jeremiah (cf. 2:18.) Matthew must get the young family to Egypt if the Massoretic reading of Hos 11:1 is to refer to Jesus, a text which in that book of prophecy has to do with the call of the people Israel ("my son") to freedom in the exodus. For Mt, Jesus is that people typically or in eminent degree. The holy family had to remain in Egypt until Herod's death, Mt writes, so that the child could return to conditions of safety (cf. vv. 19f.) Actually, getting him to his traditional place of origin in Galilee is even more the intention (cf. v. 23).

Herod died around the feast of Passover, according to Josephus, in 4 B.C. (by later calculation). Archelaus, one of his three surviving sons, received from the emperor the title of ethnarch of Judea, Samaria, and Idumea. He held on to power there for ten years when, having experienced repeated embassies to Rome by Jews and Samaritans for his barbarism, he was removed by Tiberius in disgrace. Joseph's fear of returning to Judea (v. 22) may reflect Mt's knowledge of Archelaus's earliest days in power. According to Josephus, he put down a grievance of his new subjects by slaughtering 3,000 of them before he could appear in Rome to solidify his appointment. There is even some suspicion that in order to get the lion's share over his brother Antipas (the "Herod" of Jesus' adult career) and half-brother Philip he altered his father's will days before the old king's death.

Mt's knowledge of the house of Herod is not at issue here. His account squares with the known facts. He is much more interested in explaining why the followers of Jesus are being designated *nosrim* in his day. Jesus' home town Nazareth provides the adjective *Nazôraios* to describe him (as also in 26:71; Ac 24:5; in Mk 16:6; Lk 24:19, *Nazarēnos*). Mt may be playing on the word *neser*, the "shoot" of Is 11:1. If, however, Nazareth derives from a word meaning "guard" or "protect" (*nasar*) we cannot sustain Mt's meaning in this way. A note in NAB cites Is 66:18f. and Am 9:11f. If these texts explain Mt's otherwise cryptic citation, they do so by dint of reckoning Galilee in with *Gentile* territory as the place where Jesus will make God's glory known.

The synagogue of Ben Ezra in Cairo, not far from the Nile, contains a pool from which the Pharaoh's daughter is said to have drawn out the boy Moses. Not surprisingly, it is not far from a cluster of seven Christian churches, on the site of one of which (a church in Greek Orthodox hands dedicated to Mary) the holy family stayed.

SOLEMNITY OF MARY, MOTHER OF GOD (A)
January 1—Octave of Christmas

Numbers 6:22-27. The first twenty-one verses of this chapter are concerned with the regulations laid down for Nazirites, that dedicated class the existence of which is testified to in every period of Israel's history. It has been conjectured that they got their start as protesters against Israel's having passed from a nomadic way of life to a settled, agricultural one in the new land of Canaan. The taboo in favor of sacred hair, however—much stronger than that against wine from grapes (which they can drink when the period of their vow is over, v. 20)—may tell against this theory. In this Priestly account, the regulation of the vowed Nazirites (the word *nazir* means "untrimmed" with respect to vines in Lev 25:5 and 11) is in the hands of the priests (cf. Num 6:11, 16, and 19f.). This is the only visible connection with the blessing which "Aaron and his sons" are instructed to give (v. 23) in the concluding verses of the chapter.

In its present form the blessing is postexilic but it goes back to ancient times. Fragments of it which occur in Pss 4:7 and 67:1, the latter a harvest prayer in its final verses, testify to its antiquity. Sir 50:20f. tells of the custom of the high priests' giving a blessing over the congregation, in which "the name of the LORD would be his glory." That is the way it is in the formulary of Numbers 6, where the divine name thrice repeated is the matter of the greatest significance. *Tamid* 7:2 in the Mishnah (literally "oral repetition," the collected materials of the first two Christian centuries which are at the core of the Talmud) required pronunciation of the blessing every morning at the hour of sacrifice while the temple still stood. In the temple the divine name YHWH was spoken whereas in the synagogues, in all services, Adonai ("my Lord") was said in its place. This means that Mary of Nazareth, celebrated in today's feast, would have heard the blessing many times.

Pss 77:19*b* and 97:4, where "his lightnings illumine the world," have been suggested as places to account for v. 25, but no such direct literary dependence seems called for. In its own rich language the formula is a simple invocation of protection and peace, one of the great treasures of our Hebrew inheritance.

Galatians 4:4-7. Verse 4 is often cited as the sole, fragmentary "life of Jesus" that St. Paul attempted short of his frequent reference to the last three days of Jesus' life in which our salvation was accomplished. It says only that Jesus was a Jew because born of a Jewish mother, but this is already quite a lot. The passage has more to do with our "status as adopted sons" (*huiothesian*, v. 5), however, than with Jesus' birth as a Jew. His being "born under the law" (v. 4) is far from a title of liberty for Paul. Rather, Jews and Gentiles are each in their own condition of servitude, the Gentiles as slaves to "gods not really divine" (v. 8), the Jews in their subjection to the law (cf. v. 5.) In its original form this passage may have been a creedal hymn into which Paul inserted his special concerns (viz., vv. 4*c*-5*a*).

It is a much argued question how Paul could have got himself into the state of mind whereby he thought the law repressive and impossible to keep when other rabbis of his time found perfect observance possible and even liberating. There are times when Paul seems to have felt quite equal to its demands himself (v.g., Gal 1:14). But that is not the question at the moment. He wants to establish to a mixed readership of Galatians, some of them Jews and some Gentiles, that enslavement was the condition of them all and that all are in danger of slipping back into it.

This passage is evidently directed to Jews, as the whole argument of ch. 3 had been, or if not to them then to Gentile converts who are heeding Jewish teachers, Christian or otherwise, insistent that the whole law be kept. The phrase in v. 3 about the "elements (*ta stoicheia*) of the world" is puzzling because it does not seem to fit into a Jewish context. It is more properly a reference to pagan dependence on astral bodies and the powers directing them, as is the case in v. 9. It may be that Paul wishes to put calendar-conscious Jewish observants in the same class. In any case, at the "designated time" (*to plērōma tou chronou*, v. 4) God had worked out both "deliverance" (in the sense of purchase: *hina . . . exagorasē*, v. 5) and sonship.

Modern women may be offended at Paul's male vocabulary ("adopted sons"), if redeemed status is meant to include them; but they must notice that his figure is from the realm of property inheritance (v. 1). In that culture possessions were passed on only to sons, who then had to look after womenfolk.

The inheritance Paul speaks of, returning to a theme he first took up in 3:2ff., is the gift of the spirit. Possession of the spirit—with its power enabling the believer to call on God as "Abba"—is proof for Paul that slave status is behind the Galatians and adoptive sonship upon them. Paul is acquainted with the form of address to God which uses the Aramaic diminutive of affection (rather than the Hebrew "Abh") followed by the translation in Greek. Probably this was Hellenist Jewish usage of the time. The Christian's outcry is not so important for Paul, however, as the inherited gift of God which makes it possible, namely "the spirit of his Son" (v. 6).

Luke 2:16-21. The shepherds are in that group of seven witnesses to Jesus' birth whom Luke introduces in his first two chapters and does not call on again: Zechariah, Gabriel, Elizabeth, Joseph (apart from mention in 3:23 and 4:22), the shepherds, Simeon, and Anna. It is the "manger" (*phatnē*) of v. 16 that has fixed Jesus' birth in a cave or shelter for animals. Matthew localizes the place where the Magi visit as a house (Mt 2:11). Astonishment (*ethaumasan*, v. 18) is a standard response in the gospels to the wonders performed by Jesus; in this case, to what has been reported (*tōn lalēthentōn*) of his birth. Mary's response to the marvelous events (*ta rhemata tauta*) is to store them up for reflection, while the shepherds "glorify and praise God" over them (v. 20).

The narrative in v. 21 continues the parallel with the story of John by describing circumcision on the eighth day (cf. 1:59-79.) Reference is made back to the naming of the child as "Jesus" by Gabriel in 1:31. In neither place does Luke explain the derivation of the name as Matthew does (1:21).

EPIPHANY (A)

Isaiah 60:1-6. This visionary poem is spoken in praise of Jerusalem, "city of the LORD," "Zion of the Holy One of Israel" (60:14c). Chapter 49 on which it is patterned was concerned with the return of the exiles from Babylon. This chapter is more taken up with the ingathering of the dispersed sons and daughters of Israel (v. 4). They will return not only to the homeland but to the holy mountain, "my altar" and "my house" (v. 7). In their coming, the light and glory of Israel's LORD will shine upon them (v. 1), hence upon the city. The whole people is conceived as a woman lying prostrate who is summoned to "Rise up!", in an ancient call to worship.

Darkness and thick clouds (v. 2a) evoke the image of YHWH enthroned as king (Ps 97:2) and in turn are derived from the Sinai theophany (Ex 20:18, 21). Here, however, they are a prelude to that great glory of his which will dispel them (v. 2b). The people will shine with his radiance (vv. 3, 5). Nations and kings will bask in their light. More than that, the latters' treasures will be brought in tribute from distant coastlands (v. 5b) and far-off deserts. The queen of Sheba had brought gifts to Solomon from Southern Arabia (cf. 1 Kgs 10:2). In the poet's vision dromedaries will come from Midian and Ephah (below modern Elat, east of the Sinai peninsula). Kedar is the desert of northern Saudi Arabia lying just under the fertile crescent.

Taken all together, we have in the various images a vision of Israel triumphant through her God. Psalm 72:8-11 paints much the same picture. Foreigners shall pay tribute and do homage to the LORD for his mighty deeds, while the hearts of the Israelites throb with pride (v. 5a). It has been noted that ch. 60 has verbal allusions to or quotations from the following verses in ch. 49: 1, 3, 5, 6, 7, 8, 10, 12, 14, 18, 22. So skillfully are they reworked, however, that it is a new composition to fit new circumstances.

Those circumstances are the expected assemblage of all, Israel and the nations alike, to holy Zion. The dream of the new Jerusalem was still alive when John recorded in his Revelation the vision of a city that had no need of sun or moon, into which the treasures and wealth of the nations should be brought (21:23-26; cf. Thomas Fawcett, "Light in the Darkness," pp. 71-82 of *Hebrew Myth and Christian Gospel*, SCM, 1973). It is the perennial vision of the epiphany of God to his people, and theirs to other peoples who will share in their reflected light.

Ephesians 3:2-3, 5-6. The writer of these verses is convinced that in Christ Jesus a measure of the vision of Is 60 is already fulfilled. Jews and Gentiles together are co-heirs, co-members of the body, sharers of the promise (*sygklēronoma, syssōma, symmetocha tēs epaggelias,*

v. 6). The preaching of the gospel has made a reality of what before was only a hope. The mystery (vv. 3, 4) unknown to former ages has been revealed to apostles and prophets (v. 5) who are accredited ministers for its diffusion (v. 2). Paul is surely one of them (v. 1), thanks to God's unmerited goodness (*charitos*, v. 2). The *mystērion* spoken of is what God long knew he meant to do, namely bring Jews and Gentiles together into one.

This conviction about a divine plan hitherto concealed is held by the author of Col 1, although only Ephesians uses *mystērion* to signify the Jewish-Gentile union. (See commentary on Eph 1:3-6, 11-12, p. 392f.) The Qumrân hymns (*Hodayoth*, 12) contain a similar sentiment: "In the mystery of your wisdom you have opened knowledge to me." A previous phrase had said: "I . . . know you, O my God, by the spirit you have given me, and by your Holy Spirit I have faithfully attended to your marvellous counsel."

Matthew 2:1-12. The fourth gospel attests to the tradition that the Messiah is to be Davidic and come from Bethlehem, David's city (Jn 7:42). Matthew fulfills the expectation literally as a demand of Micah 5:1. He quotes the latter verse in a way that derives from neither the Massoretic nor the Septuagint version, changing "clans of Judah" to "rulers of Judah" and "you are the least" to "you are by no means least" to heighten the messianic effect (cf. commentary on Mi 5:14, p. 277.)

The story of the magi with its strong mythological elements is as much about the threat to kingly power which Jesus constitutes (cf. Mt 27:11-31) as it is about Gentile homage (v. 11) or the prodigy of the star in the heavens (2:2, 9f.) The astronomers/astrologers became three in subsequent Christian legend because their gifts were three (v. 11); they became kings by association with Ps 72:10; Is 49:7; 60:10. This was legitimate enough since they may have come into being out of those passages.

Matthew's narrative genius is nowhere more evident than in this chapter and the one that precedes it. By the time the tale of vv. 1-12 has been told, the origins of Jesus and God's design for him have been underscored thoroughly.

The magi return to their places, their kingdoms, but no longer at ease. They had witnessed a birth that was more like death—their death.

BAPTISM OF THE LORD (A)

(First Sunday after Epiphany)

Isaiah 42:1-4, 6-7. This is the first of the four servant songs. "The Servant is conceived as an individual figure, but he is the figure who recapitulates in himself all the religious gifts and the religious mission of Israel. . . . He incorporates the dominant features of Israel's past; he has some of the traits of a new Moses, he is the spokesman of divine revelation, he is the witness of the divinity of Yahweh to Israel and to the nations, he is a prophet" (McKenzie, *The Second Isaiah*). The servant is chosen for a mission by the LORD who, having decided upon him, holds fast to him (v. 1). He has been given a measure of spirit, i.e. divine impulsion to act. The gift is for the purpose of holding out *mishpat*, "just judgment" understood as the whole Sinaitic revelation, to the Gentiles. Unlike the loud proclamations of military and civil authority, the servant's message will be quietly spoken (v. 2; cf. 58:1 for a contrast in manner.) Verse 3 contains figures describing the powerless whom the servant will not crush by coercion. Oppression will be no part of his activity as he delivers divine revelation to the farthest coastlands (v. 4), meaning either the Mediterranean shores to the north and south or distant realms never explored. The concept of a deliverance of *torah* ("teaching," v. 4) to the nations and not only to Israel occurs elsewhere in Second Isaiah. The servant is envisioned as a proclaimer of covenant law outside the boundaries of Israelite peoplehood.

Verses 5-9 are a reworking of some of the ideas of the song in simpler fashion and are often designated a response to it. Verse 5 appeals to the power of God in creation and moves on to declare the divine intent to assist and strengthen ("I formed you and set you . . .", v. 6), an echo of 41:10*b*. The servant represents Israel, under the figures of a "covenant of the people" (here *'am* is not the people Israel, as customarily) and a "light of nations" (*'ôr goyim*, the *phōs ethnōn* of LXX which Lk employs in Simeon's song, 2:32). He stands for all that *mishpat* and *torah* can mean to a Gentile world if it accepts them. The light of v. 6 does not so much go with the servant's revealing mission as deliver from figurative darkness and blindness (v. 7) those captive to ignorance of the LORD or the service of false gods.

Acts 10:34-38. The sermon of Peter which Lk inserts here corresponds in outline to the speech of ch. 2 (esp. 22-24, 32-36). Today's pericope includes only the link with the situation (vv. 34f.) and a portion of the kerygma (vv. 36-38) which goes on to v. 41. Peter "opening his mouth, said:" (v. 34), as Philip had done in 8:35, a phrase which like the *Ep' alētheias* ("in truth") of his opening utterance underlines the solemnity of the moment. This is for Lk no less than the official disclosure of the gospel to the non-Jewish world through Peter. God "shows no partiality," i.e., is not *prosōpolēmptēs* or a favorer of persons. The phrase has a history of biblical use to describe his strict justice and imperviousness to bribes (cf. Dt. 10:17; 2 Chr 19:7; Job 34:19) but without the connotation of even-handedness as regards Jews and Gentiles. "The author is not thinking of Israel's past, but of the challenge now posed by the gospel" (Haenchen).

From v. 36 on, Peter's speech parallels the presentation Lk puts on Paul's lips in Pisidian Antioch, particularly the twofold audience of Jews and "others who reverence God" (13:26); compare "the sons of Israel" of 13:36 and the God-fearers who comprised Cornelius's household. The "message" of v. 36 is a *logos* which proclaims peace between God and man. Jesus Christ, the *pantōn Kyrios*, is the intermediary who brings about salvation; he can proclaim peace because he has come to effect it. The proclamation referred to in v. 36 follows in v. 37. The widespread character of "what has been reported" (*to genomenon rhēma*) is assumed throughout Palestine, even to Caesarea. The story of Jesus began with John's preaching of baptism (v. 37) as in the Marcan account, not with his infancy as in Lk's first book. God anointed (*echrisen*, v. 38) him, just as he is reported to have done in Lk 4:18, which tells of the initiation of his ministry in the Nazareth synagogue. Jesus' "doing good works" (*euergetōn*) places him in the category of Gentile rulers who are hailed as "benefactors" (*euergetai*, Lk 22:25). When he heals "all who were in the grip of the devil" we have an echo of the cosmic struggle of Mk, the *mythos* whereby the latter interpreted his historical reminiscences. The phrase "and God was with him" recalls Mt's title "Emmanuel" (1:23).

Matthew 3:13-17. The baptismal narratives of Mk and Lk will be read on this feast in Years B and C respectively. The chief differences between this pericope and that of Mk on which it is patterned (1:9-11) are the insertion by Mt of John's demurrer on the grounds of his inferiority to Jesus (vv. 14f.) and the change of the voice from heaven from the second person ("You are my beloved son," Mk 1:11) to the third ("This is my beloved son," Mt 3:17). St. Jerome in his *Against the Pelagians* (III.2) has an interesting quotation from the *Gospel according to the Hebrews* which changes Mt's statement of John that he should be baptized by Jesus to a scruple of the sinless Jesus at accepting a baptism of repentance: "The mother of the Lord and his brothers said to him, 'John the Baptist baptizes for the forgiveness of sins; let us go and be baptized by him.' But he said to them, 'In what have I sinned that I should go and be baptized by him? Unless, perhaps, what I have just said is a sin of ignorance?' " Both Mt and this lost gospel appear to be wrestling with the problem inherent in Mk's presentation of the sinless Jesus as a candidate for John's baptism. Mt views the difficulty as one of superiority-inferiority and settles it in terms of a divine imperative: "Thus it is fitting for us to fulfill all justice" (*houtōs gar prepon estin hēmin plērōsai pasan dikaiosynēn*, v. 15). The Gospel of the Hebrews places the initiative for the plan on the shoulders of Mary and Jesus' brothers, who elsewhere in the synoptic gospels are described as concerned for his welfare (cf. Mk 3:31ff. and parallels). It sees the account as a problem for a sinless Jesus.

The *Gospel of the Ebionites* (cited in Epiphanius, *Against Heresies*, XXX. 13.8) adds these details to the canonical account: "And immediately a great light shone around the place; and John seeing it, said to him, 'Who are you, Lord?' And again a voice from heaven said to him, 'This is my beloved Son, with whom I am well pleased.' Then John, falling down before him, said, 'I beseech you, Lord, baptize me!' But he forbade him, saying, 'Let it be so; for thus it is befitting to fulfill all things.' " The same concern to keep John in a position subordinate to Jesus is evident here. Jerome quotes from the *Gospel according to the Hebrews* in another place (*Comm. on Is. 11:2*), to the following effect: "When the Lord ascended from the water, the whole fount of the Holy Spirit descended and rested on him, and said to him, 'My son, in all the prophets I was waiting for you, that you might come, and that I might rest in you. For you are my rest; and you are my firstborn son, who reigns forever.' "

Mt does not give any reason for the Baptist's attempt to dissuade Jesus (v. 14), having portrayed a Jesus who "comes" (*paraginetai*, v. 13) from Galilee for the express purpose of submitting to the rite. He is more explicit than Mk in this, who treats the event matter-of-factly. John's response ("he tried to prevent him") is described in an "imperfect of attempted action" (Stendahl). The Matthean reason why the baptism of Jesus should go forward is the righteousness of God which underlies the entire careers of John and Jesus (cf. Mt 6:33; 21:32.) It is interesting that, while Mk (1:4) and Lk (3:3) have John preaching "a baptism of repentance for the forgiveness of sins," Mt omits it from the two parallel places (3:1, 4), seemingly because he wishes to identify this work of *aphesis hamartiōn* exclusively with Jesus (cf. 26:28; Mt's usage does not occur in the eucharistic words of Mk, Lk, or 1 Cor.)

For a comment on vv. 16f. (paralleled in Mk 1:10f. and Lk 3:21*b*-22), see pp. 279f.

SUNDAYS OF THE YEAR

SECOND SUNDAY OF THE YEAR (A)

(Second Sunday after Epiphany)

Isaiah 49:3, 5-6. The first six verses make up the second of four servant songs of the Second-Isaiah (cf. 42:1-4; 50:4-9; 52:13—53:12.) It has been observed that in chs. 40-48 (at 41:8, 9; 42:1, 19; 43:10; 44:11, 21, 26, 45:4) the term "servant," or "servants," is a designation for the righteous Israel or its individual members. This people is chosen for the role of messenger, but as messenger to whom is not clear. Beginning at ch. 49 and continuing through ch. 55, a remarkable distinction is found between an Israel which is the servant or messenger of God and the rest of Israel (cf. 49:3, 5, 6; 50:10; 52:13.) This servant of the LORD would prosper, but not without being marred in appearance (52:14), stricken, smitten, and afflicted (53:4). The vocation is a corporate one, not to a specific individual despite the wording of 43:1f. The mystery of the servant's identity lies in the later distinction between the pious Israel which recognizes its call from the womb (the servant) and faithless Israel which does not heed it.

The mission of the hidden arrow in the LORD's quiver, the sword concealed in the shadow of his arm (49:2), is that it must come out of obscurity and proclaim the glory of the LORD (v. 3). YHWH has formed his *ebhedh* Jacob (Israel) from the womb. He is to bring Israel back to himself now, in a reconciliation of son to father; glory and strength are to be the new guise of the reconciled son (v. 5). The LORD asks the faithful among the Jewish people if they find their calling too modest, their role too confining (v. 6). Raising up the survivors of exile and debilitating wars is no less than seeing that Israel serves "as a light to the Gentiles" (*l^eor goyim*) and "my salvation" (*y^eshuati*) to the ends of the earth.

Arthur Waskow puts the Deutero-Isaian vision well in a review of Meir Kahane's *Our Challenge*, a book which he characterizes as unbiblical in spirit: "The Prophets in their most ecstatic calls for a return to the Land and for the great triumph of Torah throughout the world never forgot that universal peace and justice are an integral part of that triumph. Jewish particularism, certainly; Jewish nationalism perhaps; Jewish chauvinism, never."

Today's reading is a prophetic call for universal peace through its emissaries, a chosen segment of a chosen people.

1 Corinthians 1:1-3. "Grace and peace" (v. 3), a hybrid Greek and Jewish greeting, is a constant in Paul's letters (cf. Rom 1:7; 2 Cor 1:2; Gal 1:3; Phil 1:2; Col 1:2; 1 Thes 1:2; 2 Thes 1:2; Phm 1,3.) So is mention of his call as an apostle, someone "sent." The recipients at Corinth are designated as "consecrated (*hēgiasmenois*) in Christ Jesus" and "called to be saints" (lit., "summoned saints," (*klētois hagiois*, v. 2). Paul then extends his greeting to all in whatever place who call upon the name of the Lord, the Jesus Christ who is not only "our" Lord but "theirs and ours" (*tou Kyriou hēmōn . . . autōn kai hēmōn*, vv. 2, 3). In familiar binitarian fashion, Paul invokes grace and peace upon all believers from "God our Father and the Lord Jesus Christ" (v. 3).

The greeting is a summary of those blessings that Paul is convinced have been made available to humankind through God's action in Christ.

John 1:29-34. Jn's "the next day" (*tē̦ epaurion*, v. 29) seems to be part of a week in a new creation patterned on Genesis 1:1—2:4 (cf. vv. 35, 39, 43; 2:1) but the exact sequence is impossible to determine. We do not know why the Baptist describes Jesus as "the lamb of God" (*ho amnos tou Theou*, v. 29), i.e., whether he has in mind the paschal lamb, a lamb of daily sacrifice, the Yom Kippur goat of Lv 16:20ff. who was to "carry off their iniquities . . . into the desert," the lamb led to slaughter in Is 53:7, or the messianic lamb (*to arnion*) who is the leader of the 144,000 in Rev 14:1. Barrett opts for the symbolism of the Passover lamb, a Pauline usage (cf. 1 Cor 5:7), but says we cannot know whether 1:29 influenced Jn 19:31-37 (Jesus' death at the hour of slaughter on Preparation Day) or vice versa. One theory has it that an Aramaic word for servant, *talya*, underlies the gospel word for lamb but the evidence is not compelling. The Lamb is the "bearer" on his back or "carrier off" (*ho airōn*) of sin, probably the latter in the sense of the remover of human guilt. The Vulgate's *tollit* is ambivalent in the same way as the Greek.

Dodd contends that "after [me]," *opisō mou* (v. 30), never has a temporal sense in the NT but always a spatial or relational, hence that Jesus is being described as superior in importance (cf., "ranks ahead of me," "was before me," *emprosthen mou . . . prōtos mou*, v. 30); therefore it has nothing to do with their respective ages as described in Lk's prologue. The precedence of Jesus to John as to all creation, in the spirit of the Johannine prologue, cannot however be ruled out. It may even underlie the two latter adverbs of v. 30.

The testimony of the Baptizer mentioned in 1:6ff., 15 proceeds in

vv. 32ff. At first the son of Zechariah did not "recognize" Jesus (*ēdein*, from *oida*, vv. 31, 33; cf. v. 26), a knowing which for Jn connotes acceptance in faith (cf. 7:28, 29.) Verse 31 expresses the paradox of the revealer to whom the subject of his revelation must first be revealed. The Spirit's descent as a dove (v. 32) is a tradition Jn has in common with the synoptics (Mt 3:16; Mk 1:10; Lk 3:22), probably deriving from the dove of the subsided flood waters (Gn 8:11f.) The dove identifies for the Baptist the one who, unlike himself, is to baptize with holy spirit (v. 33). Having received this testimony, he gives his own. NAB follows the 3d-c. papyrus (p⁵) and Sinaiticus of a century later which read *eklektos*, the "chosen one" of God rather than the easier reading, "son" of God.

THIRD SUNDAY OF THE YEAR (A)

(Third Sunday after Epiphany)

Isaiah 9:1-4. See p. 14.

1 Corinthians 1:10-13, 17. The community of believers (*adelphoi*) is asked by Paul to come to agreement and desist from "factions" (*schismata*, v. 10). He begs for perfection in mind and judgment (*katērtismenoi en tǭ . . . noï kai en tę̄ . . . gnōmę̄*)—unanimity, as we would say. Paul identifies his informants regarding the dissension (v. 11) at Corinth. Chloe—lit., "a blade of green grass"—is not otherwise referred to in the NT.

Paul grows specific about the factionalism. There are parties in the Corinthian church claiming the names of Paul, Apollos (cf. 3:6; Ac 18:24-28), Cephas, and Christ. The first two have doubtless been the teachers of some. The citation of Cephas inclines certain scholars to think that he visited Corinth, but his representatives from the mother-church of Jerusalem would satisfy the terms. As to the naming of Christ (v. 12) in a list of apostles, Paul may be speaking scornfully or else be referring to an actual Christ-party of authoritarians who claim the highest source possible. The absurdity of the Corinthians' fragmented outlook is underscored by the questions in the *diatribē* of v. 13. A divided Christ is unthinkable to Paul, as is the substitution of an apostle's name like his own for that of the only Savior.

In verses 14f., Paul seeks to dissociate himself from the bickering of the Corinthians by naming the few he has baptized (for Stephanas, cf. 16:15, 17.) He does not think poorly of the rite; rather, his is another ministry, that of preaching. One suspects, however, that Paul conceives preaching as nobler and more unifying than any ritual activity. As soon as he has mentioned the strife over ministers of baptism he is put in mind of another folly that has reached his ears (his eyes by letter?) A portion of the church seems hot in pursuit of a "wisdom" with which he has little sympathy. The gospel for Paul is chiefly the cross, not a philosophical rhetoric that comforts seekers after *sophia*. It is a call to suffering which unsettles all who hear it. This leads to the apostle's striking antithesis between wisdom and folly, a paradox in which the world's wisdom is God's foolishness while the foolishness of the world, the cross, is supreme wisdom in God's eyes. Cf. 2:7, 9; 3:18-20; 4:10, 19; 5:12f.; 8:1-3.

Matthew 4:12-23 (longer) or 12-17 (shorter).   Mt (v. 12) follows Mk (1:14) in placing the beginning of Jesus' ministry in Galilee immediately after John's arrest. Both situate it after his temptation in the desert. Lk, in doing the same as they (4:14), is alone in having him return to Galilee "in the power of the Spirit." For Mt, Jesus "withdrew" (*anechōrēsen*, v. 12) to Galilee while, for Mk, he simply "came" (*ēlthen*, 1:14) there. The expansion of vv. 13-17 is peculiarly Mt's. He omits the exorcisms and healings in Capernaum (Mk 1:21-38), including that of Simon's mother-in-law (1:29ff.), and retains only the call of the early disciples (4:18-22=Mk 1:16-20). The several wonders performed by Jesus in Galilee according to Mk are summarized in v. 23 of Mt, where the latter reports all the teaching (*didaskōn*), proclaiming (*kēryssōn*), and healing (*therapeuōn*) of every disease (*noson*) and illness (*malakian*) accomplished there.

Mt immediately places Jesus in Capernaum rather than Nazareth as the focus of his Galilean activity (v. 13; cf. 2:23), something which Mk gets around to only in 1:21 and Lk in 4:23 and 31, in what has to be an altered sequence. The ancient "territory of Zebulun and Naphthali" is not clear in its outlines for Mt (Capernaum would have been in Naphthali, Nazareth in Zebulun), but for his purposes it encompassed Capernaum, for he wishes to cite Is 8:23—9:1 as part of his *pesher* ("solution," "compromise") technique. That book of prophecy contrasted the degradation and darkness that fell upon the region around "the seaward road and the District (*gelil*) of the Gentiles" (v. 23; AV 9:1) when Tiglath-pileser ravaged it in 733-32, with the "great light" (9:1) that would dawn on it at the accession of the child proclaimed oracularly in 9:1-6. Isaiah had intended to signify by "the way of the sea" (*derek hayyam*) the Mediterranean but Mt takes it to refer to the Sea of Galilee. The familiar Matthean rubric of fulfillment (*hina plērōthē̦*, v. 14) is here, indicating that Jesus' settling down in Capernaum was indeed the Isaian light shed upon that dark region. The people living (lit., "seated," *kathēmenos/oi*; v. 16) in darkness and the land overshadowed by death saw the light of God, namely Jesus, rise on them.

Mt (v. 17) shortens Jesus' proclamation from Mk's longer: "This is the time of fulfillment. The reign of God is at hand! Reform your lives (*metanoeite*) and believe in the gospel" (1:15). *Metanoein* renders the Hebrew word for "turn around"; not precisely "repent" and certainly not "do penance."

The changes made by Mt in Jesus' call of the two sets of brothers (vv. 18-22) from the Marcan prototype (1:16-20) are negligible, the most significant addition being "Simon *now known* (*legomenon*) as Peter" (v. 18). The "now" of NAB means the time of the gospel's writing, not of the call. "Come after me" (*deute opisō mou*, v. 19) is a technical term for discipleship, a literal following of one's teacher. "Fishers" (*haleeis*) of men" had only an eschatological meaning and a threatening, judgmental one at that until the milieu of the gospel gave it a favorable meaning. Cf. W. Wuellner, *The Meaning of "Fishers of Men"* (Westminster, 1967).

FOURTH SUNDAY OF THE YEAR (A)

(Fourth Sunday after Epiphany)

Zephaniah 2:3; 3:12-13. This late 7th c. prophecy written during Josiah's thirty-two year reign (whether before or after the deuteronomic reform of 621 we cannot say; some even think in Jehoiakim's time, 609-598) emanates from court circles and is akin to the writings of Amos and Isaiah. It predicts a day of the LORD (1:7) which will be a day of his anger (2:2, 3). From it, only justice and humility will afford protection. The court is oriented toward Assyria, hence there is much apostasy from the worship of YHWH, doubt concerning his power, and social corruption. The prophet does not foretell the destruction of all but the sparing of some—a holy remnant (3:12, 13). Princes and judges, prophets and priests have grown predatory and insolent (3:3f.) Not so the humble and lowly. They shall take refuge in the name of the LORD and speak no lies (vv. 12f.) This is the beginning of a theology of election in which not the whole people, as in former days, but the faithful, however few, are seen as the beneficiaries of the covenanted promise to Israel.

1 Corinthians 1:26-31. This passage continues the theme of vv. 17-25 (cf. the commentary of last week, pp. 30f.) that God's folly is wiser than men and his weakness more powerful than men. The fact that the Corinthian Christians (*adelphoi*) have received a call (*klēsin*, v. 26) has not altered the social fact that they number few who by a worldly standard are wise, powerful, or well-born (*sophoi . . . dynatoi . . . eugeneis*, v. 26). The elements reckoned absurd and weak (*ta mōra . . . ta asthenē*, v. 27) have been divinely chosen to humiliate the world's wise and strong. God's categories of acceptability include the low-born, the despised, and those who count for nothing (*ta mē onta*, v. 28). Through the latter he means to bring low (*katargēsē*) the world's "somebodies" (*ta onta*, v. 28). The incarnation of God's wisdom and strength in Christ Jesus should keep humanity from foolish boasting (v. 29).

Of old Jeremiah (9:22f.) had cited knowing the LORD as the sole justification for a man's glorying in his riches, his strength, or his wisdom. God has made his son our wisdom and our justice, our sanctification (*hagiasmos*) and our redemption (*apolytrōsis*, v. 30). In Christ Jesus alone, therefore, may we boast (v. 31) in the spirit of the text of Jeremiah. This pericope continues Paul's polemic against the strutting of partisan-minded Corinthians who are claiming various lofty spiritual pedigrees (cf. 1:10-13.)

Matthew 5:1-12. Both Mark (3:13) and Luke (6:13) have Jesus going up a mountain to select his disciples. Following the choice he makes of them in Lk, he enunciates two sets of four headings under which they will experience beatitude or woe according as they are faithful to him or not. The connection of the beatitudes with the naming of the first four disciples is just as prominent in Matthew (4:18-22) as the naming of all in Mk and Lk. He assembles various catechetical materials in the collection known as the sermon on the mount, presenting them as a discourse on the effects of answering the call to discipleship.

Mathew's mountain is usually a place apart (cf. 14:23; 17:1, 28:16) where Jesus goes to be with his "disciples" (a term first used in 5:1), not a site for public promulgation. The Moses typology of the sermon, long the conventional interpretation, has been challenged by two scholars as far apart on Matthean matters as Davies and Stendahl. "Matthew presents Jesus as giving a Messianic Law on a Mount, but he avoids the express concept of a New Torah and a New Sinai; he has cast around his Lord the mantle of a teacher of righteousness, but he avoids the express ascription to him of the honorific 'a new Moses'." (W. D. Davies, *The Sermon on the Mount*, p. 32)

Jesus uses the poetic form in this first teaching recorded by Matthew. A catalogue of blessedness ("happy the man," *ash^eri ha ish*) is familiar from the Psalms (e.g., 1:1; 40:5; 84:6) and the wisdom literature (Prv 3:13; Sir 14:1, 20). Matthew's emphasis is more ethical ("who show mercy . . . are single-hearted . . . are peacemakers") than Luke's, who confines himself to states of deprivation and persecution (6:20-23). The stress is nonetheless on the bliss of life under God's approaching rule rather than on an improved life (vv. 8, 9, 10). Matthew's "poor in spirit" (*ptōchoi en pneumati*, the *'anawi ruah* of Qumran's 1 QM, 14, 7), his "lowly" (*praeis*), and his "single-hearted" (*katharoi tę kardią*) are not economic classifications, least of all is the last-named concerned with chastity. All are ways to describe generous openness to the LORD in the tradition of Jewish *'anawim* piety. It is the standard Pharisee vocabulary of self-abasement.

Verse 5 bears an allusion to Ps 37:11, v. 8 to Pss 24:4; 73:1. "Seeing God" (v. 8) means final bliss in the kingdom, though in Ps 24:4 access to the mountain of the LORD is being spoken of. The key concept in all the beatitudes is the "holiness" of v. 10, not an acquired virtue but God-given righteousness (*dikaiosynē*) which for Mt is "the vindication of God's people as the goal of history" (Stendahl).

The beatitudes culminate in vv. 10-12. There, as in v. 3, God's reign is what matters. A stance of humility may lead to insult, persecution, and even martyrdom. The persecution of disciples for the sake of, or because of (*heneken*), the righteous conduct that flows from God's righteousness and because of (v. 10) "me" (v. 11), placed thus in close conjunction, indicates that persecution for behavior and for the disciples' relationship to Jesus, who is the source of their way of life, is the same thing. There is, in other words, no additional understanding of the causes of persecution in v. 11 over v. 10. The martyrdom of the prophets (cf. 23:34, 37) was a Jewish tradition. None of the three major and twelve minor prophets of the canon died a violent death but the slaughter of others, e.g. Zechariah (2 Chr 24:20f.) and Uriah (Jer 26:20-33), is reported. Elijah attributes to the people of Israel (cf. 1 Kgs 19:10, 14) rather than to Jezebel (cf. 1 Kgs 18:4) the slaying of certain unnamed prophets. Jeremiah generalizes. "Your own sword devoured your prophets" (2:30). Josephus in *Antiquities* (ix. 13.2) and later rabbinical writings show how lively the tradition of Israel's rejection of the prophets was. In Mt 5:12 (as also 22:6; 23:29-39; Ac 7:52) the Christians are interpreting the persecution of their missionaries as "the contemporary manifestation of the 'law of history' that Israel continually persecutes the messengers sent by God" (Hare).

FIFTH SUNDAY OF THE YEAR (A)

(Fifth Sunday after Epiphany)

Isaiah 58:7-10. The earlier part of this chapter takes a strong stand against acts of religion like fasting which, at the same time that they are practiced, are accompanied by no relief to the oppressed, the hungry, the naked, and the homeless. Verses 8 and 10 employ the theme of light and darkness from ch. 9 but modify it notably. Here the distress is caused by the sins of the people, not the Assyrian conqueror. The brightness of dawn (v. 8) or midday (v. 10) shall come not with a victorious king but as a result of repentance and an about-face in social conduct (vv. 6f.) The corporal works of mercy will bring vindication from the LORD (v. 8) and an answer to heretofore unanswered prayers (v. 9).

Verses 9*b* and 10*a* (in Lawyer Jaggers' phrase) "put the case that" the conditions of vv. 6f. shall be fulfilled. In this case-law form, as opposed to the apodictic form of laws, a hypothesis is stated rather than a condition demanded. Given the removal of false accusation (lit., "extending the finger") and malicious speech (lit., "uttering vain nothings"), given likewise the feeding of the hungry and the satisfying of the afflicted, darkness and gloom shall yield to the brightness of noonday.

1 Corinthians 2:1-5. The latter part of ch. 1 is important background for today's reading because in it Paul sets up important pairs of opposites: wisdom vs. folly (absurdity); signs-wisdom vs. Christ crucified; weak vs. strong; lowborn-despised vs. "somebodies" (*ta onta*, v. 28). In a word, the cross is the polar opposite of all that this world esteems, yet this sure symbol of weakness in men's eyes is the very strength of God. The experience of salvation (v. 18) is normative in Paul's argument. The only proper subject of a human boast (v. 29) is God's gift: Christ Jesus, our wisdom, our justice, our sanctification, our redemption (v. 30).

Paul then moves on, in this reading, to what seems to be troubling him. He brought to Corinth the only message that is of any lasting worth, namely God's gracious action through the cross, and now he finds the Corinthians engaged in vainglorious boasting over their apostolic pedigrees—in modern terms, their "spiritual directors" or "former pastors." He is heartily sick of it. We know from 2 Cor in particular how deeply hurt he was to be by the repudiation of his person but here he tries to keep the argument on the plane of principle, not person. His message and his preaching (*ho logos mou kai to kērygma mou*, v. 4) are the things at issue. Paul grants the shortcomings of his mode of presentation, giving us some idea of why he thinks he is being discounted as a preacher and teacher ("weakness," "fear," "trepidation," v. 3; lack of "persuasive characteristics" of "wise argumentation" [*ouk en peithoi(s) sophias (logois)*], v. 4). The Corinthians have things all wrong, by Paul's standards. For him, their values were non-values, and vice versa, from the outset. He had brought them something different, namely the "convincing power of the Spirit" (*apodeixis pneumatos*, v. 4) and they had not recognized it, as their subsequent, foolish boasting showed. The power of God, not the wisdom of men, has been the underpinning of their faith (v. 5) but they have not known this, even up to the time of the distressing reports that have reached him from Chloe's household (cf. 1:11.)

Is Paul piqued by the claims made in favor of the eloquence of the Alexandrian Jew Apollos, whom Ac 18:24 describes as *logios*, "learned" or "eloquent"? We would be able to answer in the negative, so studiously does Paul avoid any personal reference in his tirades against false wisdom (1:20, 22; 2:6f.; 3:18ff., etc.), but for one detail. In citing Is 29:14—and not following the LXX closely—he cannot be unaware of the force of the play on words involved:

Apolō (I will destroy) *tēn sophian tōn sophōn
kai tēn synesin tōn synetōn athetēsō.*

Paul has preached divine wisdom embodied in the person of the crucified Christ. He has brought the power of God "to those who are experiencing salvation" (*tois de sozomenois*, 1:19). The reports that have reached him on the misconceptions among the Corinthians, including the childish claims they are making in favor of eloquence and learning (Apollos) and an apostolic link to Jerusalem (Cephas), confirm Paul in the rightness of his course.

In 2:1 the reading *to mystērion tou theou* found in p[46], a 3d-c. Chester Beatty papyrus at Ann Arbor, seems preferably to *to martyrion*; hence, "proclaiming the divine plan, hitherto kept secret" rather than "God's testimony" as in NAB.

Matthew 5:13-16. Salt sayings are related to wisdom in rabbinic literature, a detail which ties this reading in with the first two. In common modern parlance, an insipid person (lit., one without taste or tang) is a boob. Similarly, *mōranthę* (v. 13), rendered "goes flat" in NAB, can also mean "is foolish," i.e., is characterized by the *mōria* (folly) which Paul reprobates. The "you" (*hymeis*) of v. 13 are the disciples of Jesus who presumably have not gone the way of the conventional wisdom of the Iavneh school of rabbinic interpretation. Reams have been written on "tasteless salt" as some granular compound mistaken for sodium chloride, but the internal contradiction intended would seem to be salt that has no taste. Hence, the Christian is by definition someone who provides wisdom to the interpretation of the law just as he must be an agent of light if he is to fulfill his calling.

Various salt and light sayings found in Mk and Q have been woven into this twofold (i.e., v. 13; vv. 14ff.) short parable by Mt. (Cf. Mk 9:50; 4:21; Lk 14:34f.; 8:16; 11:33.)

If the sayings are not to be understood in praise of the faithful disciples of Jesus, Mt may be couching them in the way he does to threaten the readers of his church with the dire consequences of infidelity.

LENTEN SEASON

FIRST SUNDAY OF LENT (A)

Genesis 2:7-9; 3:1-7. The six days of creation of the Priestly account and what was made on each of them are matters too well known to rehearse (cf. Gn 1:1—2:4.) The parallel creation account of the Yahwist, containing certain Elohist elements, occurs in 2:5-25. In sequence, the things formed (the normal word for a potter's work) in it are: man (v. 7), a garden in Eden (v. 8), various trees, including two especially singled out (v. 9), wild and domestic animals and birds (vv. 19f.), and woman (vv. 21ff.). The J-E narrative continues through chs. 3-4, P resuming with the "generations" (*tol^edoth*) of 5:1.

"YHWH Elohim" is used throughout, a sign of the fusion of J and E. In v. 7 he forms the man (*ha 'adham*) from the clay (*'aphar*) of earth (*'adhamah*), breathes into his nose the breath of life (*nish^emat hayyim*), and the man becomes a living being (*nephesh hayyah*). The phrase *'aphar min ha 'adhamah* has also been less aptly translated "the dust of the earth," as is well known. The cognate status of the words for "the man" and "earth" are what are of importance here. They are related to "red" (*'adhom*) and "to be red" (*'adhem*). Paul will refer to this text in 1 Cor 15:47 (cf. pp. 294f.) The P author has had male and female created together (1:26f.) In J the LORD makes man first, then woman out of his bone and flesh (2:21ff.) Man is not only the clay of earth, he lives by the breath of God himself.

Creation had succeeded a "formless wasteland" in P (*tohu wabhohu*, 1:2) which later in the same verse turns out to be a watery chaos, the "abyss" (*t^ehom*). The image employed by J is that of a parched land succeeded by an oasis with trees and rivers, a "garden in Eden (*gan be 'edh^en*), in the east." The dry earth is a Palestinian image, the lush garden one probably borrowed from an eastern mythology (cf. Ez 28:12-19, where the king of Tyre is ejected from "Eden, the garden of God" by a cherub, cast to earth, and reduced to dust; observe the occurrence of the precious stones of Gn 2:12.) "Eden" is from the Akkadian *edinu*, basically the Sumerian word *eden*, meaning "plain"; the vowel quantity of the first letter differentiates it from the Hebrew word for "pleasure" or "enjoyment" with which it was soon associated. One interesting facet of the J myth is the "stream welling up out of the earth" (v. 6) before the LORD God sent the rains. Some moisture was evidently needed to make the dust into clay for God to form man, as a potter might do.

The trees of the garden provide food and esthetic pleasure in the ordinary way (v. 9a). One is a mythical "tree of life" (v. 9b), of which nothing more is heard until Proverbs (3:18; 11:30; 13:12; 15:4). There it is a symbol of wisdom, the fruit of virtue, a wish fulfilled, and a soothing tongue. The other tree "of the knowledge of good and bad" (vv. 9b, 17) "in the middle of the garden" (3:3) employs a possessive construction unique in the Bible, whereas the objective "to know good and bad" (3:5, 22) is quite usual. It is supposed that the former derives from the latter.

The serpent was known for cunning in the ancient world (cf. "wise as serpents," Mt 10:16), not only because of his shedding his skin and starting afresh but also because of the earth-habitation which put him in touch with the spirits of ancestors. The Yahwist sets aside any connection with wisdom and healing (cf. Nm 2:8f., the "saraph of bronze"; the Canaanite god Eshmun, like the Greek Asklepios, healed with snakes entwined on a staff), and makes his cunning exclusively evil. Not everyone agrees that the Hebrew of 3:1a has interrogative force. Speiser (Anchor Bible *Genesis*) has a syntactical difficulty with a question and renders it: "Even though God told you not to eat of any tree of the garden . . ." with the woman then interrupting the serpent. The LORD's prohibition of 2:17 had only been of the "tree of knowledge of God and bad"; this the woman informs the serpent of, calling it "the tree in the middle of the garden" (3:3). The couple's knowledge of good and bad can be deduced from the outcome of shame at their nakedness (2:25; 3:7) to be something different from the general power of moral discretion. Cf. 2 Sm 19:36, where the eighty-year-old Barzillai uses the phrase to describe capacity for sense pleasure. The godlike wisdom of Enkidu in the Gilgamesh epic (Tablet I, col. iv, 11. 16ff.) is a matter of sexual knowledge, i.e., experience. Enkidu is then clothed by the woman who has seduced him, in a set of correspondences with Gn 3 that should not lightly be set aside.

The dialogue on death concerns physical death (vv. 3f.) and recalls not only the tree of life of this narrative but also the tale of Adapa and man's search for immortality which is central to the Gilgamesh epic. Utnapishtim survives the flood and Gilgamesh is briefly given a magic plant to rejuvenate him—which a serpent ultimately steals.

The dependence of the J author on Mesopotamian material is clearer than the precise use he wishes to make of it. This much is evident: man is fated to death, not deathlessness, and the secret of procreation, while shared with man and woman, remains the LORD's possession. They have "knowledge" now but in them it is no threat to the godlike wisdom of YHWH Elohim. Its acquisition is also used to explain the nomad's horror of nudity, the "shame" of which is a ritual taboo rather than a sexual one (cf. Max Weber, *Ancient Israel*, pp. 191ff.) in opposition to the orgiastic displays of the Canaanite priesthood.

See p. 250 for commentary on Gn 2:18-24 and p. 391 on Gn 3:9-15, 20.

Romans 5:12-19 (longer) or 5:12, 17-19 (shorter). Commentaries on the passages that lead up to this one are to be found on p. 335 and p. 105 (Rom 5:6-11).

Paul's paralleling of Adam and Christ has invested "the man" of Gen 1-3 with an importance in Christian catechesis that is probably far greater than that intended by the Apostle. His stress is on "the gracious gift of the one man, Jesus Christ" (v. 15)—an emphasis found everywhere in his writings—rather than on the progenitor of a sinful humanity found only here and in 1 Cor 15:22, 45. Paul has been exulting in Christ, who is our reconciliation with God (v. 11). The "therefore" with which v. 12 begins is hard to justify logically; it is probably intended as a loose link with the next argument. Certainty of future salvation has just been affirmed (vv. 9-11). The same is now done in another way: we can be as sure that the grace of God will abound for all (v. 15; later, "acquittal" and "life," v. 18; "justification," v. 19) in virtue of Christ's deed as we are that Adam's sin brought death to the world.

Some, like Bousset and Reitzenstein, have held that the Adam-Christ parallel derives from a myth of the first man as a redeemer-god. Earlier (1895), Gunkel had found traces of a Jewish belief that the events of the beginning will repeat themselves at the end. In Paul's interpretation, Christ will give life to all as Adam first brought life, then death (1 Cor 15:22). W. D. Davies presents the evidence for a cosmic conception of the "first man" in biblical, intertestamental, and rabbinic sources (*Paul and Rabbinic Judaism*), while C. K. Barrett has commented fully on Paul's analogy in *From First Adam to Last*.

Paul takes literally the Genesis story of death's following Adam's sin of disobedience (v. 12) as a punishment. He describes death as universal because sin is universal (cf. also 3:23.) The NAB's "inasmuch as" renders *eph'hǭ*, which roughly means "because." Had the Vulgate's *in quo* been the *quia* it should have been, the Christian world might have been spared the doctrine of original sin in the form in which Augustine, chiefly, passed it along, namely a transmission of guilt by virtue of physical descent from Adam. St. Paul is at pains to grant a typological initiation of all sin to Adam; in that sense he can be said to sanction the notion of "in whom." In fact, however, that is

not what he meant, since it is not what he said when he wrote
eph'hǭ.

Original sin is in Scripture in the sense that Adam the sinner
begot a race that, like him, sinned but not by way of a guilt
transmitted by physical descent. What is not to be found in Paul is
implied, however, in the extrabiblical 4 Ezra 3:4-34, especially
vv. 21f.: "For the first Adam transgressed . . . and likewise also all
who were born of him. Thus the infirmity became inveterate; the Law
indeed was in the heart of the people, but [in conjunction] with the
evil seed."

St. Paul's argument, if taken strictly, would grant immunity
from death to anyone who did not sin. He does not envisage there
having been any such person. *Hamartia*—the creature's spirit of
rebellion against the Creator—is universal, even if a law is required
for it to be "imputed" (v. 13). Such was the case in Adam's
breaking a "precept" (*parabasis*, v. 14), an act which Paul in the next
verse will call an "offense" (*paraptōma*). The distinction here, in
more familiar Bible English, is between sin and transgression, the
former a universal state of heart. The latter is a formal overstepping
of bounds which has as its result that it is charged to one's account
(the literal meaning of *ellogeitai* in v. 13).

Paul so wishes to stress the reign of death through sin from
Adam to Moses that he does not pause to note the Noachian precepts
(according to the later rabbis, against idolatry, blasphemy, incest,
murder, and robbery, and in favor of justice by way of law courts).
Surely an "offense" would have been reckoned against those who
disobeyed these demands traditional before Moses' time. Paul's main
thrust is that only by law (v. 13) is offense to be identified. It was
found worthy of condemnation (*katakrima*) in the sentence (*krima*)
passed on it in one instance (v. 16): the offense of the "one man"
(v. 17) Adam. The opposite of Adam's act of sin (*paraptōma*) will be
God's act of grace (*charisma*), words rendered as "gift" and
"offense" in NAB (v. 16). Elsewhere the gift that God gives through
the obedience of Christ is described as *dōrēma* (v. 16), *charis*, and
dōrea v. 17).

Paul's analogy is not perfect in balance at all points. His main
contrast is between the acquittal and life for many achieved by the
one deed of Christ and the offenses imputed to the many sinners who
followed the first man, whose one deed was both sin and offense (cf.
vv. 18f.) Sin brought its train of tragic effects, chiefly death (v. 21),
but grace through (*dia*) justice, its outcome, eternal life (v. 21). In
order to remove all doubt about a perfect cancelling out in his figure
of the two races of humanity, Paul says explicitly that grace has far
surpassed sin (*hypereperisseusen*=Vulg. *superabundavit*) despite the
increase (*pleonasē*, v. 20) of offense that came with the promulgation

of the law. The ill effects of the totality of sin and offense from Adam through the entire Mosaic period cannot match the good effects of the grace and gift that were given in Jesus Christ.

Matthew 4:1-11. The temptation narratives of Mk and Lk will be read on the First Sunday of Lent in Years B and C respectively. Commentary on them is printed below (pp. 189f. and 297f.). That portion should be consulted which deals with Mk 1:12f. rather than v. 14f., and the Lk commentary in its entirety since it features his emphases regarding Q material in contrast with those of Mt.

Mt 4:4 cites Dt 8:3*b*; v. 6, Ps 91:11f.; v. 10, Dt 6:13. The Q source makes specific the statement of Mk that Jesus was tempted by Satan in the desert (1:13). He probably does so in terms of the Messianic confrontation reported by Mt, which Lk modifies as the urgency of the earliest epoch yields to problems of behavior in the community.

SECOND SUNDAY OF LENT (A)

Genesis 12:1-4. Abram has been introduced as the son of Terah in 11:26, among the "generations" (*tol^edoth*; "descendants," NAB, 11:10) with which that chapter concludes. Abram's saga proper begins at 11:27. No reason is given for Terah's migration from Ur of the Chaldeans to Canaan, interrupted as it was by a protracted stay in Haran (NW Mesopotamia, modern Turkey; ca. 110 mi. northeast of Aleppo, Syria, on the River Balikh, a tributary of the Euphrates). Ancient Ur, excavated in 1929, lies south of the modern Euphrates near An Nāṣiriyah, Iraq, not far from the point where the river debouches into the lagoon Hawr al Hammār which, in turn, feeds the Persian Gulf beyond Ābādan.

There is no reason to consider Abram a fictitious character. A date of ca. 1800 B.C. is assigned to him. He is not an eponymous ancestor, i.e., no tribe or people takes its name from him. He is the first clearly delineated person to appear in the Bible, as contrasted with types like Adam and Eve, Cain, Abel, and Noah. He remains throughout the Gn account a righteous individual, a man of faith. The story of his call out of Haran upon the death of his father Terah which comprises today's pericope is the opening of his saga. One could not learn from this tale the advanced state of Canaanite civilization into which "Abram the Hebrew" (14:13) came. Only ch. 14, a later insertion, gives us any remote indication of the data that a century of archaeology has revealed to us.

The Priestly classification of three main groups of peoples, the descendants of Noah's sons Shem, Ham, and Japheth (Gn 10:1), puts Abram's ancestors in with the Semites (vv. 21f.) while the Canaanites are grouped with the largely African offspring of Ham (v. 6). The categories are clearly territorial rather than ethnic. And as S. Goitein points out, Hebrew is a "Hamitie" language in biblical categories because it was spoken by the Canaanites before the Israelites arrived. The call of Abram (12:2f.) is the first of numerous such poetic oracles. The LORD calls him to be the father of a "great nation" that shall be a "blessing" to the peoples of the earth. Later Jewish writers will see in this designation the people Israel (e.g., Is 51:2: "Look to Abraham, your father, and to Sarah, who gave you birth;/ When he was but one I called him, I blessed him and made him many"; Ez 33:24: "Abraham, though but a single individual, received possession of the land; we [the Israelites], therefore, being many, have as permanent possession the land that has been given to us.") St. Paul (cf. Rom 4:16-22) made Abraham's fatherhood consist in his faith rather than in any ethnic primacy, specifically in his belief that the word of the LORD about aged, childless Sarah's having a son (cf. Gn 18:14) would come true.

Today's reading confines itself to Abram's first trustful act in response to the divine promise, namely his proceeding with his wife and his nephew Lot (the son of his brother Haran) southwest to the land of Canaan with all the possessions and offspring that had been acquired and begotten during the stay in Haran (v. 5).

2 Timothy 1:8-10.   The counsel to the disciple-recipient of this epistle not to be ashamed (*mē oun epaischynthēs*) of his testimony to "our Lord" and to his model Paul seems to be based on the apostle's similar declaration in Rom 1:16: "I am not ashamed (*ou gar epaischynomai*) of the gospel." As to the writer's status as a prisoner, the personal information supplied in 4:10ff. might seem to presuppose Caesarea as the place of composition, with Ephesus as the residence of the addressee (cf. the route attested in Ac 20f.) A difficulty against authenticity, however, is that in 1:17 Paul is described as having been at Rome while from the data of ch. 4 he has not yet visited there. Nor would Timothy require the information supplied in v. 20, since presumably he was along. The pseudonymous author probably possesses Acts and some Pauline letters but is not interested in plotting Paul's career exactly. He does wish to feature a "share in the suffering" (*sygkakopathēson*, v. 8) which the gospel entails and declare it to be overcome by the power of God (*kata dynamin theou*).

God is a savior for the author. He has called Christians "with a holy call" (*klēsei hagia*, v. 9; cf. 1 Thes 4:7), not in response to human works but in accord with his own "design" (*prothesin*) and "grace." That grace or favor was proffered in Christ Jesus before time began (*pro chronōn aiōniōn*, v. 9) but is "now made manifest through the appearance (*dia tēs epiphaneias*) of our savior." Obviously vv. 9f. incorporate a kerygmatic statement of the kind familiar from Eph 3:4f.; 3:9ff.; Rom 16:25f., in which the present age of revelation is contrasted with a former age when all lay hidden.

The term "savior" (*sōtēr*, v. 10) for Christ, characteristic of the pastorals, appears first in Phil 3:20. It is undoubtedly a contribution of Hellenist Judaism, in which God is described as the life-giver through his appearance or manifestation. The influence of the cult of savior-deities like Asklepios, Isis, and Sarapis is not absent. The appearance (*epiphaneia*, v. 10) of hidden divinity is the operative concept: here, the Jesus of history making known (*phōtisantos*, v. 10) life and immortality "through the preaching of the gospel." The hidden God becomes God manifest through the resurrection which, proclaimed and accepted, becomes salvation to believers.

Matthew 17:1-9. The author of 2 Pt has gone on the assumption that the account of the transfiguration was an historical narrative of an anticipation of Jesus' future glory, and even inserted himself into it as an eyewitness. It is, however, much more demonstrably an affirmation by the early church that Jesus was God's chosen servant well before the cross and resurrection and anticipated as such by the great prophetic servants Moses and Elijah. The reported lack of faith in Jesus by his disciples is all but incomprehensible if they experienced divine epiphanies such as those reported at his baptism and here. Moreover, the words of God in v. 5 are almost identical with those spoken at Jesus' baptism in 3:17, telling us that the evangelist is professing the same christological doctrine in both places. His chief sources are the OT and Jewish eschatology.

Mt's version follows Mk's very closely, omitting only the phrase about the work of a bleacher (Mk 9:3), the attribution of fear to the disciples and of impetuous blurting out about booths to Peter (9:6). The disciples fall forward to the ground in awe and are raised up by Jesus in Mt only (vv. 6f.). Lk is the only evangelist to speak of Jesus' impending passage (*exodos*) which is about to be fulfilled in Jerusalem (9:31) and to anticipate the detail of the sleep of the disciples in the garden (v. 32; cf. 22:45f.) He alone, also, has the three prophetic figures enter the cloud rather than merely being overshadowed by it (v. 34).

The details of the gospel account follow closely those of Moses' being summoned apart to the mountain with Joshua his aide (Ex 24:13), the cloud's covering the mountain (v. 15), and God's calling to Moses from the midst of the cloud (v. 16) which subsequently envelops him (v. 18). The disciples experience something of God's glory as Moses had done (Ex 33:18-23). Elijah in the cave on Mt.

Horeb hears the LORD's voice (1 Kgs 18:11) but there the similarity of detail to the career of the great prophet of monotheism ends.

The evangelists have a keen interest in the three prime witnesses to the resurrection, Peter, James and John, who are shown by the transfiguration narrative to have been able retroactively to discern the glory of God present in the earthly life of Jesus. Many scholars see in this passage a post-resurrection appearance of Jesus projected back into his earthly life but, if such is the case, it does not satisfactorily account for the details. The theme of the three booths (v. 4) indicates that the evangelists were thinking of the inauguration of the New Age. Zech 14:16 identifies Booths (*Sukkoth*) with the cult of Yahweh as king while its earliest significance, the ingathering of the harvest, led to the symbolism first of the bridal bower in the sacred marriage of Yahweh and his people, then of the shelters used by the children of Israel on pilgrimage. Its conjunction in autumn with the new year in the postexilic calendar would have filled Christian believers with thoughts of a new epoch in which Jesus was enthroned as priestly messiah. Peter's satisfaction "that we are here" (v. 4) may have to do with the resting-place (*anapausis*) of the ark in Nm 10:33 and Ps 132:8—understood as Jesus, the new covenant—a Septuagintal term. 2 Clement will use it in the phrase, "rest in the coming kingdom and in eternal life" (5:5).

THIRD SUNDAY OF LENT (A)

Exodus 17:3-7. This is one of three water stories in the Bible, the others being concerned with the turning of bitter waters to fresh (Ex 15:22-27) and the contention of the people at Kadesh, not Rephidim as here (Nm 20:2-13). All are probably the same tale describing an incident late in the wanderings. *Massah* means "test" (here, the Israelites' testing the LORD, in ch. 15 his testing them); *meribah*, "quarreling." *Rephidim* ("expanses," "stretches") is probably the modern Wadi Refayid which has an oasis and is in the vicinity of Jebel Musa, the traditional Mt. Sinai south-central in the peninsula. Kadesh is up near the pre-Six-Day War Egypt-Negev border, 'Ain el Qadeis southeast of the town of El Quseima and 45 miles southwest of Be'er Sheva. The whereabouts of the desert of Sin is likewise unknown. The southern foothills of the central mountainous mass Jebel el Tih is one possibility, the desert plain on the coast near modern El 'Arish another.

In this narrative the quarreling is between the Israelites and Moses (vv. 2ff.) for having brought them out into this waterless waste. The stoning of their leader (v. 4) would be the supreme indignity and mention of it conveys Moses' state of near-despair. The "staff with which you struck the river" (v. 5) refers to his rendering the Nile polluted (cf. 7:17f.) The instrument which made the water undrinkable for the Egyptians will have the opposite effect for the Israelites. The LORD makes his promise to Moses "on the rock in Horeb" which may have been scribally induced from the mention of Mt. Hor in Nm 20:22. This was probably modern Jebel Maderah some 15 miles northeast of Kadesh. Nm 20:23 places it "on the border of the land of Edom."

The source-identity of this passage is uncertain. Stalker's selection is as follows: 1*a*, P; 1*b*-2, J; 3, ? J or E; 4-6 ? E; 7*a* and *c*, J; 7*b*, E.

Romans 5:1-2, 5-8. In the previous chapter Paul has begun his development of Abraham's justifying faith. Abraham hoped "against hope" that he would be the father of many nations as he had been promised (4:18). His faith in his role for the future was credited to him as justice (cf. Gn 15:6; Rom 4:3) just as ours will be credited to us as justice "if we believe in him who raised Jesus our Lord from the dead" (Rom 4:24). It is conventional to say of the latter verse and v. 25 (e.g., Buber, Bultmann) that Hebrew *emunah* is trust in the person of the LORD whereas Pauline *pistis* is faith in a fact, a deed that God has done in Jesus Christ. Paul would probably be shocked to learn of any such difference and say that he was incapable of thinking like a German professor. He seems to be at pains to show how the Christian believer and the patriarch Abraham are identical in all respects as regards faith in God's promise. Note that 4:24 does not praise the deed of the resurrection or ask faith in it but in him who did it. Paul cares more for the faith of the Christian in a God who will yet act than in a God who has acted.

Justification by means of faith is already, however, a reality for Paul. It means peace with God for the believer (cf. Col 1:21) achieved through Christ the reconciler (5:1; cf. 2 Cor 5:18f.) The present condition of the Christian is grace; with respect to the future it is hope for a share in God's glory. Christ is the person who has made both possible, faith the condition to which God has successfully invited us through him (cf. v. 2.) "The immediate results of Christ's work are ours through faith." (T. W. Manson)

The road to hope may be a rocky one. Paul traces it by means of stages, the stopping-points of which are affliction/endurance/tested virtue/hope (*thlipsis/hypomonē/dokimē/elpis*, vv. 3f.) The hope is not a frustrating kind because the gift of the Spirit fills our hearts with love (cf. v. 5.) *Agapē*, for Paul, is what to do until the messiah comes back.

The "love of God . . . poured out in our hearts through the Holy Spirit" (v. 5) is our present justification. It means peace with God (v. 1). It was all God's doing at his appointed time "when we were still powerless" (*ontōn hēmōn asthenōn eti*, v. 6). More than that, we were "godless" (*asebōn*, v. 6) and "sinners" (*hamartōlōn*, v. 7)—in a word, entirely helpless to save ourselves. The "appointed time" (*kata kairon*, v. 6) indicates not only a compassion on God's part but his taking the initiative to save us when we had no merits of our own. That is the whole point of vv. 7f. Rarely does anyone give his life "for a just man" (*hyper dikaiou*, v. 7). Paul breaks off his thought and starts afresh: "Possibly someone might dare to die for your good man" (*tou agathou*, v. 7). His "perhaps even" (*tacha . . . kai*) is concessive, a mere hypothesis. In the actual case the facts are all against us. God "demonstrates" (*synestēsin*, v. 8) his love for us by the fact that while we were still sinners Christ died for us. This total non-meritorious condition shows what the divine *agapē* consists in. It is prevenient, undeserved, and completely reconciling (vv. 9ff.)

See commentary on 5:6-11, p. 105.

John 4:5-42 (longer) or 4:5-15, 19-26, 39, 40-42 (shorter). Jesus' northward journey to Galilee (vv. 3f.) was on the west bank, a usual route but hazardous for the Jew because of tensions with the Samaritan population. Ancient Shechem (Heb. "shoulder") lies within modern Nablus (Vespasian's *Flavia Neapolis*, "New City" named for himself, Flavius Vespasianus), a sizeable Arab town. Jacob's well is situated within a Greek orthodox church, across the road from a large Israeli jail. A hospitable priest, accompanied by his shy little daughter, invited this commentator to drop a pebble down the shaft and listen for the splash.

Jn has portrayed Jesus as the fulfillment of ceremonial (2:6-11), liturgical (2:19), and eschatological (3:3, 5) Judaism. Jesus will now heal an ancient breach going back many centuries (cf. Josh 8:30, with "Gerizim" bowdlerized and emended to "Ebal" since Gerizim is obviously the mount of blessing of vv. 33f.; 24:1, 25, 32; 1 Kgs 12:25; 2 Kgs 17:24-41: "To this day they worship according to their ancient rites" [v. 35]; "Thus these nations venerated the LORD, but also served their idols" [v. 41]; Ez 16:51; *Ant.* 12. 5. 5 [12,259]).

Jacob's acquisition of a plot of land in Shechem (v. 5) is described in Gn 33:19; 48:22; Josh 24:32. The Greek text refers to Sychar rather than Shechem (which the Sinaitic Syriac changes to Sichem), 'Askar in modern Arabic. Jn with his love of paradox has Jesus, the giver of living water (v. 10), ask a woman and a Samaritan for a drink at the high point of thirst of the day (v. 6). Verse 9b, "Jews have nothing to do with (*ou gar sygkrōntai*) Samaritans" could just as well be translated "do not use vessels in common with," a possible reference to the Jewish scruple over purity with respect to a dipper. "God's gift" (v. 10) will be the antitype *hydōr zōn*, "flowing water" (v. 11), fulfilling the type which is the standing wellwater of Jacob. In taking Jesus literally the woman engages in the classic Johannine incomprehension preliminary to an explanation of his true meaning. He responds in vv. 13f. that his gift will slake thirst forever, being a fountain within leaping up to provide the life of the final eon (*en autō pēgē hydatos hallomenou eis zōēn aiōnion*, v. 14). She asks for it, still not comprehending his deeper meaning. He prods her by a reference to her irregular life (vv. 16ff.), a detail that may be factually based but is much more likely to refer to the Samaritan liaisons with Marduk and his consort, with Nergal, Ashima, Nivhaz and Tartak, Hadad and Anath (cf. 2 Kgs 17:30f.) Even their veneration of the LORD was vitiated (20:32f.), the probable referent of "and the man you are living with now is not your husband" (v. 18).

Jesus' second sight is a commonplace with Jn (v. 19). The ensuing exchange transcends Samaritan-Jewish differences over the locale of official cult (vv. 21f.), as so frequently happens in this gospel. The hour is "already here" (*kai nun estin*, v. 23) with the presence of Jesus when those who worship God must do so "in spirit and in truth" (*en pneumati kai alētheia*, v. 24). Jesus, in other words, represents heavenly perfection, a rising above all particular forms to what is of God, Jn's "real" and "true."

The evangelist next makes a faith declaration in Jesus' messiahship, something inconceivable on Jesus' lips from our knowledge of the first stratum of gospel material. Mk does something similar in 14:62 with his, "I am." The embarrassment of the returning disciples is true to what we know of the customs of the time (v. 27) but it is chiefly a bridge to the proclamation of faith in Jesus by a member of a non-Jewish people (v. 29).

The opaqueness of the disciples over Jesus' "food" is another exchange of the kind we have come to expect in Jn (vv. 33f.) It leads into a discourse of Jesus about harvesting in which he takes two current proverbs (vv. 35, 37), the second one popular in Greek circles, and applies them to the situation typified by the Samaritans' newfound faith (vv. 41f.). "The reaper has overcome the sower; the time of fulfillment has come" (Barrett). By the time the gospel is written, everyone is indebted to the apostles. The story ends with the statement by the Samaritans that "this man is truly the savior of the world" (v. 42). Despite the historical preeminence of the Jews to whom Jesus belongs (v. 22), a new universalism has come to prevail (cf. 3:16.)

Jesus is a man on the move (v. 43); it is the spirit of truth who will remain (cf. Jn 14:17.) Jn's "after two days" are his normal transition to a biblical third day of fulfillment. Verse 44 is one of the many indications that Jn knew various synoptic traditions but used them sparingly (par. Mk 6:4; Mt 13:57).

FOURTH SUNDAY OF LENT (A)

1 Samuel 16:1, 6-7, 10-13. The biblical tradition on the radical social change from prophetic priesthood, represented by Samuel and his sons acting as judges, to the monarchy launched with Saul, is more than ambivalent (cf. chs. 8-10.) Sorting out the historical strands is impossible. The same is true of the co-regency of Samuel and Saul, if it can be so called (cf. chs. 12-13.) The psychological inadequacy of Saul to the new role of kingship in Israel is spelled out in ch. 15, where his failure to enforce the ban (*herem* = total destruction) against the Amalekites—softened by the pious priestly explanation that he had meant to offer the best sheep and oxen in sacrifice—is identified as his downfall.

The first thirteen verses of this chapter seem to be an editorial introduction to the David saga, which is a composite of two traditions: one in which he is an unsophisticated tender of his father's sheep and the other in which he is, from earliest youth, a successful guerrilla fighter. Verses 1-5 place Samuel emotionally on the side of the faltering giant Saul (cf. 15:35) and have the LORD impelling Samuel to go and surreptitiously anoint David as he previously did Saul (9:14—10:8). His fears over a reprisal by Saul are stilled by a suggestion of the LORD whereby he is to present himself to Jesse, the boy's father, as the itinerant sacrificer of a heifer (vv. 2f., 5).

The son of Jesse the Bethlehemite whom the LORD has in mind has not been specified in v. 1, hence Samuel's wonderment on seeing a likely candidate in Eliab (vv. 6f.), the oldest. In the event, Eliab is not let in on the choice of the younger David, as his dismissal of him as one fit for the warrior's role makes clear (17:28). The word of the LORD to Samuel about appearance is surely a pious comment of the author on the unsuitability of the imposing but psychotic Saul (cf. 9:1f.)

The verses omitted from the public reading name two other of Jesse's seven sons, all instinctively rejected by Samuel.

David is finally produced by his hesitant father in the manner of such tales the world over (v. 11). The shepherding detail is far from unimportant. Instructed by the LORD that "This is he!" (v. 12), Samuel fulfills his clear duty and pours the oil. A large measure of *ruah*—the powerful breath of God—rushes down upon David, and deserts the hapless Saul in the very next verse.

The choice of a Judahite will complicate Israel's history from this point on. Saul had been of Benjamin, Judah's neighbor immediately to the north. Despite their theoretical kinship as the two southern tribes, David's habit of victory—and Saul's defeat at his hands—will succeed in aligning the men of Judah in an uneven contest against all the other tribes.

Ephesians 5:8-14. The author of Ephesians draws freely on the Pauline light-darkness theme (cf. 1 Thes 5:4f.; 2 Cor 6:14; Col 1:12f.) "Children of light" are *tekna phōtos* here (v. 8) but *huioi* (sons) *tou phōtos* in the one use of the phrase in the synoptics (Lk 16:8). The "sons of light" of Jn 12:36 appear also in the Dead Sea scrolls *Manual of Discipline* at I, 9 and III, 24.

Darkness is the realm of shameful deeds (vv. 11ff.), a commonplace figure in the ancient world. "All that then appears is light" (*pan gar to phaneroumenon phōs estin*, v. 13*b*) seems to be an equating of the good deeds of believers with the light that is Christ. We assume that in v. 14 we have a snatch of a lost baptismal hymn. The non-vigilant sleepers of the NT are not praised (cf. 1 Thes 5:6ff.; Mt 25:5; 26:40; Lk 12:37.) Here, as in some other places, they are the dead (1 Thes 5:13ff.; 1 Cor 7:39 [*ean . . . koimēthē̦*]).

A series of cautions follows: against folly (v. 15; cf. Mt 25:1-13), in favor of "ransoming the time" (*exagorazomenoi ton chairon*, v. 16; cf. Col 4:5) and discerning the will of the Lord (cf. Rom 12:2; 1 Thes 4:3; 5:18), against drunkenness (cf. 1 Tim 3:3), and in the direction of song, thanksgiving, and praise.

John 9:1-41 (longer) or 1, 6-9, 13-17, 34-38 (shorter). As is mentioned below on p. 166, Robert Fortna (*The Gospel of Signs*, 1970) thinks that this pericope was built up by the evangelist from a book of seven signs consisting of 2:1-11; 4:46*b*-54; 21:2-14; 6:1-14; 11:1-45; 9:1-8; and 5:2-9, 14, which concluded with a passion narrative. Fortna thinks that this signs-source had as its purpose proving Jesus' messiahship by his works of power.

Clearly the narrative is an expansion of the saying of 8:12: "I am the light of the world./ No follower of mine shall ever walk in darkness;/ no, he shall possess the light of life" (cf. 9:5.) The synoptic-like sabbath healing (cf. v. 14) narrative of vv. 6f. (cf. Mk 8:22-26, including the detail of saliva; 10:46-52) is introduced by a familiar Johannine dialogue (vv. 1-5) in which the ignorance of the disciples (v. 2) is removed by Jesus' illumining response. There was no sin committed to account for the handicap, he says. Rather, the blindness was permitted "so that (*hina*) God's works might be shown forth in him" (*phanerōthē̦ ta erga tou Theou en autō̦*, v. 3). Verses 8-12 represent a slight expansion of the healing narrative and 13-34 the fullscale investigation and exchange in the service of which Jn employs the cure. Verses 35-41 complete the faith-meaning of the incident.

Jesus takes the initiative, not the blind man (vv. 1, 6f.). He does God's deeds "while it is day" (v. 4), namely, before the nightfall of his death. Applied to the Johannine church ("We must do . . ."), the reference would be to a season of good deeds in Christ's eschatological presence. Jesus in the world is its light, in glory its continuing light and life.

So far as we can tell from the narrative, Jesus is still up at Jerusalem for the Feast of Booths (*Sukkoth*; cf. 7:2, 37.) The water used for its libations was drawn from the Pool of Siloam (*Shiloah*; Neh 3:15; Is 8:6), an aqueduct in the southern part of David's old city on Mt. Ophel. The verb *shalah* does indeed mean "send," and may have something to do with the etymology of the name of the pool (e.g., "sent" through Hezekiah's conduit from the Spring of Gihon, its source). This is doubtful but Jn's intent is not in doubt, viz., to identify Jesus as "one who has been sent" (*apestalmenos*, v. 7; cf. the use of the same verb, *apesteilen*, in 10:36.) Jesus sends the man to pool for a washing off of the mud paste on his eyes (v. 7). He is cured as a result of his obedience, a possible parallel with the obedience of Jesus to his mission.

The opponents of Jesus who challenge the validity of the cure are variously "the Pharisees" (vv. 13, 16, 40) and "the Jews" (vv. 18, 22). The passage is an inquiry into Jesus' motivations by unfriendly elements among his own people, in a gospel which has only one question by the high priest ("about his teaching," 18:19) in the passion narrative. J. Louis Martyn (*History and Theology in the Fourth Gospel*, 1968) thinks that Jn is operating at two levels of time here as elsewhere, the *einmalig* or unique occurrence of the historical cure and the subsequent challenge to a Jewish believer in Jesus in the Jewish quarter of some diaspora city. The elaboration, with its questions put by the Pharisees who grew in influence after Jesus' day (vv. 16, 17, 19, 24, 28f., 34), argues strongly for a confrontation of Christian Jews of a later period by others who have not accepted him.

An especially influential detail is the occurrence of the word *aposynagōgos* (v. 22), which seems to be a technical term for someone expelled from the assembly (cf. its occurrence in the plural at 12:42; 16:2.) It is nowhere to be found in secular Greek usage or the LXX. Martin thinks it a term which arose in the late 1st century period on which we have little information beyond the gospels on tensions about Jesus within the Jewish community. He ties it in with the phrase contributed to the Eighteen (*Shemone esre*) Benedictions by Simon the Small ca. A.D. 85 which prays officially against *nosrim* and *minim*, Christians and heretics (i.e., those who lead astray from worship of the one God). Cf. also, "They ejected him" (*exebalon auton exō*, v. 35), which may not be the removal envisioned by NAB's "They threw him out bodily" but an official expulsion technique similar to making a person *aposynagōgos*. If the argument and its phrasing is read in this setting it becomes more comprehensible than if it were a spontaneous exchange that took place in Jesus' lifetime. The parents, for example, seem more alerted to the possibility of a public reprisal and its nature than they would have been if the Jesus of their son's cure had appeared in their lives only immediately before. A third possibility is that of elaboration by the evangelist without any historical data from his own age. The argument against this is cumulative, both from what we know of gospel composition generally and from data found elsewhere in the fourth gospel.

The case against Jesus is that he does not keep the sabbath (v. 16), that it is being claimed of him that he is the Messiah (v. 22), that he is a sinner (v. 24), and that his origins are obscure (v. 29; cf. 7:27f.) The blind man in response confesses him to be a prophet (v. 22), calls him devout and obedient to God's will (v. 31), assumes that he is from God (v. 33), and concludes by stating his belief in Jesus, coupled with a gesture of veneration, in a verse that is missing from numerous manuscripts (38).

The polarization in the exchange is between disciples of Moses who are sure of what is possible under Mosaic revelation from Sinai down to the oral law (vv. 28f.) and disciples of Jesus, an unknown without pedigree (cf. 7:41 but also 8:23.) The man blind from birth keeps alleging the miracle he has experienced as something that God would work only through his faithful servant (vv. 11, 15, 17, 25, 30-33). This was the way the Christians of the Johannine church were arguing: from Jesus' "works" or "signs" to his messiahship.

Verses 35-41 disclose the meaning of the event. It was so that the healed man might come to believe in the Son of Man. His progress from blindness to sight was a parable of progress from not having faith to having faith. The paradox of Jesus is that through him the blind see and those who claim they see are sightless. Verses 40f. become explicit: The continuing claim "But we see" by those who do not accept Jesus is, for the evangelist Jn, the ultimate in blindness.

This pericope is especially persuasive in making the case that the fourth gospel represents an internal struggle within late 1st-c. Judaism.

FIFTH SUNDAY OF LENT (A)

Ezekiel 37:12-14. The vision of the dry bones lying on a battlefield and summoned to life at the LORD's injunction by the prophetic word of Ezekiel might seem to be about the resurrection of the individual dead. The interpretation of v. 11 makes it clear, however, that a restoration of hope to the whole house of Israel is at issue. The people will be brought back to their land from the grave (v. 12). Revivified by the breath (*ruah* = spirit) of God himself, this people of the LORD will be settled on their own land (v. 13). He will do this for them because he has promised it (v. 14).

If the preacher wishes to speak about hope in the future for apparently lost causes or the power of the word of prophecy or the necessity of God's spirit if there is to be life, he may do so from this text. Most fittingly, it applies to the hope for liberty of a nation which at present is defeated or under a conqueror's heel. For a disquisition on the dead rising again, one is better advised to turn to Dan 12:2f., which deals with that subject directly. Isaiah 26:19 is ambiguous. It may refer to personal resurrection but is more probably a hymn to faith in national vindication.

Romans 8:8-11. Just as the dry bones of Ezekiel represent a nation that has not called on God for renewal of power and restoration, so "flesh" in this passage is humanity that has not been enlivened by him while "spirit" is humanity that has. Flesh by definition is not subjected to God's law (v. 7); it serves and suits itself, hence cannot serve him. Paul's word is "please" (*aresai*, aor. inf. of *aresko*, v. 8). To please God (cf. 1 Thes 4:1) and one's neighbor (cf. Rom 15:2; 1 Cor 10:33) is to live selflessly or in the spirit for Paul. Its opposite, living to please oneself (cf. Rom 15:1, 3), is living in the flesh.

In v. 9 the apostle turns to what he assumes is the situation of the Roman Christians. They are in the spirit since the presumption is that the Spirit of God—indistinguishable for Paul from the Spirit of Christ—dwells in them. This is a new definition of Christian life which does not call on eschatological categories such as "dying and rising with Christ." Through knowing Christ in faith, one receives the Spirit. A new life—lived "in Christ"—begins. Christ within one means death to the body (*to . . . sōma*, v. 10), namely the self, the province of sin (*dia hamartian*). Cf. 7:4, "You died to the law." That death of the former, sinful self is of no consequence, however, since the spirit is alive (lit., "life") because of justice (*dia dikaiosynēn*), that is, a right relation of the whole person to God.

We are not to suppose that Paul is dividing present humanity into a dead body and a living spirit. The distinction is between a pre-baptismal dead self, whole and entire, and a body and soul now spirit-enlivened. With life in Christ came the action of God's Spirit resulting in a life of spirit—justification, to use the Pauline term that is synonymous with it.

The ultimate act of God's Spirit in the *eschaton* will be to raise up our bodies as it has already raised up Christ's. But that lies ahead. The Lord may have his dwelling in the new éon but we continue our mortal existence, however much on the edge, in the old one. Nevertheless, the one Spirit is having its effect on all that lies between the two ages. Dwelling in us, it brings our mortal bodies to life also (*zōopoiēsei kai ta thnēta sōmata*, v. 11). This will culminate in our bodily resurrection, but the present tense of the verb argues for a present spirit-quality in our lives. The Spirit in us gives a life that is spirit.

See commentary on 8:9, 11-13, p. 112.

John 11:1-45 (longer) or 3-7, 17, 20-27, 33-45 (shorter). This is the fifth of the seven signs in the order proposed for a signs source in last week's commentary: Cana, the royal official's son, the miraculous catch of fish, the loaves and the fish at Passover, the resuscitation of Lazarus, the man blind from birth, and the man at the sheep pool of Bethesda.

Today's narrative has several points in common with last week's: the announced purpose of the illness ("that through it the Son of God may be glorified," v. 4), daylight—the time of Jesus' presence in the world—as the time for the deeds of God (vv. 9f.), and the official opposition of "the Pharisees," leading in this case to a session of the Sanhedrin. The chief differences from the story of the blind man are the emphasis on acceptance of Jesus as giving *life* rather than *light* (vv. 25f.) and the belief of "many of the Jews" in him as a result of the sign (v. 45).

Lazarus has not previously appeared in this gospel. The reference to his sisters cannot presume on the reader's awareness of Lk 10:38f. (which Jn probably knows from a source common to him and Lk rather than from Lk's gospel); therefore an identification of Mary is made through an anticipation of 12:3. Some dialogue is contrived in familiar Johannine fashion about the disciples' confusion between sleep and death (vv. 11-14); Judea is identified as the region inimical to Jesus, the likely place of his dissolution (vv. 7, 16); Jesus makes his way to his dying friend after waiting a biblical three days (v. 6) to heighten the sign value of what he means to do.

The characteristics of Martha and Mary from the Lucan story are probably reflected in v. 20. Martha concurs in the Pharisee teaching on bodily resurrection on the last day (v. 24), a prelude in

Jn's technique to some soaring transcendence of the familiar. Jesus does it by making clear the sense in which belief in him brings an end to death (v. 26). He is rewarded by a faith-statement of Martha in him as the Messiah, the Son of God, and *ho erchomenos*, the "one coming into the world" to save it (v. 27), which has the ring of a creedal formulary.

Verse 25 contains the best known of the Johannine "I am" sayings (cf. 6:35, 41, 48; 8:12; 10:7, 9, 11, 14; 14:6; 15:1, 5.) A Chester Beatty papyrus (p⁴⁵), various Latin and Syriac versions, and Origen and Cyprian do not have "and the life" but the great bulk of manuscript witness favors it. The force of the saying is not that belief in Jesus is a protection against death but that whoever believes is assured of being raised to a new life.

Verse 32, Mary's view of Jesus' power, echoes that of Martha in 21 before the revelation was made to her. Jesus' troubled emotional condition in vv. 33, 38 (connoting anger for Barrett but not for all commentators) is not easily explained. Mention of it encloses the description of his weeping (*Edakrysen ho Iēsous*, which is v. 35 in its entirety) but another emotion is being described. Is it a special drain on his intercessory power to ask for the resuscitation of a fetid corpse? Is Jesus' taking on of man's last enemy, death, responsible? Does he shudder at having to provide this greatest of signs to elicit faith in him as *hē anastasis kai hē zōē*?

The "four days now" (v. 39) reflects the Jewish popular belief that the spirit or breath of a person hovered in the vicinity of the body for three days; hence Lazarus' death was complete.

Jesus utters a *berakah* or blessing of God spoken in gratitude (*Pater, eucharistō soi*, v. 41). The only other such recorded prayer is in Mt 11:25 (=Lk 10:21) where the verb is *exomologoumai*, "I praise you," a rendering of the same Hebrew verb *barak*. Of Jesus' blessing of God spoken at table before he suffered, all we know is that he spoke it, not what he said. Here he thanks the Father for having heard him, as he always does, but this time for the sake of the crowd and its belief in him (v. 42).

It has been asked whether Jn historicized the parable told of another Lazarus by Jesus in Lk 16:19-31. Probably not. His record of fidelity to synoptic material in other places tends to free him of the charge. He doubtless has a traditional account of a certain resuscitation (the synoptics have two such, although neither person is long dead) and works up the story for his usual theological purposes.

The miracle is said to have had its intended effect, namely the faith of some Jews in what they saw. The narrative provides a welcome exception to the usual employment of the term *hoi Ioudaioi* in Jn to describe the adversaries of Jesus.

PASSION SUNDAY (A)

(Palm Sunday)

Matthew 26:14—27:66 (longer) or 27:11-54 (shorter). The Judas
tradition available to Mk—which Mt follows—was one of his
complicity with religious leadership (Mk 14:10=Mt 26:14), not civil
(cf. Mk 14:43.) Mt makes Judas take the initiative for reasons of
cupidity whereas Mk does not actively supply a motive. This is in
marked contrast to Jesus' advice in 10:8*b*, "The gift you have
received, give as a gift." "Iscariot" is usually taken to be a Greek
rendering of "man of Kerioth" (cf. Josh 15:25), a Judean town,
because the Codex Beza writes *apo Karyōtou* wherever *Iskariōtēs*
occurs in the fourth gospel; Sinaiticus has the same at Jn 6:71. This
attribution of a place name may be early interpretation, however.
Torrey and Gärtner propose an Aramaic word meaning "of betrayal"
or "of falsehood," in which case it would be a clear case of *Nomen
est omen.* Mt derives the betrayal price of thirty pieces of silver from
Zech 11:12f., from which even more of the Judas story appears to
stem.

Mt 27:3-10 is an insertion into Mk between 15:1 and 2, although
the connection of Judas's death with a graveyard called Field of
Blood (27:7) is probably pre-Matthean (cf. Ac 1:15-20.) Mt tells his
story of Judas's regret and subsequent self-destruction as an elaborate
introduction to the last of the many "formula quotations" (vv. 9f.) in
his gospel. This is a stitching together of Zech 11:12f. and Jer 32:6-
15, with incidental reference to Jer 18:2f. The mention of Jeremiah
when it is the Zechariah quotation that is being fulfilled (27:9) is a
slip or else testimony to the casual mode of citation in this targumic
(i.e., paraphrasing) procedure. Basic to Mt's fusing of the two texts is
the similarity of the Hebrew words *yōtsēr* and *'ôtsār*, meaning
respectively "potter" and "treasure/treasury." The result of the
priests' action, for Mt, is the unconscious fulfillment of prophecy
since the thirty pieces of silver that could not be put in the temple
treasury (Zech 11:13) were used to buy a field. Jeremiah had bought
a field from his cousin Hanamel as a sign (Jer 32:6-15), putting the
deeds in a pottery jar (v. 14). He had also spoken of Israel under the
figure of a vessel on a potter's wheel in God's hands (18:2f.) Mt gives
what he thinks is the hidden meaning of the Zech text by an involved
procedure which results in a reading of Zech not to be found in any
Greek, Aramaic, or Hebrew text of that book.

For Mt, the last supper is a Passover meal (*to pascha*) eaten on
the first day of Unleavened Bread (*Tę . . . prōtę tōn azymōn
[massoth]*, v. 17). He adds, "My appointed time draws near" (v. 18)
to Mk as part of his conviction that everything that happens to Jesus

is part of the divine decree (cf. 26:2, 53f.: "it must happen this way," *houtōs dei genesthai.*) Mt follows Mk closely in describing the preparation of the meal at the home of an unspecified householder (*ton deina*, v. 18, literally "a certain someone"; he eliminates Mk's detail about meeting a man carrying a water jar). Verses 17-24 parallel Mk 14:12-21 until Mt adds a specific question to Jesus by Judas, "Is it I, *rabbi*?" (v. 25; previously "lord," *kyrie*, v. 22). Jesus' response is the, "It is you who have said it" (*Su eipas*) of the later exchange with the high priest (26:64).

Mt's additions to the table injunctions of Jesus (vv. 26-29 = Mk 14:22-25) are the imperatives "Eat" (v. 26) and "Drink of it, all [of you]" (v. 27), plus "with you" (v. 29) in his vow of abstention from wine until he drinks it new (*kainon*) in his Father's reign.

The passage from the supper room to the Mount of Olives and Jesus' prediction of Peter's threefold denial, preceded by his quoting Zech 13:7 on a stricken shepherd and scattered sheep, is much as in Mk (26:30-35 = Mk 14:26-31). His statement that, once raised up, he will go to Galilee ahead of them (v. 22 = Mk 14:28) is important because it conveys the conviction of both evangelists that Galilee, not Jerusalem, is the site of the origins of the gospel, i.e., the proclamation that Christ is raised from the dead. Mt eliminates "twice" (v. 34) from Mk's prediction of the cockcrow. In Gethsemane, Mt does not include the redundant "Abba" (Mk 14:36 = v. 39) in Jesus' prayer, the wording of which he alters slightly. More importantly, here and in v. 42 he prays as he has taught others to pray (cf. 6:10*b*), "Your will be done." For the rest, the prayer of Jesus, "nearly heartbroken with sorrow," is in the same three stages and three challenges to the sleeping "Peter and Zebedee's two sons" (v. 37) as in Mk (vv. 35-46 = Mk 14:32-42).

Mt removes "scribes" from the party of captors (v. 47), possibly as out of place there, but like Mk makes Judas the leader of a band of toughs "from the chief priests and elders of the people," i.e., it is an arrest by religious not civil forces. The prearranged sign of Judas's embrace may be a practical detail (even though the moon was at the full) but is meant to underscore his betrayal of friendship. His greeting in Greek is the usual *Chaire*, although as NAB indicates a Jew would have said *Shalom*. Jesus' challenge, "Friend, do what you are here for" is a Matthean touch. Its declarative form will strike the Roman clergy, reared on the Vulgate's "Amice, ad quid venisti?" as strange; similarly, Protestants familiar with the AV's, "Wherefore art thou come?" But aside from the absence of an interrogative mark in the Greek codices, Jesus' command accords better with his lordly bearing throughout Mt (cf. Jn 13:27 to Judas at the supper table: "Be quick about what you are to do.")

When Jesus rejects the use of the sword (vv. 52ff.; not found in

Mk, although Lk 22:51 has it briefly, with a healing), he speaks majestically as the Son of God who can call on more than twelve legions of angels, a peculiarly Matthean concept. He also acts on his own advice in 5:39 to offer no resistance to evil. Without his capture the scriptures cannot be fulfilled (vv. 54, 56). When the disciples forsake Jesus and flee Mt terminates the narrative there (v. 56). He does not include Mk's story of the young man in the linen cloth, perhaps anticipating mentalities like Morton Smith's in *The Secret Gospel of Mark* (1973).

Mt supplies the correct name of the high priest, Caiaphas (v. 57), missing in Mk. Mk and Lk nowhere include it, while Jn does through the Annas-Caiaphas relation (18:3) and in the puzzling follow-up on Lazarus (11:49). Mt implies, along with Mk, that the scribes and elders were convened in the residence (or courtyard, *aulē*) of the high priest. Mk has used the verb *synerchontai* (14:53) which Mt changes to *synēchthēsan* (v. 57) to bring it in line with the LXX of Ps 2:2: "The princes conspire together against the LORD and against his anointed." Mt observes of Peter somewhat ominously that he went inside, not to "warm himself at the fire" (Mk 14:54) but to "see the end" (*idein to telos*, 26:58; cf. the use of *telos*, 26:6, 14, to designate the end of the age.) This reflects Mt's certainty that this death marks the consummation of an epoch.

The Matthean account of the search for testimony against Jesus by "the chief priests, with the whole Sanhedrin" (26:59) impugns their motives even more than Mk's does by calling the testimony they were after "false testimony." He also shortens Mk, who denies that there was any agreement among the witnesses, by having two of them come forward to say the same thing (vv. 60f.) The tradition that Jesus had prophesied the destruction of the temple evidently came from an earlier period in his public life (Mk 13:2 = Mt 24:2 = Lk 21:6) and was introduced into the trial narrative as one of the chief charges of the priests against him. Mt removes Mk's adjective about temples "made by human hands" and "not made by human hands" (*cheiropoiēton . . . acheiropoiēton*), no doubt finding it a "spiritualized" version, less probable historically. This change accords with Mt's interest in continuity, for he refers to "the temple *of God*" and says "I will rebuild it," whereas Mk speaks disparagingly of "*this* temple" and says "I will build another."

Whatever the historical substrate of Jesus' saying on the temple, Mt wishes to imply that two witnesses agreed (26:60) on what had been a true prophecy of Jesus, namely that he would destroy the temple of God and rebuild it in three days. By the time the logion has reached the trial narrative it had acquired for those who believe in Jesus the Johannine meaning of "the temple of his body," even if, as spoken, it had referred to the actual edifice.

We need not go beyond Jeremiah to find a paradigm for Jesus' prophecy about destruction in Jerusalem: "The priests and prophets said to the princes and to all the people, 'This man deserves death; he has prophesied against this city, as you have heard with your own ears' " (Jer 26:11).

Mt depicts the chief priests, the scribes and elders, and the whole Sanhedrin (26:57, 59) of Jesus' day as resembling the priests and prophets of Jeremiah's time ("You must be put to death!" Jer 26:8).

Mt has the high priest attempt to put Jesus under oath (*exorkizō*) before the living God to tell whether he is "the Christ, the son of God" (26:63). The adjuration is not historically probable in its wording (the formula is Christian), but it adds to the solemnity of the occasion and leads to Jesus' practical refusal to be bound by oath. His reply, "It is you who say it" (v. 64), is probably not an evasion; certainly it is not the formulation of an oath. Hence it is neither denial nor affirmation of Jesus' status as Messiah (with which "Son of God" is taken by the evangelist to be equivalent). It is Mt who has changed the response away from the "I am" of Mk 14:62. Hence, in neither gospel is the response to be confused with a declaration of Messiahship by the historical Jesus. Most probably Jesus is being made, by the phrase "It is you who say it," to have nothing to do with an oath, and to declare at the same time what the church already knows: that he is Messiah and Son of God.

Mt (26:66) follows Mk (14:64) in having the high priest ask his colleagues their opinion (*ti hymin dokei?*) and in finding Jesus deserving of death because of the blasphemy they have supposedly just heard. He does, however, eliminate a word of Mark that may be proper to judicial sentence, *katekrinan*, satisfying himself with the neutral, "they answered" (*apokrithentes eipan*).

Mt omits the detail of blindfolding from Mk as if it were self-evident (v. 67). *Christe* (v. 68) is a taunt delivered to a false Messiah.

The alterations in account of Peter's denial are relatively few and inconsequential. He omits the detail of Peter's warming himself (Mk 14:67) and has the serving girl call Jesus "the Galilean" rather than "the Nazorean" (Mt 26:69, par. Mk 14:67), inserting "Jesus of Nazareth" later at verse 71. Mt's Peter denies Jesus "in front of everyone" (v. 70) and "with an oath" (v. 72), getting more explicit in his second denial, "I do not know the man" (*ibid.*), than in Mk. The phrase, "Even your accent gives you away" (v. 73), is a further Matthean explication. He likewise adds "bitterly" (*pikrōs*) to the account of Peter's weeping, and tidies up Mark's prophecy of a threefold denial by the time of a second cockcrow (14:72) by having a cock crow once (Mt 26:74). He then brings Jesus' prophecy into line with this change (v. 75).

Mt's account of morning activity by the Sanhedrin ignores what has happened the night before just as thoroughly as does Mk's. The chief priests and elders decide (plot?) to put Jesus to death in the same phrase, *symboulion elabon* (27:1), as that used in 12:14 and 22:15. His fate is sealed before he goes off to Pilate.

The charge on which Jesus is brought before Pilate (27:11) is the only one actionable before a civil court, namely that he is a messianic revolutionary ("Are you the king of the Jews?"). His answer is a cryptic *su legeis*, much like the *su eipas* of 26:25 and 64. In verses 12-14 Jesus remains completely silent before the accusations of the chief priests and elders. In all of this, there is no substantial departure from Mark in substance and very little in wording.

The same is true of Mt's account of Barabbas. He does not specify murder in an uprising but contents himself with calling him a "notorious prisoner" (*desmion episēmon*, v. 16). It is interesting to speculate why he should have softened the charge against Barabbas, since the latter's sentence for insurrection is presumably the same one under which Jesus will shortly fall. It is true that Mt stresses the alternative between the two as Mk has not done (v. 17). Jesus is "called (the) Messiah" in Mt (27:17), whereas in the parallel place Mk (15:9) has Pilate designate him "the king of the Jews." The Jewish people would not have called him that if they had written the title but "king of Israel" (cf. Mt. 27:42). Pilate is as aware in this gospel as in Mk's that the Jewish leaders have handed him over out of envy (*dia phthonon*, v. 18).

The improbable account of the warning Pilate's wife delivers to her husband as a result of a dream (27:19c) accords with Mt's reliance on dreams in his first two chapters. It also highlights Pilate's innocence, something which the four gospels are committed to, in contrast to the guilt of the priestly leaders and even of the "whole people" (v. 25; cf. Ac 3:13-15). For the genesis of the people's disclaimer of guilt, "Let his blood be on us and on our children," see the reference to Jer 26:15 and 51:35 and the phrase attributed to Paul, "Your blood be upon your own heads. I am not to blame" (Ac 18:6). The expression, far from being a self-inflicted curse, is a strong statement of innocence. It appears in later, mishnaic form in the tractate *Sanhedrin 37a*, where in capital cases the witness uses the invocation as a proof of his innocence. If he is lying, he is willing to have the blood of the accused fall on himself and his offspring until the end of the world. Mt has Pilate wash his hands and declare his innocence (a Jewish, not a Roman custom; cf. Deuteronomy 21:6-9; Psalms 26:6a, 73:13b) so that he may set the willing acceptance of responsibility of the "whole people," i.e. all present, against it.

Pilate yielded when he saw that his offer of Barabbas was gaining him nothing, but bringing on a riot instead (v. 24). Mt has him deliver Jesus over (*paredōken*, v. 26) as in Mk. This word is frequent in the passion accounts (Mk 14:10; 15:1; Mt 27:26; Lk 23:25) and is heavily freighted with religious symbolism in Rom 8:32.

The place of Jesus' appearance before Pilate has been indeterminate. He is now led "inside the praetorium" (v. 27) for a mocking at soldiers' hands. The royal scepter in the form of a reed (v. 29) is a peculiarly Matthean detail; so is his "scarlet military cloak" (*chlamyda kokkinēn*), Mark having reported a (royal?) purple (*porphyran*, 15:20) cloak. The mocking game of the soldiers ends in Jesus' being led away to be crucified (v. 31).

In Mt's passion, a tendency to view the Jewish leaders unfavorably is undeniable. That, however, is not primarily what the evangelist is about. He wishes to convey that the one whom he portrays as innocent and just dies. This is not, however, to be taken "in the sense of an error of justice or of an infamous judicial murder, not even to magnify the guilt of the Jews thereby, but as a profoundly necessary event in God's plan of salvation" (G. Barth). The one who dies is the Lord, the Son of God.

EASTER SEASON

EASTER VIGIL (A)

Romans 6:3-11. *See* p. 312,

Matthew 28:1-10. Matthew probably has Mark's account of the women at the tomb before him, modifying it in light of certain discrepancies from the special material at his disposal (e.g., the names of the women at the burial and at the tomb, 15:47 and 16:1; the Marcan account of burial rites completed by Joseph of Arimathea, 15:42-46). Thus, in Mt the women come "to inspect the tomb" (v. 1) rather than "to anoint Jesus" (Mk 16:1). The angel in Mt charges the women to "tell his disciples" (v. 7), eliminating "and Peter" (Mk 16:7). Mt is evidently leading up to the single appearance to all the disciples in Galilee (v. 17) for the missionary charge, hence sees no need to single out the appearances to Peter and the disciples as Mk does. Furthermore, he has no interest in Mk's theology of the messianic secret. This means that the detail of instructing women otherwise fearful and silent (Mk 16:9) to proclaim the risen Christ to Peter and the Twelve, as the final unveiling of the secret, is meaningless to him. Matthew's women cannot remain silent. "Half-overjoyed half-fearful" they run to carry the good news to his disciples. The encounter with Jesus (vv. 9f.) is a Matthean insertion into Mk's narrative. Jesus greets them, they worship him, and he repeats the angel's charge. This appearance of Christ to the women in Jerusalem is unexpected. We would have looked for his meeting the disciples in Galilee next. Mt seems to possess the tradition from some independent source and want to work it in. It may have been an appearance of an angel to the two Marys in its earliest form, since it does not occur in 1 Cor 15:5-7 or in Mk. The christophany of Jn 20:11-18 seems to be from the same tradition but independently developed. (Cf. Lk 24:22, where the women report "a vision of angels.") This christophany in Mt is the turning point of the "relocation of the primary appearances to the disciples in Jerusalem in Lk 24 and Jn 20" (Fuller). It is also the first materialization of the appearances (viz., "embraced him," "did him homage"), a departure from their mere listing as in 1 Cor 15:5f. and Mk 16:17. The borrowing of details from Mk 5:6 and 5:22, with its indiscriminate view of Jesus as a "divine man," indicates that while the appearances may be out of a primitive tradition the narratives are not.

EASTER SUNDAY (A)

Acts 10:37-43. The omission of 34*b*-36 from the lectionary is a sensitive one. It suppresses a key-concept in Lucan theology, namely his late first-century attempt at "reconciliation" of the lion and the lamb, Gentile Christianity and Judaism, which has the lamb ending up inside. God's impartiality is such that the message sent to the sons of Israel leaves them with no special distinctiveness such as they have in Paul (where theirs are "the adoption, the glory, the covenants, the law-giving, the worship, and the promises . . . the patriarchs, the Messiah [in his] human origins," Rom 9:4f.; they are "the first fruits," "the root," "the cultivated olive," Rom 11:16, 24). For Luke the sons of Israel, like the "man of any nation who fears God and acts uprightly," are merely "acceptable to him" (Ac 10:35). Luke overcomes the obstacle provided by the fact that God addressed his message to the Jews by citing Jesus' Lordship as the reason why *anyone* may now enter the messianic community of salvation.

The vision Peter has had in the house of Simon the tanner at Joppa (Ac 10:9-16) has convinced him that all foods are clean. Hence he is relieved of any scruple over dietary laws in eating with the "God-fearing" (i.e., Jewish-oriented) centurion Cornelius and his household (v. 22). Seated at ease in the midst of this Gentile company, Peter begins to share a portion of his message (*logon*, vv. 36, 44) with them.

Peter's sermons, Lucan in form, bear a remarkable resemblance to Paul's in the book of Acts, while the latter seem barely acquainted with the fundamentals of Pauline theology. They do contain, however, the basic elements of Paul's proclamation, namely the crucifixion of Jesus (Gal 3:1), his death for our sins (Gal 1:4; 1 Cor 15:3), his burial (1 Cor 15:4), his having been raised from the dead (Rom 8:34) on the third day (1 Cor 15:4) and made "son of God in power" (Rom 1:4) at the right hand of God (Rom 8:34), where he intercedes for us (*ibid.*) He who delivers us from the wrath to come (1 Thes 1; 10) is awaited from heaven (*ibid.*), at which time God will pass judgment through him on the secrets of men (Rom 2:16). For the above ideas in Paul's preaching as found in Ac, see 13; 16:41; 17:31; 26:23.

The notion of a message that brings the good news of peace and the very phrasing employed in the New Testament derive from the Septuagint versions of Nahum 2:1 (Vulgate, AV, 1:15) and Is 52:7. There the context is respectively the announcement of the smashing of

Assyria's brutal hold (v. 7c) and the proclamation to Jerusalem and Zion of the impending restoration of Israel from Babylonian captivity (v. 6c). For the Christian author of Acts the good news of peace is the final liberation proclaimed "through Jesus Christ who is Lord of all" (10:36).

A slim but influential book of C. H. Dodd published in 1936, *The Apostolic Preaching and Its Developments*, gave currency to the notion that Peter's discourse in Ac 10 provided the framework for the synoptic gospels, notably Mk. In this theory, Mark in his passion story deserts Ac 10 and takes his cue from 1 Cor 15. It is generally supposed nowadays that the literary form "gospel," which Mark invented, does not depend so neatly on the form of the apostolic preaching (*kērygma*). It simply goes in the only direction open to it. Nonetheless, the correspondence between Peter's discourse at Caesarea and the synoptic gospel sequence (Galilee, Judea, passion-resurrection) is undeniable. Galilee witnesses the initiation and the greater part of Jesus' ministry after his baptism by John, inevitably a Judean occurrence.

In his homeland he breaks the devil's grip by healings and exorcisms in proof that the reign of God has drawn near. The "land of the Jews" (v. 39) is Judea. Its inhabitants rather than Jews taken ethnically are charged with Jesus' death, although the latter idea is doubtless encompassed within the former. The high point of the sermon is the claim by Peter to be among the chosen "witnesses" to the resurrection. This is a technical term for the sharers in the eschatological meals of the earliest believers who were charged with proclaiming Jesus' rising from the dead (v. 42; Mk and the Pauline letters have him "raised up," as in v. 39). In a non-technical sense, modern Christians who partake of the Easter eucharist do so as witnesses to the resurrection. Like their apostolic forebears they have been commissioned to preach and bear witness to the Christ whom God has set apart as judge. The "testimony of all the prophets" to Jesus (v. 43), belief in whose person (= "name") brings forgiveness of sins, means the whole gamut of biblical texts collected into "books of testimonies" for preachers—texts in which the book of Acts abounds.

Colossians 3:1-4 (first alternate). This letter seems to be filled with anti-gnostic arguments (although contemporary-Jewish would do) which stress the superiority of Christ to angels (2:16), his role as first-born of all creatures and the one who continues them in being (2:15, 17), him in whom absolute fullness (*pan to plērōma*) resides (1:19), the reconciler of all on earth and in the heavens (1:20). Through him as image of the Invisible God (1:15) we have been rescued from the power of darkness and brought into "the kingdom of his beloved Son" (1:13; only a few NT phrases attribute kingly reign to Christ, e.g., 1 Cor 15:24f.; Mt 13:41; 2 Tim 4:18). The "Great Christology" of Col 1:15-23, while drawing on Jewish and possibly pagan religious writings for its vocabulary, is remarkable chiefly for its attribution of divine status to Christ at so early a period—whether during Paul's captivity at Ephesus (early 50's) or Rome (58-60), or shortly after his lifetime, as some would have it.

In any case, the assumption of the present reading is that Christians have been mystically raised up with Christ. For this reason they are to set their hearts on what pertains to "the higher realms" (to anō), an adverbial phrase found also in Jn 8:23. There the contrast is between "above" and "below." The antithesis between "the above" and "earth" in Col (3:1, 2) is more closely paralleled by the heaven-earth opposition of Jn 3:31. Gnostic terminology may be invoked, but ordinary Jewish usage on the respective abodes of God and man will do. Christ is at God's right hand for Paul (Rom 8:34) and 1 Pet (3:22); he is seated there according to the authors of Ephesians (1:20) and Hebrews (10:12).

The attention of Christians is summoned to what God has done for them in Christ, not to the other-wordly as contrasted with the this-worldly. The invitation to transcendence is issued and is expected to be accepted here, not in some ethereal realm. The contrast is between a God-centered life and one that is selfish or trivial.

The theme of death with Christ and hiddenness with him is reminiscent of Paul's reference to mystical death and burial with him in Romans (6:4) and a death to sin that parallels Christ's (6:10f.) Life in Christ as a life of faith in the Son of God is the theme of Gal 2:19f., with an echo of the same "life" after death in Phil 1:21. The actual state of being with Christ is a thing of the future for Paul (Phil 1:23; 1 Thes 4:17). He takes a strong line against the Corinthian enthusiasts who imagine that through baptism they have "risen" as much as they are going to (1 Cor 15), a view made explicit in 2 Tim 2:18. The uncharacteristic notion of Col 3:1 of being raised up with Christ in the present (Paul makes it future in virtue of a resurrection in Rom 6:5, 8, although he does not balk at the reality of new life in him now, Rom 6:11) is balanced by the anticipation of our appearance with him in glory only when he appears (Col 3:4).

This passage cannot be made into an appeal to transcend the material order. The "spiritual" of the NT always embraces the material, orienting it Godward. Only when this is not done does a man become "unspiritual"—even in his intellectual and psychic powers. When the Lord appears at the end in glory, it will be manifest how committed to the Spirit faithful Christians were. This manifestation, like that of Christ himself, has nothing to do with non-corporeality.

1 Corinthians 5:6-8 (second alternate). Paul identifies Christ as our Passover, our *transitus* from death to life. Just as in Israel's safe passage from Egypt to the desert of freedom and from the land of Sinai to the land of promise there was escape to liberty and new life, so the believer in Christ as a sacrificial victim lives again through this commemorative action. It is a second symbol of release, the Passover meal (which is not rescinded) being the first. Paul recalls to his Corinthian readers familiar with Jewish practice the rabbinic custom of destroying every available crumb containing yeast during the Passover as a means of fulfilling literally the command of Ex 13:7. Only *maṣṣoth*, yeastless loaves, are to be used during the eight-day observance. This commemorative practice makes yeast the enemy; an otherwise neutral or even helpful agent becomes the symbol of corruption and wickedness. *Maṣṣoth* in themselves are no more innocent than leavened bread, but they become the symbol of sincerity and truth. Jesus is reported as using the same figure of speech, "the yeast of the Pharisees" (Mk 8:15), to describe that portion of their teaching which he disapproved.

Deliverance for the Christian is spoken of in this passage as a present reality. It has often been asked why St. Paul inserted this reference to the Passover here. The usual response given is that he was probably writing his letter at that season. What is the boasting he warns the Corinthians against (v. 6), which is the context of his remarks? Probably their arrogance in assuming that their tolerance of incest in their community is proof that they can "handle it." This corruption doubtless is the "little yeast" of Paul's severe warning. His pastoral principle seems to be that that immoral conduct which must pass unnoticed in those who do not know Christ is not to be admitted within the Christian community.

Since the ostracism of those of irregular life has caused untold pain in the Christian church over the centuries, Paul's meaning must be pondered deeply before any too hasty conclusions are drawn from his warning.

John 20:1-9. This reading from John combines two traditions on the resurrection in the early Church, the earlier one of appearances of Christ to various persons and the later, more developed one of the empty tomb. The christophany to Mary Magdalene begins in vv. 1-2 and resumes at v. 11; v. 3, which is almost identical with v. 13 (except for its plural, which is probably a rhetorical device and does not require any other person at the sepulchre) is provided as a link to the story of the two disciples. Mary's lament to the angels is duplicated to the disciples in a transition from the more primitive discovery story (e.g., Mary Magdalene's; cf. Mt 28:1ff.; Mk 16:1ff.; Lk 24:10) to an alternative one in which John features the faith of the beloved disciple (v. 8). A second development besides that from christophanies to empty tomb may be that from the earliest appearance in Galilee to those in Jerusalem, all accomplished before the first gospel is written.

Luke has a running Peter who, alerted by the women's report, stoops down when he arrives to see the wrappings in the tomb but nothing else (24:12). In John's account, the beloved disciple outruns Peter but allows him to enter first. This preserves the tradition of Peter's primacy of discovery but leaves room for the special Johannine character of the beloved disciple: "He saw and believed" (v. 8). Mary too will stoop to look inside (v. 11). She is no more moved to believe by what she sees than is Peter. The neatness of the wrappings in an apologetic detail, hinting against the theft of the body (cf. Mt 27:64; 28:13-15) and in favor of Jesus' miraculous passage through the wrappings as through locked doors (cf. Jn 20:26.) The beloved disciple announces his faith to no one and when the disciples assemble a week later (vv. 19ff.) none of them is reported as already believing. The race to the tomb and its outcome, therefore, is for a specific Johannine editorial purpose.

Matthew 28:1-10. See p. 62.

SECOND SUNDAY OF EASTER (A)

Acts 2:42-47. Professor Jeremias is connected with the view, a commonplace by now, that in v. 42 we have the shape of a primitive eucharistic liturgy in the sequence: apostolic teaching (*didachē*), table fellowship (*koinōnia*), breaking of the bread (*klasis tou artou*), and prayers (*proseuchai*). He considers "devoted themselves" to be a verb denoting cult and thinks that Lk here uses ambiguous phrases about the eucharist to mask it from non-Christians. Against this is the difficulty that cryptic speech has not yet overtaken a community whose representative, Lk, elsewhere reports the formula, potentially damaging in a context of banqueting on human flesh: "This is my body . . . This cup is the new covenant in my blood" (Lk 22:19f.) Moreover, the temple is identified as a place where the apostles go for prayers (Ac 3:1) and teaching (5:21); the distribution of food—if, as is likely, this sharing is the meaning of *koinōnia*—is carried out apart from a worship service (6:1); and "prayers" do not merely conclude a Christian worship service. It therefore seems more likely that Lk is here using "and" to list four distinct activities of the community, one of which undoubtedly is the communal meal (cf. 2:46; 20:7, 11; 27:35). "The breaking of the bread" (cf. Lk 24:35) is already standard usage for the eschatological meal which becomes the eucharist. The term derives from the symbolic gesture with which every Jewish meal opens, although there is no evidence that it existed in Jewish circles as a usual designation for having a meal.

The summary that runs from v. 43 to v. 47, a favorite Lucan technique, anticipates those of chapters 4 and 5 (4:32-35; 5:41f.) He uses them skillfully to separate his stories. This one features the subsequently repeated phrase "signs and wonders" (5:12). The "fear" that overtakes them all is the holy awe which marks the last age and which in turn is clearly identifiable as the milieu of Lk's spirit-dominated Jerusalem community. Non-Christians presumably look on in wonder at the life of a church filled with miracles.

Community members did not divest themselves of their property but sold it as there was need (v. 45). Neither did they break with their Jewish religion, the worship center of which was the temple (v. 46), but observed what was special about their new faith in Christ through "breaking bread" at substantial meals of celebration, even "revels" (trophēs) taken in homes. All is done in a spirit of messianic joy (agalliasis, v. 47; cf. Lk 1:14, the intertestamental Enoch, and Testaments of the Twelve Patriarchs.) Luke often features the notion of praise of God (2:13, 20; 19:37; Ac 3:8) which he here (v. 47) couples with relationship to men. The entire picture of the early Jerusalem community is romanticized—eschatologized, actually—a fact which has led to much peace in Christian living. It has also accounted for a multitude of sects through literalist attempts to reproduce a world that never was.

1 Peter 1:3-9. The greeting that precedes these eight verses is addressed to the Christians scattered throughout the five Roman provinces that comprised the bulk of Asia Minor at the turn of the second century. Only south-central Pisidia and Lycaonia and Cilicia along the southern coast (plus Commagene to the far south-east) were omitted. Christian believers are described as having been providentially called to a life of "obedience to Jesus Christ and purification in his blood." A triadic scheme of divine activity is present in the greeting: foreknowledge of election is attributed to God the Father while consecration to obedience to Christ and purification in his blood are made a work of the Spirit (cf. 2 Thes 2:13.) There follows in vv. 3-5 a snatch of a Christian hymn, probably a baptismal one. Christ is described intimately as "our Lord," a usage found as early as 2 Thes 3:18 and going back to the Aramaic "Marana" (1 Cor 16:22).

Cf. Tit 3:5-7 for a common stock of ideas on which this author is drawing. God is praised as the merciful giver of "new birth unto hope," a living hope which is derived from Christ's resurrection from the dead. Our hope of rising is grounded on and guaranteed by his rising (cf. Rom 8:10f.; 1 Cor 15:12-22.) The author will make the connection between baptism and Christ's resurrection again in 3:21. The whole complexion of life—now a matter of baptismal bath, rebirth, hope—has been changed by Christ's victory over death. Paul's phrase for this reality, "living a new life" (Rom 6:4) occurs in a discussion carried on in terms of baptism, Christ's resurrection, and ours. The birth imagery is sustained by 1 Pt in 1:23 and 2:2. It occurs throughout the New Testament (e.g. Jn 3:1-8; 1 Jn 2:29; Jas 1:18) and is probably dependent verbally on the mystery cults of Isis, Cybele, and Mithra—all of which speak of the "regeneration" of their votaries—but in content on the Jewish expectation of a new creation. The baptismal hope is an "inheritance," a fitting enough figure for the newborn but also one with a long Jewish history (cf. Dt 19:10, where the inheritance is Canaan; it is God himself in Ps 16:5—the "Dominus, *pars*" that used to be recited at clerical tonsure; in Dn 12:13 it is a rising up at the end of days). Moreover, this heritage is incapable of destruction, fading, or defilement (v. 4). No matter what vicissitudes the baptized may undergo, their inheritance (*klēronomia*) will be preserved safe in heaven, to be revealed in the last days as a birth "unto salvation" (*eis sōterian*, v. 5). God, in other words, will keep the Christian from disaster and show forth his blessedness at the opportune moment.

Does 1 Pt betray a conviction, by speaking of what will happen *en kairō eschatō* (v. 5), that the last age will come soon? Those who say so cite 1:7, 13 and 4:7. Yet the epistle is full of practical advice for the conduct of ongoing life, so we must not too hastily assume that the timeless "suddenness" of eschatological discourse was taken by the author and his readers to be a temporal "soon."

The exchange of letters between Pliny, imperial legate to Pontus-Bithynia in 110, and the emperor Trajan make some think that verses 6-9 speak of a real persecution and not of the apocalyptic trial (*peirasmos, thlipsis*) that will precede the end. The genuine quality of faith, more precious than fire-tried metals, recalls Paul's usage in 1 Cor 3:11-14, where the image of the construction of each one's life on the foundation that is Christ is similar. The image of fire at the final judgment, like the judgment itself, came to Israel from Iranian sources. Here the late NT author touches on the problem (v. 8) of the fate of those who have not known Christ (cf. 2 Cor 5:7; Jn 20:29; Heb 11:27). He concentrates on love of Christ rather than of God, an idea that only begins to appear in the Johannine literature. The language of vv. 8f. is that of eschatological joy, a joy paradoxically realized in this age. Verse 9 speaks of "the salvation of your *psychōn*," meaning your persons or selves, not your souls.

John 20:19-31. This account of Jesus' appearance to his disciples is parallel to Lk's in 24:36-43. Both depend on traditions which, by the time the gospels are written, have placed the appearance to the disciples in Jerusalem rather than the earlier tradition of Galilee. Jn has changed Lk's "feet" to "side" because of his "piercing" narrative in 19:34. Both evangelists are interested in connecting this appearance with the inauguration of a mission, in Lk the preaching of penance for the remission of sins (vv. 36, 47) which is to be confirmed by "the promise of my Father" (v. 49), in Jn the forgiveness of sins (v. 23) by the breathing of the spirit (v. 22). Lk has separated the outpouring of the spirit (Ac 2:1-4) from any christophany.

There is much discussion as to whether Jn's "forgiving" and "holding bound" (v. 23) is a disciplinary injunction similar to that of the rabbinically-oriented Mt 16:19; 18:18. Even though the latter may have its origins in a post-Easter saying—the Petrine confession is thought by many to belong to the risen life—the verb Mt uses is "loose" (*luein*) rather than the "remit" (*apheinai*) of Jn, which is cognate with Lk's baptismally-oriented *aphesis* (23:47). The phrasing in Jn is very Hebraic, hence presumably primitive: a word of the Lord circulated in the Aramaic-speaking community. Fuller thinks it may even be the earliest form of the command to baptize.

Jn uses Thomas, who is just one among the Twelve in the synoptics, as a foil of misunderstanding (11:16; 14:5) and here (20:24-29) doubt, a role that Peter tends to have in the synoptics. The evangelist ties in his Thomas story with the appearance story that went before—with which it does not seem to have been connected—by modeling the "locked doors" of his linking-passage, v. 26, on v. 19. He employs the same parallel in v. 27 with v. 20.

The creedal statement, "My Lord and my God!" would be unusual for the NT but for Jn's previous, studied attempts to convey Jesus' equality with God (1:1; 5:18; 8:58; 12:45; 14:9). Throughout, he remains quite clear that God is God and Jesus the presence of God in act in the last age. Such is the case here, where Thomas's expression of faith (nominative; with vocative force?) comes in a risen life that vindicates all that Jn has claimed for Jesus in his discourses.

An interesting question is, did Thomas ever do with his finger what Jesus directed? The evangelist does not say. He is interested in the faith of believers of his time who had not seen Jesus, not so much in an apologetic against docetism.

The last two verses (30f.) are clearly the end of the book, which only heightens the puzzle of why the Galilee appearances were added in chapter 21. They were probably in a tradition that was come upon by the author of 21:24f. who is likely to have written the whole chapter, and who in any case wishes to attribute the first twenty chapters to the mysterious "disciple whom Jesus loved."

THIRD SUNDAY OF EASTER (A)

Acts 2:14, 22-28. Peter's reported discourse to "Jews" is to the people of Jerusalem, Judeans, along with festal pilgrims. Loisy called v. 14 "the solemn inauguration of Christianity." Verse 22 returns to Peter's more intimate speech after his self-defense against the charge of drunkenness and the extended quotation from Joel. Jesus is identified as *ton Nazoraion*, probably a reference to his hometown which Luke in one place calls *Nazara* (Lk 4:16), elsewhere using the adjective *Nazarēnos*. The Jewish Christians came to be known as *Nosrim* probably for this reason, although some following another derivation think it was because they were "observants." The legitimation of Jesus' mission had been accomplished by God through "miracles, wonders, and signs" (v. 23) with which the hearers were presumed to be familiar. This same verse combines the workings of God's plan and man's free, malicious choice. Some translations have the agents of Jesus' destruction "lawless men" (*anomoi*), others those who did not know Torah (*nomos*), pagans. The explanation of Jesus' death which fixed responsibility on Jews using Roman Gentiles as their instruments has already been worked out by the time of the four passion accounts. Lk's antithesis is: "you . . . killed him" (v. 23) but "God raised him up again" (v. 24). Death binds man fast: "God freed him" (*ibid.*) De la Potterie thinks *anomoi* means "wicked."

Ps 16 is attributed, in the Jewish manner, to David, God's anointed king. In context the psalmist is only expressing his confidence that God will not let him die and go down to *sheol* before his time. The Christians saw in these verses a prophecy of the raising up of God's true anointed from the grave. They were abetted in their use of these verses as a proof-text by the LXX which rendered a word that could mean security (v. 26) by "hope." Ac 13:35 will use Ps 16:10, "you will not suffer your faithful one to undergo corruption," in the same way, in conjunction with Ps 2:7 and Is 55:3. This type of interweaving of texts both here and in Peter's sermon in Ac 2 argues for the existence of collections of biblical "testimonies" for early Christian preachers. "The path to life" of Ps 16:11—upright living for the psalmist—is taken by the author of Ac to mean Christ's risen life (*hodous zōēs*, v. 28).

The use of the LXX throughout is an indication that Lk is the author of Peter's speeches, which he derives from Hellenist Christianity rather than the primitive Jerusalem community. This fact merely highlights the theologically developed condition of early Ac, with its triumphalist report of growth by leaps and bounds (2:41). The actual steps by which the gospel was spread are no less remarkable. Unfortunately, they are hidden from us.

1 Peter 1:17-21. The widespread assumption that 1 Pt 1:1-4, 11 is a baptismal homily (Preisker, F. L. Cross), while probably not correct, is at least contributed to by this hortatory segment which culminates in cryptic references to "having purified yourselves" (v. 22) and "rebirth" (v. 23). The passage also undoubtedly contains embryonic creedal formulas or christological hymns (vv. 20, 21). Ps 34:10 ("Fear the Lord, you his holy ones") probably underlies vv. 15-17. God is identified in v. 17 as a Father who judges, a usage that derives from coupling the notions of his perfect justice (Dt 10:17f.) and his fatherhood (Jer 3:19; Mal 1:6). Awareness of his total impartiality should result in fear of the Lord (*yirath Yahweh*, Is 11:2), here expressed as "conducting yourselves reverently" (*en phobǭ*, v. 17) during the time of your "sojourn in a strange land." The latter phrase renders *paroikia*, an echo of the author's "strangers" (*parepidēmoi*) of 1:1. Both words connote transitory residence without a citizen's rights. The Israelites are *paroikoi* in the Septuagint of Lv 25:23 and elsewhere, in Ac 13:17, their stay in Egypt is a *paroikia*. Such is the earthly pilgrimage of the Christian.

The epistle tells its readers, in what seems to be a catechetical formulation from its introduction in v. 18, that they have been released from the traditional and "futile way of life" of their fathers. This is almost certainly a reference to their once pagan status, for the LXX version uses the word "futile" scornfully of the heathen (cf. also Eph 4:17.) Deliverance comes to the Christian not by silver or gold but by the precious ("beyond all price") blood of Christ. The verb "delivered" in v. 18 is redolent of the ransom imagery of both testaments of Scripture: Is 52:3; Ti 2:14; 1 Tim 2:6; Heb 9:12; Mk 10:45. The blood is not paid *to* anyone as in later Christian theology, least of all to the devil. God is the referent rather than the recipient. He acts as deliverer and rescuer of the baptized, the same role he had as regards Israel's deliverance from the hands of the Egyptians in Ex 6:6. The author shifts easily in v. 19 from the ransom figure to one of sacrifice. Silver and gold have a price; Christ's blood is priceless because, as eternally elect, he is a "spotless, unblemished lamb." The second adjective reflects the ritual requirements for beasts in Ex 29:1; Lv 22:17-25 while the first (*aspilos*) has no LXX counterpart. He who, for long ages, was chosen is now revealed. The familiar creedal God "who raised him from the dead" (cf. Rom 3:11; 2 Cor 4:14; 1 Thes 1:10) is, through Christ, the author of the "faith and hope" (v. 21) of the baptized—the latter two a coordinate meaning total confidence in God rather than two distinct theological virtues. Christians are reminded at Easter that they are not simply believers in God, theists, but believers in the God who raised Christ up from the dead.

Luke 24:13-35. Visitors to Israel today see a sign at Latrūn, as they drive to Jerusalem from the Lod airport, pointing to Imwās. This is one identification of the Emmaus of Luke's gospel but unfortunately it is more like fourteen miles from Jerusalem than seven. The medieval Franciscans hit upon modern Al Qubeiba which is the designated "sixty stadia" from the city and more sharply to the northeast. The garrison town of Vespasian called Ammous by Josephus (modern Kaloniye), is a third possibility, though the best textual witness to his mention of it in *Jewish War* places it only thirty stadia from Jerusalem. Exact geographical reference, however, is meaningless to Luke. There is also the question of whether the place name and that of Cleopas (v. 18) crept into the account later.

The story is a model of the story-teller's art. The empty-tomb account (vv. 22f.) and that of the assembled company in Jerusalem (v. 33) have evidently been combined with Emmaus, as a reading from v. 21a to 25 and an examining of the link comprised by vv. 33-35 will show. The last-cited verse contains mention, by way of a flashback, of the primary appearance to Simon (cf. the primitive appearance-account in 1 Cor 15:5.) As in Jn 20:7, Peter in Lk 24:12 did not see Jesus at the tomb. The longer ending of Mk (16:9-20), which is made up of portions of the canonical risen-life accounts, reports the Emmaus story in vv. 12f. Taken all together, the tale reminds us of angels visiting earth in human form (Gn 18:1 and 19:1; Heb 13:2).

The latter part of v. 19 and v. 20 strongly resemble a kerygmatic speech in Ac, while vv. 25-27 conform perfectly to the Lucan theology of glory through suffering. The poignant, "We were hoping . . . ," of v. 21 has been much preached upon, echoing as it does the probable actual state of the dispirited community. Central to the story is the identity of the two in relation to St. Paul's listing of appearances. Since the story is one of a later appearance in Jerusalem rather than an earlier one in Galilee, it seems that they should be identified somehow with the "all the apostles" of 1 Cor 15:7. We would be surer of this if the name Cleopas (Greek for the Jewish Clopas) means a particular apostolic personage.

Luke sets the disciples' recognition of Jesus in the context of a meal (v. 30), using the standard liturgical vocabulary fixed by his time. This joining of the narration of appearances to table fellowship is to be expected and occurs elsewhere (Lk 24:41-42; Ac 10:41; Jn 21:9-14).

In the dialogue on the road, the identification of Jesus as a prophet (v. 19; cf. Dt 18:15) may mean that the narrative derives from earliest christology. That he will "set Israel free" (*lytrousthai*, v. 21) is an idea that will recur in 1 Pet 1:18, commented on above. In Lk it may be a historical reminiscence of the dashed political hopes of some. Vv. 25, 26, and 27 contain the idea of the fulfillment of Scripture found in 1 Cor 15:3f. All in all, the Emmaus story is a remarkable interweaving of Easter traditions made newly meaningful by Lucan theology.

FOURTH SUNDAY OF EASTER (A)

Acts 2:14, 36-41. Peter's "standing up with the Eleven," means taking a stance for purposes of speaking publicly. The numbering of the group exclusive of Peter acknowledges the recent election of Matthias. Today's reading takes for granted the first reading of last week up to v. 28, hence omits the argument that David in Ps 16 must have been speaking of Jesus as God's faithful one who will not be let undergo corruption. It also assumes that Ps 110:1 is speaking of Jesus' heavenly glorification as the Christ, not of any earthly enthronement of a Davidic king (its original sense).

The conclusion Luke has Peter draw from his citation of Joel and the two psalms is that the crucified Jesus is beyond doubt Lord and Messiah, for in what other age has God's spirit been poured out so profusely and who but Jesus has escaped death and corruption? Peter is made to charge his Jerusalem hearers (whom he addresses biblically as "Beth Israel") with the death of Christ, in the phrase, "whom you crucified" (v. 36). This interpretation of Calvary is part of the tradition by this time, as the three synoptic passion narratives demonstrate. Yet Luke uses the charge to connote personal guilt rather than group guilt. The sins of those who were called to be believers had brought on Jesus' death. The response proper to them is repentance and baptism for the forgiveness of their sins, a rite which would bring the gift of the spirit (v. 38). Baptism "in the name of Jesus Christ" (*ibid.*) is the formula Luke is familiar with in his own community. There is no mention of ecstatic behavior as a result of the gift of the spirit as in 1:5; 2:4; 10:44; 19:2-6. Hence it is a misreading of Ac to understand "baptism in the spirit" as if extraordinary behavior such as speaking in tongues were essential to it. Here as in 8:16f. the gift of the spirit (62 times in Ac) does not have such observable effects. In the account of Peter and John at Samaria (8:16f.) the gift of the spirit is described as separable from the rite of baptism in Christ's name.

The result of Peter's preaching—reported as if it were given only fragmentarily ("many other arguments," v. 40)—is mass acceptance of the message and of baptism. By his use of scriptural proofs derived from the Septuagint version Lk establishes that he is not reporting on primitive happenings in Jerusalem, an Aramaic-speaking church. His Peter does not depend on wonders (as at Pentecost) but on careful arguments. Luke in his various sermons is probably following the typical preaching pattern of his age (ca. 90?) It includes an introduction suited to the needs of the hearers, the *kērygma* of Jesus' life, death, and resurrection, stress on the witness function of the disciples, scriptural proof, and an exhortation to repentance. Numerous examples of it are found in chapters 2, 3, 5, 10, and 13 of Ac. In every case there is a legitimation of Jesus' mission by the signs that accompanied it, culminating in the resurrection, and an explanation of his shameful death in terms of the guilt of those who murdered him.

1 Peter 2:20-25. "Putting up with suffering" is identified as the vocation of Christians, household slaves in this case (v. 18). This underlines one of the main objectives of the letter, namely to strengthen the reader's spirit in time of adversity. The latter need not be persecution at imperial hands; petty harassment by local magistrates will do. It is not suffering in itself that is the virtue but "enduring it patiently" (*hypomeneite*, v. 20). Christ's suffering "for you" is provided as the reason for the Christian's calling. The pattern or example (*hypogrammon*, lit., "a child's letter-tracing," v. 21) of the sinless Jesus (v. 22, citing Is 53:9) is put forward as a motive for following in his footsteps. The use of the fourth servant song (Is 52:11—53:11) identifies Christ as the supreme example of the innocent sufferer. Some commentators think this whole passage an extract from a hymn, although the abrupt switch from the second person to the third in v. 21 indicates that a tag-line from a creed (cf. 3:18; 1 Cor 15:3) has been inserted here.

The point of vv. 22f. is that Jesus left his vindication to God, hence unjustly dealt-with slaves should do the same. That Jesus "brought his sins to the cross" (*xylos*, lit. "tree," the gallows of Dt 21:23) may simply mean "bore our sins," in the sense of Is 53:12— "bear," "take away," since the Greek phrasing is identical.

The preposition with the accusative conveys the idea of motion toward. Does the author have some figure of transferred guilt in mind, like that of an offering on an altar or the symbolic deliverance of sins onto a scapegoat? Grammatically, "on" the cross is as justifiable as "to" the cross. "God's will" (v. 24) is the familiar *dikaiosynē*, "righteousness," here a high standard of moral behavior. The "wounds" of v. 25 (from Is 53:5) are actually bruises or stripes, an apt figure for slaves. The main point of the use of the servant song is probably the intimation to sufferers that, just as Christ's wounds were beneficial to many, so their endurance may also have a vicarious quality. The "flock" and "guardians" (v. 25) are coupled in Paul's speech to the elders at Miletus, Ac 20:28. God is described in various places in the LXX as *poimēn* and *episkopos*; 1 Pt so designates Christ. "Your souls" are "yourselves."

John 10:1-10. The first five verses of this reading are the only parable (*paroimia*, v. 6) in the fourth gospel, properly speaking. Even then, it may be understood to have allegorical elements since its follow-up in vv. 7-10 is pure allegory; but without reading the subsequent elaboration back into it, it can stand by itself as a parable. Some scholars (like J. A. T. Robinson) think that two parables have been fused, the first ending at 3*a* with "the keeper opens the gate for him" and the second, which begins at 3*b*, following immediately without benefit of the opening it once had. In the first half the contrast is between the shepherd and the thief (also called a "marauder," [*lēstēs*, v. 1]), in the second half between the shepherd and the "stranger" (*allotrios*, v. 5). This opposition between two characters is standard in the synoptic parables (cf. the Pharisee and the tax collector, Lk 18:9-14; the two builders, Mt 7:24-27). The introduction of a third character, the gatekeeper, is not unusual (cf. the father in the parables of the two sons, Mt 21:28-31 and the prodigal son, Lk 15:11-32). The shepherd figure of Jn is familiar from a number of places in the synoptics (Mt 25:32; Mt 18:12f.; Mt 9:36). At all points in the gospels the descriptions of grazing practice are true to the realities of Palestine. "Calling his own by name" (v. 3) is a phrase for knowing the sheep individually, just as the shepherds of the synoptics are spoken of as solicitous for individual sheep. The gatekeeper of v. 3 appears as (*thyrōras*) in the parable of the waiting servants (Mk 13:34), where he is in a position of trust with respect to the master of the house like that of his relation to the shepherd. Jn's "thief" (v. 1) appears as a housebreaker in Mt 24:43f. and Lk 12:39f., parables of servants waiting for their master, though the element of surprise does not figure in Jn. The latter is interested in the fact that the gatekeeper admits the rightful entrant.

Jn in vv. 1-5 calls on material from a reservoir of tradition similar but not identical to that available to the synoptic authors. He then uses it, characteristically, as a point of departure for his own development. In it, Jesus becomes the gate (*thyra*) and unnamed predecessors (probably the Jewish leadership, a favorite target of Jn) thieves and marauders. The usage is like that of the many Johannine "I am" statements—among them way, truth, life, vine, shepherds. The thief comes to steal, slaughter, and destroy; such is his purpose. Jesus' purpose in coming is that "they might have life . . . to the full" (v. 10). Like all the I-sayings in the fourth gospel, this one may well have had a creedal history in the third person.

The gift is life, a common Johannine theme, in this instance a natural complement to the figure of pasturing.

FIFTH SUNDAY OF EASTER (A)

Acts 6:1-7. The revival of the permanent or lifetime diaconate in the Roman Church has created new interest in that church in the question: "Who were the Seven?" The disciples (a self-designation of Palestinian Jewish Christians, taken over by Lk but never found in Paul) were divided among Greek-speaking Jews (*Hellēnistai*) and Aramaic-speaking Jews (*Hebraioi*). The former were probably settlers in Jerusalem from the diaspora. Widows among them could have been numerous because of the tendency of the aged to gravitate toward the holy city. They would also have been dependent as a class. The daily distribution (*diakonia*) of v. 1 is unlike any Jewish scheme of poor-relief we know of from the times. Extant data tell of the distribution of food on Friday for indigent residents and daily for transients. If these accounts and Luke's are dependable, a period of time is required for some evolution to have taken place.

The term "the Twelve" appears only here (v. 2) in Acts, although it may be deduced from 1:26 and 2:14. 1 Cor 15:3-5 (ca. A.D. 54) is its first occurrence in the New Testament. An assembly is called (cf. 4:23) to solve the inequity of the neglect of preaching by the Twelve to wait on tables. It is not a question of fixing blame but of remedying a situation. Num 27:16ff. in the LXX provides the verbal model—Moses' choice of Joshua, a "man of spirit." Luke requires prudence (*sophia*) as well, understood as administrative ability (v. 4). The passage suggests the requirements for bishops and deacons in 1 Tim 3:7ff. Luke does not use the word *diakonos* but it is fairly inferred from *diakonia* (vv. 1 and 4) and *diakonein* (v. 2). The group seems, from Ac 21:3, to have become known as "the Seven," possibly on a Jewish community model, "The Seven of the Town." It is the community that chooses them (v. 5) but the apostles who install them ritually (v. 6). The latter are seen here as men of prayer, as in 1:14 and 3:1, but also given to preaching and teaching (v. 4). Stephen is singled out for his fullness of faith and the holy spirit, Nicolaus as a convert (i.e., proselyte) of Antioch, hence perhaps the only non-Jew of the Seven (v. 5).

In his passage of conclusion and transition (v. 7), Lk speaks of the growth of the community in terms of Jewish priests, a sign of God's blessing. These were probably the numerous impecunious priests of the twenty-four classes among whom Zechariah was numbered (Lk 1:5), not the high priests whom Lk will identify as enemies of the gospel.

The Greek names of the Seven—Stephen prominent among them—help identify them as Jews from the diaspora. Whenever we encounter them again they are preachers, not servants at table. This means that Lk has used the story to account for a distinct Stephen-party which is provoking the wrath of certain Jews in Jerusalem (v. 15) and elsewhere (11:19f.) Diaspora Jews were also among Stephen's opponents (6:9). The cause of division was evidently a considerable freedom adopted by the Stephen-party with respect to the law (cf. the charges of v. 13), culminating in the acceptance of gentiles in Syrian Antioch (11:19-24). This move is described as winning the approval of the Jerusalem community (v. 22) but in Ac 6:8-15 it resulted in Stephen's being apprehended and stoned to death. Already the interpretation of the law in Jesus' sense, reported in the gospels, is resulting in persecution, not only by the Sanhedrin (6, 12) but by other Christians as well. This division would account for the poor treatment of the Hellenist widows and the separate scheme for their relief. By the time Lk comes on the tradition there has already developed in the community a segregation on the basis of language and ideology.

1 Peter 2:4-9. The writer wishes to support his readers in their persecuted state by reminding them of their splendid vocation as the baptized. He does this through a variety of figures developed in midrashic form (i.e., through recondite elaboration on biblical texts). Having described them as infants (2:2), he proceeds to speak of them as living stones, a holy priesthood, and a people God claims for his own. He is convinced of their elite status and assurance of God's special protection. Verse 4 combines Ps 118:22 (cited in full in v. 7) and Is 28:16, two favorite texts of the early Church (cf. Ac 4:11; Mk 12:10). The first identifies Israel as discarded by the world-powers but nonetheless marvelously exalted by God. The Christians, influenced by what may have been a Jewish messianic reading of this text, saw

Jesus in the place of Israel. The "precious cornerstone in Zion" of the Isaian text is laid in right and justice, not lies or falsehood, and consists of Yahweh's assurance of salvation, this time against the Assyrian threat. "Living stone(s)" in vv. 4 and 5, for Christ and the baptized, is not biblical in origin; it doubtless derives from the Lord's risen status (from the tomb?) and is related to the imagery of Christ as the new temple (cf. Mk 14:58; Jn 2:21) and believers as a similar edifice (cf. 2 Cor 6:16; Eph 2:20), an "edifice of spirit" (v. 5).

They are not only a temple but a priesthood offering spiritual sacrifices—if coupled with Rom 12:1 the "*oblationem rationabilem acceptabilemque*" of the Roman canon (cf. Heb 13:15f.) The author of 1 Pt uses the texts from Ps 118 and Is 28 as if their authors had a personal messiah in mind, which is not the case. He then employs the phrase from Is 8:14, "an obstacle and a stumbling stone," to describe what Jesus will be to those who "refuse obedience to the gospel of God" (4:17). Such is their predestined role, even as others are called by God's foreknowledge to obedience (2:1; cf. 1 Thes 5:9.) Verse 9 is a conflation of Ex 19:6 and Is 43:20f. from the LXX. The praise meted out by 1 Pt is corporate rather than individual and conveys the clear conviction that the baptized have a corporate, priestly function. The "glorious works" of God, his "mighty deeds" of Ac 2:11, are chiefly the raising up of Christ from the dead. God's call out of darkness into light is not only the familiar biblical antithesis of the two, here the eschatological light (cf. Jn 12:35; Rom 13:12; Eph 5:14), but also a probable reference to baptism which would shortly come to be known as *photismos*, "enlightenment" (cf. Heb 6:4; 10:32.)

John 14:1-12. Jesus' discourse after the departure of Judas (13:30f.) is punctuated by questions by Simon Peter (13:36), Thomas (14:5), and Philip (14:8). All act as foils for Jesus in familiar Johannine style. The concern of this part of the discourse is imminent separation (v. 2) which is to be followed by reunion (v. 3). During the separation the disciples will be able to "know God" (v. 7) and do "far greater works" than any Jesus has done (v. 12). One comes to the Father only through Jesus (v. 6). Seeing Jesus is seeing the Father (v. 9). Jesus is in the Father and the Father is in Jesus (v. 11). Here we have a compendium of Johannine "realized eschatology" in which the believer is already in possession of the benefits of the last age. He "sees," "knows," "comes to know," and "recognizes" the reality of the Father through the son. The futurist eschatology of the synoptics is not abandoned in Jn (cf. 14:2f.) but it is subordinated to the present experience of God which "faith in me" (vv. 1, 12) brings. Jesus will again speak of his return to the Father in 16:5, 7, 17 where there is mention of the Paraclete, as there will be in 14:16f. The striking parallels between portions of chs. 15-17 and 14 have convinced many that we have here alternative versions of the last discourse placed in sequence (some would say a different sequence), unedited.

Jesus' departure will be accompanied by his return to the believer through the gift of "another paraclete" (v. 16). Since Jesus is "the way" (v. 6), to know him is to know the way that leads where he goes (v. 4). It is also to see the Father (v. 7) who speaks and works through the Jesus in whom he lives (v. 10).

The many "dwelling places" (*monai*, from *menein*) of v. 2 is related to Jewish belief in compartments or abodes in heaven (cf. 1 Enoch 39:4; 2 Enoch 61:2). Jesus "going" for Jn (v. 2) is always his death and resurrection to his Father's house. This "passion and glorification . . . is the means by which believers are admitted to the heavenly life" (Barrett). Similarly his "coming back" to take his disciples with him (v. 3) means something more in Jn than the synoptic *parousia.*

Verse 10a and 10b will recur in 17:21 and other passages of the prayer of that chapter. Later theology will see "circumincession" here. For Jn there is never a perfect reciprocity of Father and son. The son always depends on the Father and can do nothing apart from him; the Father is in no such dependent condition. He lives in Jesus and accomplishes his works in him (v. 10) but merely as a mode of self-disclosure. Belief in Jesus should come first; failing that, belief in the testimony afforded by his works (cf. 2:11; 5:26; 10:18.) It is always the Father who accomplishes them.

SIXTH SUNDAY OF EASTER (A)

Acts 8:5-8, 14-17. Luke began his story of Stephen's *passio* as if it had been a set of legal proceedings before the Sanhedrin (Ac 6:12) presided over by the high priest (7:1). He ends it as if he knows nothing of procedures in a legal execution by stoning (on which we have detailed information from the Mishnaic tractate *Sanhedrin;* boulders were dropped on the condemned man from a height). What he describes, rather, is the action of an infuriated mob which ends in Stephen's death. He identifies the event as one which triggers "a great persecution of the church in Jerusalem" (8:1) and brings about a psychological change in Saul, not easily believable, from consenting bystander (v. 1) to prosecuting zealot (v. 3).

In today's reading Lk, having left the apostles in Jerusalem to assure continuity, describes the spread of the gospel in terms of the dispersion of all the rest: literally (v. 4), "Here Comes Everybody." The "countryside" of 4:1 is the two provinces named, not the rural districts, for the act of evangelizing is centered on the town of Samaria—probably Sebaste though perhaps Shechem—until v. 25, when there is mention of "villages" on the return journey. The Philip of v. 5 is one of the Seven (cf. 6:5) who preaches to dispersed Hellenists, going "down" (north) from elevated Jerusalem. He reappears at Caesarea as the father of four virgin daughters (21:8), and may have become one of the Twelve in Jn 12:20f., where he brings the Greeks (*Hellēnes*) to see Jesus. The confusion between the two Philips is complete by the time of the erection of the basilica of St. Philip at the site of his martyrdom in Hierapolis, Asia Minor. Parenthetically, the traditional site of Stephen's stoning is marked by the latest of several churches named for him, in the École Biblique complex on the Nablus Road in East Jerusalem.

Philip's preaching is accompanied by visible and audible ("shrieking loudly") wonders—v. 7. The result is eschatological joy (*chara*), and with this familiar Lucan cachet the scene closes. The episode of Simon, the practitioner of magic, intervenes. The narrative thread is resumed at v. 14. Samaria "accepts the word of God" in the New Testament sense that some converts are made there. Apostolic presence, in the persons of Peter and John, sets the seal on Philip's evangelizing efforts, but even the apostles are subordinated to the gift of *pneuma hagion* (v. 15). Here, holy spirit is distinguished from baptism in the name of the Lord Jesus as an additional gift. Its mode of transmission is the imposition (*epithesis*) of hands, a rite which will barely survive in baptism—though it still exists in Tertullian's time (d. after 220) as witnessed in his *De Baptismo*. It will be transferred to what is later called "the sealing" and still later "confirmation."

1 Peter 3:15-18. The context of this reading is the suffering that may come to those of upright life for their very commitment to what is good (cf. vv. 13f.) They have been promised, in the above two verses, that no harm can come to them (cf. Is 50:9; Mt 10:28; 8:31) and told that if their *dikaiosynē* brings on pain their condition is blessed (*makarioi*, v. 14)—the word used in the beatitudes. There is no promise, however, of immunity from physical abuse: vulnerability and the likelihood that its consequences will overtake believers have already been conceded (2:20). It is a person's inner integrity that will be retained through all calamities if he/she remains faithful. Verses 14f. are an adaptation of Is 8:12f., the Asian persecutors now being understood to replace the Assyrians of Isaiah's time and "the Lord, that is, Christ" proposed as the object of blessing rather than

Yahweh. In the christology of 1 Pt Christ is freely called "*Kyrios*," the LXX translation of "Yahweh." The latter it was in early Isaiah who would be Israel's dread, not the fear brought on by the king of Assyria. "Venerate" in v. 16 is literally "acknowledge as holy," as in Is 29:23 and Mt 6:9. Faith and reverence rather than fear are to reside in the Asian Christians' hearts. The reply they should be ready to make is *apologia*, a legal term for defense; the "reason" they give, *logos*. Both terms can have a juridical flavor, conjuring up the interrogations of Ac 25:16 and the account that must be given before God in Rom 14:12. A less formal explanation of one's position is a possibility, however. Rabbi Eleazar in *The Sayings of the Fathers* (2:18) similarly proposes that students of the Law be able to answer an Epicurean, typical of pagan philosophers. The Christian's response is to be such in tone (the "respect" of v. 16 being toward God rather than the challenger) that the libelous will be shamed. If Providence has suffering in store, it should at least be unmerited by evil deeds.

John 14:15-21.   Dodd finds in the "asking in my name" of vv. 13f. immediately preceding a similarity to the synoptic tradition of two or three "gathered in my name." When they ask for anything it will be granted by the Father (cf. Mt 18:19f.) An important difference is that in Jn prayer is addressed to Christ, who will grant what is asked ("I will do," v. 14), rather than to the Father as in Mt (but cf. Lk 24:49.) In today's reading from Jn, the best gift of the Father is "another paraclete" (v. 16), to be given on condition of love and obedience to Christ's commandments (v. 15). The "intercessor" of 1 Jn 2:1, namely Jesus Christ, renders "*paraklētos*." At first it seems that this counselor of Jn 14 will be bestowed in Christ's absence, as with the gifts of holy spirit (Lk 12:12) and words (lit., "a mouth") and wisdom (Lk 21:15), for purposes of giving witness. But v. 18 seems to equate the paraclete's "remaining" and "being with you" (v. 17) with Jesus' coming (v. 18). The text does not say "coming again," however, only "*erchomai*" without "*pain*." The injunction to love Jesus and keep his commandments occurs three times in 14:15, 21, 23f. (in the last-cited verse, "words"). Some commentators see a threefold presence in those who love and obey: Paraclete/Spirit (vv. 16f.), Jesus (vv. 18-21), and the Father (v. 23). Yet the pattern is not perfect, for verse 23 speaks of a presence of both the Father and Jesus. It has been conjectured that the three modes of divine presence stem from three different stages of the Johannine tradition, here woven together. In such a supposition, "often the sayings about God's presence through and in the Paraclete are thought to be the latest [stage]" (Brown).

Love for Jesus is not a common NT theme. It occurs largely but not exclusively in the Johannine writings (cf. Eph 6:24; 1 Cor 16:22; 1 Pt 1:8). It has been suggested that, as Jesus comes to be seen in a covenant relation with believers, so he is portrayed as demanding exclusive love for himself after the model of the Sinai covenant (Dt 6:5). Such love and obedience toward him as was asked by Israel's God will bring the gift of a mysterious figure (*paraklētos*; in the Old Latin and Vulgate versions *advocatus* and *consolator* respectively) who is variously witness (Jn 15:26), instructor (14:26), encouraging friend (16:6f.), guide (16:13), and prover of the world wrong (16:8-11). The functions of such a one derive from the angelology of the late biblical and intertestamental periods. Only in the Qumrân literature is the title "spirit of truth" found in the pre-Christian period (*Community Rule* [*Manual of Discipline*], 1QS iv, 23-24), where it denotes either an angel or a way of life. Some lines above this we read: "The nature of all the children of men is ruled by these [two spirits] . . . . Truth abhors the works of falsehood and falsehood all the ways of truth." Jn follows the standard Jewish usages of having two figures in a complementary relation, the second of whom completes the work of the first; the transmission of the spirit of the main figure of these two through the second one; and a personal, angelic spirit who leads others and guides them to truth as contrasted with an opposing spirit who leads to darkness and destruction. All these images Jn puts in the service of the idea of the paraclete, who stands for the personal presence of Jesus in the Christian while Jesus is with the Father.

The idea of being "orphaned" (v. 18) is found in rabbinic writings with respect to disciples at the death of their teachers.

Vv. 15-17 and 18-21 can be shown to contain two sets of parallel features, as between the coming and remaining of the paraclete and the coming and remaining of Jesus (both have the necessary conditions: the recognition of this spirit and Jesus by the disciples and the failure of the world to recognize them; the resultant "being within" the disciples of the spirit and Jesus). The same features occur in 1 Jn 3 at vv. 2, 15-17, 23-24. The phrases "a little while" (v. 19) and "On that day" (v. 20) do not fit exactly either the parousia or Christ's resurrection appearances. The Johannine outlook here stresses the continued, intimate presence of Christ to the believing Christian "to the end of time" (*eis ton aiōna*, v. 16) in a love on Christ's part that is self-revealing (v. 21).

ASCENSION (A)
(Thursday after Sixth Sunday of Easter)

Acts 1:1-11. Lk 1:1-4 is a preface to Lk-Ac in its entirety, addressed to the unidentified, highly placed (*"kratiste"*) Theophilus. Ac 1:1-5 is a preface to this book only, which reviews certain materials found in Lk 22. Among these are Jesus' being taken up to heaven (v. 2; cf. Lk 22:51); his appearing to "the apostles" over the course of forty days (v. 3; cf. Lk 22:15f., 30f., 36); his suffering (*to pathein*, v. 3) of which he spoke in Lk 22:25ff. and 44-47; and his meeting (eating) with his disciples (v. 4; cf. Lk 22:41-43) at which time he told them not to leave Jerusalem (v. 4; cf. Lk 22:49). The order of events in the preface to Ac is obviously different but this does not alter or minimize their importance, namely as links between Lk's "first account" (*prōton logon*, Ac 1:1) and his second. Jesus' life, death, and glorification prepare for his Father's promise (Lk 22:49; Ac 1:4f) to be sent down: "power from on high" (Lk) or "being baptized with holy spirit" which will bring "power" (Ac). The detail of forty days (v. 3) does not appear in Lk. This sacred space of time (cf. Gn 7:12; 8:6; Ex 24:18; 1 Kgs 19:8) gives ample room for the demonstration "in many convincing ways" (v. 3) of his state as living (*zōnta*). Lk's gospel, conversely, seems to describe Jesus as leaving the Eleven after having blessed them (24:51) on the evening of the day he was raised up. (Cf. vv. 9, 13, 36, 50 for indications of the sequence.) The difference is of no consequence; least of all is it to be settled by recourse to a theory of Jesus' earthly visitations from his new home in heaven. The two things being affirmed are the reality of his being taken from his friends into glory and his conversations with them about God's reign (v. 4), which for Lk will begin with the parousia. For him the life of the spirit-directed church is a separate matter. The affirmations against gnostic docetism (Lk 24:43; Ac 10:41) were probably later developments. "All that Jesus did and taught" (v. 1) describes Jesus' earthly life, while the risen-life instruction (lit., "command," from *enteilamenos*) he gave the chosen apostles (v. 2) corresponds to Lk 24:44. It is in their chosenness "through the holy spirit" (v. 2) that they have been given authority to teach in the ways that will follow in Ac.

Luke's word for Jesus' being taken up in v. 2 (*anelēmphthē*) has already been used in its noun form in his gospel (9:51) for the same purpose. It seems to derive from the LXX of 2 Kgs. 2:11 where Elijah—for Lk, a type of Christ—is taken up in a chariot of fire.

Only in Mk 13:11 and its parallel in Mt (not Lk, interestingly) does Jesus speak of the spirit in the synoptics. In Ac 1:5 and again in

11:16, a saying attributed to John the Baptizer is put on Jesus' lips (Mt 3:11; Lk 3:16). Lk will later have Paul make the same distinction in Ephesus between the water-baptism of John and the spirit-baptism of Jesus (Ac 19:1-6) as is made in v. 5.

The apostles' query about when Israel will have the *basileia* restored to it (v. 6) is answered in terms of undivulgeable mystery (v. 7) and missionary command (v. 8). Mk 13:32 (par. Mt 24:36) contains a *logion* of Jesus like that of v. 7 which Lk had not used in his gospel, saving it for here. It is calculated to relieve disappointment in the Christian community over the non-realization of the parousial hope (cf. 2 Pt 3:3ff.) By Lk's time the question is not even to be raised; a new relationship to the world has been arrived at: life in the holy community. The notion of witnessing to Jesus, viz., to his resurrection, is common throughout Ac. Jesus' sending of the apostles "to the ends of the earth" (v. 8) will only mean getting Paul as far as Rome in this book, but it is at least a divine sanction on his mission. Peter and John travel as far as Samaria.

There is no final blessing by Jesus in Ac as in Lk 24:50 (cf. Sir 50:20f.) He is taken up swiftly in the apostles' sight (v. 9), a detail which constitutes them witnesses of the ascension. Livy tells of Romulus' being swept up in a cloud, while the intertestamental book of Enoch has that prophet say the same of himself. The two men in white (v. 10) resemble those in Lk's empty-tomb account (24:4). They administer a rebuke intended for the whole church. All expectation of the imminent return of Jesus is to be reprobated. It is a reality of the future but one that has about it no precise connotation of time.

Ephesians 1:17-23.   Eph, after its initial greeting, begins with a blessing of God (*Eulogētos ho theos*, v. 3) in vv. 3-14—the traditional Jewish *berakah*—and moves on to a thanksgiving in vv. 15-23 (*eucharistōn*, v. 16). The anonymous author, usually known as "the Ephesian continuator," doubtless includes both forms because such was Paul's practice at various times. The technique, while redundant, is nonetheless to be found in Dn 2:20 and 23. The hope expressed in the present passage is that the wisdom bestowed on Gentile Christians (v. 9) may be effectively received by them (v. 17). A heritage has been given, the wealth of which (v. 18) is comprised of wisdom and understanding (v. 9). This inheritance (v. 14) is not yet fully given but exists at present by way of pledge or first payment (*arrabōn*), to be rendered in its entirety when the full redemption (*apolytrōsis*) of God's personal possession—his people (cf. 1 Pt 2:9)—has been bestowed. Such time will be after the parousia. The acceptance of the inheritance by believers is required if it is to be a completed reality. That Christians may know the hope to which they are called, the "eyes of their hearts" must be enlightened (v. 18). God's power in the believer is likened to the strength he showed in Christ when raising him from the dead and seating him at God's right hand (v. 20). The importance of verse 20 is that it distinguishes between the resurrection and the subsequent exaltation of Christ, something that Paul does not do. He thinks in terms of a single act of glorification while Lk-Ac resembles Eph in its division of the mystery into two episodes.

Mention of the Ephesians' faith (v. 15) is a Pauline touch, but this theological treatise in epistolary form does not much resemble the communication of someone who lived among the recipients for quite a while. Paul knew this congregation as well as any and did not need to learn of its faith by hearsay.

The anti-gnostic or anti-angelic-hierarchy tone of Colossians is caught in vv. 21-23 and again in 6:12. Christ is high above the choirs of angels. Four of the traditional intertestamental nine are here named: *archai, exousiai, dynameis*, and *kyriotētes* (Col 1:16 has "thrones" in place of "virtues," *dynameis*). The headship of Christ here (vv. 22f.) is over his body, the church, whereas in 1:10 it had been over all things in the heavens and on earth, and over principalities and powers in Col 2:10. The important declaration of faith in Christ (as in Col 2:9) is that he has been made the *plēroma* of him who fulfills everything in the universe, namely God. Col says that in Christ the *plēroma* of God dwells in bodily form. Both writers mean to challenge all gnostic and angelic hierarchies that lay claim to *plēroma* status and put in their place the ascended, exalted Christ and him alone.

Matthew 28:16-20. This concluding section of Mt with its command to make disciples of all the nations (a proper ending such as no other gospel has), is a departure from the description of Jesus' ministry to Israel attributed to him in 15:24. The evangelist's pattern for Christ's "all authority" (v. 18) is no doubt the authority given to "one like a son of man" in Dn 7:14, LXX: *kai edothē autōi exousia, kai panta ta ethnē tēs gēs kata genē kai pasa doxa . . . .* Mt has used an earlier part of the Daniel text in 26:64. The concluding vision of the book of Isaiah cannot be far from his mind; in it, God's glory shall be proclaimed to the nations (cf. Is 66:19) and Israel's brothers from all the nations (v. 20) shall be brought as an offering to the Lord. The "in" of v. 19 is literally "into" (*eis*), connoting entrance into the messianic community understood as fellowship with the Father and the son and the holy spirit. Mt has spoken only of the kingship of the son of man and the Father's glory so far (16:27f.) In adding the holy spirit he follows a lead already given him by Paul in 1 Cor 12:4-6 and 2 Cor 13:14 (used in the new *Ordo Missae*), later to be found in

1 Pt 1:2. Mt is probably citing a baptismal formula from his Palestinian churches. It is, in any case, found again in the first-century *Didachē* (7), where "running water" is prescribed. The phrase "to the end of the *aiōn*" (v. 20), used also in Mt 13:39 and 40 and 24:3, is of some help in establishing the primitive character of the tradition on which it is based.

SEVENTH SUNDAY OF EASTER (A)

Acts 1:12-14. Zech 14:4 describes the feet of the Lord as resting upon the Mount of Olives on the day of a mighty battle between Jerusalem and all the nations. *Ho kyrios* (v. 1, LXX) is here taken to be Jesus rather than YHWH. A sabbath's journey, the distance a Jew might travel without breaking the commandment to stay at home on that day (Ex 16:29), was reckoned at 2000 ells or 960 yards, somewhat over the athlete's 880 or half-mile. The "Eleven and the rest of the company" had been led out near Bethany (Lk 24:50) by Jesus to witness his being taken up into heaven, but that town's modern site is a couple of miles beyond Olivet. Luke is unconcerned here, as elsewhere, with a topography he does not know.

Having made his point calmly about possible idle speculation concerning the parousia (v. 11), he returns the Eleven—whom he names—to the city and the upstairs room (*hyperōion*) of their regular stay. The word is new. The place may be the upstairs room (*anagaion*) of Lk 22:12. Lk 24:53 brings them back to the temple (cf. Ac 2:46) but this does not seem sufficient reason to locate the *hyperōion* there. The list of disciples is not identical in order with that of Lk 6:4-16; the three groups of four remain, but in different sequences in the first two cases, while Judas Iscariot is missing from the last. "The women" of Lk 24:10 were three who are named plus "the other women"; in 8:3 Susanna appears but not Mary the mother of James. Mk 6:3 names James, Joses, Judas, and Simon as Jesus' brothers. These, together with Jesus' mother, give us a sizeable nucleus, especially if the men's wives are included. Such was the company that devoted itself steadfastly to prayer "together" (*homothymadon*, a favorite Lucan adverb for acting in concert). Luke is trying to identify the earliest congregation—probably made up of women of means (cf. Lk 8:3) and Jesus' more plebeian family members.

1 Peter 4:13-16. This letter has brought home to its readers the idea that the Christian calling is one of suffering after the example of

Christ (2:21), and that to have suffered in the flesh like him is to have broken with sin (4:1). Today's passage is a return to that theme. To suffer is to have cause for present rejoicing, just as at the revelation which his parousia will be (*apokalypsis*) there will be reason to rejoice anew. Cf. Rom 8:17; 2 Tim 2:11, for the same sentiment, a commonplace in NT writings. Verse 14 is reminiscent of Mt 5:11 and uses the same word, *makarioi*, to describe the happiness of those insulted for the sake (lit., "name") of Christ. "The spirit of the Father will be speaking in you" was Jesus' word to those handed over to authority (Mt 10:20). Stephen, too, "filled with the holy spirit . . . saw the glory of God" (Ac 7:55). The spirit resting on the Christian here (v. 14) is "the glory" of the OT (as in Ex 33:9f.). The God who comes now will be given to sufferers in his fullness at the end.

The shift to vv. 15f. is puzzling in its harshness. The point made seems to be that suffering for being a *Christianos* (the word occurs only in Acts 11:26 and 26:28) is noble, whereas a Christian's suffering for his sins is something else again. The list of heinous crimes seems to be a stock one—more rhetorical than actual as regards the community members in question. If there is a practical lesson to be learned it is that believers long adept at crying "foul" need to be sure that none of their suffering is fair.

John 17:1-11. Some scholars (notably Käsemann) see in the prayer of Jesus of chapter 17 the climax of the final discourse, an epilogue to his public life provided by the evangelist to match the prologue. Thus, "a glory I had with you before the world began" (17:5) speaks to the "glory of an only Son" which "we have seen" of 1:14. The prayer of Christ, which is the form this chapter takes, is a proclamation and a thanksgiving, not a petition. Jesus earlier uttered a *berakah* (*eucharistia*) "for the sake of the crowd," for "I know that you always hear me" (Jn 11:42). The prayer of chapter 17 is at once a concluding testament and a farewell speech—like Moses' song and blessing on the tribes (Dt 32 and 33), the Testaments of the Twelve Patriarchs, and Paul's charge to the elders of Ephesus at Miletus (Ac 20). "The speaker is not a needy petitioner," Käsemann writes, "but the divine revealer and therefore the prayer moves over into being an address, admonition, consolation, and prophecy." Later in the chapter Jesus will pray for his disciples and for all believers. In the early portion he makes a proclamation of his fidelity to his charge: "I have . . . finished the work you gave me to do" (v. 4), "I have made your name known" (v. 6), "I entrusted to them the message you entrusted to me" (v. 8). The Johannine Christ has been obedient to his Father in sharing a knowledge of the Father's glory. His obedience has been this glory incarnated and made manifest. The result of his embassy will be eternal life to believers (*aiōnios zōē*, v. 3; the life proper to the final *aiōn*) and a resumption of glory at his Father's side (*ibid.*) Heavenly glory has broken in upon men with Jesus' teaching.

As Jesus prepares to return to the realm from which he came, men are invited, in their sphere, to pass from death to life. *Gnōsis* is their means of doing this (cf. Wis 15:3), a knowledge of the only true God and him whom he has sent (v. 3). Having received the entrusted message (v. 8), they continue to have the presence of Christ. The message is the Father's possession (v. 10); believers in it are likewise his possession (v. 9); their belief in the message contributes to Jesus' glory: "It is in them that I have been glorified" (v. 10). He stakes out a portion of "the world," which by definition is *not* his Father's realm, as a place that becomes such by the very presence of believers in it (v. 11*a*). As Jesus comes to his Father he leaves a portion of the Father's glory behind: the community of faith.

The differences between Jn's conception of Jesus' person and mission and that of the synoptics is clear. For them he is a person of earth exalted to God's right hand by his obedience to his calling. For John he is a visitor from above who goes back to where he was before to enjoy the (now augmented) glory that was his.

PENTECOST (A)

Acts 2:1-11. Those who are gathered in one place are "all," in the Greek text—the one hundred and twenty of 1:15. They assemble on the Jewish feast of Weeks, Shabhuoth, which comes at the completion of seven weeks, "beginning with the day after the sabbath of the wave-offering sheaf of Passover" (Lv 23:15f.; cf. Dt 16:9-12.) This makes it the fiftieth day: in Greek, *pentēkostēs*. The noise heard by the gathering resembles that of a driving wind (*pnoēs*, cognate with *pneuma*). All in the "house" hear it. Whatever the sizeable building indicated here may be it is probably not the temple, for which Luke always uses a proper word. The parted, fiery tongues (or "tons of fire," in the reading provided by a child in an early Corita print) appear in the intertestamental Enoch at 14:8-15 and 71:5. There, however, they convey divinity without connoting differences of language. Individual flames rest on the believers (v. 3), filling each of them with holy spirit (v. 4). Their expression in speech is solemn or inspired, not ecstatic (*apophtheggesthai*, v. 4); the "other" tongues (*heteroi*) are foreign rather than various, as *dialektos* in v. 8 will show. The utterance the disciples begin to engage in is proclamation (*lalein*) rather than conversation or ordinary discourse. There is no indication of ecstatic spirit-language. Such speech would mean nothing to hearers who were not yet believers and hence would defeat the purpose.

Authorities differ on whether the Jews "staying in Jerusalem" (v. 5) were pilgrims (Billerbeck) or regular residents (Haenchen). A multi-lingual population from the diaspora of both Jews and proselytes (cf. v. 10) is indicated, whichever the case. They are attracted by "the sound" (*phonē*, v. 6), but whether this is the *ēchos* caused by the wind of v. 2 or the diverse speech of the assembly of believers it is impossible to say.

Confusion and utter amazement are the reactions (vv. 6f.) of the crowd to the marvel of Galilean Jews speaking in the variety of languages listed (vv. 8ff.). The author inserts their query, beginning at v. 7, as a means of conveying the wonder that was taking place. He is not interested in an exact analysis of the linguistic occurrence, just as throughout he is creating the mood of the spirit's visitation rather than writing a documentary. Yet one point that he wishes to convey is that the disciples are not speaking a spirit-language which all could follow. The marvel consists in the variety of languages spoken, all of them comprehensible to the hearers.

The Medes and the Elamites (v. 10) were a historical memory by the time of the writing so they must have been borrowed from the LXX to convey the idea of remote distances. If Judea is removed from v. 9, twelve regions remain in vv. 9-10. These undoubtedly corresponded to the signs of the zodiac, as Cumont's researches (1909) showed. In such a scheme, Persia was *aries*, Syria *capra*, etc., (cf. Dn 8:20f.) Lk has rendered Persia as Parthia, a military threat that was on everyone's lips in his day. Aquarius was Egypt. Each country named possessed a Jewish population. Missing from the list in Ac are Armenia (unless Pontus is meant in its place) and Hellas-Ionia. Luke makes up his twelve—Libya Cyrenaica is eleventh—by adding Phrygia and Pamphylia, provinces of Asia Minor. The "Cretans and Arabs" (v. 11) fall outside the zodiacal scheme of twelve and, like "Judea," are a later addition. Lk's ordering is presumably calculated. It begins with the specter of Parthia and ends in Rome (Italy=*scorpio*), where his book will also conclude. A reason for various inclusions may be that Aquila and Priscilla came from Pontus (Ac 18:2), Apollos from Egypt (18:4), and Lucius from Cyrene (13:1) along with various unnamed others (11:20). In any event, the author of Acts wants to make it clear that the spread of the gospel to far-flung parts existed germinally on Pentecost day through the Jews and proselytes assembled in Jerusalem. We should not look for a Gentile witness here. That is to be inaugurated, for Lk, with the conversion of the household of Cornelius in Ac 10:45.

The disciples celebrated in speech God's marvels (*ta megaleia*,

v. 11), a generic term which Peter will spell out in his description of the career and glorification of Jesus immediately following.

1 Corinthians 12:3-7, 12-13. The context of the earliest and briefest of creedal statements, "Jesus is Lord" (v. 3*b*), is a discussion by Paul of spiritual gifts (v. 1). The chief *pneumatikon* has been the progress made by Corinthian Gentile Christians from their worship of mute idols to that of the living God through Christ. The ability to proclaim Jesus' lordship is a gift of the spirit; nothing else will adequately account for it. In what circumstances might Christians declare him accursed (*anathema*, v. 3*a*)? These are hard to conceive. Paul may simply need a balance for his contention that faith in Jesus expressed by ecstatic utterance is a work of the spirit. Some have thought that he had in mind the weakness of Christians hailed before civil or synagogue authority. If these were to yield to pressure and say "Cursed be Jesus!" as commanded, this could not be an utterance of the spirit. Again, according to others, if frenzied speech in the community—the "tongues" of 13:8 about which the entire discussion of chapter 14 is concerned—should result in such a contradictory utterance, Paul is holding here that it is to be judged immediately by its content. The statement is false, hence the spirit of God can not be its author.

At no time does Paul deny the reality of ecstatic speech or behavior. He assumes it, simply wishing to provide norms for the discernment of claims made for the spirit. Gifts differ (*charismata*, v. 4); so do ministries (*diakoniai*, v. 5) and works (*energēmata*, v. 6). They are all the doing of the same spirit. A manifestation of the spirit to an individual is always made with the same purpose, namely mutual profit or "the common good." Scholastic language will later speak of such gifts as *gratiae gratis datae* meaning freely given— church offices, for example—for the purpose of further transmission of the divine gift. Paul judges all such endowments as personal but communal in God's design. He is rejecting strongly the idea that God could act in such a way for the benefit of the individual only. This brief passage provides the principle which he will specify at length later: while each member of the church has his gift and none is excluded, none has received his for private use but for the good of all. As Paul will make clear in chapter 14, any contest between tongues and teaching is to be settled in favor of the latter. *Propheteia* is demonstrably in the common interest; *glōssai* may or may not be. The one thing that can be clearly shown about the latter is that they are a gift to the individual. Hence any speaking in tongues must yield to an intelligible exposition of its meaning.

John 20:19-23. See pp. 70f.

TRINITY SUNDAY (A)

(First Sunday after Pentecost)

Exodus 34:4-6, 8-9. Martin Noth reconstructs the original J (Yahwist) narrative as follows: chapter 19, then some part of 24:12-15*a* according to which Moses was summoned up the mountain, followed immediately by chapter 34 with its reference to the broken tablets (v. 1). The latter verse was inserted to take into account Moses' wrathful response to the golden calf episode (32:19). This chapter with its religious laws is very explicit about the terms of the covenant YHWH makes with his people (34:10, 17). Only in appearance is it concerned with covenant-renewal. Moses, summoned up the mountain to receive the stone tablets on which the Lord had written (24:12ff.), makes the ascent in chapter 34 armed with two new tablets which he had cut (34:4). Yahweh has announced that he will write on them (v. 1) and has told Moses to "get ready for tomorrow" (v. 2), probably by some cultic preparation like that described in 19:10f. The mountain is to be free of anyone but Moses, including flocks and herds (v. 3). The ritual sacredness (i.e., separateness) of the mountain is to be strictly preserved.

Moses makes his way to the top as instructed in v. 2 and YHWH descends in a cloud, standing next to him. It is not easy to determine whether the speaker in vv. 5-7 is Moses or the Lord. In whichever case, the sacred name of YHWH is proclaimed and he is celebrated for his mercy and justice in stereotyped phrases (cf. Ps 103:8f.; Ex 20:5.) It is to be noted that the Lord's "passing before" Moses and calling out to him from a cloud (v. 6) is suspect as authentic J material, being closer to the less anthropomorphic 33:18-23. Verse 8 describes the natural, awestruck reaction of Moses to the Lord's passing by. The purpose of the account of the theophany is to underscore the common lot of YHWH and Israel despite the latter's sins (v. 9). Moses sets the condition: "If I find favor with you." His function is mediatory. The presence of the Lord effected by the covenant with Israel is not distant: "Do come along in our company . . . Receive us as your own."

The Vulgate, from which the lectionary is taken, has "Dominator, Domine Deus" at v. 6 for the Hebrew "Yahweh, Yahweh El." One can only suppose that this verbal coincidence accounts for the use of the passage on Trinity Sunday.

2 Corinthians 13:11-13. Chapters 10-13 of this epistle are as severe a polemic against anyone as Paul indulges in, with the strictures they contain against the "super apostles" (11:5). Whether 13:11-13 is a conclusion to an independent letter (the epistle written "with copious tears" of 2:4) or concludes the one letter written in several different moods (1-7; 8, 9; 10-13), these three verses are an unmistakable Pauline valedictory. They contain a charge to the Corinthians to mend their ways (*katartizesthe*, lit. "set in order"), to provide mutual encouragement, to think harmoniously, and to live in peace (v. 11). The reward of such behavior will be a dwelling with them of the God of love and peace (*ibid.*) The holy kiss (*philēma*) of v. 12 is the ordinary Eastern embrace, not the mouth-to-mouth kiss of the West. It is, at the same time, the model of the restored exchange of peace in the Roman liturgy (*eirēneuete*, v. 11). The "holy ones" or "saints" of v. 12 are ordinary believers—standard NT usage.

Paul's farewell culminates in a triadic invocation in which *charis* is connected with the Lord Jesus Christ, *agapē* with God, and *koinōnia* with the Holy Spirit. Is the threefold usage conscious with Paul? Undoubtedly it is. Does he have three gifts in search of tutelary patrons, like Pirandello's characters in search of an author? It is much more likely that he is carried on from the mention of Christ as *Kyrios* to the *Theos* from whom the Lord comes and then to the *hagion pneuma* without whom nothing in the order of grace is accomplished. All three are indiscriminately tied to the three gifts. There is, however, a sense in which God is the author of selfless *love* which he shares through the *grace* of his deed in Christ, the result for believers being a *fellowship* in the Holy Spirit.

John 3:16-18. This brief segment of the Johannine kerygma centers on God's son as the eschatological revealer—the one sent by the Father not for the condemnation of the world but, because of his great love for it, its salvation. The use of the first person does not occur here or in the conclusion of the discourse (vv. 31-36), unlike the usage in the solemn declarations of 5:19, 24, 25. The absence of the phrase "I am," found in all the other great discourses, does not however mean that John is not presenting a revelation of God by the son. The evangelist's "We are testifying to what we have seen" (3:11), is his way of identifying himself completely with the testimony of the eschatological revealer about what goes on in heaven. He has "transposed it into his testimony as preacher" (Schnackenburg). The question whether Christ or the evangelist is the speaker would be falsely put. The latter's vocabulary of "seeing," "knowing," and "testifying" indicates that what Christ has revealed he, John, transmits unaltered.

Verse 16 sums up the whole message of redemption in memorable form. 1 Jn 4:9f. will repeat it, with the added note of Christ's uniqueness as son supplied by the Greek word order. The giving of v. 16 is the sending of v. 17, not the delivering over (*paradidomi*) of the passion account (cf. Jn 18:30, 35, 36; 19:11, 16).

The purpose of the giving is belief unto eternal life, not rejection unto death (*apolētai*, lit. "destruction," "ruin"). The "world" of v. 16 is the world of mankind separated from God and in need, which will divide itself by its response to God's revealer into an inimical "world" and a community of salvation. *Krisis*—adverse judgment, condemnation—is not what God intends in sending his son. Lack of faith in him will result in it, but what God has in mind is that the world may be saved through him (v. 17). The life and death may be literal life and death for John in the manner of the Hebrew Bible, just as condemnation and rescue are literally that. The believer escapes condemnation; the unbeliever is already (*ēdē*) condemned by the fact of his unbelief. He should have committed himself over to God's only son (*eis to onoma*). Instead, judgment overtakes him here and now in an eschaton that has arrived.

John's basic scheme of salvation is binitarian rather than trinitarian. He is familiar with a begetting spirit (v. 8), who in a subsequent passage will be seen as an enveloping light (v. 20) and truth (v. 21). His great concern, however, is with a son who reveals the Father in an invitation to belief. The invitation can only be accepted if an unseen *pneuma* is let blow where it will (v. 8). In such case, spirit will beget spirit (v. 6). The alternative is a begetting of flesh by flesh, which means world, condemnation.

The spurious "Johannine comma" of 1 Jn 5:7, a 3d-c. Latin interpolation of the African church and then the Spanish, identified the three witnesses in heaven as "Father, word, and spirit," a needless explicitation taking its lead from the threefold witness of "spirit, water, and blood." The interpreters and copyists of the patristic age were unwise not to let well enough alone. All three witnesses are, in effect, set aside by 1 Jn as human testimony inferior to God's much greater testimony on his son's behalf: the testimony possessed in the heart by the fact of belief. If Father, word, and spirit are witnesses there is nothing left to witness *to*. The Johannine triad is much more subtle—and much more clearly a dyad.

CORPUS CHRISTI (A)

(Sunday after Trinity Sunday)

Deuteronomy 8:2-3, 14-16. "Deuteronomy" takes its name from Dt 17:18 where the Greek word renders the Hebrew phrase, "a copy of this law." It is cast in the form of three addresses given by Moses on the plains of Moab (1:1—4:43; 4:44—28:68; 29:1—30:20), followed by a series of appendices in chapters 31—34. He begins to speak "on the first day of the eleventh month" (1:3) and dies on Mt. Nebo (34:4). A thirty-day period of mourning follows (34:8). By the tenth day of the first month the Israelites under Joshua are camped near Jericho (Jos 4:19). This works out to a forty-day period for Moses' discourse. The book probably emanated from priestly circles in the north rather than Jerusalem and under the influence of 8th-century prophets like Hosea and Jeremiah. Critical scholarship relates the book to the reform of King Josiah in 621. The book is much more likely to have been the cause of such a reform than the result (cf. the tradition of the discovery of the "book of the law" in 2 Kgs 22—23, taken by many to be Dt 12—26, 28, but possibly even Dt 4:44—30:20.) Linguistically Dt has affinities with the E stratum of the first four books of the Torah.

Chapter 8, from which this reading is taken, is central to the book. It names obedience to God as the condition of Israel's prosperity and warns against idolatry as the path to ruin: "It is the Lord your God who gives you the power to acquire wealth . . . But if you forget [him], and follow other gods . . . you will perish utterly" (vv. 18f.) Today's reading has Moses reminding Israel of the Lord's protective care during the forty years of desert journeying and his testing of the people's intent to remain obedient by the afflictions he has sent (v. 2). They are reminded of the manna (cf. Ex 16:15, where a popular etymology renders *man hu* by "What is this?", *man* doing double duty as the late Aramaic "what?" and "manna"). The mysterious "food unknown to your fathers" (Dt 8:3) is the sweet, sticky sap of a tree (the Arabic *Tarfa*, tamarisk?) which has passed through the bodies of insects. The point the Deuteronomist wishes to make is that a contemporary of his who is too sophisticated to revert to idol-worship as in desert days may credit himself with his own achievements and thereby "promote himself to the divine vacancy" (Henton Davies).

The sense of the antithesis "bread alone" and "every word that comes from the mouth of the Lord" is not material vs. spiritual—the interpretation generally put upon it, especially since its attribution to Jesus (Mt 4:4; cf. Lk 4:4)—so much as it is between one kind of sustenance and another that is more lasting. If the latter is accepted, namely God's words of command, then every benefit of life both spiritual and material will come to Israel.

Matthew has Jesus quoting Dt accurately according to sense, for the intent of the temptation narrative is to show that he counsels living trustfully by God's word as did the levitical preacher. This, presumably, Israel failed to do in its time of temptation.

The typology of manna for the eucharist on the feast of Corpus Christi should be clear. The fourth evangelist employed it with respect to the person of Christ (cf. Jn 6:48ff. and see commentary below).

The Roman liturgy uses the manna/eucharist typology in the familiar antiphon, "Panem de caelo praestitisti eis" (from Wis 16:20, where the Vulgate has "illis"). Unfortunately the isolation of the manna-theme in this truncated reading (returned to in v. 16) obscures the central point of the chapter: the very richness of Canaan, with its potential for agriculture (v. 8) and its iron and copper (v. 9), will provide occasion for the self-delusion that says, "It is my own power and the strength of my own hand that has obtained for me this wealth" (v. 17). The editing of this pericope is a reminder of how unbiblical it can be to preach about bread from heaven as a type of providential care without reference to the idolatry of self latent in certain economic patterns. The omitted portion is important for the meaning of the whole.

1 Corinthians 10:16-17. St. Paul is counseling his formerly pagan Corinthian Christians to be wary of trafficking with demons (cf. Dt 32:17) in eating meats sacrificed to idols (vv. 14, 19-21). Such is the context of his statement that participating in the cup and in the bread means sharing in Christ's body and blood. A *koinōnia* with those whom the food represents—whether Christ or demons—is taken for granted; this is the assumption which underlies his argument. The union with Christ which Paul claims for participants in the eschatological meal is more than a merely moral one; it is metaphysical or mystical-real. "Cup of blessing" (*to potērion tēs eulogias*) is a technical term found in Jewish sources for the cup of wine drunk at the end of a meal to close it formally (cf. 11:25.) The blessing is a thanksgiving or grace addressed to God, similar in wording to the prayer spoken at the offering of the wine in the new *Ordo Missae*. The "sharing" of v. 16 is not meant to be in the blood and in the body only. It is also a common participation among those who drink and eat. Their sharing in the one Lord is at the same time a sharing with each other.

The order cup-bread rather than the more familiar bread-cup of the synoptics (the problems of Lk 22:17-20 are special) is not significant. Paul is not recording a liturgy here but framing a theological argument. He wants the bread/body symbolism to come in second place as a lead into his use of the one *artos* (v. 17) to illustrate the fact that we, "many as we are" (*hoi polloi esmen*), are all (*pantes*) "one body" (*hen sōma*). By the shared body (*sōmatos*, v. 16) of Christ is probably meant the church (cf. 1 Cor 12:27; Rom 12:5.) The specification, "in the body of his flesh" of Col 1:22 (NAB, "his mortal body"), does not settle Paul's meaning in 1 Cor, since here the *sōma* could easily be Christ's glory body, a sharing in which makes us to be one body-church. Eating this loaf means having a share in that company which "has by anticipation entered upon the new age which lies beyond the resurrection" (Barrett). The question "Is not . . .?" (*ouchi*) of v. 16 means that Paul is appealing to a eucharistic faith which he can count on his Corinthians to hold as a result of the teaching he brought them. In v. 17 he means to develop the tradition further—the link is "because" (*hoti*)—by deducing that, since one loaf is broken and distributed, those who partake of it are, despite their plurality, one body. The argument resembles that of 5:7f., where Christians become unleavened loaves, as it were, through having been united with their Passover, Christ. Paul's theoretical argument is in the service of a practical purpose: he wants to keep his converts free from demon-worship as contrasted with the mere eating of food sacrificed to idols, which could be done inculpably. He also wants to put the eucharist on a basis of personal faith and loyalty to Christ rather than have it thought of as achieving anything in itself through mere eating and drinking. This insistence is, of course, the chief importance of the passage to people of this age who are unlikely to be moved by the reference to food offered to idols.

John 6:51-59. Bultmann's lack of sympathy for sacramentalism has led him to conclude that 6:51*b*-58*b*, which he thinks refers without any doubt to the eucharist, has been taken from a quite different circle of ideas than that of 6:27-51*a* and has been added by an ecclesiastical editor. The hand that has written "and I will raise him up on the last day" (v. 54) has added the same phrase, he thinks, at vv. 39, 40, and 44, as a means of imposing unity on the whole discourse. Bultmann finds the background for our present passage in the Hellenistic mysteries, where the food taken is the god himself.

If we take the "ecclesiastical editor" to be the final redactor or evangelist, it is clear that this John means to interpret the foregoing discourse on Jesus as the bread of life in terms of his redemptive death ("the bread . . . is my flesh, for the life of the world," v. 51) and of the eating and drinking that characterizes the Lord's supper. The *sōma-haima* of the eucharistic accounts elsewhere in the NT (Mk 14:22-25 and parallels; 1 Cor 11:23ff.) becomes *sarx-haima* in Jn; this will be the usage of Ignatius and Justin.

Jn inserts the quarreling of his familiar opponents of Jesus, "the Jews," to show that the reality of Jesus' suggestion ("the bread I will give is my flesh") is understood and rejected as absurd. Jesus replies solemnly with the double "Amen" characteristic of Jn, referring to eucharistic practice clearly by adding mention of the drinking of blood to the eating of flesh (v. 54). The former would be found especially revolting in Jewish circles in light of the stern prohibition of Lv 17:10ff. Eating the Lord's supper is understood to be the necessary means to life (v. 54); those who partake of this meal bear the power within them that guarantees their resurrection. The food and drink of Jesus' flesh and blood are "real" (*alēthēs*), a familiar Johannine designation. Eating and drinking them leads to coinherence in Christ (*menei*, v. 56). "Feeds on" in vv. 56 and 58 is the participle *trōgōn*, meaning "munching" or "gnawing" as if to stress the reality of the eating over some spiritual type of ingestion. The evangelist is affirming that the sacrament alone truly nourishes for life; all other eating leads ultimately to death (v. 58). The transmission of the Father's life through the son is to be accomplished sacramentally only (v. 57). The phrase describing union with Christ, "he in me and I in him" (v. 56), is found elsewhere in Jn at 15:4f. and 17:21ff. The living power of Jesus (cf. 5:21, 26) is made the basis of the power of the sacrament. The talk that is "hard to endure" (*sklēros . . . ho logos*, v. 61) is not only that which features eating and drinking flesh and blood, although this seems to trigger the response. It is the total stujbling-block provided by Jesus, God's revealer "coming down" (*katabainōn*, vv. 50, 51, 58) from heaven.

SUNDAYS OF THE YEAR

NINTH SUNDAY OF THE YEAR (A)

(Second Sunday after Pentecost)

Deuteronomy 11:18, 26-28. Verses 18-20 repeat 6:6-9 (cf. p. 212), with v. 18*b* containing the injunction of 6:8 to bind the words of the LORD on the wrist and wear them as a pendant on the forehead. Both are literalist interpretations of Ex 13:9, where the "sign on your hand" has to do with a signet ring and the "memorial between the eyes" with the tatoo on the forehead of many Middle Eastern tribes. In Ex the week-long eating of unleavened bread was to serve as the remembrance rite for the deliverance from Egypt in place of these customs of Israel's neighbors. The Passover (*Pesaḥ*) *maṣṣoth* prevailed, of course, but so did the wearing of four portions of Torah in leather pillboxes (*t*^e*phillin*) strapped to wrist (*shel yad*) and forehead (*shel rosh*) in a cartridge affixed to the doorpost (*mezuzah*). Whether this custom goes back to Dt we do not know. The Bible quotations enclosed were Ex. 13:1-10, 11-16 and Dt 6:4-9; 11:13-21, containing the basics of Judaism: the uniqueness of God, loving obedience to his commands, his deliverance from captivity, and the redemption of the first-born. For instructions on making modern *t*^e*phillin* and binding them to the body with straps, and the correct days of usage, see *The Jewish Catalogue* (1973), pp. 58-61.

The choice offered to Israel between a blessing and a curse (vv. 26ff.) is of primary importance in this reading. The LORD has made choice of Israel. It, in turn, is to make choice of him in the new land. Like Dt 11:29, Dt 27 dramatizes the election of the one God and reprobation of false gods by making Gerizim the mount of blessing and Ebal the mount of cursing (vv. 12f.) The same story is told in Josh 8:30-35, where Joshua acts out the renewal of the Mosaic covenant from atop the two hills that dominated Shechem. Surely Gerizim appeared primitively as the site of the covenant altar in 8:30 (also in Dt 27:4) in place of Ebal, as the Samaritan Pentateuch has it. The scribal alteration was part of Judah's later repudiation of the "false worship" carried out on that site. The unique status of YHWH was the matter of earliest concern. The Deuteronomic hand made it a matter of commandments.

Romans 3:21-25, 28.   Paul's theme in Gal (e.g., 2:16) has been that the justice of God as a gracious gift to man goes back to Abraham, when faith in the promise first made it operative. He repeats it here. This righteousness (*dikaiosynē*) is not bound to the law as Paul's rabbinic opponents—and he himself before he knew Christ—held. It is true, of course, that the law and the prophets give testimony to God's justice (v. 21). It works now through faith in Jesus Christ for all who believe (v. 22). Universal sinfulness is a fact. Its result is universal deprivation of any title to the divine glory (v. 23). God now gives a gift (*dōrean*) to all through the grace of universal redemption (*apolytrōsis*, v. 24). The blood of Christ is what achieves the "expiation" (*hilastērion*, v. 25; it is the LXX word for the ancient propitiatory or mercy-seat, *kipporeth*). God thereby shows forth his justice in the present (v. 26) and remits all sins of the past (v. 25): in the former instance by the overlooking (*paresis*, v. 25) of sins and the latter by forbearance (*anochē*, v. 26). The mode of remission is not so important; Paul simply needs two separate words to describe the two periods. The blood of Christ, the effective sign of God's justifying intent, is operative as expiatory for both.

Verse 28 is the great watchword of Christian faith to describe the way redemption is available. Paul did not mean by it to drive a wedge between Christians and all Jews forever or between Catholics and Reformed Christians, but this in fact is what has been made of it. It is a simple declaration of the need for total trust in God's action.

Matthew 7:21-27.   Matthew's sermon on the mount (chs. 5-7) has been setting forth the terms of a more perfect righteousness for Jewish Christians than that proposed by the rabbis of Iavneh in their "academy" reconstituted there after the fall of Jerusalem. The concluding verses (24-27) frame a brief parable which are a key to the discourse (*tous logous toutous*, v. 28) as a whole. The latter contains rock-solid teaching. Fidelity to these words is a practical assurance that the law and the prophets are being fulfilled (*plērōsai*, 5:17) properly.

A warning is directed in vv. 15-23 against quite another group, the charismatic Christian prophets who in Mt's view are predatory as a class (v. 15). He will refer to them again in 24:11 and 24. Presumably they have no affinity with the patterns of community (*ekklēsia*) organization of the evangelist (cf. 16:18ff.; 18:15-18; 28:18b-19a). He proposes the test of deeds as a means to deal with them (vv. 16-20). Their stock in trade seems to be the multiplying of invocations of Jesus as "Lord." This verbalizing will prove profitless on "that day" (v. 22), the day of the Lord or judgment. Jesus will be the judge for Mt, as we know from 25:31-46. Exorcisms and miracles will have no meaning then (v. 22). Whomever Mt has in mind, their works are evil (vv. 16-20, 23). They may therefore expect to be destroyed in the eschatological fire.

TENTH SUNDAY OF THE YEAR (A)

(Third Sunday after Pentecost)

Hosea 6:3-6. Hosea was an 8th-century prophet of the northern kingdom, Israel, which he most often designates Ephraim. His chief concern was the failure of leadership during the reign of Jeroboam 11 (781-753) and after, down through the period of Assyrian expansion under Tiglath-Pileser III (745-27). In the first three autobiographical chapters of the book we learn of Hosea's marriage to his wife Gomer, of the symbolic names he gives his children, and of his love for an adulteress (3:1)—his wife or some other. Fact and figure are so interwoven in the imagery of the prophet's wife as harlot that the only thing clear is that Israel is being accused symbolically of infidelity.

The first six verses of Hosea's chapter 6 provided the once-familiar first reading of the Good Friday liturgy known inexactly as the "Mass of the Presanctified." It was perhaps this passage about Israel's woes, with its phrases, "He has struck us, but he will bind our wounds. / he will revive us after two days; / on the third day he will raise us up" (Hos 6:1f.), that was alluded to in the Pauline "gospel" of 1 Cor 15:4: "that he was buried and, in accordance with the scriptures, rose on the third day" (but cf. Ex 9:11). In the Hosean context, Israel's confession of sin is insincere. She expects God to provide relief after a short time, namely the three days that mark a divine healing (cf. 2 Kgs 20:5.)

It could well be that a Baal-like fertility cult is indicated, in which the "rending" of 3:1 is a reference to the violence done to nature by the dry summer season. The god dies and goes into the nether world only to be revived by the winter "rain" of v. 1 followed by the "spring rain" (*ibid.*) which matures the crops. In any event the irony of the prophet in this passage—which features the cheap grace of feigned repentance as a means to swift restoration—is muted in the use made of it, out of context, by the lectionary. Here it seems to convey a sure knowledge of God and his coming ("as certain as the dawn").

Yet the sense of the reproach of the Lord is retained. He addresses both the north and the south in v. 4, reprobating their piety as no more substantial than morning clouds or dew which the sun will dispel. His exasperated response will be to slay his people with a prophetic word (v. 5), smiting them with the demand (v. 6) for love (*ḥesed*) and a profound knowledge (*da'ath*) of God rather than sacrifice (*zabah*) and holocausts (*'oloth*). This verse is the key to the message of Hosea. It will be picked up by Mt in 9:13 and 12:7 to be used as a saying of Jesus. The strong statement of Hosea in favor of covenant love cannot be taken as a rejection of temple sacrifice (cf. Is 1:11-17; Am 5:21-24.) It is a strong preference for interior disposition over external observance. "Shall I give my first-born for my crime, / the fruit of my body for the sin of my soul? / You have been told, O man, what is good, / and what the Lord requires of you: / Only to do the right and to love goodness, / and to walk humbly with your God" (Mi 6:7f.)

Romans 4:18-25. This passage validates Abraham's faith, which was "credited to him as justice" (*dikaiosynē*, v. 22), just as ours will be credited to us as justice (v. 24). The difference lies in the object of faith, not its quality. Abraham was asked to believe in God's promise that he would be the father of many nations (i.e., Gentiles; v. 24). We are asked to believe in God "who raised up Jesus our Lord from the dead" (*ibid.*) Paul's allusion in v. 18 is to Gn 17:5 and 15:5. The phrase in that verse, "Hoping against hope," is literally, "against hope, in hope," the first being human expectation, the second a reliance on the unseen things that God will accomplish (cf. 8:24f.) St. Paul has identified the God who creates as the reason for Abraham's faith (v. 17), not any human potential.

The advanced age of the couple represents death (vv. 19f.) The promise of God not only strengthens Abraham's faith but represents life (vv. 20f.) Abraham never doubted (v. 20); he was full of conviction (v. 21; the verb is *plēropherein*) that God would do what he had promised. Abraham's confidence gave glory to God (v. 20), as those who did not believe in him failed to do (1:21). Trust in God's power as God is the essence of faith. The opposite is a reliance on human possibility, whether by way of total fidelity to the Law or being intimidated by the fact of human limitation, in this case the infertility of the aging Abraham and Sarai (who would be called Sarah only as a mother-to-be, Gn 17:15).

Faith for Paul grows stronger (v. 20) in the measure in which it is not mixed with reliance on "any thing or any one other than God himself" (Barrett). Verse 22 returns to the quotation of Gn 15:6 with which the argument began in 4:3: "It was credited to him as an act of righteousness." Paul is dealing with Abraham not as an historical figure but as the father of all believers; hence it is that the words from Genesis were "intended for us too" (v. 24). In our case it is not faith in the son Isaac who comes forth from a dead womb but in God's Son Jesus who comes forth from the tomb.

Paul does not seem to be making use of the rabbinic theme *aqedath Yishak* ("the binding of Isaac") in v. 25, although he may be alluding to it in 8:32. He centers his attention on Jesus and what God has accomplished through him. Jesus is the new and more effective sign of power than the one made manifest in Abraham. The pericope, and with it chapter 4, ends in what seems to be a creedal formula. We do not have any clues regarding it, nor can we be sure if the "handed over" (v. 25) is a reference to the LXX of Is 53:12. The deed of Christ is taken as one, and as accomplishing the one effect. Thus, it is not to be supposed that Paul conceives the crucifixion as meeting the challenge of our sins while the award of the justification we stood in need of is deferred until his resurrection, indeed, through it. The phrasing is rather a rhetorical antithesis which does not mean to separate the death and resurrection of Christ in terms of the one effect achieved, namely our justified status.

Matthew 9:9-13. The attribution of the authorship of Matthew's gospel to a disciple of Jesus is almost certainly a device employed by the pseudonymous author. This is not to say that the designation "According to Matthew" may not have gone back to the time of the writing. This pericope is the story of the calling of one known as Matthew. He will appear in the gospel only once again (at 10:3) in a listing of the "twelve apostles." Mt has omitted Mk 2:13, which describes Jesus walking along the lakeshore teaching. He transmits the content of Mk 2:14, with the important change that "Levi the son of Alphaeus" becomes "Matthew." When Mk composes his list of twelve, Levi does not appear but Matthew does (3:18). "James the son of Alphaeus" occurs in both lists. We do not know a reason for the change from Levi to Matthew in Mt. Tradition has made Matthew Levi's name as a Christian, in a historical tidying-up process. It is much more likely that the author Mt, using the Marcan account of Levi's call, made it a story of "Matthew" (taken from Mk's list) to tie in his gospel with the apostle most closely connected with the church to which he belonged.

Simon, Andrew, James, and John had been called to follow Jesus (Mt 4:18-22) without his giving them any reason; no more is a motive supplied here. The disciples receive a gift (10:8) which they are expected in turn to give. Merit is no part of the calling.

Tax gatherers (*telōnai*) were in the pay of Rome, hence assumed to be dishonest and "sinners," i.e. voluntarily outside the Law. The importance of their inclusion in Jesus' table-fellowship is crucial (cf. Gal 2:12.) He is not concerned about observance or works. The messianic banquet, which the meals taken with Jesus foreshadow, has no such condition as this attached. Sickness is a symbol for sin in v. 20. The evangelist explains what has happened at this meal that includes tax gatherers and other undesirables by appending Hos 6:6, as he will do again at 12:7 (with respect to the charge that his disciples "harvested," in plucking grain; cf. Ex 20:8, interpreted by the rabbis in the spirit of Lv 25:4.) The covenant relation is held out, not to the self-righteous but to "sinners," whether their offense be ethical or ritual. The conditions of acceptance as part of the covenant people, in other words, are notably altered in Mt's understanding of Jesus' call.

ELEVENTH SUNDAY OF THE YEAR (A)

(Fourth Sunday after Pentecost)

Exodus 19:2-6. Although the itinerary is Priestly (resumed from 17:1), a Deuteronomist hand has inserted the words of the LORD in 3*b*-6 into the E narrative here. The encouragement is cognate with that of the poetry of Dt 32:10f. but the prose of Ex has a stronger beauty. *Rephidim* ("supports"?) is related to the narrative of the battle with Amalek in 17:11f. It is not known where "the front of the mountain" may be. The present Jebel Musa (7,500 ft.) has been identified as Mt. Sinai since the 4th c. Ex 17:1-7 and Num 20:2-13 situate the mountain near Kadesh, which would satisfy the requirement of the Amalekites' proximity (cf. Gen 14:7; 1 Sam 15:7; 27:8.) In the Kadesh region—about 60 miles due south of Gaza on the Mediterranean—the likeliest candidate for Sinai-Horeb is Jebel Helal (3,000 ft.), which is about 25 miles west of the Kadesh oasis.

The point of this pericope is God's readiness to rescue his people, as an eagle might do in swooping down to catch its little ones that have fallen from the nest. Elsewhere Israel is described as the Lord's "special possession" (19:5); among the passages are Dt 7:6; 14:2; 26:18f. Moreover, in all three the people is "sacred" to him. This notion is similar to that of the kingdom of priests and holy people in that it means set apart or separated rather than ethically upright, while including, however, the latter notion. Holiness in the biblical sense was likeness to deity, specifically to Yahweh, and it consisted in being distinct from all that surrounded it. The separated character of the priests is here expanded to include the entire people. 1 Pt 2:5f. will contain the same idea as regards the baptized. The condition of such corporate priestliness for the Deuteronomist author is obedience to the covenant, the terms of which are shortly to follow (chapters 20ff.)

Romans 5:6-11. The predilection of God for his people Israel in the previous reading is matched in this one by his concern for "us godless men" (v. 6), the race of "sinners" (v. 8) for whom Christ died. The "love of God" (v. 5) which has been poured out in our hearts through the holy spirit is doubtless a subjective genitive meaning God's love for us, the idea found in v. 8. The spirit has been given at some time in the past (v. 5) such as the first call to belief or the event of baptism. Similarly the death of Christ can be dated; it has happened "at the appointed time." Its providential occurrence took place within that long period when man was "godless" (v. 6), i.e., powerless to remedy his sinful state. The appointed time is the eschatological moment which brings the wait of centuries to an end (cf. Gal 4:4.) God has taken the initiative on our behalf in terms of fidelity to his own commitment. "For us" employs the familiar preposition *hypér* of passages describing the reality of the redemption such as Jn 10:11; 1 Cor 11:24; Gal 2:20; Heb 2:9. St. Paul compares God's action favorably with that of man who is not likely to die for his fellows (v. 7). Courage like this is displayed rarely enough, and when it is, the manifestation is usually in behalf of "a good type" (such being the sense of the phrase, which has the article in Greek), not merely a good individual. God, acting in Christ, is undeterred by the general unworthiness of his beneficiaries. His historical action is the proof of "his love for us" (v. 8). The holy spirit was given to us (cf. v. 5) while we were still sinners.

Since Christ's blood was the price of our justification, freedom from God's wrath may be expected in the future (v. 9), even as peace is the effect of justification in the present. The former situation of enmity has led to reconciliation; the present reconciliation may be expected to lead to being saved (v. 10). It was Christ's death that achieved the first. It will be his life as risen that accomplishes the second. In this discussion Paul speaks of the tension between God and man under two figures, reconciliation to terminate enmity and justification to terminate a legal dispute (vv. 9f.) The two, however, are one. Similarly, there are not two distinct entities spoken of as accomplished by his death and by his life (v. 10). The two steps or moments of importance are not Christ's (1) death and (2) resurrection, but (1) the manifestation of God's love in the one historical deed which includes both, laid hold of by faith, and (2) the later salvation of all believers when history shall have been brought to a close. The second step is "all the more certain" because, whereas our first condition was totally unmeritorious, now God may be presumed to finish gloriously what he has begun. Concluding this thought in v. 11, Paul makes God's anticipated action in Christ the subject of a boast (v. 11). Such boasting had only been a hope in v. 2.

The "now" of v. 11 is the reconciled condition of Christians in the present which justifies Paul in exulting about the favorable outcome in the future.

Matthew 9:36—10:8. This pericope is the introduction to the second of five collections of Jesus' sayings in Matthew, all of which end with a summary like that of 11:1. It consists of a statement about the needs of the people (v. 36) to whom Jesus, moved with pity, was proclaiming the gospel and whom he was likewise curing. It also includes Jesus' charge to pray for laborers (9:37f.), his empowerment of the twelve to exorcise and heal (10:1), and his naming of "twelve apostles" (10:2-4). Israel in the Bible is a nation of "sheep without a shepherd," a phrase found in Num 27:17; 1 Kgs 22:17; and Zech 10:2. The substitution of Jesus for YHWH is a staple of New Testament christology; he, rather than Israel's LORD, will be the shepherd of Mt 25:32 (the judgment scene). He appears again as shepherd in 26:31 (which quotes the "Song of the Sword" of Zech 13 about an associate of the LORD of hosts, a stricken shepherd). Hos 6:11 and Jl 4:13 use the figure of the harvest as a time when God will settle accounts with his world in judgment. Such is the spirit of Mt 13:30 and 39, whereas here the harvest is a gathering of the just. For this holy work, laborers are needed (cf. 1 Tim 5:18 for the term *ergatēs*, found also in Phil 2:3 and 2 Cor 11:13 to describe false apostolic laborers.)

The twelve apostles are probably chosen to correspond to the number of the tribes of Israel (cf. Mt 19:28.) Mt derives his list from Mk 3:16-19, reordering the names slightly. Andrew is brought forward and put directly after Simon; Mk's "Matthew and Thomas" are reversed. The word "apostles" occurs in Mt only here (10:2), just as in Mk only once (6:30). It will be used in the early church to describe others than the twelve. Literally it means those "sent." "The Zealot Party member" (10:4) renders *ho Kananaios*, a rendering of the Aramaic *qane'an* meaning zealous. Whether this group, committed to the ejection of Rome by force, so designated themselves at this time is not sure. Iscariot (v. 4), according to the researches of C. C. Torrey, cannot mean "man of Kerioth" (Josh 15:25; Jer 48:24) or be a corruption of *sikarios*, "assassin." It has to be a Greek transliteration of some Aramaic designation. He holds for *ishqaryā'*, "the false one," from the adjective *sheqaryā'*.

Jesus has been sent by his Father to preach, teach, and heal. He now sends out the twelve with a similar authority (*exousia*, 10:1).

Verses 5-7 have no parallel in Mk or Lk. They confine Jesus' missionary charge to the Jewish people. The shepherd of Israel is described as having no interest in (literally) going "toward the road of the Gentiles" or any Samaritan town (v. 7). This command is in marked contrast to that of 28:19, which probably reflects the actual practice of the Matthean community, however tentative, distinct from this earlier theological construct. Mt 10:6 accords better than 28:19 with the hesitant stories outside Jewish circles reported in Ac 11:1ff. and 11:19, a tradition that would never have been preserved in the Jerusalem community if there had been an authentic logion of Jesus like 28:19.

The apostles are instructed to preach and heal. The command to "raise the dead" may be meant metaphorically for bringing life and salvation to the world. Cf. Eph 2:1f. In any case, others are to be treated as the disciples have been in receiving God's gifts without charge.

TWELFTH SUNDAY OF THE YEAR (A)

(Fifth Sunday after Pentecost)

Jeremiah 20:10-13. The word "jeremiad" derives from the attribution of the five Lamentations to the prophet, the result of a misreading of 2 Chr 35:25 and the LXX preface to Lam. (The Hebrew canon does not associate the book with the prophet.) Today's reading, however, is from a poem which, with 20:14-18; 15:15-21; and 17:14-18, reveals the heart of Jeremiah in his deepest distress. In his struggle with the temple administrator, Pashhur, which is given as the setting of his outcry, he expresses chagrin at the mockery heaped upon him for his repeated, doom-filled message, "Violence and outrage!" (v. 8). This description of the realities of the situation is too much for the optimists in residence who are winding down the war. But the word of the LORD has become like a fire burning in his heart (v. 9). He cannot be silent. Jeremiah renames Pashhur *Magor missabhibh*, "Terror on every side" (v. 3), to indicate that the harassing visited by his temple police on the prophet (v. 10) will ultimately be visited on him by the nation's enemies. Some have thought that Jeremiah's prophecy of 19:14f. was inspired by the defeat of Egypt by the Babylonians at Carchemish on the Euphrates in 605 (cf. 46:2; 36:1ff.) In any case, he knows he is being watched like a hawk at every step (v. 10) for any false prophecy, at which point he will be apprehended and dispatched. He feels totally secure, however. Yahweh is his "mighty champion" (v. 11). The prophet's enemies will fail and be put to shame as a result of the vengeance taken by the LORD (v. 12). This portion of the psalm ends with an expression of confidence in final vindication (v. 13), a convention in this type of writing (cf. Ps 22:23-31.) In v. 14 Jeremiah will return to an expression of despair which has become classic in the world's literature, showing the alternation of moods possible in a man of great faith.

Romans 5:12-15. This passage follows immediately upon that of last Sunday. For commentary, cf. pp. 40ff.

Matthew 10:26-33. Matthew's exhortation to fearless confession is not from Mk but Q (Lucan parallel, 12:2-9). The logion of Mt. 10:26 occurs in Mk 4:22, that of Mt 10:33 in Mk 8:38. This preparation for persecution at the hands of "synagogues . . . rulers and kings" (10:17f.; cf. Lk 12:11, "synagogues, rulers, and authorities") is employed in the same way, by and large, by the two evangelists. Jesus has been warning his disciples in Mt that the pupil should not expect a better fate than the teacher nor the slave than the master (v. 24). Proclamation of Jesus' teaching is obligatory for his disciples (vv. 26f.) but it should be expected to bring the same sanctions that will be (at the time the gospels were written, have been) leveled at him. Three times the disciples are enjoined not to fear (vv. 26, 28, 31). Persecution may bring death but it can do nothing worse. Denial of the message can bring destruction of soul and body *en Geennē*, a figure of destruction by fire taken from the Valley of Hinnom south of Jerusalem where refuse was burned—and where popular Jewish belief located the last judgment (cf. Mt 5:22; Mk 9:49; Is 66:24.)

The remaining logia are only loosely connected, being expressions of providential care (vv. 29ff.) which the author of Q saw fit to insert in this context of persecution. The Lucan phrasing of Mt 10:32ff. is more primitive, "the son of man will acknowledge him" (12:8) and [he] "will be disowned" (v. 9) having a more authentic ring in their third person and (divine) passive voice than Mt's identification of the son of man with Jesus and conversion to the active "I will disown." All of this heightens the puzzle of the greater Hebraic character of certain sayings in Luke, and has led R. L. Lindsey (*A Hebrew Translation of the Gospel of Mark*) to the unusual conclusion that Lk was written first from a primitive narrative and Q.

THIRTEENTH SUNDAY OF THE YEAR (A)

(Sixth Sunday after Pentecost)

2 Kings 4:8-11, 14-16. Elisha is one of God's prophets, hence a man possessed of spirit, capable of intercessory influence with the divine. Shunem is in the land of Issachar (later Galilee) at the southeastern tip of the Plain of Jezreel, about five miles south of Nain. A miracle of resuscitation was later to be reported of Jesus at Nain (cf. Lk 7:11f.) like the one (2 Kgs 4:32-37) which this passage leads up to and that related of Elijah on which it is patterned (1 Kgs 17:17-23). This is not surprising because of Lk's consistent attempts to make Jesus an Elijah-figure.

In v. 13, which the lectionary eliminates, the prophet asks what he can do to repay her hospitality to him and his servant. She replies with some spirit, "I am living among my own people," an indication of the strength of her clan. Here was a wife who had the backing of her family, hence needed no favors from the king or the military (v. 13). The prophet's promise of childbirth within a year, and a son at that, may be what prompts her to cry out in grief a dozen years or so later, when the boy has died in the fields: "Did I ask my lord for a son? . . . Did I not beg you not to deceive me?" (v. 28).

The story is one which ultimately reflects Hebrew belief in the communication of power by direct contact, but today's pericope contents itself with a prophecy of the birth of a son in response to the wealthy woman's hospitality.

Romans 6:3-4, 8-11. Paul has been holding that our wrongdoing provides proof of God's justice (3:5) and that "my falsehood brings to light God's truth" (3:7). He hears his teaching slanderously reported as condoning "doing evil that good may come of it" (3:8). This has made him very sensitive concerning all matters that touch on the Law and grace. In chapter 6 and the two that follow he tries to set the record straight. He is not, he feels he must insist, for continuing in sin that grace may abound (6:1). This sounds like the taunt of libertinism from his enemies: it forces him to express the Christian ethic in its fullness.

His response is that the old self of the Christian is just as dead in baptism as Jesus was on the cross, just as buried in its waters as he was in the tomb, and just as much living a new life (the familiar Hebraism "walking—*peripatēsōmen*—in newness of life") as Jesus was raised from the dead. Moreover, both occurrences were caused by "the glory of the Father" (v. 4), meaning his power—possibly a snatch from a creed (cf. 2 Thes 1:9.) It is evident that Paul can count on a knowledge of this baptismal doctrine in a community he has not instructed.

The religious terminology of Oriental cults is often cited in this connection but the content of the doctrine is Jewish: an identification with the messiah in tribulation as a prelude to the age to come. Paul is careful not to suggest that the baptized Christian has come up out of the waters to the fullness of this age, only to a "new life" (v. 4). The baptismal rite is the effective symbol of the reality of Christ's death and resurrection. It achieves likeness to the former perfectly, to the latter only inchoately. The tense of our living with Christ (v. 8) is future (*syzēsōmen*), not present. Our rising with him is something we believe (v. 8), hence which lies in the eschatological future; his death and its finality is something we know (v. 9).

This certainty that Christ will never die again affirms his conquest of death as anticipatory of the general resurrection in the last age. The death of the obedient Christ, although in a context of sin ("God made him who did not know sin to be sin," 2 Cor 5:21), achieved his final break with sin (v. 10). His risen life was life "for God" in the sense that the former identification with sin was behind him. The Christian must similarly consider himself dead to sin, but Paul is realistic enough to know that his being alive is by way of a new relation to God, even though outward appearance continues as it was. The transition from the this age (*ha 'olam ha zeh*) to the age to come (*ha 'olam habbah*) is accomplished "in Christ Jesus" (v. 11) in that being alive to God is something that cannot be seen.

Matthew 10:37-42. Elisha restored the Shunammite woman's son to life by God's power. God does the same for both his dead son Jesus and all those who, believing in him, die to sin. Matthew's gospel in this passage spells out certain conditions of life in the new age. The disciple must love Jesus more than his own kinship circle (v. 37). In accepting the cross (v. 38) he must take on the shame of being an outcast ("God's curse rests on him who hangs on a tree," Dt 21:23). Verses 38f. are a doublet of Mt 16:24f. In the former the verbs are find—destroy; destroy—find and in the latter, wish to save—destroy; destroy—find.

Verses 40ff. bring the discourse, which has been a charge of Jesus to his disciples, to an end. Verse 40 is reminiscent of the Mishnaic passage *Berakoth* 5, 5: "A man's emissary is like the man himself." It is an identification of preachers of Christ with Christ, stress being laid on the roles of *prophētēs* and *dikaios*, the *nabi* and *saddik* of the Matthean milieu (v. 41). Church ethics are stressed here. They comprise a set of understandings about behavior that Paul would stigmatize as "works" if they were thought to be saving of themselves.

FOURTEENTH SUNDAY OF THE YEAR (A)

(Seventh Sunday after Pentecost)

Zechariah 9:9-10. The king through whom the Lord is to save Israel will be a peaceful ruler, unlike other strivers after world sovereignty who attempt their conquest by force. Aram (Syria), Phoenicia with its cities of Tyre and Sidon, the Philistine cities of Ashkelon, Gaza, Ekron, and Ashdod will all be reduced to domesticity, according to the oracle immediately preceding this one. The pride of the nations will be broken; from the Philistine's mouth "his bloody meat will be taken" (v. 7a). The prophets restored the popular figure of the king of peace from the age of paradise (cf. Is 9:5f.; 11:1ff.; Jer 23:5f.) Judah's offspring, who shall hold the scepter and mace forever, will tether his ass to the vine (Gen 49:11; cf. Jgs 5:10; 10:4.)

The ass suited Israel's poor economy. Horses, by contrast, were like rocketry next to infantry. There were brief periods of splendor, as in Solomon's time (1 Kgs 10:26-29) or when the last kings of Judah entered the gates of Jerusalem in chariots and on horses (Jer 17:25; 22:4). In the present passage the savior king of the future will do God's will and put an end to national self-seeking. This messiah will have no part in the wars and revolutions of the monarchy. He will terminate all violence with his kingdom of peace.

The collection of oracles that make up Zech 9—14 cannot be shown to be postexilic as clearly as can 1—8. Whatever the date of authorship, the notion of hope for the future through a kingly figure or the house of David largely ceases after the references in Zech 9:9f. and 12:1 through 13:6. The idea of a messiah does not die entirely but he does not play a particularly central role in Jewish eschatology. Messiah and suffering servant may blend in 9:9f. (and in 12:10?— "they shall look on him whom they have thrust through, and they shall mourn for him as one mourns for an only son") but it cannot be demonstrated, only inferred. These Zecharian oracles, indeed, are the only trace of a meek and humble redeemer we have from the postexilic period, even though Israel never lost sight of submissiveness and humility as her vocation.

Verse 9 has a parallel in Is 62:11. An "ass . . . the foal of an ass" is poetic parallelism; the phrase does not speak of two beasts.

Matthew's free rendering of this passage (21:5) adds an additional "and," thereby contributing a second little donkey who trails behind in Christian art. The king and "just savior" of 9:9*b* will eliminate the war-making potential of both north and south (10*a*). His peace to the nations will be universal—from the Euphrates to the waters supposedly at the ends of the earth (cf. Ps 72:8 and Mic 5:3 for the same cosmic promise). He will strip warriors of the bow, as in Ps 146:10, or the better known promise of Is 2:4 about the recycling of the swords and spears.

Romans 8:9, 11-13. In St. Paul's flesh-spirit opposition the sex passion of a giant of a man can be spirit and the intellect of a person of genius flesh. He is concerned with *sarx* as human resistance to God and *pneuma* as docility to him, or, better, to his *pneuma.* In v. 9 Paul assumes the possession of the spirit of God—which is the same as the spirit of Christ—by his Roman readers, which means that, as a result, their existence is *en pneumati* in its totality. They are not *en sarki* like those of v. 8, persons who cannot please God because they are busy pleasing themselves.

It might be better to say that the spirit of Christ possesses them than is possessed by them. It is only through Christ that the spirit is known and received. The effect of the spirit's action is to make one "Christ's" (*autou*, v. 9).

The spirit who raised up Christ as the first deed of the final age will give life to mortal bodies in this same age (v. 11). His quickening activity is a reality of now. What has been put to death for those in whom Christ dwells is their sin-body; what has risen to justice is their mortal body as spirit (v. 10). The transformation takes place gradually —"from glory to glory"—by the action of the risen Lord who is now not in the least flesh but totally spirit (cf. 2 Cor 3:18.) It can only occur in the baptized through a lifetime of free choices. The indebtedness referred to in v. 12 is the obligation we are under through having been raised up in baptism. Life according to *sarx* will bring death. Life guided by the spirit is death-dealing to the deeds (NAB renders *ta praxeis* "evil deeds") of the body (v. 13), a phrase like "whatever in your nature is rooted in earth" (*ta melē ta epi tēs gēs*) of Col 3:5.

Matthew 11:25-30. The first two verses are a *berakah*, a hymn in praise of God like that described in Jesus' multiplication of the loaves and his prayer over bread at table. Such prayers are the essence of all *eucharistiai* (*eulogiai*) which later become anaphoras and canons. They are in three parts: thanksgiving to the Father for a revelation received, a statement of its content, and an invitation to a course of action. Chapter 11 has spoken in praise of John the Baptizer (vv. 7-15) but in reproach of the present generation whom no preacher can please (vv. 16-19) and of the unrepentant towns of Galilee (vv. 20-24). By contrast, the "merest children" (*nēpioi*, v. 25) have had revealed to them no less than the Father himself, at the good pleasure of the son (v. 27).

Verse 27*a* closely resembles Jn 3:35 except for its active voice; 27*b* is like Jn 10:15*a*. This similarity of wording in two otherwise dissimilar writings leads to the supposition that Jesus' actual expression has been reworked by the two different communities or schools. The revelation of God to the simple, which the learned and clever have had withheld from them (v. 25), is entirely a matter of his gracious design (*eudokia*, v. 26). This sovereign freedom of the Father to reveal is a Matthean theme which will recur at 16:17. In Jn, Jesus is more clearly the revealer of the Father than in Mt; nonetheless, the whole sermon on the mount is an instance of Jesus' teaching with authority (7:29). Jesus is God's son in Mt (cf. 3:17) without any of the Johannine implication of divine preexistence, yet his possession of everything (*panta*, v. 27) in common with the Father is indistinguishable in the two gospels.

Wisdom invites the untutored to partake of her food and drink (Sir 51:24), even saying: "Submit your neck to her yoke" (v. 26). Jesus becomes personified wisdom in the present pericope, a Matthean theme which will reappear in 23:37ff., where Jesus' lament over Jerusalem "bears unmistakable traces of the idea of Wisdom's rejection by men" (M. Jack Suggs, *Wisdom, Christology, and Law in Matthew's Gospel*, p. 31; the book is largely about the six verses of this reading).

Accepting the yoke of Torah was described by the rabbis as giving rest and ease. First-century Rabbi Nehunia ben ha-Kanah wrote: "Everyone who receives upon him the yoke of Torah, they remove from him the yoke of the kingdom and the yoke of worldly occupation. And everyone who breaks off from him the yoke of Torah, they lay upon him the yoke of the kingdom and the yoke of worldly occupation." Verses 29*c* and 30 appear as saying 90 of the Gospel according to Thomas: "Jesus said: Come to me, for easy (*chrēstos;* the Coptic borrows from the Greek) is my yoke and my lordship is gentle, and you shall find repose (*anapausis*, as in Mt) for yourselves." The heavy loads which the scribes and Pharisees put on others (Mt 23:4) are here replaced by the teaching of Jesus. He does this as the meek one (*praüs*) who fulfills all justice, acting side by side with sinners to bring them into fellowship with himself. The result is rest for the weary and heavily burdened (vv. 28, 29; cf. Is 28:12; Jer 6:16.) Christ's yoke and burden (which are *chrēstos kai*

. . . *elaphros*, v. 30) are his interpretation of the Torah, demanding yet endurable.

Didache 6, 2 employs these verses in a more explicitly understanding spirit than any encountered in the NT: "If you can bear the Lord's full yoke you will be perfect. But if you cannot, then do what you can."

FIFTEENTH SUNDAY OF THE YEAR (A)

(Eighth Sunday after Pentecost)

Isaiah 55:10-11. This chapter is at first addressed indiscriminately to all who are thirsty (v. 1), even though it centers around covenant-renewal offered to the people of David, the "leader and commander of nations" (vv. 3, 4) by "the Holy One of Israel, who has glorified you" (5*d*). Verses 8 and 9 stress the transcendence of Israel's LORD and his differences from his people, yet 10 and 11 suggest his way of closing this great gap. Under an agricultural figure that would mean much to a people dependent on moisture and soil (vv. 10*a*, 10*b*), the prophet speaks of God's word (11*a*) as effective in intent (11*b*) and fruitful in result (10*c*). Is 45:23 has referred to God's oath regarding his unalterable word. This word is to be fulfilled simply because it contains the power of God and the will of God which brooks no interference. His word and his plan are one.

The theme of invincible intention has appeared in Deutero-Isaiah before: "Cyrus: My shepherd, / who fulfills my every wish" (44:28); "I say that my plan shall stand, / I accomplish my every purpose" (46:10); "and the will of the LORD shall be accomplished through him" (53:10). God does not expect to utter a single word to his people without its achieving its purpose. He is as certain in the successive fulfillment of his design as the seasons.

Romans 8:18-23. Sin has its victories in the present age: sufferings (v. 18), subjection to futility (v. 20), slavery to corruption (v. 21), groanings and agony (v. 22). All continue right up to Paul's day despite eager awaiting (v. 19), hope (v. 20), and the spirit as first fruits (v. 23). The latter figure (*aparchē*; Heb. *bikkurim*) describes the initial green shoots which presage a harvest; they are a pledge of all that is to follow (cf. 11:16; 16:5.) The chief contrast in this passage is between the hardships of the present and the "glory to be revealed in us" (v. 18; cf. 3:23; 5:2.)

If "the whole created world" of v. 19 (*ktisis*) means mankind rather than the cosmos, it becomes easier to understand the hoped-for passing of "the world itself" (v. 21) from bondage to full freedom. Manson suggests that mankind is in three stages rather than two: that segment subject to futility (v. 20) and corruption (v. 21) through not knowing Christ; believers in him who have the first fruits of the spirit (v. 23); and an already redeemed humanity which is confident it will live in a transformed universe (vv. 18, 19, 21). It appears that Christians are not the only ones who "groan inwardly" while awaiting the *apolytrōsis* of "the body" (v. 23; here the body of the individual, not the church). The whole created world is in similar condition (v. 22), having the same agony but not the same hope.

Believers in Christ have in prospect their being identified (*apokalypsis*, v. 19) as sons of God, the eschatological revelation referred to in 2:5; 1 Cor 1:7; 2 Thes 1:7. It will bring to consummation the revelation of the gospel which has already been accomplished after long ages (cf. Rom 16:25.)

This entire pericope seems to be influenced, at least verbally, by current gnostic thought-patterns with their claimed influence of heavenly bodies on the lives of men. God is in control throughout, however; he is not locked in combat with some opposite dualistic force. It is he "who once subjected" the world to futility (v. 20), not Adam or Satan, although the story of Adam's sin as an explanation of the world's woes is probably understood here.

Matthew 13:1-23. The parable told in 4-9 (par. Mk 2:8) is chiefly about the mild frustrations of the farmer who sows his seed broadcast, secure in the knowledge that he will nonetheless reap a rich harvest. The details are secondary and are included to make a good story of it. The early church, missing the simplicity of the tale with its single point, appears to have allegorized it (Mt 13:19-23; par. Mk 4:14-20). That single point is the conviction of Jesus that the consummation of all is God's work and that it is bound to come despite "every failure and opposition, from hopeless beginnings." (J. Jeremias) The superabundant return from good soil in v. 8 is a figure of eschatological richness; it describes not so much a portion of the field as another point in time, the end. Like so many of Jesus' stories this is a contrast-parable, in this case between what man expects in view of many setbacks and what God will surprisingly accomplish.

The explanatory conclusion of vv. 19-23 can be shown to be the work of the early church by its use of the technical term *ho logos* for the gospel (cf. Mk 4:33; Lk 1:2; Ac 4:4; Gal 6:6; Col 4:3 and many other places; it is used by Jesus in this sense only in the interpretation of the parable of the sower); by the occurrence within it of a number of words which are not found elsewhere in the synoptics but are common in the rest of NT literature; and by the use of the verb for sowing (*speirein*) for preaching, a usage not characteristic of Jesus in other sayings attributed to him. More to the point, perhaps, the interpretation appended alters the meaning of the parable from its original eschatological one to a psychological. It exhorts early converts to examine their states of mind and heart and give thought to perseverance.

Verse 12 was originally an isolated logion of Jesus which Mt tacks on because it seems to echo the abundant outcome reported in v. 8.

In his explanation of Jesus' use of parables (vv. 10f., 13-17), Mt follows Mk (4:10-12) who is committed to the distinction between the mystery entrusted by Jesus to the disciples and the mystification of "the others outside." This introduces the "hardening theory" which holds that Jesus used parables precisely in order that onlookers and hearers of his teaching might neither see nor understand it. Mk quotes the Targum version of Is 6:9f. which ends, "lest perhaps they repent and be forgiven," while Mt quotes the Isaiah passage from the LXX (as does Acts 28:26f.)

Jeremias argues that Targumic use establishes that the Greek word for "lest" in Is and Mk (*mēpote*) renders the Aramaic *dil^ema* meaning "unless," followed by the divine passive *aphethē*. If so, the meaning would be, "unless they turn and God will forgive them." This leads him to conclude that Mk introduced the Targumic version of Is 6:10 not to explain Jesus' use of the parable form but to account for reaction to his teaching in general, i.e., "the mystery of the reign of God" (Mk 4:11). Outsiders find Jesus' words obscure but if they repent all will go well: they will find forgiveness. The "mystery" is the breaking in of God on men in the teaching and action of Jesus.

Even if Jeremias is right, Matthew with his "because" (*hoti*, v. 13) is explaining the use of parables not as a pedagogical device— which they were—but as part of the working out of God's plan. Verse 35, which quotes Ps 78:2, will do the same. Mt's inclusion of vv. 16f. in this context (par. Lk 10:23f.) confirms this view. Prophets and saints from Israel's past could not have known those mysteries, a knowledge of which has been given "to you," the disciples (v. 11).

In the allegorized explanation (vv. 18-23), Mt ties the various types of men in with an understanding of the word (v. 17); and it is to be noted that he does not make Jesus the sower.

SIXTEENTH SUNDAY OF THE YEAR (A)

(Ninth Sunday after Pentecost)

Wisdom 12:13, 16-19. The first-century B.C. Alexandrian author takes a view of the Canaanites in vv. 3-6 not unlike that of those "varmints" and "pesky redskins" held by citizens of the Righteous Empire.

"They were a race accursed from the beginning" (v. 11), he says. Therefore YHWH's conduct could only be reckoned magnanimous as Israel gradually exterminated them. "Condemning them bit by bit, you gave them space for repentance. / You were not unaware that their race was wicked / and their malice ingrained, / And that their dispositions would never change" (v. 10). Because of God's omnipotent rule, he need not explain himself to anyone; his conduct may be presumed just (cf. v. 13.) His might is his justice, his sovereign power his leniency (v. 16). Never so clearly does the might of the LORD shine forth as when it is challenged (v. 17). Yet it is always tempered with mercy and his justice with clemency.

The entire passage is a lesson in the noble restrains of power. Israel is to learn from her God that, like him, she can afford to be just because of her strength.

Romans 8:26-27. The spirit was the life-principle common to the messiah and his people in this final age of outpouring. He led the community out of slavery into adoption as sons (vv. 14f.) The new condition of believers as children and heirs enabled them, in the spirit, to address God as "Father" (vv. 15c-17). In this pericope the spirit is not only a witness with our spirit but strengthener and enabler in the work of prayer (v. 26). Because he is somehow distinct from God he can intercede for us (v. 26), an office which Christ will be described as performing in v. 34. The spirit's inarticulate groanings (*stenagmois alalētois*) are related to the agonized outcries (*systenazei, stenazomen*) of creation and even of Christians (vv. 22, 23). God, who is the searcher of hearts, can alone interpret the intercession for believers which the spirit makes from within them. The spirit speaks to God who is spirit from the depths of man's spirit.

Matthew 13:24-43. The parable of the weeds and the wheat (vv. 24-30) occurs in Mt only among the evangelists, although the Gospel of Thomas 57 gives it as well. There the ending is abrupt and no allegorization follows: "On the day of harvest the weeds will appear.

They will pull them and burn them." The agricultural vendetta reported, strange to us, was evidently quite conceivable in ancient times. The weeding of a wheat field described in v. 28 was also a commonplace.

As it stands, this parable of Jesus was told to impress on the impatient the need for patience. The elaboration found in v. 30a beyond the phrasing of Thomas shows that Mt is preparing the way for an allegorical interpretation. The parable of the mustard seed is taken almost verbatim from Mk (4:30-32) while the presence of the brief parable about the woman with the three measures of flour is from Q (cf. Lk 13:20-21.) These two parables show the future magnitude of God's realm despite humble beginnings and also the inexorable character of his rule. His work among men cannot be stopped, any more than the growth of a tree or the action of yeast in the dough. The quotation of Psalm 78:2 in explanation of why Jesus taught in parables is found in Mt alone. The *mashal* or comparison in terms of which the psalmist chooses to speak, his "mysteries" (*hidoth*) from of old, are the history of Israel's desert wanderings told in detail, concluding with events down to David's day. The evangelist has no special interest in the psalm as it develops, only in its early affirmation that the speaker will teach by multiplying examples.

The vocabulary of the allegorical explanation in vv. 37-43 is distinctly Matthean, as can be seen by the more than three dozen words that are his. Jesus never speaks of his kingdom (v. 41); other terms like *poneros* for the evil one, *diabolos* for Satan, and *kosmos* for the world are not part of the first layer of gospel tradition. They all represent development of vocabulary in church circles. Mt in his explanation accounts for seven categories in the story, one after the other (vv. 37-39). He then appends a "little apocalypse" (vv. 40-43) which tells us the fate of the wicked and the just at the final judgment.

Mt bypasses the point of the parable about patient waiting until the end, so intent is he on moralizing about the fact that believers (members of the church) and unbelievers must live side by side, and about the ultimate fate of each at the separation that will characterize the judgment. He warns against false security and promises apostates and evildoers a bad end (v. 41). The holy ones will fare much better (v. 43).

Thus, even as early as the year 85 the urgent note in Jesus' tales which asks the hearer to recognize an eschatology that is in the process of realization has been lost. In its place has been put a moralizing about persecution and falling away in apocalyptic dress.

SEVENTEENTH SUNDAY OF THE YEAR (A)

(Tenth Sunday after Pentecost)

1 Kings 3:5, 7-12. Solomon is a boy-king when he succeeds his father David on the throne ("twelve years old" according to the LXX at 2:12; Josephus says aged fourteen). This dream story, heavily edited by the pious Deuteronomist, is told to account for Solomon's wisdom—even though in 2:6 he is said by David to possess it natively. Gibeon, where the dream occurrence is located, is six miles northwest of Jerusalem in Benjaminite territory. The king had gone there to offer sacrifice at the formerly Canaanite "high place," probably to mend a few political fences with his Benjaminite and Canaanite neighbors. The Deuteronomist editor regrets his presence at this sanctuary which took the place of Nob a short distance to the south after Saul's vengeful slaughter of the priests there (2 Sam 22:18f.), and balances it off by situating Solomon at Jerusalem for sacrifice before the ark in v. 15.

The temple had, of course, not been built yet, nor had public worship been consolidated at one place only. Still, the Deuteronomist is uneasy over Solomon's presence at the Gibeonite shrine. He is more at ease in accounting for Solomon's astuteness regarding men and affairs (vv. 11, 12), which will lead to riches and glory (v. 13). The story of the two harlots (vv. 16-28) is told to illustrate Solomon's sagacity. Unfortunately, his carrying on of a blood feud with Joab and Shimei until he destroys them, attributed to his father's counsel (2:5-9, 34-46), is also cited as proof of his wisdom.

For dreams as a way whereby a worshipper at a shrine might be communicated with by God, cf. Gn 28:12, 31:10f.; 1 Sam 3:1-18.

Romans 8:28-30. NEB makes "the Spirit" of vv. 26f. the subject of *synergei* (v. 28); thus: "And in everything, as we know, he co-operates for good," etc. On the other hand, it is God who "works for good" (RSV) or "makes all things work together for . . . good" (NAB), on the supposition that God is required by the context as the subject of the sentence (cf. v. 29.) In some MSS (including Chester Beatty p⁴⁶, Vaticanus, and Alexandrinus) *theos* occurs after *synergei* (as in KJ). The Vulgate makes *panta* the subject of *synergei*; thus, *omnia cooperantur in bonum*. If, however, *panta* is an accusative of specification, we have the "in everything God works for good" of RSV. NAB understands God to be the subject of *synergei* and *panta* its object.

While Paul's statement about God's providence regarding believers is subjective as regards their love, he puts the greater stress on their being objects of God's love since they are called as a result of his decree (*prothesis*, v. 28). In the working out of the divine plan the stages are: God's foreknowledge (v. 29*a*); man's sharing in the image of God's son who serves as the model ("the first-born of many brothers," 29*b*); and the calling of the predestined (30*a*) who are first justified (30*b*), then glorified (30*c*). The last stage, glorification, lies in the future but Paul, with the certainty of one who knows how the plan is meant to work, uses *edoxasen*, an aorist with the sense of completed action.

There is undoubtedly the notion of predestination in this passage but it is a predestination (*proōrisen*, v. 30, from *proorizō*) to glory, not to reprobation. God's decree inspires confidence, not fear, because it is above all a saving decree.

Matthew 13:44-52. The parables of the buried treasure, the pearl, and the dragnet do not occur in Mk or Lk, but Thomas has the first two as sayings 109 and 76. Thomas's story has a parallel in a rabbinic midrash on the Song of Songs. In the former the man who finds a treasure on his land lends money at interest to whomever he pleases; in the latter, the seller of the land grows choleric at the sight of the prosperity of the buyer. Jesus in Mt seems to be using a folktale to describe the supreme value of the reign of God, which is worth all that a man has and more. Thomas 76 on the pearl is substantially the same as Mt plus the content of Mt 6:19f. on a treasure immune to moth and rust (in Thomas, moth and worm). Mt makes the merchant sell all he has to establish a parallelism with v. 44. In Thomas he merely sells "the merchandise." The key phrase for both parables is "rejoicing" (*apo tēs charas*, v. 44), the joy being eschatological as part of a true estimate of what is of worth in this life.

The parable of the dragnet (vv. 47f.) has its close parallel in Thomas 8 except for the detail of one large, fine fish in Thomas. It is much like the story of the wheat and the weeds (Mt 13:24-30) in its ending about a separation at the judgment. The "useless" fish (*ta sapra*) would be those without fins or scales of Lv 11:10f. and the shellfish which Jesus' contemporaries did not eat. Again, separation is left to the end and to God's angelic agents, both because men do not know how to distinguish the worthy from the unworthy (v. 29) and, more importantly, because the fullness of time decreed by God must be reached: *ēn hote eplērōthē*, v. 48 ("when it was full").

The householder who brings forth new and old from his store, to whom Matthew compares the scribe learned in the reign of God, can be reckoned as the subject of a brief parable but most commentators consider it merely a simile.

Verse 53 contains the rubric, "When Jesus had finished these parables" (elsewhere "words" or "giving this instruction": 7:28; 11:1; 19:1; 26:1), with which five of his major discourses in Mt conclude.

EIGHTEENTH SUNDAY OF THE YEAR (A)

(Eleventh Sunday after Pentecost)

Isaiah 55:1-3. This pericope occurs in the second collection of oracles of the Deutero-Isaiah (chs. 49-55), the entire chapter serving as the climax. In it the author sees the return of the exiles to the land for covenant renewal (vv. 3*b*, 12), a land to which fertility shall be restored (v. 13) if this condition is fulfilled. In Hos 2:10f. the LORD is Israel's provider. Heeding him means rich fare and life (vv. 1ff.; cf. Prv 9:1-6), failing to do so villainy and wickedness (v. 7). The people are summoned to return to the LORD in a new land of promise. The benefits assured to David for covenant fidelity will be theirs in this age (v. 3*b*) if they represent YHWH to the nations as David once did (vv. 4f.)

Romans 8:35, 37-39. Verses 31-39 are a hymn of praise to "the love of God that comes to us in Jesus Christ" (v. 39) which is made effective in the intercession of Christ, dead but now raised up "at the right hand of God" (v. 34, obviously a creedal fragment). God has predestined his elect, i.e., those who in fact are being saved, to glory (v. 30). Neither God (v. 33) nor Christ (v. 34) is conceivable in an adversary relation, a figure from the courts of law. The suppressed personal accuser of v. 31 can be taken either as Satan (cf. Jb 1:6) or the law of Moses. No one, in any case, can make a successful prosecution, so strong will the defense be (v. 29f.) For a comment on vv. 31-34, see p. 191.

Persecution is a real contender for separating Christ from his chosen. Paul doubtless has his own trials in mind (cf. 5:2ff.; 1 Thes 3:3f.; 2 Cor 11:23-33.) Verse 36 quotes Ps 44:23. Yet God's personal love (v. 37) is superior to death and life, to all human and angelic powers (v. 38). "Neither height nor depth," that is to say, the positioning of heavenly bodies, can defeat this love. No creature is thinkable who has the power to contend with the overmastering divine love (v. 39).

Matthew 14:13-21. For a parallel to this first feeding of the multitude, see the commentary on Lk's only account (9:11-17), p. 338. As is remarked there, the Lucan narrative is sufficiently like Mk

6:30-44, from which today's pericope is derived, that it could have come from it as its sole source (cf. in particular Lk 9:16f. and Mk 6:41ff.) The words of blessing and distribution (v. 19) are close to those attributed to Jesus at the last supper (26:26), which means that the eucharistic meal practice of the Matthean church is mirrored in both accounts.

The point of the story is not that Jesus has moved the hearts of the crowd to the point where they share voluntarily, as was being maintained by various gospel-as-ethics schools earlier in this century, but that he performs a Moses-like work of power. Numerous colorful Marcan elements are removed from the story (e.g., the phrase "on the green grass in groups or parties," Mk 6:39) but the specifically eucharistic usage remains (*artoi, klasmata, klasas* = "loaves," "fragments," "breaking"). Mt also heightens the miraculous by reporting the detail that the 5,000 who were fed did not include women and children.

Like Mk, Mt has the fragments gathered up into twelve baskets, symbolic of the completion of elect peoplehood.

NINETEENTH SUNDAY OF THE YEAR (A)

(Twelfth Sunday after Pentecost)

1 Kings 19:9, 11-13. Elijah's victory over the prophets of Baal is complete and the drought comes to a close with a heavy rain, bringing to an end the famine in the land (chapter 18). This should have pleased King Ahab but his wife Jezebel, apprised of the slit throats of her 450 co-religionists, is moved to murderous reprisal. Elijah hears of her intent and flees for his life, discouraged. The action of the LORD in sending rain has not made his life quite so easy as he expected. He makes his journey of forty days and forty nights to Horeb (as it is called in the D and E sources; Sinai, in J) on the strength of the hearth cake and the water miraculously provided (vv. 5f.)

The conversation between the LORD and his prophet in the cave reveals a state of mind not unlike that of the sulking Jonah. Elijah is far from Israel where he belongs and is reproached for his flight (v. 9*b*). In a burst of self-pity he complains of his reverses as if only he, of all Israel, has kept faith. "As though Carmel had never happened!" one commentator puts it.

Strong wind, earthquake, and fire supervene but none of this is the sign of God's power. Rather, a "tiny whispering sound"—the "still, small voice" of KJ. Vv. 13f. are an obvious doublet of 9f., with the difference that Elijah is sent back to the Aramean desert to anoint King Hazael in the second case rather than outside the cave to "stand on the mountain before the LORD" (v. 11). When Elijah recognizes Yahweh's speech in the tiny whispering sound he hides his face, as Moses had done in similar circumstances (cf. Ex 3:6.) The passage is a powerful parable of the unexpected way of God's action. Popular understanding has taken the "still, small voice" as having to do with conscience. It is, in fact, concerned with God's action in ordinary ways, not the flamboyant extraordinary.

Romans 9:1-5. Paul can be separated by nothing from God's love in Christ (8:38f.) but that does not mean that he feels no pain of separation. The great grief of his life is separation from his Jewish brothers over the gospel. He could even wish, *per impossibile*, to reverse the course of things and be separated from Christ in order to be joined with his kinsmen (v. 3), enduring the one for the sake of the other. Paul lists the irrevocable benefits to his own people (v. 4), among them "the glory." This *k^ebhod Yahweh* dwelling in their midst (cf. Ex 40:34f.) was the epitome of all the rest. Whose were Abraham, Isaac, and Jacob if not Israel's, and whose the blood line from which sprang that messiah who, in Paul's faith, is Jesus (v. 5)? Overwhelmed at the irreversible course of history with its gifts to his own people, Paul can only conclude with a *berakah*, a prayer that singles out the blessedness of God responsible for it all. (NAB cuts a grammatical Gordian knot in its rendition of 5*b* according to sense; the "blessed" one could be Christ, but barely.)

In the first eight chapters of this epistle Paul has been speaking in praise of God's freely bestowed love for sinful man. With these opening verses the epistle goes in a new direction. Paul begins to reflect that despite all Israel's privileges of the past (and his energies on her behalf), there is in prospect indeed a present reality, the refusal of the love. Paul speaks the truth of the matter not on his own but "in Christ"; his conscience bears him witness "in the holy spirit" (v. 1). For the phrase "separated [by a curse] from Christ" (*anathema . . . apo tou Christou*, v. 3), see 1 Cor 16:22; Gal 1:8f. To be apart from Christ for Paul is to be consigned to destruction, *anathema* being the LXX rendering of the OT *ḥerem* or ban. His "kinsmen" are specifically *syggenōn mou kata sarka*, his human, not yet Christian kinsmen. Paul can no longer claim kinship with them *kata pneuma.* He will make the same qualification in v. 5 as here in 3 with respect to the Jewishness of the messiah; it, too, is a matter of his "human origins." Israelite sonship of God is such by adoption (*hyiothesia*, v. 4), as if some new status were acquired at the exodus (cf. Ex 4:22; Hos 11:1.) God's purpose in choosing Israel as the scene

of man's salvation seems temporarily thwarted. It is with this
paradox that Paul will wrestle in the next three chapters.

Matthew 14:22-33. Matthew takes the account of Jesus' walking on
the sea from Mk 6:45-52 but puts it to quite different use by adding
vv. 28-31, the section about the saving of Peter, and omitting Mk's
v. 52. This provides an important illustration of redaction criticism,
the editorial use of traditional materials to serve an overall
theological purpose. Both evangelists have Jesus separate his disciples
from the crowd after the feeding miracle but, whereas Mk uses the
appearance of Jesus on the stormy waters to heighten their lack of
understanding (in this case, about the loaves, v. 52), Mt employs it as
a confession of the Lord who has marvelously appeared to them
(v. 33). It is, in other words, construed as an illustration of faith in
the latter case and lack of faith in the former.

In both gospels the disciples are described as terrified at Jesus'
appearance (Mt 14:26; Mk 6:50*a*). Not even his comforting words in
Mk (v. 50*b*) can dispel their fears; if anything, the latter seem to be
heightened as the pericope ends (v. 51*b*). The disciples' early terror in
Mt, however (v. 26), is replaced by a trust in him which goes as far
as confessing him to be "the son of God" (v. 33).

Mt in his insertion of vv. 28-31 (his use of *ta hydata* for water as
in 8:32 rather than the *thalassa* found in Mk at 6:48f. and copied by
Mt in 14:25, plus the characteristically Matthean *kyrie* [vv. 28, 30],
certifies that it is an insertion) uses the epiphany of Jesus to "set
them free to exercise a fearless faith." (Held) Mt understandably has
Peter crying for help in words very close to the disciples' cry during
the storm on the sea (8:25). The "It is I" of v. 27 is joined by "if it
is you" as a faith-link. Jesus has said "Do not be afraid!" in both
gospels (Mk 6:50; Mt 14:17) but only in Mt do they heed his
injunction.

Mt uses his Petrine insertion for a double purpose. It shows the
promise made to faith in a context of discipleship, a theme that runs
throughout his gospel. It also underscores the disciple Peter's inability
to remain firm on his own during a time of testing. It is Jesus who
gives his disciples the power to follow him. Without that there is only
dismay and fear at his prowess, and destruction as the fruit of
misplaced trust in oneself.

The scene is ecclesiological as is usual in Mt, not only
christological. Jesus looks for a community of believers that is not,
like Peter, of "little faith" (*oligopiste*, v. 31*b*). He means to transmit
his authority, signified by the power to walk on water, to those whom
he sends in his name.

TWENTIETH SUNDAY OF THE YEAR (A)
(Thirteenth Sunday after Pentecost)

Isaiah 56:1, 6-7. This chapter marks the opening of the third book in the collection known as Isaiah which spans two centuries. The Babylonian exile is over and the people Israel is back in the homeland. Perhaps the temple has already been rebuilt (520-16 B.C.). Deutero-Isaiah had been a gospel of promised salvation; the restored community must now be enjoined in an institutional spirit to "observe" and to "do" (v. 1) Trito-Isaiah tries hard to be faithful to the outlook and even the vocabulary of his predecessor. Verse 1 is like 46:13a and 51:5a as to wording but the spirit is different. The LORD's "justice" that is about to be revealed—even to foreigners and to the previously excluded eunuchs (Dt 23:2)—is a matter of observing sabbaths (2b, 4a, 6c), holding fast to the terms of the covenant (4b, 6c), and offering sacrifices and holocausts on God's altar (7b). It is understandable that in exile sabbath observance would have come to the fore since temple sacrifice and other cultic forms were impossible to keep (cf. 58:13.) Still, the new demand for observance on priestly terms is somewhat disturbing in light of the great Isaian prophetic tradition.

Second-Isaiah had spoken marvelously of Egyptians, Ethiopians, and Sabeans who would come to Israel joining her in chains (45:14), of every knee bending to the LORD (45:23b), and nations who knew her not running to Israel because of her LORD (55:5). Verses 6 and 7 attempt an "opening to the left" by welcoming proselyte Gentiles and the castrated into the worshiping community on condition that they keep the sabbath and make the proper offerings in the temple on Mt. Zion.

Eunuchs had been disbarred probably because of their inability to have offspring. Here, their fidelity to observance is accepted in place of the perpetuation of their names in their children. The foreigners "ministering" to the LORD (a priestly term) may be proselytes who, in virtue of circumcision, become the mysterious "temple slaves" (*ethinim*) of 1 Chr 9:2 and Ezr 8:17, 20.

The ringing prophecy of Is 2:2-4 and of chapters 40-55 is somehow fulfilled in v. 7. The bold term "house of prayer" is one of several descriptive titles to which this author is partial (cf. 58:12; 60:14, 18; 62:4, 12.) All are triumphalist ways of describing the return from the exile, depressingly like modern church pronouncements to the effect that promised reforms have now been achieved.

Romans 11:13-15, 29-32. St. Paul's wrestling with the theological problem of the refusal of his fellow Jews to accept the gospel he has preached to them, carried on over chapters 9-11, culminates in the seven verses of this reading. He has already pressed his conviction that there is a "chosen remnant" (11:5), a nation within a nation made up of Christian Jews. As to those who do not accept the choice made of them by grace but persist in works and their own "seeking" (v. 7)—by far the greater number—Paul's argument concerning them takes the familiar *a fortiori* form.

He writes to the Gentiles of Rome as one conscious of his special apostolate to Gentiles (cf. Gal 2:7, 9), explaining why his concern for fellow-Jews nonetheless persists. He says quite frankly that the greater his efforts to evangelize the uncircumcised, the greater is the likelihood that the circumcised will be moved by envy. His goal is modest, "to save some of them" (v. 14), as if he now realizes that while he may witness a few conversions, the acceptance of Christ by all Jews is an eschatological event (cf. v. 25) at the farther limit of history. If the rejection (*apobolē*) of Jewish people has meant reconciliation (*katallagē*) for the world—the world of Jews and Gentiles as in Eph 2:16? the world of alienated Gentiles to God? —how much more will their acceptance (*proslēmpsis*) mean. It will be an event of the end time, however, and the "life from the dead" it signals is no less than the final resurrection of all. Paul's theology here is one of happy fault. There is no telling what progress, if any, the gospel might have made among the Gentiles but for Jewish resistance. That obduracy has triggered a modest stage one. Consider, then,—he suggests—on the hypothesis of Jewish openness to the gospel—the magnitude of stage two.

Verses 29-32 put the same argument another way. Gentile disobedience may have been responded to by the divine mercy but Jewish disobedience was the very condition of it. Now that the Jews have slipped back into the helpless state of the Gentiles, they may expect rescue on the same terms. Disobedience all around means mercy all around. In fact, had the Jews not fallen to the Gentiles' low estate, there is no telling how rescue would have come their way. It is something like the alcoholic who has to go all the way to the bottom before he recognizes he needs help from outside himself.

God does not go back on his gifts and his calling (*charismata kai klēsis*, v. 29). Apparently, however, the unbelief of the Jews regarding Christ is, for Paul, a necessary stage on their way to faith. God's mercy is the key to all human need, whatever a people's spiritual history or lack of it may have been.

Matthew 15:21-28. Matthew follows Mk 7:24-30 quite closely in this pericope, omitting chiefly the characteristic note of secrecy in Mk's v.

24b. He calls the woman a Canaanite rather than a Syrophoenician and adds the detail of the disciples' attempt to be rid of her, which merits in response the important logion, "My mission was only to the lost sheep of the house of Israel" (v. 24). This phrase is simply an explicitation of the Marcan exchange. The remaining alterations in Mt are small and verbal only, not substantive.

Mark's situating of Jesus outside Jewish territory (this occurrence on the Phoenician coast is followed by his appearance in the Decapolis, 7:31) seems to be a brief "Gentile ministry" calculated to meet the needs of Mk's Gentile readers. The overall tradition does not appear to support any such extensive stay, however. It may have taken its rise largely from Mk's universalist inclinations.

The main thrust of the story, as Mt tells it, lies not in the healing but in the initial silence (v. 23a) and then the conversation (vv. 25-28a) which precede the miracle. Jesus' answer to the woman's plea indicates that his powers are conceived by the evangelists as specific spiritual powers in aid of God's establishment of his reign among his Jewish people. The Gentile woman is described as accepting this without difficulty (the harsh term "dogs" was the ordinary religious obloquy of the times for any less favored group than one's own). She is portrayed as accepting the divine division of things as between Jews and Gentiles. By her persistence and in her speech she acknowledges Jesus as Israel's messiah ("Lord, Son of David . . .", v. 22). The point of the tale is not so much her spirited response as her concurrence in the Jewish reading of the providential plan of salvation.

Briefly, Jesus is described by his followers as having regarded his commission and, later, theirs as one that was confined to Israel. As *Jewish* messiah, however, he would have been aware of the many prophecies which spoke of the Gentiles as participants in Israel's saved condition. (Cf. Is 19:19-25; 60; 66:19f.; Mi 4:1f.; Zech 8:20ff.) That was to be a matter of the last days, however. Any anticipation, as in St. Paul's reading of the data in Rom above, was exceptional. The relative places of Jew and Gentile in the order of salvation were fixed.

The resurrection changed this perspective somewhat. Only the adventures of the gospel in Jewish circles over four decades brought about serious reconsideration of this position. Meanwhile, Mt the evangelist to Jews tells the story of the Canaanite woman's cure in support of the position that nothing has been changed (cf. v. 24) as between Jewish and Gentile election.

TWENTY-FIRST SUNDAY OF THE YEAR (A)

(Fourteenth Sunday after Pentecost)

Isaiah 22:19-23. We do not know who Shebna was (v. 15) aside from being a political upstart who had feathered his own nest, in this case a sepulcher hewn from the rock. The prophet in consigning him to oblivion has given him a surer place in history than he would have had through his career or his memorial. "Master of the palace" was his title (v. 15), an office we know of from 1 Kgs 4:6. Shebna probably also served as chief cabinet minister in the court of King Hezekiah of Judah (716-687 B.C.). The present incident is to be dated some time before the happenings of chapters 37-39, which are usually put at 701.

The LORD will eject Shebna from his office (v. 19), deprive him access to the government car-pool (the vehicles are chariots), and replace him by the trustworthy Eliakim. The virtues of this son of Hilkiah are specified in v. 21. The divine wrath was evidently only moderately effective against Shebna, who continued to function as the king's "scribe" (36:3; 37:2; cf. 1 Kgs 4:3; Jer 36:12), an office of cabinet rank.

The importance of the passage to Christian literature—for in itself it merely describes a faithful public servant—is the use made of it in Rev 3:7. Writing to the *aggelos* or "presiding spirit" of the church of Philadelphia in Asia Minor, the Apocalyptist applies the Isaian text to Christ as "the holy One, the true." From here it makes its way into the *Magnificat* antiphon of December 20, "O clavis David." The symbol of Peter's keys in Mt 16:19 may also be drawn from this mention of a key, carried slung from the shoulder and symbolizing authority.

An appendix to the poetic oracle of vv. 15-24 written by another hand in prose indicates that Eliakim, fixed "like a peg in a sure spot" (v. 23), will regrettably "break off and fall" (v. 25), a cryptic reference to one more politician's inability to withstand the pressures of office. It is generally assumed that the weight of the cloak referred to some offense like nepotism or trading in favors to hangers-on.

Romans 11:33-36. This passage follows immediately upon that of last Sunday which was a highly compressed version of St. Paul's view of God's mercy shown to Jews and Gentiles alike, each of whom were disobedient in their own way. In today's reading, the concluding segment of his argument, Paul praises the inscrutable design of God. He has already alluded to the wealth of God's kindness and forbearance (2:4) and of his glory as contrasted with his wrath (9:23). Cf. Col 1:27, where the "glory beyond price" of God's mystery in Christ is *to ploutos tēs doxēs tou mystēriou toutou.* Here, God is rich in wisdom and knowledge (v. 33). Paul's exclamation in v. 33*b* has a Job-like quality. The next verses, 34 and 35, are quotations, one from the Septuagint (Is 40:13) and the other not (Jb 41:11). No one acts as the LORD's counselor; moreover no one is a donor to him in such a way that a claim can be lodged against him. At all points he is the initiator in his mercy.

All things are from, to, and for God for a Jewish believer like Paul (v. 36*a*). There is a phrase not unlike this in Marcus Aurelius' *Meditations* (4, 23), after he has apostrophized the Universe and Nature: "From you are all things, in you are all things, unto you are all things." Such verbal usage was probably a convention in the Hellenistic Judaism from which Paul sprang.

He ends in an ascription of glory to God for the richness of his gift (v. 36*b*).

Matthew 16:13-20. As we have come to expect, Mt adds to Mk (8:27-30) for his special confessional and ecclesial purposes. He has Jesus call himself "the son of man" in v. 13 (interchangeable with the "I" of Mk 8:27*b*), adds the name of Jeremiah (v. 14) and the phrase, "the son of the living God" to "Christ" (v. 16), and finally inserts vv. 17-19 about Peter as the rock into the Marcan account. Caesarea Philippi, modern Banyas near Dan at the northern extremity of Israel, is of no OT significance, hence doubtless existed in the historical tradition as it came to Mk. It was the site of a shrine to the god Pan still clearly distinguishable, hence its Greek name. A wall of rock rises almost sheer, if not high, as part of the foothills below distant Mt. Hermon.

Mk's parallel passage (v. 29) has the disciples recognizing Jesus as the Messiah for the first time, with Peter as their spokesman. Mk is chiefly interested in the first prediction of the passion, which culminates in the rebuke delivered to Peter (v. 33) and, through him, to all. Mt retains this idea, adding that Peter is a hindrance (*skandalon*) who threatens to make Jesus "trip and fall" by his resistance to the idea of his suffering (v. 23). Jesus has previously been recognized as the son of God in Mt (14:33) but this is his first designation there as the Christ or Messiah.

The verses 17-19 include, among other things, a Matthean explanation of Simon's name Peter. The latter cognomen is generally Cepha[s] in Paul as also in Jn 1:42 but Peter in the synoptics. The Aramaic *Kēpha*, Hellenized by the addition of an "s", means rock (just as *sur* does in Hebrew, the modern way to say Peter). In the gospels the name says nothing about Peter's character; indeed, Mt takes the pains to deny any special human qualification to him and attribute all to God (v. 17). The rock figure clearly has something to do with Simon's office of spiritual leadership with respect to the community (*ekklēsia*, v. 18, found again at 18:17), referred to in terms of faith in Lk 22:32f. and love in Jn 21:15-19.

The church spoken of as an edifice has interesting parallels in the *Qumrân Community Rule* (8:7): "[The council of the community] shall be established in truth. It shall be . . . a house of holiness for Israel . . . It shall be that tried wall, that precious corner-stone, whose foundations shall neither rock nor sway in their place" (cf. Is 28:16.) The *Testament of Levi* at 2:3-5, which occurs in an Aramaic fragment at Qumrân, says that "unrighteousness had built itself walls and lawlessness sat upon towers." In a dream, Levi says, "I beheld a high mountain, and I was upon it." He had this vision while feeding the flocks in Abel-Maul (the Abel-meholah of Jgs 7:22, generally situated in Samaria near the Jordan). Stendahl speculates that this fragment may provide a parallel to the country around Caesarea Philippi, "since this area played a role in Jewish apocalypticism as a place of revelation and as a meeting-place for the upper and the lower world." What the geographic link with *Test. Levi* may be he does not say.

Peter's binding and loosing under the figure of keys can refer to the ordinary judgments of a rabbi in determining the measure in which people are bound to rules in following *halakah*, the way, or it can refer to church order. Probably the former is intended in Matthew. An important question is, did Jesus envision in his lifetime an *ekklēsia* or community of followers, or was such simply the reality from Mt's time? The evidence of Qumrân favors the notion of organization as a Jewish reality whereas much that we know of Jesus from his other sayings is against it. A community of faith in him was real, however, in his lifetime.

Peter is to be the "Rock" (v. 18) in his own person through his faith. Cullmann has shown that most attempts to have the term describe this firm *trust* of Peter but not his *person* stem from Protestant bias. At the same time not every claim made for the chief bishopric in the faith-community—not many, one is tempted to say, only an important few—can be traced to the intent of Mt in this crucial passage.

Bornkamm holds, against Cullmann and Oepke, that the saying of vv. 17ff. belongs to the period after Easter. The *ekklēsia* of v. 18 is an eschatological entity but one of future, earthly time. It "bears throughout an institutional character, characterised by the authority in doctrine and discipline of a particular apostle." Decisions about doctrine and discipline in this church will be confirmed, ratified, in the coming *basileia* or reign of God. Mt has changed the rejection of Peter's confession by Jesus in Mk into a confession of Peter endorsed by Jesus as the ground for making him the rock of the church.

TWENTY-SECOND SUNDAY OF THE YEAR (A)
(Fifteenth Sunday after Pentecost)

Jeremiah 20:7-9. This passage immediately precedes the first reading for the Twelfth Sunday of the Year in Cycle A. See, the commentary on Jer 20:10-13, for some background material.

Verses 7-13 comprise a literary unit, a psalm which has as its burden the prophet's awful suspicion that he has been taken in by the LORD. In context it comes after a declaration that the temple administrator Pashhur will be captured by Babylon and carried off into exile (v. 6) much in the way he inflicts beatings and forcible restraints (v. 2) on the prophet. The psalm could serve, of course, as a more general outcry of the heart stemming from Jeremiah's anguish at having to be a prophet of doom. His role is an unenviable one. The prognosticator of impending tragedy is thought to wish it to come on whereas those who deny its likelihood are confused with people who have no desire for it. The prophetic stance is even more painful for the one forced to assume it if he is by nature cheerful and gregarious. His only burden is that of clear vision. He will not compromise his integrity by remaining silent.

But even Jeremiah, being a truthful man, is subject to doubts. Like any popular teacher with an unpopular message, he needs some response, some "feedback," to indicate that he may be on the right track. Hearing none he begins to wonder if he may be one of the false prophets described in 1 Kgs 22:19-23. There, "lying spirits" are described by Micaiah as sent by the LORD into certain prophets' mouths, a part of Micaiah's strategy to deter Ahab from his foolish plan of attack. Jeremiah suffers the ultimate doubt. Has counsel been taken in heaven resulting in the choice of him as the mouthpiece of a lying spirit? One is reminded of the tortures of the saints who wondered if it was the devil who was acting through them.

Jeremiah concludes that he must be duped by the LORD because he is the object of such mockery and derision (vv. 7, 8). His message, "Violence and outrage!" (8*a*), has come true only in Pashhur's mishandling of him, not as between Judah and Babylon. The entire sequence is remarkably modern.

Then a ploy occurs to him: absolute silence about the LORD (9*a*). He will act the mute so as to stay out of trouble. But it won't work. Such action would make him a false prophet. He could not endure the pain of holding in what he knows to be true (9*c*). "Thy love is like a burning fire / Within my very soul" might serve as a paraphrase of 9*b*. Better to wear out in prophetic truth-telling than rust out in lying silence.

Romans 12:1-2. Although these two verses follow those of last week's reading, the epistle goes in a new direction with the opening of chapter 12. Perhaps better put, Paul begins to list the practical moral implications for his brothers (i.e., those in Christ like himself) of the fact that God has willed to "have mercy on all" (11:32). His doctrinal teaching concluded, he proceeds to spell out its necessary ethical consequences; hence the "And now" of v. 1 (*oun*, "therefore").

God's mercy (*tōn oiktirmōn*, the *rachᵉmim* or "compassion" of the Hebrew Bible) is Paul's point of appeal. The way God has expressed it has been sketched in the epistle up until now, chs. 9-11 in particular. The proper response to these mercies is self-surrender. "Your bodies" (v. 1) means your whole selves. The vocabulary is that of formal worship (*latreian*), specifically a sacrifice (*thysian*) which is holy and acceptable (*hagian, euareston*). The worship is to be spiritual (*logikēn*; cf. 1 Pt 2:2; in v. 5, *pneumatikas thysias*), that is, a movement of man's whole inner *logos* or spiritual self. The notion is familiar from the *Miserere*, which speaks of a contrite spirit as the psalmist's sacrifice (Ps 51:19). There is also the idea of loving and serving God with one's whole heart (cf. Dt 11:13.) However biblical Paul's thought may be, his term *logikē* to describe the Christian's sacrifice is Stoic usage current in Hellenist Jewish circles.

Paul's exhortation in v. 2 is eschatological. Christians may not take the present *aiōn* as their standard of conduct, "this age" being understood as one still ruled by demonic powers despite Christ's death and resurrection. Those "in Christ" have entered upon the new age of the Spirit (cf. 8:12, 23) but Paul never speaks of the age to come as if it has arrived except by foreshadowings. The renewal of mind which will qualify believers to judge God's will for them rightly and tell what is *agathon, euareston,* and *teleion* in their regard is a fruit of life in the Spirit, hence of the new age. The renewal (*metamorphousthai*) spoken of is total, beginning at baptism and proceeding with every conscious choice throughout life. It is with this renewed *nous* that Paul serves the law of God but with its opposite, *sarx*, that he serves the law of sin (cf. 7:25.) Nothing else can pass judgment on what is good, pleasing, and perfect. The latter adjective is related to the concept of Christ as the end (*telos*) of the law (10:4).

Matthew 16:21-27. Last Sunday's reading and commentary will have alerted us to Matthew's special use of Marcan material. In today's pericope he gives us the text of Peter's rebuke (v. 22), whereas Mk had been satisfied to record the fact (8:32). Mt adds the word *skandalon* (v. 23), "make me trip and fall," and removes Mk's "crowd" (8:34) so as to constitute v. 24 a charge to the disciples alone. In v. 27 he features the repayment of faithful acknowledgement by Jesus when he comes in glory at the end, much in the manner of the later judgment scene (25:31-46). Mk is content (v. 38) to let the shame which disciples experience over Jesus be countered by his being ashamed of them. For the rest, the two narratives are largely alike.

In both gospels Peter's confession of faith in Jesus serves as the context of the first prophecy of suffering (Mk 8:31; Mt 16:21). Mt highlights the relation of the two more than Mk with his phrase, "From then on" (Mk's link between the two narratives had been "And . . .") Similarly, Mt employs a favorite word, "then" (*tote*), in v. 24 to show clearly that the doctrine of the cross for disciples follows from Jesus' prophecy of his own suffering.

In Mk Jesus makes Peter's confession nothing but an occasion for an injunction to silence (8:30). Mt on the other hand gives it an importance in itself (16:17-19). Having inserted the promise to Peter, he might well have reduced the tension caused by the rebuke of Peter by eliminating it. Instead, he heightens it by providing the wording of Peter's remonstrance ("May you be spared . . . , God forbid . . .", v. 22) which Mk does not do. Mt has no special interest in Mk's deferral of a disclosure of Jesus' glory until after Easter, even though he knows about it (v. 20). His concern is to have Jesus endorse Peter's confession of faith in him and use it as the ground for making him the rock of the church.

Mt's theology is such that he does not tone down Mk's contrast between the glory of Jesus as the Christ and his sufferings as Son of Man on earth. He too wishes to place the disciples on the way of suffering imitation (cf. 16:24ff.) The judge who will come to repay them according to their fidelity (v. 27) is none other than this suffering Son of God and Son of Man.

The promise of the keys to Peter is clearly a church tradition, one which may even go back to a post-Easter appearance. Mt's making it a pre-Easter story, particularly in the context provided by Mk, shows his determination to teach that the church with its power of the keys is subject to the law of suffering of the earthly Jesus. Jesus will sustain the church's decisions in the coming judgment if its binding and loosing (v. 19) have been carried on in imitation of Christ's sufferings and fidelity to his vocation. The norm for the church is, "When he does [come], he will repay each man according to his conduct" (v. 27).

Concern with Mt's *ekklēsia*-theology may have its thousands but Jesus' words in vv. 24-26 (cf. Mk 8:34-37) have their tens of thousands. One is hard pressed to find their like in all literature to express the place of personal integrity in man's search for meaning, discipleship of Jesus quite apart.

TWENTY-THIRD SUNDAY OF THE YEAR (A)

(Sixteenth Sunday after Pentecost)

Ezekiel 33:7-9. These verses repeat 3:17-19, as part of the parallelism between the two parts of this book, chs. 1-24 and 25-48. The beginning of the second half (chs. 25-32) is made up of prophecies against Moab, Tyre, Sidon, and Egypt, while from ch. 32 onward there are messages of comfort and salvation for Israel.

The parable of the watchman concerns the prophet, whose favorite designation for himself is "son of man." He interprets his role as one involving heavy public responsibility. Just as the negligent guard or sentry can expect the death sentence for his failure, so Ezekiel feels he must warn his people of their perilous condition under pain of his life. Anyone who falls before the oncoming Chaldean army has only himself to blame if he disregards the prophetic trumpet (vv. 4-6). The passage makes clear that, although it is based on the imagery of a city taken by surprise, its chief thrust is ethical. The prophet is not a political or military man—even though he should prove to be one indirectly—but a moral teacher. A person's or a nation's sin is Ezekiel's concern (v. 6). Dissuading the wicked from their guilt is his task (v. 8). Once the prophet has delivered himself of his warning he is free of responsibility; it now lies with the other. The prophet, having done his work, can rest secure (v. 9).

The parable is a powerful example of Hebrew (hence Christian) morality which holds that the religious man must be a public man.

Romans 13:8-10. The first seven verses of this chapter contain Paul's theory of obedience to legitimate authority. Conceivably it was penned in a spirit of "Rome papers please copy" to win for the Roman Christian community the benefits Judaism enjoyed as a *religio licita*. It is more likely, however, that the passage represents Paul's deepest convictions on the power of the state as an arm of God's providence. The empire acts as a regulating and even a restraining force (cf. 2 Thes 2:6f.) to ensure the spread of the gospel until Christ shall return in glory. No law-abiding Christian whose conscience is clear need fear reprisals, writes Paul. His is the simplicity of one who has not yet learned how few rivals the ancient (or modern) state will endure.

Turning in v. 8 to the morality of interaction among Christians as contrasted with that regarding the government, Paul counsels that all go free of debt. The obvious exception is the obligation to mutual love, a debt that no one can be free of. This is doubtless an injunction to practice *agapē* (the noun and verb forms of which Paul uses) in the community. He is on record as not being interested in

Christians' loving Christians only (cf. 12:14, 17, 19ff.) but he seems to understand "neighbor" here (vv. 8, 10) as Lv 19:18 did, namely fellow-countryman in a community of faith. Yet he takes pains to designate the recipient of this love as *heteron*, "another" (v. 8) rather than the *plēsion* or "neighbor" of the LXX in v. 9, 10, as if to highlight difference or distinction, not likemindedness. Perhaps not too much should be made of this (NAB renders both by "neighbor") since *hetera entolē* in v. 9 will mean simply "any other commandment."

Verse 8 speaks of fulfilling the law, a phrase which has its meaning clarified by v. 9. As was the case with Jesus when quoted by Mk on the decalogue (10:19), Paul does not name the prohibitions in the order given in either Ex (20:13-17) or Dt (5:17-21). He says that keeping them fulfills the law with regard to our neighbor, a matter adequately summed up in Lv 19:18. Mk 12:31 and parallels indicate that there was contemporary rabbinic usage to this effect. Paul does not identify this usage as a "word of the Lord" as he does elsewhere (1 Cor 7:10; 1 Thes 4:15). It either has not come to him as such or else he wants to favor the sentiment without quoting Jesus, thereby running the risk of a new legalism.

If one loves he cannot wrong his neighbor (v. 10), hence is free of any offense against ethical demand. Love is the fulfillment (*plēroma*) of the law in the sense that it keeps it, not that it dispenses from the need to keep it. Paul's usage in v. 9 establishes this. The Christian's *agapē* fulfills Lv 19:18 and all that is summed up by it.

Matthew 18:15-20. The lectionary proceeds from the *ekklēsia*-oriented passage of Mt 16 read on the last two Sundays to the only other one in his gospel that uses the term. Prevailing as the notion of church is in Mt, the word occurs in these two places only (16:18; 18:17). As we might expect, there is no parallel place in Mk. (Lk has a saying in 17:3 that somewhat resembles 15a but that is all.)

We are not too far wrong in seeing in this passage a portion of a manual of discipline for the community like that of Qumrân or chs. 7-15 of the *Didachē* addressed to church leaders. There is, indeed, a striking resemblance between Mt 18:16 and *MD* vi, 1: "When he has a charge against his neighbor, he is to proffer it on that very day and not render himself liable to a penalty by nursing a grudge. Furthermore, no man is to bring a charge publicly against his neighbor except he prove it by witnesses." Both obviously derive from Lv 19:17. A little earlier in Qumrân's community rule (v. 24) an annual review of spiritual attitudes which should end in promotion or demotion is proposed.

Mt is of course a gospel featuring catechetical elements for beginners but it has disciplinary counsel for the leadership as well, as today's pericope indicates.

Recalcitrance is tested in three stages: as between individuals (v. 15), before witnesses (16), and in the presence of the assembly, *ekklēsia* (17). If it persists beyond the last stage it is to end in formal excommunication, such being the force of the reference to Gentiles and tax-brokers. Mt 18:18 is repeated from 16:19 but in a quite different sense. There it was the promulgation of *halakah* (practice) and had the force of giving Peter authority as the chief rabbi, i.e., arbiter. Here it is repeated precisely to alter its implications in the direction of disciplinary action.

The sayings on prayer, whatever their original significance might have been, are employed by Mt as a means whereby two or three witnesses can count on Christ's presence to support their disciplinary action. The technique proposed is not unlike that suggested by Paul against the incestuous Corinthian (1 Cor 5:4f.). Verses 21ff. which follow today's reading exhort to an even more generous handling of church disciplinary problems than Lk 17:4 with its "seven times."

Verse 20 has a long history of being cited in Christian circles, whether in favor of community prayer, against formal liturgical prayer, or as testimony to Jesus' mystical presence. Mt's concern that the gathered two or three are there to settle thorny interpersonal problems in the congregation does not negate its more widespread application, needless to say, though one becomes uncomfortable with interpretations the farther they depart from the Matthean context.

TWENTY-FOURTH SUNDAY OF THE YEAR (A)

(Seventeenth Sunday after Pentecost)

Sirach 27:30—28:7. Jesus ben Sirach, the author of this book, is identified as the first of the sapiental authors—the psalmists here not included—to identify wisdom with the law (cf. 28:7.) Previous biblical wisdom writers, unlike the priests, had been unconcerned with institutional religion or a covenantal concern with YHWH. One achieves wisdom, ben Sirach holds, by frequenting the company of the elders (6:34) and men of prudence (36) and meditating constantly on the LORD's precepts and commandments (37).

Vengeance is not in man's province; it belongs to the LORD (28:1). This is the teaching of the law (Lv 19:18; Dt 32:35, 39, 41*b*). Man's part is to forgive—even injustice—and he may expect the same from God in return (v. 2). Here, as in the teaching of a later Jesus, forgiving others is the condition of receiving forgiveness (cf. Mt 6:12,

14; 18:21f.; Mk 11:25.) Our Lord illustrates v. 4 with a parable in Mt 18:23-35.

Perhaps the most telling advice in the passage occurs at v. 7: "Overlook faults." The Bible contains no loftier counsel.

The motivation provided is the thought of death the great leveler, and of the covenantal relation in which the believer stands to Israel's God (vv. 6, 7).

Romans 14:7-19. St. Paul cannot conceive of a human situation in which the believer escapes being the Lord's, that is, Jesus Christ's. He is his special possession. Whether in death or in life one is under God's judgment; hence one is unwise to judge another before appearing at the judgment seat himself (v. 10). Christ risen is Lord of all (v. 9).

Paul enunciates his certainty, expressed elsewhere, that no foods defile (1 Cor 10:25), just as no diet or abstention brings us closer to God (1 Cor 8:8). Yet he is as sensitive here as he was in 1 Cor (8:9-13; 10:23-30) to the plight of the weak brother who could come to ruin or commit blasphemy at the sight of a Christian whose acts show he is more liberated than he is (vv. 15, 16). Dietary laws are not what the kingdom of God is about (v. 17), rather the spirit's gifts of justice, peace, and joy. But working for peace and mutual strength (v. 19) in the community may mean staying away from certain foods which are harmless in themselves (vv. 20ff.) Paul shows no awareness here of knowing any teaching of Jesus in similar vein (e.g., Mk 7:15).

There is a paradox in this teaching in that the judgments of fellowmen should not determine anyone's course of action; it is God alone whose judgment counts (vv. 10-12). Yet if a strong man boasts of his superiority and despises the weak he has fallen under judgment. So one's conduct with respect to one's brother turns out to be of supreme importance. The other both is and is not the determiner of one's actions.

Paul has already laid it down in Rom that the supreme command is love (13:8ff.; 12:9f.). In this passage he suggests some practical implications of this love in a world where not all are strong.

Matthew 18:21-35. We spoke last week of the enlargement of the need for forgiveness in Mt over the norm provided in Lk 17:4: "If he sins against you seven times a day, and seven times a day turns back to you saying, 'I am sorry,' forgive him."

Only Mt has this parable of the merciless *doulos*. The central figure in the tale, like all his companions, is a slave but the amount he owes is so great that he must be thought of as having some large position of trust. That is not the point, of course, but rather the huge discrepancy between his indebtedness (literally "ten thousand talents") and the tiny sum that is owed him ("a hundred denarii"). It is as if we should speak of a billion dollars and a fifty-cent piece.

The application of the parable is probably Matthew's; in any event it is one which dulls its effect considerably. ("My heavenly Father" is a Matthean term.) Forgiveness is not a matter of speech only but something that comes from the heart (cf. Mt 15:8.) This is a parable of the last judgment at which the merciful may expect forgiveness but the unmerciful strict justice.

TWENTY-FIFTH SUNDAY OF THE YEAR (A)

(Eighteenth Sunday after Pentecost)

Isaiah 55:6-9. The oracles of the postexilic Trito-Isaiah have opened with ch. 55. (See the commentary on the Fifteenth Sunday of the Year, Cycle A, p. 114.) Israel's God, her Holy One, will summon the Gentiles who will come running to her. But there is a condition. This LORD must first be sought by his own people. Only their identification with him will make him attractive to the nations.

Today's passage shows how he is to be called on, namely in repentance and conversion (7a and b). An evil man thinks vengeful thoughts. Reprisal, "getting even," is his stock in trade. Not so the LORD, who is as different from man in the way he thinks as the heavens are far removed from the earth (v. 9).

Man tends to look for repayment or at least psychic satisfaction. God offers mercy (7b).

Man is slow to reconcile and expects apologies. God is generous in forgiving (7b).

The invitation of Isaiah 55 is to be like God, not like men. It is a message of the nearness of salvation but couched within it is a warning to turn away from sin and back to the LORD in his mercy.

Philippians 1:20-24, 27. In last week's second reading Paul had said that "in life and death we are the Lord's" (14:8). Today's selection opens with the same thought. Christ is exalted in the believer whether he lives or dies (v. 20c). Both life and death are alike under Christ's dominion. This passage is noteworthy because in it Paul faces the prospect of his own death, something he had failed to do in 1 Thes 4:17, 2 Thes 2:1, and left an open question in 2 Cor 5:2-5. In the latter place it cannot be determined how he thinks the "heavenly dwelling" will envelop him with mortality giving way to life, whether by death or by some eschatological overtaking of the living.

In Philippians he is quite specific. Life (zōē) and Christ are the same thing for St. Paul; dying would put him in possession of that life much more fully (v. 21). Continued survival means that the hard work of evangelizing will continue (v. 22). Paul is ready for either and attracted to both, the former because of the immediate improvement of his personal situation and the latter for the sake of those he serves (v. 23). He ends by opting for continuing on in the body in terms of the Philippians' need of him (vv. 24f.) They should be prouder to have him as a live companion than a dead hero (v. 26), even though his present availability to them is minimal. (We do not know if his imprisonment, mentioned in 1:13, is at Caesarea—A.D. 56/58—or Rome—58/60.) He leaves the question of his return to them open, as indeed a man in jail must (v. 27). Stone walls do not a prison make but they tend to create an impression. What he pleads for from the Philippians is continued fidelity to the gospel of Christ. In the same way, the Isaiah oracle above has asked for fidelity to the understandings of the covenant (55:3b).

Matthew 20:1-16. NAB has no verse 16b, "For many are called but few are chosen," following Sinaiticus, Vaticanus, and other early manuscripts. Mt alone has the parable. He inserts it after a Marcan saying about the first and the last (Mk 10:31), showing that for him it represents the reversal that will take place on the last day. In its original form, however, it scarcely ended with 16a. This phrase is demanded by the context Matthew assigns it. The generalized conclusion mentioned above as missing no doubt made its way back in some MSS. from Mt 22:14.

The details are not important. They simply reflect agricultural labor practice of the time. It is a mistake to take the owner of the vineyard to be God or to worry over the equitable character of his action at the day's end. The proletariat of Jesus' day was familiar with such high-handed procedures.

Rabbinical literature has an almost identical parable concerning Rabbi Bun bar Hiyya (d. ca. AD 325).

The lesson of Jesus' simple, powerful tale is a single one: in the reign of an openhanded and generous God there is equality of reward.

TWENTY-SIXTH SUNDAY OF THE YEAR (A)

(Nineteenth Sunday after Pentecost)

Ezekiel 18:25-28. The prophet acts as a pastoral theologian in this chapter, spelling out a code of personal responsibility that goes counter to the theory of corporate guilt and innocence implicit in the proverb of v. 2. Ezekiel rejects the proverb utterly, viewing it as a rationalized attempt to escape responsibility for one's own acts. The father is accountable for what he was done; likewise the son. Neither one can have imputed to him the virtues or vices of the other. The doctrine of personal responsibility is not new with Ezekiel (cf. Dt 24:16; 2 Kgs 14:6) but he is its clearest exponent up to his own day (cf. 3:16-21; 14:12-20; 33:1-20.)

Today's passage deals with Israel's complaint that God acts unfairly whereas actually it is its own injustice that keeps it from discerning his righteousness. Two cases are cited in support of God's acting, the punishment that overtakes the man who departs from the path of virtue and the new life that is his who repents of his wickedness. Ezekiel does not argue the cases, he simply states them. He implies that only the person of ill will would claim that the LORD had not acted fairly in both instances. God's righteousness is self-evident for the prophet. The unrighteousness of the man who has difficulty comprehending it is equally so.

When Ezekiel speaks of life and death as the divine sanction on human behavior (cf. Dt 30:15ff.; Jer 21:8) he means it literally. He conceives continued earthly existence or its lack as the sign of God's judgment as his ancestors had done. Nonetheless, since he is making a breakthrough with respect to which acts are culpable and which inculpable, he may be expected to have new insights into reward and punishment. And he does. A man's survival or his imminent destruction are doubtless in Ezekiel's mind as modes of God's judgment, but he does not rule out life for the just and death for the unjust here and now. If a man experiences illness, suffering, or other setbacks he knows a mitigated form of death. Likewise happiness, peace, and prosperity are experienced as amplified forms of life. These are the ways in which God responds to ethical choices even when they constitute a sharp break in a person's life from what has gone before. He takes a man's freely arrived at decisions with complete seriousness and in so doing, says Ezekiel, is utterly fair.

Philippians 2:1-11. Paul writes to the first church he founded on the European continent from some situation of imprisonment (1:7, 17). He asks for a unanimity of spirit in Philippi (i.e., that the Christians there be *sympsychoi*, and hold fast to *agapē*, v. 2). In order to impel them to "fellowship in spirit"—which could just as well be translated "of the Spirit"—he cites the humble attitude of Christ as it is expressed in a hymn. Whereas some, like Cerfaux, think that the hymn is Pauline, most find the language too unlike Paul's to wish to attribute it to him.

The sacred song of vv. 6-11 was probably of Jewish origin and may have had a prior history in gnostic circles. Some attribute its content and even its wording to the fourth Servant Song (Is 52:13—53:12), accounting for small differences like *doulos* (v. 7) for *pais* by recourse to Aquila's translation rather than the LXX. J. Jeremias, one of those who holds for the dependence of Phil 2:6-11 on Isaiah, says that its use of the Hebrew text of the servant song and not the LXX takes care of most difficulties.

Other scholars feel that this explanation does not take sufficiently seriously development in Jewish thought since the time of Deutero-Isaiah. Thus, Schweizer holds that the humiliation/exaltation theme was expressed by a fusion of the Servant with the apocalyptic Son of Man into a suffering Righteous One who would be like to God (i.e., his *eikōn*; someone in his *morphē*). Still others see the late Jewish hypostatization of wisdom or speculations about the two Adams, Anthropos and Kyrios, behind this hymn. For Käsemann the underlying motif is Hellenistic. There was, he thinks, a myth of the divine primal man which the Christian author took over, making it describe one who once was the same as God but has now become the same as man. For his obedience he is placed in the highest position, made lord of the cosmos, that is, set over all cosmic powers (v. 10). As enthroned redeemer he becomes the "reconciler of all" (cf. Col 1:20.)

The arrangement of the hymn in NAB is basically the widely accepted one of Lohmeyer, viz. a hymn in two stanzas (vv. 6-8 and 9-11) of three strophes each, three lines to a strophe. Jeremias favors grouping vv. 6-7a, 7b-8, and 9-11 for reasons of Hebrew "parallelism of members." This would yield three stanzas, one devoted to the redeemer's pre- (earthly) existence, another to his earthly existence, and a third to his post-earthly existence.

What the "form" (*morphē*) of God is we cannot be sure (v. 6). "Status," "stamp," and "specific character" have all been proposed. In any case, the notion is that of Christ as heavenly man. Again, when being equal to God (*isa theō*) is spoken of as not thought "something to be grasped at" (*harpagmon*, the "robbery" of AV and Douay), it is not clear whether this treasure is conceived by Paul as *res rapienda*, something to be achieved, or *res rapta*, something already achieved. The grasping is more probably of the latter kind. That is, the pre-existent Christ possessed equality with God but did not deem it something that could not be let go of should the providential design require this.

Christ's emptying of himself (*heauton ekenōsen*, v. 7) is not to be understood metaphysically but as a figure for the nadir of abasement he endured. His status as a slave is surely an echo of the

Isaian Servant Song. His being "of human estate" (*hōs anthrōpos*) may reflect the "one like a son of man" (*hōs huios anthrōpou*) of Dan 7:13, LXX. The fullness of his humiliation comes with death (v. 8). "Death on a cross" is probably a Pauline addition to the hymn.

Exaltation results from this obedient self-abnegation. At Jesus' name the powers of heaven and earth acknowledge his lordship in phrases patterned on Isaiah 45:23. It is his resurrection which has won him this acknowledgment, the fullness of which will come with the parousia.

It is not the divine Christ as pre-existent word who is being hymned here. It is the servant son of man, previously existent in some kind of equality to God, now hailed as Lord in glory.

The Christian mind, dogmatically formed, is prone to read Phil 2:6-11 as a description of an eternal, divine son whose emptying consisted in his taking on human nature. The early hymn is incapable of this concept, however. It only knows of a man with God who did not hold fast to the glory that was his in that association but accepted the conditions of human life, then death, and was raised even higher than before for his obedient conformity to the divine plan.

Matthew 21:28-32. This parable, found in Matthew only, may be derived from the same source that gives us the Lucan prodigal son (11:15-32). It is told against those who profess to be servants of God keeping the law but who fail to do so, in contrast with those reckoned ungodly (the non-observants, Gentiles) who nonetheless do the Father's will. There may be some notion here of the law offered to the Gentiles who refused it at the time of Sinai whereas Israel at the time gave a fervent "yes." Jesus tells his tale to convey his conviction that the roles are now reversed.

Verse 32 is an editorial addition, as we know from the existence of the logion as independent in Lk 7:29f. It changes the parable from one which had as its original purpose the ultimate vindication of the good news (the despised will receive and accept God's invitation which the self-proclaimed observants reject) to one which is interested in who will be saved at the end and who will not (cf. Matthew's parables of the tenants, 21:33-44, and the wedding banquet, 22:1-14.)

The pious put no trust in John. So much the worse for them. Tax-gatherers and prostitutes do. God will know how to reward them.

TWENTY-SEVENTH SUNDAY OF THE YEAR (A)

(Twentieth Sunday after Pentecost)

Isaiah 5:1-7. Psalm 80 is familiar with the image of Israel as a "vine transplanted from Egypt." Verses 9-16 of that psalm end with the plea to the LORD: "Take care of this vine, and protect what your right hand has planted." Ezekiel knows the figure too. "Your mother was like a vine . . . stately . . . and tall . . . but she was torn up in fury and flung to the ground"; now she is planted in the desert (19:10-14). There is the possibility that Isaiah's song of the vine was originally a piece of love poetry, as testified to in the Song of Songs. There (8:11f.), the bride says of her body, "My vineyard is at my own disposal." She addresses her beloved as Solomon, saying that all the fruits of her vineyard are his to deal with, just as Israel's king had had the disposition of his extensive fields of grapes at Baal-hamon.

As the song appears in Isaiah it is a plea to the populace, Judah itself, to pass judgment between the owner and his recalcitrant vineyard, standing for the LORD and his people. Jesus' parables similarly put the auditor in the role of judge. He even tells one (Mk 12:1-11; Mt 21:33-44; Lk 20:9-18) that seems to derive from Isaiah 5, although the spoilers are not the vines but the tenant farmers who mistreat the collectors of produce. (See gospel commentary below.)

YHWH, the plaintiff, asks for judgment in his favor against the "choicest of vines" (v. 2*a*) he planted which yield only "wild grapes" (v. 2*c*). Literally, these *b^eoshim* are "stinking things," perhaps overripe fruit, in any case inedible. There is a play on words in the pairings "judgment—bloodshed, justice—outcry" in verse 7 (*mishpat —mispah, sedakah—se'akah*). There is no choice for Judah but to concur in the sentence against the vineyard which is itself.

This parabolic song introduces a catalogue of woes against a people guilty of injustices of every sort (vv. 8-23) and ends in a threat concerning the form the LORD's wrath against them will take (vv. 24-30). He will summon a far-off nation—Assyria—by whistling to it. It will come with bows and arrows, horses and chariots, roaring like a lion bent on destruction.

Philippians 4:6-9. This brief passage follows the call to rejoice (v. 4) familiar as the entrance song of Gaudete Sunday. Joy and rejoicing are recurrent themes in this epistle (cf. 1:18f.; 2:17f., 28; 3:1; 4:10.) Verse 6 proposes that the prayer of gratitude (*eucharistias*) be offered to God as an antidote to anxiety. Paul expresses the latter notion by using the verb *merimnate*, the one employed with reference to concern over clothing (Mt 6:28), worry about what to say when handed over to give witness (Mt 10:19), and anxiety about the numerous details of housekeeping (Lk 10:41). Presenting one's needs to God in prayer will bring peace, says Paul. It was v. 7 that moved King James I to remark that "Dr. Donne's verses are like the peace of God; they pass all understanding." The incomprehensible nature of God's peace is the fact that it is bestowed in the midst of difficulties. It is given "in Christ Jesus," that is, in the mystery of our salvation through his cross and resurrection.

The list of adjectives in the neuter plural describing virtuous states and conditions which Paul recommends for serious thought (*tauta logizesthe*) in v. 8 comprised a commonplace of Hellenistic ethics. He takes them over completely, here as in so many places, secure in the knowledge that life in Christ incorporates whatever is good in human life. Again, he does not hesitate to propose imitation of his own teaching and conduct as a means to ensure the presence, "not of the peace of God but of the God of peace" (v. 9).

Matthew 21:33-43. Matthew follows Mark carefully in the parable of the tenants, where it is already an allegory. This makes it unique among Jesus' parables. It occurs in Thomas 65 in the form servant-servant-son, the latter identified as the heir (*klēronomos*). An important difference is that the details about the hedge, vat (Mk; Mt has winepress), and tower, taken from Is 5:1f. have not yet been incorporated. This shows editorial activity as early as Mk. Interestingly, Lk (20:9) omits the Isaian touches along with Thomas. The use by Mk and Mt of phrases from Isaiah's song puts beyond all doubt the thought that Israel's LORD is represented by the owner, but the killing of the son and heir as the last in a series is already enough to establish the story's allegorical character.

The succession of emissaries beaten and killed (in Mk 12:5 "many others") is an expansion of Jesus' original parable referring to the prophets and their fate. Luke tells the story with the most restraint, but whether as a result of his stylistic superiority or the tradition available to him it is hard to say.

Mark had given the story a christological twist by calling the son "my beloved son" (12:6), a detail which Mt omits. Mt has the killing occur outside the vineyard (21:39), probably a reference to Jesus' execution outside the city walls (cf. Jn 19:17; Heb 13:12f.) In Jesus' original narration an identification was made between himself and God's son—something that would not have struck his hearers as an ordinary way to speak of the messiah. Moreover, the destruction of that figure of the messianic age simply was not contemplated. Jeremias reports on the rabbinic form of the parable (*Sifre* Dt 32:9,

312) in which the son is taken to be Jacob representing the people Israel. The people can suffer; not the messiah.

Verse 42 provides one of the early church's favorite proof texts for the vindication of a rejected Christ, Ps 118:22f. (cf. Ac 4:11; 1 Pt 2:7.) This text referred originally to the tiny nation despised by the powerful ones, for which God nonetheless had a plan.

The explicit threat to the Jewish people of v. 43 is peculiar to Matthew, himself a Jew, in the manner of the threats of the prophets. Verse 44, more graphic still, is textually doubtful.

TWENTY-EIGHTH SUNDAY OF THE YEAR (A)

(Twenty-First Sunday after Pentecost)

Isaiah 25:6-10. This passage tells of a coronation feast for Israel's LORD which he himself will provide for the Gentiles on Mt. Zion. They will be served the best of food and drink. The "web" and the "veil" to be removed (v. 7) are probably those of mourning since the context is one of death, which the LORD "will destroy forever" (v. 8). One thinks of the antiphon from *Tenebrae* in the former liturgy of Holy Week: "*O mors, ero mors tua.*" A reference to the Canaanite god of death Mot, similar to the Hebrew words for death and dying, may be intended (cf. Ps 49:15*b*.) There will be an end to sorrow as the LORD wipes away the tears from every face (v. 8), a phrase quoted twice in Revelation (7:17; 21:4). The hostility which God's people have experienced they will experience no more "on that day" (v. 9), an indication that the last day is meant.

The LORD will then be seen to be the savior of his people. To this the only fitting response is joy. "We looked to him to save us," and indeed he has.

Philippians 4:12-14. Paul's sentiment echoes that of Isaiah in that he acknowledges the Lord, in this case Jesus, as the source of his abundance and strength. The Philippians' assistance to him has been unexplainedly interrupted but is resumed once more (v. 10). He is grateful but he wants to make the point that he can do without it.

An old saw says: "I' been rich and I' been poor, and believe me, rich is better." Paul says that neither is better. He has learned to cope with both through being inwardly self-sufficient (*autarkēs*, v. 11, a Stoic term occurring only here in the NT). Paul can do all things in him who strengthens him (v. 13). Despite this claim of inner divine resources, the apostle does not wish to appear ungrateful to the generous Philippians (v. 14). He seems to be using their gift as the occasion for a moral lesson. They are a source of strength to him. The Lord is an even greater one.

Matthew 22:1-14. The lector who terminates today's reading at verse 10 will have read one parable of Mt while the one who elects the longer version will read a second one, the parable of the guest without a wedding garment. The first, the wedding banquet, occurs in this allegorized form here alone while Luke 14:16-24 and Thomas 64 report it more simply as a dinner from which guests absent themselves (Mt also has this feature) by a variety of excuses. In the latter telling it is a story of a full complement of guests assembled as a result of the host's insistence, while the invited who are disinterested must forego the feast. Thomas concludes with the special allegorical ending, turning it into a parable of the last judgment: "The buyers and the merchants will not enter the places of my father."

In Mt, that is its character throughout. The host is a king. He gives a wedding banquet for his son. There are two refusals of his invitation, the second one marked by violence which he meets with murderous reprisal. Probably Mt intends to convey the reception accorded the prophets by the first group of servants (v. 3), that given to preachers of the gospel by the second (v. 4) including their persecution (v. 6), and the destruction of Jerusalem by the fate of "those murderers" whose city is to be burned (v. 7). Verses 9f., on such supposition, describe the Gentile mission. We know from 21:43 with which last Sunday's reading concluded that Mt is interested in having Jesus' stories illustrate the eschatological plan of salvation.

The second, appended parable (vv. 11-14) would then have to do with baptism (vv. 11f.), the last judgment, and hell (cf. 8:12; 25:30.) Mt's allegory of the plan of redemption is thus complete.

TWENTY-NINTH SUNDAY OF THE YEAR (A)

(Twenty-Second Sunday after Pentecost)

Isaiah 45:1, 4-6. The poetic oracles of the Second Isaiah (chapters 40-55), at least those contained in chapters 40-48, were composed in Babylon on the brink of release from captivity in 538 B.C. Chapters 49-55 may represent the work of the prophet's disciples upon their return to Jerusalem; otherwise, at a later period in the last stages of the captivity.

Cyrus, king of Persia, is hailed as the LORD's anointed (*mashiah*, v. 1). This is the only instance in the OT in which the term is applied to anyone outside the faith-community of Israel. Normally it designated a kingly figure but there are also cases of its use to describe the anointed priest and patriarch. The term did not at any time have the significance which Christianity gave it, although in later Judaism it began to describe a leading figure or figures of the messianic age. The concept of such an epoch is much more prominent in the Hebrew scriptures than that of a single person who would dominate it.

The author of Second Isaiah portrays Cyrus after the manner of Abraham because he wishes to describe a return to the land of Israel from the east and the north, the route of the patriarch. Abraham has been called the LORD's "attendant" and the "champion of justice" (41:2), the friend of God (v. 8) and father of "Israel, my servant" (v. 8). Cyrus, in turn, is described as someone whom "I have stirred up from the north, and he comes; / from the east I summon him by name" (v. 25). This chosen one shall trample down the rulers like a potter treading the clay (v. 25).

If Israel is the LORD's servant in one sense, Cyrus surely is in another. (Some scholars have seen a contrived antithesis in which the author-editor of the Servant Poems sets the humble Israel in contrast to the noisy, conquering Cyrus, but this is doubtful.) We have an inscription on a clay barrel, the so-called Cyrus Cylinder, which contains that sovereign's pledged loyalty to Marduk, "the great lord," who "pronounced his name [i.e., declared him] to be(come) the ruler of all the world" (cf. James Pritchard, *Ancient Near Eastern Texts*, p. 315.) RSV, following AV, renders 41:25; "he shall call on my name." NEB translates the phrase better as "I summon him by name" (NAB: "in my name"), it being entirely unlikely that the biblical author is attributing Yahwist faith to this instrument of Yahweh's purpose. The initiative is the LORD's throughout. Both Cyrus and the servant Israel merely respond to it. Cf. 45:3*d*: "the God of Israel, who calls you by your name."

Verse 1*b* and *c* of ch. 45 echoes the prowess of the LORD through Abraham (41:2f.) and Cyrus (41:25). It is a declaration of intent to keep the promises made in 42:13ff. and 43:5 ("Fear not, for I am with you; from the east I will bring back your descendants, from the west I will gather you.") The LORD is made to explain in v. 4 his usage of "anointed" in v. 1: "I have called you by your name, giving you a title though you knew me not." There follows in vv. 5f. a familiar declaration of the absolute uniqueness of Israel's LORD (cf. Dt 32:39; Mal 1:11*a*.) He alone arms Cyrus, as he says to him, "though you know me not" (5*b*).

1 Thessalonians 1:1-5. This greeting, which precedes the first of Paul's letters we have, is a summary of how he thinks divine election works. God first made choice of this community in the Macedonian seaport and then sent Paul and Silas (Silvanus) to work among them (Acts 17:1-9; probably Timothy too, cf. 16:3.) As a result of their preaching in power and in the holy spirit (v. 5), the community began to live lives of faith which led to love and were carried on in hope (v. 3). Corresponding to these three gifts of God, *pistis, agapē*, and *elpis* are the efforts of the Thessalonians, characterized as *ergon, kopos*, and *hypomonē* respectively. A literal translation would be, "the work of your faith, the labor of your love, and the steadfastness of your hope." This combination of the three Christian graces probably precedes Paul, who uses it also in 1 Cor 13:13. His distinction between what faith and love accomplish may be that between daily living (faith) and the spread of the gospel (love). Hope looks for the return of the Lord Jesus, hence is patient in endurance.

Paul finds the survival and fruitfulness of his gospel in this busy commercial capital a marvel. He will not attribute this success to the force of his words; his preaching derives its power from God (v. 5*ab*). Verse 5*c* proposes the generous service of Paul and his companions to the Thessalonian community as an essential part of the *euaggelion*.

Matthew 22:15-21. This pericope follows immediately the one used as last Sunday's gospel. Mt alters his Marcan source (12:13-17) only by an occasional change of word, notably the designation of Jesus' enemies as "you hypocrites." The latter is the familiar Matthean stigma of the Jewish establishment (6:2, 5, 16) which is also found in the *Didachē* (8:1f.) The presence of the Herodians (v. 16) heightens the notion of a political trap.

Matthew favors Pharisee teaching but not its practice in his day (cf. 23:3). In this discussion and the next two on the resurrection of the dead (vv. 23-33) and the greatest commandment (vv. 34-46). Jesus gives unexceptionable answers. He silences the Pharisees if he does not satisfy them and he downs the Sadducees, at least by a Pharisee standard.

The challengers flatter Jesus for his sincerity and his fidelity to *halakah* ("God's way," v. 16). Then they question him on the rightness of a Jew's subjecting himself to a foreign (Gentile) ruler by paying imperial taxes. Not only was the tribute exacted onerous but it had attached to it the shame of being required in coinage that bore the emperor's "graven image" and inscriptions proclaiming his cult. The coins of Tiberius, the Caesar of Jesus' adult lifetime, bore the titles *divus* and *pontifex maximus*.

Jesus makes his first point by not having such a coin in his possession whereas his opponents do (v. 19). They hand him a *dēnarios*, the coin with which the tax is paid (*to nomisma tou kēnsou*). He makes them spell out whose *eikōn* and *epigraphē* are to be found on it (v. 20), following which they are told to give it back (*apodote*) to Caesar. The cleverness of Jesus' response is complete. The coins are to be out of Jewish hands and into Gentile ones with all possible speed; therefore Jesus cannot be faulted as an offender against Torah (Ex 20:4f.) No more is he to be charged with political subversion. The Zealots, the left wing of the Pharisee party, favored armed revolt whereas the Pharisees waited for God in his good time to set Israel free. Jesus in his response aligns himself with the Pharisees.

Centuries of interpretation have made this text read as a clear delimitation of the claims of religion and the body politic. But what belongs to each sphere? Primarily Jesus holds out a choice between two forms of worship. In Tillich's term, what will be a person's "ultimate concern"? Will he or she choose money, the state, a religious establishment at ease with both? Or will there be transcendence of these extensions of the self and a choice made of God?

THIRTIETH SUNDAY OF THE YEAR (A)

(Twenty-Third Sunday after Pentecost)

Exodus 22:20-26. This portion of social morality from the law code of Israel reflects some recurrent biblical concerns. The people was constantly reminding itself of its obligation to windows, orphans, and non-Israelites (*gerim*) who lived in its midst (cf. Lv 1:16; Dt 10:18; Zech 7:10; Jer 7:6.) From Yahweh's first call of Moses to a new covenantal relation, the setting free of his people in a rich land is tied to their release from Egyptian enslavement (cf. Ex 3:7-10.) They could do no less for others than was done for them. The divine punishment for the neglect of orphans and widows would be warfare ("I will kill you with the sword," v. 23) which would convert the wives and children of Israel's offending men into widows and orphans in turn.

The prohibition of money-lending is one against exploitation of people in their need, whether this take the form of interest that is extorted unfairly (v. 24) or a man's only cloak to keep him warm (vv. 25f.) Such lending at interest, moreover, is forbidden with respect to fellow countrymen but allowed in the case of foreigners (very specifically in Dt 23:20f.) Dt gives as the reason for this the economic solidarity necessary for the Israelites to "make it" in the new land.

Moneylending by Jews to Gentiles in the middle ages, something they were forced to do for survival because land-owning and the trades were closed to them, was well within Mosaic law so long as no usurious practice (in the sense of excessive) accompanied it. No borrower feels kindly toward the lender when he falls behind in his payments, no matter how upright the latter may be. Hence Christians persecuted Jews for reasons besides the initial one which led to the relationship in the first place, namely economic necessity. The entire matter was complicated by the scholastic teaching which departed from the patristic and held that goods consumed by use (*fungibilia*) were unproductive. Money was "sterile" in Aristotle's view, hence a charge could be made for its use only under some extrinsic title. Over the course of centuries numerous such titles were devised. Meanwhile, however, moneylending Jews had an additional reason to suffer at Christian hands.

Amos 2:7c-8a grows wrathful at those who do not keep the prescription of v. 26: "Son and father go to the same prostitute, profaning my holy name. / Upon garments taken in pledge they recline beside any altar."

The compassion of the LORD (v. 26c) must be emulated by the compassion of men. This is the basis of the entire morality of Torah.

1 Thessalonians 1:5-10. St. Paul does not hesitate to couple messengers of the gospel like himself with the Lord (v. 6) as fit models for the Thessalonian community. These Macedonians have been through numerous trials (*en thlipsei pollē*) for their faith but the result has been joy (*chara*). Paul keeps hearing from various places in Macedonia and Achaia, the two provinces which comprise eastern and southern Greece, how strong the faith of the Thessalonians is (vv. 7f.) Evidently large numbers of them have been pagans and not Jews (v. 9). The contrast in their objects of worship is between lifeless idols of wood and stone and the living God.

The new, Christian life is one serving him (*douleuein Theōi zōnti*, v. 9) and awaiting (*anamenein*) his Son's return—Jesus the deliverer from the coming wrath, *orgē*. This blazing anger will be directed toward the wicked in the last age. The linking of pagan Greeks to Jewish eschatological motifs shows us that primitive Christian preaching made few cultural concessions. Jewish thought patterns were the narrow door for all.

Matthew 22:34-40. After the silencing of the Sadducees on bodily resurrection which the lectionary omits (vv. 23-33), the Pharisees return to the testing of Jesus. A "lawyer" is a "scribe" and vice versa. Here he is called *nomikos*, normally a Lucan word. Mt uses *grammateus* in every other place.

As does Mk, Mt has Jesus bring together the love of God (Dt 6:5) and the love of neighbor (Lv 19:18). Lk (10:27) has them already combined (cf. Mt 19:19), a Jewish catechetical practice which we know about from the *Testament of Issachar* (5:2). The summing of the 613 positive and negative precepts found in the law under a few headings (v. 40) was common practice in Jesus' day. It is not cited here as a matter of dispute but of agreement between him and his opponents. They ask a received question and are given a received answer. Mt's point is that they can make no capital of his unexceptionable rabbinic response.

THIRTY-FIRST SUNDAY OF THE YEAR (A)

(Twenty-Sixth Sunday after Pentecost, Lutheran;
Twenty-Fourth Sunday after Pentecost, COCU)

Malachi 1:14—2:2, 8-10. Not all was "life and peace" in the postexilic community. In particular, the priesthood had its sins to answer for.

Sheshbazzar and Zerubbabel had first bravely got an altar up and then the foundations of a rebuilt temple. This was in the Zionist movement of return of the 530's and '20s. But the old men cried in sorrow. The new structure was such a poor patch on the temple of Solomon they had known. Others cried out with joy. The one sound could not be distinguished from the other (cf. Ezra 1—3.) The inhabitants of the land provided every kind of resistance to the work of resettlement. It went ahead nonetheless. Ezra the scribe came from Babylon in 459, Nehemiah the civil servant of Persia from Susa in 446. Together they laid the foundations of what we now call Judaism. Temple worship flourished; the priesthood was strengthened. The scribes—the learned class—were theoretically subordinated to the priests and influential laymen.

In fact, however, when the priests grew rich through sharp practice (cf. Mal 1:6-14) the scribes were moved to action. By the mid-fifth century, the mid-point as well of the reign of the supportive Artaxerxes I (465-25), priestly abuses reached a crescendo. Taking the pseudonym Malachi ("my messenger"), a bold, prophetic spirit lashed out at the sins of the priesthood. He might have been a priest himself; he need not have been a scribe. He was, in any case, an anti-establishment theologian zealous for the honor of the LORD.

Malachi's threat is not a novel one. All the prophets had uttered it before him. If the abuses continue, he says, the LORD will desert Israel's covenanted Levites and turn to the Gentile nations. Among them his "name will be feared" (1:14*b*). There he can expect sacrifice and a pure offering, the acknowledgement of his name from the rising of the sun even to its setting (cf. 1:11.)

The offense of the priests is twofold. They should have taught the people well but instead they taught them falsely (about a God interested in generous donations, a magnificent structure, religious display?) They further showed partiality, presumably to the rich but also and above all to themselves.

The results are in full view, says Malachi. The unjust, venal ways of the priests have become familiar. The people hold them in contempt.

1 Thessalonians 2:7-9, 13. Paul's boast is in a direction completely contrary to the practice of the fifth-century priests. While in Thessalonica, he had worked and worked hard, not *at* preaching the gospel but *while* preaching the gospel. He not only made no money from the works of religion; he supported himself while recommending them. What a nursing mother does for her baby, Paul had done for his Macedonian converts: he supported new life from his very self. The good tidings of Christ had thus imposed no burden. God's grace was *gratis*. There were no handling charges.

This self-support aspect of Paul's teaching ministry was not incidental to it but at the heart and center.

Matthew 23:1-12. Jesus continues the tradition of Malachi here. The offenders are not priests, eating the shoulder-cut of beef while offering blind and lame beasts in sacrifice (cf. Mal 2:3; 1:8.) Yet like the priests they lead people astray by their teaching. In Mt's day (i.e., after the fall of Jerusalem) the Sadducees who held power in the temple are no longer the enemy; the scribes and Pharisees (cf. 23:2) are. Does this teaching reflect Mt's day only and not the conflicts of Jesus' time? Lk 11:46; 20:46; 11:52; and 11:47 lead us to believe that these sayings derive from historical tradition and not merely from the situation of the Matthean church.

The opposition between church and teachers within Judaism is such as to be stylized by the time this gospel is written (cf. Mt 6:16 and the "hypocrites" of *Didachē* 8:1.) All the same, the resistance of Jesus to teachers who laid burdens on others while lifting not a finger to help them (v. 4) was a fact of his lifetime. His sharp criticism of certain Pharisee teachers is duplicated in the talmudic writings which that very tradition produced. Whereas the Jewish world was taught to distinguish among its Pharisees as we are among our doctors, lawyers, and businessmen, the gospels blurred distinctions and taught the Christian world to mistrust the Pharisees as a whole. This is as unfortunate as mistrusting all politicians, all clergymen as practicers of duplicity.

The *Moÿseōs kathedra* (v. 2) was a piece of ancient synagogue furniture, as real as a modern pulpit, from which the rabbi taught. Verse 3 about "doing everything they teach" is a puzzle in light of vv. 16 and 18, where the teaching selected serves only to highlight its untrustworthy character. The earlier verse is therefore probably a dramatic way of distinguishing between the nobility of the scribal office and the low estate to which it has fallen. Vigorous efforts to proselytize in this debased spirit (cf. v. 15*b*) only heighten the evil.

Jesus accuses the teachers of interpreting the law to suit themselves. Vanity of office accompanied their practice in the forms of dress and behavior (v. 5; cf. 6:1-18.) Phylacteries represented an interpretation of the phrases "ready to hand" and "in mind," already literalized by the time of Ex 13:16 and Dt 6:8. Snatches of the law (from Ex 13 and Dt 6 and 11) were encased in leather boxes strapped to the wrists and the forehead. Tassels were prescribed for the garments of the pious in Nm 15:38-41 and Dt 22:12. Jesus wore the latter (cf. Mt 14:36), presumably with a becoming ordinariness.

The titles "rabbi" (which Mt equates with *didaskalos*), "father," and "teacher" (*kathēgētēs*, doubtless for *moreh*) were evidently coming into use in rabbinical circles. Mt repudiates them all in highlighting the uniqueness of God and Christ. Jesus is *the* Teacher, like Qumrân's "Teacher of Righteousness" (*moreh haṣṣedeq*). Taking Jesus at his word by expunging the titles from use would be falling into the trap of literalism that he warned against. The early church did not do this. Yet following his spirit on signs and titles of office is something concerning which the church has never had a distinguished record.

Mt concludes the passage with one repeated saying on humility (cf. 20:26 for a parallel to v. 11) and a new one (v. 12)—which Lk will use twice (14:11; 18:14).

THIRTY-SECOND SUNDAY OF THE YEAR (A)

**(Twenty-Fourth Sunday after Pentecost, Lutheran;
Twenty-Sixth Sunday after Pentecost, COCU)**

Wisdom 6:13-17. The wisdom here personified is an attribute of God. This literary convention is found in Job (28), Proverbs (1:20-33), and Sirach (24:1-21), among other places. God's spirit, his word, and his justice are likewise spoken of in other sapiential writings as if they were persons. Wisdom resulted from possession of the spirit of God, in the earlier literature. The present, 1st-c. book of "the Wisdom of Solomon" makes the two identical, spirit-wisdom becoming the principle behind the universe which sustains all human life and action.

Today's passage contains echoes of Prv 1:20-22 and 8:1-36, especially the references to wisdom's crying out in the streets and appearing at the city gates. Her clothing is royal since she is of God (v. 12). She goes out of her way to make herself known (vv. 13-16). Like the father of the wastrel son in Jesus' parable, she runs out to meet those in need of her. But the best guarantee of her ministrations is that one should be a seeker. She responds most generously to those who search her out.

The earliest concept of wisdom in the biblical books was one of mental skill or ability. It yielded to that of ethical discernment, with God serving as the universal moral standard to whom all could appeal. This later notion is found in the Hellenist book of Wisdom; to it is joined the idea of *hokmah* as an all-pervasive logos which confers meaning and order on the world.

1 Thessalonians 4:13-18. Former altar-servers may well carry around in their heads the rhythmic cadences of this passage in Latin, ending in a sonorous, "*Itaque consolamini invicem in verbis istis,*" from the days when the daily Mass of requiem dominated their lives. Paul's message of consolation which he proposed for regular exchange (cf. v. 18) was that we should be with the Lord "unceasingly" (*pantote*, v. 17).

His categories are those of Jewish eschatology, the distinctive feature being that when the living are caught up into the air with the risen dead (cf. vv. 16f.) all should "meet the Lord," namely Jesus. Paul seems to have no doubt that we will be among the living, so sure is he of his vocation to preach Christ until his glorious return.

The obvious thrust of the passage is comfort for the survivors of the Thessalonian dead, about whose fate Paul seems to have left no clear message. The "hope" (v. 13) of Christians is Christ dead, risen, and expected back again. They are perfectly free to mourn their dead but their grief cannot resemble that of those who have no such hope. Christ, moreover, did not rise for himself alone but for the raising up of all who died believing in him. The second question raised by the Thessalonians seems to have been, Will not the living enjoy some special advantage over the dead? No, says Paul, it will all take place "in proper order" (cf. 1 Cor 15:23), the dead first (v. 16), then the living (v. 17), but not in such a way as to constitute an advantage for the latter.

Paul is sure of his response. It is not as if he had given a private opinion, like his counsel to remain unmarried in 1 Cor 7:25. He teaches here "as if the Lord himself had said it" (*en logǫ Kyriou,*

v. 15). The fate of the dead and of the living was therefore a part of the substance of the tradition, traceable back to Jesus and the Church's earliest preaching. What is sure is the nature of Christian hope. No such claim is being made for the imaginative details. These Paul borrows freely from the Jewish picture of the end-event, simply inserting Christ as the summoner in the skies in place of God.

Matthew 25:1-13. The gospel parable echoes the first reading. Its stress, however, is on prudential care rather than wisdom. NAB renders *phronimoi* "sensible" though "common-sensical" would be better, if there were such a word, and "prudent" best of all had it not been devalued in current speech to mean "timid" or "cautious." The world's literature has thoughtlessly taken the two companies of bridesmaids to be wise or foolish over the preservation of their virginity, but Jesus was interested in something quite different. His concern was over preparedness for the end. The tale is eschatological, like all his *basileia* parables. This one is cast in the future: "the reign of God *will be* like" (*homoiōthēsetai*, v. 1), not "is like" as in the parables of ch. 13.

The marriage between the LORD and Israel (or Jerusalem or Zion), his virgin bride, is a familiar biblical theme. We are not surprised to encounter it as a motif for the consummation of all at the end. Mt has told a previous parable of a wedding-banquet that ends unhappily (20:11-14). If he had given us a story of the return of the groom *and his bride*, as some manuscripts have it, it would be a simple tale of being on the alert. The fact that all ten fell asleep (v. 5) makes the praise of vigilance in v. 13 inapplicable.

No doubt Jesus' original story, like all that he told, had a single point: "Be ready!" As Mt tells the story it is an allegory, the groom inevitably suggesting Christ and the two groups of women with their two outlooks those fated to enjoy the *parousia* ("presence" of the Lord) and those not. The delay in the groom's coming establishes with certainty the allegorical nature of Mt's version. This is fortified by the activities of the two groups of bridesmaids who stand for waiting Christians. Some take prudent measures while they wait. Others relax their vigilance.

As in all such parables of the reign, the people Israel was understood as early as the 2d c. to represent one group of bridesmaids and the Gentiles the other (as in the fable of the hare and the tortoise). Such could scarcely have been Jesus' meaning. He was not so labored a teacher as Matthew and his other followers. His stories were true-to-life, fleshed out with appropriate detail, and seldom said more than one thing.

In this case, as in so many others, it is: "Be ready!"

THIRTY-THIRD SUNDAY OF THE YEAR (A)

(Twenty-Fifth Sunday after Pentecost, Lutheran [2d and 3d readings]
Twenty-Sixth Sunday, Presbyterian/UCC [1st reading]
Twenty-Seventh Sunday, COCU [2d and 3d readings]

Proverbs 31; 10-13, 19-20, 30-31. Elements of this poem in praise of
a good wife were echoed by Pope Paul in an address of 1972 when,
in deploring a widespread eroticism, he commended (as the English-
language dispatches reported it) the "lyrical and generous gift of self"
to another.

It is clear what the worthy wife was giving in that male-dominat-
ed culture, not so clear what her husband's gift was. One presumes
fidelity as the bare minimum. The husband's praise of her is cited
(vv. 28f.) but it is neutralized by the poet's view of a good wife as a
man's possession and his prize (vv. 10f.)

There are but two modern touches in this eulogy, deeply flawed
as it is by its good intentions. One is the reality of the hard labor of
a wife and mother. The other is the counsel in the first part of v. 31,
"Give her a reward for her labors." This cannot come about
contemporarily by "letting her works praise her at the city gates"
(husband's shirts always starched, children neat at school clutching
their lunch money). It can only come about by the whole culture's
repudiating the picture of womanhood represented by vv. 10-31.

Preaching homilies on vv. 1-9 would be a good start in this
direction, especially v. 8: "Open your mouth in behalf of . . . the
rights of the destitute." Wives know something about the drinking
that makes their men forget what the law decrees (v. 5) and the vigor
given to other women (v. 3). The praise of the wife and mother, in
Prv 31, even in its abbreviated form, can be infuriating to a
thoughtful woman because it depersonalizes her thoroughly and tells
her (boob of a poet!) that charm and beauty count for nothing so
long as the linen closet stays full. Enter the vigor bestowed on other
women.

1 Thessalonians 5:1-6. St. Paul was fully committed to the biblical
reality of the "day of the LORD" (which becomes, for him, the "day
of Christ," Phil 2:16) but like any wise rabbinic teacher of his time
he knew enough not to name specific *chronoi* or *chairoi* (v. 1) in
connection with it. It was a certainty and a certainty of the future.
That was enough for him. The chief feature of the onset of the last
days (*ha aharith*) would be its suddenness. The figures of a thief in
the night and labor pains were not new with Paul but current coin
(cf. Mk 13:8, 32; Mt 24:8, 43f.)

The criers of "Peace and security!" in Thessalonica are

purveyors of the false assurance that was being hawked in Jeremiah's time (cf. Jer 6:14; 8:11.) Paul expects a little ruin (v. 3); he just doesn't want it to fall on his Thessalonian Christians unaware. They are children (lit. "sons") of *phōs* and *hēmera*, not of *nyx* and *skotos*. He gets somewhat lost in his imagery when he says in v. 4 that *hē hēmera* ("the Day," meaning the day of Christ) should not catch off guard those whose proper medium is daylight rather than the darkness that shields the thief. But "the Day" that will overtake the daylight is not his meaning. He simply names vigilance and sobriety as the best preparedness for any untoward cosmic occurrences—at the center of which will be the coming of Jesus as Lord.

Matthew 25:14-30. Differences could be pointed out between Mt's parable where the *talanton* is the monetary unit and Lk's (19:12-27) which features the far less valuable *mna*, but they would not be especially instructive. Suffice it to say that Lk's story seems to be our parable conflated with another about an unpopular ruler (Archelaus, 4 B.C.—6 A.D.?), which he uses to explain why the *parousia* is delayed.

Mt's version is clearly the earlier one but even it has undergone some development. He interprets Jesus' story as a *parousia*-parable, although not incorrectly like Lk (cf. its setting in the context of 24:32 —25:13 and 25:31-46.) The watchfulness enjoined in v. 13 provides the cue, a fact obscured in English by the understandable omission of the postpositive *gar* of v. 14 (which begins, literally, "For, like a man going on a journey, . . .")

Without its allegorical additions the story tells of a rich man who expects the successful investment of his funds in his absence. Failure to invest by his slaves is interpreted as laziness, the offender receiving the kind of obloquy that the little man is used to from the rich and powerful: "Why didn't you take some initiative since I never encouraged you to take any initiative?" Jesus' original tale had to do with self-preservation as the first law of life and inertia as the first step toward economic death. Mt's interpretation (v. 29) of Jesus' meaning is not too wide of the mark: "Them as has, gits."

The evangelist cannot restrain himself, however, from adding some allegorical details about Christ and the eschaton. Thus, in vv. 21 and 23, in the phrase, "Come share your master's joy!" the *kyrios* in question is surely Christ, the *chara*, the bliss of the final age. Similarly, the command to "throw this worthless servant into the darkness outside" is not the utterance of an exasperated businessman but of Christ, the arbiter of reward and punishment in the Last Age.

Once again, the principle is sustained that Jesus told marvelous stories before he began to get a little help from his friends.

FEAST OF CHRIST THE KING (A)

(Last Sunday after Pentecost)

Ezekiel 34:11-12, 15-17. This chapter contains a severe indictment of Israel's rulers under the figure of shepherds (for this verbal convention, cf. 1 Kgs 22:17; Jer 23:16; Mi 5:3.) Their crime was that they fleeced and slaughtered their flocks for their own gain. Ch. 34 was probably written retrospectively with reference to the fall of Jerusalem. In the present pericope the LORD says that he himself will do what the rulers failed to do: retrieve his scattered flock from "clouds and darkness"—signs of a threatening "day of the LORD"— and bring them to good pastures on the mountain heights of Israel. The first 18 vv. of Jn 10 may derive from this passage. Surely today's gospel reading from Mt, whatever its original form, was beholden to v. 17.

It is interesting to observe that the LORD will not judge between sheep and goats (who often pasture side by side) but between sheep and sheep, between tough old rams and goats. Some scholars have seen in this passage a reference to the mid-5th c. situation described in Neh 5:1-5. There, Jew preys upon Jew by letting the (Persian) king's tax be levied on a landless peasantry. As a result, the latter have to pawn off their own children in order to eat. In Ezekiel's image the emphasis is on predators of the same stock or kind, not two different kinds.

The Roman lectionary surely includes this passage in order to set the stage for the second and third readings on the last judgment. The final verse (17) acts as a special cue for the gospel pericope.

1 Corinthians 15:20-26, 28. St. Paul has been dealing earlier in this chapter with the special problem of the Corinthian enthusiasts, namely their conviction that they need not die and rise since, by faith and baptism, they already live "risen lives." After arguing carefully the causal relationship between Christ's having been upraised and their need to be, he moves on to today's passage.

In v. 20 he uses the agricultural figure *aparchē* (Heb., *bikkurim*), the early presage of a grain harvest. Possibly he is thinking of the actual season of Passover, at which time the first-fruits of grain are being offered in the temple. It was at this mid-point of the month Nisan that Christ rose from the dead. Paul will return later (Rom 5:12-17) to his theme of an unredeemed humanity from Adam, who fathered it in death, and a redeemed one whose begetter to life is Christ (v. 22).

Paul's vision of the final resurrection is of an event that will be both orderly (*Hekastos de en tǭ idiǭ tagmati*, v. 23) and in stages

(*Christos, epeita* . . . , v. 23; *eita*, v. 24; *hotan* . . . *tote*, v. 28—a succession of adverbs of time preceded by Christ's coming.) The "end" (*to telos*) follows the destruction of all cosmic powers inimical to God (v. 25), of which death is the last (v. 26). There is evidently, therefore, a period of the intermediate reign of Christ. The "end" will bring the final and total reign of God. Verse 27 quotes Ps 8:6 while v. 25 is redolent of Ps 110:1.

The imagery contained here is very probably that of several Jewish apocalypses which envision first, "the days of the Messiah," then "the age to come" or "the end." It is clear that, at Christ's coming, "all those who belong to him" (v. 23) will be raised up. There is no teaching about the fate of the reprobate, if in fact there are any—those not "in Christ." This fact has led some to read into the passage a second, general resurrection but to do so they must translate *to telos* (v. 24), not as "the end" but as "the rest," "the remainder." The translation, while defensible on the basis of certain Greek writings, is unlikely.

Needless to say, vv. 24-28 had a lively history in the subordinationist controversies of the 4th century. C. S. C. Williams traces the creedal phrase "and of his kingdom there shall be no end" to a refutation of Marcellus of Ancyra who held that v. 24 meant that there would be an end to Christ's kingdom.

God's being *ta panta en pasin* (v. 8) is Paul's way of expressing his complete dominion. There is no need to deny nervously that this will be achieved by the total interpenetration by God of his creation. What is needed to make it a final reality is the submission of "even our rebellious wills."

Matthew 25:31-46. This passage offers a vision of God's judgment "through a man he has appointed" (Ac 17:31). The Son of Man, come in his glory (v. 31), is the king (v. 31) and the judge (v. 32). His action answers perfectly the problem posed by Matthew's gospel, What should the community addressed by it be doing about discipleship until the Lord returns? The answer lies in helping those in need. They represent the Lord. All that Israel's rulers did not do (cf. commentary on Ezekiel above), this segment of Israel must do. Their performance, even if totally acceptable to Christ, will be so "secular" and natural that they will not be aware of its virtuous character (cf. vv. 37ff.) The same is true of the unacceptable behavior of the negligent (v. 44). If the severe judgment on them is to be just, they must have heard another word of Jesus: "On judgment day people will be held accountable for every unguarded word they speak" (Mt 12:36).

The norm of judgment is works of mercy. It accords well with

Mt's concern for the "little ones" (18:6, 10, 14) who will find forgiveness only if "each . . . forgives his brother from his heart" (v. 35). The norm creates a problem for those Christians who consider faith alone as saving and are scandalized by a "Jewish concern" for works.

A second problem arises: Is this a vision of the final judgment of mankind or only of the judgment of Christians? Matthew only intended to answer the question of what to do till the messiah comes. He has unconsciously given God's answer concerning all. Serving one's fellowman is the behavior that leads to salvation, even if one happens to be in that great company that has never heard of a saving gospel.

It seems fitting to observe, in conclusion, how well the framers of the new lectionary have caught the spirit of the kingship (i.e., messiahship) of Christ in biblical categories.

YEAR B

ADVENT SEASON

FIRST SUNDAY OF ADVENT (B)

Isaiah 63:16-17; 64:1, 3-8. This passage, part of a long prayer of intercession which runs from 63:7 to 64:11, is noteworthy chiefly for the use made of 3*b* and *c* by St. Paul in 1 Cor 2:9: "No ear has ever heard, no eye ever seen, any God but you / doing such deeds for those who wait for him." The postexilic prophet centers his attention on what God has done in recent times. Paul makes the verse refer to God's mysterious, hidden wisdom which planned all that happened in Christ not long before. The preparation God has made for all who love him includes for Paul the mystery of the cross and resurrection. Many have been invited by God's recent revelation to share in this wisdom. The verse of the Third Isaiah and the use Paul makes of it are therefore not too far separated. The one plan of God has been revealed in two stages. The unintended but widely held conclusion that a life to come is being spoken of by Paul would be still a third.

The "invasion of the holy place" and "trampling in the sanctuary" of v. 18 could provide a valuable clue to dating the prayer if the event were able to be identified; the same is true of v. 9, "Zion is a desert, Jerusalem a waste." A deserted city anywhere between 586 and 520 is as close as we are likely to come.

Verse 16 praises God for his faithful fatherhood even though the patriarchs Abraham and Israel (Jacob), who gave the people its name, should desert them. Cf. 49:15 for the similar figure of a mother forgetting the child of her womb. No longer do the tribes fear the LORD (v. 17); the prophet pleads that the hardening of hearts which "causes" this should stop.

This intercessory prayer contains not only historical reminiscence (63:11f.) but praise of God as well. The LORD is reminded by the composer of his triumphs in the past (64:2) so that he will wreak a little havoc in the present (v. 1). There is, however, a catch which keeps him from acting. The sinfulness of the people prevents it. They have forgotten their father (v. 7), him who works them like a potter his clay (v. 7.)

The appeal in this prayer is based on an election made long ago. The LORD is Israel's age-old ransomer (*go'el*, v. 17; cf. 43:3; 63:1) who comes to save. He does so neither by a messenger nor an angel but by coming himself (63:9*b*). The people grieve his holy spirit

(vv. 10*a*, 11*c*) which he has sent to guide them (v. 14). Nothing good can be hoped for until he turns back (v. 17*c*) for the sake of his servants.

1 Corinthians 1:3-9. Verse 3 of Paul's introduction grows increasingly familiar to the modern ear as a greeting of priest to people in the revised Roman liturgy.

The reason for Paul's continued expression of thanks in v. 4 (*Efcharistō* is "Thanks" in modern Greek, just as *Parakalō* is "Please") is the favor (*charis*) bestowed in Christ Jesus. Speech (*logos*) and knowledge (*gnōsis*) are part of the resulting enrichment (v. 5). God has followed up Paul's initial witness in Corinth with gifts of every sort (v. 6) bestowed on a community that awaits Christ's being finally revealed (*apokalypsis*, v. 7). The strength God gives will find the Corinthians blameless "on the Day" (v. 8). The initial call was to have all things in common with Christ (*koinōnia*, v. 9); God's utter fidelity will ensure this.

Despite the concentration on Christ and the gifts given in him, Paul's thanksgivings, like his theology, remain theocentric.

Mark 13:33-37. Jesus' eschatological injunction to watchfulness (cf. Mt 24:42; 25:13) is illustrated by two short parables, that of v. 34 (cf. Mt 25:14) and that of vv. 35f. (cf. Lk 12:38.) The first also bears resemblances to Lk 19:12f. God's reign will come when it is least expected.

SECOND SUNDAY OF ADVENT (B)

Isaiah 40:1-5, 9-11. The opening poem in the collection of oracles (chs. 40-55) that hail the rise of Cyrus and the imminent liberation of Israel (538 BC) features the coming of God with power. His release of the people Israel from captivity is spoken of under the figures of "ruling by his strong arm" (v. 10), "feeding his flock," and "carrying the lambs in his bosom" (v. 11). Salvation is imminent. Release from exile is predicted as certain.

The Second Isaiah in v. 2 counsels gentleness toward Jerusalem, meaning the people in its exiled condition. The punishment, which was brought on by the LORD "to refine your dross in the furnace, removing all your alloy" (1:25), is described as twice as severe as the crime. The LORD was the sentencing judge but he is also the pardoner: "For a brief moment I abandoned you, / but with great tenderness I will take you back" (54:7).

The voice that speaks to the prophet is that of some kind of herald from the heavenly court (v. 3). It introduces the theme of a royal road (*derek YHWH*), a highway (*mesilla*) which the LORD will traverse at the head of his people. The road-building operation of v. 4 is required for the theophany to follow, the manifestation of "the glory of the LORD" (*kebhod YHWH*, v. 5). All mankind, despite its weak condition (vv. 6f.), will witness it in a display of unity and solidarity. The word of God will supply strength to human weakness (v. 8).

A portion of the people ("Zion," "Jerusalem," v. 9) is selected to transmit the glad tidings of deliverance to the whole people. There is no place for fear. The coming of the LORD God with power rules it out (v. 10).

2 Peter 3:8-14. The author of this tract, self-consciously derivative from Jude and the latest NT book to be received into the canon, attempts to assure his readers ("dear friends," v. 8) about the delay of the *parousia*. What some call delay is not that at all (v. 9), he says, since the Lord's time-schedule is so unlike that of men (v. 8); Ps 90:4 is quoted here. Rather than being neglectful of the world, the Lord is providing ample opportunity for repentance. His delay or slowness (*bradytēta*, v. 9) is simply an example of his forbearance.

Jesus had likened the coming of the son of man to a thief breaking in (Mt 24:43; Lk 12:39); the figure turns up as a staple in early catechesis (1 Thes 5:2; Rev 3:3; 16:16). When the surprise occurrence of the end takes place it will be marked by cosmic catastrophe. Only in 2 Pt in the NT does the idea appear that the world will be destroyed by fire (vv. 7, 10), an Iranian eschatological conception found in late Jewish lore in the Sibylline Oracles and the Qumrân writings, and in Stoic literature (the doctrine of *ekpyrōsis*). This impending catastrophe is held out as a motivation for living well (vv. 11f.) It will be succeeded by "new heavens and a new earth" (cf. Is 65:17; 66:22), the setting for a period of God's justice. The certain coming of the new order requires special efforts on the part of believers to be found without stain and at peace (v. 14).

Mark 1:1-8. Mark is the inventor of the literary form "gospel"— sayings interwoven with a continuous narrative. He even uses the term (1:1), deriving it from Second-Isaiah's use of *euaggelizesthai* (see the first pericope above) but also probably with a view to the Roman imperial cult. An inscription of 9 B.C. from Priene south of Ephesus reads: "The birthday of the god was for the world the beginning of the tidings of joy [*euaggelion*] on his account." Mark is convinced that Jesus is a person deserving divine honors, the very "son of God" (1:1).

He cites Isaiah but quotes a conflated version of Mal 3:1 and Is 40:3, probably taken from some early preacher's handbook or "book of testimonies." The messenger of preparation for the last age was popularly taken to be Elijah. Certainly John is described in terms reminiscent of the Tishbite (cf. 2 Kgs 1:8; Zech 13:4.) His message is one of repentance. The one "more powerful (*ischyroteros*) than I" in the struggle against the common foe is Jesus. Later (3:27, following Is 49:24ff.) Mk will designate Satan as "the strong one" against whom Jesus struggles and whom he succeeds in binding and plundering. The plunging of penitents in the River Jordan is but a prelude, says Mk, to the baptism in the holy spirit of the last age.

Perhaps the most remarkable parallel to Mk's baptismal narrative is the 2d-c. B.C. *Testament of Levi*, a Hebrew document which probably contains Christian interpolations: "The heavens shall be opened, and from the temple of glory shall come upon him sanctification, with the Father's voice as from Abraham to Isaac. And the glory of the Most High shall be uttered over him, and the spirit of understanding and sanctification shall rest upon him. . . . And Beliar shall be bound by him, and he shall give power to his children to tread upon evil spirits" (cf. vv. 10f.)

In short, Mk's opening verses convey his conviction that the cosmic struggle is joined and with it the preparation for the messianic age inaugurated.

THIRD SUNDAY OF ADVENT (B)

Isaiah 61:1-2, 10-11. The postexilic poet-prophet views himself as one invested with God's spirit, an anointed individual who has been sent (the latter verb is *shalah*, from which *shaliah*, an "apostle," derives). The "lowly" of v. 1, *anawim*, are the pious poor rather than the economically depressed. The glad tidings brought to them are those of freedom in the ancient homeland, discouraging though the daily work of restoration may be. The Third-Isaiah is perhaps capitalizing on an actual year of jubilee in v. 2 (cf. Lv 25:10) to teach the true nature of redemption. Comfort is in store for the mourners in Zion. The year 538 was a year of vindication in a special way but God's continuing, providential care is such a figurative year. In verses 10-11 the jubilant bride decked out for her wedding and the fruitful earth are the symbols of salvation, justice, and peace. This lyrical outburst is different in quality from the verses with which the chapter opens but it hymns the same reality: a release from the hardships and inequities of postexilic life.

1 Thessalonians 5:16-24. The apostle's invitation to rejoice is the same word in the plural as Gabriel's greeting to Mary in Lk 1:28, *chairete* (v. 16). This injunction to eschatological joy derives from LXX usage. Paul goes on to suggest unceasing prayer and thanksgiving as God's will for believers (vv. 17f.) He hints at trials (3:13) and the grief of loss (4:13) in the Thessalonians' lives. The counsel given about testing the spirit (19ff.) may be a general one but it may also hint at resistance to claims for special gifts of prophecy. Paul does not wish them to be rejected out of hand. He does propose, however, a critical spirit with regard to them.

God is faithful (*pistos*, v. 24). Therefore he who first called the Thessalonians will preserve them until the Lord's return. "Spirit, soul, and body" (*to pneuma kai hē psyche kai to sōma*, v. 23) was the ordinary way of the times to say "whole and entire." We would say "in soul and body."

John 1:6-8, 19-28. The lectionary separates out some verses (but not all; cf. 12*b*, 13, 15, 17-18) which are widely thought to be prose insertions into a poem adapted by the editor of the gospel to refer to Jesus Christ (v. 17).

A distinction is made between John, son of Zechariah, as witness to the light and Christ "the real light" (*to phōs to alēthin*, v. 9). The light is real or true both in the Platonic sense of a heavenly paradigm and the Hebraic sense of that which God has done. NAB has the "light . . . coming into the world," v. 9, but since *erchomenon* agrees with both *anthrōpon* in the accusative and the neuter *phōs* in the nominative, other translations have the light giving light to "every man coming into the world." Context alone suggests a choice. Verse 10 has the "real light" "in the world," which makes it reasonable to assume that the previous verse has described his coming into the world.

The catechetical exchange between John and "priests and Levites" from Jerusalem (v. 19) is an early indication that the fourth gospel may preserve the better historical reminiscence of Jesus' traditional opponents in that city. The synoptics, beginning with Mark, feature "scribes and Pharisees," a probable echo of later opponents to believers in Jesus. The questioners are *hoi Ioudaioi*. NAB renders this as "the Jews" but the translation is inadequate. In a few places in John's gospel it means simply that (e.g., 11:19). More often, however, it is the evangelist's syncopated way of saying "those Jews who opposed Jesus." At times it appears that it should be rendered simply "the Judeans." The evangelist's first chapter builds up to a succession of titles of Jesus (vv. 34-51), including "messiah" (v. 41). Here that title is denied to John (v. 20), as are "Elijah" come back to life (v. 21; cf. Mal 4:5) and "the prophet" (cf. Dt 18:15; Ac 3:22.)

John is made to quote Is 40:3 in testimony to himself, he becoming the herald's "voice." He baptizes with water (v. 26) in performance of a lesser task. After him will come the greater (v. 27) who baptizes in the Holy Spirit (v. 33).

See commentary on Jn 1:1-18, pp. 17f.

FOURTH SUNDAY OF ADVENT (B)

2 Samuel 7:1-5, 8-12, 14, 16. This pericope contains the so-called "dynastic oracle" which legitimated the throne and house of David for all time to come. It occurs in a chapter that stands apart from the rest of the book in which it appears. David was a commoner (1 Sam 16:12f.) who, after the murder of Ishbaal, son of Saul (2 Sam 4:7), was anointed king (5:1-5). The prophet Nathan is here described as David's intermediary with God. No priest is consulted; indeed, David himself has worn the priestly apron (*ephod*, 6:14) while dancing before the ark of the LORD.

The word for house (*beith*) has at least a twofold meaning: dwelling-place and temple. It can also signify family line. The Lord tells Nathan that he has never had a *beith* (dwelling place) in all his desert wanderings (vv. 6f.) but now he will establish a *beith* for him (v. 11*b*) in the sense of offspring or posterity (*zera'*, v. 12*b*). David is promised that he will be God's son (v. 14*a*). The divine favor will never pass from him as it did from Saul (v. 15); it will somehow be permanent in character.

Texts like 2 Sam 23:5, Ps 89:28f., and Is 55:3 show how the tradition of the commitment of the LORD to David and his house has entered into the religious-political life of the people with the force of a covenant like that made with the patriarchs of old.

Romans 16:25-27. These three verses come at the conclusion of the epistle. They take the form of a doxology in which glory is invoked upon God forever through Jesus Christ, in familiar Pauline binitarian fashion. As part of the description of the God who strengthens, mention is made of the *mystērion* long hidden but now made known to the Gentiles. This is none other than the plan, counsel, or will of Eph 1:9 (where it is also called a "mystery") and the mystery of Col 1:26, 27; 2:2. It signifies what God long intended to do and now has done: manifest himself through a death and resurrection culminating in "Christ in you, your hope of glory" (Col 1:27).

The Pauline literature, broadly taken, has the term "mystery" in twenty-one places. This secret of God is now gloriously being revealed among the Gentiles through the preaching of the apostles.

Luke 1:26-38. See commentary, p. 393.

CHRISTMAS SEASON

CHRISTMAS—MASS AT MIDNIGHT (B)

Isaiah 9:1-6. See commentary, p. 14.

Titus 2:11-14. See commentary, pp. 14f.

Luke 2:1-14. See commentary, pp. 15f.

FIRST SUNDAY AFTER CHRISTMAS (B)
Holy Family

Sirach 3:3-7, 14-17; Colossians 3:12-21; Luke 2:22-40. See pp. 18f.

SOLEMNITY OF MARY, MOTHER OF GOD (B)
(January 1—Octave of Christmas)

Numbers 6:22-27; Galatians 4:4-7; Luke 2:16-21. See pp. 20f.

EPIPHANY (B)

Isaiah 60:1-6; Ephesians 3:2-3, 5-6; Matthew 2:1-12. See pp. 23f.

BAPTISM OF THE LORD (B)
(First Sunday after Epiphany)

Isaiah 42:1-4, 6-7; Acts 10:34-38; Mark 1:9-11. See pp. 24ff.

SUNDAYS OF THE YEAR

SECOND SUNDAY OF THE YEAR (B)
(Second Sunday after Epiphany)

1 Samuel 3:3-10, 19. This reading describes an oracle of the LORD which overtakes the boy Samuel in sleep, calling him to forceful priestly leadership. He is awakened from his place near the ark, where he slept close to the old priest Eli. The author underlines the fact that at this period "a revelation of the LORD was uncommon and vision infrequent" (v. 1). Ex 25:10-22 describes the ark, a chest of acacia wood forty-five inches long by two feet wide by twenty-seven inches high, slung on poles for carrying purposes. On top of it were two cherubs of beaten gold facing in toward the propitiatory, an oblong surface of gold designated to receive the sprinkled blood of bullock and goat for sin-offering on the Day of Atonement (cf. Lv 16:1-19.) The ark was made to hold the tables of the law. Its chief characteristic was mobility: it went where the people did as a sign of the LORD's presence to them in their wanderings. For the moment the ark was stationary at Shiloh where the sons of Eli carried on their wicked traffic (2:12-17). It was, moreover, in the temple (*heikal*, v. 3) of the LORD.

The story hints at the many communications in store for Samuel later in his career (v. 7). He is aroused by a call that comes to him three times, the ordinary ritual pattern. Upon instruction, he tells the LORD to speak, for his servant is listening (v. 9). The message containing a threat against Eli for his failure to reprove his sons (vv. 11-18) is repressed in this reading, with its noble acceptance by the old man of the LORD's sentence. Rather, the reading is made to conclude with the young Samuel's growth to manhood under the watchful eye of the LORD who (literally) "let none of his words fall to the ground" (v. 19).

1 Corinthians 6:13-15, 17-20. It is clear from other passages in St. Paul that he believes that the resurrection body will be a transformed body (cf. 15:35-44; 2 Cor 5:1-5; Phil 3:21.) Here he affirms his faith in human resurrection at the hands of the same divine power that raised Jesus up as Lord (v. 14).

In the present context he is inveighing against sexual immorality. Paul willingly admits the naturalness of digestive processes and the inevitability of death, quoting what seems to be a familiar saw (v. 13). The sense of the proverb that precedes it (v. 12) may be that no activities of the body can have everlasting consequences. This Paul takes special pains to deny. The body (sōma) means humanity as a whole for Paul, not just material organs and processes. The argument he appears to be refuting is that illicit sexual activity is no more lasting in its consequences than food intake and excretion. Since Paul allows freedom there, how can he restrict it in matters like fornication? His response is that the proper correlative of the body (the self) is the Lord; in other words, in the matter of sex there is nothing like the natural correlation that there is between humanity and digestion or disposal.

Human bodies are human persons. They are as if members of Christ's body (v. 15a). The elimination of 15bc and 16 from the lectionary (out of delicacy?) makes what follows even harder for the hearer to understand. The man who lies with a prostitute is understood to become one body with her, and because the choice is wrong, one "flesh" in the pejorative sense, in the marriage image of Gn 2:24. Paul may be overestimating the character of such a union, particularly if it is transient, for rhetorical purposes. But he obviously means to contrast that sōma-to-sōma union with the pneuma-to-pneuma union of Christ and the believer in him (v. 17).

Paul's strong charge to the Corinthians to shun lewd conduct (v. 18) has as its appended reason the statement that fornication implicates the body as no other sin does. Strictly speaking, that is not so. One has only to think of suicide, alcohol and drug abuse, and self-mutilation. Yet Paul's point remains in general true. The giving over of one's body-person to a prostitute when it should be committed to the Lord subjects it to a unique indignity.

Each man is destined for the spirit's indwelling (v. 19), not a prostitute's caresses. One should act, therefore, so as to give God the glory. This, for Paul, is quite readily done in the body since he sees no opposition whatever between the action of physical members and a life in the spirit (for him, no different than the spirit).

John 1:35-42. Interrupting this reading after v. 42 destroys its force since the Johannine "call of the disciples" is made the vehicle of successive titles of Jesus. The christology of the gospel to follow is built around the designations "lamb of God" (v. 36), "rabbi" (v. 38), "messiah" (v. 41), "the one Moses spoke of in the law—the prophets too—" (v. 45), "son of God . . . king of Israel" (v. 49), and as a culmination, "son of man" (v. 51). The fourth evangelist possesses the historical tradition of Simon's change of name to Cephas (Peter). He also connects the calling of Jesus' followers with discipleship of John, vv. 28-35, as the synoptic authors do not do (but cf. Luke's "one of those who was of our company while the Lord Jesus moved among us, from the baptism of John," Ac 1:21f.)

The pericope is part of a complex sequence of symbolic days in a week (cf. "the next day" in vv. 29, 35, 41 and "about four in the afternoon," v. 39, as a possible prelude to Sabbath rest, the unaccounted-for day of their staying with him.) The "Where do you stay?" (*pou meneis*) of v. 38 has been suggested as an echo of God's dwelling with his people forever (cf. Dn 6:27.) The verb *eskēnōsen*, "made his dwelling," in 1:14, has likewise been suggested as word play on *shakan^eti* of Ex 25:8, "I shall dwell (among them)"; cf. the LXX of Sir 24, where wisdom first dwells (*kateskēnōsa*, v. 4) in the highest heavens, then pitches her tent (*skēnēn, kataskēnōson*, v. 8) in Israel.

John is the only evangelist who gives the Aramaic original of the Greek name Peter, *Kephas* (the Greek adding a final *sigma*). Note the mutual designations of messiah and Kepha in v. 42, found elsewhere only in Matthew (16:18) in the setting of Caesarea Philippi.

THIRD SUNDAY OF THE YEAR (B)

(Third Sunday after Epiphany)

Jonah 3:1-5, 10. This postexilic tale challenges the earlier biblical notion that God's protective care necessarily excludes all the enemies of Israel. It is written as if the grandeur of the Assyrian capital Nineveh (destroyed in 612) is by now a memory. The archaeological evidence is that Nineveh was about three miles wide. This size, unusual for the ancient world, has become a matter of a three days' journey across (v. 3).

Very probably the seed of this drama in miniature is the declaration of Jer 18:7f.: "Sometimes I threaten to uproot and tear down and destroy a nation or a kingdom. But if that nation which I have threatened turns from its evil, I also repent of the evil which I threatened to do." The identity of a certain prophet Jonah son of Amittai, unknown except for mention in a context of the spread of the northern kingdom's boundaries in the reign of Jeroboam II (783-43), has been preempted for purposes of the tale. He preaches to the Ninevites in the name of his God, the LORD. Far from resisting the message as Israel consistently does, they repent and put on sackcloth, man and boy. The king declares a fast so that God may relent and forgive. God in turn does as Jeremiah says he will do by reconsidering the punishment he has threatened and not carrying it out (v. 10).

Chapter 4 appears to be based on Elijah's flight in terror to the cave of Horeb, followed by his pique at the Israelites because he alone was faithful (1 Kgs 19:10, 14). The repentance of the Ninevites is the "sign of Jonah" of the first stratum of gospel material (Mt 12:39, 41; 16:4; Lk 11:30) which a later tradition read (misread?) in terms of the whale's belly and Jesus' "three days and three nights in the bowels of the earth" (Mt 12:40).

1 Corinthians 7:29-31. As in Mark's so-called little apocalypse where the Lord "has shortened the days" for the sake of those he has chosen (13:20), so here what Paul actually says is that the time before the end "is shortened" (v. 29). His meaning is the simple one that there is little time left. In that which remains ("From now on," *to loipon*), people should conduct themselves in all aspects of life as though they were not (*hōs mē*) married, weeping, rejoicing, owning things, or using the world. Paul gives as the reason for such detachment the fact that the world "as we know it" (meaning its outward appearance, *schēma*, v. 31*b*) is passing away.

He has made clear in 7:2-5 that he does not expect the married to live apart from each other while awaiting the end. Similarly, he does not counsel here a Stoic suppression of tears or laughter. (Recall Rom 12:15: "Rejoice with those who rejoice, weep with those who weep.") Least of all does he wish sham behavior: acting one way while inwardly feeling another. His point is not that marriage and family life and business are transient but that all human institutions will shortly be transformed. At the Lord's coming, people will devote themselves entirely to him. Paul is asking for a wholehearted anticipation of this now (cf. v. 31).

Mark 1:14-20. Mark gets John off the scene in order to launch Jesus on his ministry. The son of Zechariah has heralded the messiah and baptized him. Now Jesus appears in order to proclaim the good news of God (v. 14). He preaches the reform of people's lives (*metanoiete*, v. 15), related to the repentance or turning about (*metanoia*, v. 4) of his predecessor, and faith in the new tidings as well. This is Mk's programmatic statement of Jesus' ministry—an end to the time of waiting and the arrival of God's sovereign rule (*peplērōtai ho kairos*).

The "fishers of men" story is illustrative of Christian call and response, a narrative of divine power. In rabbinic literature nets and fishermen are related to judgment, not to "catching" in a cause.

FOURTH SUNDAY OF THE YEAR (B)

(Fourth Sunday after Epiphany)

Deuteronomy 18:15-20.   Deuteronomy, the work of levitical priests, emanated from some northern sanctuary but was connected with public proclamation at Jerusalem in Josiah's reign (621). It attempted a regulation of the duties of the king (17:14-20) and priests (18:1-8) before turning to the function of prophets (9-22). The part on prophets concludes with a criterion for recognizing a genuine oracle of the LORD, namely that it be fulfilled (vv. 21f.) Verses 15-20 are set in a polemic against Canaanite priests and their magical rites. Soothsaying, necromancy, and fortunetelling are declared abominations; the practice of child sacrifice is also suggested (v. 10). Opposed to all this is the proper attitude which is one of utter candor toward the LORD (v. 13). He will abide no traffic with the spirit-world (v. 14).

The LORD is made to tell Moses he means to raise up a succession of teachers like him. The Deuteronomist goes on to describe a collective prophetism (vv. 15, 18). Subsequent generations will take this to refer to one man (cf. Jn 6:14; 7:40.) That a singular collective is intended by vv. 20ff. is clear. Such a one may be a true prophet or a false. In the former case he will speak as the LORD has commanded him; in the latter, presumptuously, either in another vein or in the names of other gods.

1 Corinthians 7:32-35.   This reading immediately follows last Sunday's. St. Paul expresses the hope that his Corinthians should be anxiety-free (*amerimnous*) as they wait for the Lord. He does not wish their lives to be wrapped up in family life or commerce, in possessions or relationships. Paul may be speaking in v. 32*b* of the form the anxiety of the unmarried man takes, in v. 33 that of the married man. He may, again, be using the verb form *merimna* in two different senses, "is busy with" (v. 32) and, uncomplimentarily, "is caught up in" (v. 33). In either case he is contrasting, unfavorably, pleasing one's wife with pleasing the Lord.

The Christian husband by definition is committed to pleasing both the Lord and his wife. This means that he is divided but in a good way. If he were to be devoted to the world's demands and to pleasing his wife, he would be divided in a bad way. The question is, does Paul classify a wife with "the world" and against the Lord? Not necessarily. He does think, however, that there is bound to be division of some kind. He seems unwilling to identify pleasing one's wife with pleasing the Lord, if only because they are distinct, each making personal demands. That the wife's will should coincide with the Lord's will or that pleasing the wife should be identical with doing the Lord's will is a possibility Paul does not entertain.

Rather, he goes on the assumption that, being free from marital obligations, a man (v. 32) or woman (v. 34) will be free for "holiness in body and spirit." The latter sentiment may be one held by the Corinthian ascetical party, as 7:1b undoubtedly is, hence properly set in quotation marks. In such case, Paul is identifying himself with the opinion. Yet we know from other expressions of view that he does not confine holiness in the body to the unmarried but considers it the vocation of all (cf. Rom 6:12; 12:1; 1 Cor 6:13.)

Paul requires that one be detached in all matters. He never says that the unmarried or the virginal have, *ipso facto*, achieved detachment. He merely intimates that they have a running start on the problem.

Mark 1:21-28. According to Mark, Capernaum was the center of Jesus' ministry. It lay on the northwest shore of the Sea of Galilee. A ruined synagogue of Capernaum is there to be visited, but this edifice did not stand in Jesus' day. Mark is not so much interested in *what* Jesus taught (he transmits little of his teaching, compared to Mt and Lk) as he is in the effect it had on his hearers. He is especially concerned to report that Jesus taught with authority (*exousia*, v. 22), not like the scribes, and that people were spellbound by his teaching. The "authority" in question is not that of the well-informed teacher, the layman who, although without rabbinic training, discourses like a master. For Mark it is rather the divine authority of the son of God (cf. 1:1, 11b.)

The cosmic struggle between God and superhuman powers which is a feature of Mk's gospel is first introduced in this passage. Jesus deals not merely with a sick man but with an unclean spirit or demon who shrieks at him, convulses the victim, and then at Jesus' sharp command leaves him. The spirit (who speaks in the plural: ". . . to destroy us") addresses Jesus in fear, not in respect. He recognizes him as "God's holy one." The adversaries are thus here joined: God's chosen one and the troubler of humanity.

The demons' search to express Jesus' identity does not include utterance of his name. The title arrived at is thought by scholars to be an attempt to gain power over Jesus (as in various Jewish magical papyri, where possession of the victim's name gives such power). If so, it is an unsuccessful attempt. Jesus speaks a simple word of command. The Greek verbs for "rebuked" and "be quiet" have a history in exorcism formulas of the time. The crowd is amazed by Jesus' authoritative stance. It is all that is needed to convince the people of the whole region (*holēn tēn perichōron*) of Galilee that God's emissary has taken up residence in their midst. Mk achieves his initial purpose by portraying Jesus as one who has come to usher in the new eon by stripping the rulers of the former age of their power.

FIFTH SUNDAY OF THE YEAR (B)

(Fifth Sunday after Epiphany)

Job 7:1-4, 6-7. This chapter, a continuation of the preceding one, contains Job's response to Eliphaz, the first of his troublesome comforters. Job has been describing his brothers as having no more dependability or staying power than desert streams in the summer sun (cf. 6:15-17.) His three visitors are terrified at the adversities in his life with which he confronts them (v. 21). He wants nothing from them but a little instruction, some convincing argument about the meaning of his present distress (vv. 24f.) They can supply him with none. *Their* words they take as proof but his desperate utterance as wind (v. 26). Job plows ahead in what, for him, is the only sincere and truthful appraisal of the state of things.

Man's life, he says, is like that of the field worker who owns nothing and never will. He waits for the sun's heat to abate and the day to end, for the next payday, for the relief of nightfall. But night does not bring sleep, only restless, insomniac tossing (vv. 3f.) The days are long and the nights longer but paradoxically it is all over in an instant and without hope. The shuttle flies, the thread is snapped, the cloth is finished. Yet nothing is done.

Benjamin King's *Pessimist* said there was,

> Nothing to do but work,
> Nothing to eat but food
> Nothing to wear but clothes
> To keep from going nude.

Job is weary of having nowhere to stand but on. He wants Eliphaz to know that there's nowhere to fall but off.

1 Corinthians 9:16-19, 22-23. The one thing Paul most holds in horror is that boasting which his opponents in the spread of the gospel glory in. *Kauchaomai* is a verb he uses about 35 times, plus its cognate nouns *kauchēma* and *kauchēsis*. The sounds are onomatopoeic in their resemblance to the cawing of crows. Priding himself on externals has no appeal for Paul. If he has to boast it will be in Christ Jesus with respect to his relationship to God (cf. Rom 15:17.)

The context of Paul's remarks here is that he has never exacted support from the Corinthians, even though in principle "those who preach the gospel should live by the gospel" (1 Cor 9:14). He does not press these rights lest anyone rob him of his "boast," that is, deprive him of the possibility of preaching the gospel untrammelled (v. 15). On reflection, however, Paul concludes that he is not so much free with respect to the gospel as constrained. He has to preach it; failure to do so would spell his ruin (v. 16). Free or unfree, he cannot make the responsibility go away. He is gospel-haunted, God-ridden. The payment (*misthos*) he receives consists in presenting the gospel free of charge and thereby retaining his liberty (v. 18). Pressing its full authority (*exousia*) on his hearers might bring an end to this, so Paul forbears.

The apostle Paul is not only free at last, he is free (*eleutheros*) first and always (v. 19). Yet his liberty is a happy servitude in the cause of convincing others of the truth of the gospel.

Verses 20-21 are omitted from the reading with a commendable delicacy. The framers of the lectionary are seemingly sensitive to the long history of proselytizing directed against the Jews. Paul the observant Jew could press on fellow-Jews his convictions about his freedom from the law in a way that no Gentile can, yet many, offensively, have.

The "weak" of this passage may be Jews of his time who cannot bear the burden of freedom from the law and feel they must conform to it. Paul is sympathetic toward them. He does not bully them into a freedom which for them would be no freedom at all. His *tois pasin . . . panta* stance, "all things to all men" (v. 22), has been both praised over the ages as resiliency of spirit and reviled as chameleon-like strategy or low cunning. It is probably none of these. It is an open declaration of conscious motivation, made specific in v. 23. Paul does all that he does for the sake of (*dia*) the gospel. His interest, he admits disarmingly, is self-interest. He wants some share, some commonality (*sygkoinōnos*), in its benefits. He knows no better way than to offer participation in the saving message to others on any terms that may prove congenial to them.

Mark 1:29-39. Jesus, for Mark, shows his power over the forces inimical to man not only by ejecting the shrieking unclean spirit but also by healing the fever-ridden mother of Simon's wife. The fact of her immediately beginning to wait on them (v. 31) has nothing much to do with the domestic chauvinism of the times, however marked that might have been. It is, rather, Mark's familiar cachet signifying the return to normalcy after a wondrous deed has been performed by Jesus. The chaos in nature has been overcome. The order that speaks of God's power succeeds it.

Mark distinguishes between the unwell and the possessed (vv. 32, 34). This helps give the lie to the modern supposition that the ancient world attributed all otherwise unexplained pathology to demonism. Still, Mark is insistent on the common feature in all human suffering. Man is under the influence of a baleful enemy so powerful that only the "holy one of God" (v. 24) can break his hold. Jesus for Mark is the man who by God's power puts the strong one under restraint in order to despoil his property and plunder his house (cf. 3:27.) Satan's household is not a house internally divided. Jesus in his holiness is laying seige to it from without.

Jesus' reduction of the demons to silence (v. 34) is conceivably a historical reminiscence but more demonstrably a narrative technique of Mark. Their knowledge of Jesus is not the knowledge of faith but of hatred, just as their acknowledgment of his identity is a shrieking (*anakrazein*), not a proclamation (*kēryssein*). Mark reserves genuine epiphanies of Jesus for later times (cf. 8:30; 9:2-7; 14:62; 16:6.)

The desert for Jesus is a place of testing by inimical forces (1:13), in Mark's theology of geographical setting. Its solitude is also, however, a place of prayer and recovered strength (1:35; 6:31; 8:4), not to mention protection (1:45). But, as is so often reported, the crowds seek Jesus out and remind him of his vocation. He has come for proclamation (*hina . . . kēryxō*, v. 38; *kēryssōn*, v. 39).

Mark's Galilee is the favorable region where the gospel is preached and demons are expelled. In Judea, Jesus engages in polemic, is plotted against, and meets his death (cf. 10:32; 11:27f.; 12:13; 14:1; 15:37.)

SIXTH SUNDAY OF THE YEAR (B)

(Sixth Sunday after Epiphany)

Leviticus 13:1-2, 44-46 (Hebrew 45-46). Biblical leprosy (*sara'ath*, literally a "striking down" or "laying low"; in Greek, *lepra*) is not necessarily Hansen's disease but more often something closer to psoriasis or ringworm. Sufferers from Hansen's disease have been caused untold anguish as a result of the false conclusion from biblical data that their disease is a divine punishment for wrongdoing. The priests are charged by the Mosaic legislation with acting as public health officers. Verses 3-44 in the Hebrew text may be repulsive and unfit for public reading in their clinical detail but they have been much praised for the diagnosis of symptoms they propose. It is as up-to-date as that of any modern practitioner in a dispensary.

The isolation technique of vv. 44-45 is primarily to provide protection for the healthy but also contains elements of a crude hygiene for the afflicted. The latter's cry of "Unclean!" (*tame'*) had to do with the ritual impurity resulting from their physiological condition. Because of the lack of distinction made between ritual and moral imperfection in the early biblical period, this warning technique, whatever its effectiveness, came to be taken in the popular mind as synonymous with moral offense. Thus, the adjective *tame'* of vv. 45 and 46 becomes *akathartos* in the Septuagint, the same word as that used to describe "unclean spirits" in Mk 1:23, 26, 27. The segregation of those with infectious diseases (and Hansen's disease is barely such) therefore ceases to be a public protection and takes on the character of moral stigma. Purists may say that any such notion is "unbiblical" but the popular misconception seems to be a fact (cf. 2 Kgs 5:27; Jn 9:2f.)

1 Corinthians 10:31—11:1. St. Paul here provides his converts with an overarching principle for the conduct of their everyday lives, just as in last week's pericope he had supplied one to account for all that he did in his attempts to spread the gospel. Today's passage comes as the summary of his lengthy discussion of the legitimacy of eating meat which has been sacrificed to idols (as most of that available in Corinthian markets had). His conclusion transcends all the counsel he has given in individual cases: Do all that you do for God's glory. The way to achieve that is to avoid personal offense whenever possible. The person comes first for Paul. Being solicitous for his needs, whatever his particularities (Jew, Greek, weak, strong, of tough mind or tender conscience) has the highest priority. Seeking the advantage of the other rather than oneself is the means to ensure both his salvation and God's glory.

Volumes have been written on Paul's final sentence: "Imitate me as I imitate Christ" (11:1). He has already hinted at a good, practical norm for the conduct of others (9:22). Now he makes it explicit. The suggestion that his conduct might have about it some exemplary character has come up in previous letters (1 Thes 1:6; 2 Thes 3:7, 9; Phil 3:17). Part of his special calling as an apostle is to show in an especially clear way the demands of Christian life (cf. 1 Cor 4:9-13.) Paul does not hesitate to propose that people imitate Christ directly (Rom 15:2f.) but he is convinced that, since that is what he is doing, others are safe to follow him. There is no implication that a mediated discipleship is a necessary or even a better one, only the realistic view that the remembrance of Paul's presence provides a more accessible model than the historical life of Jesus.

Mark 1:40-45. This gospel reading, consecutive with last week's, shows why today's selection from Leviticus was chosen as necessary background material. The detail of the leper's kneeling down (v. 40) is consistent with Mark's view of Jesus as son of God. Mark has Jesus heal with a touch, thereby showing his power (v. 41); then he enjoins silence (v. 44) as part of the Marcan technique of combating the "divine man" Christology that probably characterized the chief source on which he drew. Jesus conforms fully to the levitical prescription (v. 45). The evangelist may be ironical if the phrase "a proof (*martyrion*) for them" is intended to go with the phrase about the offering rather than with the ritual of the leper's presenting himself.

SEVENTH SUNDAY OF THE YEAR (B)
(Seventh Sunday after Epiphany)

Isaiah 43:18-19, 21-22, 24-25. The poet employs the Exodus theme in verses 16-17 with the usual references to a path in the sea and chariots and horsemen lying prostrate, never to rise, only to admonish his reader to forget all this imagery (v. 18). Jer 16:14f. likewise hints that in the popular mind the memory of the Exodus will fade and yield to that of deliverance from Babylon. Israel's God is doing something new. He is making a way in the desert and, in the wasteland, rivers (the Dead Sea MS of Isaiah seems to read "paths," a reading followed by NEB). His own people have water to drink in the desert but Israel, instead of praising God, grows weary of him. The lesson of the new deliverance is lost on the people, the LORD complains. They weigh him down with sins and crimes instead of offering sheep and fatlings and sweet cane on their sacrificial altars. He does not remember their sins but wipes them out.

Would they have a true audit? They had better go along with his forgiveness, for they could not stand a day in court.

2 Corinthians 1:18-22. Many scholars consider 1:1—6:13 part of a letter written in Macedonia which should follow the fragments of correspondence represented by 6:14—7:1 and 10:1—13:10. After 6:13 would come 7:2 through 9:15, with 13:11-14 comprising the conclusion to chs. 7—9.

St. Paul has been speaking of his sincerity in having had the intention of visiting the Corinthians twice, once on his way to Macedonia and again coming back. Only consideration for them restrained him from doing so (1:23). He insists that he keeps his word even as God himself does (v. 18). This prompts Paul to describe Jesus Christ as the great affirmative. The Greek word for a strong "Yes" is *Nai*, which strikes our ear as strange. That is what Christ is, though: the fulfillment of all God's promises. And that is why it makes sense to associate oneself with Christ at the great "Amen" of the assembly of worshipers (*pros doxan*). "Amen" means "It is firm," a usage which prompts Paul to describe God as "firmly establishing" him (Paul) along with the Corinthians in Christ. The three aorist participles (*chrisas, sphragisamenos, dous*) which speak of anointing, sealing, and depositing the first payment of the spirit in our hearts (vv. 21f.) may be early baptismal vocabulary, although non-sacramentally oriented Christian scholars tend to refer the "Amen" addressed through Christ to God to the response to preaching, namely faith. One thing that is certain is the legal nature of the figure of "down payment" or "pledge" (*arrabōn*, v. 22; it occurs also in 5:5). Like the agricultural figure "first fruits" of Rom 8:23 it describes the gift of the spirit, following Christ's resurrection, which serves as the first installment of the new age that is to come.

God, the firm establisher, is likewise the giver of the gift.

Mark 2:1-12. Capernaum is the center of Jesus' Galilean activity for Mark. Crowds gather around his door (v. 2). Here, as characteristically, the reality in the onlookers that elicits the miracle is their "faith" (v. 5). The faith of the healing stories is neither faith in God (as in Mk 11:22) nor faith in Jesus (as in Mt 18:6) but something absolute—a power that is the power of God himself arising from the encounter with Jesus (cf. "faith" in the healing stories of Mk 5:25-34 par.; 5:21-24, 35-43; 7:24-30 par. Mt 15:28; Mk 9:14-29; 10:46-52 par.; Mt 8:5-13 par.; Mt 9:27-31; Lk 17:11-19.) The stories of healing are basically not stories of healing at all but exemplary stories of the power of faith which is elicited through Jesus. The healing is not the object of faith; God is, with Jesus as the instrument.

Mark has Jesus forgive the man's sins, as the church of his day is doing. He is then charged with blasphemy and is made by Mk to use the power of the healing (v. 11) to justify the possession of still greater authority.

EIGHTH SUNDAY OF THE YEAR (B)

(Eighth Sunday after Epiphany)

Hosea 2:16, 17, 21-22. The God of Israel has been made a fool of, time and again, by the adulterous adventures of his wife. What no man in Israel has had to endure he stands ready, even willing, to undergo. He will take back this self-seeking spouse who callously gives as the reason she intends to return, "I was better off with him than I am now" (v. 9). The LORD divulges his strategy in today's pericope. He will re-create the situation in which he first won his bride by leading her out into the desert of Sinai and there wooing her afresh (v. 16*b*). Nowhere is the Canaanite idea of the sacred marriage better made use of.

Adlai Stevenson, in conceding defeat on the night of one of his unsuccessful tries for the presidency, confused the newmen thoroughly by quoting 1:17*a* (AV, 1:15). The morning papers went to press before any of them had located the quotation he used about making the Valley of Achor (i.e., trouble) a door of hope. Emek-Achor was a western entry into Canaan where Achan was stoned for pillage (Jos 7:24ff.) The early Zionist settlers named one of their first towns, now a thriving city, *Pethah-tikvah*, "Gate of Hope," out of this verse in Hosea.

The prophet looks for a response from the people such as Israel made in the days of her youth. Right and justice, love, mercy, and fidelity are all favorite words of Hosea. They are the terms of the renewed and lasting marriage which he envisions. Crowning all is a particularly sublime Hosean concept: "You shall know the LORD," again derived from the intimacy of marriage.

2 Corinthians 3:1-6. Throughout this portion of the letter Paul stresses the purity of his motivation. He has said that he is a noxious odor to those on their way to destruction but a breath of life to those who are being saved (2:15f.) He is no Christ-monger, with the gospel his stock in trade. Veiled reference to other preachers is apparent. St. Paul knows his Corinthians so well that he scoffs at the idea of needing to be introduced to them. The letter-technique has presumably been reported to him of others. The "letter written on your hearts" refers to the new covenant (cf. 1 Cor 11:25) spoken of in Jer 31:33, though the tablets of stone go back to Ex 24:12; 31:18; 32:15f. Paul, here as elsewhere, is not proposing a new Mosaic dispensation in place of the first one but is suggesting that a written form of words cannot contain the richness of God's intent. Only his life-giving spirit can do that. The written law "kills" only in the sense that it literally does not allow breathing-space. It informs the believer from without what he is held to. The spirit tells him from within what he is capable of.

Here there is no question of two distinct covenants but of one which is renewed by the gift of the spirit. Neither is there thought of a spirit which underlies written rules. This is a spirit who interprets and makes possible the observance of written rules, removing all despair over the inability to do so.

The "entitled" of verse 5 in NAB is *hikanoi*, just as "credit" is *hikanotēs* and "made qualified" is *hikanōsen*, all words meaning "sufficient." The Greek translations of the Bible by Aquila, Symmachus, and Theodotion rendered the divine title Shaddai by *hikanos*, relying on a doubtful etymology. Paul may have this in mind as he declares God and not ourselves our great sufficiency. He it is who has made us ministers (*diakonous*) of a covenant of spirit, the one covenant in which a life-giving spirit instructs us.

Mark 2:18-22. This passage appears not only in Mk but also in Mt and Lk, as a substantial portion of Mk does (cf. Mt 9:14-15; Lk 5:33-35.) The brief narrative of v. 18 provides the setting for the saying of Jesus found in 19*a*: "How can the guests at a wedding fast as long as the groom is still among them?" This question is the center of gravity of the passage. Mention of fasting and the use of wedding imagery suggest that the saying originated in Jewish circumstances. Yet 19*b* indicates a break with the practice of fasting. *Today* is a wedding; the groom is with them; there is no mention in this phrase of future expectation. These features suggest a modification of the Jewish setting.

Nothing in 18-19*a* expresses the Church's faith in the resurrection or the theological interpretation of Jesus' mission which grew out of that faith. Hence we are right to take it, in its reflection of contemporary Judaism, as something coming from the setting of Jesus' lifetime. Verse 20 (and perhaps 19*b*) is a different matter. It comes from a later time, for it is evident that in it the death of Jesus is very important for Mark. Not only does his death assume a prominent place in his gospel but it occurs as a "plot to destroy him" in 3:6, the summary conclusion to all the conflict stories with Jewish authorities collected between 2:1 and 3:6, of which today's pericope is one. The slight allusion to Jesus' death in 2:20 "anticipates the more direct hint in 3:6, which in turn prepares for the definite predictions of Jesus' death which begin at 8:31." (D. O. Via)

Verses 21-22 express the joy of newness, an anticipation of the resurrection. In the five verses of this reading two major matters are expressed: Mk's presentation of reasons for Jesus' death—he challenged the established order—and Mk's understanding of the significance of Jesus' death and resurrection—a new day of celebration has dawned. Believers are being told that they are free of ritual requirement. They may fast or not as they choose.

NINTH SUNDAY OF THE YEAR (B)

(Ninth Sunday after Epiphany)

Deuteronomy 5:12-15. Students of the Hebrew Bible like Ackroyd, de Vaux, and Rowley assume that the religious observance of the sabbath came into prominence during the exile, in default of other ritual possibilities in Babylon. This is not to say that the sabbath originated there but only that sacred time probably took on more importance with the loss of sacred place. While the Priestly writings tend to support this view, the evidence is by no means such as to make it certain. What is clear is that the sabbath loomed large for the P author. Genesis 1:1—2:4 reaches a first climax in the creation narrative in the account of the sabbath, an anticipation of the final climax, which is the picture of the tabernacle as the center of a worshipping community. Again, the materials used by P in this account may be presumed to have preceded its sixth-century composition.

The Exodus 20:8-11 account of the "fourth word" in the Hebrew division of verses in the decalogue—E expanded by additions from P —connects the term "sabbath" (*shabbath*) with the Hebrew root for "to rest," *shabhath. The* original meaning of the word, which is also found in the Babylonian (*šapattu*), is disputed. The latter is the 15th of the month, the day of the full moon. The observance of phases of the moon, hence of a period of four weeks, is very old. Assyria seems to have forbidden work to the king and priests on the 7th, 14th, 21st, and 28th days because these were unlucky. It was only in ancient Israel that work was stopped on a religious principle.

There are small differences between the sabbath precept in Dt and that in Ex. Dt has "keep" (*shamor*, v. 12) rather than the "remember" of Ex (*zakor*, v. 8). There are small additions in vv. 12*b* and 14. Dt (5:15) links the sabbath with the exodus rather than with the creation of the P author of Ex (20:11). This choice illustrates the Deuteronomist's general historical concern. He relates the fourth word, with its prohibition of labor, to the LORD's clemency in delivering Israel from its forced labor in Israel.

Perhaps no custom besides circumcision so separated the Jewish community from the Gentile after the fall of Jerusalem as sabbath observance. This means that the option of the Gentile church, as contrasted with Jewish Christianity, to worship on the first day contributed to making the breach with Judaism final. The various sabbatarian restorations of the Reformers and those who came after them are well known—on the rest principle (Puritans like Nicholas Bownde) and on the seventh-day principle (Adventists like the much later William Miller and Ellen White).

Religious considerations quite apart, it is clear that ancient Israel gave the globe the legacy of a day of freedom from its week of toil. This immense contribution has made prayer and re-creation possible for all who are not bound by economic servitude, a condition which too often is the result of cupidity by observants of a weekly free day.

2 Corinthians 4:6-11. Paul in this section of the collection of letters that has come to be known as 2 Corinthians (the unit is probably 2:14—7:4) writes as a theologian against discouragement in the Church (cf. 4:1.) He proclaims the truth openly; it is not veiled. He views the splendor of the gospel as a light shining out of darkness (vv. 4, 6, the latter referring to Gen 1:3 and Is 9:1). The treasure carried in earthen vessels is an ability to proclaim the Moses-like "glory of God shining on the face of Christ" (v. 6; cf. Ex 34:29-35; Heb 1:3.) It is made possible, in the first instance, by the light shining in our hearts.

This is God's doing and not ours (v. 7), as the present afflictions of apostles like Paul amply demonstrate (vv. 8-10). Nothing short of divine power could send such beams of light from lamps of human clay. The master stroke is the paradox of Christ's life being revealed and made accessible by the daily mortality of those who proclaim it. The dying are themselves the life-giving principle. In Thompson's words, "The Slain hath the gain, and the Victor hath the rout."

Only those headed for destruction, those who actively resist the gospel, are in a "veiled" condition for Paul (v. 3). He takes his stand against any esoteric character of the message. It is a beacon in the manner of the pre-cosmic wisdom of God in Hellenist Jewish thought —Paul's favorite exemplar for Christ.

Mark 2:23—3:6. These are the final two conflict stories of the collection that runs from 2:1 to 3:6. Mark wants his reader to see in Jesus of Nazareth "the eschatological messenger who restores the true understanding of God's will in the End Time" (Kee). Mark spells out this role in relation to specific issues, here the precedence of human need over sabbath observance. The evangelist presents Jesus as one whose ministry was characterized by the work of interpreting God's law anew. Repristination of the law was one of the eschatological functions expected in late Judaism to occur in the Last Age. At Qumrân the Teacher of Righteousness was to fulfill this role. For Mark it was Jesus.

Jesus' disciples are accused of offending against the prohibition of harvesting on the sabbath in Ex 34:21, as interpreted in strict Pharisee circles. Jesus counters with a question of his own in approved rabbinic fashion, citing 1 Sam 21:1-6. Ahimelech was high priest at the time of the incident but his son Abiathar, better known through his association with David, is evidently the one of whom the anecdote is being told in some circles. Mark uses the exchange to show the transcendent character of human need (verse 27, a rabbinic maxim, may well have been abroad in Jesus' day) and identify Jesus as having the authority to set aside the venerable sabbath law. Even if the phrase "the son of man" means simply a man here, the power of Jesus remains Mark's main thrust.

The second story likewise arose out of Christian debates about sabbath observance, since it is not primarily a healing story. The Christians are clearly on the side of Hillel whose interpretation of sabbath requirements was more humanely oriented than that of Shammai. The latter's school permitted only the saving of a life on the sabbath. Jesus here identifies disease as incipient death.

The plot against Jesus' life reported in 3:6 is not to be thought of as being hatched early in his ministry; there are no rubrics of time in Mark. It is characteristic of this evangelist to sum up a section in such fashion. The verse sets the stage for Mark's preoccupation with the desire of "the chief priests and scribes" to entrap and kill Jesus (14:1). Its presence here is chiefly a matter of dramatic anticipation.

LENTEN SEASON

FIRST SUNDAY OF LENT (B)

Genesis 9:8-15. This Priestly narrative contains the first biblical mention of the idea of a covenant (*bᵉrith*). It is also marked by the initial appearance of a biblical "sign" (*'oth*, v. 12), which is any event interpreted as the entrance of God into human affairs (cf. Jgs 6:36-40; Ex 4:2-8.) The tale is obviously designed to account for the origin of the rainbow—a sign of God's compact with all living creatures, available after every rainfall. By it, God commits himself never again to wreak the devastation of the earth by flood. The rainbow will appear as a symbol of divine splendor again in Ez 1:28 and Rev 4:3.

The covenant made with Noah has a universality about it unlike the particular one with Abraham which is to follow (15:9-21). The Noachean covenant embraces all humanity and all living creatures. Men are to have complete discretion over the lives of animals but not over human life. Human blood is not to be shed under any circumstances (v. 6). Neither is the blood of animals to be eaten. The latter cultic taboo is here validated in terms of a covenant that supposedly went back to the time after the flood, well before Abram's call. Because of its antiquity it is thought of as binding on all humanity and not just on the circumcised (Gen 17). The rationale is that, since blood is the symbol of life, it is sacred because all life is sacred.

The LORD has committed himself to all mortal creatures including the subhuman. No one of them whether wild or tame escapes his solicitous care.

1 Peter 3:18-22. The writer has been speaking in the previous passage about persecution and the equanimity with which it should be faced. Here he turns to the reason why Christians should be confident, namely the victory over evil which Christ has won by his resurrection, a victory made accessible through faith and the saving waters of baptism (v. 21).

The compression of phrasing in parts of this passage, its careful balance, and the introduction by the particle *hoti* ("For") all contribute to the impression that a liturgical hymn or catechetical formula has been inserted here. Verses 18 and 22 are evidently phrases that have been sung in praise of Christ, more clearly so than the labored figure developed in between. The author obviously wants to relate "Noah's fludde" to baptism. He does it by identifying water as the means of salvation in both cases. Noah and his wife, the three sons and their wives, were the eight saved by God's patience (v. 20). The same kind of effect is possible today, says the writer: not the removal of physical stain by water but life in Christ, bestowed on condition of the pledge of a good conscience (v. 21).

The author of 1 Pt prefers the verb "suffered" to "died", which means that the latter's use in v. 18 comes as a surprise; as a matter of fact, "died" occurs as a textual variant in some MSS. Cf. the similar creedal formula in 1 Cor 15:3. "Once for all" (*hapax*) is reminiscent of Rom 6:10 and various appearances in Hebrews (7:27; 9:12, 26, 28; 10:10). The author favors antithesis, as is evident from his use of just/unjust and flesh/spirit. The latter occurs in Rom 1:3f. and 1 Tim 3:16. "Spirit," of course, means the corporeal Christ in his heavenly or exalted sphere of existence as contrasted with his previous career as a man among men.

"The spirits who had disobeyed" are probably the wicked angels of Gen 6:1-4 who lusted after the daughters of men, who in turn begot giants by them. The exploits of these perverse spirits are a commonplace in post-biblical literature, including the Dead Sea Scrolls. The dovetailing of this tale with that of the flood in Gen 6:4-5 can be seen to be very close. The "prison" of v. 19 is probably not the *sheol* or underworld of biblical literature but the second of seven heavens postulated by 1 and 2 Enoch, up to which the risen Christ ascended to preach. Why this proclamation to wicked spirits? It is not a preaching of the gospel but a proclaiming by Christ, the new Enoch, that their power is finally broken.

Mark 1:12-15. Jesus is driven by the spirit, in Mark, into the desert. This rocky wasteland is the home of jackals and mountain lions (cf. Is 34:11-15) and is also the traditional dwelling-place of spirits inimical to man. Jesus' testing here described is not one of interior struggle. It is a joining of eschatological forces: the holiness of God versus all that is opposed to it. Mark has it in mind to assure his Christian readership that their resistance to hostile forces is part of the same, ongoing battle. Mastery of the wild beasts was part of the equipment of the righteous man, as in the Adam story, Job 5:22, and *Testament of Benjamin* 5:2; cf. also the expectation that in the messianic age the animals would live in harmony, Is 11:6ff., Hos 2:20. In Ps 91:11-13 dominion over the wild beasts goes hand in hand with service by angels. "St Mark probably means that by his victory over Satan Jesus has reversed Adam's defeat and begun the process of restoring paradise" (Nineham). The forty-day period without any hunger that is being reported on is clearly eschatological. Perhaps Mark has in mind the feeding of Elijah by angels and his forty-day flight to Horeb (1 Kgs 19).

Verse 14 marks the beginning of Jesus' Galilean ministry, his public declaration of himself once the messianic herald John is off the scene. Mark saves the details of the Baptizer's detention until ch. 6; here he simply has him "handed over." John's work is finished. The time has come for Jesus' mission to begin. Verses 14-15 are a manifesto or summing up of the entire ministry of Jesus. The proclamation of the good news of God (b*e*sorah, Gk. kērygma; cf. Is 40:9; 52:7; 61:1) meant that the time of waiting was over and that God's reign (malkuth; Gk. basileia) had, in some form, arrived. Mark here has Jesus proclaim himself as the messianic bringer of the kingdom, but in his gospel he portrays Jesus as muting or down-playing this role. This stems from his theological conviction that Jesus is no mere wonder-worker but the son of God who must nonetheless suffer and die as son of man.

He uses the language of later Christian evangelism in giving a summary of Jesus' public activity. This includes terms like "the fulfillment of time" (peplērōtai ho kairos), "the coming near of God's sovereign rule" (ēggiken hē basileia), and the commands to "repent" (metanoiete) and "believe in the gospel" (pisteuete tǭ euaggeliǭ).

SECOND SUNDAY OF LENT (B)

Genesis 22:1-2, 9, 10-13, 15-18. This narrative is so rich that no amount of reflection can exhaust it. It is dear to Jews, Christians, and Muslims alike. For Jews Abraham is the first of the patriarchs, the father of an elect and covenanted people. For Christians he is the progenitor of all regardless of peoplehood who cleave to God in faith, understood as a spirit of complete trust. The world of Islam venerates him as al Khalil, God's "friend"—the name by which it knows the town of Hebron.

Aetiologically (i.e., in the realm of causes or origins) the tale is probably rooted in polemic against Canaanite human sacrifice. The Hebrews—Jacob, to become Israel, is as yet unborn—are to sacrifice animals as burnt offerings, not children. "God himself will provide the sheep for the holocaust" (v. 7; cf. Mic 6:7.) The site is important. "Moriah" is related in popular etymology to vision from a height (cf. "the LORD will see," yireh, v. 14.) The Elohist writer speaks of Jeruel (2 Chr 20:16), a wilderness near Tekoa which satisfies the condition of Abraham's three-days' journey. Later the mountain will be identified in folklore with Mt. Zion in Jerusalem. If the better rendering of v. 14 is "on the mountain the LORD is seen" or "it is provided," there is already reference to the temple.

Abraham's prompt obedience is consistent with his leaving his kinsfolk and his father's house in Haran (Gen 12:1). His binding of Isaac (*aqedath Yiṣḥaq*) and placing him on the wood of the altar (v. 9) is thought of by Jewish scholars like Lévi, Schoeps, and Spiegel to have supplied St. Paul with the rabbinic paradigm which led to his development of Jesus' expiatory sacrifice. Since there had been no tradition that the Messiah would die, mention of the binding of "your own beloved son" (or "your only son") would have served Paul as the necessary bridge. Vermes has shown that an expiatory view of Isaac's sacrifice was widely held in the Jerusalem of the first century. It cannot be established that Paul originated the doctrine of the atonement on his own.

This is to get far ahead of the Yahwist's narrative. He is at pains to describe the high point in the spiritual pilgrimage of Abraham. The patriarch survives admirably the testing he is put to. His complete spirit of surrender is a symbolic passing through death, a sealing of the covenant that has been "cut" in ch. 15.

Romans 8:31-34. See p. 121 for the passage immediately following this one. The condition Paul puts is, "If God is for us." If it is fulfilled our salvation is assured, despite difficulties and opposition of every sort. But it is fulfilled. Jesus Christ is the proof. To him we must adhere in faith. Verse 32 seems to contain a reference to Gn 22:16 above, where the LXX word "spared" (*epheisato*) is used by Paul. It may also echo Is 53:11.

Paul's questions in vv. 33f. are rhetorical and probably ironic. God's "chosen ones" is unusual for him (cf. 16; 13; also Col 3:12.) The obvious answer to the question in v. 33, in the context of a law court or the final assize, is Satan. The patent absurdity of the justifying God or the resurrected and interceding Christ taking a stand against the elect on whose behalf they have labored seems to be the force of Paul's interrogative responses. He may have Is 50:7ff. in mind here, a passage in which the innocent sufferer is confident of the LORD's support.

Mark 9:1-9. Verse 1 probably reflects this evangelist's conviction that the *parousia* will occur in his lifetime, or if not that, that the Gentile mission will succeed sufficiently to vindicate his words. The transfiguration narrative which follows at the very least supports the claim that Jesus is the Messiah. The literary resemblance of v. 7 to

1:11 of the baptismal account is evident but it is not certain, as some hold, that this is a resurrection narrative placed back in Jesus' earthly life. Moses and Elijah represent the law and the prophets, hence the totality of foreshadowing. Elijah was also connected with the coming of the Messiah (Mal 3:23f.) Matthew will describe the occurrence as a vision (17:9). The booths proposed by Peter are like the *sukkoth* of the autumn harvest feast of Tabernacles. Jesus' injunction to silence in v. 9 is part of the Markan design to build up to the final climax of 16:16.

THIRD SUNDAY OF LENT (B)

Exodus 20:1-17. Dt 4:13 and 10:4, also Ex 34:28, refer to the ten "words." The commandments interrupt the flow of the narrative, which leaves the people at the foot of the mountain in 19:17 and returns to them, in fear and trembling there, in 20:18. The decalogue is not a law code so much as a designation of the spirit underlying all the laws that will follow.

Jewish tradition makes v. 2 the first word and then groups vv. 3 and 4 as the second. Philo, Josephus, the Greek Church, and Calvin reckon v. 3 as the first word, vv. 4-6 on graven images the second, and so on until the tenth word, which is all of v. 17. The Catholic division of commandments, which Luther continued to use, derives from St. Augustine. In it, vv. 2 through 6 comprise the first word, the prohibition against idolatrous images being subsumed under the command to adore only the LORD. The second commandment is v. 7, and so on, until nine and ten, which are v. 17 divided into coveting one's neighbor's wife and his goods, following the order of Dt 5:21 (in Ex "house" comes before "wife", in Dt vice versa).

In postexilic times Israel was clearly monotheistic in the strict sense. In an earlier period, as testified to by vv. 2-6, the Israelite concern like that of its polytheistic neighbors was that its God was supreme over all the others. The command to practice monolatry led in time to theoretical monotheism. The LORD's "jealousy" comes to have as its practical consequence the meting out of punishment and mercy according as the Israelites' "hate" or "love" him.

No human image or indeed any image can be carved, including representations of heavenly bodies, the beasts of the earth, and the fish of the sea. A tradition of images continued in Israel long after Moses' time (e.g., the mentions in Jgs 8:27; Num 21:8f.; 1 Kgs 12:28ff.) Nonetheless, no representation of YHWH has ever been found from the earliest period, nor of anything resembling a consort.

Verse 7 stresses the sanctity of God's being as it is represented by his name. The prohibition is not against oath-taking but against spells, incantations, and the loose invocation of the divine name in attestation of the truth. On vv. 8-11, cf. the commentary on Dt 5:12-15 for the Ninth Sunday of the Year above, p. 185. In Ex, as has been noted, the LORD's six days of creative activity are given as the motive for imitating him in his rest.

Respect for parents by sons and daughters of any age comes after respect for God in Israelite piety. Cf. Ex 21:7 for the punishment of a serious breach of filial concern. The reward for decency to parents is longevity, both to the individual and to the people for its corporate fidelity to family life. " 'Honor your father and mother' is the first commandment to carry a promise with it," says Eph 6:2.

What is proscribed by v. 13 is murder, killing in war being specifically allowed in this crude culture (Dt 20:13) and capital punishment as well (Ex 21:12-17). The commandment not to kill is concerned with the sanctity of human life, the next three with the sanctity of marriage (cf. Lv 18:20), property, and good name. The terms of perjury in the law courts, a matter prohibited by v. 16, are spelled out in Dt 19:16-21.

Israel's ethical requirements, unlike those of her neighbors, are rooted in God's will. They are apodictically addressed to individuals in the second person singular, not couched casuistically as in the common law of other ancient peoples: "If a man should . . . then thus and so." There is no magical component to these commands. It is a simple matter of fidelity in behavior. If there is moral lapse, no curses or plagues are promised, but the LORD will desert his people as he has said he will do.

1 Corinthians 1:22-25. St. Paul describes the proclamation of the gospel (v. 23) as satisfactory to neither Jews nor Greeks in the states of mind he ascribes to them. Like most epigrams, this one derives its power from generalization. Putting God to the test or retreating skeptically into gnostic categories cannot be met satisfactorily with the *skandalon* of the cross. Paul in vv. 24f., as in v. 31, draws on Jer 9:22f., but he adapts the passage considerably. God's address to the "called" (*klētois*) makes all the difference in what is real power and wisdom, real folly and weakness. We must prescind from what seems to be a slur on two ethnic groups to arrive at Paul's real meaning. He is describing the powerlessness of God before egocentric concern, wherever it may be found. God's action in Christ is such that it goes against all conventional wisdoms. We would err grievously if we thought that the Apostle was addressing himself to two peoples long since dead. He is speaking to a mentality alive in every age.

John 2:13-25. Robert Fortna in *The Gospel of Signs* develops the view that the source which the fourth evangelist used was composed of seven sign narratives and a passion account. The seven miraculous signs, he thinks, were described in shorter versions of the following passages: 2:1-11; 4:46b-54; 21:2-14; 6:1-14; 11:1-45; 9:1-8; 5:2-9, 14. The prelude to the passion account, as in the synoptics, was originally today's reading: 2:14-16, 18-19. Verses 11:47a and 53 formed a bridge, after which came the anointing at Bethany and the entry into Jerusalem of ch. 12. Jesus' arrest, in this view, began at 18:1 and events proceeded from there on in the familiar order, through to the end of ch. 20.

Fortna is of the opinion that John's signs-source consistently proved Jesus' messiahship by his works of power. Hence, the request of v. 18 for a sign authorizing Jesus to do these things is answered by, "Destroy this temple and in three days I will raise it up (*egerō*, v. 19)." John alone makes Jesus the subject of this verb (here and in 12:1). Elsewhere in the NT it is God who does the raising.

The transition between 2:12a and 4:46b seems to be a natural one. To introduce the cleansing pericope, clearly an intrusion followed by the stories of Nicodemus and the Samaritan woman, John employs one of the stereotyped editorial formulas interspersed throughout his gospel (v. 13). Vv. 14-16, derived from John's source and unaltered by him, are close to but not identical with the same material in the synoptics. Their account culminates in Jesus' direct quotation from Is 56:7 (cf. Mk 11:17; shorter version found in Mt 21:13 and Lk 19:46) with a snatch of Jer 7:11 appended. Jn's v. 16 *may* be an allusion to Zech 14:21 but it is more probably the composition of the author of the source to meet the situation. The evangelist's comment on the meaning of the event is contained in v. 17, where his citation of Ps 69:10 tells what the disciples made of the cleansing when they later came to believe (cf. 2:22; 12:16.)

John makes Jesus' opponents "the Jews" (v. 18), as he does characteristically. In his source it may have been "the chief priests and the scribes and the elders" of Mk 11:27 (cf. Jn 18:3: "the chief priests and the Pharisees.")

The challenge put in v. 18 resembles that of Mk 8:11; Mt 12:38 = Lk 11:16. The Johannine source has Jesus answer in terms of a miracle of power (v. 19). "Unbelief asks for a sign so that it can dare to believe, as is clearly expressed in 6:30" (Bultmann). The destruction of the temple and the building of a new temple will be that sign: the eschatological catastrophe which brings judgment to unbelievers and salvation to believers. Mk 13:2 and Acts 6:14 refer to a saying of Jesus in which he prophesies only destruction. This, coupled with the testimony reported of his appearance before priestly authority that he was responsible for such an utterance (Mk 14:58 = Mt 26:61), leads us to believe that a historical tradition underlay it.

The phrase "in three days" is a biblical expression for God's setting things right after catastrophe (cf. Ex 19:11; 2 Kgs 20:5; Hos 6:2.) The evangelist interprets the "temple" in terms of Jesus' risen body (v. 21), which for him is not distinct from the believers raised up with him to new life. It is possible that the author of the source was wrestling with the problem of the meaning of the destruction of the temple (in A.D. 70), as we know Jewish writers of the time did. He could have tied it in with the death of Jesus, the evangelist then making it an explicit reference to the resurrection. Another possibility is that the story contains an attack on the Jewish temple cult.

Verses 23-25 concludes the narrative with a familiar Johannine motif. Many believed in Jesus as a result of the signs he performed, inadequate though this faith was (cf. 4:48; 14:11.) Jesus has no illusions about popular acceptance (cf. 6:15.)

FOURTH SUNDAY OF LENT (B)

2 Chronicles 36:14-17, 19-23. This passage concludes the Chronicler's re-telling of the fall of Jerusalem to the Babylonians in 586 B.C. recounted in 2 Kgs 24-25. There (24:17) we learn that Mattaniah, the twenty-one year old uncle of King Jehoiachin, had his name changed to Zedekiah by Nebuchadnezzar, king of Babylon, who placed him on the throne of Judah. A son of King Josiah by Hamutal (2 Kgs 23:30f.; 24:18), he adopted a throne name when he was made the agent of the Babylonian king. His nephew Jehoiachin (whom 2 Chr 36:10 calls his "brother" or kinsman) had been deported to Babylon along with his family, functionaries, and chief men of the land (2 Kgs 24:15).

The Chronicler sees in Zedekiah's reign eleven years of indiscriminate resistance to the prophet Jeremiah (v. 12), King Nebuchadnezzar (v. 13), and all of God's messengers and prophets (v. 16). The eighteen-month siege of Jerusalem by the king of the Chaldeans (v. 17), i.e., the Babylonian Nebuchadnezzar, came as a result of this conduct in the eyes of the Chronicler (cf. 2 Kgs 25:1-7.) The temple, indeed the whole city, was put to the torch (2 Chr 36:19; cf. 2 Kgs 25:9.) Jeremiah's counsel to Zedekiah on this occasion is famous, namely that he should capitulate to the king of Babylon so that the people might live and not see the city become a heap of ruins (Jer 27:12, 17). Equally well known is his castigation of the prophet Hananiah for having raised false confidence in the hearts of the people and "preached rebellion against the LORD" (Jer 28:15-17). This line of public policy goes entirely counter to that of Isaiah during the Assyrian threat.

The last two verses of the present pericope (22f.) are taken verbatim from the first three of the book of Ezra. Their brief account of the restoration under King Cyrus of the Persians fifty years later keeps the book from ending in defeat and destruction, with Jeremiah's prophecy of v. 21 (cf. Jer 25:9-12.) The best 2 Kgs can do about the problem is tell, in conclusion, of Jehoiachin's release from prison to "eat at the king's table" (25:29). After thirty-seven years of Jehoiachin's captivity (562 B.C.), Evilmerodach, successor of Nebuchadnezzar, sets free the rightful king who has been kept a hostage all those years.

The Chronicler, through the book of Ezra, makes Cyrus out to be a believer in the LORD, the God of heaven (Ezr 1:2; 2 Chr 36:23). The addition of the doublet (vv. 22f.) was required because Ezra and Nehemiah were placed before 2 Chr in the Hebrew Bible. In it the last named is the book with which the "Writings" (kethubhim) and with them the whole collection ends. The pious Chronicler stresses the LORD's compassion (v. 15) but says that his anger finally blazed forth against the people for their recalcitrance (v. 16). The key to the passage is the prophecy attributed to Jeremiah (v. 21), which makes the observance of the sabbath, a detail absent from the book of Jeremiah, the key to the termination of seventy years under foreign dominion. Actually it was more like sixty, counting the initial siege.

Ephesians 2:4-10. God's mercy in restoring his people is the theme of this reading as of the previous one, only this time "death in sin" is a handicap experienced by the entire race over all its years of existence (lit., "we were by nature children of wrath," v. 3). The agency of restoration is God's "favor" or "grace" (charis, vv. 5, 7, 8), which is a totally unmerited gift (v. 8) and not a reward (v. 9). The NT charis is a development of the idea of divine favor over the more usual Septuagintal eleos to convey "mercy" (Heb., ḥesed).

The perfect participle is used in vv. 5 and 8 to express the fact that the baptized have already been saved (este sesosmenoi), a strong touch of realized eschatology. The holy spirit has earlier been declared the pledge and first payment of full redemption (1:14), which means that completion lies well in the future. Here the notion is different, namely the present glory of Christians, which was featured in some Hellenist circles. Thus we read: "he raised us up and gave us a place in the heavens" (v. 6). Despite the mention of "ages to come" (v. 7), the emphasis here is on the present authority enjoyed with

Christ over angels, who are the normal inhabitants of *epouraniois* (v. 6). This thought pattern is not only uncharacteristic of Paul but one which he constantly opposed, notably among the "Corinthian enthusiasts." When he speaks in his epistles of the present action of God he usually balances it off with what God will do at the end (cf. Rom 6:1-11; Col 3:1-4 does the same).

Vv. 5 and 6 feature three *syn*-verbs: God has "brought us to life with Christ," "raised us up with," and "seated us with" him (*senezōopoiesen, synēgeiren, synekathisen*). This is a doctrine of fellowship with Christ rather than incorporation into him, as in the Rom 6 passage cited above and Col 2:10-13. The Pauline notion of union with Christ in his death and burial is absent.

Boasting ("priding oneself," v. 9) is unthinkable to anyone who has received salvation by grace since it is all God's doing (cf. Phil 3:3; Rom 4:2; 1 Cor 1:28ff.) It is not easy to determine whether we are being called God's "handiwork . . . in Christ" (v. 10) at our creation or our redemption. As God's wisdom, Christ is as much an agent of the former as the latter. What is clear is the balance between the "good deeds" (*epi ergois agathois*) we are expected to devote a lifetime to, which God "made preparation for in advance" (*proētoimasen*), and the gift of God which makes them possible. The preparation spoken of culminated in our being his "handiwork, created in Christ Jesus" (*poiēma, ktisthentes en Christǭ Iesou*). Despite our responsibility to do good works, it is inconceivable that we should do them on our own or boastfully claim them as our own.

John 3:14-21. The gospel reading, like the first two readings, has God as the healer or restorer of his people. What was done in desert days through the effective sign of the serpent of bronze, John here has God accomplish through the believer's gazing in faith on the uplifted son of man. *Hypsōsthēnai* ("raise," "lift up") does double duty for crucifixion and resurrection in John. Belief in Christ begets eternal life, not death; favorable judgment, not condemnation. Acting in truth brings one into the light and out of darkness. A total Johannine theology is available in this passage. Set against the deeds of the realm below (*katō*) are the deeds of the realm above (*anō*): *krisis, skotia, ponēra ta erga,* versus *hina sōthē ho kosmos, phōs, ta erga . . . en Theǭ . . . eirgasmena*; condemnation, darkness, wicked deeds, as against God's sending his son that the world might be saved, light, deeds done in God.

It is an uneven contest for John. God through his son is already the victor.

FIFTH SUNDAY OF LENT (B)

Jeremiah 31:31-34. Ostborn's 1945 study, *Torā in the Old Testament*, traces the theme that in the ideal future, however conceived, God or some chosen agent of his will impart Torah ("instruction" or "revelation" rather than "law"). The implication is that the new covenant (*bᵉrith ḥᵃdhāshā*, v. 31) to be formulated in days to come will be drawn up on the basis of the existing Torah. A difference will be that men will "know the LORD" without the necessity of teachers from among friends and family (v. 34).

It is not to be assumed that Jeremiah wrote these verses as part of his opposition to the Deuteronomist reform party. Some among the latter edited his prophecies; moreover, both he and they insist on the need for a "circumcision of the heart" (Jer 4:4; Dt 10:16; 30:6). The principal edition of Deuteronomy is marked by pleas for inward obedience, much as in the writings of the prophet. Jeremiah was not disaffected with written Torah so much as he was unhappy over mere words confined to the scrolls of a book or impressed with a stylus on baked clay ("tablets of stone"). He wanted written Torah to be enshrined in the heart universally and looked forward to a time when such would be the case.

The notion here expressed by Jeremiah is found elsewhere in the Bible, notably Pss 37:31 and 40:8. The first verse reads, "The law of his God is in his heart,/ and his steps do not falter"; the second, "To do your will, O my God, is my delight, / and your law is within my heart." Even if both psalms were to have been written after Jeremiah's time and under the influence of the present passage, they only establish that their authors, like him, reconciled a new covenant with written Torah. All three pericopes say that whoever now have the law in their hearts will enjoy messianic blessings in the future.

Christians have at times mistakenly supposed, because of their belief in Christ or their knowledge of Paul's view of the abrogation of the binding force of the law, that in these verses Torah is being prophesied as transcended or set aside. There is no ground given by the text for such a conclusion. A better referent for Jeremiah than Paul is Ezekiel. There, a "new heart" and a "new spirit" (36:26) will be given by the LORD in place of hearts of stone to "make you live by my statutes, carefully observing my decrees" (v. 27). Any contrast between law and love is alien to Jeremiah's thought. The giving of the law was a mark of YHWH's love. The covenant of the future envisioned by the prophet involves observance of Torah on an inner, spontaneous principle. "For Jeremiah the New Covenant would probably demand both the letter and the Spirit" (Davies).

Hebrews 5:7-9. These three verses provide what may be the New Testament's clearest picture of Jesus' suffering as one of us "in the days of his flesh" (v. 7). They contain a principle of salvation that modern soteriology is rediscovering. Once perfected (*teleiōtheis*) by the obedience he had learned from what he suffered, Christ has become the cause of eternal salvation (*aitios sōterias aiōniou*) for those obedient to him. Jesus' "loud cries and tears" are the sign that he is facing the implications of perfect acceptance of the divine will. He saves us in both an exemplary and a more directly effective way, the obedience we are called to being in the same order as his.

The reference to God's ability to save Jesus from death and Jesus' being heard is puzzling. Evidently the author does not have the passion in mind but the reverent stance (*eulabeia*) of Jesus throughout his life that saved him in every instance but the last. Jesus' unique sonship (v. 8) is a primary datum for the author of Hebrews. It provides Jesus with no immunity from suffering but equips him in a special way for the high priestly office to which he is called (v. 10).

The motif of suffering followed by glory, so pervasive in the primitive *kērygma*, is evident here.

John 12:20-33. The "Greeks" (*Hellēnes*) of v. 20 appear but once in this gospel, not to be mentioned again. It is warmly disputed who, exactly, they were. Only at 7:35 does John use the term elsewhere, speaking of "the diaspora among the Greeks." The Vulgate renders this "*Gentes*," and for many that is what is meant here ("*Gentiles*"). Others are convinced that in this passage Greek-speaking Jews are indicated, in contrast to Aramaic-speaking Jews. Whoever they are, they are in Jerusalem for a specifically Jewish reason. An approach is made to Jesus through Philip, presumably a Jew with a Greek name whose home, Bethsaida, on the north shore of the lake Kinnereth (Sea of Galilee), is in the Greek-speaking diaspora.

There is no suggestion in the fourth gospel that the heritage of Israel is to be given to the Gentiles. The disciples are never spoken of as appearing before them, as in the synoptics. Nowhere are they held up for favorable comparison with the Jews. Jesus does not leave Jewish soil in this gospel; "there is no mention of a gentile mission, nor anything about their coming in, even after his glorification" (J.A.T. Robinson). Hence, while it is possible that Gentiles may be making a single appearance in the narrative at this point, it is quite unlikely that that is what the evangelist means by "some Greeks." This is not to say that John is narrowly nationalistic. He has, throughout, a cosmic perspective. Still, he never distinguishes between Gentiles who come to the light and Jews who do not. Many Jews come to believe in Jesus (cf. 2:23; 7:31; 8:31; 10:42; 11:45; 12:11.) We do not seem to have in the present passage a case of Gentiles seeking enlightenment while Jews do not but of Jews from Galilee in a search for the light ("to see Jesus," v. 21, connotes faith for John, not simply looking at Jesus).

Jesus addresses himself to these Jews who are *Hellēnes* as he does to all: in terms of the impending hour of his glorification, of life through death, of "loving" life and losing it versus "hating" it and keeping it. Being a servant (*diakonos*) of the son, serving (*ean tis diakonē*) him, means that the Father will respond by honoring (*timēsei*) one who so conducts himself.

Jesus' soul is troubled (*tetaraktai*) at the prospect of suffering (v. 27). He is tempted to pray for deliverance from it, as in the prayer reported in Mk 14:36. He forbears. As in similar passages in the synoptics (e.g., Mt. 10:39; Lk 14:26f.; 17:33), he does not ask his disciples to do anything he will not do himself. The Father speaks out from the heavens, confirming the glory that will be given to Jesus in his death and exaltation. John the Baptizer has already given his testimony that the spirit, like a dove, has come to rest on Jesus (1:32). Many people have accepted in faith John's witness concerning him, even though it was accompanied by no "sign" (10:41f.) Now a sign is given, not for Jesus' sake but that of the bystanders (12:30). The voice like thunder sets up a debate as to whether an angel has spoken. The Johannine passage has elements of the Sinai narrative, which is in keeping with the evangelist's picture of Jesus as messiah delivering Torah in new circumstances.

The judgment (*krisis*, v. 31) that has come on the world may be related to the dispute over whether or not it is God's voice that has been heard. The prince (*archōn*) of this world will be driven out as Jesus is raised up from the earth in crucifixion and exaltation. *Krisis*, condemnation, will come upon all who do not look upon him in faith. Those who *do* so view him, he will draw (*elkysō*, v. 32) to himself.

The editorial comment of v. 33 appears to be the work of the final redactor of the gospel who has added ch. 21 and who, throughout, shows a tendency to allow little to chance. He dots all the i's, crosses all the t's, and in general reminds the reader at intervals how the story turned out.

PASSION SUNDAY (B)
(PALM SUNDAY)

Isaiah 50:4-7. These four verses make up the bulk of the third of four "servant songs," generally identified as Is 42:1-7; 49:1-6; 50:4-9;

52:13 to 53:12. In all four the "servant of the LORD" seems to be Israel (cf. esp. 49:3), although a case can be made for an individual representing the people as the subject of the fourth song. In the present one, Yahweh acts as a schoolmaster to the servant "morning after morning" (v. 4). The servant is given "the tongue of the learned" to speak a word that will rouse the weary (v. 4); further, like Moses (Ex 32), he suffers contradiction (v. 7). Yet the two details together do not seem sufficient to make us see in him a giver of Torah in the last age. The servant is "the one despised, whom the nations abhor" (49:7), someone beaten, buffeted, and treated shamefully (cf. 50:6.) We have here a picture of Israel's prophetic function which can only be exercised at great cost in pain. Accepting the training in consolatory and encouraging speech which the LORD offers and refusing to rebel against him are ways Israel can express its fidelity to God. The picture of the humiliation meted out to the servant may derive from the actual career of Jeremiah, thrown into the stocks (Jer 20:2) and a dungeon (chs. 37-38). The servant's trust is in God rather than idols.

God will not fail this people (cf. Is 41:11; 42:17; 45:24; 49:23.)

Philippians 2:6-11. See pp. 140ff.

Mark 14:1—15:47. In place of either the longer or the shorter reading, a selection like Mk 15:33-39 might better be chosen since it contains the Marcan core: Jesus' death in fulfillment of Scripture, the cosmic nature of the event, and Mk's faith conviction of who he was.

The compelling reason to substitute for the readings proposed is not merely that their length precludes the preaching of a homily adequate to the problems they raise. It is rather that, in the evangelist's first-century attempt to arouse sympathy for Jesus in his innocent suffering, he almost inevitably gives the twentieth-century hearer the impression that he knows exactly where human responsibility for Jesus' death lay.

In fact, Mark does not know. As a vehicle for his christological concern he constructs his moving account from fragmentary historical reminiscences (he probably possesses a primitive narrative of arrest, appearance before some representatives of the Sanhedrin, condemnation by Pilate, journey to Calvary, and crucifixion and death) and biblical sources (Pss 21, 41; Zech 13:17; Ps 110:1; Dn 7:13). Of the two sets of sources, the latter are better suited to his theological purpose. Such historical traditions as he possesses he puts in the service of a portrait of a Christ who is to come as the victorious Son of man, having become such by way of ignominious suffering. The latter is Jesus' Marcan title for readers oriented to Jewish apocalyptic writing (cf. 14:62.) For the more Hellenized, "this man was the son of God" (15:39). Mk has been occupied throughout to identify Jesus in the latter way (1:1, 3:11; 5:7; 15:34), but he does it by challenging readers to discipleship "in the context of the prospect of the coming Son of Man" (Perrin).

Jesus' meal with his disciples is a Passover meal for Mk (14:12, 16), eaten after sundown on the 14th Nisan. John locates it earlier (13:1), putting Jesus' death on the day before the feast of Passover (18:28). Mk wishes to situate Jesus' glorification and the origins of the Gentile ministry in Galilee (14:28, 16:7). For Lk (24:47) and Jn (ch. 20) it is a Jerusalem mystery (but for the author of Jn 21, a Galilean one).

Mk has two traditions on Jesus' appearance before the Sanhedrin. Of these, that in 15:1 is likely to be historical while the "night trial" (14:55-64) is probably an example of Mk's "sandwich-structure," an insertion into the story of Peter's denial in the high priest's courtyard to fill up a space of time. In 15:1, *poiesantes* is a better reading for the *etoimasantes* followed by NAB, hence "made their plans" rather than "reached a decision."

Mk's christology demands an affirmation of Jesus' messiahship and sonship of God, which he puts squarely on his lips (14:62; only in this gospel does Jesus answer "I am"). Jesus "seated" derives from Ps 110:1, "coming" from Dn 7:13, probably a conflation to meet two different parousial hopes in the primitive church. The "blasphemy" of v. 64—since Jesus has not uttered the divine name—may well be the charge on which disciples of Jesus in the Marcan church are being found guilty as a result of their claims about him in relation to God.

The passion narrative is chiefly interested in making faith affirmations about Jesus in a context of the biblical-type humiliations he endured. This earnest effort has been badly misconstrued over the centuries as reporting Jewish guilt and Roman compassion (15:2-15). There is no good reason to continue the confusion in the minds of contemporary Christians.

If a parish wishes to devote a lenten series of lectures to a form-critical and redaction-critical treatment of the passion narratives, it should be encouraged to do so. As proclamation, however, these portions of the gospels can serve to pour fuel on the Christian fire of anti-Jewish sentiment.

EASTER SEASON

EASTER VIGIL (B)

Romans 6:3-11. See pp. 312f.

Mark 16:1-8. Assuming that we have in this pericope the conclusion of the gospel as it came from Mk (vv. 9-20, while canonical, being the work of another hand), we see immediately that the evangelist makes the story of an empty tomb "the place where they laid him" of v. 7, central to his narrative. Paul's account of Jesus' being raised, presumably primitive, centers on the earliest witnesses to the event (1 Cor 15:5-7) and makes no mention of the tomb. Mk has had the highly placed Joseph of Arimathea bury Jesus according to Jewish custom and roll a stone across the entrance of the tomb (15:46). Both details render the eight verses of Mk's final chapter puzzling. Why was a further embalming necessary, and why was there a tomb story at all? To complicate matters further, there is the ambiguity of who the second Mary was (cf. 15:40, 47, and 16:1 for the conflicting details; NAB makes her the mother of Joses and James (cf. 6:3) in the latter two verses, thereby conforming to the first, but the genitive case denotes wifehood more readily than motherhood). Also, Salome appears in 15:40 and 16:1 but is missing from 15:47.

The transition from v. 6 to v. 8 is an easy one, confirming the impression that v. 7 is an insertion into a preexistent narrative. Mk's theology requires Galilee as the place of parousial glorification, or if not that, the central place of the Christian movement. The trembling and bewilderment (*tromos kai ekstasis*) of v. 8 are normal responses to the appearance of an angel (cf. Lk 1:12, 29.) If this appearance to women was not part of the original narrative, it and the empty-tomb story could have been added at the same time. The announcement of an angel (*neaniskos*, lit., "young man") would have been central to a cultic recitation, much like the *Quem quaeritis?* tropes of medieval drama.

The mention of the stone's having been rolled back (*anakekylistai*, v. 4, is probably a "divine passive" denoting action by God) is confirmed in Jn 20:1, where it occurs apart from any angelic appearance. This leads us to suppose that the stone rolled away was a detail of the earliest telling of the empty tomb story. A tradition retained in Acts (13:29) identifies Jesus' opponents as those who laid him in the tomb, leading to the speculation that legendary accretion made a certain member of the Sanhedrin a disciple of Jesus (Mt 27:57; Lk 23:50; Jn 19:38 describes him as a disciple "in secret" like Nicodemus). If the story of burial by Joseph is late and legendary, it leaves the account of a visit by the woman (originally Mary Magdalene alone; cf. John 20:1) intact. The disciples came back from their experiences of the risen Jesus in Galilee and receive a confirmation of them from the Magdalene's story of an empty tomb. The angel's, "He has been raised up. He is not here" (v. 6), is not a report of a bodily resuscitation but of a new eschatological existence. He has been resurrected or has ascended from a grave to a transcendent life, in which mode of being his disciples experience him. Mk has the women keep silent, a familiar theme of his (v. 8). The gospel breaks off abruptly, "For they were afraid," perhaps to heighten completion in the future by parousial encounter.

See commentary on Mt 28:1-10, p. 62, which derives in part from this Marcan pericope.

EASTER SUNDAY (B)

Acts 10:34, 37-43; Colossians 3:1-4 (first alternate); 1 Corinthians 5:6-8 (second alternate); John 20:1-9. See pp. 63-67.

SECOND SUNDAY OF EASTER (B)

Acts 4:32-35. The respect which the apostles were universally accorded in Jerusalem (v. 34) is essential to Lk's idealized conception. The community members lived in peace, holding all things in common and distributing "to each according to his need from each according to his means." No one went without the necessities. The apostles were the first distributors of goods (v. 35) until the number of disciples grew so large as to make the designation of assistants necessary (6:2f.) The account is so heavily romanticized that the appearance of Ananias and Sapphira (5:1-11), with its little touch of larceny found in all of us, comes almost as a relief in the otherwise oppressive idyll.

The narrative conveys successfully a pervasive charity and mutual support which is the work of the Holy Spirit.

1 John 5:1-6. It is our faith that conquers the world (v. 4), a faith which for 1 Jn is our acceptance of Jesus as the Christ (v. 1) and son of God (v. 5). This faith confers divine sonship on us. Love of God and obedience to his commands, which are no burden, brings in its wake love of all who are his progeny by faith (v. 2). Some of these ideas have occurred previously in this letter in 2:13; 3:1f., 10; 4:4.

A new idea is introduced in v. 6, namely that of Jesus' coming "in water and blood" to which the spirit testifies. Probably his baptism and his death are meant in all their historical reality, his "flesh" having existed between these two *termini*. Conceivably, although less likely, the reference here is to Christian baptism and eucharist (cf. Jn 6:54.) The spirit, who is truth (v. 6), testifies to the reality of Jesus both in the gospel accounts of his baptism and transfiguration and in the post-Easter spread of the gospel, which is achieved only by the spirit's power.

John 20:19-31. See above, pp. 70f.

THIRD SUNDAY OF EASTER (B)

Acts 3:13-15, 17-19. Abraham Lincoln once proposed to Salmon P. Chase, his Secretary of the Treasury, that the Union in its inability to pay its military creditors should produce script bearing Peter's words to the cripple at the Beautiful Gate: "Silver and gold I have none, but what I have I give thee" (3:6). Peter's reported speech, in extension of the healing miracle, is Luke's composition, hence contains the view found in his gospel that the Jews handed Jesus over (*paredōkate*) and disowned him (*ērnesasthe*) while Pilate was for releasing him. The main point of Peter's discourse is not ascription of guilt but that the same God who raised Jesus from the dead healed the cripple; therefore the miracle is not to be attributed to any "power or holiness" of Peter and John (v. 12). Peter's description of God (v. 13) in relation to the patriarchs is the LORD's self-description in Ex 3:7, 15. The "glorification of his servant" is an echo of Is 52:13 at the beginning of the fourth servant song (*ho pais mou hypsōthēsetai kai doxasthēsetai*). God has glorified Jesus through the miracle of healing, not through raising him from the dead, which is first mentioned in v. 15. The designation of Jesus as servant (*pais=ebhedh*) seems to derive from an early stratum of Palestinian usage, after "Jewish prayers, in which great men of God, especially David" are so denominated (Haenchen). It is Luke's way of saying "son of God." The term will recur in the Didache 9:2f., 1 Clement 59:2-4, and Mart. Polycarp 14.1.

Verse 14 is a reference to the Barabbas episode in Lk's gospel (23:17-25). In v. 15 this murderer is contrasted with Jesus who is described as *ton archēgon tēs zōēs*. The first one upraised from the dead, Jesus gives life to all. The chief emphasis of Peter's speech is on the phrase, "God raised him from the dead," which negates the known fact (for Luke) that the holy and just one was put to death in the place of a murderer. Being a witness to Christ's resurrection (v. 16) is, again for Luke, the cachet of an apostle.

Peter addresses the crowd in v. 17 as "my brothers," the ordinary term for Christian believers, as if to indicate that the ignorance (*agnoia*) that underlay the crucifixion can easily be mended by repentance. Some think this a reference to the "unintended sins" of the Hebrew Scriptures (e.g., Lv 22:14; Num 15:22-31). It is, in any event, an echo of exculpation of the Jews that was probably part of the tradition of missionary preaching by Luke's time. Cf. Jesus' word from the cross in Lk 23:24 (missing from many early MSS); also Ac 13:27 and 17:30. In the last two passages, God is spoken of as overlooking the deed because the rulers of the Jews did not "know" or "recognize" Jesus. Verse 18 reflects the common assumption of the apostolic company that all the prophets were united in prophesying the suffering of the messiah. Since this is nowhere said by any of them, the tradition must derive from coupling the identification of Jesus as the messiah with the various plights of the righteous sufferer in Hosea, Isaiah, Jeremiah, and the Psalms. The invitation to repent and turn to God (v. 19) is the climax of the speech. Only by going in a new direction can there be forgiveness of sins, new life coming from the LORD who "sends you Jesus" (v. 20).

1 John 2:1-5. The address "my little ones" (*teknia mou*) is an ordinary affectionate term used by a father of his children. The Damascus Document (Zadokite Fragment) of Qumrân employs it in the Johannine sense at 2:14. 1 Jn has denied that anyone is sinless (1:8) yet he writes to help the reader stay clear of sin (2:1). He has a category of sin he calls "deadly" (*pros thanaton*, 5:16f.) from which he does not think recovery is possible. All other sin is remediable through the offices of Jesus Christ as intercessor (*paraklētos*). It is because he is just and in the presence of the Father that he can succeed in the role of defense counsel. 1 Jn, like the author of Hebrews, ties Jesus' powerful advocacy in with his death. It is a universal expiatory offering (*hilasmos*, v. 2; cf. 4:10). Paul has spoken of Jesus' death as the "means of expiation for all who believe," using the cognate word *hilastērion*, the LXX's normal rendering of *kaporeth*, "mercy-seat" (Ex 25:17). The propitiation that heals the breach is thus a personal life freely laid down (cf. 3:16.) The sure way of "knowing" Christ (in the Johannine sense, i.e., cleaving to him in faith) is keeping his commandments (v. 3). Any claim to knowledge without the obedience of love is a flagrant lie (v. 4). Keeping Christ's word means bringing to perfection the love the believer has for God, which originated in God's love for him (v. 5a).

It is much disputed whether the *agapē* of the Johannine literature is confined to the brotherhood (a gnostic dualist circle, in Käsemann's view; cf. *The Testament of Jesus*, pp. 40, 46f.) or is extended to all the world. Dodd thinks that "our brothers" of 3:16 is to be interpreted in light of 4:14 which calls the son "the savior of the world."

Luke 24:35-48. The commentary on Lk 24:13-35 found on p. 73 may provide helpful background for today's reading. The two Emmaus-road disciples have returned to Jerusalem to recount their experience of the risen Lord to the Eleven (vv. 33ff.), telling how they had come to "know him in the breaking of bread." That *klasis tou artou* (v. 35) has become a technical term for the table fellowship of Christians by Lk's time. Joining it to the narration of appearances of the risen Christ occurs also in Lk 24:41f., Ac 10:41, and Jn 21:9-14.

Verses 36-43 are concerned with proving the truth of the resurrection, while vv. 44-49 are an instruction on Jesus as suffering and risen messiah derived from the Hebrew Bible, composed of "the law, the prophets, and the psalms" (synecdoche for the "writings") of v. 44. The mention of "cooked fish" in v. 42 is an indication of the Galilean origins of this narrative (cf. Jn 21:1-14) but vv. 33 and 47 situate it in Jerusalem. Fuller suggests that it may be the second appearance of Jesus of 1 Cor 15:5, namely to the Twelve, here "pedantically corrected to eleven" by a pre-Lucan link. Luke, like Mk and Mt, uses this appearance, not for a church-founding purpose as Paul has done but for a mission-inaugurating one (cf. v. 47.)

The motif of doubt, absent from Paul, is introduced into this narrative as in Mt 28:17, Jn 20:25, and the addition to Mk, 16:11, 13, 14. Joined to it is the note of physical proof of the resurrection, something quite contrary to the eschatological character of Christ's "spiritual body" of 1 Cor 15:35ff. which Paul labors so hard to underline in extension of his resurrection-kerygma found earlier in that chapter (vv. 4-8). This indicates the development which the narratives of Jesus' appearances have undergone (cf., for example, Mt 28:9 which is much more realistic than the narrative of Jesus' resurrection of the first seven verses, told in apocalyptic terms.) Clearly, Lk wishes to identify the risen Lord of the church in Acts with the earthly Jesus who could be touched and seen and who ate fish. In place of the triumphant climax of "proof" that may have existed in the pre-Lucan source, Lk inserts the Christ-kerygma of vv. 44-49.

In 4:18-21, Lk has Jesus expounding Is 61:1 as referring to himself. This attempt of the earthly Jesus was evidently not successful, for minds must be opened once again (v. 45) to the meaning of the Scriptures as at 24:27. Verses 26 and 46 are very close in intent, the title "Christ" and the word "suffer" being the common elements. Luke's concern is not with history but with salvation-history, hence the actual location of the appearances is of less importance to him than that the commission to preach penance to all the nations (v. 47) should have originated in Jerusalem.

The "rest of the company" with the Eleven (*tous syn autois*) of v. 33 have been forgotten by v. 48, so intent is Lk in centering on the apostles as "witness" (cf. Ac 1:8, 22.) The ministry, death, and resurrection of Jesus have been interpreted by Jesus the risen one as eschatological fulfillment of prophecy. It must now be preached, worldwide.

FOURTH SUNDAY OF EASTER (B)

Acts 4:8-12. Detained over night in jail by the temple guard, presumably for preaching "the resurrection of the dead in the person of Jesus," Peter and John appear before a representative high priestly group to face interrogation. The apostles' offense is their anti-Sadducee proclamation of a resurrection in the flesh (cf. Ac 23:8.) This alignment of forces is essential to Luke's historical picture. He holds throughout that the Christians were opposed not by the Pharisees but by one group only, the "party (*hairesis*) of the Sadducees" (Ac 5:17). Actually, the latter were not a sect or group but those aristocratic circles that kept aloof from the popular Pharisee movement toward reform and renewal.

It cannot be established whether Luke has any exact information about an appearance of Peter and John before an official body. He does know something of the composition of the Sanhedrin or Great Council, the elders (*presbyteroi*) tending to be Sadducees and the scribes (*grammateis*) Pharisees (v. 5). The same confusion persists here as in the gospels over Annas, whose high priesthood had run from A.D. 6 to 15. Joseph called Caiphas, his son-in-law, held the office around the years A.D. 17 to 36. Perhaps all that Luke intends to convey is the uniting of all religious power-figures and mentalities against the apostolic company.

Peter is filled with holy spirit, as had been promised in Lk 12:11f. He makes a spirited defense to authority in response to the charge of healing ("he was restored to health," *sesōstai*, v. 8). Peter's point is not only that a good deed is not fitting as a charge but that restoration or healing is the very matter that Jesus is come for. He whom God raised from the dead has rendered "this man before you perfectly sound" (v. 10). Psalm 118:22 is quoted in v. 11, as has already been done in Mk 12:10 (par. Lk 20:17). Here, however, Luke follows another tradition. Men have rejected Jesus as Scripture foretold. (In the context of the Psalm, it is the people Israel that is being described). God has responded by making him a person of greatest importance. Only in Jesus' name is salvation to be found. The healing of the cripple and of all humanity is attributable to the same name of Jesus and power of God.

1 John 3:1-2. The biblical writer is lost in amazement at the gift of divine sonship in the present, yet there is more to come. He explains the undistinguished appearance of Christians in terms of the non-recognition of the son for what he was (v. 1). Perhaps v. 2 is a response to a position which holds that total likeness to God is the condition of the believer now. If so, John is at pains to refute it, the present situation of humanity being neither one of the direct vision of God nor inability to sin (cf. 1:8.) Remaining in the son who takes away sins and in whom there is nothing sinful (v. 5) is the best guarantee of not sinning (v. 6). At the same time, being like God and seeing him as he is are future realities, not present ones (v. 2).

Jn 10:11-18. This pericope follows the selection for the Fourth Sunday of Easter in last year's cycle, commented on on p. 76. The key to the long allegorical parable(s) of Jn 10 is Ezekiel 34 in which Israel's rulers, indicted as false shepherds, are deposed in vision and replaced by a Davidic shepherd-king. John finds in the Jewish leadership of his time and place hireling shepherds, with whom the good (literally, "honorable," "beautiful," *kalos*) shepherd is contrasted. For John, Jesus is the one messiah-deliverer. He gives his life. Hired hands run away in face of persecution. Wages are their only concern (v. 13), not the welfare of the sheep.

Mutual knowledge of the kind that characterizes Father and son marks sheep and shepherd. It is the Johannine "knowledge" which is the same as "seeing." Who are the "other sheep"? The readiest answer is the Gentiles, but as was pointed out in these pages (p. 199), these are no concern of the fourth evangelist. Probably they are the Jews who, at the time of the writing, have not accepted Jesus. The vision of "one flock, one shepherd" may be taken as an eschatological fulfillment of Ez 34:23 which speaks of one supreme shepherd of God's flock, "my servant David."

The climax of the discourse is the statement of Jesus' freedom in laying down his life (vv. 17f.), a freedom that takes the form of obeying a command or charge (*entolē*) of the Father. This freedom in "laying down" and "taking his life (*psychē*) up again" will divide Jesus' hearers in the way that Johannine discourses do.

FIFTH SUNDAY OF EASTER (B)

Acts 9:26-31. In St. Paul's account of his ejection from Damascus, he says he was let down the city wall in a basket by the ethnarch of King Aretas IV of Nabatea (2 Cor 11:32f.) This leads us to conclude that the king ruled Damascus through a governor at that time. The tradition that Luke possesses has forgotten the enmity of this monarch—the father of the wife of Herod Antipas whom Antipas repudiated in favor of Herodias—to Saul for his missionary activity in the Damascus area, and ascribes the plot to his customary later enemies, "the Jews." Luke wants to put the seal of approval on Saul by having him consort freely with the apostles in Jerusalem. This accords ill with Paul's later solemn declaration in Gal 1:18ff. that he visited Jerusalem for the first time three years after his Arabia-Damascus stay, there meeting Cephas and James but no others. "The communities of Christ in Judea had no idea what I looked like; they had only heard that "he who was formerly persecuting us is now preaching the faith he tried to destroy' " (Gal 1:22f.) Luke's narrative requires the intermediary offices of Barnabas, however, and the preaching activity of Saul in Jerusalem where he early incurs Jewish wrath (Ac 9:29). Saul is thus bundled off to Tarsus via Caesarea (v. 30), whereas by his own account he makes his way back to his native Cilicia with no help or even knowledge of the Judean community (Gal 1:21).

Verse 31 is a familiar Lucan-type summary of the church at peace, enjoying "the increased consolation of the holy spirit."

1 John 3:18-24. This epistle has been speaking against the failure to love (v. 14) and closing one's heart to one's brother in need (v. 17). The present passage proposes deeds of love rather than words as the way to know we are "of the truth" (*ek tēs alētheias*, v. 19). God's knowledge of our hearts and his greatness are sufficient to overcome any reproach of conscience within us (v. 20). "God is with us," literally, "we are free to speak (*parrēsian*) to him" (v. 21). Pleasing him and keeping his commands, specifically believing in his son and loving one another (v. 23), ensure our receiving from him all that we ask. This fidelity to commandment is the certain way to abide (*menein*) in God and him in us (cf. 3:11 and 4:7.)

John 15:1-8. The Hebrew Bible in several places uses the figure of vines and vineyards to refer to Israel (cf. Ps 80:8-15; Jer 2:21; Ez 15:1-18; 19:10-14.) The synoptic gospels do the same, especially at Mk 14:25 and parallels: "I will never again drink of the fruit of the vine until the day when I drink it new in the reign of God."

The messiah Jesus, by the shedding of his blood, makes possible the true people of God. The agricultural processes of trimming and pruning (vv. 2f., 6) are ways to describe the fruitfulness the Father has brought about in Jesus' disciples. St. Paul uses a similar figure in the grafting of wild olive branches into the trunk of the olive tree (Rom 11:17). Jesus' word of truth is the means of pruning away what is useless (v. 3). Living on in Jesus (*ean meinēte en emoi*, v. 7; cf. v. 4) provides assurance that whatever is asked will be given, that God will be glorified in the fruitfulness (*karpon polyn pherēte*, v. 8) of his disciples.

SIXTH SUNDAY OF EASTER (B)

Acts 10:25-26, 34-35, 44-48. This chapter contains the story of the conversion of the first Gentile. Cornelius is a Roman army officer with a hundred men under his command (*hekatontärchēs*, v. 1). He is "God-fearing," a technical term for someone not a full proselyte (i.e., a circumcised Gentile who observes the whole law) but a respectful participant in synagogue services who espouses the Jewish world-view and ethos. He is garrisoned in the harbor town of Straton's Tower, renamed some decades before *Kaisareia Sebastē* by Herod the Great to honor his patron Augustus. Caesarea was the seat of the Roman proconsul (*praefectus*), Pontius Pilatus until A.D. 36. The narrative that precedes today's reading attempts to make Peter aware by means of a vision that the line between fit (*kosher*) and unfit foods has been erased. One immediate consequence is that table fellowship with Gentiles which was frowned on for observant Jews because of its side-effects, is now allowed to participants in the table fellowship of Christ such as Peter. We know from St. Paul that it was Peter's practice to eat with Gentiles when he came to Antioch (Gal 2:12), even when others came "who were from James," i.e., Jewish Christians from

Jerusalem; this even though Peter later lost his courage and fell into pretense (v. 13).

Cornelius drops to his knees respectfully (vv. 25f.) but Peter resists the gesture, as Paul is later reported having done at Lystra (14:15). Luke stresses Peter's affability in the midst of this family gathering. Today's reading resumes with Peter's discourse, which begins with a declaration that God is not a respecter of persons (*prosōpolēmptēs*, v. 34). The word literally means a "face-taker," a term not unlike our "name-dropper." The notion of God's total impartiality occurs in Dt. 10:17, 1 Sam 16:7, and Wis 6:7, the same phrase in Rom 2:11 (*prosōpolēmpsia*) and Gal 2:6 (*prosōpon ho theos anthrōpou ou lambanei*). Peter's point is that God looks at respect for God and righteous deeds irrespective of ethnicity, in the hope of finding a man acceptable (*dektos*, v. 35).

The reading omits Peter's kerygma, which is on the same model as Paul's at Pisidian Antioch. It resumes with the spirit's action, which follows upon the close of the exhortation to repentance for the forgiveness of sins (v. 44). The circumcised Jews in Peter's party are surprised that the Gentiles are speaking in tongues (v. 46). Peter sees no barrier to their baptism in water—the practice familiar to Luke (v. 47). And so it is done (v. 48). The narrative illustrates the Lucan theology of peaceful coexistence of Jews and Gentiles in the primitive church. Paul's account in his epistles conveys considerable strain, as does the story of Stephen in Ac 6-7, which Luke nonetheless incorporates.

1 John 4:7-10. The love (*agapē*) that John hymns has its origin in God, not in men. Its clearest manifestation is the sending of his son for our sins (vv. 10, 9). The son came that we might have life through him (v. 9). To love is to have one's existence from God, just as it is to know him (v. 7). The loveless man is the man not possessed of God-knowledge (v. 8). God and love are the one (v. 8). Because love is something of God, we should love one another (v. 7). Love for one another is the author's great concern. He never says that love is God, only that God is love.

In these four verses we have a perfect compendium of Johannine theology.

John 15:9-17. Today's gospel reading continues last Sunday's, saying the same sublime things without employing the allegory of the vine and branches. The son loves his disciples with the Father's love for him, and is faithful to his Father's commands with the fidelity he exacts of his disciples. A revelation is being made in the son to bring about the fullness of eschatological joy (*chara*). What is revealed is the way of friendship, not of servitude. Perfect friends die for each other. Election means to have fruitfulness as its outcome. The great command is mutual love.

ASCENSION (B)

(Thursday after Sixth Sunday of Easter)

Acts 1:1-11; Ephesians 1:17-23. See pp. 84ff.

Mark 16:15-20. Verses 9-20 of chapter 16 give every evidence of having been written by someone other than Mk. W.R. Farmer, *The Last Twelve Verses of Mark*, 1974, considers the question still open, after reviewing the external and internal evidence. They are often called "the longer ending" in contrast to a shorter one of two verses found in certain MSS (and given in NAB, NEB, RSV, and JB). Non-Marcan though they are, vv. 9-20 have been considered canonical from early times. Besides the occurrence of the canonical ending in numerous earlier codices, it is testified to from the mid-2d c. on by Justin, Irenaeus, and Tatian among others. Eusebius and Jerome in the 4th c. say that it is missing from almost all the better MSS. Codex Washingtonensis ("W" in the Freer Gallery of the Smithsonian Institution) has a 2d- or 3d-c. insertion between vv. 14 and 15 which softens the condemnation of the Eleven. In it Christ explains the mystery of the atonement in the first person.

The canonical ending has often been designated the first harmonized version of material from the four gospels. It may be helpful to indicate here the parallels of all the verses, not just the final six of today's reading. The Marcan verse numbers follow in parentheses: (9) appearance to Mary Magdalene, Jn 20:16, who had seven devils, Lk 8:2; (10) her bringing the news to the Eleven, Jn 20:18—although Mk only has her "grieving and weeping"; (11) the disciples' unwillingness to believe the women, Lk 24:11; (12) the manifestation to two disciples walking toward Emmaus, Lk 24:13-32; (13) the report they brought to the other disciples, Lk 24:33-35—although the renewed disbelief of the latter is proper to Mk; (14) Jesus' appearance to "the Twelve" at table, Lk 24:36-41, Jn 20:19-21; Mt 28:16-20—Lk says "they thought they were seeing a ghost" and are upbraided by Jesus for it, but his scolding is severest in Mk for the lesser matter of doubting witnesses to the resurrection; (15) the command to preach everywhere, Mt 28:19f., (16) the necessity of baptism, Mt 28:19; (17f.) the signs which shall accompany the gospel,

Ac 1:8, including the gift of speaking in tongues, Ac 2:4; immunity from snakebites, Ac 28:5; exorcism, Mk 9:37; healing, Mk 6:13; (19) the ascension of Jesus, Luke 24:51, and his exaltation at his Father's right hand, Acts 2:33; (20) a summary of the spread of the gospel from the glorification of Jesus as Lord and Christ down to the time of the writing.

The commonly accepted view of the canonical ending as an artificial summary of the appearance stories in the other gospels has been challenged by scholars like Dodd and Goguel, who compare its chronological sequence of appearances with those in 1 Cor 15:5ff. Dodd thinks that its author is composing freely from tradition, with supplementary material from Mt and Lk. He points out the following distinguishing characteristics: (1) the appearance to the Eleven occurs while they are at table, a difference from Lk and Jn; (2) the Emmaus story is situated at table but to *two* disciples; (3) bread and fish are distributed to *seven* disciples in Jn 21:13; (4) only here does the risen one reproach the disciples for their disbelief in testimony to his risen state.

The purpose of the Marcan list of persons to whom Jesus appears is not the same as in 1 Cor 15, viz., to authenticate the resurrection kerygma, but to prepare the way for the great commission in vv. 15-18, which is not paralleled in wording in the other gospels. The statement of the ascension in v. 19 is the only one to echo 2 Kgs 2:11 and Ps 110:1.

All in all, then, the Marcan ending contains independent traditions on the ascension, the missionary charge, and the command to baptize; and it summarizes appearances of Jesus from the other gospels in its own fashion.

SEVENTH SUNDAY OF EASTER (B)

Acts 1:15-17, 20-26. Acts 1:2-8 sums up the appearances of Jesus and the reconstituting of the apostolic group which is to act as witnesses to Jesus "in Jerusalem, throughout Judea and Samaria, yes, even to the ends of the earth" (v. 8). The passage looks back to the twelve he had selected from among his disciples to be his apostles (cf. Lk 6:13.) The twelve are witnesses of the resurrection, though clearly the number that could be so designated was larger than twelve, as the account of the choice of Matthias over Joseph Barsabbas shows (vv. 22f.) Luke's interest, here as elsewhere, is to forge a link between Jesus in his lifetime and the church's beginning and continuation in history. The names of eleven are given (v. 13), whose special significance is that they are not twelve.

The defection of Judas has destroyed the eschatological symbolism of the number of the tribes, which would befit a mission to Israel. Since nothing is done later to replace the martyred James (cf. Ac 12:2), we can only conclude that while he is removed from the work of the others, he is not removed from their number. The flaw of Judas' departure was that it made him a non-witness of the resurrection, hence the early chain between Luke's Israel and newly constituted Israel was incomplete. Soon after Pentecost, Luke lets the twelve disappear from the stage. They are still intact as a group in 6:2; hence presumably the twelve are meant in 4:33, 36; 5:2, 12. In 6:3-6, the twelve are obviously superior in church organization to the seven, who just as obviously are leaders "of a divergent, or at least of a distinct, wing of the church" (Barrett, *The Signs of an Apostle* 1970). The latter author points out that when the apostles are mentioned again in 8:1, 14, 18; 9:27; 11:1; 15:2, 4, 6, 22, 23; 16:4 a closed group is indicated, distinguished at times from "the brothers" (11:1; cf. 1:15) and at other times from "the elders" (cf. the citations in chs. 15 and 16 above.)

The Psalms quotation which the lectionary retains (109:8; it omits the quotation of Ps 69:26) speaks of the total repudiation of an anonymous sufferer. Another has taken his "office" (*episkopē*, the LXX term for *pᵉkuda*) or responsibility, besides widowing his wife and orphaning his children. The apostles utter a prayer asking God to help them choose a replacement (*topos*) for the apostolic ministry (*tēs diakonias tautēs kai apostolēs*) of Judas (v. 25). In the drawing of lots (*klērous*) the choice (*klēros*) falls on Matthias (v. 26). It is the Greek word that has given us "clergy" but there is no connection with games of chance. The derivation is closer to the *meris tēs klēronomias* of Ps 16:5, the "Dominus pars hereditatis meae" of the now suppressed rite of clerical tonsure. The LORD is the psalmist's lot, his inheritance, and his cup, just as the Lord Jesus becomes the lot of apostle, cleric, and Christian believer generally.

1 John 4:11-16. Mutual love among believers is the corollary of God's initial love for us (v. 11). The biblical denial that any man sees God and lives (Ex 33:20) is repeated here (v. 12) in preparation for affirming the believer's dwelling (*menei*) in God and God in him (vv. 12, 15, 16). Anyone's acknowledging (*hos ean homologēsē̄*, v. 15) that Jesus is the son of God brings this mutual indwelling. The recognition of Jesus' sonship results in a knowing and believing in God's gift of love (*agapē*), a love that is none other than God himself (v. 16). The love is not inchoate but one brought to perfection (*teteleiōmenē*, v. 12; *teteleiōtai*, v. 17).

John 17:11-19. Chapter 17, Jesus' final discourse to those near to him, is interested in his glorification (vv. 1, 5), just as the prologue had been (cf. 1:14.) In the Johannine community everyone is commissioned to authority and discipleship (cf. 17:18ff.) Unlike the situation in Lk-Acts, in Jn the theological significance of the apostles as a distinct group is not to be found. The word apostle in its technical sense does not occur in Jn. Jesus gives his peace and the breath of holy spirit to his "disciples" (20:20ff.) An office is really conferred, but on a wider group than the twelve. "The world-wide commission and mission of the Church and the duty of every individual believer to participate in it are all presupposed" (Käsemann, *The Testament of Jesus*). The call to discipleship includes being sent into the world as Jesus was sent (cf. v. 18.) Christian life as such is mission. It is mission to the world, an alien realm (vv. 16ff.) Like Jesus, his disciples are pilgrims and sojourners below, visitors from a heavenly sphere of existence.

The Father is asked by Jesus to protect his friends from the evil one (v. 15). No one was lost in his careful watch over them except "him who was destined to be lost (*ho huios tēs apoleias*, literally, "the son of ruin, loss")—in fulfillment of Scripture" (v. 12). This providential view of the defection of Judas is not unlike that of Ac, where the guide of "those that arrested Jesus" is likewise seen to have been prophesied in Scripture (cf Ac 1:16-20.)

The reason for the revelation represented by the "word" Jesus spoke and will speak (vv. 14, 20) is that his disciples may share his joy completely (*hina echōsin tēn charan tēn emēn peplērōmenēn en autois*, v. 13). This joy will be at the same time a unity among all believers, who will be united in Father and son as they are in each other (cf. v. 21.)

PENTECOST (B)

Acts 2:1-11; 1 Cor 12:3-7, 12-13. See pp. 89ff.

John 20:19-23. See p. 70.

TRINITY SUNDAY (B; LUTHERAN A)
(First Sunday after Pentecost)

Deuteronomy 4:32-34, 39-40. This reading is taken from the concluding part of Moses' first address of three, represented by the Levitical author as having been spoken east of the Jordan, on the brink of Israel's entry into Canaan (1:1—4:43; 4:44—28:68, the heart of the 7th-c. Josian reform; 29:1—30:20). Chapter 4 is practical and hortatory in tone, coming as it does after a review of events between the deliverance of the commandments on Mt. Horeb and the defeat of the Amorites, Edomites, Moabites, and Ammonites. Heshbon and Bashan are the last to be conquered, along with their kings Sihon and Og. Moses climbs Mt. Pisgah, to be told there: "Look well, for you shall not cross this Jordan" (3:27). He reviews, instead, the statutes and ordinances he is teaching the people to observe. His chief message is that in the new land, with its complex civilization, this nomadic people is not to forget the revelation made at Horeb and fall into idolatry. Abandoning the covenant will bring quick destruction in Canaan by the LORD, a jealous God.

Verse 31 describes the LORD as a merciful and remembering God. The verses that follow (32-38) spell out his deeds of mercy, unparalleled in human history. Who has ever heard of such prodigies as those reported in the theophany of Horeb—the voice of God from the midst of fire without the destruction of the people addressed (v. 33), the snatching of Israel from the power of Egypt, which is terrified by the strength of YHWH's outstretched arm (v. 34), the delivering over, by the conquest of more powerful nations, of Canaan as a heritage, "as it is today" (v. 38, the latter phrase betraying the lateness of authorship)?

This great display of divine power and solicitude had but a single purpose: to fix in Israel's heart the truth that the LORD is God and there is no other (vv. 35, 39). Heretofore, other gods and their representations were forbidden (Ex 20:3). Nothing was to be made to rank with the LORD (Ex 20:23). Now for the first time he is described as the only God. The claim will be reiterated two chapters later in what is to become the opening phrases of the daily prayer the

Sh^ema: "Hear, O Israel! The LORD is our God, the LORD alone!"
(Dt 6:4)

The framers of the lectionary wish to underline the conviction of
Christians that they have not deserted Israel's ancient, monotheist
faith. Despite a mystery of son and spirit there is for them no
plurality of gods nor any plurality in God. He is one. There is no
other (v. 39). Moreover, the revelation of his oneness has as its
consequence the lodging of stern ethical and cultic demands (v. 40).

Romans 8:14-17. The second reading is a splendid example of what
later came to be designated trinitarian thought. For Paul, the spirit
of God is a spirit of his adoption (*huiothesia*) of men and women
along with Christ, whose sonship of God is primary. Christ's status as
heir (*klēronomos*) is such by right of proper sonship, ours a matter
of becoming heirs with him (*sygklēronomoi*, v. 17). There was no
scheme of legal adoption in the biblical period. It was an
arrangement of the Hellenistic age, having largely to do in the Near
East with inheritance. The context of Paul's remarks has been life
"according to the flesh" (vv. 12, 13), meaning life lived apart from
God. The natural consequence of such foolish autonomy is death
(v. 13), its concomitant, slavery (v. 15). In opposition to it Paul puts
life in the spirit. The spirit has been received (v. 15) but the gift is
not yet perfect in its effects. In its fullness it is something we look
forward to. Now we possess the spirit as first-fruits (v. 23). If we
suffer with Christ we shall be glorified with him (v. 17). Hence the
testimony which the spirit renders along with our spirit (*symmartyrei*,
v. 16) is to an eschatological event already made present in some
measure. "Children of God" that we are (*techna Theou*, v. 16), we
can address him as "Abba!" an Aramaic word found elsewhere in
Mk 14:36 and Gal 4:6. Paul may derive it from Jesus' own usage, as
it appears in the opening phrase of the Lord's prayer in Lk (11:2).

Father, son, and spirit work together to achieve the sonship of
the human race in the New Testament. They comprise a mystery of
human salvation and describe God at work, not as he is "in himself."

Matthew 28:16-20. In illustration of the point made immediately
above, there is mention of the Father and the son and the spirit in
conjunction with the immersion in water which will signal the
disciples to be drawn from all nations. The "mountain to which Jesus
had summoned them" (v. 16) is in Galilee, as part of the evangelist
Mt's intent to designate this locality the center of origin of the
Christian movement. The doubts of some (cf. Jn 20:24-29) are
overcome; they do the risen Christ reverence (v. 17) and receive the
command. He is not described as to his person, as he was in the

transfiguration narrative (Mt 17:1-8). He speaks, that is all. His words form the only proper conclusion we have to a gospel, Mk and Jn having been given endings by other hands which thought the gospels not well enough concluded and Lk supplying only a bridge to Acts.

In virtue of his full authority (*exousia=moshel*, as of the messianic king, Zech 9:10), pointed to by the "therefore" of v. 19, Christ tells the eleven disciples to go and make disciples (*mathēteusate*) of all nations. This charge to approach the Gentiles has not occurred previously in Mt. It comes with Jesus' glorified state as messiah. Neither is there any mention in the synoptic gospels of Jesus' disciples baptizing (cf., however, Jn 4:1-2.) Baptism elsewhere in the NT is performed in the name of the Lord Jesus (Ac 2:38; 8:16). Hence it is supposed that we have here a church formulation rather than a phrase from the lips of Christ. The trinitarian formula is found in the Didache 7:3, a writing which, in the form it has reached us, knows Matthew's gospel. Christ's teaching is summarized as "all that I have commanded you" (*panta hosa eneteilamēn hymin*), an echo of the farewell speeches of Moses in Dt. These commandments could include the injunction to take the eucharistic meal (26:26ff.) and other matters like the specifics of church order (18:15-22). Christ's promise that he will be with his disciples always, "until the consummation of the age" (*heōs tēs synteleias tou aiōnos*, v. 20)— for Mt the period of the church—makes clear that this is a testament, a farewell speech. As in 18:20 there is the assurance that Christ will be in the midst of his church sustaining the actions its members take.

Here again, as in Paul's letter to the Romans, Christian life under the one God has a "trinitarian" character (to use the much later term deriving from Tertullian, *trinitas*; Theophilus, *trias*).

CORPUS CHRISTI (B)

(Sunday after Trinity Sunday)

Exodus 24:3-8. This pericope is an Elohist tradition (E) inserted between two Yahwist (J) ones, 1-2 and 9-11. E resumes with 12-15*a*. The result of the combination is the appearance of a ratification of the covenant in two stages, the first in a sprinkling of blood and the second in a meal. In the J tradition the people are not to come near the LORD since they are represented by Moses and the seventy elders. In E, although a similar awe is reported (cf. 20:18), Moses and the people are solidified in a blood rite in which he acts as their priest (v. 6). The present narrative follows that of the designation of Moses by the people as their spokesman (20:19) and their being told to construct an altar of earth or unhewn stone (vv. 24ff.)

The "words and ordinances" (v. 3) reported by Moses to the people are the E material which makes up chs. 21 and 22 plus ch. 23 with its inserted passages (4-5, 6-9, 10-19, 22b-24 J, 27 J, 29-31a J). The spirit of respectful awe which characterized the people in 20:20 is found again in their declaration that they will do everything the LORD has told them (v. 3). The "book of the covenant" (v. 7) is presumably "all the words of the LORD" (v. 4) which Moses wrote down, i.e., the collection of laws contained in 20:23—23:33.

The altar and twelve pillars, which signify the twelve tribes (contrast the reprobated Canaanite pillars, 23:24), were erected at the foot of the mountain in order to prepare for the act of slaughter. In ancient Israel the priests did not do the slaughtering but offered up the blood of bulls by splashing it on the sides of the altar, placed the meat on top of the wood and embers on the altar, and burnt the whole offering (viz., made a "holocaust"; cf. Lev 1:5-9.) Moses associates certain young men with him in the priestly act of offering (v. 5). The institutionalization of priesthood through Aaron's sons has not yet been achieved. The symbolism of blood sprinkled on the altar and the people while the "book of the covenant" is being read is self-evident. The rite solemnly ratifies the acceptance by the people of the terms of the covenant. The people are sealed in fidelity to the written words, just as they are to the LORD to whom sacrifice has been offered in blood on the altar. The "blood of the covenant" (v. 8) is the blood which ratifies the covenant (cf. Zech 9:11.)

The inner disposition of the Israelites is described as one of utter fidelity to the prescriptions of YHWH which are written in the book of the covenant. The sprinkled, sacrificial blood stands for this fidelity as a sign.

Hebrews 9:11-15. Many scholars doubt that this book was intended for Hebrew-speaking Christians, thinking Hellenists or God-fearers of the diaspora far more likely as the intended recipients. The title of the epistle (which actually is a theological treatise) is deduced from its contents. Its author knows the LXX version of the Bible thoroughly and wishes to relate Jesus to temple priesthood and sacrifice. The case is usually made for post-A.D. 70 authorship, on the supposition that the Christian author is accounting for the succession of levitical priests by Christ in the providential plan. Some scholars, however, see in the christology of the book, with its stress on Jesus' being made perfect in humanness through what he suffered (cf. 2:10;

5:9; 7:28), indications of pre-70 authorship. This would date the work before the composition of the canonical gospels, all of which betray signs of a "pressure" of Jesus' divine status on his human, something that Hebrews does not. There are also Platonizing touches discoverable within it which have made some relate its authorship to Alexandria.

Heb is intent on the effect of Jesus' death (cf. v. 15) through the shedding of his blood (v. 12), hence the fittingness of this reading on the feast of "the Body of Christ." The "perfect tabernacle (*teleioteras skēnēs*) not made by hands" (v. 11) is the heavenly abode of God (cf. Ac 7:48) where Jesus now dwells. He has entered as high priest into the sanctuary (*ta hagia*, v. 12) located there. The good things "which have come to be" (*genomenōn*, v. 11) is a better reading than "yet to come" (*mellontōn*), following p[46] (*genamenōn*), Vaticanus, and other MSS against Sinaiticus and Alexandrinus. This indicates the author's concern with the benefits of an eternal redemption (*aiōnian lytrōsin*, v. 12) which have been made available by Christ's priestly activity.

The author's argument in vv. 13f. is a simple one of the rabbinic type *qal vahomer*, lit., "light and heavy" (in the West, *a fortiori*). If temple sacrifice (cf. Lev 16:14) has as its function the removal of ritual defilement, how much more potent is the blood of Christ which "cleanses our conscience (*syneidēsin*) from dead works to worship the living God!" (v. 14). His deed is rendered effective "through the eternal spirit (or "Spirit," which would be much the same thing from the Platonic outlook). Christ is offerer and offered, priest and victim. He is such effectively because his *pneuma* is *aiōnion*, everlasting, like the spirit of God itself; hence the redemption he achieved is everlasting. The argument of Heb seems to be that ritual sacrifice achieves ritual purification whereas the deep personal involvement of Christ, in which eternal spirit has a part, reaches deep into human consciences to set them free of personal sins. "Dead works" are not any works but deeds done apart from God's *pneuma*. Thus set free, the Christian can "worship (*latreuein*) the living God" (v. 14), a not unexpected figure of speech in a document so cultically oriented.

Verse 15 identifies the precise role of Christ as "mediator (*mesitēs*) of a new covenant." His death accomplishes deliverance from "transgressions" (*parabaseōn*) committed under the "first covenant" (of Ex 24:7f., understood), that those called may receive the promised eternal inheritance. These two stages appear to be an echo of Jer 31:32, now made explicit in terms of faith in Christ. Deliverance has prepared the way for promise, ransom for inheritance, *apolytrōsis* for *epaggelian . . . tēs aiōniou klēronomias*. Jesus' priestly action, therefore, is a boon in two parts, the first of which is the necessary link with the initial, Mosaic covenant.

Mark 14:12-16, 22-26. Vincent Taylor finds two streams in the Marcan passion narrative, one which is fairly continuous, characterized by classical Greek words and Latinisms, the other made of narratives and shorter passages filled with possible Semitisms. The latter (B, as he terms it) is intercalated into or appended to A. In this schematization, vv. 12-16 by their detail and use of the term "disciples" (*mathētai*) suggest that they are a later addition to the A narrative, although Taylor will not say with certainty that they were absent from it as it was first framed. He assigns vv. 22-25 to the Semitic B narrative ("blessed and broke . . . the bread," "this my body," "this my blood," "blood of the covenant," "poured out for many," "Amen"; "fruit of the vine" and "reign of God" in the vow of v. 25); vv. 26-31 he assigns to A.

The phrase "the first day of *azymōn* (*maṣṣoth*)" is puzzling. This is not normal usage for the day of preparation on which paschal lambs were slaughtered and offered (cf. Ex 12:6), normally Nisan 14. It has been suggested that the Aramaic tradition that lay behind the Greek had said "the day of preparation." The narrative at vv. 13f. hints at a greater familiarity of Jesus in a Jerusalem setting than Mk would have us believe. There is nothing preternatural about the sign. Jesus knows a peculiarity of someone who may either be a friend or have a public accommodation for hire. The guest room (*katalyma*, v. 14, Lk's word for a traveler's lodge at 2:7) is situated off the ground (*anagaion*, v. 15). At Passover time thousands of families and companies of villagers would be making similar arrangements.

A lengthy Passover meal with its ritual order (*seder*) is not reported, only the liturgical formula of what has become the commemorative Christian meal. It cannot be determined from Mk whether a true Passover supper is being described, although some like Jeremias maintain it. Bread is broken and a blessing offered "while they were eating" (*esthiontōn autōn*, v. 22), not before as is customary at Jewish meals generally. Moreover, the blessing over the cup follows immediately, not as if it is one of the four interspersed through the Passover meal. The two verbs used for blessing (*eulogēsas*, v. 22 and *eucharistēsas*, v. 23) are not different in meaning; both translate *barak*. It is God who is blessed rather than the food, for his goodness in a particular action: in ordinary meals that goodness takes the form of bringing forth food and drink from the earth; at the Passover, deliverance from Egypt; at the Christian eucharist, saving us through the death and resurrection of his son.

The phrase "this is my blood of the covenant poured out for

many" is a clear reference to Ex 24:8, indicating the way the first Christians conceived Jesus' death as priestly and atoning. The phrase "on behalf of many" (*hyper pollōn*, v. 24) is an echo of Is 53:6 and 12 even though the exact prepositional phrase does not occur. The Nazirite-like vow of abstention from wine until a deed is done (v. 25) resembles the vow-tradition which underlies Lk 22:16, 18. This, coupled with the cup-bread-cup order in Lk, is part of the evidence that has led some scholars to think that this eschatological saying of Jesus with its future orientation was primitive in the Christian meal and the retrospective aspect of a body given and blood shed a later development. All this would have happened in the two decades between Jesus' death and Paul's account of the tradition he had received by the time he wrote 1 Cor (cf. 11:23-29.) By this time the meal is looking back to the night on which Jesus was betrayed, even while it remains a proclamation of the death of the Lord "until he come."

The songs of praise sung (*hymnēsantes*, v. 26) are the *hallel*, Psalms 114-18, or 115-18 according to another usage, with the acclamation *Halleluiah* interspersed between each half-verse; again, such is the case if a Passover meal is being described by Mk.

SUNDAYS OF THE YEAR

TWELFTH SUNDAY OF THE YEAR (B)

(Fifth Sunday after Pentecost)

Job 38:1, 8-11. The closest parallel to this biblical book in Near Eastern literature is the Akkadian text from ca. 1000 B.C. known as The Babylonian Theodicy, a dialogue about human suffering and divine justice. There the sufferer is answered by one friend only, not three "troublesome comforters" with an Elihu added in (chs. 32-37). The present pericope occurs early in the "Theophany" or "YHWH speeches" (38:1—42:6), the fourth part of this unevenly divided five-part book. Neither the dialogue of chs. 3-31 nor the Elihu speeches use the divine name YHWH found in 38:1. It occurs in the Prologue and Epilogue (the first and fifth parts) and in this section at 40:1, 3, 6 and 42:1.

In 31:35-37 Job has cried out: "Oh, that I had one to hear my case," followed by the more familiar (AV rendering), "and that mine adversary had written a book." The fact that the LORD answers him and not Elihu here (v. 1) strengthens the hypothesis that the latter's speeches are an interpolation. The divine answer "out of the storm" is a detail associated with theophanies (cf. Ps 18:8-16; Zech 9:14; Ex 19:16) and perhaps derives from the cult of the weather god.

The LORD has quelled the sea in 7:12 and 26:12. Here he challenges Job in terms of his own power in binding up the newborn and vigorous, infant sea-god in swaddling bands (v. 9). The motif does not appear elsewhere in Near Eastern epic writing, although the Mesopotamian and Ugaritic creation myths have the waters defeated and held back by victorious opponents. In the former, Marduk slays the sea dragon Tiamat, creates the primeval seas from him, and holds them back in place with a bar. The Ugaritic Baal defeats the sea god Yamm and holds him captive. In Job YHWH set limits for the sea and "fastened the bar of its door" (v. 10). The command to the waves, "Thus far and no further," has taken hold in the popular imagination in the legend of King Canute. Actually, it derives from v. 11.

2 Corinthians 5:14-17. The "love of Christ" (v. 14) is almost certainly a subjective genitive here: Christ's love for us. The context of these remarks is Paul's career of attempts to persuade men in his rôle as apostle. If any Christians are inclined to boast of him as someone caught up in ecstasy (v. 13), he will by no means discourage it. God, who "knows what we are" (v. 11), is the reason, in any case, behind external appearances and what lies in the heart (v. 12). The love of Christ acts as the impelling, controlling force in Paul's life (*synechei=urget*, the Greek verb being found elsewhere only in Phil 1:23, "I am attracted, drawn"). Christ's love is proved by his death (cf. Rom 5:8; Gal 2:20) "on behalf of all" (*hyper pantōn*, v. 15), an axiom found in the tradition at 1 Cor 15:3. "He died for all. Therefore (*ara*) all died" is the literal rendering of v. 14. Paul repeats the phrase in v. 15, then gives the reason for this death with Christ, which is obviously a mystical and not a physical death: "so that those who live [their physical status] may live no longer for themselves but for him." Christ died to sin. Those who have done the same live not selfishly as Adam did but "in indebtedness and obedience to Christ" (Barrett). His risen life to God is the paradigm of the selfless lives of the baptized, which ideally have Christ as their center.

As a consequence (*hōste*, v. 16), from the death and upraising of Christ (v. 15) onward (*apo to nun*, v. 16) Paul looks upon no one, not even Christ, "in terms of mere human judgment" (*kata sarka*, v. 16). This phrase is commonly taken by Bultmann and others to mean a ruling out of consideration of the historical, earthly Jesus. In fact, however, Paul rejects by the phrase the making over of Christ as a Messiah in any human image. He confesses his erroneous view of Christ before his conversion and says that he now sees him and all humanity in a new eschatological way, as a "new creation" (v. 17). Of Jesus' earthly days nothing is being affirmed; the *sarx* of the phrase is an unredeemed race of men, its condition before the death and upraising of v. 15. Verse 17 states positively what v. 16 has put negatively. Paul celebrates the new act of creation (*kainē ktisis*, v. 17) comprised by God's act in Christ. The old age has passed (cf. Rev 21:4) and a new one has come to birth. The Christian still has to live amidst the old creation but he does so in terms of the new; in Eliot's phrase, "no longer at ease."

Mark 4:35-40. This chapter has been taken up entirely with parables, including those of the sower (vv. 3-8) and its allegorical explanation (vv. 13-20), the seed growing on its own (vv. 26-29), and the mustard seed (vv. 31f.) A brief sayings collection which Mt and Lk will employ in other contexts acts as a bridge between the first and second parables (vv. 21-25). The pericope of the stilling of the storm

(vv. 35-41) is used by Mk as a challenge of Jesus to the disciples' faith in "the mystery of the reign of God" (v. 11), which for the evangelist is bound up with Jesus' person and his power (v. 41). It does not stand on its own, however—the chapter division coming from the medieval church—but forms a unity with the deeds of power in ch. 5, the expulsion of the legion of unclean spirits in Gerasa, the healing of the hemorrhaging woman, and Jesus' victory over death in the case of Jairus's daughter. As such, the stilling of the storm initiates that group of four (or three) miracle stories more than it concludes the Marcan day of parables.

Jesus' power over wind and wave is part of the larger confrontation basic to Mk's gospel in which Jesus takes on the cosmic powers of evil, replacing chaos and death with divine order and life. The normally placid Lake Kinnereth (Sea of Galilee) resembles in its brief squalls the Mediterranean lashing the coast—the "deep" (*tehom*) of the Bible, which typifies all that is inimical to humankind. The Marcan penchant for detail is evident in the narrative. The "bad squall" of v. 37 is *lailaps megalē anemou*, lit., "a fierce gale of wind." Even the seasoned fishermen were terrified (v. 38). Jesus' word of power (v. 39) resembles in its sovereignty that of the God of Israel (cf. Ps 65:8; 77:17; 107:25-30; Jb 12:15.) His "rebuking" (*epetimēsen*) the wind is the same verb used to describe Jesus' dealing with the demons at 3:12 and 9:25 and closely parallels the wording of the exorcism in 1:25.

The challenge of Jesus to his disciples in v. 40 is the first of a series in Mk (cf. 7:18; 8:17f., 21, 32f.; 9:19). They have been confided in at 4:11 and 34 over the meaning of parables but have not yet (*oupō* for *ouk* or *pōs ouk* in some MSS) arrived at faith. At this point in the gospel, faith in Jesus is taken to be the same as faith in God.

THIRTEENTH SUNDAY OF THE YEAR (B)

(Sixth Sunday after Pentecost)

Wisdom 1:13-15; 2:23-25. In these early chapters the postexilic sage (*ḥakam*) argues the question of reward for the just and punishment for the wicked, two states determined by having recourse to wisdom or spurning it. Verse 13 is redolent of the Deuteronomic charge to choose life (30:19*c*) while v. 14 is more philosophical in tone than anything found in Torah. What God creates is life-sustaining; there is nothing in common between man's home, the earth, and the abode of the dead (v. 14). God's justice is deathless and leads to deathlessness

(v. 15). The influence of 2:18 on the passion narratives seems evident ("If the just one be the son of God he will defend him/ and deliver him from the hand of his foes"). The railing continues in vv. 19ff. but the wicked have not counted on God's hidden counsels. The effect of being created in his image (cf. Gn 1:26f.) is imperishability, *aphtharsia*, and God means to bring it about. Only primordial tragedy has set the divine plan in disarray. It is impossible to know if the author has in mind Gn 3, in which case the tempting snake is here first identified as the devil, or the story of Cain's murder of Abel in Gn 4. John's gospel (8:44) thinks like Wis but provides no clue as to *how* the devil brought death to man from the beginning.

The case has been made, with the aid of the silence of Wis on bodily resurrection, for the author's interest in spiritual death like that of Rev (2:10; 21:8) and his corresponding interest in a blessed immortality, i.e., with Israel's God. While the latter is undoubtedly his concern, it seems from 3:1-12 that he is wrestling with the problem of real death and the subsequent fate of the just and the wicked.

2 Corinthians 8:7, 9, 13-15. Paul's prevailing sentiment toward the Corinthians despite the way they have tried his patience is affection and respect. He is not being ironical in v. 7 any more than he was in his opening prayer of thanks in 1 Cor 1:4-7. The Corinthians possess the riches of faith and speech and knowledge they do because he brought them the gospel in the first place. Why they should seek any of these gifts from another source both eludes and pains him.

The context of his remarks is the collection for the Jerusalem church, a matter in which Titus is Paul's agent. The latter holds up for emulation the generosity of the Macedonians who are none too well off themselves (8:1-5). The chiastic figure of riches and poverty in Christ's life resembles the hymn of Phil 2:5-11 and is not too unlike the paradoxes of wisdom and folly, strength and weakness in early 1 Cor.

Paul then turns to practical advice. He is not proposing any giving which leaves the donors unable to provide for their own needs (vv. 13ff.) Everything will balance out, he suggests, if the churches continue in a spirit of mutual support. If the economics of this proposal do not satisfy, Paul is ready with a biblical citation (v. 15; Ex 16:18). The manna miracle provided a sufficiency all around. Only the greedy saw their manna hoarded for the next day turn wormy and corrupt.

Mark 5:21-43. The basic Marcan story is about Jesus' mastery of man's enemy, death, with a word. The pericope corresponds admirably to the first reading. Mk's "inclusion technique" accounts for the miracle-within-a-miracle, vv. 25-34. Mk doubtless inserts the cure of the menstruous woman for his usual reason, namely to fill up a space of time in the narrative. The girl first reported ill (v. 23) is later described as dead (v. 35) as a result of Jesus' delay. Faith (meaning trust) is named as the condition of the cure in both instances (vv. 34, 36). Jesus is powerful with the power of God for those who will acknowledge it. He confesses to the loss of "healing power" (*dynamin*, v. 30) akin to the "portion of spirit" possessed and transmitted by the ancient prophets. Dialogue turns the "fearing and trembling" woman (v. 33) into a person of faith, even as Jesus proposes faith in place of fear (v. 36) to ensure the resuscitation of the twelve-year old girl (*talitha*).

FOURTEENTH SUNDAY OF THE YEAR (B)

(Seventh Sunday after Pentecost)

Ezekiel 2:2-5. This passage describes the restoration to normalcy of the priest Ezekiel after his vision of chapter 1, experienced in Babylonian exile some time after the year 597. It is the beginning of the commission by the LORD to his "son of man" (i.e., mortal creature) to be a teacher of his people. They may be rebellious (v. 5) but he must be obedient (v. 8) and even courageous in the face of contradiction and rebellion (v. 6).

The pericope should be preached on in Christian circumstances only in the context of the rebelliousness of Christians to their Lord and his heavenly Father. Otherwise it will have proven itself an unwise choice of the framers of the lectionary. The passage makes eminent sense as a paradigm of everyone's call by God to speak the truth in a prophetic spirit to refractory listeners in one's own circle.

2 Corinthians 12:7-10. This is part of Paul's "severe letter" to the Corinthians (10:1—13:10). In the present passage he feels compelled to boast of his weaknesses whereby the power of Christ is brought to perfection in him. It is in his native powerlessness that he is strongest (v. 10). The rapture of fourteen years before (v. 2ff.), which he feels he must boast of as a deed of God and not of himself (v. 5), was a great turning-point in Paul's life. It brought an end to whatever dream he may have entertained of "power, predominance, and conspicuous success" (Dodd). From this point on, all that has mattered is the grace of Christ (*charis mou*, v. 9) which is sufficient for Paul despite mistreatment, distress, persecutions, and difficulties (v. 10).

We have no clue as to Paul's "thorn in the flesh" (*skolops tē sarki*, v. 7). The ordinary word for stake, thorn, or splinter, *skolops* is here used figuratively for some recurrent misfortune calculated to keep Paul low. An impairment of vision (cf. Gal 4:13ff.), epilepsy, malaria, and stammering have all been proposed—none with any compelling reason.

The "extraordinary revelations" of v. 7 answer to those of Ezekiel above—in both cases, for transmission to the people in their interests and not as private endowments.

Mark 6:1-6. The third reading continues the theme of the first two of gifts to the prophetic teacher, in this case wisdom and miraculous deeds, for the sake of those whom he will teach. Jesus' family circumstances are well known to the villagers in "his own part of the country" (*patris autou*, v. 1). Matthew will change "the carpenter" (v. 3) to "the son of the carpenter" (Mk 13:55). Naming a man by designating his mother is unusual Jewish practice. Here it may refer to the traditions surrounding Jesus' birth.

"They found him too much for them" (*eskandalizonto en autō*, v. 3) is Mk's laconic comment on this display of power by a familiar. A saying attributed to Jesus in the Gospel of Thomas combines two logia from the canonical gospels: "No prophet is acceptable in his village, no physician heals those who know him" (31).

The inability of Jesus to heal any more than a few because of his distress at the lack of faith of those of his own region (vv. 5f.) is often cited as proof of the primitive and unretouched character of the tradition Mk here employs.

FIFTEENTH SUNDAY OF THE YEAR (B)

(Eighth Sunday after Pentecost)

Amos 7:12-15. Jeroboam II, king of Israel, ruled ca. 783-43. The activity of Amos is placed toward the end of his reign (ca. 750). It seems to have been a brief enough career; its termination is recorded in Am 7:10f. Tiglath Pileser would come to the Assyrian throne in 745, hence Amos was right in speaking of impending doom. In the first half of the 8th c., however, Assyria had been weak and the two kingdoms, Israel and Judah, prosperous as a result.

Bethel was an ancient shrine going back in its foundations to Jacob's time (cf. Gen 28:10-19.) It was the last town of consequence in the northern kingdom on the road to Jerusalem. Today there is a tiny Muslim village on its site. Jeroboam II (931-10) tried to set it up, along with Dan in the far north, as a rival shrine to Zion in Jerusalem. Amaziah, its priest, thinks that Amos is guilty of *lèse majesté* by prophesying the king's violent death and Israel's exile from its land (v. 11). He takes the utterance to be politically seditious and a sufficient reason for rejecting Amos to his southern (cf. 1:1) homeland. The form of address, "visionary" (*hozeh*), is not pejorative but the assumption that Amos earns his living by prophesying is (v. 12). Amos denies the imputation by describing himself as a herdsman-farmer. The biblical sycamore (*shikmim*, v. 14) is a kind of mulberry tree the fruit of which requires bruising to encourage ripening. Amos says he is not a *ben-nabhi*, literally "the son of a prophet", or as NAB renders it, a member of a roving band whose religious authenticity was very much in doubt.

The "was" of v. 14 is supplied, there being no verb of any tense in the Hebrew. Amos' point is that he received his call to prophesy while going about his ordinary rural tasks. He has no personal stake in prophecy, as Amaziah hints against him. It is the LORD's doing that he is engaged in it. All it will net him is reproach and expulsion from the territory of Israel.

Ephesians 1:3-14. This epistle, a theological manifesto, is concerned with "the catholicity and divine origin of the Church" (Chadwick) which seems to replace interest in the *parousia*. The document progresses toward notions like the building of "a holy temple in the Lord" (2:21), "that perfect man who is Christ come to full stature" (4:13), and "the whole body . . . [which] builds itself up in love" (4:16) rather than the imminently expected return of Christ.

For commentary on vv. 3-12, see pp. 392f.

The link between the life of the baptized believer, hymned in vv. 3-14, and the future consummation of that "glorious heritage" (v. 18) is found in the last two verses of today's pericope, 13f. It is the seal (*sphragis*) of the promised holy spirit given as a pledge of our inheritance (*arrabōn tes klēronomias*, v. 14). "The first payment" of NAB is redundant for *arrabōn*, leading to the twofold *eis*: "*against* the full redemption of a people . . . [lit.] *unto* the praise of his glory." The first installment, which promises future payment in full, is already present to the Christian in the seal of the spirit.

Mark 6:7-13. Jesus' instructions to the Twelve are followed quite closely by Mt (10:1, 9-11, 14) and Lk (9:1-6). The latter two differ slightly as to equipment and add the healing of diseases to Mk's exorcism in v. 7 and Lk's omission of the preaching of repentance and exorcising from Mk's vv. 12f. The mission of the Twelve has been prepared for in 3:14-19. The message of repentance they preached (v. 12) must have been related to Jesus' gospel of 1:14f. The instructions, including the sensitivity about money—the "traveling bag," *pēra*, v. 8, may be a begging bag—reflect later apostolic practice. So does the symbolic shaking of dust from the feet (cf. Ac 13:51), and anointing the sick with oil (cf. Jas 5:14; in Lk 10:34 the context is different). These details indicate a set of guidelines for Palestinian preachers of the post-Easter period set in the context of Jesus' lifetime. His sending them is not in doubt but rather the specifics of his instructions. Barrett thinks that Lk retains something like the original Q form of the charge in 10:2-16 (esp. 4-11) and that the complex, edited charge of Mt 10:5-42 proves the case for lateness (*The Signs of an Apostle*, p. 32).

Sending out messengers in pairs was a regular custom in Judaism, though it cannot be demonstrated to be as early as the Hebrew Bible. It was both a protective measure and an application of the legal clause of Dt 17:6; 19:15, originally judicial, which ensured the trustworthiness of two witnesses and provided a spokesman with a confirmatory partner. The prohibition of *duō chitōnas* (v. 9) probably meant no cloak over a robe and would have made sleeping out overnight a hardship.

Josephus writes in praise of the Essenes (*Jewish War* 2, 125 [2.7.4]): "They carry nothing whatever with them on their journeys, except arms as a protection against brigands. In every city there is one of the order expressly appointed to attend to strangers, who provides them with clothing and other necessities."

SIXTEENTH SUNDAY OF THE YEAR (B)

(Ninth Sunday after Pentecost)

Jeremiah 23:1-6. The prophet first deplores the weakness of Judah's kings (vv. 1-4) and then pronounces an oracle, probably to the discredit of Zedekiah (598-87) whom Nebuchadnezzar put on the throne in place of the young man's uncle Jehoaichin. (Cf. the commentary on 2 Chr 36:14-17, 19-23, p. 195.) Jeremiah's contempt for Jehoaichin, who ruled during 598 only, was near total. His view of Zedekiah was not much better. In place of the latter, whose throne name means "The LORD is righteous" (*sedhek*), will come a "righteous shoot" (*semah saddik*, v. 5), a future king whose justice is to be such that Judah and Israel will be able to give him the name, "The Lord our justice" (*YHWH sidhk^enu*, v. 6).

See Ez 34 for an extended parable on governance and leadership under the figure of "shepherds who mislead and scatter the flock of my pasture" (Jer 23:1).

Ephesians 2:13-18. Verses 14-16 are a christological hymn which Schlier thinks reflects the gnostic concept of a redeemer who destroys the hostile wall between the godhead and those who are to be redeemed. As to the setting of the hymn, those "once far off" (v. 13) are the Gentiles, in a reference to Is 57:19 where peace and healing are promised to the far and the near. Christ's blood is the reconciling agent between Jew and Gentile (cf. Col 1:20-23; Rom 5:10f.) The "barrier of hostility" (v. 14) may be Torah, a wall at once standing between Jew and Gentile and between man and God. Perhaps a barrier between heavenly and earthly realms is meant (cf. 1 Enoch 14.9.) The writer of Eph sees Christ, not as the end or fulfillment, but the evacuator of the law (*katargēsas*, v. 15; "he cancelled, nullified the law.") Jews and Gentiles come to the Father together in the spirit as "one new man" in Christ. The Mosaic commands and precepts are taken by the author to be instruments of division of Jew from Gentile.

St. Paul sees the one God justifying the circumcised and the uncircumcised alike on the basis of faith (Rom 3:29f.) He flatly denies, however, that he is abolishing the law by means of faith. "On the contrary, we are confirming the law" (v. 31).

"One new man," "one body," "one spirit" all indicate that there is to be no enmity or alienating division in the redeemed community that is the church.

Mark 6:30-34. Mark is not followed by Mt (14:13f.) or Lk (9:10f.) in reporting the impossibility the disciples experienced in finding time to eat. Similarly, he alone has Jesus issuing the invitation to "come to an out-of-the-way place (*eis erēmon topon*) and rest a little," v. 31.

The disciples have been away from Jesus preaching (6:12f.) and Mark must get them back on the scene. It is also essential to his story of the feeding with loaves and fish that it occur in a deserted place (cf. vv. 31, 32, 35) like the desert of the exodus. Finally, people must be there in numbers to witness it (v. 33). This pericope of five verses is a mere link for Mk in his narrative. It is doubtless chosen to respond to the reading from Jer; both speak of a leaderless people "without a shepherd." The phrase is found in Num 27:17 and Ez 34:5.

SEVENTEENTH SUNDAY OF THE YEAR (B)

(Tenth Sunday after Pentecost)

2 Kings 4:42-44. This brief tale from the Elisha cycle has a famine in the land as its setting (v. 38) and follows immediately upon a story of some noxious food rendered harmless by the prophet's throwing meal into the pot which contains it. The present narrative tells of the multiplication of barley-loaves made from first-fruits, which are normally the portion of priests. The hundred men in this case may have been cultic prophets associated with Elisha at a shrine. Baal-shalisha in ancient Ephraim is in modern Shomeron, south-west of Nablus.

Ephesians 4:1-6. The writer has designated himself a "prisoner for Christ Jesus" in 3:1. Col 1:10 has a parallel phrase to the exhortation, "lead a life worthy," not of "the calling you have received" (*tēs klēseōs hēs eklēthēte*, v. 1), but of "the Lord." Verses 2f. bear a close resemblance to Col 3:12-15. There love is the bond that sustains perfection whereas here it is peace—a major concern of the author. As in 2:16, the starting point is "one body" which doubtless means the church but can also refer to the crucified body of Christ that brought us into one.

The closest parallel to vv. 4-6 is 1 Cor 12:4-11 which speaks of a diversity of spiritual gifts. There are six examples of things that are "one" leading up to the seventh, "one God and Father of all" (v. 6). It was a familiar rabbinic device of the time to heighten the unity and the uniqueness of God by enumerating things that were one and reflected his oneness. Thus: "One people, one temple, one God." The groupings were usually of three, five, or seven members. Mention of Spirit, Lord, and God is no doubt intentional. It is not so certain that body consciously goes with Spirit, hope with Lord, and faith and baptism with God, although a case can be made for it.

The concluding phrase, "who is over all, and works through all, and is in all," is an echo of Stoicism (via Hellenist Judaism) which saw divinity everywhere. The "all" is a genitive and dative plural so it is impossible to tell if "everything" or "everybody" is intended. Probably the former, on a parallel with 1:23 where Christ fills "all in all" (*ta panta en pasin*), rendered by NAB as "the universe in all its parts."

John 6:1-15. This multiplication of loaves and dried fish is one of Jesus' signs (v. 14) for John. It led to speculation that he might be the eschatological prophet hinted at in Dt 18:15 and also a threat to carry him off as king. Dodd sees in Jn 6:1—7:1 a shadow of the

Marcan order in 8:1—9:30. At the same time, this feeding corresponds in some respects, including the numbers, to Mk 6:34-44. The next incident in both is the walking on the water (Jn 6:16-21; Mk 6:47-51). John 6, situated in Galilee, comes puzzlingly after chapter 5 which has Jerusalem as its setting. Attempts have been made to put 6 after 4 and before 5 but it seems clear that the evangelist wrote in this order for theological reasons, whatever order he may have found in his source.

This sign is reported to have taken place close to the second Passover of Jesus' public career (v. 4; for the first, cf. 2:13, the third, 12:55). The dating may be chronologically based but it clearly has theological significance, as his subsequent words "in a synagogue instruction at Capernaum" (v. 59) underscore. The Passover commemorated the desert experience. John's Jesus describes himself as the *real* manna come down from heaven (vv. 31-35, 51, 58).

The verbs of v. 11, "took," "gave thanks," and "passed around" are those of the last supper accounts but matters are complicated by their applicability to any Jewish meal. Similarly, John's "gather up" and "go to waste" (v. 12) are his normal verbs for the gathering and perishing of men (cf. 11:52; 17:12.)

The people conclude from the sign that Jesus is the messiah.

EIGHTEENTH SUNDAY OF THE YEAR (B)

(Eleventh Sunday after Pentecost)

Exodus 16:2-4, 12-15. The story of the manna and the quail also occurs in Num 11:4-35, quite different as to detail. This leads to the theory of an independent Moses saga, featuring the murmuring of the people, as the source of both narratives. (Cf. Ex 15:22-27; 17:1b-7 and Num 20:2-13 for two treatments of the theme of finding water.) Most of this chapter is from P but vv. 4-5, 13b-15a, 27-30 are probably from J, although some scholars catalogue today's pericope as E material.

The Israelites are described in 16:1 as having been on their desert journey one month since their departure from Egypt. The desert of Sin (Zin? cf. Num 13:21) is south of the Negev and northeast of Kadesh-barnea if the shorter, due eastward route of the exodus is assumed rather than the longer, southward journey toward traditional Mt. Sinai. The "bread from heaven" of v. 4 is not the allegorized "spiritual food" of 1 Cor 10:3, "heaven" being simply "sky" in Exodus. The sufficiency for a single day of v. 4 was later elaborated on (v. 5) in an edifying lesson geared to sabbath observance. "Fleshpots" were for the cooking of meat and came to connote a sybaritic existence only in the minds of moderns for whom "flesh" in any context vaguely connotes sex. The murmuring theme (vv. 3-4) occurs everywhere in the exodus accounts.

Manna and quail are natural phenomena of the northern Sinai desert, the former being an excretion of plant-lice resembling a resinous gum called bdellium (Num 11:7) or coriander seed (cf. Ex 16:31). The latter are migrant birds from Europe which arrived exhausted on Egyptian shores and were easily netted. The mention of quail inclines us still further toward a northern location for the Desert of Sin on the Sinai peninsula.

The J account of the quail in Num 11:31-34 seems to have been incorporated into Ex 16:13*a* by the P author. The flakes left on the ground by the morning dew prompted the question, "*Man hu?*", Aramaic for "What this?" (reminiscent of *New Yorker* editor Harold Ross's marginal query to non-specific writers, "Who he?"). The etymology proposed by the J author is improbable. "Manna" was doubtless the traditional local name of the providentially available food.

The tale is one of nature's bounty, interpreted by the entire believing community (*kol-edhath*, v. 1) in terms of the special care exerted by its LORD on their behalf.

Ephesians 4:17, 20-24.   Verse 17 is a turning-point in the epistle, taking it in an ethical direction without any desertion of the earlier doctrinal themes. The two are fairly closely integrated. The Gentiles are warned against, as peoples dwelling in mental futility (*en mataiotēti tou noos autōn*, v. 17) and alienation from God (*apēllotriōmenoi tēs zoēs tou theou*, v. 18). "Old self" (v. 22) is literally "old man" in parallel with the "new man" of v. 23. The appeal of Ephesians is to fidelity to the days when "you learned Christ" (v. 20), as presumably happened when "you were taught in him in accord with the truth which is in Jesus" (v. 21). The "new man" is the whole body of Christ, Jewish and Gentile, that "perfect man who is Christ come to full stature" (vv. 13-16). No specific ethical crisis is contemplated, contrary to the usual case in Pauline letters. We have here a general exhortation to Gentiles to a life lived in Christ. "Illusion and desire" (*epithymias tēs apatēs*, v. 22) are to be left behind, to yield to a life in God's likeness (*kata theon*) marked by justice and piety (*dikaiosynē kai hosiotēs*, v. 24). Both qualities stem from truth (*alētheia*).

Note that the incorporation into Christ of Eph is not quite as complete as that of Rom 5:12-19 and 1 Cor 15:20-28. In this epistle Christ remains distinct from his people who "grow up into him" (Eph 4:15).

John 6:24-35. In the Capernaum discourse Jn identifies Jesus as the "real heavenly bread" (v. 32), true manna for the life of the world (cf. v. 33.) The familiar Johannine typology is present. What went before in Israel's history was a foreshadowing. The occurrence in the life of Jesus is genuine, authentic (*alēthinos*). The sign, the work provided by God to authenticate Jesus, is Jesus himself. "It is on him that God has set his seal" (*touton gar ho patēr esphragisen ho theos*, v. 27).

NINETEENTH SUNDAY OF THE YEAR (B)

(Twelfth Sunday after Pentecost)

1 Kings 19:4-8. Elijah is in flight for his life because of Jezebel's threat to destroy him (vv. 2-3). The rains have come and YHWH's honor has been vindicated. The prophet is a fugitive in the southern desert, nonetheless. A day's journey from Beersheba he is accosted by a *melek* of the LORD, a term of the J and E writers to describe the presence of God in human form. He is roused from his despair by this messenger and twice prevailed upon to eat. In the strength provided by the hearth cake and water he proceeds on foot to Mt. Horeb. (Such is the designation of D and E; J calls the mountain Sinai).

Ephesians 4:30—5:2. The holy spirit of God is personified here more than elsewhere in the epistle. Cf. 1:13, probably an echo of Ez 9:4ff. and likewise a hint of baptismal practice. The exhortation, coupled with mention of the spirit "with whom you were sealed" (*esphragisthēte*, 1:13), indicates that a baptismal homily may have been the setting. The "day of redemption" (*apolytrōsis*) is the last day. We might have expected "salvation" rather than "redemption" in a Pauline letter.

Lists of vices and virtues like those of vv. 31 and 32, a convention of the ancient world, are to be found in Rom 1:29ff.; Gal 5:19ff.; 1 Cor 6:9f.; Eph 5:3-5; outside Paul, in 1 Pt 4:3 and Rev 21:8. They are not typical of the Hebrew Scriptures or rabbinic Judaism but were adopted from the Stoics by way of Hellenistic Judaism.

The charge to be imitators of God resembles Paul's counsel to imitate him (cf. 1 Cor 4:16 and 11:1.) The phrase "dear children" has been used in 1 Cor 4:14 with reference to Paul's fatherhood rather than to God's, as here. There are echoes of Christ's giving himself in love, in the phrases of Eph 5:25 and Gal 2:20.

Verse 2 employs the LXX's language of sacrifice, a "gift of pleasing fragrance" (*eis osmēn euōdias*) which occurs in Ex 29:18 and Lev 2:9. Here it refers to Christ's offering of himself to God, whereas in Phil 4:18 Paul uses it to refer to the gifts that Epaphroditus has brought him from the Philippian community.

John 6:41-51. Verse 42 is usually taken to be a synoptic parallel (cf. Mk 6:3; Mt 13:55; Lk 4:22), not unlike that of 4:43ff. The fourth evangelist does not know of a tradition about the virginal conception of Jesus. His opponents in this exchange situated in Galilee are "the Jews," the usual designation for Jesus' hostile opponents in Jerusalem. Public readers would do well to read "the crowd" in vv. 41 and 52 since that is what is meant, not Jewish people generally, as would be connoted by the translation of *hoi Ioudaioi* as "the Jews." The "murmuring" of the crowd is the normal LXX word for the grumbling of the period of the exodus.

The Father's drawing of people to Jesus (v. 44) echoes a rabbinic phrase in which God attracts people to the Torah (cf. the parallel phrase in v. 65.) The raising up of believers on the last day will have a similarity in 12:32, where the Jesus lifted up from the earth in crucifixion/exaltation draws all men to himself.

"They shall all be taught of God" (v. 45) would appear to be a slightly different rendering of Is 54:13 than the Masoretic and Septuagint readings which speak of "all your sons." Verse 46 puts Jesus in a position superior to Moses, as 1:18 has done. "Your ancestors," like "your law" (8:17) and "your father Abraham" (8:56), resembles the psychic distancing of an angry father in today's world who speaks to his wife of "your son." The phrases are not to be credited to the earthly Jesus, being rather the polemic speech of the evangelist in his day.

The "belief" of v. 47 is acceptance of Jesus as God's son, the only one who has "seen the Father" (v. 46). "Eating" (i.e., believing in) him brings deathlessness; *zoēn aionion* (v. 47) is the life proper to the final *aiōn* or age. "My flesh for the life of the world" (v. 51) is the body of Christ raised up from the earth. To look upon it in faith is to live forever. He is the manna (cf. Ex 16:15), the life-giving principle, of the last age.

The prospect of eating flesh, taken literally, would be as shocking to hearers of Jesus' day as to us—the more especially as it had connotations of the cultic practices of the heathen. John employs his familiar technique of uncomprehending audience-reaction to provide the opportunity for a further word from Jesus. In responding, Jesus is made out to be even more insensitive to Jewish reaction. "Drinking his blood" (v. 53) is doubly repulsive because of the specific Mosaic prohibition of eating meat from which the blood has not been removed (Lv 3:17; 17:10). "Flesh and blood" is a Hebraic idiom for manhood, whole and entire. Total acceptance of Jesus in faith is surely intended, with possible further reference to a two-part eucharistic meal known to the Johannine community. There may also be veiled mention of the blood of the covenant of Sinai (cf. Ex 24:8), in line with "my blood, the blood of the covenant" in Mk 14:24 (pars. Mt 26:28; Lk 22:20; 1 Cor 11:25).

The "eating" (*phagēte*) of v. 53 becomes "feeding" (*trogōn*) in v. 54 but we cannot be sure whether a difference is intended by the second, cruder verb. It may be graphic speech to connote the taking in of Jesus in his entirety by the believer, whose daily feeding upon him places the Christian above his fathers nourished by the manna of old.

TWENTIETH SUNDAY OF THE YEAR (B)

(Thirteenth Sunday after Pentecost)

Proverbs 9:1-6. Wisdom has appeared in 1:20-33 and 8:1-21 as a good woman issuing an invitation (cf. Is 53:1-3.) Here she appeals for a hearing on the grounds of her priceless worth and her prime place in the created order of the world. She and Folly "are personified as rival hostesses inviting men to very different kinds of banquets" (R.B.Y. Scott). The injunction, "Forsake foolishness and find life" is found elsewhere in Proverbs at 4:4; 7:2; 11:19; 12:28, and is not unlike Amos' charge, "Seek the LORD that you may live" (5:4, 6) or "Seek good and not evil, that you may live" (5:14). The note in NAB on these seven verses provides a helpful summary: "Wisdom offers the food and drink of divine doctrine and virtue which give life. Unstable and senseless folly furnishes the stolen bread and water of deceit and vice which bring death to her guests."

The house of Wisdom (v. 1) may be an ordinary dwelling but pillars ordinarily marked palaces or the homes of the mighty, while the number seven suggests cosmic significance. Wisdom, after all, was present at the creation as the LORD's model and craftsman (cf. 8:22-31.) Rabbinic tradition has the cosmos resting on either twelve or seven pillars; the Pseudo-Clementine Homilies speak of seven. The Babylonian planetary deities have also been proposed as the exemplar. Wisdom in such case would supplant Ishtar, the "queen of the heavens."

It is the simple, those who lack understanding, whom Wisdom invites (cf. vv. 4, 16.) She has no message for the wise or the arrogant.

Ephesians 5:15-20. Verses 15-16 bear a resemblance to Col 4:5, which warns against dealings with outsiders, while verses 19-20 largely reproduce the content of Col 3:16-17. We learn nothing of the circumstances of the writing from the phrase "these are evil days" (v. 16) since it is a standard one with moralists. Folly, ignorance, drunkenness, and debauchery are deplored. Celebration in song and gratitude to God in Christ are praised.

"Make the most of the present opportunity" (*exagorazomenoi ton kairon*, v. 16) is the *Ransoming the Time* of Maritain's title, recalling Horace's watchword, "Carpe diem!"

John 6:51-58. Consult the commentary for the previous Sunday, above, since few new ideas are introduced in these verses. The chain of the transmission of life (*zōē*) is direct: from the Father to Jesus, the son; from the son to the man who "feeds on him," on "his flesh," or on "this bread" (vv. 56, 57, 58). The insistence of the evangelist on the quality of the eating (NAB's verb "feed," as was indicated in last week's commentary, being equally capable of the translation "munch" or "gnaw," vv. 54, 56, 58), has led some to see an unquestionable reference to the eucharist here, others a polemic against gnostic denials of the reality of Jesus' manhood. Either may be the case but a taking in of the person of Jesus in faith will satisfy the text just as well. Such "eating" or "drinking" of him will result in his remaining (abiding) in the believer and the believer in him.

TWENTY-FIRST SUNDAY OF THE YEAR (B)

(Fourteenth Sunday after Pentecost)

Joshua 24:1-2, 15-18. The parallel between this chapter and ch. 23 is evident, and even more so that with 8:30-35 (D). The present description of the promulgation of the covenant at Shechem seems to be out of place since ch. 23 has reported a valedictory of Joshua. In this chapter only the place and the participants are named. In 8:30f. the law written by Moses is inscribed on an altar of unhewn stones which is built on Mt. Ebal. Half of the Israelites face it while the other half face Mt. Gerizim to the south; the valley in which Shechem is situated lies in between. The death and burial of Joshua will be told twice: in 24:29-31 and again in the Deuteromic book of Judges at 2:6-9. Shechem seems to be historical as a covenant-site after the conquest, related to the presence of a Canaanite temple of covenant there (cf. Gen 12:6) known variously as that of Baal ("Baal of B^{e}rith," Jgs 9:4) and of El ("El-b^{e}rith," Jgs 9:46). Placing the people on Ebal from which they gaze at Gerizim betrays a later, anti-Samaritan editorial hand. Likewise, the subsequent deemphasis of Shechem as a place of sacrifice and emphasis on Mt. Zion in Jerusalem is part of anti-Israelite or anti-Ephraimite bias on the part of editors from the southern tribes, Benjamin and Judah.

The reminiscence reported of Joshua in v. 12 harks back to Gn 11:26-28 with its mention of Abram's father Terah and his brothers Nahor and Haran. The "River" of vv. 2, 3 is the Euphrates. Verses 3-12 review the conquest and culminate in v. 13 which praises the stability and agricultural accomplishments of the Canaanites—now an Israelite possession. The choice the patriarch offers is between the LORD, whose cult derives from the polytheism of Abram's ancestors in Ur, and the local gods of the Amurru or Amorites (lit., "Westerners," as the Syrians and Mesopotamians called them).

Since the Israelites' God brought them out of slavery, watched them safely through the desert, and drove the Amorite dwellers in the new land out before them, the people elect to serve him as their God (cf. v. 18.) They will never forsake him for other gods, they say (v. 16). Such are the terms of the covenant to which they commit themselves in the new, God-given territory.

Ephesians 5:21-32. The morality of the new man includes a conjugal morality of mutual deference and service. Reverence for Christ is proposed as the reason (v. 21). The Pauline ordering of the cosmos is apparent here: Lord Jesus-church-man-woman, the wife appearing in a relation of submission to her husband as the church is to Christ (vv. 23f.) The philosophical notion of a cosmic marriage between spirit and matter is probably influential here. The relative positions of the sexes would be intolerable to contemporaries were it not for what follows, namely the constant solicitude of husband for wife (vv. 25-29). The imagery of vv. 26f. is that of the preparation of an oriental bride for marriage, something that was not the groom's task but performed by other women. The author wishes, however, to feature the idea of Christ's service to his church. The giving over of himself, followed by the sanctifying and purifying of believers in the word-energized water of baptism, requires the figure of a groom immediately engaged in preparing his spotless bride. Christ's care for his church is the reality that governs the rhetoric (vv. 29f.)

St. Paul has the concept of Christ as a second Adam (cf. Rom 5, 1 Cor 15.) The exegesis of Gn 2:24 proposed in vv. 31ff. is that the clear reference to human marriage has symbolic sense. It is a "foreshadowing" (*mystērion*; Vulgate, *sacramentum*) of Christ's union with the church, which would be Eve. Some see in this passage a veiled response to some gnostic system like that of Valentinus featuring heavenly eons in male and female pairs. The author of Ephesians gets back to his main point in v. 33, which is that of the mutual respect and support of spouses.

John 6:60-69. John reports Jesus as largely having failed in his Galilean ministry except for Peter's confession of faith in him (vv. 68f.), which probably derives from traditional material. The people murmur as they had done against Moses in the desert (v. 61). Jesus proposes his ascent to "where he was before" as an even greater test of faith in him than the feeding at the lakeshore and the challenge to believe which he evoked from it. John provides his special view of flesh as "useless" when contrasted with the spirit and life represented by Jesus' words (v. 63). This seems to be a precaution against the reader's understanding the eating of flesh and blood in any gross sense. Access to Jesus, which is belief, is a gift of the Father (v. 65). The Twelve have received the gift (v. 69). The "holy one of God" means simply the Christ for John, but it does have a synoptic ring (cf. Mk 1:24.)

TWENTY-SECOND SUNDAY OF THE YEAR (B)

(Fifteenth Sunday after Pentecost)

Deuteronomy 4:1-2, 6-8. The first three chapters of Deuteronomy have been devoted to a recapitulation of the final wanderings of the Israelites. The narrative has taken them from Kadesh-barnea (south of Beersheba in the Negev desert) to the Moabite and Ammonite highlands. The journey is described as a matter of thirty-eight years (cf. 2:14), so as to get them into the promised land, under Joshua's leadership, in forty. Chapter 4 spells out the moral of the story of safe passage told in the first three chapters. In the present passage Moses, who has been the speaker, tells Israel that fidelity to the LORD's statutes and decrees is the condition of possessing the new land. Such observance alone can guarantee life there. The implication is that the Canaanite-held territory will become holy if the LORD's commandments are neither added to nor subtracted from but only adhered to. The Deuteronomist's stress on Torah as a collection of precepts rather than globally as the instruction of God which accompanies the covenant is, of course, a postexilic development.

Wisdom and intelligence, understood as canny prudence, were much prized in Egypt and Mesopotamia. It was from these cultures that Israel had derived her notion of wisdom (*hokmah*). The incoming

conquerors are therefore described as superior to the pagan nations in
these endowments—somewhat anachronistically, of course, since the
full flowering of the wisdom concept came after the exile. The
proximity of God, the intimacy between the LORD and his people
are featured in vv. 7-8, as they will be again in 30:10-14. The book of
the law is fully available; it is not something up in the sky or across
the sea. All that this people has to do is carry it out. The
distinguishing feature of the decrees and statutes is their justice (4:8).
Everything about them bespeaks the wisdom, the moral superiority,
the loving care of Israel's God.

The Bible has no author to rival the Deuteronomist in hymning
the glories of the law.

James 1:17-18, 21-22, 27. The Father who gives gifts from above in
this puzzling introductory phrase is the changeless deity of Stoic
philosophy, not the constantly active God of Israel. Yet, as the source
of benefits to man, he is distinguished from the heavenly bodies he
has created, in a familiar Hellenist-Jewish apologetic convention.
Some scholars think that, because of the context, being brought to
birth with a word of truth (v. 18) has to do with the act of creation
only, or at most with the instruction comprised by Torah if the
epistle had a Jewish pre-history. The weight of opinion, however,
favors reference to the new birth that results from acceptance of the
gospel. This view is reinforced by reference in v. 18 to "us" as first
fruits (cf. Lv 23:11; Rom 8:23; 1 Cor 15:20, and the comment on the
aparchē of 1 Corinthians on p. 292. The much argued "implanted
word" (*ton emphyton logon*, v. 21) has the power to save, but only if
hearers becomes doers (*poiētai*, v. 22). Failure to act on this word
comprises self-deceit. The teaching, as often in James, is redolent of
words of the Lord: here the parable of the wise man and the fool
who built, respectively, on rock and sand as they did or did not put
Jesus' teaching into practice (cf. Mt 7:24-27.)

Doing the works of mercy and keeping free of worldly blemish
(*aspilon . . . apo tou kosmou*) constitute the pure and stainless
worship of God (*thrēskeia kathara kai amiantos*, v. 27). Again, we
are reminded of Jesus' pronouncement of final judgment in Matthew
on the basis of deeds (25:31-46); also, of the word of 1 John on
loving God through the brother one sees (4:20). This concern with
ethical choices has distressed some Pauline faith-alone purists by its
"Jewishness" but it is part of the fabric of New Testament teaching.
Jesus never deserted *halakah*, the way of conduct as a means to
please God. Both he and Paul, like many of the rabbis before them,
were insistent on purity of intent.

Mark 7:1-8, 14-15, 21-23. Mark explains Pharisee ritual washings to his Gentile audience (vv. 3-4), something which Matthew omits in the parallel place (15:1-9) as needless for his readership. Both are describing the repudiation of certain aspects of the oral tradition of the ancients (*presbyteroi*, vv. 3, 5), i.e., the rabbis of the past century, which characterized Hellenist Jewish Christianity and which probably went back to a word of Jesus himself. The citation of Is 29:13 (vv. 6-7) is probably the evangelist's doing. God's "commandment" (v. 8) is presumably the deliverance of Torah and is distinguished from "human tradition" (*tēn paradosin tōn anthrōpōn*). This distinction the Pharisee party did not honor because of its conviction that the oral law, which was a modern interpretation of ancient material, was on an equal footing with the written law.

The exchange is made the basis of an explicit teaching of Jesus which rescinds dietary observance (vv. 14-15). Only that which comes out of a man—spelled out in a Hellenist catalogue of evils (v. 22)—renders him impure (*koinoi*, v. 23). The latter two verses probably reflect early church teaching but there is no reason to think that Jesus did not speak on the subject of rabbinic practices concerning food. We know from other places in the synoptics his support of the law of Moses. The distinction between what God intended and what men have perversely made of it is at the heart of many of the conflict-stories reported of him.

The Christian would do ill to think of Jesus as the first or the only rabbinic teacher to stress interiority in matters of Mosaic observance. What is clear is that he did so consistently, and that a tradition which had as its final outcome desertion of all such observance was traced to him.

TWENTY-THIRD SUNDAY OF THE YEAR (B)
(Sixteenth Sunday after Pentecost)

Isaiah 35:4-7. See commentary on p. 8, on Is 35:1-6, 10.

James 2:1-5. It has been hotly debated whether the gold-ringed man is a Christian in Gentile circumstances or Jewish, or a wealthy pagan who visits the Christian assembly, and whether the assembly envisaged (*synagogēn*, v. 2) is a law-court or a worship assembly. Bo Reicke's speculations about the alignment of the Jewish poor with Roman patricians are receiving a wide hearing through his Anchor Bible commentary but not an acceptance to match. The assumption in possession is that *synagogē* (v. 2) means the religious assembly, even though the arguments in favor of a Jewish court of law are not unimpressive. The point of the passage is clear. Some Christians are practicing favoritism (*prosōpolēmpsia*, "acceptance of persons," v. 1). The discriminatory tactic is reprobated by the author as being no better than the maneuverings of corrupt judges.

This world's poor (*ptōchous*) are fated to be rich (*plousious*) in faith and as heirs of the kingdom, according to James. Martin Dibelius introduced into the world of scholarship a half-century ago the notion of *Armenfrommigkeit* (*Armenstolz*), a piety of the poor testified to by James. James's audience was thought to be forerunners of those Jewish Christians later known as Ebionites, the "poor" used as a technical term of self-description by early Christians. A recent doctoral study done for the present writer by F. Kelly seems to dispel any such notion. It shows, contrariwise, that early Christianity, like Judaism, did not propose poverty as an ideal to be sought but viewed it as an evil to be relieved. It favored simplicity of life and deplored riches because of the evils attendant on amassing them.

Here the stress of James is not on exploitation of the poor by the rich, as seems to be the case at first blush (cf. vv. 6-7.) The offense, rather, is dealing unfairly with respect to the various baptized for reasons of unequal social status. All are viewed as equal by James, as had been the case with all who stood before Mosaic law. The rabbis fulminate against favoritism. So, too, does James (cf. v. 9.)

Mark 7:31-37. This reading obviously corresponds to the first one from Isaiah with its multiplication of signs of the messianic era. It is not only the framers of the lectionary who have the correspondence in mind; the evangelist seems to as well. The geography of v. 31 has been likened to a journey from New York to Philadelphia by way of Boston. If "Sidon" were a misreading for "Bethsaida" (and there is scant textual evidence for it) the situation would be relieved somewhat but not greatly. Mk may wish to keep Jesus out of Herod Antipas' territory but his contrivance of the "secret" (cf. vv. 33, 36) until he is ready to reveal Jesus as the messiah in the narrative of the trial, passion, and resurrection would account for Jesus' sequestration sufficiently.

Mt uses the Markan summary of 7:37 in 15:31 but does not tell the healing story. The detail of the saliva has caused uneasiness, as if some magic were being attributed to Jesus. John at 9:6 has Jesus using a mud paste to cure a blind man. The action may be taken as a parable in sign rather than word, such as Israel's prophets employed. Its occurrence in pagan healing narratives as well as Jewish is, at the same time, undeniable. This fact does not diminish its impact. Jesus inaugurates the messianic age for Mk by works of healing. The deaf hear and the mute speak at the hands of him who does all things well (*kalōs*, lit. "beautifully," "admirably," v. 37).

TWENTY-FOURTH SUNDAY OF THE YEAR (B)
(Seventeenth Sunday after Pentecost)

Isaiah 50:5-9. Zion complains in her state of defeat:
> The LORD has forsaken me;
> my lord has forgotten me. (49:14)

He responds in the first four verses of ch. 50 that, although for its sins and crimes Israel's mother has been divorced and the nation's children sold to creditors (the Babylonians), his hand is not too short to ransom. Verses 4-9 comprise the third servant song, a response in faith to the present adversity of the exiled nation.

The servant people or its paradigmatic individual Jew knows it has not lost the role of teacher. Consolation is a daily task but one that can only be discharged after a faithful hearing of what the LORD has to say (v. 4); the servant can claim perseverance (vv. 5, 7) in the face of humiliating treatment (v. 6). The latter verse may be patterned on the personal sufferings of Jeremiah. It probably contributed to the accounts of mockery in Jesus' trial narrative. The servant's trust in God is so firm that he volunteers to take on all challengers (vv. 8-9a). The LORD will hear his voice and make an end of them—wear them out like a garment (cf. Ps 102:27), consume them like a moth. In a word, his vindication of his servant will be complete.

James 2:14-18. James returns to his theme of the necessity of testifying to religious faith with deeds. Faith that is professed without being practiced has no power to save one (*sōsai auton*, v. 14). A "brother" or a "sister" is a Christian. "Goodbye and good luck!" is literally, "Go in peace," a fact inclining some scholars to think that a liturgical dismissal is in question. Ordinary well-wishing in the Jewish manner would satisfy the requirement of the phrase. Clearly what is required is a matter of solicitude in word but not in fact. The author calls such faith without works dead (*he pistis, ean mē echē erga, nekra estin*, v. 17). The contest of v. 18 is unequal, stacked as it is against the person of faith alone, in his stance of moral superiority. He is challenged as one having faith without (*chōris*) works whereas the other, representing the author's point of view, has a faith to declare that underlies his works (*ek tōn ergōn mou tēn pistin*).

James is solidly in the Jewish tradition when he claims the need of deeds in proof of faith. Neither does he contravene Paul, who is by no means disinterested in an ethical life in favor of the brother. He only resists works when they are made the subject of a boast in lieu of saving faith in Jesus Christ.

Was James writing a polemic against Paul or against a Pauline position originating in the Gentile Christian world? Possibly the latter but not, of course, if his letter preceded Paul's first epistle (1 Thes) as some think. A twofold understanding of *pistis* has been proposed as the solution: in the Hebraic sense of trust in James (*emunah*) but of Hellenic belief in a saving deed in Paul. Such a variant understanding in part may be the case but it does not seem required as a way out of the difficulty. Paul's "faith working through love" as that which counts for something (Gal 5:6) should be acceptable to James. Paul never uses the words "faith alone" in sequence. James does (*ek pisteos monon*, 2:24), only to deny it as saving. He attributes salvation to works but not to works alone.

The two writers are engaged in emphasizing different matters. Neither denies what the other affirms. Paul would challenge James on the sense in which works justify and doubtless elicit from him a soteriology he would find woefully deficient. But Paul cannot be shown to favor a faith unaccompanied by works as saving, the matter James is at such pains to deny. He does so only if his individual statements are taken out of the context of his entire teaching on the subject.

Mark 8:27-35. Mk's Caesarea Philippi account differs from Mt's (16:13-20) in having Jesus describe himself as "I," in omitting mention of Jeremiah, and in not attributing to [Simon] Peter faith in the "son of the living God," but above all in failing to use the confession of faith ecclesially as a means to underscore Peter's subsequent role. Mk underscores the "secret" aspect of Jesus' messiahship, v. 30 (Mt will follow him in this, 16:20).

In both evangelists, the prophecy of suffering is used as the setting for an elenchus of sayings on the self-abnegating life of the Christian (cf. Mk 8:34-38.) These are already church sayings in Mk but vv. 35-37, being eschatological, could well have originated with Jesus.

This pericope forms a turning point in Mk's gospel and concludes the first half. We are wrong in concluding anything about what the confession of faith meant in Jesus' career. Mk has no interest in a historical sequence, only in a faith narrative, the framework of which is entirely his doing.

TWENTY-FIFTH SUNDAY OF THE YEAR (B)
(Eighteenth Sunday after Pentecost)

Wisdom 2:12, 17-20. The earlier portion of this chapter spells out a full-scale program of hedonism, the claims of might over right and youthful vigor over infirm old age. Needless to say, the author considers this to be anything but right thinking (cf. 2:1.) It serves as a backdrop, however, for his sketch of the just one, that "child of the Lord" (v. 13*b*) and "son of God" (v. 18*a*) who seems to be the eternal victim of the man of power but in fact is his moral superior. The titles were ordinary designations for the pious in that period.

The antithesis spells out a parable of human life in general but its graphic character made the early church conclude that it contained specific prophecy. The mocking of the bystanders at the cross in the passion narratives derives from v. 18, although not exclusively from there. Another contributor is the poetry of the righteous sufferer developed long before in sources such as Jeremiah 20 and Lamentations 3.

The chapter concludes with the reflection that the shameful death to which the wicked consign the just man (cf. v. 20) will not be lasting. Man was formed by God to be imperishable (v. 23). Recompense and reward lie in store for the innocent (v. 22). In the hidden counsels of God they will be given to them to thwart death, which was brought on by the envy of the devil (v. 24). The latter notion derives from a rabbinic midrash which makes the serpent of Genesis the devil and the seducer of Eve, by whom she begot Cain.

James 3:16—4:3. Jealousy and strife bring a variety of evils in their train. Wisdom produces a harvest of justice, peace, and every other virtue. Cravings (*hēdonōn*, v. 1) produce inner struggle in the individual (cf. Rom 7:19 for a statement of the same axiom.) Frustrated desires lead to murder and violent quarreling. The "asking" and "receiving" of v. 3 seem at first to be describing a better means of acquiring goods than murderous plunder but on inspection prove to be the suggestion of recourse to prayer. The antinomy in the writer's mind is that between God and world or God and devil. Submission to the divine will (v. 7) will elevate the lowly, turn tears into laughter, and in general restore the balance of a disordered universe.

Mark 9:30-37. This pericope contains the second prediction of the passion in Mk, as last Sunday's reading did the first. (The third will occur in 10:33f.) All three include reference to his rising again (*anastēsetai*, v. 31) not—as elsewhere in the synoptics—his being raised up. (Jn 20:9 also has "rise"). The secrecy theme (v. 30) is explained by Jesus' desire to instruct his disciples in particular (v. 31). This shorter prophecy than that of 8:31 introduces the notion of the son of man's being "delivered over" (*paradidotai*, v. 30; cf. Ac 2:23; Rom 8:32), which connotes the plan and foreknowledge of God more than any handing over of Jesus by means of the deed of Judas or his captors. As on the previous occasion, Mark portrays the disciples as stunned at the disclosure—uncomprehending more than resistant. Whatever their actual thoughts on Jesus' death were (if indeed he prophesied it) we cannot know. Mk's literary construct conceals this from us even while seeming to reveal it.

A series of sayings on discipleship follow (illustrative of the suffering principle?) The first two deal with ambition and humility, though the saying in 36f. does not follow especially from that in 35. The Aramaic word *ṭalyā* which does duty as both "servant" and "child" (*diakonos* and *paidion*) has been proposed as the link. Later sayings in the collection are linked up by a word such as "salt" or "fire." A greater puzzle than the contiguity of vv. 36 and 37 is the separation of v. 37 from 10:14f., not only because of the children theme but because the two sets of sayings have in common a word unusual in the gospels, "embracing" (*enagkalisamenos*, 9:36; 10:16).

TWENTY-SIXTH SUNDAY OF THE YEAR (B)

(Nineteenth Sunday after Pentecost)

Numbers 11:25-29. The best-known anecdote in the American experience paralleling Moses' reply is that of President Lincoln who said, when apprised of Ulysses Grant's drinking habits, that he wished the rest of the Union generals drank the same brand of whiskey. Moses responds briskly to the protective Joshua that "spirit" is a gift of the LORD freely given and his only regret is that it is not universal among the Israelites. About its distribution beyond the seventy elders (if that is where the missing Eldad and Medad fell), Moses has no problem.

The appointment of the seventy comes in the wake of the people's complaints to Moses about the surfeit of manna (11:6) and the shortage of meat (v. 13). The LORD provides a company of authorities to share responsibility with Moses, even as he promises food so abundant that it will come out their nostrils (v. 20) and thereby remove the cause of complaint. The manna story is paralleled in the E-tradition (this is P, as is three-fourths of the book of

Numbers) in Ex 16:3-35 and in the account of the selection of the elders in Ex 18:17-27, where Jethro makes the suggestion. "Spirit" is conceived in the early period as divisible, a kind of *mana* (in the Polynesian, Melanesian sense) whereby spiritual power is concentrated on individuals. In Israel, prophets who had a portion of spirit from God were at times moved to frenzied behavior (cf. 1 Sam 19:20-24.) Here its primary result would be wisdom for judgment but the seventy thus endowed also prophesied (vv. 26, 29).

We are not told why Eldad and Medad were detained in the camp and were not in the assembly. If ritual uncleanness were the explanation, Joshua would have an additional reason for his scruple. Their absence from "around the tent" (v. 24) would, however, suffice. Joshua tries to protect Moses' office and reputation, in the manner of aides everywhere, and is repulsed for his pains. Moses has a far less protective view of his office, a proof of his greatness. He sees himself as a channel of God's spirit and not an exclusive one at that. The tale is one of incalculable importance for the exercise of power in God's name over all succeeding ages.

James 5:1-6. This excoriation of the rich, not because they are rich but because they defraud the poor (are there other ways to get rich?) is in the best tradition of the 8th- and 7th-c. prophets. The just LORD hears the cries of the farm-workers, who are unorganized. The owners have not stopped at litigation and murder. The language of the corrosive effects of wealth may be stereotyped but it is no less powerful for that. There has been no justice for the impoverished and exploited just ("decent, hard-working people," we would say). They will receive justice, says James, in the last days (v. 3). He is by no means proposing, however, that in principle justice be deferred until then. In wrath he wants it now.

Mark 9:38-43, 45, 47-48. Verses 44 and 46 of the Vulgate do not occur in the Greek, so the editors of the lectionary are proposing no omissions. The dependence of the first three verses of the pericope upon Numbers above is obvious. In vv. 37, 38, 39, 41, the phrase "in my name" is common to all and ties them together (the prepositions are *epi, en, epi,* a matter of no consequence: the same is true of the modifiers, "my." "his," "my," and in v. 41 simply *en onomati*). Whether the deed is receiving a child, exorcising demons, or giving a cup of water "because you are Christ's" (*hoti Christou este,* v. 41), it is good because of its personal ascription—undoubtedly the work of the church, not a saying of Jesus—and will not go unrewarded. Contrariwise, the scandalizing of simple believers is an offense deserving of drastic punishment. No play on words remains in Greek but similar-sounding Aramaic words for stumbling-stone and millstone (v. 43) may be assumed.

The punitive sayings of vv. 43-47 are inserted by Mt into the sermon on the mount in a context of lustful gazes (5:29f.) The speech is figurative as attested to by the existence of an actual Gehenna, a blazing refuse-dump in the valley of Hinnom southwest of Jerusalem. The warning is nonetheless serious. The worm and the fire of v. 48 derive immediately from Is 66:24, where the fate of the corpses of God's enemies is in question.

Taking figurative language literally (severing limbs, plucking out eyes, anticipating worms or fire) is destructive of its meaning. Taking it seriously is understanding its meaning.

TWENTY-SEVENTH SUNDAY OF THE YEAR (B)

(Twentieth Sunday after Pentecost)

Genesis 2:18-24. Verses 4b-24 of this chapter are part of the J account, which centers on man (cf. "the earth and the heavens," v. 4b; "the heavens and the earth" of 1:1 betrays a cosmic concern.) God has formed the man out of the clods in the soil (v. 7), settled him in the garden of Eden to till and tend it (v. 15), and allowed him to eat of the fruit of any tree except that "of knowledge of good and bad" (v. 17). The present passage attempts to account for the names, i.e., the different species, of beasts and birds and the origin and purpose of marriage. The "suitable partner" to man is literally an "aid" or "help" alongside him. The traditional "help meet for him" in early translations is cognate with the English word "helpmate."

The distinguishing feature of the "living creatures" of v. 19 (Speiser thinks this phrase a later gloss because it does violence to Hebrew syntax in this position) is that, despite their variety, none is "help fit for him" (v. 20). The unsuitability is remedied. A rib (*sela'*) taken from the man (*ha 'adham*) is built up into a woman, who is brought to the man (vv. 21f.) The poetic couplet of v. 23 relies on the similar sounds of the Hebrew words for "woman" (*ishsha*) and "man" (*ish*), different as to their consonantal make-up and unrelated. The English "woman," derived from "wife of man," actually makes the point better, philologically. The two become one "body" (lit., "flesh," *basar*) through union, a fitting arrangement in the author's mind since they had originally been the one creature, man and rib.

The concrete, earthy character of this Yahwist (J) account betrays its origins from Mesopotamian sources, as the presence of loanwords for "well up" (v. 6) and "Eden" (v. 8), found in both

Akkadian and Sumerian, help to establish. There are numerous details in common like the harlot-lass who mates with Enkidu the hunter in the Gilgamesh Epic, making him forget the wild beasts of the steppe (Tablet I, iv). Yet the Priestly account can also be shown to derive from Mesopotamian traditions about the beginnings of the world. Despite the differences of emphasis in the P account of Gen 1 and the J account of Gen 2, "the traditions involved must go back . . . to the oldest cultural stratum of Mesopotamia" (Speiser).

The motif of the tree of knowledge (v. 17) likewise betrays certain Mesopotamian links. There is nothing strange in the biblical authors' use of these concepts, since each is writing a primeval history which is a preface to a story that comes to life in Mesopotamia. That land alone provides the necessary historical and cultural records.

Hebrews 2:9-11.   The subjection of all things to Jesus is not a matter of present experience (v. 8) as it will be in the vision of the end which St. Paul spells out in 1 Cor 15:25-28. Hebrews has that much in common with Paul. More than Paul, however, Hebrews centers on the role of Jesus as "leader" (v. 10) or pioneer in the human necessity of becoming perfect through suffering. Glory and honor have come to him because he underwent death (v. 9). By that same path men will follow him in obedience (cf. 5:8f.), coming at last to where he is, through the "veil" of his flesh (cf. 10:20). Jesus is not exempted from the route of pain to glory any more than his "brothers" are (v. 11).

Hebrews quotes Ps 8:6f. verbatim from the Septuagint, omitting only 7a. J. A. T. Robinson points out the almost universal English rendering of *brachy ti* (Vulgate, *modico*) by "for a short while" under the influence of subsequent christology (*The Human Face of God*, pp. 159f.). But nothing in the adverbial phrase requires this translation connoting time. It is rather a matter of degree, as the normal translation of the identical psalm verse in the OT indicates: "little less than the angels" (NAB, the NT translation of which, at Heb 2:9, Robinson does not cite although it follows the others). He espouses Westcott's view that *brachy ti* is used here of magnitude and not of time, as the unambiguous Hebrew bears out. The point is important in conveying the christology of Hebrews accurately. Its author is not saying that Jesus started higher than the angels and for a brief space was lower but that "in him (and as yet in no other man) we see fulfilled the ultimate *destiny* of man" (Robinson, p. 160). Christ *became* superior to them "when he . . . took his seat at the right hand of the Majesty in heaven" (1:3).

Jesus' present enthronement (v. 9) marks him out for future supremacy over all. Meanwhile, he has the fatherhood of God as his possession along with all those whom he consecrates (*hagiazōn*, v. 11). This expresses a common lot between Jesus and the rest of humanity while preserving his distinctiveness which neither Paul nor the evangelists achieve as well.

A weakly attested reading gives *chōris theou* for *chariti theou.* In it, "apart from God" would refer to the "all things" of v. 8 or the "all men" of v. 9 rather than speak of a work done "through God's gracious will." In terms of sense, it seems unlikely that this was the primitive reading.

Mark 10:2-16. This account of Jesus' opposition to divorce does not appear in the Q material, hence it is not in Luke. Bultmann and Streeter find Mark's version awkward, artificial, and inferior to Mt in terms of Jewish usage. Mk's account seems to Bultmann to have been thoroughly rearranged from an earlier controversy-story. First comes the Mosaic legislation permitting divorce (v. 4, quoting Dt 24:1). This is put on the lips of the Pharisees, strangely, who may be presumed to have known it well. Even stranger is their question (v. 2) which asks if divorce is permissible—a difficulty they could not possibly have had in that form. Jesus puts Moses' concession down to stubbornness (v. 5) and cites against them the unequivocal divine will (vv. 7f.) expressed in Genesis 2:24. Verse 9 sums up Jesus' teaching; verses 11f. make it fully explicit, as if enunciating a fundamental law for the disciples who will act as missionaries to the Gentiles.

Jesus' final comment, given to the disciples "in the house," is a positive regulation laid down for the wider church. Mk has in view only Christian readers and hearers; for them he sets out the Lord's teaching which unequivocally prohibits divorce followed by remarriage. It is highly likely that this final logion (vv. 11f.) had an existence independent of the story, which is complete without it. Cf. Mt 5:32 and Lk 16:18 for its attestation in Q. Some, like Dungan, think that the final saying existed as an abstract of the story.

Mt's dependence on Mk or Mk's on Mt in this narrative cannot be settled on form-critical grounds. What is clear is Mk's intention to answer his own question for the church, "Shall there be divorce at all?" with a strong "No." The question was one that arose in Hellenistic churches, as is clear from the absence of all the Palestinian Pharisaic overtones found in Mt's account. The special mention of the woman "who divorces her husband" (v. 12) gives proof of this. Mk's version is frequently taken to be more primitive than Mt's because Mt's "exceptive clauses" (at 5:32 and 19:9) are taken to be interpretative relaxations in a Jewish milieu. Whether they place lesser demands on those who dismiss or leave their partners than in the Marcan form is another question. The bulk of

NT scholarship seems to think so, and with this conclusion Orthodox and Protestant church practice is in accord. Catholic practice did not follow scholarship in the matter so much as the apparently more restrictive of the two NT teachings.

A modern view that has had currency among Catholic exegetes particularly is that the *porneia* of Mt's two clauses is the adulterous conduct that justifies dismissal but that Mt has remarriage no more in view than Mk does. Some have held *porneia* to mean an incestuous union which would comprise a clear exception, but the Matthean context does not give this view much support.

As to the next pericope, on Jesus and the children (vv. 13-16), it need only be said that, except for 9:36f., no passage in early Christian literature attends to the condition of childhood in any special way. The separation of this narrative from the other of the previous chapter has already been remarked (cf. pp. 247f. on Mk 9:36f.) The child, in trusting openness, becomes the norm for all acceptance of the reign of God by the more suspicious and sophisticated adult.

TWENTY-EIGHTH SUNDAY OF THE YEAR (B)

(Twenty-First Sunday after Pentecost; 2d reading of COCU includes that of next Sunday)

Wisdom 7:7-11. Beginning at 6:22 the author has been speaking as if he were a king in search of wisdom. He is no better than the rest in his common humanity (7:1-6) but the search for wisdom should set him apart. The prayer and plea of v. 7 evoke the tale in 1 Kgs 3:5-15 of Solomon's dream at Gibeon where he begged for "an understanding heart to judge your people and to distinguish right from wrong" (v. 9). Solomon's wealth, particularly his possession of gold, is highlighted in 1 Kgs 10:14-17; 21-23. In immediate context, however, there is placed (by an editorial hand?) his pursuit of wisdom, v. 24. That juxtaposition, by way of contrast, is central to the present pericope. Gold, silver, health, beauty—even the great treasure of light itself in the unillumined ancient world—are as nothing compared to prudence and wisdom.

The bloom is taken off the rose somewhat by the practical conclusion (after all, a king is a king) that all good things and countless riches come in wisdom's train (v. 11). Prv 8:21 has said the same. Uneasy, evidently, lies the unwise head that wears a crown, whereas the possession of *ḥokmah* finds the king in the counting-house, counting out his money. Yet such rewards "were insignificant compared to the supreme benefit of 'friendship with God' " (cf.

v. 14.) R. B. Y. Scott, just quoted, observes that the author's "only wish now is that his thoughts and words should be worthy of this theme" (cf. vv. 15f.)

Hebrews 4:12-13. The author has been engaged in a disquisition on fidelity and infidelity, obedience and disobedience, with Jesus proposed as the supreme example of both virtues. For his completion of the work God gave him to do, Christ enjoys the heavenly rest (*katapausis*) of the LORD himself (Gen 2:2; cf. Heb 4:4.) It was not given to the Israelites of old, even though it was promised them (cf. 3:18f.; 4:6), because of unbelief. Psalm 95 on which these two chapters are a commentary, especially the recurring vv. 7*b*-8 (cf. Heb 3:7f., 15; 4:7), represents a renewal of the promise in David's day (4:7). "Therefore a sabbath rest still remains for the people of God" (v. 9). Failing, in faith, in imitation of the unbelief of the people of old, is the great sin which this Christian author warns against.

In today's reading of two verses, self-deceit is warned against. All lies bare and open before God (v. 13). He judges the reflections and thoughts of the heart by the sword of his word (v. 12). God's "word" here is his communicating power, not particularly the *logos* of the Johannine prologue nor the rational element in creation nor even the Hebrew scriptures. It is his speaking to his people in prophecy and act (cf. Rom 9:6), a communication the substance of which is eminently conveyed by preaching (cf. 1 Cor 14:36; 2 Tim 2:9.) The sword figure seems to derive from Wis 18:15f. Eph speaks in allegory of "the sword of the spirit" (6:17) and Rev (19:15) of a sharp sword coming from the mouth of "the king of kings." The all-seeing eye of God is the theme of Job 34:21f.; Ps 90:8; 139:2-6, 16.

The sword of God's word is alive and active (*zōn . . . kai energēs*, v. 12). Its penetration and division of "soul and spirit, joints and marrow" (*psychēs kai pneumatos, harmon te kai myelōn*) is a way of describing penetration to one's innermost being. Nothing physiological is intended, least of all a real separation of the members named. Perhaps the closest NT parallel to this passage is found in Simeon's words to Mary, Lk 2:35. For Hebrews, God's word represents "the dynamic activity of the omnipresent God" (H. Montefiore).

Mark 10:17-30. The detail of the journey (v. 17) is used by Mk as a link with what has gone before. The mention of "kneeling" and the form of address, "Good Teacher," betray obsequiousness, a stance which Jesus will not allow (v. 18; Mt nervously changes this to "Why do you ask me about what is good?" 19:17). The story underscores Jesus' respect for the various commandments—cited from Dt 5:16-21 with "do not defraud" summarizing the last two and the one on parents placed at the end. At the same time, Mk wishes to put becoming a follower of Jesus (v. 21) above perfect observance. Detachment from riches is a condition of such discipleship (v. 21). This enunciation leads to a special explanation to the disciples, in Marcan fashion (v. 23). Verse 25 comes before v. 24 in some MSS, the probable order. God is so powerful that he can save even the rich (v. 27). Peter's plaintive declaration of insufficient funds (v. 28) was probably a separate saying originally which here serves as a link to still another independent *logion* (vv. 29f.) The "hundredfold" of v. 30 represents the conviction of the Marcan church that its members had made a good bargain. Adhering to Christ was infinitely rewarding; compared with it, any wrench experienced by separation from family or property was as nothing.

TWENTY-NINTH SUNDAY OF THE YEAR (B)

(Twenty-Second Sunday after Pentecost; 2d reading, Lutheran, occurs in next Sunday's Roman Lectionary)

Isaiah 53:10-11. These verses are part of the fourth "servant-of-the-LORD" oracle which runs from 52:13 to 53:12. The first (42:1-4) describes a just and gentle figure who acts like a king, the second and third (49:1-7; 50:4-11) someone cast more in the prophetic mold. Here the servant is to be exalted above the kings of earth (52:15) after a humiliation (v. 14) that ends in his death (53:8ff.) It is likely that the Second Isaiah had in mind the "death" of Abraham's seed in undergoing Babylonian exile, which is still a reality as he writes. Thus the "wicked" and the "evildoers" of v. 9 would be the pagans among whom the exiled believers dwelt.

The crushed servant will, in the future, see his seed ("descendants," v. 10) long-lived as a result of his proffering his life (literally, "spirit," v. 10) as a sacrifice of reparation ("offering for sin," *'asham*). *'Asham* means first an offense, then the means by which the offense is righted, and finally a sacrifice of reparation. Confusion in the Bible between this expiatory rite and a sin offering, *hatta'th*, is nearly total. We must say, at least, that the offense of the *'asham* is a measurable one and that Second Isaiah is proposing the life of the servant as a compensation for the people's sins. The servant (the exiled portion of the people?) acts on behalf of all the rest. To "see the light" means to enjoy happiness, as a footnote in NAB observes; the noun "light" must be supplied to the Hebrew from the LXX and Qumrân. The servant, described as "my just servant" in Hebrew, will render many just by his suffering (lit., his "knowledge" or "experience").

"Their guilt he shall bear" is again an expression of the author's conviction that the servant's humiliation and death acts as a reparation for sin.

Hebrews 4:14-16. The author at this point resumes his theme that Jesus is the faithful apostle and high priest who founded a house of faith (cf. 2:17—3:6.) He was tested through what he suffered (2:18). This makes him sympathetic toward us and a model for all who are tempted as he was (2:18; 4:15). The phrase "apart from sin" (*chōris hamartias*, v. 15) does not negate the fact that Jesus was "beset by weakness" (5:2). It does concur in the theological judgment of all the New Testament writers who consider the question—it cannot be a historical judgment—that Jesus never sinned (cf. 2 Cor 5:21; 1 Pt 2:22; Heb 7:26); that he was an unblemished victim (cf. 1 Pt 1:19; Heb 9:14.) For Jesus' temptation to have been real, he must have known "from within the existential meaning of human sinfulness . . . [while] not consenting" (J. Knox). Otherwise he was not tempted as men are. To feel the pull of evil one must see it, under some aspects at least, as more attractive than the good. The "set" of Jesus' will therefore "remains constant in its direction . . . [although like a battle-weary soldier] physically—even mentally—he may consent to the relief he longs for" (Moule).

Confidence is recommended to those who approach the "throne of grace" (located in the "sanctuary," 10:19, "higher than the heavens," 7:26, where Jesus "rests from his work," 4:10). Mercy, grace, and help are available there "at the suitable time" (*eis eukairon*, v. 16).

Mark 10:35-45. The third of Mk's three predictions of the passion has intervened since last Sunday's reading. Mt has the mother of the sons of Zebedee speak for them (20:20) but Mk is never protective of the disciples; if anything, the contrary. Mt also eliminates the phrase about being baptized with Jesus' baptism (Mk 10:39), retaining only mention of the cup. The placement of this story of selfishness after Jesus' reiteration of his need to suffer is surely intended by Mk as part of his having the disciples consistently miss the point. Verses 35-40 seem to be the original unit, with 41-55 woven out of individual *logia* appended to it as Mk's commentary.

Verses 38f. seem to say that martyrdom has a priority in the kingdom (Jesus' "cup" being death) but it may only mean to highlight the disciples' need to suffer like the master as the precondition of glory, the very point made by Hebrews above.

Luke's use of the sayings of vv. 42-44 (Lk 22:24-27) shows that they were originally concerned with authority and service in the community. The final Marcan word on Jesus' life as a ransom for "the many" (the *rabbim* of Is 53:11) closes the pericope on a soteriological note.

THIRTIETH SUNDAY OF THE YEAR (B)

(Twenty-Third Sunday after Pentecost)

Jeremiah 31:7-9.   Here we have a vision of the return from exile which forms part of the "Book of Consolation," made up of chapters 30-33, of which chapters 30-31 are a distinct part. Jacob (Israel) stands for the exiled people, specifically the northern tribes. Deliverance has come. The remnant of Israel will be brought back from the land to the north (v. 8) across the fertile crescent. The throng shall include the diminished (blind and lame) and the increased (childing mothers). Sorrow marked their going (v. 9). Their return shall be on a level road with the wadis full of water at their feet. It has to be so since the LORD is Israel's father and Ephraim—son of Joseph—is his "first-born," a term of affection for the northern kingdom (cf. v. 20.)

Verses 2-6 and 15-22 of this chapter seem to have been addressed by Jeremiah to northern Israel early in his career, when Josiah was pressing his reforms in the north (622 B.C.; cf. 2 Kgs 23:15-20.) Verses 7-9 may have been composed in similar circumstances and modified later to refer to the exiles living in Babylon. They bear a striking similarity, in any case, to the later chapters of Isaiah. In particular there is a relation between vv. 8-9 and Is 35; 40:3-5, 11; 41:18-20; 42:16; 43:-17; 44:3f.; 48:20f.; 49:9-13.

Hebrews 5:1-6.   Having declared Jesus the perfect high priest because of his sympathy with our weakness and his being himself tempted (4:14ff.), the author goes on to discuss the office theoretically. He does so in idealized terms from sources such as Ex 28:1; Num 18:7; Lev 4:3-12; 9:7; 16:6, 11. It is almost as if he knew nothing of the debased process of selection of high priests in his day, or was totally disinterested in current Jewish views of the office. The author concentrates exclusively on the high priest's representative function in worship. He ignores completely his contemporary role as presiding officer of the Sanhedrin. The words for "gifts" and "sacrifices" (v. 1) are used interchangeably in the LXX, so no case can be made for a description of cereal offerings in contradistinction to blood sacrifices. Heb is interested in expiatory sacrifices "for sins," a phrase used in the plural with respect to Yom Kippur only in the Bible. The transition from the selection process (v. 1), which *de facto* is confined to Aaronite stock (Num 18:1-7), to the sympathetic stance of the non-Aaronite Christ (v. 2) is imperceptible. "Erring sinners" (v. 2) are literally the "ignorant and the straying," a single class of unconscious offenders whose sins need expiatory sacrifice for remission. Lev 4:3-12 describes the offering of a bullock in cases where the priest himself is an inadvertent sinner (i.e., a transgressor of a ritual taboo); there is mention of a priest's sacrifice for his own sins as well as those of the people in Lev 9:7, while 16:11 speaks of the necessity of his doing so in a context of the annual observance of the Day of Atonement. All of the above is background for Heb 5:3.

For v. 4, cf. Ex 28:1. The offense of Korah the Levite, Dathan, and Abiram, described at length in Num 16, was their leadership of 250 Levites, who aspired to the priestly office on the ground that the whole nation was holy. The ground did not sustain them (cf. vv. 31f.) The author of Heb, like the Hebrew scriptures, requires a divine vocation for the priestly office. Since he is presumably aware of Christ's non-priestly origins, he situates his calling to the office of high priest in two psalm verses, 2:7 and 110:4. It is God who calls him "Son" (v. 5; cf. 1:5), then designates him a priest forever in a Melchisedekian sense (v. 6).

Whence did Heb derive its central theme of Jesus as high priest? Other NT authors use Ps 2:7 in support of Jesus' special sonship of God (cf. Ac 13:33; also, the verse's probable use as underlying Mk 1:1, 9:7; Mt 3:17; Lk 3:22.) The author of Hebrews acts like a conscious innovator in the way he develops the argument for Christ's priesthood in ch. 7 (cf. also 6:20.) Yet he may have been started on his train of thought—Christ as a priest like the pre-Aaronite Melchisedek—by meditating on the use of Ps 110:1 in Mk 12:36 (pars. Mt 22:44, Lk 20:42). There the verse is attributed to Jesus, arguing in behalf of his own status as a son of David who is at the same time his "Lord." The author of Heb might have gone on from this tradition to examine the implications of v. 4 of the psalm. It is clear from 10:5 that he thinks Jesus' whole career one of a call to sacrifice. The non-Aaronite priesthood of Jesus was separated by a world from the usurping Hasmonean prince exercising the priestly office whom the author of Ps 110 probably had in mind. No matter. The words are right to describe Jesus Christ, so far as the author is concerned, because it is he who is being directly addressed by God in v. 4.

Mark 10:46-52. Mk seems to have come upon a story in the tradition in which Jesus was already leaving Jericho (not the ancient city; a town near it rebuilt as a Roman garrison by Herod the Great). This would account for the strange "came" and "were leaving" of v. 46. The characters in the first-level of tradition in the healing narratives are nameless, which causes some to think that an original story came to be connected with a known figure in the Marcan church, Bartimaeus of Jericho. The awkward introduction of the parenthetical explanation of the meaning of the name probably identifies it as an early textual gloss. The point of the story is the messianic title "Son of David" (vv. 47, 48) coupled with that of alacrity in becoming a follower of Jesus (vv. 50, 52). The "healed" (*sesōken*) of v. 52 is studiedly ambiguous for "cured" and "saved." It is attributed to the beggar's "faith" (*pistis*), again ambivalently his trust in Jesus' power to heal him and the state of the later disciple regarding Jesus as the Christ (cf. Mk 5:34, par. Lk 7:50; 17:19; Mk 2:5.) The element of personal trust in these healing narratives is probably historical.

The pericope is transitional in Mk between the unit of the third prediction of the passion (10:33-45) and the entry into Jerusalem (ch. 11). Jesus is the sight-giving Son of David whom Marcan church members are following. He is also the one who suffers, as they must suffer, in Mk's studied correction of the false christology abroad which viewed Jesus only as a "divine man" (*theios anēr*), or thaumaturge.

THIRTY-FIRST SUNDAY OF THE YEAR (B)

(Twenty-Fourth Sunday after Pentecost)

Deuteronomy 6:2-6. The previous chapter has contained the commandments delivered in the covenant of Horeb. These are to be observed faithfully in the land of Canaan, which Israel is about to conquer (vv. 1-3). There, milk and honey will flow on condition of perfect observance. The promise of the LORD will be fulfilled if the terms of the covenant are kept.

"Hear, O Israel!" (*Sh͏ema' Yis͏eroel*) introduces the expressed conviction that the LORD is Israel's God and he alone, and that he is to be loved totally and exclusively. The four words of the formula can be rendered in various ways. Of these, the best known alternative to that of NAB (which *The Torah* of the Jewish Publication Society of America also follows; *BJ*, like it, has, "est le seul Yahvé"), is that of RSV and JB, "The Lord our God is one LORD." NEB adopts still another position: "The Lord is our God, one LORD." Whether the Hebrew text means to emphasize his unity or his uniqueness, it is clear that identifying Israel's God by his proper name is paramount and that he is the exclusive object of the people's devotion. This creedal statement, as it rightly or wrongly is frequently called, means to distinguish the LORD from all the gods of Canaan. The command to cleave closely to him ("heart," "soul," and "strength" expressing the ideas of interior will, person, and intensity or "muchness") is to be taken to heart (vv. 5f.)

The passages Dt 6:4-9, 11:13-21, and Num 15:37-41 came to be written on small scrolls and recited daily as the *Shᵉma'*. In later times they were inserted in leather boxes (*tᵉphillin*) worn on wrist and forehead, or in a cartridge (*mᵉzuzah*) affixed to the doorpost, in literal fulfillment of vv. 8f. (cf. p. 99.)

Hebrews 7:23-28. The commentaries on the four readings from Hebrews in the previous month should be consulted, especially that on Heb 4:14-16 (p. 256) where Christ's sinlessness despite his temptations is discussed, and that of the Thirtieth Sunday, where the text (5:1-6) underscores the personal sins of the ordinary high priest.

Today's passage refers to Christ's unique status (v. 23) as high priest continuing forever (vv. 24f.), while returning to the theme of his sinlessness (v. 26; cf. 4:15 and elsewhere, 2 Cor 5:21; 1 Pet 2:22.) A new idea is introduced in v. 27, namely the definitive character ("once for all," *ephapax*) of his self-offering. The necessity the ordinary high priest labors under of offering sacrifices for his own sins as well as those of the people, found in v. 27, has been alleged in 5:3. Here, mention of Christ's exempt status is repeated. It is only the people's sins that do not require remission by repeated offering. His self-offering did not take away any sins of his own "once for all," since this Son appointed priest was "made perfect forever" (*eis ton aiōna teteleiōmenon*, v. 28). The "oath" is that of Ps 110:4, superseding the law which sets up a priesthood marked by weakness. The parallel of the line of argument here with that of Paul in Gal 3:19-22 and Rom 5:20-22, though without the law's function of increasing offenses or locking all things under the constraint of sin, is inescapable.

There is no biblical mention of the high priest's offering sacrifice daily (*kath'hēmeran anagkēn*, v. 7) but only on the Day of Atonement (Lv 16:6). The Septuagint rendering of Lv 6:13, however, has the priest sons of Aaron making a grain-offering "continually" or "regularly" (*dia pantos*), while v. 12 in the Hebrew describes fat burning on a wood fire, made fresh by a priest every morning. Philo reports a tradition of daily sacrifice by the high priest; Ben Sirach has a richly vested priest offering sacrifice twice daily (45:14).

Mark 12:28-34. Frequently Mk describes Jesus as having taught the crowds but, except for the parables of ch. 4, not much of his teaching is reported in the first nine chapters. Not until 9:33, with the second of the three predictions of the passion behind him, does Mk provide any sizable blocks of teaching besides the parables. From that point on teaching begins to proliferate, especially after the entry into Jerusalem at the beginning of ch. 11. Chapter 12 features the parable of the tenants and the exchanges with the Pharisees over tribute to the emperor and the Sadducees on the resurrection of the body.

Today's pericope does not report struggle but agreement. A scribe, presumably of Pharisaic bent, has found Jesus' response to the Sadducees "skillful," predictably enough. The link in v. 28 to what precedes it is awkward but it is doubtless Mk's way of following one story with another. The question was usual enough in rabbinic circles, where the search for the weightiest commandment of the law was constant. Jesus responds by reciting the opening phrases of the *Sh*e*ma'*, Israel's daily prayer. The phrase, "all your *mind*" (*dianoias sou*) is not found in the Hebrew text or the LXX, which at Dt 6:5 has *dynameōs* for "strength" rather than Mk's *ischyos*. The two details lead to the speculation that this version of Dt 6:5 came from a church which was no longer reciting the prayer. How Lv 19:18 (v. 31) is a "second" commandment is not clear. Mt takes the pains to explain that the second is "like" (*homoia*, 22:39) the first, hence presumably on an equal footing, while Luke runs them together uninterruptedly (10:27). Mk's comment in 31*b* has the same net effect: the two are inseparable. Yet he alone of the three evangelists precedes his answer with the summons to reflect on the LORD's uniqueness in Israel's life. This inclusion has the effect of underscoring the LORD as the source of the possibility of love, whether of himself or of one's neighbor.

Jesus' Jewish contemporary Philo places the two together as "duties" (*Special Laws* 2, 63). The commandments are found side by side in the Testaments of the Twelve Patriarchs (Iss 5:2; 7:6; cf. Dan 5:3; Zeb 5:1; Benj 3:3). In rabbinic times the conjunction was a commonplace. We cannot know how original Jesus was in placing the two together, nor is it important.

Verse 32 is the sole instance in the gospels of a teacher agreeing with Jesus. The latter's favorable view of the scribe's response contradicts Mk's usual opinion of teachers of the law (cf. 2:6f.; 3:22; 7:1ff.; 12:38ff.) While these details have led some to think that the story arose in the church, its unusual character tells in favor of its genuineness.

Jesus and the scribe concur in the importance of love over ritual requirements, a biblical theme (cf. 1 Sam 15:22; Hos 6:6; Is 1:11; Prv

21:3); they are followed by many of the rabbis. In approving the scribe's answer, however, Jesus does not say that he is under God's rule. He is not far (*ou makran*) from that *basileia*. There is still a gap, which in his response of v. 34 Jesus invites the scribe to close. This means that the reign Jesus envisages does not lie in an eschatological future but can be achieved now. As Schweizer remarks, "Salvation and judgment are accomplished when one meets Jesus."

THIRTY-SECOND SUNDAY OF THE YEAR (B)

(Twenty-Fifth Sunday after Pentecost)

1 Kings 17:10-16. Zarephath, the Sarepta of the New Testament, is the first Phoenician city to yield up its treasures—an event of 1970 under the expert hand of James Pritchard of the University Museum, University of Pennsylvania. It is about ten miles south of Sidon on the seacoast and some fifteen north of ancient Tyre. Elijah is introduced as the adversary of King Ahab (874/3-853) who threatens him with drought (17:1) because Ahab has married Jezebel, daughter of the king of Sidon, and erected a statue of the chief deity or baal of that country, Melkart, in Samaria (16:31f.)

The Elijah cycle comes to us unedited by the Deuteronomist's hand, probably from before the mid-8th-c. period of Amos and Hosea. The miraculous element of the tales is part of their fabric. It shows forth the LORD's power in his servant Elijah, who will challenge the Phoenician cult and culture which threatens that of Israel. The prophet is probably in flight from Ahab when we first encounter him, hence his hiding in the Wadi Ḥerith. Ravens, no friend to other species, feed him. A Phoenician woman, no friend to Israelites, does the same. She even accedes to his demand to feed him before herself and her son, and in her obedience ensures the life of this unlikely trio for a year (v. 15). The drought was doubtless the cause of the famine and the widow's starvation. She is promised flour and oil in unending supply until the rains come (v. 14).

Hebrews 9:24-28. The author reiterates his point (see the commentary on 7:27 above) that Christ is a high priest who was offered up but once (*hapax*, v. 28). As the death of humankind generally is unrepeatable, so is his. But whereas judgment faces the normal individual after death (v. 27), in Christ's case there will follow his return to save; not to take away the sins of the many—that has already been done—but to bring final salvation.

The sanctuary Christ has entered into is not made by human hands (*ou . . . cheiropoiēta eisēlthen hagia*, v. 24), a concept already encountered in 9:11 with respect to the tabernacle (*skēnē*). The term "made with hands" was a Jewish way of stigmatizing idolatry in the Hellenist world (cf. Ac 17:24.) It appears in the NT as a description of the temple (Mk 14:58; Ac 7:48). In its negative form, *acheiropoiēton*, it is a term of praise designating Christ's resurrection body (Mk 14:58), the church (2 Cor 5:1), and baptism as compared favorably with circumcision (Col 2:11; cf. Eph 2:11)—all achieved by God rather than men. Christ did not enter a sanctuary which, like that in Jerusalem, was a "mere copy" (*antitypa*) of the heavenly or "true" one (*alēthinōn*, v. 24; cf. 8:2.) Heaven is here identified for the first time as the sanctuary where Christ's sacrifice is offered. His appearing before God now on our behalf suffices (v. 24). There is no repetition in any sense akin to the annually repeated rite of Yom Kippur (v. 25). His sacrifice occurred once at the end of the ages (v. 26; cf. 10:24); repeated deaths of Jesus would be an absurdity. We are left to conclude that his continued appearing before God as intercessor is effective because of the acceptability of his once-for-all sacrifice.

Mark 12:38-44. We can find as severe a condemnation of the conduct of religious functionaries in Jewish sources as in vv. 38-41. Mark clearly means to distinguish, however, between the usual mode of behavior of the self-consciously religious and those who follow in the footsteps of Jesus. (Cf. pars. Mt 23:1-7; Lk 11:43; 20:45ff.) There is some grammatical evidence that v. 40 had circulated as a separate saying but been appended to 38f. in a pre-Marcan source.

The same is true of 41-44, although the transfer from a public occurrence to an admonition of the disciples in 43a is probably an editorial addition. Mark sees in the widow's generosity an example of Jewish piety like that of most in the crowd. They heard Jesus with delight (v. 37), in contrast to leaders of the type described in vv. 38ff.

Stories like that of the widow's mite are told in many traditions. Note that she could have kept one of the coins, but did not. A *lepton* is something like one tenth of a cent, indicating her marginal status if two were "all that she had to live on."

THIRTY-THIRD SUNDAY OF THE YEAR (B)
(Twenty-Sixth Sunday after Pentecost)

Daniel 12:1-3. The book of Daniel is concerned with "the greatest calamity that has ever occurred under heaven" (9:4), the humiliation of Jerusalem by "a little horn [on the ram that was Greece] which kept growing toward the south," namely Antiochus IV (8:9; cf. vv. 23-26.) The interruption of temple sacrifice achieved by his desecration (cf. 11:31) ran from 168 to 165 B.C., according to 1 Mc (1:54 and 4:52). Gabriel, the first angel to be mentioned in the Hebrew canon by name (Dan 8:16), explains to Daniel the meaning of his visions. Michael, the second (10:13), is the "prince" of Israel. Persia (v. 13) and Greece (v. 20) have their own protective princes. Chapter 11 describes conflict between the king of the north, Antiochus, and the king of the south, Ptolemy, son of the Egyptian monarch who was the brother of Antiochus, Seleucus IV (d. 175). It peaks in its description of Antiochus' blasphemies, which include desertion of the gods of his fathers (vv. 36-39). Verses 40-45 presumably describe the resolution of the struggle, but at this point the author deserts history for eschatology. There was no such overwhelming of Egypt as v. 40 describes, nor do we know what the pitching of the royal pavilion between the Mediterranean and Mt. Zion (v. 45) signifies. It may have been the beginning of the siege of Jerusalem. We do know that Antiochus IV "came to his end" (v. 45) in Persia, a matter concerning which the author has either no knowledge or no interest. He does care, however, about the fate of the victims of the unparalleled distress he describes (12:1).

Michael shall take care of his people "at that time." Those who escape, "everyone found written in the book" (v. 1), are presumably the Jews who remain faithful. There is no implication, however, that the heroic dead in the Maccabean uprising are unfaithful. They are projected as living forever in the flesh while the betrayers of the cause live on in shame (v. 2). The "wise" who "lead the many to justice" (v. 3) are the national heroes who counseled and took part in the resistance.

Undoubtedly life after death is being spoken of here but without any detail as to its conditions. The Jewish scriptures have been largely silent on the point until now (Is 26:19 and Ez 37 are probably only prefigurative of the last age). Their fear of foreign mythologies about rising deities may have been influential. But here there is a clear statement of faith in the lot of those who took part in the resistance to the Greeks. They will awaken to life or to horror in relation to their deeds.

Hebrews 10:11-14, 18. This passage returns to the theme of the last two Sundays' readings and those of the preceding month. A new argument is proposed in support of the preeminence of Christ's priesthood. He is seated, as in Ps 110:1 (cf. David's posture in 2 Sm 7:18.) The temple priests stand (cf. Nm 16:9.) The visual lesson provided by the cathedral at Aachen comes to mind, the "triple church" where a seated Charlemagne observed from his throne the activity of the bishop standing at the altar below him. The positioning is a matter of significance.

Jesus has performed his priestly work once and finally, and sits at the right hand of God (v. 12). He continues as a priest; that role will last forever (cf. 7:16f.) He exercises his priestly function now by renewed intercession (cf. 7:25; 9:24.) Enemies are placed beneath his feet (v. 13) as in the footstool metaphor of Ps 110:1. Paul in 1 Cor 15:24-28 uses a similar figure to describe Christ's victory at the end, even if verbally he relies on Ps 8:7 rather than 110. There, a more general dominion of man over nature is described. The enthroned Christ need not move about like the Aaronic priests, since his work is done. It is not as though the sanctified (v. 14; cf. 2:11) had been perfected in every respect, even though from the standpoint of Christ's sacrifice, a perfect act, they are. The perfection lies in Christ, the cause, rather than in the effect in the consecrated. The same idea recurs in v. 18. The forgiveness of sinners in Christ means that no further offering will be required on his part, not that none will be necessitated on theirs.

Mark 13:24-32. The evangelist describes the end-time but his real interest is in the church living in his own age. "During that period" (v. 24) is identical in Greek with "in those days" of v. 17, a favorite Marcan phrase (cf. 1:9; 8:1) which serves as a link between narratives but does not connote proximity in time to what preceded. There will be trials (*thlipsin*), presumably in Judea and somehow related to the "abominable and destructive presence" (v. 14). This phrase is rendered in Today's English Version by "the Awful Horror." The same version personifies the neuter *bdelygma*, "where *he* should not be," though *deî* is impersonal. Evidently the horror is taken to be that of an individual's presence. Caligula's desecration of the temple by erecting statues of himself is most often presumed here (his actual throne name, A.D. 37-41, was Gaius; "Caligula" means "Little Boots"). In the midst of cataclysm, the son of man will appear. His coming will be sudden, like the burst of summer in Palestine (v. 28). Encountering him is not a matter for distant generations but for this one (v. 30).

The apocalyptic setting of the passage is not so important as the coming of the son of man. His assembly of his chosen "from the farthest bounds of sea and sky" (v. 27) is a detail from Dt 30:4f. and Is 60:4ff. (cf. Mi 4:1f.) The ingathering is of the chosen, as in 12:25, not the resurrection of all the dead or the judgment of the good and evil. In contrast to other apocalypses of the period like the *Assumption of Moses*, there is no mention of the annihilation of enemies. The goal of the prophetic narrative is the great power and glory of the Son of Man, in which the dispersed will be joined with him in ultimate fellowship with their God.

Verses 28f. are a parable which, in its original independent form, was not referring by "these things" to what has preceded in vv. 24-27. "All these things" of v. 30 (which is seemingly a separate saying) may refer to Jesus' activity (cf. 9:1.) In any case the *tauta* and *genētai* of the two logia is what brought them together. Similarly, 31 has been joined to 30 only because of the catchword "pass away" (*parelthē/pareleusontai*). Verse 31 is similar in meaning to Mt 5:18 except that here it is Jesus' words that have the staying power, a development beyond the Matthean attribution of such perdurance to the law.

Verse 32 was also a separate saying originally. It is in a quite different spirit from 29f. and is unique in Mk for its mention of "the Father" and "the son." If it is a genuine saying of Jesus—as its reference to limits to his knowledge hints—it is his only reference to himself as the son. Whatever the case, it sets him apart from other mortals and puts him in company with the angels in his ignorance. If, on the other hand, Jesus cannot be thought of as calling himself the son, the saying could be one of the early church to express the fact that it had no word from him about when these things would happen. The gathering of the chosen to the Son of Man, in its circumstances, was an absolute mystery of God.

FEAST OF CHRIST THE KING (B)

(Last Sunday after Pentecost)

Daniel 7:13-14. A "son of man" means an individual human being in Hebrew. The author wishes to distinguish the one like a man in his visions (who probably stands for Israel) from the beasts who had preceded him (the empires of the Babylonians, Medes, Persians, and Greeks, vv. 3-7). The man-like figure comes on the clouds of heaven, an indication that something angelic is intended. To him the Ancient One, Israel's God, turns over peoples of every sort. Later it is the "holy ones" of that same God who receive the kingship (cf. vv. 18,

22). The author of Dn does not connect the angelic being as man with the concept of Messiah. The reference to kingship should provide a link, however (m^{e}shiah = anointed king). An eschatological appearance is intended, of one who is a man but who has a representative function both with respect to Israel and Israel's God. Later Jewish apocalypses like the *Book of Enoch* and *IV Ezra* featured in detail visions and revelations given to "my son," "my elect one," and "the man." The activities of Dn's "one like a son of man" are restrained in comparison. He is chiefly the recipient of everlasting dominion (v. 14) from the Ancient One (v. 13): Israel sovereign among the nations.

Revelation 1:5-8. Verse 4 has introduced the letters to the seven churches. John, the author, is God's servant (v. 1). The letters come as a message from the LORD (cf. Ex 3:14 LXX, for the unchanged *ho ōn* to render "who is") and from Jesus Christ (v. 5). "Faithful witness" is from Ps 89:38, referring to the moon in the sky, "first-born" from the same psalm at v. 28. The author leaves them in the nominative, not bringing them into line with the genitive of "Jesus Christ" as good style requires. Paul, whose epistles some commentators think Rev was familiar with, uses the phrase "first-born of many brothers" (Rom 8:29) and "first fruits of those who have fallen asleep" (1 Cor 15:20). Col 1:18 uses the same words as Rev, "first-born from the dead." "Ruler (LXX has *hypsēlon*, the highest) of the kings of earth" is, again, from Ps 89:28. The psalm is speaking of David. Rev modifies it to describe Christ as Lord of the living and the dead. The author has God freeing us by his blood in a past action; his continuing love is expressed by the present tense.

Verse 6a quotes Ex 19:6 and 7a quotes Dn 7:13, both in Theodotion's version rather than the LXX. Verses 5b and 6 are a doxology to Christ who is credited with making us "a royal nation of priests," a work of the LORD in Exodus. Mt 26:28 and Heb 10:19, like v. 4, have theologies of the saving character of Jesus' blood, as do 1 Pt 1:19 and 1 Jn 1:7. Theodotion describes the one like a son of man as coming "amid (*meta*) the clouds," LXX "on (*epi*)" them. Verse 7, after quoting one brief line from Dn 7:13, immediately turns to Zech 12:10 and 14, paraphrased and used selectively, for its picture of a sufferer who has been run through by a sword or spear and is bitterly lamented. Jn 19:37 likewise quotes a portion of v. 10, "They shall look upon him whom they have pierced." "So it is to be! Amen! (*nai, amēn*)" are words saying the same thing in Greek and Hebrew. "Amen" will become a proper name of Christ in 3:14 but here it is more the strong affirmation of the saving work of God that occurs in 2 Cor 1:20.

The separation of "God (*ho theos*)" from "the Almighty (*ho pantokratōr*)" which occurs in v. 8 is unusual in Rev (cf. 4:8; 11:17; 15:3; 16:7; 21:22.) The author will use the first and last letters of the alphabet to describe Jesus Christ again in 21:6 and 22:13. He repeats himself from v. 4, *ho ōn kai ho ēn kai ho erchomenos*, as if to enclose his christology within two brackets that declare Israel's faith in the everlasting nature of her God.

John 18:33-37. The fourth evangelist does here what he does throughout, namely hang a profound theological reflection on a peg of history. The peg is the fact derived from the tradition that Jesus was sentenced to death by Pilate. Despite the apparent trustworthiness of Jn in certain other details of the passion narrative, the fact of sentencing appears to be the sole *datum* behind this exchange. One other possible historical reminiscence is Pilate's question, "Are you the king of the Jews?" (v. 33) found in Mk's more primitive stratum at 15:2 and Lk 23:3. The title has no subsequent history in the church but it did have a nationalist political connotation, hence could have derived from historical tradition. Only Jn troubles to answer the charge that Jesus' kingship—the *basileia* that he preached and the term *basileus* that enthusiasts attributed to him—was non-political.

Verses 34, 36, and 37 are clearly Johannine developments. V. 35 contains the theme of "handing over" (*paredōkan*), so dear to the synoptics. In 34, Jn has Jesus distinguish between the Roman and the Jewish notions of kingship, the latter with its profoundly religious component. "My kingdom" (v. 36) does not accord fully with the synoptics' "kingdom of God." "Only those who belong to the truth can understand in what sense Jesus has a kingdom and is a king" (R. E. Brown).

Pilate declares Jesus not guilty (v. 38*b*; cf. 19:6) but inexplicably hands him over to be crucified (v. 16). Jn must be concluding thereby that Pilate is not "of the truth." Pilate's favorable view of Jesus in John is usually identified as part of the Christian apologia before the empire. He may, however, as Bultmann suggests, merely be employing Pilate as a symbol of the vacillating "world." At first he accepts Jesus when, paradoxically, the Johannine *Ioudaioi* do not, but ultimately the worldliness of power prevails.

YEAR C

ADVENT SEASON

FIRST SUNDAY OF ADVENT (C)

Jeremiah 33:14-16. This passage is from the final chapter of the
Book of Consolation (chs. 30-33) which spells out how things shall be
after the return from the exile in 538. It is part of a dynastic oracle
which builds on that of Nathan (1 Sm 7:11-16) and adds the notion
of perpetual sacrifice by a Levitical priesthood (v. 18). Today's
reading with which the complete passage (vv. 14-26) opens is the
rephrasing, by a postexilic author, of Jer 23:5-6 (cf. page 231.) There
the prophet was playing on the throne name of Zedekiah (598-87),
meaning "The LORD is righteous," by promising a wise Davidic king
in time to come who would fittingly be called, "The LORD our
justice" (*YHWH ṣidhk^enu*). In the original oracle the predicted king
was the subject of such attribution. Here the subject is Judah and
Jerusalem (v. 16). The "just shoot" (*ṣemaḥ ṣaddiḳ, ṣ^edaḳah*) of the
two passages (23:5; 33:15) resembles Is 11:1, which describes a green
shoot (*ḥoṭer*) and bud (or "branch," *neṣer*) sprouting from the stump
and root of Jesse.

The endowments of such a sovereign are listed in Is 11:2-5. His
preeminent justice in judging described there (vv. 3b-5) is a theme
developed at length in Ps 72:1-4, 12ff.

1 Thessalonians 3:12—4:2. This prayer of Paul for abounding
mutual love asks for hearts that are blameless and holy (*amemptous
en hagiōsynē*) before God at the *parousia* of Christ "with all his
holy ones." The last phrase is doubtless an echo of the one describing
those who accompany the son of man in Daniel's vision (cf. Dn 7:18,
21, 25), the faithful Jews in the Maccabean revolt. Paul makes his
love for his converts the norm for theirs (v. 12) as is his frequent
practice. They have learned from him how to please God (4:1); they
must do so yet more. His "instructions" of v. 2 mean strict orders in
ordinary Greek but here they stand for Paul's preaching.

Luke 21:25-28, 34-36. Luke's apocalyptic discourse parallels Mk
13:24-26 and Mt 24:29-30 in vv. 25-26. Verse 28 is special to him. He
omits the falling of the stars from heaven found in the other two,
speaking instead of signs in "the sun, the moon, and the stars"
(v. 25). Is 13:10 seems to be the source of cosmic disturbance for all

three synoptics. Ps 65:8 provides Luke, uniquely, with his image of the roaring sea and the waves. The fright seems to derive from v. 9 of the psalm, where "dwellers at the earth's ends," and not Judaea only, are in fear. Lampe suggests that the "powers in the heavens," i.e., the stars, are the *astra* of Is 34:4 in LXX—a "host" that shall wither away, in the Hebrew.

The climax of the passage occurs after the signs of v. 25, with the coming of the Danielic son of man "in a cloud" (Mk: "in clouds"), resembling Theodotion's "with clouds." Mt has "on clouds," following LXX. The singular "cloud" in Luke may be the middle member of a series of three, in which the usage as to number occurs in the transfiguration (9:35) and ascension (Ac 1:9) accounts as well. Luke omits the apocalyptic detail of the angels sent out to gather the elect from the four winds and puts in its place a word of comfort about the certainty of impending deliverance (*apolytrōsis*, v. 28).

Again, Lk's conclusion to the discourse is special to him in its present form. It probably draws on Mk's exhortation to watchfulness (13:33-37) without including its parable. Such a parable has already been used by Lk in a form he might have deemed sufficient (12:35-40). Is 24:18 probably lies behind Lk's image of a self-indulgent people caught in a trap (v. 34).

SECOND SUNDAY OF ADVENT

Baruch 5:1-9. A poem of consolation for Jerusalem and her captive children runs from 4:5 to 5:9, coming after another poem characteristic of the later sapiential school which equates wisdom with the Torah (3:9—4:4). It is impossible to date the one from which today's pericope comes. Most choose the Maccabean period as that in which the whole collection was composed. (The prayer of 1:15—3:8 derives strongly from Dan 9:4-19; Belshazzar is made Nebuchadnezzar's son in both books). Clearly the catastrophes of a later time are being described as if they took place in the days of Jeremiah's well known secretary Baruch. Some have even opted for the period after the sack of Jerusalem in 70, the two Persian kings being thought code names for the father and son Vespasian and Titus. Thus, submission to Rome (the "nation from afar" of 4:15?), in the interests of peace, may be the course of action counseled in 1:12: "That we may live under the protective shadow of Nebuchadnezzar . . . and . . . Belshazzar, his son, and serve them long, finding favor in their sight." If so, however, the detail of sacrifice on "the altar of the LORD our God" (v. 10) is an anachronism.

The sins of Israel are the cause of God's destructive wrath (4:5-13) but he promises his deliverance (vv. 18, 21, 27, 29). Jerusalem is told to look to the east for liberation (vv. 36f.), a reconstruction of the events of 538 B.C. The latter happenings pervade the remainder of the poem (5:1-9), since its details depend heavily on Is 35:1-2; 40: 4; 49:22-23. Jerusalem is to dress in her finest, no longer in the clothes of mourning. Her children were once led off captive on foot but now they come back borne on thrones. Ps Sol 11:2-7, probably from A.D. 1st c., contains phrases in common with this portion of Baruch: "Stand on the height, O Jerusalem, and behold your children,/ From the East and the West, gathered together by the LORD;/ . . . High mountains has he made as a plain for them . . . / Every sweet-smelling tree God caused to spring up for them . . . / Put on, O Jerusalem, your glorious garments; make ready your holy robe."

The whole poem is an exhortation to hope. The Roman liturgy uses this deuterocanonical book in Advent with a view to the song of Zechariah in Lk 1, the east as the provenance of Matthew's astrologers (2:1) and the star at its rising (v. 3), all portents of joy for Jerusalem.

Philippians 1:4-6, 8-11. Verses 3-11 are the prayer of thanksgiving, familiar from other epistles, with which Paul sets the tone of what is to follow by reviewing recent happenings—often the deeds of the recipients of the epistle—for which he is grateful to God. He says he prays constantly (*pantote*) and joyfully (*meta charas*) for the Philippians (v. 4) because of the way they promote the gospel in partnership with him (v. 5). The *koinōnia* spoken of may be either financial or by way of fellowship; it probably connotes both. Later in this letter the apostle will mention Epaphroditus whom the Philippians have sent to take care of his needs (2:25). Elsewhere, he writes of the unique generosity of this Macedonian community in supporting him (4:15-16), and his willing acceptance of that support (2 Cor 11:9). Since he constantly underscores his fiscal independence in his dealings with the other churches, the Philippian case must be an exception in his mind: not "support" so much as taking part in a common enterprise.

NAB renders v. 3 as though the remembrance (*mneia*) is Paul's of the Philippians but the *hymōn* that modifies it could just as well be subjective as objective, i.e., their keeping him in mind.

The "first day" of v. 5 is that of the Philippians' initial coming to believe and is contrasted with the "day of Christ Jesus" (v. 6), the hoped-for consummation of faith.

It is unclear which imprisonment Paul refers to in vv. 7, 13f., and 17. Ephesus and Caesarea both had praetorian guards (cf. v. 13), like the traditional favorite, Rome. Whatever the case, he writes of his lively hope that he will be rejoined to the Philippians (vv. 8, 26). He prays for their growth in *agapē* accompanied by understanding (*epignōsis*) and insight (*aisthēsis*) so that they may value the things that matter (v. 10), again *eis hēmeran Christou*, "up to the day of Christ." The eschatological assize is never far from Paul's thoughts. He wishes to find his converts laden with the fruit of justice when that day comes, with God's glory and praise as necessary concomitants.

Luke 3:1-6. The third evangelist is alone in setting his gospel in the context of contemporary events. His dating by Tiberius' fifteenth year makes it A.D. 28-29. Pilate was *praefectus*—later the title was changed to *procurator*—from 26 to 36. The Galilean Herod is Antipas, a half-brother to Herod Philip. Both are sons of Herod the Great. "Tetrarch" is a title that once designated rule over the fourth part of a kingdom but it was not so in this case. The empire divided Palestine in A.D. 6, ten years after the old king's death, into three parts: Galilee and Perea (east of the Jordan and south of the lake), the area well east of the lake designated "Ituraea and Trachonitis" by Lk, and the praefecture of Judaea under a Roman of equestrian rank who looked to a senatorial legate in Syria as his superior. Historical sources confirm all this but are silent on any Lysanias of Abilene (west of Damascus, lying between Ituraea to the west and Trachonitis to the east). A century before, that territory had had a king so named; this may be another Lysanias.

There was no "priesthood of Annas and Caiaphas" but the former (A.D. 6-15), father-in-law to the latter (A.D. 18-36), continued to wield such influence that Lk's phrasing is pardonable.

John's preaching is in the prophetic mold (cf. Jer 1:2.) He calls for reform of life and proposes an immersion in water as the sign of repentance. Lk seems to follow Mk in his quotation of Is 40:3, lengthening it to include vv. 4-5. This fits in with his universal concern ("all mankind"); perhaps "the entire region of the Jordan" (v. 3) is a similar trace. For Lk as for the other synoptists John is the forerunner of Jesus, in a christological pattern they all find important.

THIRD SUNDAY OF ADVENT (C)

Zephaniah 3:14-18. This book of prophecy dates to the closing years of the 7th c. Its author is much influenced by Amos and Isaiah. The first two chapters speak of the destruction of all mankind (1:2-18) and, specifically, judgment on the heathen nations (2:1-15). The third chapter holds out hope for a righteous remnant, "a people humble and lowly" (3:12). The concluding verses of the oracle, which make up the bulk of today's reading, are thought to be by another hand than Zephaniah's. They celebrate the LORD's presence in Israel's midst and call for rejoicing; the sentiments are very much in the mold of Second-Isaiah and various enthronement psalms. The joyous conclusion to the book, probably derived from the period of the restoration (6th-5th c.), serves the purposes of an Advent liturgy admirably, however little it may accord with the somber note struck by the earlier prophetic oracles.

Philippians 4:4-7. This reading as employed in the Latin *introit* provides the familiar title, "Gaudete Sunday." In Greek the Pauline injunction to rejoice is LXX's eschatological greeting, *Chairete Kyriǭ*. Earlier (v. 1) Paul has called the Philippian community his joy and his crown. He enjoins its members to display their *epieikes*, unselfishness ("magnanimity," NAB; "tolerance," JB; "forbearance RSV; *modestia vestra*, ineradicably, to generations brought up on the Vulgate). It is the one sure sign that the Lord Jesus is (or draws; the Greek has no verb) near—again, a reference to the final age.

Joy and rejoicing are recurrent themes in this epistle (cf. 1:18f.; 2:17f., 28; 3:1; 4:10.) Verse 6 proposes that the prayer of gratitude (*eucharistias*) be offered to God as an antidote to anxiety. Paul expresses the latter notion by using the verb *merimnate*, the one employed with reference to concern over clothing (Mt 6:28), worry about what to say when handed over to give witness (Mt 10:19), and anxiety about the numerous details of housekeeping (Lk 10:41). Presenting one's needs to God in prayer will bring peace, says Paul. The incomprehensible nature of God's peace is the fact that it is bestowed in the midst of difficulties. It is given "in Christ Jesus," that is, in the mystery of our salvation through his cross and resurrection.

Luke 3:10-18. Verses 10-14 are not to be found in the other evangelists' accounts of the preaching of John. They immediately remind the reader of the picture of sharing in the Jerusalem community in early Acts. The two coats (*chitōnas*) of v. 11 may depend on the *logion* of Mt 5:40 which uses the same word along with *himation*, the outer garment proposed as the sign of more generous giving. (Lk preserves the Matthean gesture of divesting in 6:29 but in reverse order: coat-shirt rather than shirt-coat.) Tobit 4:16 may be the source for both. The tender conscience of the *telonēs* Zacchaeus reported in 19:8 is the standard proposed in v. 13, just as the *strateuomenoi* of v. 14—not necessarily Roman soldiers, probably Herodian—are enjoined to conduct themselves like the God-fearer Cornelius (Ac 10:1ff.)

Mk's "one more powerful than I" (7:1) is made explicit by Lk in v. 15. He spells out the mood of popular anticipation somewhat as John does in 1:20f. This may be a polemic against a still flourishing sect of baptizers, though not necessarily so (cf. Ac 18:25 for John's baptism as the only one known to Apollos despite his being "instructed in the new way of the Lord.") Josephus' reference to the preaching and the execution of John (*Antiquities* 18. 116-19) shows how influential he was. All four evangelists place Jesus above him as a result of their faith conviction, but whether in terms of a direct apologetic is hard to say. Verse 16 is a conflation of Marcan and Q elements (Mk 1:7f.; Mt 3:11), v. 17 is from Q (Mt 3:12). The theme of the purification of Israel by the refiner's fire occurs in Mal 3:2f., of stubble in a blazing oven 3:19 (Massoretic text, 4:1).

The final verse, 18, is a summary proper to Lk. He has John preaching good news to the people (*euēggelizeto ton laon*), an indication of his desire to associate the Baptizer with the new age (cf. 16:16.) At the same time, Lk notes John's imprisonment at this point, unlike Mk (6:17f.) and Mt (14:3f.), to clear the stage for the appearance of Jesus. Conzelmann has called attention to Lk's epochal scheme (cf. Ac 10:37; 13:24f.) in which he puts the activity of John in the age of the prophets (*The Theology of St. Luke*, pp. 22-27). The "centre of history" is the age of Jesus' preaching. It takes place largely in Galilee, Jerusalem being the scene of the inauguration of the third age of world history (Lk 24:47ff.; Ac 1:1-11). Lk in 24:6 alters Mk 16:7 = Mt 28:7 to make Galilee the scene of a former prophecy of Jesus, not the geographic center of the new age as Mk does. Cf. Conzelmann, pp. 202-06. Lk will reintroduce John into his narrative at 7:18, but his summary at vv. 29f. tends to support Conzelmann's contention that, despite Jesus' lavish praise of John, Lk means to situate him in the former epoch rather than "*die Mitte der Zeit*," the central age.

FOURTH SUNDAY OF ADVENT (C)

Micah 5:1-4. This 8th-c. prophet was active in the reigns of Ahaz (733-21 B.C.) and Hezekiah (720-693). Only the first three chapters of the book are thought to be authentically his. Chapters 4 and 5 date to the exile and the postexilic period; the same is true of part three (chs. 6 and 7), with the possible exception of 6:6—7:4 as genuinely Mican material. Today's passage seems to refer to the exile as past in speaking of the "giving up" of the people and the return of "the rest of his brothers" (v. 2) but reverts to the 8th c. in its mention of the Assyrian threat (vv. 4f.) The thrust of vv. 1-3 is in the direction of a restored monarchy of the line of David, an ancient family which had its origins in Bethlehem-Ephrathah. Ez 34:23f. and Am 9:11 contain similar promises of a restoration of the fallen house or "hut" (*sukkoth*) of David. The LORD will abandon Israel and Judah until a woman has borne such a ruler, says the oracle (v. 3).

The "seven shepherds" and "eight men of royal rank" are the bold defenders of Israel against Assyria, the numerical progression being a biblical device to show strength (cf. Am 1:3.)

The lectionary probably retains v. 4, which derives from the earlier period, because it has the word "shepherds" in common with the Davidic prophecy.

Matthew (2:6) employs the Micah prophecy in a form which is neither that of LXX nor the Massoretic text. The Bible has featured Bethlehem's insignificance in Judah, despite which a great principle of leadership emerges from it. Mt reads quite the opposite: "You . . . are by no means the least" (v. 6). Stendahl shows in *The School of St. Matthew* that this text is one of eleven "formula quotations" which adapts biblical material in the *pesher* or interpretative tradition, used also by the Qumrân sect (cf. pp. 99f.) The concluding phrase in v. 6, "who is to shepherd my people Israel," is added from 2 Sm 5:2 (LXX), although v. 3 of Micah suggests the same idea in other words: "he shall . . . shepherd his flock by the strength of the LORD." Matthew's interpretation of the Micah text clearly has a specific object, namely to point out the fulfillment in Christ. He is not at all deterred from putting such a reading in the mouths of "all the chief priests and the scribes of the people" since he is convinced of the truth of the interpretation.

Hebrews 10:5-10. The author of Hebrews quotes Ps 40:7-9*a* in LXX (39) which reads, "but ears you readied for me" (v. 7), changing it to "a body you have prepared for me" as better suited to his purpose. There is very small possibility of a textual error: *sōma* in place of *ōtia* (one Syriac MS has the marginal correction *ōta*); nor is the suggestion of synecdoche helpful here, i.e., the whole substituted for the part. It seems a clear case of alteration in the *pesher* tradition. The verb *eudokēsas*, "gave [you] no pleasure" (Hebrews) in place of *ēthelēsas*, "you did not will" (LXX) is a minor matter; the variant reading *ezētēsas* occurs in the MS tradition of both Pss and Heb. The psalmist has declared himself ready to do God's will in preference to all blood sacrifices and Heb attributes the sentiment to Jesus in the flesh. The "book" is either Torah or the whole collection (*Tanak*, an acronym for *Torah, nebhiim, ketubhim*). All Scripture speaks of Jesus for him.

Verse 8 is a rearrangement of Ps 40:7 with an eye to 1 Sm 15:22, naming the four main classes of Levitical offerings as the psalm verse does. Verse 9*a* is from Ps 40:8f. and declares the obedience of the man Jesus to be preferable to temple sacrifice. In its reading of Jer 31:31ff. (9*b*) it is less nuanced than Paul in Romans (9:3-6; 11:1f., 14, 32)) bearing a closer resemblance to his "new covenant" in 2 Cor 3:6. The author of Hebrews is quite convinced that Christ has taken away (*anairei*, v. 9) the first covenant and established the second by his blood (cf. 9:15-28.) In 10:19, 29 the effective agent of redemption is Christ's blood. Here (v. 10) it is his body, an echo of the *sōma*, of v. 5 which is at the same time a Hebraic means of designating his entire person.

Luke 1:39-45. This pericope follows immediately that employed as the gospel in the feast of the Immaculate Conception, p. 393. It is a part of the longer reading proposed for the feast of the Assumption (Lk 1:39-56). In Lk's theology, Jesus is "Lord" from before his birth (1:43). The infancy and boyhood narratives of the first two chapters indicate what Jesus will become through what he already is. When he passes through death to glory and is made Lord and Messiah he will be no other than he was proclaimed to be at the beginning.

The story of the meeting of Mary and Elizabeth is part of Lk's John-Jesus diptych, the Baptist being identified as a prophet and witness to Jesus from before his birth. Lk may have in mind the oracle of Gn 25:23 in which the elder twin in Rebekah's womb, Esau, is fated to serve Jacob, the younger.

The "hill country" (*oreinē*) of Judah is indeterminate (v. 39). Ain Karem is a centuries-later attribution of no special merit except for its natural beauty. The baby's leaping in Elizabeth's womb may derive from the call of Jeremiah: "Before I called you in the womb I knew you, / before you were born I dedicated you, / a prophet to the nations I appointed you" (Jer 1:5). The spirit of prophecy, the Holy Spirit, is active throughout the Lucan account. Elizabeth acts the prophetess in praising the faith of Mary, her younger kinswoman (v. 45).

CHRISTMAS SEASON

CHRISTMAS—MASS AT MIDNIGHT (C)

Isaiah 9:1-6; Titus 2:11-14; Luke 2:1-14. See pp. 14ff.

SUNDAY IN THE OCTAVE OF CHRISTMAS (C)
Holy Family

Sirach 3:3-7, 14-17; Colossians 3:12-21; Matthew 2:13-15, 19-23. See pp. 18ff.

SOLEMNITY OF MARY, MOTHER OF GOD (C)
(January 1—Octave of Christmas)

Numbers 6:22-27; Galatians 4:4-7; Luke 2:16-21. See pp. 20ff.

EPIPHANY (C)

Isaiah 60:1-6; Ephesians 3:2-3, 5-6; Matthew 2:1-12. See pp. 23f.

BAPTISM OF THE LORD (C)

Isaiah 42:1-4, 6-7; Acts 10:34-38. See pp. 25f.

Luke 3:15-16, 21-22. Lk is unique among the synoptics but resembles Jn (1:20, 25) in putting bluntly the question entertained inwardly by "all" as to whether John might be *ho Christos* (v. 15). Jn's use of the title is the same in this context; he alone of the evangelists uses *Messias* (at 1:41 and 4:25), translating it *Christos* each time. The Baptizer's response to direct inquiry in Lk, v. 16c, most closely resembles Mk 1:7. Verse 16d, "He will baptize you in the Holy Spirit and in fire," is verbally identical with Mt 3:11c. Lk then appends v. 17 from Q in a form identical with Mt 3:12 except for the smallest stylistic changes. His vv. 18-20 are proper to him, probably because he wishes to get John safely into prison (v. 20) before he brings Jesus onto the scene. Verse 18 constitutes a difficulty for Conzelmann's theory of a clean break in epochs between that of the law, the prophets, and John (16:16 is the critical verse) and that of God's kingdom as preached by Jesus, "the center of history." It is an embarrassment because Lk 3:18 has the Baptizer preaching good news (*euēggelizeto*) to the people, presumably the prerogative of Jesus in the new age.

Lk's "When all the people were baptized" (v. 21) is his own, and here Conzelmann is right in seeing him interested in closing the John chapter before opening the Jesus one. In the remainder of v. 21 he gives his edited version of Mk (1:9f.) and Q (Mt 3:16). Verse 22 follows Mk 10f. closely, adding only that the dove was "in bodily form" (*somatikǭ eidei*) and retaining Mk's direct address of the voice to Jesus. "On you my favor rests," rather than the Matthean, "My favor rests on him" (3:17).

The Q version of the Baptizer's ministry includes baptism with fire, not just the Holy Spirit, and interprets his preaching in terms of eschatological judgment (Mt 3:11f./Lk 3:16f.) For long Q has been thought to reflect the historical tradition of John's ministry better than Mk because of its supposed freedom from theological presuppositions. Mk's "historical Baptist," however, while reflecting the New Covenant pattern of Ez 26:24-28 (and IQS 3, 9), and showing the influence of the Elijah typology, is "only tangentially related to Mark's theological interests" (Parrott). This would indicate the greater historical reliability of Mk's account of John's preaching, which Jn confirms by his omission of the Lucan (Q) development of the theme of final judgment.

SUNDAYS OF THE YEAR

SECOND SUNDAY OF THE YEAR (C)

Isaiah 62:1-5. The entire chapter can be taken as a single poem in the collection known as Third-Isaiah (chs. 56-66; cf. commentary on Is 56:1-7, page 125.) These five verses may also be viewed as separate. The affinities with the poem that makes up ch. 60 are evident (cf. commentary on Is 60:1-6, page 23.) The similes of the dawn and a burning torch are complementary to the light images of 60:1-3, 5a. The "new name" of v. 2b has been given in 60:14—two of them, in fact. Ezekiel has likewise renamed the new Jerusalem, "The LORD is here" (48:35). The city is a crown and a diadem. It is also a "delight" (Heb. *Hephzibah*) and its land "espoused" (Heb. *Beulah*). The theme of marriage between the LORD and his virgin bride occurs in Hos 2:4-7; Jer 3:1, 8f.; Ez 16. Your "Builder" (*banai*) requires an emendation of the Massoretic text reading "your sons," since it is impossible in the context for Jerusalem to be espoused to her own offspring. God is a bridegroom (*ḥathan*) who takes joy in Zion his bride.

1 Corinthians 12:4-11. The Corinthian community is torn over "spiritual gifts" (*pneumatika*, v. 1, with *charismata* from v. 4 understood). Paul in this epistle supplies a radical criterion for discriminating among them: it is the spirit of God bearing witness to the lordship of Christ (vv. 3f.) In "holy spirit" (v. 4) alone can one acknowledge in speech that Jesus is Lord. Various other spirits are available, Paul intimates, to account for ecstatic utterances like the puzzling *anathēma Iēsous*, which Christians might cry out in the assembly while "resisting the trance of ecstasy they felt coming upon them" (Barrett).

Having dealt with the criterion for judging inspired, ecstatic speech, Paul moves on to a general discussion of gifts and persons. "One and the same spirit" (v. 11) is responsible for putting them all into operation in everyone (*en pasin*, v. 6), distributing them individually as he sees fit. His sole purpose is the "common good" (*pros to sympheron*, v. 7). The various "distributions" (*diaireseis*, vv. 4, 5, 6) are his doing. "Ministries" (*diakoniōn*, v. 5) are here probably any services, not ministerial functions; "works" (v. 6), the ways in which divine power is applied. A "manifestation" of the spirit is just that: *hē phanerōsis* (v. 7); one receives such a manifestation to put this gift of the spirit in the service of all.

Further gifts are a *logos* of wisdom and one of knowledge (v. 8). This gift of discourse in two situations varies more as to Paul's word use than in reality. The "faith" of v. 9 cannot be the saving *pistis* found in all believers but must be related to the special gift of 13:2 which can "move mountains," i.e., work miracles. "Healings" (v. 9) and "miracles" (v. 10) are given to different persons, just as one can utter *propheteia* (v. 10; intelligible speech in ch. 14), another, things said unintelligibly in tongues, and still another interpretation (*hermēneia*, v. 10) of what is thus uttered. "All these [gifts]" (*panta de tauta*, v. 11) have been given by the one spirit, not to divide the community but to bring it into unity through diversity.

John 2:1-12. The Cana miracle is the first of Jesus' signs (v. 11). Jn seems to forget his own count (cf. 4:54) unless he is using the word *semeia* in a discriminating sense that escapes us. Despite ingenious attempts by scholars like Boismard (*Du Baptème à Cana*, 1956) to plot a symbolic six-day week of Jesus' activity (cf. 1:29, 35, 43), there is a good likelihood that "on the third day" is primarily intended as the biblical designation of divine activity (cf. 4:43.) The sign is calculated to reveal Jesus' *doxa* so that his disciples may believe in him. Such is the announced purpose of the gospel (20:30f.) as it comes from the hand of the last redactor but one. Even with the working of this sign, it is not Jesus' "hour" (v. 4) as his raising up on the cross will be (19:27). The "woman" (*gynē*) addressed in this first sign anticipates the "woman" of the last sign (19:26). Jesus' question to his mother in v. 4, literally, "What to me and to you?" occurs in biblical Hebrew in just this form to express a difference between two —for Jn, her solicitude in human affairs and Jesus' intent in the divine dispensation. Operation thus at two levels is a favorite Johannine device.

Dodd has written eloquently of the six jars of ritual purification, not seven, signs of the old order, to be replaced by the wine of teaching, not water, in the new order. The levels of meaning intended by the evangelist are multiple here, as throughout.

THIRD SUNDAY OF THE YEAR (C)

(Third Sunday after Epiphany)

Nehemiah 8:2-4, 5-6, 8-10. The framers of the lectionary cannot have known of any special reasons for omitting v. 3 from public reading when they were at work on their task of selection. At that time, Vatican funds had been invested heavily in the development venture responsible for the Watergate complex (Vulgate, *porta aquarum*) on the Potomac. Public disclosures resulted in the Holy See's withdrawing its financial stake.

Unlike the modern situation, the open space before the Water Gate in Ezra's 4th c. witnessed the full disclosure of a document of record: the law in its Deuteronomic form. The "Chronicler" responsible for 1 and 2 Chr is the author of the two books of postexilic history known as Ezra and Nehemiah. The latter have had a very complex literary history, their contents having once formed a single book which became two recensions in the transmission process. Ezra is described as a scribe of the exiled people in Persia, possibly a court secretary for Jewish affairs, sent to Judah to promulgate an already existing law (Ezra 7:14, 25f.) His mission may be placed around 400 B.C. in the reign of Artaxerxes II, who came to the throne in 404. His chief responsibility in Judah was to enforce the prohibition of mixed marriages for Jews which had been in force since Zerubbabel's time (Ezra 9-10). The law promulgated in Neh 8 is not the Priestly Code, as scholars once thought, nor the entire Pentateuch (Wellhausen's view), but D or a combination of JED.

The old people wept for joy at the restoration of their people's great treasure, the law. The celebration of it at the end of the feast of Booths (modern *Simḥath Torah*; cf. Dt 31:11) is reported in vv. 8-12. A description of this autumn feast itself, which is Deuteronomic not Priestly, follows. The scene is one of joyous religious renewal after the repudiation of foreign wives, and a fitting penance for that offense, have been achieved.

Modern Christians do well to grasp the exultant spirit that marks the possession of Torah, even to this day. It is not a burden or a curse for the pious Jew but all that is liberative and restorative.

1 Corinthians 12:12-30. Paul teaches in this section that all in the church are a body and that the body is that of Christ (v. 27) who is its Lord (v. 3). The context of the passage is the dispute in Corinth over the possession of spiritual gifts. Paul engages in his elaborate figure of the diversity of parts in the human body, and their mutual dependence, to hammer home the lesson that not all can do everything. His rhetorical questions in vv. 29f. call for a negative answer, possibly as a refutation of certain Corinthian "spirituals" who are claiming omnicompetence. No one can do anything except in the one spirit (v. 13) who, in the sign of baptism, made many diverse types to be one body of believers. Differences remain in the Corinthian church ("Jew," "Greek," "slave," "free") but they must now contribute to a higher unity, as in the functioning of parts of a body. Their having been "given to drink of the one spirit" (v. 13) requires this.

The body figure is an old one in rhetoric (cf. Plato, *Protagoras* 330A.) "And so it is with Christ" (v. 12*b*) contains a surprising leap, collapsing the argument of v. 27. All who are "in Christ" are members of the body which has its purpose and direction from him. Verses 14-20 spell out the necessity of distinction of function, while vv. 21-25 stress complementarity with an excursus into the less important (lit. "weaker," v. 22) and less presentable (vv. 23f.) parts— the latter the occasion for a rationale of clothing (v. 23). In v. 26 St. Paul deserts his figure for the reality of members as actual people who suffer, are honored, and rejoice.

Having made his case for the essential nature of supportive contrariety, the apostle then deals with offices: the big three first, which deal with the all-important ministry of the word. "Apostles" is impossible to identify specifically from other Pauline usage beyond itinerant proclaimers, while "prophets" and "teachers" are stable members of local communities. Perhaps prophets are the bearers of revelation as contrasted with teachers who spell out its implications for Christian life. In modern parlance these would be, respectively, preachers and theologians. NAB attributes the gifts of second rank to persons but in Paul they are the gifts themselves: "miracles," "gifts of healing," "support," "administrative direction," "kinds of tongues." The third and fourth resemble what later emerged as the offices of deacon and bishop, both of them local ministries in contrast to the traveling ministries of apostles. Barrett notes that "Gifts of a self-assertive kind, *direction* and *tongues*, which appear to have suited the Corinthian taste, are placed at the end of the list."

As rhetoric Paul's presentation is marked by small inconsistencies and *non sequiturs*. As pastoral counsel to a troubled church it is impeccable.

Luke 1:1-4; 4:14-21. The identity of Theophilus (v. 3; cf. 1:1) is unknown. He is more likely to have been the actual patron of Luke's two-volume work than an anonymous "lover of God" (something like the "gentle reader" of nineteenth-century fiction). The high-born title of address, *kratiste*, accords with the presumption of wealth. The first four verses are a classical rhetorical prologue announcing the purpose of the entire work, probably with the opening verses of Acts a simple reminder of the flow of the narrative. The "fulfillment" of v. 1 may mean no more than that the events took place but the accomplishment of divine promise is also possible, especially in light of chs. 1-2. The stress in "eye-witnesses and ministers of the word" (*autoptai kai hypēretai*, v. 2) is on the transmission of apostolic testimony; the latter term connotes official church designation of some sort (cf. 4:20; Ac 26:16; it is the gospel word for the apprehenders of Jesus, Jn 18:3, and the retinue of a household, Mt 26:58). Lk has investigated matters carefully (*akribōs*) from the beginning (*anōthen*), namely the progress of God's word from Jerusalem—for him the place of origin of the revelation made in Jesus Christ (cf. Lk 1:5-23)—to Rome (cf. Ac 28:14). Theophilus has probably been "instructed" (*katēchēthēs*) in these matters previously rather than merely informed. In any case, the *asphaleia* provided in the writing to follow, which NAB translates adjectivally as "reliable" (NEB, "authentic knowledge"; 1941 CCD, "certainty"; RSV, "truth"), is intended to confirm Theophilus in his present state of knowledge. The testimonies of the next two chapters in particular "spring from and seek to elicit shouts of joy and hymns of praise on the part of the devout community, which knows itself dependent on God's saving power. The term *proof* is alien to that milieu" (Minear).

Lk effects the transition from the first of his epochs, the time of the law and the prophets up to John, to the second, the ministry of Jesus, in the sermon in the synagogue in Nazareth (4:16-30). "Their" synagogues (v. 15) conveys Lk's psychic distance from the Palestinian reality, whereas the popular acceptance of Jesus in Galilee comes from the tradition. Lk's word-picture of a postexilic synagogue is accurate—a layman with something to say being asked to comment on a reading from Scripture—but its position as programmatic for all that Jesus does (cf. Mk 6, Lk's source) is all-important. Kee calls the sermon and its immediate sequel Janus-like: "The passage looks back to the Old Testament, whose prophecies are seen as being fulfilled in Jesus, and it looks forward to the events of Jesus' ministry, in which the fulfillment itself takes place."

Is 61:1-2, the passage chosen to be read, is one of the great eschatological poems of the Hebrew collection. The speaker, Third-Isaiah, describes himself as anointed for his prophetic mission of announcing glad tidings to the poor. Lk 3:21f. has described just such a figurative anointing of Jesus by the Spirit. For Luke, all that the Isaian author has proposed as the work of the final age, Jesus will do. Of special importance is the concluding phrase "a year of favor from the Lord" (v. 19) because it fits in so well with Lk's periodization-scheme. History unfolds for him in accord with that divine plan which the prophetic scroll announces. Lk links up prophecy and fulfillment in v. 21 in the person and ministry of Jesus.

FOURTH SUNDAY OF THE YEAR (C)

(Fourth Sunday after Epiphany)

Jeremiah 1:4-5, 17-19. We know nothing of the circumstances of Jeremiah's upbringing in a priestly family in Anathoth of the land of Benjamin (1:1). We may presume that it was pious. He never married, according to 16:1-4, as if he had some intimation of disaster "in this place" too great for a wife and children, to bear. He was probably somewhat younger than King Josiah who came to the throne as an eight-year-old boy in 640. The incident of his call as a prophet occurred in the thirteenth year of Josiah's reign (v. 2), hence 628. The almost fifty years of King Asshurbanapal on Assyria's throne were drawing to a close, to yield to a neo-Babylonian dynasty. Nineveh would be destroyed in 612 and the Assyrian empire ended by Nebupolassar in 606. Nebuchadnezzar, who figured so prominently in Jeremiah's book of prophecy, came to rule in Babylonia in 604. Jeremiah lived on until that sovereign's conquest of Jerusalem (587), following which he was carried off to Egypt despite his strong protest (43:7f.)

Jeremiah's protest that he was too young to prophesy (v. 6) was probably compounded by fear of the "awful cost of prophetic office" (Bright). The LORD dismissed his scruples (vv. 7f.), telling the young priest that he had made him "a fortified city,/ A pillar of iron, a wall of brass, against the whole land" (v. 18). Despite these assurances, Jeremiah never seemed fully at ease in the prophet's role. In part this was because of the extreme distaste he felt for the company of prophets who, as a class, soothed with soft words those who despised the word of the LORD (cf. 23:16-22.) He was conscious, however, of a divine call that went back to before the time of his birth and he accepted it. He had no course but to answer it and so, all his life long, he spoke the word which the LORD had spoken to him (cf. 23:21.)

1 Corinthians 12:31—13:13. The Corinthians put a high value on speaking in tongues while Paul regarded it as one of the lowest of the gifts. Prophecy and teaching ranked well ahead of it, following the norm of service to the community. But now the Apostle comes to the way "which surpasses all the others" (*kath' hyperbolēn*, v. 31), the way of *agapē*. Since the introduction of ch. 13 by v. 31*b* is awkward and the transition between v. 31*a* and 14:1 smooth, some have come to think ch. 13 an independent unit. A few scholars attribute authorship to another hand, but most suppose it to have been composed by Paul and inserted here because so apposite to the situation at Corinth. Verse 14:1 seems to set love apart from the "spiritual gifts" (*ta pneumatika*), as if every Christian should have it no matter how individuals might otherwise be endowed.

Verses 1-3 contrast love with other gifts and attitudes; vv. 4-8*a* describe it largely but not entirely by the *via negationis*; vv. 8*b*-13 contrast love in its future fullness with its present immature and partial state. In v. 1 St. Paul reverts to the question in the previous chapter of speaking in tongues, which he can do well (14:18) but is indifferent to. The "tongues of angels" perhaps describes such unintelligible speech. "Gong" (lit. "brass" or "copper") and "cymbal" may have once referred to pagan worship but have become by Paul's time a figure for meaningless noise. Prophecy, knowledge, and the faith that works miracles (v. 2) are great gifts but they can be equally hollow if they are not exercised in love. "Knowing all mysteries" is probably a way to describe grasping the church's eschatological situation, just as giving relief to the poor and practicing self-immolation, perhaps with a view to Dan 3, are colorful figures for religious zeal. Without love, all endowments and activities come to naught.

The description of love turns out to be not something abstract but the concrete behavior of a person who loves (vv. 4-7). "Love's forbearance" of v. 7 is, literally, "love supports (*stegei*) all things." This may be related to the saying of Simeon the Just in *Pirqe Aboth* 2, 1 that the world is supported by three things: Torah, temple-worship, and the doing of kindnesses (*gemiloth = agapē*?) Only God's love is indefectible, yet Paul describes it as it is found in humanity. It never fails (lit. "falls," v. 8) in the sense that perseverance under the Spirit's guidance brings with it the dependability of God himself.

Prophecies, knowledge, and tongues (vv. 8f.) are all imperfect revelations of God. When he comes they go, the imperfect yielding to the perfect (v. 10). Our knowledge of him now is indirect (*en ainigmati*, v. 12), like all mirror-imagery. Paul thinks of our present state of God-knowledge as that of childhood, with adulthood to come, not as something already here as the Corinthians conceived it. As he knows us, we shall know him (v. 12). Love will last (v. 13) because, unlike faith and hope, it is the property of God himself.

Luke 4:21-30. Luke's source is Mk 6 (Lk 4:24 = Mk 6:4) but he places the incident at the beginning of Jesus' public activity instead of later on, as programmatic for his ministry. (See last week's commentary on vv. 14-21.) Lk describes the popular acceptance of Jesus in his hometown synagogue as favorable (vv. 21-22*a*), not merely a cause for wonderment (cf. Mk 6:2*b*.) The proverb and challenge of v. 23 are peculiarly Lukan. He answers the opposition which Jesus aroused by having him cite God's deeds to non-Israelites through Elijah and Elisha (vv. 25ff.; cf. 1 Kgs 17:8-16 and 2 Kgs 5:1-14.) This implicit criticism of Israel's lack of faith angers his audience, whose members threaten violence. A walk from the center of Nazareth to the nearest "brow of the hill on which it was built" should have cooled the indignation of the townsfolk—the distance is about a mile—but Lk's intent is theological. Thus early in his narrative he wishes to describe Jewish rejection of Jesus, as a prelude to Gentile acceptance in "a year of favor from the LORD" (v. 19).

Verse 31 picks up from 14f. and is parallel to Mk 1:21. Lk has indicated in vv. 16-30 how his story will come out, hence he can proceed to the actual beginnings of Jesus' Galilean ministry.

FIFTH SUNDAY OF THE YEAR (C)

(Fifth Sunday after Epiphany)

Isaiah 6:1-2, 3-8. Last week featured the call of Jeremiah to the prophet's office, this week that of Isaiah more than a century earlier. The death date of King Uzziah of Judah was 742. Isaiah expresses an initial reluctance to serve, on the ground of being unfit in speech (v. 5). His "wickedness" and "sin" are ritually purged away by a glowing coal from the temple altar (vv. 6f.) The proclaimer of the gospel in the Roman rite prays for fitness of speech in Isaian terms: *Munda cor meum, ac labia mea, omnipotens Deus, qui labia Isaiae prophetae calculo mundasti ignito . . .*

Presumably the oracles of the first five chapters were written down after this majestic, inaugural vision. It is described as if taking place in the temple (v. 1), the house of the Holy One of Israel. The LORD is seated on a throne like an Oriental king. Seraphim (lit. "burning ones") do not appear elsewhere in the Bible. Their winged condition and their sacred song reveal them as angelic creatures in the heavenly court. The incense-smoke and the shaking edifice are intended to convey the awesomeness of the Sinai theophany (cf. Ex 40:34.) The threefold chant of the seraphim highlights the LORD's perfection of holiness (i.e., separateness) and the title "LORD of hosts" his character as warrior, from the days when the Ark accompanied Israel's armies into battle.

One of the seraphim flies from the golden altar of perfumes (cf. 1 Kgs 6:20f.; 7:48; 2 Chr 26:16) in front of the sanctuary (*debhir*), the only altar inside the temple, putting an ember to the prophet's mouth. Thus cleansed, he is in a condition of readiness to do the LORD's bidding as his spokesman (v. 8). That Isaiah experienced the vision while the majestic temple liturgy was in progress is a *Sitz im Leben des Propheten* that cannot be verified. It is safer to assert merely that the prophet-to-be framed his terrifying vision of the King (v. 5; cf. Ex 33:20) in his earthly dwelling place.

This commission of Isaiah occurs as the prelude to the Immanuel prophecies (6:1-12:6) which touched on the events of the Aram-Ephraim crisis of 735-33 (cf. 1 Kgs 15:29; 16:19) in which Ahaz disregarded Isaiah's advice and sought an alliance with Tiglath-pileser III of Assyria.

1 Corinthians 15:1-11. St. Paul inserts a traditional reading of the kerygma ("I handed on to you what I myself received," v. 3) for the benefit of his innovating Corinthians, as if to link them up with the churches of Damascus and Antioch in which he had confirmed the tradition he received by revelation (cf. Gal 1:12.) His introductory terms *parelabon* and *paredōka* in v. 3 are equivalent to the Hebrew rabbinical terms *qibbel min* and *masar l*^{e}. What follows is marked by numerous non-Pauline words, as Seeberg pointed out in 1903. Among them are the Greek for: "for our sins," "he was raised," "on the third day," and "the Twelve." All of these are terms which the synoptics incorporated from the tradition. Paul cites anew the gospel he has preached (v. 1) lest the Corinthians believe "in vain" (*eikē*, v. 2). Their faith would be purposeless if it did not include the conviction that Christ was raised up so that the dead might be raised up in turn (vv. 15f.) The conviction of the Corinthian spirituals that they were already sufficiently risen in baptism, hence had no need to be raised up at the *parousia*, elicits the traditional account of the appearances of the Risen One to the appointed witnesses.

Important to observe in the earliest written account we have of the appearances is the omission of any mention of the empty tomb (although cf. "he was buried," *etaphē*, v. 4), of appearances to the women, and of an angelophany. Paul's account uses the divine passive, *egēgertai*, which Mk, the next one to write, will also employ ("he has been raised up," *ēgerthē*, 16:6). All the linguistic evidence points to a creedal formula worked up by a Hellenistic Jewish community, perhaps at Damascus, from a tradition that goes back to the earliest Aramaic-speaking church. It consists in vv. 3b-6a, 6b seemingly being Paul's editorial comment. The witnesses are in two groups of three: Cephas, the Twelve, 500 brothers; then James, all the apostles, and Paul. Throughout, the verb used is *ōphthē*, "was seen" (vv. 5, 6, 7, 8). This, coupled with Paul's verb *apokalyptein* in Gal 1:16 ("[God] chose to reveal his Son to me") has led to the conclusion that the kerygma describes the disclosure by God of the eschatologically resurrected *Christos*.

Fuller's theory that the first three appearances (vv. 5-6a) were concerned with the church as eschatological community and the second three (vv. 7-8) with the inauguration of the apostolic mission of the church has not found immediate favor (cf. Brown, Donfried, *et al.*, *Peter in the New Testament*, pp. 34f.) There is nothing geographical about the appearances, although we may connect Cephas and the Twelve with Galilee; the 500, James, and the apostles with Jerusalem; and Paul with the road to Damascus. They are spread over at least three years, lending support to the notion of resurrection and ascension as a single mystery separated only by Lk for narrative purposes (cf. Ac 1:3, 9.)

Paul describes his own call to witness the risen Christ under the figure of a miscarriage (*ektrōmati*, v. 8). In v. 9 he reports the only sin he ever seems conscious of, persecuting God's church (cf. Gal 1:13; with Stendahl we take his graphic account of human weakness in Rom 7:15-25 to be non-autobiographical). Besides Paul's having seen Christ last of all (v. 8), he calls himself the least of the apostles even though he has worked harder than any of them (vv. 9, 10). This self-deprecation is possible only because he is so confident of his status as an apostle (1 Cor 1:1; Gal 1:1, 15f.; 2:7f.) It is God's favor (*charis*, v. 10) that has achieved this role and subsequent evangelical activity in him. His concession in v. 11 that "I or they" may have brought the apostolic preaching to them supports the view that Cephas may also have preached in Corinth (cf. 1:12) or, if not that, emissaries from Cephas or James. Paul wishes to stress above all the harmony of the apostolic preaching and to eliminate claims of spiritual parentage as a cause of strife in the Corinthian church.

Luke 5:1-11. Luke places the call of Simon, James, and John in the setting of a miraculous catch, unlike the more prosaic accounts of the call of the first disciples in Mk (1:16-20) and Mt (4:18-22). He has already met Simon in the preceding chapter at the healing of his mother-in-law, a narrative that comes after the call in the other synoptics. The remarkable similarity of this account to Simon Peter's miraculous catch of fish in Jn 21:1-13, even to some identical vocabulary, has been observed. The two evangelists have preserved the same miracle story independently rather than borrowed from one another. Lk's account has undergone more development in certain details (nets almost breaking, v. 6; two boats almost sinking, v. 7), while in others (the enumeration of 153 fish) Jn's is more developed. It is impossible to settle whether the story first arose in Jesus' ministry or as a post-resurrection appearance. Inclining us toward the latter are the "O Lord" of v. 8 and Jesus' "Do not be afraid" of v. 10b (cf. Mt 28:10; Lk 24:37f.) If such is the case, then Lk acts here as Mt seems to do in 16:16*b*-19 by forming the Petrine dialogue from post-resurrectional material. That he has changed the locale is clear from v. 8, where Simon's kneeling and his "Leave me, Lord" are details that originally doubtless took place on land rather than in a boat.

Lk makes the abundant catch of fish a symbol of Simon's future catching of men, a prefiguring in Jesus' lifetime of the missionary activity of Peter in Acts. Simon has caught nothing by his own power during the night (a symbol of darkness, Lk 5:5). By day and in the power of Jesus this sinful man has an abundant catch. James and John will also catch men (v. 10) but, in directing the Lord's promise to Simon alone, Luke is preparing for the dominant role he will have in Acts.

SIXTH SUNDAY OF THE YEAR (C)

(Sixth Sunday after Epiphany)

Jeremiah 17:5-8. The contents of this chapter are a kind of editor's miscellany, including poetry and prose on sabbath observance (vv. 19-27, probably not from the prophet's own hand), against persecutors (vv. 14-18, and on true wisdom and the LORD who is its source (vv. 5-13). More specifically, the present pericope (vv. 5-8) is a bit of wisdom poetry very close in spirit to Psalm 1. Verses 9-10 reflect on the deceits of the human heart and v. 11 is a proverb on unjust acquisitions.

The great sin of "flesh" (*basar*) is that it trusts in men and not in God. This misplaced confidence makes it like a scrubby bush in the desert. Were humanity to trust in the Lord, the "source of living waters" (v. 13), its leaves would stay green in every season; fruit would adorn its branches even in time of drought.

1 Corinthians 15:12, 16-20. This continuation of last week's reading brings us to the reason why St. Paul has reviewed for his converts the gospel he preached to them when he was in Corinth. Some are saying that there is no resurrection of the dead (v. 12). They are not resisting it on the Sadducean principle (viz., that the five books of Moses, which alone they reckoned as scripture, did not teach it) or because of a Greek sense of horror at a notion of eternal life that would implicate the body. They are rejecting resurrection of the dead as future because they already experience it as present.

The Christian preaching, at least in the condensed form reported by Paul, has not incorporated a promise of individual resurrection or immortality as Greek promises of salvation did. The former is there by implication from the fact of the death and resurrection of Jesus Christ. As an anticipation of the eschatological reality for all the just, his resurrection made eminent sense in the Jewish circles where it had originated. In Corinth it needed to be spelled out, as Paul has recently learned to his woe. The preaching of Christ raised from the dead, a matter common to all the apostles (vv. 11f.), demands the implication of resurrection for all believers. The apostolic preaching would be pointless (v. 14) if, having proclaimed something about God's deed in Christ, it said nothing about what he meant to achieve in Christians. Paul's starting-point is that the Corinthians' present experience of risenness is illusory.

The "some of you" (v. 12) who hold this position may conceivably be believers in immortality, Greek-style, rather than in the Jewish reading of the mystery. Lietzmann, for example, held that Paul simply misread their fatith. A rereading of 4:8, however, reveals his scorn for their present state of satisfaction as already rich (*eploutēsate*) and reigning (*ebasileusate*). His charge against them is precisely that they "limit [their] hopes in Christ to this life only" (v. 19). The mentality of two Christians named Hymenaeus and Philetus is made explicit in 2 Tim 2:17f.: they "have gone far wide of the truth in saying that the resurrection has already taken place." Paul himself teaches new life in Christ as a resurrection in some sense (cf. Rom 6:5-11; 2 Cor 5:15; Gal 2:19f.; also Col 3:1-4.) In 1 Cor 15 he is dismayed that his strong figurative language has been taken literally and that his teaching on bodily resurrection has not been understood as *future*.

Verse 16 sums up the three verses omitted from the reading. If we had done the writing, we might have framed the argument in reverse: "If Christ was not raised, then the dead are not raised." Paul makes the center of gravity the resurrection of the dead. If that is not to happen, then Christ's resurrection "did not take place" in the sense that it was a pointless display of God's power. Paul's sole argument against his opponents is the absurdity of a God who has acted to no purpose.

He goes on to threaten the Corinthians with the practical consequences of their misconception. The faith on which they pride themselves as saving is worthless (*mataia*, v. 17) in that it does not remit their sins. It has been reposed in a risen Christ whose risenness does not ensure their own in the future. But there is no such risen Christ as that. Therefore their faith is misplaced; it is not saving. It leaves them still in a condition of sinfulness. Paul faces them with the hypothetical reality of sin's victory, not faith's victory. As if that were not enough, he taunts them with the lack of hope of rising which would be the present state of their dead (v. 18). He then faces them with the absolute wretchedness of their own condition in terms of their theology (v. 19). They are bearing the dying of Jesus in their bodies (cf. 2 Cor 4:10) without the prospect of the life of Jesus being revealed in them—at least in no lasting way that outlives this life.

Having taken the Corinthians to the brink of despair by his logic, Paul then snatches them back by proclaiming the true gospel. Christ *is* raised and precisely as "first fruits"—the early harvest which anticipates the raising up of all the dead (v. 20).

Note that Paul's argument does not make salvation depend on the historical fact of the resurrection but on right faith in what God has accomplished in this mystery.

Luke 6:17, 20-26. Luke's sermon is on the plain (v. 17), where the people remained behind while he selected his disciples in prayer on the mountain (v. 12; cf. Mk 3:13-19, where likewise the mountain is the place of revelation as to who his associates will be.) The "mountain" in Lk is a place where the people cannot come (cf. 9:37.) It is a place of communion with God, leading to the Mount of Olives (22:39); Mk and Mt situate his agony only at "a place called Gethsemane." The "level stretch" of Lk consequently attains a special character as the place of meeting with people. Jesus' disciples, Galileans, are described as accompanied by a large crowd from Judea and Jerusalem, Tyre and Sidon (v. 17). This may be a reiteration from 5:17 of the area covered by Jesus' ministry.

He presents four states of blessedness ("macarisms") in the second person, derived from his Q source. Mt seems to have added other beatitudes from another place. Verse 20*b* parallels Mt 5:3; vv. 21*a*, Mt 5:6 but with the Jewish reference to righteousness (*sedaka*) eliminated, vv. 22f., Mt 5:11f. Lk has the title Son of Man (v. 22) and adds the blessing for weepers who shall laugh (v. 21*b*), probably another version of the mourners who shall be comforted (Mt 5:4). The woes (vv. 24ff.) are his own and consist in an exact role-reversal of those mentioned in the beatitudes. He has done the same thing about deposition of God's enemies in the Magnificat (1:52ff.) The framing of the woes is a little clumsy, as the resumption of the narrative in v. 27 shows.

It is not easy to make a case for Lk's deemphasis of futurist eschatology from this passage, or to speak of his disinterest in poverty as an ideal. Quite simply, he retains the teaching of Jesus as he finds it in Q, editing it only slightly for a Gentile readership. The overturning of all received values is a historical theme in Jesus' preaching of God's reign and not merely a Lucan theme.

SEVENTH SUNDAY OF THE YEAR (C)

(Seventh Sunday after Epiphany)

1 Samuel 26:2, 7-9, 12-13, 22-23. The lectionary makes judicious omissions in the earlier part of this story which do nothing to slow its tempo. Then, by leaving out vv. 14-21, it alters its tenor completely. The taunts of David—a man fighting for his life—shouted across the ravine, his curse of the evil counselors of Saul who have exiled him from his people and his God, and Saul's compunction over having acted the fool in David's regard are details omitted at a high price. What remains is merely an edifying tale featuring David's respect for the divine office of kingship and his readiness to forgive. Surely no lector will destroy the narrative by eliminating the latter part with such memorable phrases as: "For the king of Israel has come out to seek a single flea as if he were hunting partridge in the mountains."

The tale told here in ch. 26 may well be another version of that in ch. 24. Both describe David's betrayal by Ziphites (cf. 23:19; 26:1) and speak of Saul's picked force as being of three thousand men. David's awe at the prospect of harming the king is repeated (cf. 24:11; 26:11.) So is Saul's admission that David will succeed him (cf. 24:21; 26:25)—in the second case, in the form of a blessing on all the young man's endeavors.

Clearly the shape of this narrative is determined by its outcome. It is official military history sanctioned by the soldier-king who achieved the coup. Hence, David's youthful awe at Saul's kingship may be a much later device to encourage respect for his own. It is hard but not impossible to read between the lines of the stories in the David cycle and come to some conclusions about the complex characters of the two men. Surely 1 Sm reports on one of the most delicate struggles for power in history, complicated—as is so often the case—by religious sentiment, possibly even by faith.

1 Corinthians 15:45-49. Gen 2:7 has: "And so man became a living being" (*nephesh ḥayyah*). St. Paul adds "first" because he will designate Christ as the last Adam in the same verse. He also supplies the designation "Adam" (lit., "man"). The first man was merely a *psyché zōsa*, an animate creature. Christ by contrast is a *pneuma zōopoioun*, a man of spirit who enlivens in the spirit (cf. Jn 6:63.) The adjective "natural" (*psychikon*) in v. 44 has preceded the description of Adam as *psyché*. He is the begetter of a race of ordinary humanity while Christ leads off a humanity indwelt by spirit. Earth and dust are the components of the unredeemed race whereas the principle of redemption comes from heaven (v. 47). This parentage tells, in that the two progenies are respectively earthly (*koïkoi*) and heavenly (*epouranioi*, v. 48). Redeemed men of earth that we are, we bear the likeness or image (*eikōn*) of both the man of earth and the man of heaven (vv. 48f.)

Paul undoubtedly profited by the rabbinic developments of a cosmic or heavenly man who was to be complementary to the father of the race. Here, as so often in the use of Christ as antitype, the apostle is able to specify the myth by supplying an actual historical figure. For Paul, Christ was filled with the Spirit in power at his resurrection (cf. Rom 1:4.) The Lord qualifies perfectly as justifier of the eschatological hope for all because, as Spirit-filled, he becomes the archetype of those who will be raised up on the last day. It is the Spirit they already possess in measure who will accomplish this. Paul's main theme in this chapter is bodies, not the moral likeness of the just to Christ. Hence he describes the different kinds of bodies there are (cf. Phil 3:21), with special reference to the future reality of the resurrected body. It is this reality which some in Corinth deny.

Luke 6:27-38. Luke's development of the love of one's enemies is derived from Q (cf. Mt 5:44; 39-42; 7:12; 5:46f., 45, 48; 7:1f.) His special material which is not contained in Mt includes: "Do good to those who hate you; bless those who curse you" (v. 27), where also Lk has "maltreat" for Mt's "persecute"; he omits mention of going two miles rather than one (Mt 5:41) and the Matthean equation of the golden rule with "the law and the prophets" (Mt 7:41). Where Mt has even Gentiles doing as much, Lk has sinners (Lk 6:33 = Mt 5:47); Lk also changes greeting your brothers in public to doing good to others.

Verses 34f. are proper to Lk, with an echo at the end of Mt's rained-upon "just and unjust" (5:45). Lk asks for a compassion like that of the Father (v. 36) whereas Mt wishes disciples to be perfect. Lastly, the graphic figure of a full measure of grain poured into one's garment is proper to Lk only.

In general, the supposition regarding this passage is that Lk has "gentilized" Q for his purposes just as Mt has "rabbinized" it for his. The spirit of Jesus shines through both, namely doing more than is asked or expected.

LENTEN SEASON

FIRST SUNDAY OF LENT (C)

Deuteronomy 26:4-10. Earlier in this biblical book, a similar
historical summary of reasons for belief has occurred at 6:20-25. The
present rite of thanksgiving for harvest with the credo it contains
(vv. 5b-10a) comes at the end of the laws section of Dt (12:1—26:19).
The law enjoining the presentation of first fruits is probably very
early; here it serves as the introduction to the faith-statement
concerning deliverance from Egypt and blessedness in the new land.

"Some first fruits" are to be brought to the presiding priest in
the central sanctuary in acknowledgment of the LORD's bounty. In
v. 10 the worshiper himself deposits the offering rather than the priest
as in v. 4.

The declaration of vv. 5b-10a is thought to be very old. It
summarizes the contents of Genesis through Judges. The individual
Israelite's "father" (v. 5) is Jacob who bestowed his name on the
people. NAB suggests that "Aramean" either refers to the origin of
the patriarchs in Aram Naharaim (cf. Gn 24:10; 25:20; 28:5, 31, 20,
24), the region around Haran on the River Balikh, modern Turkey,
or is used merely in the sense of "nomad." Of importance here is the
joining of history to harvest festival or, as G. Henton Davies
describes it, "the combination of rite and creed [which] sets the
pattern for Israel's feasts." Jews are not fond of the Christian word
"creed," understandably. A better description of vv. 5b-10a might be
"a summary of God's beneficent intervention in Israel's history."

Romans 10:8-13. In vv. 5-13 a contrast is set up between the
righteousness which comes through the law and that which is based
on faith. Dt 30:11-14 refers to God's command to Israel, and speaks
in praise of its accessibility and the ease with which it can be carried
out (*poiēsomen*, v. 13). St. Paul accommodates this passage by
making the Deuteronomic *mitzvah* the word of faith which he
preaches (v. 8). The creedal formula, "Jesus [Christ] is Lord" has
already appeared in 1 Cor 12:3 and Phil 2:11. Here it is made the
central affirmation of faith. Paul is not contrasting profession of
Jesus' lordship "on the lips" with belief in his resurrection "in the
heart." The two are complementary aspects of the one mystery of
Christ. The same is true of "justification" and "salvation" (v. 10).

They are not successive steps or stages but part of a chiastic, i.e. X-like, rhetorical device to convey a single reality; thus: confess—believe; believe (eis dikaiosynēn)—confess (eis sōtērian).

Paul quotes the Deuteronomist in a version close to but not identical with the LXX (v. 8 = Dt 30:14). Dt "is full of the notion that God's relations with his people rest on grace" (Barrett), so it is doubtful that fulfillment of God's word (rhēma) is understood by the Deuteronomist as mere observance of a command (entolē). Paul has quoted Lv 18:5 in v. 5, which says of God's statutes and decrees that "the man who carries them out will find life through them." He employs this nomistic understanding of fulfillment (as again at Gal 3:12) to summarize in the law's own words what he understands the law to mean. Even though the Levitical author's view of the law is that it is life-giving, Paul feels that he must contrast Lv unfavorably with Dt, making the former speak of the "justice that comes from the Law" but the latter of "justice that comes from faith." Since Bar 3:29 interprets Dt 30:11-14 to refer to heavenly wisdom, Paul is on solid ground in applying these verses to Christ, who for him is the wisdom of God.

The "word of faith" (v. 8) is the gospel as Paul preaches it. It is immediately available to those to whom it has been brought. It is the occasion for a faith which justifies, a creedal confession (homologia) which saves. Neither Jew nor Greek has the advantage over the other since this gift of faith is available indiscriminately to both. Paul concludes with the triumphant declaration from Joel (3:5 = Mt 2:32) that all who call on the name of the LORD—viz., with faith in Christ—will be saved.

Luke 4:1-13. The Marcan temptation narrative is brief (1:12f.) and is characterized by signs of eschatological consummation—community between man and beast, ministering angels, "the desert as the place of Yahweh's marriage with Israel as well as the Satanic temptations" (Flender). Mt begins the tendency to use it as instructive for the Christian under temptation. Lk, drawing on Q like Mt, goes further in providing community members with an example for their own behavior. He omits the details of the devil's taking Jesus up a very high mountain (v. 5 = Mt 4:8) and the ministry of angels (v. 13 = Mt 4:11), possibly because these are messianic signs. Instead, Lk portrays Jesus as the new Adam (cf. 3:38), prototype of every Christian in temptation and in victory over it. Satan tempts Jesus less as the messiah (cf. Mt's heavy dependence on Dt 6 and 8 and Ps 91 for Israel's failure where Jesus the Messiah succeeds) than as an ordinary man by subjecting him to "every temptation" (panta peirasmon, v. 13). Lk has Satan leave Jesus alone "to await another opportunity" (*achri kairou*, v. 13). That time comes in 22:3 when Satan takes possession of Judas, and at the supper table when Jesus commends the disciples for standing by him in his "temptations" (*en tois peirasmois mou*, v. 28).

Lk places the second and third scenes in reverse order from Mt, putting the parapet of the temple last. Perhaps it is his preoccupation with Jerusalem which accounts for this.

SECOND SUNDAY OF LENT (C)

Genesis 15:5-12, 17-18. The nobility of Abraham's character has been underscored in the previous chapter. He will not take "a thread or a sandal strap" in spoil from the king of Sodom whom he has successfully defended against Chedorlaomer king of Elam and his three allies. Bera king of Sodom made the famous offer of booty to the Hebrews if he might have all the civilian captives. In its Vulgate rendering this became a Christian charter of zeal for souls: "Da mihi animas, cetera tolle tibi" (14:21). Abram's determination not to profit by the military skill he displayed in behalf of his nephew Lot, who was living in Sodom at the time, is made by the Yahwist author to lead into the LORD's offer of a covenant.

Verses 4 and 5 are from the E narrative but all the rest of today's reading is J material.

The promise of a son for Abraham, hinted at in 13:16, is reiterated in Gn 22:17; 28:14 (where, as in 13:16, the dust of the earth is substituted for the stars of the heavens); Ex 32:13; Dt 1:10. Abram "put his faith" (*he^{e}min*) in the LORD, who credited it to him as "an act of righteousness" (*ṣedaka*, v. 6). His right attitude toward God, in other words, gave him title to the fulfillment of God's promise. He will have his own boundless issue as his heir and not have to fall back, childless, on his steward Eliezer.

The LORD authorizes the possession of Canaan by Abram (v. 7) and suggests as a sign of it a covenant (*b^{e}rith*) to be cut (*karath*) with Abram (cf. v. 18). This mysterious, symbolic action is illumined somewhat by Jer 34:18ff., where violators of the pact are promised they will be split like the calf and their corpses left for the beasts and birds of prey (cf. Gn 15:11.) Abram undergoes a trance (*tardemah*) like the sleep of Adam as darkness falls, fascinated by the mystery before which he trembles in awe (v. 12).

The brazier and the torch which pass between the divided parts of the carcasses (v. 17) are a consuming fire which represents the LORD. He repeats his promise (v. 18), saying that Abram's descendants (lit. "seed") will possess the land from Egypt to the Euphrates. Righteousness is basically his—a gift to humankind. The LORD passes symbolically through the covenant to show unmistakably that he means to keep it.

Philippians 3:17—4:1. St. Paul has no hesitancy in proposing himself and those who are faithful to his example as guides for the conduct of the Philippians. As Christ lives in Paul, so should he live in Paul's converts. The apostle deplores any departure from this standard (v. 18) somewhat in the way that 1 Jn does in describing members who leave the ranks of believers (2:18f.)

Verse 19 has often been popularly taken to describe gormandizers, but the belly as god may have more to do with dietary observance than with gastronomic indulgence, just as the "glory" (*doxa*) spoken of may refer to circumcision, which to Paul is "shame" (*aischynē*) if it is made the subject of a boast. Another possibility is that "belly" (*koilia*; also "womb") is a Pauline euphemism for lustful conduct. All that lies in store for such offenders is *apōleia*, the type of disaster that connotes utter destruction. It is possible that the "things of this world" (*ta epigeia*) are material benefits but equally likely that we have in the term a contrast with the "heavenly" (*ta epourania*), namely the gifts available in Christ through faith. The earthbound among the Philippians are, in that sense, fools from Paul's point of view. They are not friends of the cross of Christ but its enemies since they do not accept it in faith (v. 18).

Christians have their true citizenship in heaven, Paul says, since it is from here that Christ shall come to assert his lordship (v. 20). The language is political in that Christ is the redeeming emperor. His power (*energeia*, v. 21) will be exercised only in such a way, however, as to transform our bodies from their present lowliness (*tapeinōsis*, the word rendered by *humilitas* in Mary's Magnificat) into the form of "bodies of glory" (cf. 1 Cor 15:35-49; 2 Cor 5:1-5.) The last phrase of v. 21 resembles the picture of final consummation in 1 Cor 15:24-28.

In the intensity of his exhortation to the Philippians to stand firm in the Lord he calls them "beloved" (*agapētoi*) twice in the same sentence (4:1). They can be his joy and crown in the *eschaton* only if they live heavenly, not earthly lives, i.e., in the Lord.

Luke 9:28-36. Luke substitutes eight days for the six of Mk's interval, probably to relate it to the resurrection by making the eighth day the beginning of a new week. He expands the basically Marcan transfiguration narrative (Mk 9:2-8) by having Moses and Elijah, who "appear in glory," discuss the departure (*exodos*) he was about to fulfill in Jerusalem (v. 31). His account looks forward to Jesus' anticipatory glorification on another mount than this one, that of Olives (19:37), his agony in the same place (19:45), and his ascent into heaven from there (Ac 1:12). In Lk's gospel there is a heavenly apparition (22:43) as in the transfiguration; also his disciples—not named in Lk, unlike Mk and Mt—who sleep during his agony sleep here before awakening to the vision (v. 32; no parallels).

The disciples are caught up into the cloud and are afraid (v. 34; again, Lk only). They keep silence about what they have seen (v. 36; cf. vv. 21f., referred to by some as the "passion secret in Luke.")

"Listen to him" (v. 35) was the injunction concerning the Moses-like prophet of Dt 18:19. Jesus for Lk is this prophet.

THIRD SUNDAY OF LENT (C)

Exodus 3:1-8, 13-15. Morton Smith writes that, "The Old Testament is primarily concerned with the cult of the god Yahweh. It undertakes to show how this cult was established, [and] to outline the rules for its practice. . . . In sum, the purposes of the Bible are to tell the worshipers of Yahweh what they should do and to persuade them that they had better do it." Smith goes on to remark that even if we accept the Bible's story that all Israel came out of Egypt, that story knows of the mixed multitude that accompanied the Israelites, of the peoples—Midianites and Moabites—who became associated with them in the desert, and of the others—enumerated in v. 8—who joined them after their entrance into the promised land.

Verses 1-5, 7, 13-14 have been identified as Priestly, vv. 6, 8-12 as Yahwist, and vv. 15-20*a* as Elohist. Jethro, the Midianite priest of P, seems to be the Reuel of 2:16, 18 (J, or Yahwist), who some scholars think was originally Hobab the Kenite (cf. Num 10:29; Jgs 4:11) of the clan of Reuel. Midian in ancient sources is the strip of land along the east side of the Gulf of Aqaba south of modern Elat, today the northwest extremity of Saudi Arabia. It is the only area in the entire region where there have been active volcanoes in historical times. This would tell in its favor as the location of Sinai (cf. Ex 19:16, 18) except for the fact that so many other indications favor the Sinai peninsula.

The mountain Horeb (v. 1) of E and D is evidently the Sinai of J and P where the law was given (cf. 19:10-23.) As has been frequently pointed out in this commentary, this mountain is unlikely to have been the massive peak near the tip of the Sinai peninsula singled out as Jebel Musa since the 4th c. of the Christian era. The actual Mt. Sinai probably lay NW of the Gulf of Aqaba on the northern part of the peninsula, modern Jebel Helal, with the nomadic Midianites found in the region of Kadesh-barnea east of it. They seemed to have no scruple worshiping the LORD along with the Israelites at the "mountain of God" (cf. 19:1-12), and may even have brought from their homeland the tradition of volcanic activity at a sacred peak.

An angel of the LORD (*malak* = "messenger," v. 1) is a characteristic of E but appears here in J. The word for a thornbush (*s^{e}ne*) resembles Sinai, perhaps as an intended ingredient of the theophany. The phenomenon known as St. Elmo's fire, in which pointed objects seem to emit static electricity during a storm, may have underlain the original narrative. In any event, fire or lightning is the sign of the LORD's activity (cf. Gen 15:17; Ex 13:21; 19:16), made more remarkable by the fact that here the bush goes unconsumed (v. 2). The occurrence is mentioned again in the Bible only at Dt 33:16, in the blessing of Moses spoken over Joseph. Jesus refers to the LORD's self-identification as God of the patriarchs as having been spoken "at the bush" (Mk 12:26 = Lk 20:37) since there was no citation by chapter and verse in his day.

Moses cannot "look at God." He hides his face and removes his sandals as signs of his awe (vv. 5f.) God (*Elohim*, a generic term for deity) speaks of himself as the same one whom Abraham, Isaac, and Jacob acknowledged. He will bring to completion the deliverance of the Israelites from Egyptian oppression (vv. 7f.) The name he gives to Moses will serve as proof of his intention: "I am who am" (*ehyeh asher ehyeh*, 14*a*) or, more simply, "I am" (*ehyeh*, 14*b*). Earlier (v. 12), the same verb form has connoted God's intent to be with his people, which leads some to render the divine name as "I will be." The hope in such a translation is to convey a sense of dynamic presence rather than metaphysical self-existence. The latter Greek concept was contributed to much later by the Septuagintal translation, *ho ōn*, the "one who is." The word-play on the Hebrew verb "to be" (*hayah*) is an example of the familiar popular etymology of the Bible. The actual origins of the name YHWH are unknown but are at least traceable back to "Yah" or "Yahu." Some take this to be an onomatopoeic shout to acknowledge divinity.

This passage marks the first occurrence in E of the proper name of God, "The LORD," whereas J represents it as having been known and used before the flood (cf. Gen 4:26.)

1 Corinthians 10:1-6, 10-12. St. Paul is here issuing a warning to the Corinthian church against presumption, the great offense he finds its members guilty of. In adopting the style of a Hellenistic synagogue homily, he presumes a sufficient knowledge of rabbinic midrash in some readers to refer to the extra-biblical legend of the LORD's having followed Israel as a rock (ṣur=petra, v. 4; cf. Tosefta, Sukkah 3, 11.) Even if this is lost on most, he expects them to know the basic Exodus symbolism of sea and cloud, manna, water struck from the rock (i.e., a potable spring in a sun-baked mud flat), and poisonous snakes (cf. Ex 16 and 17, Num 20, Dt 8:3.) Food, drink, and rock are all "spiritual" (pneumatikos, v. 4; RSV, "supernatural"), meaning symbolic. Paul exhorts his converts not to be "desirous of evil things," his term for idolatry and lewd conduct. For "desirous" he uses the word found in the LXX at Num 11:4, 34; Ps 78:29f. to describe the greedy craving of the Israelites for meat in the desert: epithymeō, epithymia.

The Massoretic text contains the story of a plague in Nm 16:36-50 after the tale of the destruction of Korah, Dathan, and Abiram, which the LXX does not have. NAB and BJ follow the latter as the older textual tradition, RSV and NEB the former, hence including at vv. 47ff. the account of the 14,700 who were felled for murmuring in sympathy with the three who infringed on priestly prerogatives. This is the reference to the destroying angel (olothreutēs) found in 10:10, which might prove puzzling to anyone schooled in the more recent tradition of Catholic biblical criticism. Those familiar with the traditions of the Authorized or Douay-Rheims versions should recognize the reference immediately.

Paul thinks of his own time as "the end of the ages" (v. 11), consequently that period of history which all biblical events were meant to illumine. The Corinthians should read the Exodus accounts of disobedience and grumbling with great care, with a view to finding warnings there on their own perilous condition.

Luke 13:1-9. Neither synoptic gospel other than Lk, nor Jn, has this material, although some have speculated that Jesus' cursing of the fig tree (Mk 11:12ff., 20f.=Mt 21:18f., 20ff.) originated from a parable like the one that Lk tells here. It is impossible to identify the bloody suppression of a Galilean revolt by Pilate with any of the several such events reported by Josephus. Lk's normal care with sources has led most commentators to suppose that he is reporting a historical reminiscence. The same is true of the accident at the tower of Siloam, presumably near the pool of that name below David's city on Mt. Ophel, the terminus of Hezekiah's aqueduct leading from the Gihon Spring.

The point Jesus makes about the innocence of victims of violence and accident resembles his declaration in Jn 9:2f. that neither the blind man nor his parents were guilty of a sin that caused the blindness. It is also related to his consistent treatment of the possessed as if they were guilty of no wrong. The theme of ch. 13 is the fate of Jerusalem and the Jews, starting with a call to repentance (vv. 1-5) which leads into a parable (vv. 6-9). Lk likes to set sayings of Jesus in a dialogue situation as he does here in v. 1. The audience raises the question of God's justice: Lk has Jesus elevate the discussion to the level of personal response, charging the hearers with the same phrase at vv. 3 and 5 (only the tense of the verb "reform" is different). "All" will perish similarly unless they repent—not merely all who hear him on this occasion but an unlimited population. Even if Jesus had in mind only his Jewish hearers both here and in the parable (which derives from Isaiah's song of the vineyard, 5:1-7), Lk broadens it out to the Christian community. Jerusalem has already been destroyed at the time of the writing, so the threat of judgment in the absence of reform is a threat to all.

As the chapter continues, so does the theme of accepting or rejecting salvation. The question in v. 23 is a Lucan formation. The "you" of v. 28 is the reader, not the "sons of the kingdom" as in Mt 8:12. The chapter concludes (vv. 34f.) with a reminder to the Christian reader of Lk's day that what happened to Jerusalem for its putting to death of the prophet Jesus can happen to him. He can avoid God's judgment only if he learns a lesson from the past and repents.

FOURTH SUNDAY OF LENT (C)

Joshua 5:9-12. The sanctuaries of early Israel such as Shiloh, Gilgal, and Shechem were the repositories of ancient narratives. It is thought that the stories of the conquest contained in Joshua had their origins there. Verses 2-8 contain the account of the circumcision of the men and boys born during the forty years of journeying in the desert. This is obviously a cultic tale which has as its object the prescription of fitness (removal of the "reproach of Egypt") for all males who would worship in the new land. "Gilgal" probably means "circle of stone shafts" (like those at Stonehenge, though not nearly so massive). As a note in NAB points out, the name is connected by popular etymology with "I have removed," *gallothi* in Hebrew (v. 9). The circle of stones from the river that make up the memorial at the shrine (cf. 4:5) are matched by another twelve commemorative stones in the river bed (4:9), one for each of the Israelite tribes.

Gilgal is thought to have been northeast across the river from Jericho. The author of the early portion of Joshua has a priestly interest in feasts as well as sanctuaries. He ties the observance of Passover in with the entry into Canaan, a natural and possibly even historical link, since the motifs of the crossing of the Sea of Reeds and the River Jordan are so similar. The manna of the old epoch ceases abruptly (v. 12) as the unleavened cakes and the parched grain of the new epoch begin (v. 11). The Israelites are described as entering immediately into a stable agricultural life. This may not be so fanciful if, in fact, they adopted a spring agricultural festival of the Canaanites as the symbol of their deliverance and safe entry into Canaan. The "season of the harvest" of 3:15 is a month straddling March and April, Nisan in New Testament times but in the earlier calendar Abhibh, the first month of the year.

The Hebrew word for Passover (*Pesaḥ*) is made up of the same three letters as the verb for "leap" or "hop," and "limp" (cf. 1 Kgs 18:26.) This has led to the speculation that a pre-Israelite feast marked by dancing might have given its name to the festivities.

2 Corinthians 5:17-21. The love of Christ on behalf of all has changed Paul's perspective on everything (v. 14). He has had to desert the "merely human point of view" (*kata sarka*, v. 16) which he once had on everyone, even Christ. The reference is undoubtedly to his days as a persecutor (cf. Gal 1:3) when he thought of the crucified Jesus as accursed rather than as a deliverer from the power of a curse (cf. Gal 3:13.) Now that he is "in Christ," Paul is sure that he is part of a renewed creation (*kainē ktisis*, v. 17). The new epoch succeeds the old; the latter has passed into history. The inscription on the great seal of the United States *Novus Ordo Seclorum*, while it is not biblical, partakes of this epochal mode of Semitic thought.

It is God who has achieved the change in history, not men. The believers' lot as a result of the change is a ministry of "reconciliation" (*katallagēs*, v. 18), a service-role that follows from God's work of reconciling a sinful humanity to himself. This he did by abandoning the role of injured party. Men's transgressions (*paraptōmata*) were simply not reckoned any longer (v. 19). It is clear to Paul that humanity continues the task of reconciliation by a similar disregard of offense. We are ambassadors for Christ (*presbeuomen*, lit. "we exercise a representative function," v. 20), with God making his appeal (*parakalountos*, part of a genitive absolute) through us. The apostle is thinking, in the first place, of himself and others with a charge like his. Therefore he calls upon the Corinthians to be reconciled to God, as presumably some are not (v. 21*b*). After that has been achieved, the continuing work of representing Christ will be theirs.

The concreteness of the final verse of this pericope is a striking and deservedly famous Pauline utterance. The personally sinless Christ "was made sin" (*hamartian epoiēsen*) for us that we might become the very righteousness of God in him. "Sin" here is not personal offense so much as the condition of alienated humanity. *Dikaiosynē* is the condition of reconciled humanity. Christ assumed the one so that he might give us the other. Needless to say, he does not remain "sin" but in his exaltation becomes the depositary of divine justice insofar as it can reside in a man. Through him it is given to all.

Luke 15:1-3, 11-32. Luke features the journey motif in his gospel and, along with it, that of the hospitality accorded to Jesus. Jesus is the wanderer in whose guise God visits his people (cf. 1:73, 7:16; 5:27-38; 19:9; 24:13-35.) The complaint of "Pharisees and scribes" (v. 2) against his welcoming tax gatherers and sinners (v. 1) underlines the soteriological aspect of the guest motif. "Fellowship with Jesus means forgiveness of sins and newness of life" (Flender).

The principle in two-edged parables is that the main trust lies in the second part. Verses 11-21, the wastrel son, and 22-32, the father's treatment of the elder resentful son were probably originally two parables in Lk's source. Linguistically, he has made them both his own.

The custom prevailed in the ancient world of deeding one's property to one's heirs while keeping the rent from it as income during one's lifetime. The younger son achieved this settlement from his father but also the control of his inheritance, rather than having to wait until the father died. The phrase spoken to the elder son, "everything I have is yours" (v. 31), would reflect the normal arrangement, while that with the younger son (v. 12b) the abnormal. The elder son's lively imagination, in his anger, supplies a career of loose living to the younger for which he has no evidence (v. 30). All we are told is that he was reduced to the supreme indignity of tending pigs for a Gentile master. Beside this, eating carob-pods was as nothing.

The father's initiative in forgiveness is the operative detail in the first part of the parable (v. 20bc). He does not stop to discuss the son's confession of faults but cites his return as in itself sufficient cause for new clothing, a ring (sign of authority in the household), and the order for a celebration (vv. 22ff.)

In Jesus' telling of the parable it would have been a tale of the repentance of the social outcast directed at the self-righteous observant Jew. Lk always sees the Christian mission directed first to the Jews, then to the Gentiles. We are therefore right in finding in the younger son's prodigality—his "death" and lostness—an image of the condition of Gentiles *vis-à-vis* Israel, the elder brother, who is with God without interruption and whose patrimony is always his by right. The story is another and perhaps the best illustration of the theme Lk puts so strongly on Jesus' lips: that God can forgive and accept whom he wishes, when and how he wishes.

FIFTH SUNDAY OF LENT (C)

Isaiah 43:16-21. The Chaldeans of v. 14 are that tribe which settled in Lower Mesopotamia during the period of Assyria's domination, founding the Neo-Babylonian kingdom. The context of this passage is the anticipation of deliverance from Babylon (late 6th c.) as something actually accomplished. Verses 16f. rehearse the Reed Sea episode during the Exodus. In what follows, the Jews are invited not to dwell overly on those marvels from the past (v. 18) since the LORD intends to do a new and greater thing (v. 19), namely deliver his people from Babylon and send them back through the desert (vv. 19f.) This new exodus will make the first one pale by comparison, as a desert road is laid down (cf. 35:8ff., 40:3f.) and springs and rivers make it green with vegetation (cf. 35:6f.; 41:18f.) God's providential care will be such that inimical birds and beasts will be subdued and the desert itself—unlike the Sinai peninsula of old—transformed into a rich land. The sign of fulfillment of this marvel will be greater still: the transformation of Israel into a people of praise (v. 21).

The powerful imagery of Second-Isaiah, never literally fulfilled, was of course realized in the conquest of the desert that lay under the Fertile Crescent. The restoration of God's people to their homeland validated the wildest claims of poetic imagination.

Philippians 3:8-14. John Henry Newman's novel *Loss and Gain* is about the Pauline loss (*zēmia*, v. 8) of all things which brings indescribable gain (*kerdēsō*, future of *kerdainō*) in the form of the knowledge of Jesus Christ as Lord. Paul's careful consideration (*hēgoumai* twice, translated in NAB as "rate" and "account") leads him to conclude that everything—but chiefly any trust in righteousness based on legal observance—is garbage (*skybala*, plural) in contrast with this wealth. Paul seems to be challenging the two chief claims made in the Philippian community: that in favor of observance of the law and that of special knowledge, as justifying. God alone justifies through faith (v. 9), in Christ's sufferings no less than in the power of his resurrection (v. 10). Sharing in his sufferings constitutes being "in Christ," Paul's well-known form of mystical union. This shared knowledge of sufferings (*pathēmatōn*) is experiential. Being formed in the pattern of the Lord's death is the precondition for attaining to his resurrection (vv. 10f.)

The "justice" Paul possesses (v. 9) is his right relation with God. None of this is of his doing or earning. God holds out the mystery of his son's dying and rising to be shared in by a lived faith. On condition of the latter, not of circumcision or perfect conformity, the believer may hope ultimately to achieve personal resurrection from the dead.

The apostle hastens to add that he does not yet possess resurrection but looks forward to it (v. 12a). This is an echo of the problem of the Corinthian enthusiasts examined in the commentary for the Sixth Sunday of the Year (Cycle C, pp. 291ff.) Paul claims that he has not as yet "been perfected" (*teteleiōmai*, 12), probably a word taken from gnostic vocabulary. Using the language of what today's world of sports would call track events, he contrasts grasping the award—a laurel wreath at the finish line—with being grasped (*katelēmphthēn*, v. 12) by Christ. He is still in the race, his thoughts not at all on his progress up to this point but on the prize that lies ahead: an "upward call" (*anō klēsis*, v. 14) to be "in Christ Jesus." This awareness of the award alone comprises spiritual maturity (v. 15). Only those who have such maturity can aspire to the title coveted in Graeco-Roman gnostic cults, "the perfect."

John 8:1-11. This is one of the most justly famous passages of the New Testament, yet it has an unusual textual history. It is bracketed in NAB and omitted entirely from many other translations because it is missing from John in the best manuscripts. Others have it after Lk 21:38. Its lateness, or interpolation into Jn, do not make it an unauthentic tradition. No doubt the story has been inserted here because of Jesus' declaration in 8:15 that he passes judgment on no one, or v. 26 where he says he forbears from making statements in condemnation.

The similarities to the story of Susanna and the elders are evident (cf. Dn 13.) There the young Daniel would have "no part in the death of this woman" (v. 46) but examined the two witnesses separately and caught them at their perjury (v. 61). Nowhere is the woman taken in adultery in Jn 8 exonerated from the guilt of her shameful deed. Jesus is not flouting the law or its by then archaic prescription for adultery, the death penalty. He is interested more in the motives of her accusers. For her there is compassion and the admonition not to commit this sin again; for them, judgment on their hypocrisy.

An early memory of the present writer is of H. B. Warner in *The King of Kings* tracing in the dust the Aramaic words for "lust," "extortion," and "greed," which turned into English forthwith— movie-style. As each one was completed, another man slipped away into the crowd, dropping the stone he held. It was pure DeMille but the memory remains.

PASSION SUNDAY (C)
(Palm Sunday)

Isaiah 50:4-7. See pp. 240f.

Philippians 2:6-11. See pp. 140ff.

Luke 22:14—23:56 (longer) or 23:1-49 (shorter). Luke relies on traditions (he probably possesses a primitive narrative of arrest, appearance before some representatives of the Sanhedrin, condemnation by Pilate, journey to Calvary, and crucifixion and death) and biblical sources (Pss 21, 41; Is 50:6; 53:12; Hos 6:1ff.; 10:8*b*, 11f., 14; Am 8:9). Such historical sources as he possesses he puts in the service of a portrait of Jesus as an innocent sufferer "counted among the wicked." He seems to have a tradition on the primitive eucharist superior to that of Mk/Mt; likewise, one that omits the Marcan inquiry by priests at night and also that gives the political charges before Pilate which probably led to Jesus' condemnation by Rome (23:2).

We adopt the theory, with Taylor and others, that Lk edited a special passion source at his disposal with the aid of Mk rather than revised Mk in the light of his source. Lk has Jesus eating with "the apostles," not "the twelve disciples" (Mk 14:17; Mt 26:20) and introduces in vv. 15-18—probably from his source—Jesus' twofold vow of abstention from food and drink until the reign of God has come. The eschatological concern of the vow recalls Paul's primitive sense of the eucharistic meal, which is to be eaten by Christians "until he comes" (1 Cor 11:26). The signs of food and drink will be fulfilled only when the *basileia* arrives. Verses 19*b*-20 have long been disputed textually, not because the manuscript attestation was weak but because they were thought to be an interpolation of 1 Cor 11. Through the researches of Schürmann in particular they are coming to be widely accepted as genuine. Both they and Paul's supper account are thought to derive from the same source, of which Lk's version is presumed to be the earlier. The place of origin hazarded is

Antioch, somewhere between 30 and 40. Part of the reason why vv. 19b-20 were thought non-genuine was the supposition that later copyists, nervous over the sequence cup-bread in vv. 17-19a, inserted 19b-20 to supply the more familiar bread-cup sequence. Lk probably did this on his own, however, having first provided the eschatological development he was more interested in.

Verses 24-27, the disciples' dispute over precedence, seems to come from the special Lucan source; similarly 28-30 and 31-33 (but cf. Mk 8:33; Jn 21:15-19), with v. 34 a later Marcan addition to the narrative as v. 22 had been. Verses 35-38 are entirely peculiar to Lk, looking back as they do to 10:4 when everything was different with the disciples as regards preparedness for their mission.

Jesus' suggestion about selling his coat to buy a sword must be a metaphor to describe hostility to the gospel. Taken as referring to a future time of privation and opposition it is completely serious. Jesus terminates the literal misconstruing of his meaning by the disciples impatiently (*hikanon estin*, "Enough!"; certainly not "Two are enough.") His healing action in vv. 49ff. makes this abundantly clear. Conceivably the puzzling sword-saying of v. 36 was not a *logion* of Jesus but an early apostolic practice which Lk takes the pains to refute by reporting the Master's peaceful spirit. We have some extra-biblical data on traveling Jewish teachers.

The story of the agony in the garden (vv. 39-46) is non-Marcan, all but 46b (cf. Mk 14:38) and perhaps vv. 41f. where the wording is not in Mk's style.

Verses 52b-53a give every indication of being a Marcan insertion (from Mk 14:48f.) into a non-Marcan source—Lk 22:47-54a—about the arrest of Jesus, although word-study would indicate that Lk did his editing with Mk before him (thus, 47a=Mk 14:43).

Lk's denial of Jesus by Peter (22:54b-61) suggests reliance on Mk chiefly (cf. 14:54, 66-72). It is an evening occurrence in both gospels but Lk will not let it serve as the framework for a night-inquiry by the priests as Mk does. See the commentary on Mk's passion narrative on pp. 201f. Lk's two challengers to Peter subsequent to the servant girl (vv. 58, 59) are males in Greek, unlike the parallel places, and the piercing look of Jesus in 61a is likewise proper to him. His own editorial activity could account for this without the need to posit a special written source. The mocking scene (vv. 63ff.) appears to derive from elsewhere than Mk 14:65, though the vocabulary shows that Lk has made it his own. It is much more likely that the men guarding Jesus mocked him, as in Lk, than that the priests should have done it (cf. Mk 14:65.)

Aside from the probable dependence of v. 69 on Mk 14:62 and v. 71 on 63b (with mention of blasphemy omitted), Lk's account of a morning appearance of Jesus before "their council" (v. 66) is so different from Mk 14:53-65 that dependence on another source seems most likely. David Flusser in *Jesus* (1969) concludes that while Lk does not hesitate to report the delivery of Jesus to Pilate by Jewish authorities, he is working from materials that precede Mk's dramatized attempt at popularization. Such is also the burden of D. R. Catchpole's *The Trial of Jesus* (1971).

In 18:32 Lk has had Jesus prophesy his deliverance to the Gentiles only. When the evangelist places Jesus before the Roman prefect (23:1-5) the dialogue is peculiarly Lk's except for v. 3; this he derives from Mk, taking the equivocal response of Jesus as not leaving the meaning open (Mk's and Mt's technique) but as denying the charge, for shortly Pilate will declare that he finds "no charge against him arising from your allegations" (v. 14). Verses 6-16, the examination before Herod, is Lk's special composition, one that will be echoed in Ac 4:27. Lk shows some knowledge of Johannine tradition throughout, as for example Pilate's threefold declaration of Jesus' innocence (23:4, 15, 22 = Jn 18:38b; 19:4-6).

It is hard to tell whether Lk's account of Barabbas is his own or a modification of Mk's. Chances favor the former, with v. 25 perhaps a version of Mk 15:15 finishing off the section with a carefully constructed summary. The historicity of the Barabbas tale is all but impossible to establish. Pilate's offer to release a convicted insurgent —and we know nothing of a practice of amnesty at Passover—is highly improbable on the face of it. Yet some report of a *lēstēs* who went free while the innocent Jesus died has lingered in the popular memory.

Pilate passes sentence on Jesus in Lk alone (*epekrinen*, "he decreed," v. 24), yet even here the burden of guilt is transferred to the shoulders of Jewish leadership: He "delivered Jesus up to their wishes" (v. 25).

The journey to the cross (vv. 26-32) is non-Marcan except for the first verse which derives from Mk 15:21, the drafting of Simon of Cyrene. Lk's crucifixion narrative (vv. 33-49) is similarly his own except for these insertions from Mk: 23:34b, 38, 44f., 49. The word of Jesus from the cross in 34a is textually doubtful and may have been inspired by Ac 7:60. Mk is Lk's source for the burial narrative (vv. 50-54) "without any clear sign of a second source except a knowledge of Johannine tradition" (Vincent Taylor, *The Passion Narrative of St. Luke* [1972], p. 101). Lk has the women take a more active part in the interment of Jesus than the other evangelists (v. 56), perhaps as a means to forge a link with 24:1.

The passion narrative is chiefly interested in making faith affirmations about Jesus in a context of the biblical-type humiliations he endured. This earnest effort has been badly misconstrued over the centuries as a historical report on Jewish guilt and Roman compassion (22:70—23:22). There is no good reason to continue the confusion in the minds of contemporary Christians.

If a parish wishes to devote a lenten series of lectures to a form-critical and redaction-critical treatment of the passion narratives, it should be encouraged to do so. As proclamation, however, these portions of the gospels can only serve to pour fuel on the Christian fire of anti-Jewish sentiment.

A book that may prove helpful on the entire question is the present writer's *Jesus on Trial* (Fortress, 1973), pp. 89-109. Cf. also John Bowker, *Jesus and the Pharisees* (Cambridge, 1973).

EASTER SEASON

EASTER VIGIL (C)

Romans 6:3-11. St. Paul returns in this passage to a matter he had raised in 3:8, where he attributes the question to slanderous opponents of the gospel: If grace in Christ Jesus is so abundant, may not a life of sin be allowed and even cultivated as a way to prove God's power to justify? (Cf. 6:1f.) He is resoundingly opposed to any such perverse interpretation of "grace" or "faith" (of which confused antinomian Christians may be guilty) and here he spells out the reasons for his opposition. His rhetorical questions in vv. 1 and 3 are characteristics of the style of the *diatribē*. They may reflect questions that have been put to Paul elsewhere. He has not yet visited Rome, hence cannot know the difficulties of Roman Christians.

Paul has denied flatly in v. 2 that those who precisely as Christians (*hoitines*) have died to sin can go on living in it. The first reason in his chain of argument occurs in that verse: "we died" (*apethanomen*, aorist), that is, at a specific time in the past there was death to sin. His subsequent development reveals that he has the day of baptism in mind. Continued life (*zēsomen*, future, v. 2) in sin is not a possibility for the dead. He proceeds to a second argument in v. 3 by beginning with an "Or" (*ē*) which NAB does not translate. Barrett is so convinced that it means "secondly" that he renders it, "Or (if you want further proof) . . ."

We cannot know how much awareness (v. 3) of the effect of baptism Paul can count on in a church he has not instructed. Enough, at least, for him to assume that its members are a baptized community *eis Christon Iēsoun*, elliptical for "in the name of Christ Jesus." Whether they are conscious before reading his epistle of a burial with Christ "into death" (the Greek does not have "his" death) which renders them dead to sin, even as Jesus' death brought an end to his human condition as "sin" (cf. 2 Cor 5:21), we cannot know. We need not take for granted here as common to all in the diaspora the concept of a mystical union of the baptized with Christ. The model of an initiation into pagan mysteries which brought about union with the god of the devotee is widely assumed in NT scholarly writing, especially in theological circles unhappy with sacraments.

Paul may well be saying a simpler, Jewish thing, namely that baptism should be recognized by all as a turning-point, a beginning of life in the new age (Heb., 'ōlām).

There followed upon death in Christ's case his being raised up "by the glory of the Father," in our case the "living of a new life" (v. 4; literally "walking in newness of life," a Semitic echo of practicing halakah, viz., walking in the way of the commandments). The notion of baptism "in a name" has occurred in 1 Cor 1:13 and 10:2 and is sufficiently explicable in terms of the current practice of Jewish baptist sects without turning to a Greek model. Paul must be careful here, as in all such expositions, to distinguish between Christ's having entered on the life of the new age and Christians' being only at its threshold, with suffering and resurrection yet to come. This he does in the present chapter by consistently using the future tense or the imperative. His experience with the Corinthians on this point has made him chary of any vocabulary of anticipated eschatology. The new resurrection-life for the believer is both present (v. 4) and future (vv. 5, 8).

Paul's verb for "united" in v. 5 means literally "grown together" (solved by the Vulgate by the rendering complantati) but he uses it figuratively here. His word for likeness, homoiōma, seems to have a history of connoting similarity to divinity in Greek religion, although the LXX rendering of Gen 1:26 (homoiōsis) would suffice. The imaging in baptism is twofold, both of death and resurrection. Interestingly, the apostle does not attend to the primary property of water as washing but only as immersing ("we were buried with him," v. 4); hence the quarrel of some Catholics with today's catechists is more with the Scriptures—which nowhere speak of Christian baptism as a washing away of sin—than with any supposed innovation. All New Testament washing in a baptismal sense, the lotio pedum of Jn 13 and the references to the Baptist apart, is in the blood of the Lamb.

The "old self" of v. 6 is literally the "old man," Adamic man who died with Christ on the cross. St. Paul calls for a consideration of ourselves (v. 11) as dead to sin in that sense. Human nature as sinful (to sōma tēs hamartias, v. 6) has been destroyed by Christ, but not necessarily for us as individuals. We must conduct ourselves in faith as members of the new, Christ-headed race. Death brings an end to actual slavery because it ends the life of the one enslaved (vv. 6f.) Death ended finally and forever Jesus' human life in the likeness of sin (vv. 9f.) It should do no less for us. The dead man is freed (dedikaiōtai, v. 7) from sin. He must therefore be and act like Christ, "alive to God." In his case, this comes about through being "in Christ Jesus" (v. 11).

Luke 24:1-12. "The women who had come with him from Galilee" (23:55) is the subject of the sentence in 24:1. They have prepared spices and perfumes before the sabbath (23:56), which they now bring. They find the stone rolled back but no body. The question put by the "men" about searching for the Living One among the dead does not occur elsewhere (cf. Is 8:19.) Verse 6*a* (=Mk 16:6*b*) is missing from Codex D (6th c.) and many MSS of the Vulgate. Unlike Mk and Mt, where the "young man" or "angel" directs the women to bring the disciples the message that Jesus is going before them to Galilee, Lk has the men reminisce about the passion prediction (v. 7; cf. 9:22, 44; 18:32f.) Jesus made "while he was still in Galilee" (v. 6). The place of glorification and starting-point of the message is Jerusalem (cf. 24:49), for Lk as for Jn (ch. 20). The other synoptics and the author of Jn 21 situate it in Galilee. The same point of fulfillment of prophecy will be made in the Emmaus story later in this chapter, at vv. 25-27; 32-35. The "sinful men" (*hamartōloi*) of v. 7 are no doubt the "pagans" (*anomoi*) of Ac 2:23, "Gentile sinners" (one word, like "damnyankees") who in Luke's view did the bidding of the Jewish leaders.

The women act as bearers of a message to the disciples in Lk and Mt (28:8). In Mk they say nothing to anyone out of fear (16:8). Jn alone has Mary Magdalene report to the men what the risen Lord has told her (20:18).

"Mary the mother of James" (v. 10; cf. Mk 15:40; 16:1) is "Mary of James" in Greek. The other possibility is that she is the daughter of a man so named, but not the wife. As to identifying the James in question, he may be "the younger" of Mk 15:40 but it is impossible to know. Only Lk reports on Joanna, here as in 8:3. Verse 10*b* seems to conflate with the tradition on "the Eleven and the others" (v. 9) another tradition on the "apostles."

Verse 12 is missing from the Western text of Lk. If genuine, it reflects a tradition which Jn also has (20:3-10). Verse 24 presupposes something like it, while v. 34 reports an appearance of Jesus to Peter not otherwise recorded in the gospels but found in the tradition Paul passes on in 1 Cor 15:5.

It is a characteristic of Luke's risen-life account that he has everything take place not only in Jerusalem but on the same day (cf. vv. 1, 13, 36, 50), possibly for reasons of later community liturgical observance. His report of Jesus' appearances "over the course of forty days" (Ac 1:3) is not at odds with ch. 24 of the gospel because it is a symbolic, biblical forty days. It simply fills up the time until the Pentecost he wishes to report upon in 2:1. Lk-Acts stresses the exaltation of the Lord to God's right hand rather than his character as risen.

EASTER SUNDAY (C)

Acts 10:34, 37-43; Colossians 3:1-4 (first alternate); 1 Corinthians 5:6-8 (second alternate); John 20:1-9. See pp. 63-67.

SECOND SUNDAY OF EASTER (C)

Acts 5:12-16. This is one of three summaries of community and apostolic activity found in early Acts, the others being 2:42-47 and 4:32-35. They are not unlike certain summations of Jesus' healing activity in Mk (e.g., 6:56). Benoit thinks vv. 12b-14 of the present pericope the work of a redactor (thus, also, 2:43ff. and 4:33). In his theory, 12b is taken from 2:46a and 3:11; 13 from 2:47a; and 14 from 2:47b. If he is correct, Luke is somewhat absolved of the ambiguity of who "they (all, *hapantes*)" are in v. 12. NAB opts for the apostles rather than the people, as the natural subject of the sentence; the same would apply to "them" in v. 13. Who, then, are the others of "no one else" (*tōn de loipōn oudeis*)? It would be easier to identify them as Jerusalemites motivated by fear if the ones they "did not dare join" were, not the apostles but the whole church. But the next verse, 14, describes many who were not thus inhibited and who did become believers. Torrey thought that "no one else" meant none of the elders as contrasted with the common people. The NAB rendition hints at a holding back of ordinary church members from associating themselves actively with the apostles in their "signs and wonders" (v. 12), which are an answer to the prayer of 4:29f. The problem may be caused by an early corruption of the text, *loipōn* not having been the original reading.

The power of Peter here is balanced by the attribution of a similar gift of healing to Paul (19:12). Whenever a shadow falls (*episkiasē*, v. 16) in the New Testament it is a work of divine power (cf. Lk 1:35; 9:34; Mk 9:7.) What God once did for Mary in her conceiving and for Jesus in his transfiguration is now at work in the apostles in their ministry. See the discussion of charismatic healers in Judaism, particularly the 1st-c. A.D. Galilean *ḥasid* Ḥanina ben Dosa, in Geza Vermes' *Jesus the Jew*, pp. 72-80.

Revelation 1:9-13, 17-19. Jesus Christ as the one who was once dead but now lives "forever and ever" (v. 18) accounts for the occurrence of this reading on the Sunday after Easter. His appearance in glory to the visionary author John, exiled on Patmos because he "proclaimed God's word and bore witness to Jesus" (v. 9), is not unlike his appearances to the chosen witnesses in the gospels and to Paul (Gal 1:16; 1 Cor 15:8; 2 Cor 12:2-5). It more resembles the last-cited Pauline rapture than any other NT account, although the apocalyptic details of vv. 13-16—in the spirit of Ez 1:26; 9:2; 43:2 and Dn 7:9; 10:6—are nowhere to be found in the christophanies of the risen life.

After a prologue (vv. 1-3), the author of Revelation provides a covering letter (vv. 4-20) for the epistles to the seven churches in the province of Asia, modern Turkey across from Istanbul, which will follow (chs. 2-3). It is from this introductory epistle to the Christians of Ephesus, Smyrna, Pergamum, Thyatira, Sardis, Philadelphia, and Laodicaea that today's reading is taken. The cities lie clockwise around a Roman road that is still discoverable, e.g., at the ruins of Sardis and Laodicaea. The cities are not far separated. The present writer did all but Pergamum and Thyatira (modern Akhisar) to the north in a day out of Izmir (Smyrna) by car, and could have done them all without stopping if this doubtful achievement were to have made any sense. A visit to Honaz (Colossae) near Laodicaea but, much more, a disastrous road-diversion to the ruins of Aphrodisias consumed many hours. Philadelphia is Alaşehir, Ephesus Selçuk— the former a dusty Muslim town, the latter a treasure-house to be returned to again and again. Only Pergamum and Sardis rival it as excavations, but neither for size or splendor.

The title John adopts for himself is not apostle, overseer, or elder but "brother," and this because he has a share with fellow-Christians in the distress (*thlipsis*), kingly reign (*basileia*), and endurance (*hypomonē*) that are their lot (v. 9). Patmos is an island of six by ten miles which lies some thirty-seven miles WSW of Miletos. Despite its proximity to the Turkish coast it belongs, like most of the offshore islands, to Greece. Nearby Naxos, Kalimnos, and Cos outshine it as tourist attractions. It was a penal colony for political prisoners in Roman times. We know of a campaign of emperor-worship in Ephesus during Domitian's reign (81-96). Even so, the martyrdom of Antipas of Pergamum (2:13) is hard to set in any known context.

The author dates his ecstasy (lit., "I was in spirit") on the Lord's day as a cachet of its genuineness (v. 9). The number seven, already introduced with reference to the churches, will be a constant in this book. It appears early as referring to the lampstands (*lychniai*, v. 13, the biblical *menoroth*), which in v. 20 are to be identified as symbolic of the churches.

"One like a Son of Man" in Dn 13 refers to a human figure who represents Israel, as contrasted with the beasts who are other empires. Non-canonical apocalyptic literature made a specific individual of him. The author probably has Dn 10:9ff. in mind, as the seer falls prostrate and is raised up reassuringly (cf. Ez 1:28—2:1). For "I am the First and the Last" (v. 17; cf. v. 8), see Is 44:6 and 48:12, where it is Israel's God who makes the claim. Here and in 2:8; 22:13 the title is transferred to Christ, victorious over death and the never world (*hadēs=sheol*, the abode of the dead). Mt 16:18 uses the same figure for death, *hadēs*, but there Peter's keys do not admit to it but to the "reign of the heavens (i.e., God)." Christ in glory has this power in that, at the end, he will unlock the doors to every tomb and release the faithful dead from their imprisonment.

Verse 19 contains the seer's charter to inscribe in this book all that he has seen or will see.

John 20:19-31. See pp. 70f.

THIRD SUNDAY OF EASTER (C)

Acts 5:27-41. The framers of the lectionary seem more interested in the ill-treatment of the apostles at the hands of the Sanhedrin "for the sake of the Name" (v. 41) than in their spirited and intelligent defense by Gamaliel (vv. 33-39). No lector alert to the reality of Jewish-Christian tensions should follow their lead and omit these seven verses. The historical dependability of Ac, a book which very much "looks" like history, is a doubtful matter at many points. Hence the introduction of the name of the much respected Pharisee Gamaliel and the historical reminiscence attributed to him should by no means be omitted, if only to serve as a corrective for the stereotyped concept of "Pharisee" that stalks the gospels. In Lk certain Pharisees warn Jesus of Herod Antipas' enmity (cf. 13:31) while in Ac the alliance of Pharisees and followers of Jesus is quite explicit (cf., besides the present passage, 15:5; 23:6-9; 26:5f.)

Gamaliel is Gamaliel I (fl. A.D. 20-40), the leader of the Jerusalem Pharisees and, according to the Talmud, grandson of Hillel. The Judas of Galilee he speaks of (v. 37) is probably Judas of Gamala, a town east of the Golan Heights, who in the census under Quirinius, at the beginning of Coponius' term as the first prefect of Judaea (A.D. 6), joined with a Pharisee named Zadok to resist paying taxes to Rome (cf. Josephus, *Antiquities*, 18, 1, 1). These are the roots of the religious party of the Zealots, so that the statement of 37*b* is hardly true. Two of Judas' sons were crucified under the Romanized Jewish procurator Tiberius Julius Alexander (46-48); the last son Menahem captured Masada from the Romans in 66; and the latter's nephew

Eleazar was the legendary captain of that mountain fortress, who led in holding out until 73 when all were slaughtered. Of the identity of the Theudas referred to in v. 36 we cannot be sure. Either he is the self-proclaimed prophet of the procuratorship of Cuspius Fadus, A.D. 44-46 (*Ant.* 20, 5, 1), whose story Luke anachronistically inserts here, or the unknown bearer of a name common in those times. Theudas may be a shortened form of Theodoros, "gift of God" (Heb.: Mattanyāh = Matthias), in which case a visionary of the latter name described in *Ant.* 17, 6, 2 becomes a candidate. But this is pure speculation.

The actual, formal attention of the supreme council of Judaism to the Christian movement within a year or two of Jesus' execution is problematical. Stephen is described as summoned by this tribunal (6:12-15; 7:54). So is Paul (22:30-23:30). All of the accounts labor under the same difficulties as those in the gospels of Jesus' appearance before the Sanhedrin and its presiding high priest. Here, as in that case, a historical reminiscence of official Jewish displeasure over a long period should suffice to account for the summonings in legal form which Luke describes. It is impossible at this distance to distinguish the historical reality—whatever it may have been—from Luke's determination to make the Sanhedrin "responsible for *that* man's blood" (v. 28).

The claim of the apostles to a higher obedience (v. 29) has already appeared in 4:19. Lampe wonders whether Luke has Plato's *Apology* 29D in mind. The speech of Peter in vv. 29-32 is an echo of the longer one reported in 3:13-26. Both are early *kerygmata* which deal with Israel's history and its fulfillment in Jesus Christ as one continuous narrative. The "tree" of v. 30 is a stake of execution and derives from Dt 21:22 ('*es*=*xylon*). "Savior" is confined to Lk-Ac in NT usage, as a title congenial to the Greek world. Jesus is a "leader" (*archēgos*) here, as in 3:15. In both cases the connotation is of a Moses-like figure who initiates a journey from death to life. Heb 2:10 brings the two concepts together in the phrase "leader [in the work] of salvation"; Jesus is the "inspirer" (*archēgos*) of our faith in Heb 12:2. Bringing Israel to "repentance and the forgiveness of sins" is God's gift through Jesus and also the entire purpose of the gospel, in Lk's view (v. 31). The apostles and the holy spirit testify jointly to this reality.

"This speech persuaded them" (v. 39*b*), followed immediately by a report of flogging, recalls the behavior of Pilate (Lk 23:14ff., 22*c*; for the practice as a contemporary form of punishment, see 2 Cor 11:24; Ac 22:19.)

The complicated question of the historical dependability of the various traditions in Acts referred to above may require skepticism as to a formal action by Jerusalem's highest authority. It does not impugn confrontation of any sort. The intervention reported of Gamaliel is consonant with all we know of a respected sage, the more so as this one represents the Pharisee outlook in a body where priestly Sadducees were probably in control.

Revelation 5:11-14. The ministering thousands (v. 11) in this vision of a heavenly liturgy derive from the description of the court of the Ancient One in Dn 7:10. Those purchased from every race and tongue, people and nation (cf. Dn 3:4, 7) in the new community of believers are a kingdom of priests in the manner of Ex 10:6. They call out in praise of the slain Lamb (*arnion*, v. 12; 28 times in this book) the imperial acclamation *Axios!*, "Worthy!" Before the One seated on the throne (vv. 7, 13), there is the Lamb who is standing (v. 6). He may be the Passover lamb (Ex 12:5) or the slaughtered innocent of Is 53:7f. but he is more than that. His seven horns (v. 6) make him a ram at the very least (a symbol of power in Dn 8:3 even if Alexander the Great, the he-goat, takes the measure of the ram with two horns, Media and Persia). There is the further possibility that a ram of Jewish apocalyptic literature is intended, a strong leader of the flock of Israel. Rev 14:1 would support this interpretation.

All creation, every possible category of creature (v. 13), sings the praises of God and the Lamb. Christ has won the victory and sits beside his Father on the throne (3:21). The four living creatures (cf. 4:6b-8) and the twenty-four elders (cf. 4:4) coupled in 5:14 fall down in worship. The symbolism of both is obscure. The safest thing to say is that the totality of God's people (the twenty-four priestly courses? a reference to some non-Jewish mythology?) and of the world's empires bow low before the Lamb and hymn his victory. The "new song" (v. 9) they sing celebrates him who has come to make all things new (cf. 21:1, 5.)

John 21:1-19. The "disciple whom Jesus loved" (21:20) is the great authority-figure for the author of this final, appended chapter. This disciple is the dependable witness, even in writing, to "all these things" that happened to Jesus—only a fraction of which the author recorded. We do not know why the composer of ch. 21 (who is seemingly the redactor of the whole gospel; cf. 13:23; 19:26; 20:2) gave his independent witness to appearances of the risen Jesus in Galilee. The author of the first twenty chapters has situated his three christophanies in Jerusalem. Probably the author of ch. 21 simply possesses certain traditions—found scattered around the synoptics in other forms (cf. Lk 5:1-11; Mt 16:17-19; Lk 22:31f.; 24:31, 34f., 41b-

43; Mk 14:29ff.)—and preserves them in tribute to the great hero of his community whom Jesus loved (*ho mathētēs hon ēgapa ho Iēsous*).

This disciple is described in v. 20 as one of the seven present (cf. v. 2) in such a way that he seems to be one of the unnamed "two others" rather than a son of Zebedee, viz., John. Jesus has performed two of his Johannine "signs" in Galilee but in the fourth gospel the time he spends there is minimal. Only ch. 6 has the lake as its locale, specifically the Tiberias-Capernaum crossing where modern ferries ply the choppy waters.

The unsuccessful night of fishing resembles what is told in Lk 5:4-7. (See p. 290.) "As at 20:8, [the beloved disciple] is the quicker in perception, but as at 20:6, Peter is the more impulsive in action" (Barrett). The size of the catch which did not tear the net (v. 11) is put down by some as a trustworthy remembrance because meaningless in itself. These commentators scarcely reckon with the numerological symbolism of the Johannine school. St. Jerome volunteers the information that 153 species of fish were listed by the natural historians of his time. Or again, it is a number arrived at by adding all the digits from 1 to 17; but 10 and 7, equalling 17, are signs of perfection in the Jewish world. We can be sure, at least, that these fishers of men are making a catch of "sizable fish" (v. 11) while doing no harm to the net that takes them.

The distinction between lambs and sheep in vv. 15, 16, 17 (*arnia, probata, probata*) and the verbs for pasturing and tending (*boske, poimaine, boske*) do not seem significant. The thrust lies rather in the threefold challenge, the verbal variation being incidental. The same is true of the verbs *agapan* and *philein*. This profession of love elicited from Peter rights the offense of his threefold denial (18:17, 25, 27). He is told, moreover, that he can now follow Jesus (*Akolouthei moi*, v. 19) even to martyrdom—apparently the tradition on his end which the author has—as once he was told he could not follow Jesus (cf. 13:36ff.)

The poetic form in which v. 18 is cast by NAB, following Brown and others, betrays the conviction that it is a hymnic fragment.

FOURTH SUNDAY OF EASTER (C)

Acts 13:14, 43-52. The occurrence described in this reading is Luke's theological interpretation of the increasing gentilization of the churches of Paul. It is not to be presumed literally historical, except in the sense that his source could well have recorded turbulence in the

Jewish community of Phrygian Antioch. Luke uses this as the setting of a definitive shift of Pauline interest, by way of declared policy (vv. 46f.) What evolved over many years, despite Paul's consistent and unremitting efforts to preach Christ to fellow Jews, Acts describes as a matter of Jewish rejection of salvation and correlative Gentile acceptance. It is hard to think of a passage that is pastorally less apt for public reading, given the modern temper of literalism and total unreadiness for theological history of a Lucan kind. The homilist, if he refers to the reading at all, must identify the excitement caused by Paul here as elsewhere as divisive, but hardly decisive in the way described. We may not underestimate the impact on Paul and Barnabas of their early discovery of Gentile interest in the gospel. They were doubtless unprepared for the paradox of resistance in synagogues and a friendly hearing by the wider populace ("the whole city," v. 44). Yet, the modern Christian needs to be more critical than Luke in his estimate of what is going on here.

The diaspora Jew had long borne the burden of the day's heat. His patient, plodding efforts with converts (the *polloi . . . tōn sebomenōn prosēlytōn* of v. 43, probably a mixture of many "devout" worshipers and far fewer circumcised proselytes) were well known to him. So was the enthusiasm of a day in a Greek populace with which he was well familiar. The agitation of the Jewish community reported in v. 50 would be fully understandable if, after a week's reflection, its members saw the social threat represented by Barnabas and Paul. An equal place in the Jewish community for proselytes, God-fearers, and straight-out Gentiles more numerous than Jews would have destroyed the fabric of religious community life. They are therefore to be applauded for perception rather than reviled for lack of faith. The speech framed for the apostolic pair by Luke (vv. 46f.) is the early Christian understanding of Is 49:6. Israel's enlightenment of the nations has, ever since the time of the Second Isaiah, been understood by Jews in terms of themselves as a moral and religious influence on the non-Jewish world through Torah. Verses 48-49 are a summary of apostolic activity in liturgical form.

This narrative occurs toward the beginning of the first of three missionary journeys of Paul which Luke has constructed. The immediate progress from Perga on the sea-coast to the northern plateau where Antioch lies is unexplained. The author's far greater interest is in God's grace (v. 43) and its action. For him it begets contradiction of God and violent abuse (*antelegon . . . blasphemountes*, v. 45) on the part of some; delight, praise, and belief (*echairon kai edoxazon . . . kai episteusan*, v. 48) on the part of others. Leading personages of both sexes in the Jewish community are cast in the role of *provocateurs/ses*.

Revelation 7:9, 14-17. The crowd from every "nation and race, people and tongue" of v. 9 have previously appeared in 5:9, having originated in an older Aramaic text of Dn 3:4 (according to R. H. Charles). Palm branches are a symbol of victory after war; the long white robes (*stolas leukas*, v. 9) are identified as possible baptismal vesture. It has been observed by many that the substitution of "Lamb" for God in vv. 9, 10, and 14 would be all that would be necessary to transform this from a paean celebrating Jewish martyrs into a Christian one, on the assumption that "white" (v. 14) is a generic term to convey purification.

The problem of the lack of information on any widespread early persecution of Christians has been referred to in the commentary on Rev 1:9-19 (See Second Sunday of Easter above, pp. 315ff.). The "great trial" (*thlipsis megalē*, v. 14) is probably an eschatological rather than a historical conflict, especially if the original version of the chapter is Jewish. The washing of garments (v. 14) occurs in Gn 49:11, a washing to the whiteness of wool in Is 1:18. The shelter God will give (*skēnōsei*, v. 15) is an echo of the "made his dwelling among us" (*eskēnōsen*, Jn 1:14) of the Johannine prologue. Both have been connected with the cloud above the propitiatory (cf. Lv 16:2) but the tent of Dwelling which God pitched in the midst of his people (cf. Ex 26) seems the likelier biblical type.

Freedom from thirst and the sun's heat (v. 16) is bliss for parched Israel (cf. Is 49:10), freedom from hunger a reminiscence of the privations of the exodus. The Lamb as shepherd (v. 17) evokes Ez 34:23, among many biblical places, while the springs of flowing water are from Jer 2:13 and the wiping away of every tear from Is 28:8. "Springs of life-giving water" are literally "waters of life," a phrase which recalls all that the fourth gospel does with "running water" (*hydōr zōn*, Jn 4:10).

John 10:27-30. Using the figure of YHWH as the shepherd of Israel so familiar from the Bible, Jn creates with swift strokes a picture of the bond between Jesus and his flock. The time is the season of Hanukkah (v. 22), December, a detail which does not seem to be included for any symbolic significance. The shepherd Jesus gives sustenance, the life of the final age (*zōēn aiōnion*, v. 28), and protection. He gives what he has been given by him with whom he is intimately united. No one can snatch this gift of life away. One supposes that this latter is a polemical aside, telegraphed by the evangelist to any outside the Johannine circle who would come between God and his elect in Jesus.

FIFTH SUNDAY OF EASTER (C)

Acts 14:21-27. At Lystra in Lycaonia Paul and Barnabas had been accorded divine honors by the native pagan populace as a result of the cure of a man crippled from birth (14:11-13). Despite their vigorous demurrers, they were apparently thought by some Jews from Antioch and Iconium, to the west, to have acceded to it. These reacted violently (v. 19). The stoning reported of Paul would be the one which he himself says he received (cf. 2 Cor 11:25.) Derbe (vv. 20f.) was to be the farthest east he would penetrate into Asia Minor. With Barnabas he could have elected to return overland to Syria from which they had set out. Instead they retraced their steps westward to check on the progress of their new converts (v. 22). Entering "into the reign of God," like "persevering in the faith," means for Luke living the life of the new age. It is something achieved only after many trials, whether for the Christian (cf. Lk 21:16-19) or for Christ (cf. Lk 24:26.) St. Paul's use of the concept of God's reign (*basileia*) is infrequent (cf. Rom 14:17; 1 Cor 4:20.) When he does employ the term it is as something popularly misconceived: "eating and drinking" and "talk" rather than what it is in fact, the justice, peace, and joy given by the Spirit, or his power.

The installation of officers in the local communities is done ritually (v. 23), by way of a solemn charge. These elders (*presbyteroi*), chosen on the Jewish model, need not have been senior citizens; wisdom was the chief requirement. Testimony to a similar practice in Ephesus will be found in 20:17; in v. 28 they are called those who keep watch (*episkopoi*), with the task of shepherding. In Paul's letters, the only reference to such local incumbents is the mention of *episkopoi* and *diakonoi* in Phil 1:1. This sparseness of reference has created the problem of the exact nature of local congregational government in his lifetime. The deutero-Pauline letters are specific about personal qualifications but do not remove the uncertainty of who was designated to do what (cf. 1 Tim 3:1-13; Ti 1:5-8.) In the two latter references the titles *episkopoi, presbyteroi,* and *diakonoi* appear but not in any one place. All that can be fairly deduced is that the latter class included women and that the mono-episcopate, so-called, was not a feature of the Pauline churches.

Verses 27f. describe the report of the two apostles to the congregation (*ekklēsia*) that had sent them out. A point is probably being made of their unawareness of any obligation to make a report to the church of Jerusalem. In any case, it serves as an introduction to the tension reported between Judaea and Antioch in the next chapter. The "door of faith" recalls Paul's language (cf. 1 Cor 16:9.)

No explanation is offered as to why the pair set sail from Attalia without returning to visit Salamis and Paphos in Cyprus (cf. 13:4-12.)

Revelation 21:1-5. This passage is a vision of renewed heavens and a renewed earth. It is important to be clear that Jewish apocalyptic eschatology concentrated on an age to follow this one after cataclysmic purification. The popular and incorrect view is that such literature featured the destruction of humanity or the end of the world (i.e., universe). Only one passage in the Qumrân scrolls can be adduced which envisions the "end" as an actual destruction by fire (*Hodayoth* [Hymns] col. III, 29-33). The whole tenor of this style of writing was one of redemption and hope for a new life on earth. Thus, the "sea [the abyss in ancient mythology, man's enemy] was no longer."

The new Jerusalem of this chapter is probably not the dwelling-place of God transferred to this sphere but the center of Christ's activity during some millennial period to come or the community of believers present in the world—on the assumption that they will respond to their lofty vocation. The bride image, descriptive of Israel faithful to her husband YHWH, sustains the latter view, for it was very much a hoped-for reality of earthly existence.

Verse 3 derives from Ez 37:27; 4*a* from Is 25:8; 4*b* less directly from Is 35:10. Portions of vv. 4 and 5 recall 2 Cor 5:17 strikingly.

John 13:31-35. These verses introduce the soliloquy of chapters 14-16 and the prayer of Jesus with which it closes, the latter an epilogue which balances off the prologue of 1:1-18.

The glorification spoken of in v. 31*b* is an anticipation of Jesus' sufferings, which for Jn are none other than his glory. Some have suggested that the specific reference is to the just concluded washing of feet as a sign of all that is to follow; or it may be that Judas' deed, which will set all the rest in motion, is intended. This means that the glory that is to come "soon" (*euthys*, v. 32) need not signify resurrection but the mystery of crucifixion and glorification taken as one.

Jn's "children" (*teknia*, v. 33) are the believers of his community, who are reminded here as at 7:33; 8:21; 20:29*c* that belief includes separation from the glorified Christ who is not seen.

The "new commandment" is such in its role as the sign of the new age. The injunctions to love in Lv 19:18 and Mt 5:44 have not been superseded by a further one. That general command is lived out in the Johannine church, with Jesus' love for his disciples now established as the norm of all interpersonal loves (vv. 34f.) It is the badge of discipleship.

The "Jews" of v. 33 are our familiar out-group of the fourth gospel: all who, unlike the Johannine circle, do not accept Jesus. Jn's community is likewise made up of Jews. Some go so far as to hold that Jn, unlike the synoptics, has no interest in an outreach to the Gentiles.

SIXTH SUNDAY OF EASTER (C)

Acts 15:1-2, 22-29. Luke's account of the "council of Jerusalem" is notoriously difficult to square with Paul's version of what seem to be certain of the same events and, indeed, with anything we know of the mentality of Jerusalem Christians. Peter's speech (vv. 7-11) and James's (vv. 13-21) are pure Lucan discourse, as evidenced by the improbable exegesis of LXX texts by James. The narrative is probably a fusion of two accounts, one of a dispute on circumcision and the other about food laws in cases where kosher-observing and non-kosher-observing Christians mingled in the same churches.

A delegation made up of Paul, Barnabas, and others went up (southward, since everything is "down" from Mt. Zion) from Antioch to Jerusalem to discuss differences over circumcision practice with regard to Gentile converts to the Christian way (cf. vv. 1f.) This journey seems to be the one described by Paul in Gal 2:1-10, on the occasion when he sought and achieved a favorable settlement on his decision not to circumcise Titus or Gentiles like him. Paul describes the visit as the result of a revelation but he includes the detail from Acts about provocation by infiltrators from Judea, whom he calls "false claimants to the title of brother" (*pseudadelphoi*). The sole stipulation on that occasion, according to him, was care for the poor (Gal 2:10). Acts 15 has nothing to say about this. Moreover, the occasion was only Paul's second visit to Jerusalem by his reckoning (cf. Gal 1:18; 2:1), whereas Acts 15 makes it the third (cf. Ac 9:26; 11:30.) The so-called "famine visit" by Barnabas and Saul in 11:30 contains an echo of Paul's Galatian testimony about care for the (Judean Christian) poor.

Since Peter's acceptance at Caesarea of the uncircumcized to baptism and his promulgation of full table fellowship with them thereafter (cf. Ac 10 and 11) seems not to have convinced all Pharisee and priestly Christians in Judea, Lk requires a formalization of the understanding like the one he records. The practice of Paul, which he says in his letters that he follows, indicates that he either came away with a wholly different understanding or, more likely, that there was no letter drafted like that of vv. 23-29.

We should have no difficulty in classifying it as a Lucan construct since the speeches of Peter, Paul, and James are already in that category. All represent theological charters, as it were, for the settlements that were subsequently arrived at over a long period. This is not to say that there is no possibility of historical reminiscence of a delegation to the church at Antioch which included the Judeans Judas and Silas (v. 22).

The pairing of "apostles and elders" (v. 23) is significant in light of last week's discussion of v. 23. It is Lk's way of describing both those roving bearers of the message outside any jurisdiction and the officers of the local church, a distinction made even in Jerusalem. Since Antioch is named in the greeting rather than Damascus or Tarsus, it can be seen as the recognized center of Gentile Christianity, as previously in Acts (cf. esp. 13:1-3.) Verse 24 distinguishes between the official status of the letter-writers and the unauthorized character of those who created the initial dissension in Antioch (cf. 15:1f.) Judas and Silas are the accredited interpreters of the authentic Jerusalem spirit, here understood to be that voiced by Peter and James earlier in the chapter and in ch. 10 (see p. 10f.) The coupling of the Holy Spirit with the human makers of the decision (v. 28) bears the cachet of Lucan theology. The four out of seven traditional Noachide precepts of the settlement, repeated from v. 20, are the only burden imposed on Gentile converts.

The probable OT sources for the four prohibitions enjoined, ritual rather than ethical, are: meat sacrificed to idols (Lv 17:8f.), blood remaining in meat (Lv 17:10ff.), the ritual slaughter of animals (Lv 17:13), and sex within close degrees of kinship (Lv 18:6-18). These four occur among the seven proposed by later rabbis as a *derek ereṣ* or law of the land which bound all the descendants of Noah until the law was given, and the resident aliens among the Jews thereafter. The seven prohibitions constituted a minimum for the Torah-oriented community. This was probably incomprehensible to later Christians, with the result that the variant Western text of Acts omits "what is strangled" from v. 20 and many MSS add the golden rule in the prevailing negative form. *Porneia* is omitted from some texts as out of place among dietary rules, or understood as prohibiting unchaste conduct generally rather than the Levitical incest taboo. Similarly, the prohibition against blood comes to be taken as a forbidding of bloodshed, i.e., murder, in line with later church discipline.

St. Paul is well familiar with the problems arising from eating foods not slaughtered ritually or sacrificed to idols (cf. Rom 14:14-17; 1 Cor 8:9-13; 10:23-30 and the corresponding commentaries on pp. 137 and 96f.) He does not give counsel as if the decree of Ac 15 bound him, although if it were drawn up in any such form he could argue that the problems in Corinth and Rome were different from those of Antioch, Syria, and Tarsus.

The settlement on foods recorded in Acts is probably documented in some Jerusalem-church source which Luke has come upon. It does not accord with Paul's practice but Luke, the great reconciler, makes it do so. As to the one great reconciling element in Paul's mind, the relief of the Judean poor, Luke seems to have no documentation on that.

Revelation 21:10-14. This vision of a Jerusalem descending from on high takes its departure from the bride figure of v. 2 (cf. v. 9) but concentrates on a city of precious stones. The author is undoubtedly influenced by Ez, whose ch. 40 seems to have four gates, one facing in each direction. They become twelve named for the twelve tribes in 48:30-35. Ephesians has a similar conception, namely of a temple made up of believers which rises "on the foundation of the prophets and the apostles" (2:20). The twelve names of the twelve tribes and the tutelary angel for each in Revelation are details that connote the perfect character of the believing community, at least in conception. The New Jerusalem is a perfect cube (vv. 15f.), making the same point. This city is an earthly reality but it partakes of the heavenly nature of the abode of God from which it derives (v. 10).

John 14:23-29. The fourth evangelist cannot get over the marvel of faith in Jesus as the Messiah of his faith community. The opposite reality of a "world" that has not accepted him is likewise never far from his thoughts. This pericope comes in answer to a problem posed as a personal difficulty of the disciple Jude (the Jewish people?) but doubtless very real in Jn's time: how is it that Jesus has revealed himself to those who believe in him but not successfully to a hostile world?

The answer proposed is in terms of being true to Jesus' word (*ton logon mou tērēsei*, v. 23) and the love common to the Father, Jesus, and the believer that comes as the fruit of this fidelity. The word of Jesus is from the Father, just as he is from the Father. Both God and Jesus will come to dwell with anyone who accepts the word (v. 23).

The holy spirit of God will be sent by the Father as *Paraklētos* (counselor or advocate) in a surrogate position for the departed Jesus. His function will be to instruct (*didaxei*, v. 26) and to remind (*hypomnēsei*) with respect to all that Jesus told the disciples, not to bring new teaching.

Jesus gives as his parting gift a deep and abiding *shalom*—not, presumably, the thoughtless word of farewell that is on the lips of people constantly. It is quite the opposite of the world's "Peace."

There is no place in the believer's heart for distress or fear at separation from Jesus (v. 27c). The separation is temporary (v. 28a). True love will rejoice that Jesus is with the Father, where he belongs. The Father is "greater" (*meizōn*, 28c) in the sense that he is before Jesus as before all; his will must prevail.

The revelation of Jesus' impending departure serves as a preparation for belief. There must be no hesitancy in faith because he is away from his friends. Just as later in 20:29, the non-seeing believer is praised here above the one who, like Thomas, sees.

ASCENSION (C)

(Thursday after Sixth Sunday of Easter)

Acts 1:1-11. Lk 1:1-4 is a preface to Luke-Acts in its entirety, addressed to the unidentified, highly placed ("*kratiste*") Theophilus. Ac 1:1-5 is a preface to this book only, which reviews certain materials found in Lk 22. Among these are Jesus' being taken up to heaven (v. 2; cf. Lk 22:51); his appearing to "the apostles" over the course of forty days (v. 3; cf. Lk 22:15f., 30f., 36), his suffering (*to pathein*, v. 3) of which he spoke in Lk 22:25ff. and 44-47; and his meeting (eating) with his disciples (v. 4; cf. Lk 22:41-43), at which time he told them not to leave Jerusalem (v. 4; cf. Lk 22:49). The order of events in the preface to Ac is obviously different but this does not alter or minimize the importance of the events, namely as links between Luke's "first account" (*prōton logon*, Ac 1:1) and his second. Jesus' life, death, and glorification prepare for his Father's promise (Lk 22:49; Ac 1:4f.) to be sent down: "power from on high" (Lk) or "being baptized with the Holy Spirit" which will bring "power" (Ac). The detail of forty days (v. 3 does not appear in Lk. This sacred space of time (cf. Gn 7:12; 8:6; Ex 24:18; 1 Kgs 19:8) gives ample room for the demonstration "in many convincing ways" (v. 3) of his state as living (*zōnta*). Lk's gospel, conversely, seems to describe Jesus as leaving the Eleven after having blessed them (24:51) on the evening of the day he was raised up. (Cf. vv. 9, 13, 36, 50 for indications of the sequence.) The difference is of no consequence; least of all is it to be settled by recourse to the theory of Jesus' earthly visitations from his new home in heaven. The two things being affirmed are the reality of his being taken from his friends into glory and his conversations with them about God's reign (v. 4), which for Lk will begin with the parousia. For him the life of the Spirit-directed church is a separate matter. The affirmations against gnostic docetism (Lk 24:43; Ac 10:41) were probably later developments. "All that Jesus did and taught" (v. 1) describes Jesus' earthly life, while the risen-life instruction (lit. "command," from *enteilamenos*) he gave the chosen apostles (v. 2) corresponds to Lk 24:44. It is in their chosenness "through the Holy Spirit" (v. 2) that they have been given authority to teach in the ways that will follow in Ac.

Luke's word for Jesus' taking up in v. 2 (*anelēmphthē*) has already been used in its noun form in his gospel (9:51) for the same purpose. It seems to derive from the LXX of 2 Kgs 2:11 where Elijah —a type of Christ for Lk—is taken up in a chariot of fire.

Only in Mk 13:11 and its parallel in Mt (not Lk, interestingly) does Jesus speak of the Spirit in the synoptics. In Ac 1:5 and again in 11:16, a saying attributed to John the Baptizer (Mt 3:11; Lk 3:16) is put on Jesus' lips. Luke will later have Paul make the same distinction in Ephesus between the water-baptism of John and the Spirit-baptism of Jesus (Ac 19:1-6) as is made in v. 5.

The apostles' query about when Israel will have the *basileia* restored to it (v. 6) is answered in terms of undivulgeable mystery (v. 7) and missionary command (v. 8). Mk 13:32 (par. Mt 24:36) contains a *logion* of Jesus like that of v. 7 which Lk had not used in his gospel, saving it for here. It is calculated to relieve disappointment in the Christian community over the non-realization of the parousial hope (cf. 1 Pt 3:3ff.) By Lk's time the question is not even to be raised; a new relationship to the world has been arrived at: life in the holy community. The notion of witnessing to Jesus, viz., to his resurrection, is common throughout Acts. Jesus' sending of the apostles "to the ends of the earth" (v. 8) will only mean getting Paul as far as Rome in this book, but it is at least a divine sanction on his mission. Peter and John travel as far as Samaria.

There is no final blessing by Jesus in Ac as in Lk 24:50 (cf. Sir 50:20f.) He is taken up swiftly in the sight of the apostles (v. 9), a detail which constitutes them witnesses of the ascension. Livy tells of Romulus' being swept up in a cloud, while the intertestamental book of Enoch has that prophet say the same of himself. The two men in white (v. 10) resemble those in Lk's empty-tomb account (24:4). They administer a rebuke intended for the whole church. All expectation of the imminent return of Jesus is to be reprobated. It is a reality of the future but one that has about it no precise connotation of time.

Ephesians 1:17-23. Eph, after its initial greeting, begins with a blessing of God (*Eulogētos ho theos*, v. 3) in vv. 3-14—the traditional Jewish *berakah*—and moves on to a thanksgiving in vv. 15-23 (*eucharistōn*, v. 16). The anonymous author, usually known as "the Ephesian continuator," doubtless includes both forms because the use of each was Paul's practice at various times. The technique, while redundant, is nonetheless to be found in Dn 2:20 and 23. The hope expressed in the present passage is that the wisdom bestowed on Gentile Christians (v. 9) may be effectively received by them (v. 17). A heritage has been given, the wealth of which (v. 18) is comprised of wisdom and understanding (v. 9). This inheritance (v. 14) is not yet fully given but exists at present by way of pledge or first payment (*arrabōn*), to be rendered in its entirety when the full redemption (*apolytrōsis*) of God's personal possession—his people (cf. 1 Pt 2:9) —has been bestowed. Such time will be after the *parousia*. The acceptance of the inheritance by believers is required if it is to be a completed reality. That Christians may know the hope to which they are called, the "eyes of their hearts" must be enlightened (v. 18). God's power in the believer is likened to the strength he showed in Christ when raising him from the dead and seating him at God's right hand (v. 20). The importance of v. 20 is that it distinguishes between the resurrection and the subsequent exaltation of Christ, something that Paul does not do. He thinks in terms of a single act of glorification while Lk-Ac resembles Eph in its division of the mystery into two episodes.

Mention of the Ephesians' faith (v. 15) is a Pauline touch, but this theological treatise in epistolary form does not much resemble the communication of someone who has lived quite a while among the recipients. Paul knew this congregation as well as any and did not need to learn of its faith by hearsay.

The anti-gnostic or anti-angelic-hierarchy tone of Colossians is caught here in vv. 21-23 and again in 6:12. Christ is high above the choirs of angels. Four of the traditional intertestamental nine are here named: *archai, exousiai, dynameis*, and *kyriotētes* (Col 1:16 has "thrones" in place of "virtues," *dynameis*). The headship of Christ is over his body, the church, here (vv. 22f.), whereas in 1:10 it has been over all things in the heavens and on earth, over principalities and powers in Col 2:10. The important declaration of faith in Christ (as in Col 2:9) is that he has been made the *plērōma* of him who fulfills everything in the universe, namely God. Colossians says that in Christ the *plērōma* of God dwells in bodily form. Both writers mean to challenge all gnostic and angelic hierarchies that lay claim to *plērōma* status and put in their place the ascended, exalted Christ and him alone.

Luke 24:46-53. Christ's concluding charge to his disciples has him interpreting to them the prophetic message of the Scriptures (v. 45), just as he did to the two at Emmaus (v. 27). Verse 46 has already appeared in longer form in 9:22. Penance and the remission of sins must be preached worldwide in the name of Christ (v. 47; cf. Mk 13:10) because he has suffered and risen. The latter is the content of the gospel, the former its practical consequence. Jerusalem, not Galilee, is for Lk the *locus originis* of the new faith. It is the place where the disciples do the witnessing they must now proclaim (v. 48). The promise and power of God from on high has come down like the spirit on all flesh and specifically to this city (v. 49).

The direct mention of Jesus' being taken up (v. 51) is referred to again in Ac 1:2 as the link between the two books. Lk's gospel ends as it has begun, in Jerusalem's temple (vv. 52f.) He is ready to begin the complementary narrative of how the gospel was first lived and then carried abroad. He will proceed from its fate in Jewish circumstances to Gentile to make his point that the transfer was providential, in the sense of totally foreseen by God. Lk's great theme is that the Jews had their chance and, as we might say in terms of a contemporary hermeneutic, blew it. The Christian must read him with caution.

SEVENTH SUNDAY OF EASTER (C)

Acts 7:55-60. The speech which Luke puts on Stephen's lips ends with a direct, harsh accusation addressed to the Sanhedrin (Ac 6:12) and the high priest (7:1), whom he associates with their fathers, the murderers of the prophets (v. 52). Told that their offense is failure to observe the law (v. 53), they are understandably enraged (v. 54; cf. Ps. 35:16.) The commentary on Ac 8:5-8, 14-17 (6th Sunday of Easter, p. 80) speaks of the reported action of the infuriated mob (vv. 57f.) as bearing no relation to anything we know from the Mishnaic tractate *Sanhedrin*. In that document, compiled with the rest around A.D. 200, the "place of stoning is twice the height of a man." The victim is lain supine and finished off with a stone "dropped on his heart" by either a first or a second "witness." The mention of "witnesses" in v. 58 suggests a juridical process in an otherwise extra-legal account.

Today's pericope is as much about Stephen's vision in vindication of his witness to Jesus, the Just One, as it is about the circumstances of his death. Possession of the Holy Spirit has been named earlier as characteristic of him (6:5). Here (v. 55) it is the condition of his being strengthened for death. A vision of divine glory before execution is conventional in Jewish accounts of martyrdom. Acts uses it to confirm the fact of Jesus' standing at the right hand of God (v. 56).

Cf. Lk 22:69, where he is seated; the phrase betrays Lk's ignorance of the Jewish term "the Power" for God, similar to "the Glory" in v. 55.

Luke is familiar with the designation "son of man," as we know from his gospel. He does not employ it anywhere in Ac but here (v. 56), perhaps to signalize the transition from a Jewish to a Gentile church. The question has been raised whether Lk has in mind an advocate's role for Jesus, patterned on that of God in Job 16:19: "Even now, behold, my witness is in heaven, / and my spokesman is on high." Jesus' reception of Stephen, standing, recalls Luke's view of immediate glorification promised to the repentant brigand in Lk 23:43.

The similarities in the deaths of Jesus and Stephen are evident (cf. Lk 23:46 and 34a if it is genuine; also the detail of the witnesses' garments, 34b.) The role of the Sanhedrin in Stephen's death, as in that of Jesus, is entirely problematical. So too is the intimation of blasphemy in both cases (Mk 14:64; "holding their hands over the ears," Ac 7:57). *Sanhedrin* 1.5 speaks of one's being a false prophet as an offense actionable before this body; 4.5 of witnesses in capital cases; 6.4 of blasphemy and idolatry as two capital cases. The uncertainty as to whether Rome had withdrawn capital punishment from the jurisdiction of the Sanhedrin in the days of the prefects of Judea is well known. For an extended discussion see Paul Winter, *On the Trial of Jesus.*

Revelation 22:12-14, 16-17, 20.   This is the concluding passage of the revelation given by God to Jesus Christ, reported by John on Patmos (1:1). The valedictory (v. 21) is eliminated from the public reading, probably because v. 20 provides a stronger ending. Verse 12 is repeated from v. 7 and four of Jesus' six titles are taken from those of God in 21:6 (cf. 1:8, 17; 2:8; Is 44:6.) Jesus promises that the end will come soon (*tachy*, v. 12). In eschatological perspective this is not a precise time word and may just as well mean swiftly or suddenly. Upon his return he will act as judge.

The seer, John, is Jesus' messenger (*aggelos*, v. 16) who has given his witness regarding the state of the churches (v. 16). The title "Root of David" occurs in 5:5 while "Morning Star" (*ho aster ho proïnos*) without its adjective "bright" (*ho lampros*) appears in 2:28. Those who have washed their robes (cf. Gn 49:11) and may enter the city are presumably the martyrs, or perhaps merely the just of 3:4, 7:14. The figure of the tree of life from Gn 2:9; 3:22 is cited here the only time in the New Testament. These writings in general show little interest in the "sin of our first parents" which looms so large in catechetical history (cf. Jn 8:44?; 2 Cor 11:3; in another category are

1 Cor 15:22, 45; Rom 5:14f.)

The song *Twelve Gates to the City* will be a contact point for many for last week's reading and this. It is a song about entry into life.

God's spirit speaks through the visionary authors (v. 17). He is not alone in issuing an invitation to drink of the waters of life. It is also uttered by the bride of the Lamb (cf. 19:7*b*-8), the community of God's saints. The life-giving water is traceable to Is 55:1 and occurs frequently in the Johannine literature. *Uisge beatha* and *eau de vie* are the *hydōr zōēs* of v. 17 but clearly distinguishable from the biblical draught: they are not free (*dōrean*), although they may at times be duty-free.

Christ promises a speedy (sudden?) advent and the author of the book confirms this with a grateful "Amen." He concludes with a phrase in Greek (*erchou Kyrie lēsou*, v. 20) which we know in transliterated Aramaic from 1 Cor 16:22 and also from the *Didachē: Maran atha*, "Our Lord, come!" This was evidently a liturgical phrase used in Greek-speaking churches as a remnant, like *Kyrie eleison, Hosanna*, and *Sabaoth* in the Roman rite.

Verse 21 provides the farewell blessing which seems to be missing from all seven letters to the churches of chapters 2-3.

John 17:20-26. Verses 9-19 of Jesus' final apostrophe to the Father upon completing his work have been a prayer for the needs of the disciples. In these concluding verses (20-26) he prays for all who believe in him through the disciples' witnessing word. This prayer is one for unity among believers (v. 21) and for their acceptance of Jesus' legacy of love (v. 26). The bond of personal interpenetration between Jesus and the Father is proposed as a model for unity among believers. Jesus' prayer is that they may be in God and him, as he and God are in each other (v. 21). More than that, the presence of believers to God and Jesus (*en hēmin*; the *hen* of "[one] in us," v. 21, is lacking in the best MSS) is the sign proposed by Jesus "*that* the world may believe that you sent me." Nothing can convert a hostile world, in other words, but its experience of Christians who are in God and Christ.

Jesus possesses a fullness (1:16) and a glory (1:14; 8:54) from the Father that he is able to transmit to others. This glory (*doxa*) was God's gift to him "before the foundation of the world" (v. 24). Here he would have them see it (*theōrōsin*, v. 24), whereas a few phrases above he says he has given it (*dedōka*, v. 22). The Vulgate renders the gift as *claritas* rather than *gloria*, a divine luminosity bestowed first on Jesus, then on all who associate themselves with him in intimacy with the Father. Jesus lives in his friends and God lives in him (v. 23); therefore God lives in them. This, it is hoped, will bring to completion a unity (*hina ōsin teteleiōmenoi eis hen*, v. 23) among them, with no distinction drawn as to who is one with whom: the Father, Jesus, all believers. The picture is one of mystical union in faith of God and man, with Jesus as the first beneficiary of a plan that originates in the depths of godhead.

Jesus wills that where he is, those whom the Father has given him may be along with him (*thelō hina hopou eimi egō kakeinoi ōsin met' emou*, v. 24) to see his glory. This is all part of the futurist thrust of Johannine eschatology which some would deny to it. Massey Shepherd draws attention to the opinion that this prayer with which ch. 17 concludes is an exposition of the succinct Lord's prayer in Mt and Lk, and observes in both "a curious lack of reference to the Spirit."

God is a righteous (*dikaie*, v. 25) Father for Jesus, the source of all righteousness (Heb. ṣedaka). Jn knows Jesus as primarily a Moses-like prophet who reveals God to men, but now in the fullest way possible (cf. 1:17f.; 17:26.) Ever at the Father's side (lit., "deep in his bosom," 1:18), he has been sent (17:25) by God to reveal his name (v. 26). His work of revealing will not cease. It will continue, so that the Father's love for Jesus may continue as life in Jesus' friends.

PENTECOST (C)

Acts 2:1-11; 1 Corinthians 12:3-7, 12-13; John 20:9-23. See pp. 89ff., 70f.

TRINITY SUNDAY (C)

(First Sunday after Pentecost)

Proverbs 8:22-31. Wisdom is the speaker throughout this chapter, beginning at v. 4. Ruling, governance, and justice are within her province (cf. vv. 15f.) Wealth and prosperity follow in her train (cf. v. 18) for those who walk the path of duty and righteousness (cf. v. 20.)

Wisdom had the status of a creature for the Jews, not an eternal one but a manifestation of the creative act of God at every stage in human history. The phrases "of long ago" (v. 22) and "of old" (v. 23) convey the primeval, a notion taken up in the subsequent phrases which describe the formation of the earth (cf. vv. 24-26.) Wisdom was there before there were depths or springs, mountains, clods of earth, or fields. She was with God at the foundation of the heavens and the pillars of the earth (cf. vv. 27f.) and at the decreeing of the tides (cf. v. 29.) Wisdom is from God and at his side (v. 30) but she becomes the companion and the playmate of humankind (cf. v. 31.)

The recurring phrases "when," "before," and "while as yet" of vv. 24ff. are to be found in the Babylonian creation epic *Enuma elish.* The adoption of the mythology of this composition is nearly total, but when it comes to causality the author of Prv is firm. The LORD made all through the agency of wisdom. Wisdom preceded the creation but very clearly she came after the creator God.

Romans 5:1-5. In the previous chapter Paul has begun his development of Abraham's justifying faith. Abraham hoped "against hope" that he would be the father of many nations as he had been promised (4:18). His faith in his role for the future was credited to him as justice (cf. Gn 15:6; Rom 4:3) just as ours will be credited to us as justice "if we believe in him who raised Jesus our Lord from the dead" (Rom 4:24). It is conventional to say of the latter verse and v. 25 (e.g., Buber, Bultmann) that Hebrew *emunah* is trust in the person of the LORD whereas Pauline *pistis* is faith in a fact, a deed that God has done in Jesus Christ. Paul would probably be shocked to learn of any such difference and say that he was incapable of thinking like a German professor. He seems to be at pains to show how the Christian believer and the patriarch Abraham are identical in all respects as regards faith in God's promise. Note that 4:24 does not praise the deed of the resurrection or ask faith in *it* but in him who did it. Paul cares more for the faith of the Christian in a God who will yet act than in a God who has acted.

Justification by means of faith is already, however, a reality for Paul. It means peace with God for the believer (cf. Col 1:21) achieved through Christ the reconciler (5:1; cf. 2 Cor 5:18f.) The present condition of the Christian is grace; with respect to the future it is hope for a share in God's glory. Christ is the person who has made both possible, faith the condition to which God has successfully invited us through him (cf. v. 2.) "The immediate results of Christ's work are ours through faith" (T. W. Manson).

The road to hope may be a rocky one. Paul traces it by means of stages, the stopping-points of which are affliction/endurance/tested virtue/hope (*thlipsis/hypomonē/dokimē/elpis,* vv. 3f.) The hope is not a frustrating kind because the gift of the Spirit fills our hearts with love (cf. v. 5.) *Agapē,* for Paul, is what to do until the messiah comes.

John 16:12-15. If God's wisdom is the principle of the creation (cf. Proverbs above) and justifying faith together with hope and love the proper response to his work of salvation (cf. Romans above), the guidance of the spirit of truth is the personal assurance that trust in God through Christ has not been misplaced (cf. Jn 16:13.)

This pericope has a long history in trinitarian debate, notably—and regrettably—in the "filioque" controversy ("All that the Father has belongs to me" taken as the fullness of godhead transmitted to the Son, who in turn "sends [the Paraclete] to you," 16:7, as he could not do unless he had him, any more than the Father could send him "in my name," 14:26, unless the Paraclete proceeded from the Son). This report on 9th c. debates, resurrected in the 13th and 15th at Lyons and Florence with new emphasis, would no doubt confuse the fourth evangelist. He would probably point out that he had spoken only of what would take place among men in the world, not about what went on eternally in the godhead. But he would assent vigorously to a common possession of a message from God by Jesus and the spirit of truth. The latter would not deviate from it by a hair's breadth.

While this passage says nothing directly about trinitarian theology it says everything about Jesus' message as God's own truth. Jesus will be glorified by the spirit's total fidelity to his message (cf. v. 14.) Since Jesus' teaching has had God as its source, any spirit that is of God can do no other than adhere to it fully (cf. v. 15.)

While there is current debate about the suitability of the words "infallibility" and "indefectibility" with respect to human possession of the "all" that is "announced" (*panta hosa . . . anaggelei*, v. 15), it is clear that Jn is interested in the question from another point of view. His concern is the divinity of the source, the transmitter of all that is proclaimed—Jesus—and its guarantor the spirit. He assumes but does not say that faith will receive the message in proportion as the message is given.

CORPUS CHRISTI (C)

(Sunday after Trinity Sunday)

Genesis 14:18-20. Benjamin Disraeli's quip about the mule which has neither pride of ancestry nor hope of posterity is too well known for rehearsal. Does it have any application to Melchizedek, whose activity is recorded as mysteriously as that of a bird flying through the night? Probably not, since the pious Yahwist author makes all the use possible of the historical fragment he posseses. If the designation reached the J author as *melek Shalem*, "king of Salem," it is clear why he should have wished to have the father of the Jews blessed by the king of this Jebusite city on the slope of Mt. Zion. A note in NAB suggests that the original reading may have been *melek shelomo*, "a king allied to him." We do not even know with certainty that ancient Salem was the site of Jerusalem. The operative concept in J's use of the Melchizedek story comes from Ps 133:3: "For there [the mountains of Zion] the LORD has pronounced his blessing, life forever."

Melchizedek venerates his Canaanite deity El-elyon, "The Most High God." The Gn author has the priest-king invoke on Abram a blessing of his God, designating him "the creator of heaven and earth." He also makes El-elyon responsible for Abram's victory. There is the possibility that Abram acquired the notion of God as creator from this Canaanite diety, just as he worshipped him under the title El-shaddai, the name of another Canaanite deity (cf. 17:1 where the title is translated "the Almighty"; it may mean "the mountain god" but we do not have certainty on this.) The designation "the LORD" dates to Moses' time (cf. Ex 3:13ff.), despite the Yahwist's claim (in Gn 4:26) that it was used before the flood. Ps 91:1 puts the two ancient titles *elyon* and *shaddai* together in the service of YHWH: "You who dwell in the shelter of the Most High,/ who abide in the shadow of the Almighty,/ Say to the LORD. . . ." Two other divine titles follow, "refuge" and "fortress," the latter giving us the place name Masada.

The Yahwist wants to portray the king of Salem as subservient to the patriarch Abraham. He reveals him as a learner about the creator who wins victories for those who trust in him.

For a note on the matters that precede and follow this pericope, see pp. 298, 353.

1 Corinthians 11:23-26. It was mentioned in the commentary on Lk's chs. 22 and 23 (cf. Passion Sunday C, pp. 308-11) that more recent opinion considers Lk's account of the last supper and Paul's in this pericope to have derived from a common source (Antioch practice in the years 30-40?), with Lk's version probably the earlier. Previously, many thought Lk 22:19b-20 an interpolation from 1 Cor 11:24-25a because of the similarity in wording, not for any lack of textual attestation of the passage in Lk.

For a commentary on the words of institution in Mk (14:22-26), see pp. 222f.

St. Paul uses in v. 23 the rubric on dependable transmission of tradition which he will employ again in 15:3. "From (*apo*) the Lord" probably means from oral or church tradition about the Lord, not direct revelation to Paul. "I received" (*parelabon*) is the rabbinic formula *qibbel min*; "what I handed on" (*paredōka*), *masar l*^{e}. 1 Cor alone of the four accounts of the supper situates it "on the night he was betrayed." This may be word play, *paredideto* echoing the recently occurring *paredōka*. It may also be a chronological precision. Those who follow Mlle. Jaubert in her chronology of the last days of Jesus' life, where the supper is placed on Tuesday night, point to this verb "betrayed," saying that it is an unwarranted conclusion from the Mk/Mt accounts that he ate with his friends the night before he died. The Roman canon's "*pridie quam pateretur*" is not biblical (the Vulgate for Paul is "*tradebatur*"); it seems to be a deliberate straddle, since Jesus' *pathein* could be taken as either his death or all that led up to it.

Jesus' three actions upon taking the bread in hand are blessing God (*eucharistēsas*), breaking the bread (*eklasen*), and saying (*eipen*) the words. The Marcan and Lucan traditions also have Jesus giving (*edōken*) the bread and cup to his friends. Verbs for bless, break, and give occur in both of Mk's accounts of the multiplication of the loaves (6:41 and 8:6), on which the supper account is patterned, or vice versa. The presumption is that actual eucharistic practice in the churches provided the vocabulary for both. Paul's familiar liturgy, like Lk's, has Jesus' body being given—without that Lucan verb— "for you," in contrast with the Mk/Mt blood shed "for many" (cf. Mk 14:24; Mt 26:28.) Paul's remembrance phrase, attached to both bread and cup, occurs in Lk in connection with the bread only (cf. 22:19*b*.) *Eis tēn emēn anamnēsin* is the Hebrew *l*^{e} *zikkaron*, "in remembrance."

The meal as proclamation of the Lord's death "until he come" (v. 26) is an echo of its presumably primitive status as eschatological in emphasis (cf. the wording of Jesus' vow of abstention in Lk 22:16, 18.) It is widely supposed that Christians ate this forward-looking meal in connection with Jesus' death and composed the liturgies of which we possess NT fragments only later.

Lk 9:11-17. This feeding of the multitude, the only one in Lk, parallels the first one in Mk (6:30-44) and Mt (14:13-21) more closely than the second. Lk situates it in relation to Bethsaida (v. 10), as they do not. His account could be an edited version of Mk's; no independent source is demanded. The identity of vocabulary between this miracle-narrative and the last supper accounts explains the iconographic representation of the eucharist in catacomb art. There, fish and wicker baskets are just as prominent as loaves, with the cup often missing. The "breaking of bread" (*hē klasis tou artou*) is an early name for the Christian eucharist (cf. *kateklasen*, v. 16, the same in Mk 6:41; Mt 14:19 gives the particle *klasas*). The *Didachē* speaks of the "fragments scattered on the hillside" as *klasmata*, forerunner of the modern "particles."

Lk changes Mk's groups (lit., garden plots) of "hundreds and fifties" (*prasiai prasiai kata hekaton kai kata pentēkonta*, Mk 6:40) to "groups of fifty or so." Mk probably got the phrase from Jethro's plan for the government of the people by upright judges (cf. Ex 18:21.) The story was likely influenced in the telling by Elisha's feeding of a hundred men with twenty barley loaves (cf. 2 Kgs 4:42ff.) but it must have had some historical basis in Jesus' career. The actual event was no doubt viewed as an anticipation of the banquet of the end-time, as evidenced by the development in Jn 6.

For a commentary on what immediately precedes this pericope in Mk 6:30-34, see p. 232, as well as the treatment by Jn of what is apparently the same incident, on pp. 233f.

SUNDAYS OF THE YEAR

ELEVENTH SUNDAY OF THE YEAR (C)
(Fourth Sunday after Pentecost)

2 Samuel 12:7-10, 13. Reading Nathan's charge to David, "You are the man!" could be meaningless to hearers except that the king's covetous, murderous conduct is recalled in the succeeding verses. The use the author makes of David's lapse is instructive. The king has chosen to live by the sword; his house will therefore die by the sword, or at least be plagued by its persistent presence.

The *dénouement* of this tale is brief. David repents and for this is told that he will not have to pay with his life. The price exacted is the life of the adulterously conceived child.

Jesus taught his hearers not to make easy correspondences between human tragedy and moral fault as its cause (cf. Lk 13:1-5.) The tendency is so deeply ingrained, however, that not even the savior of Christians succeeded in eradicating it. There may be no swift one-to-one retribution such as 2 Sm envisions but his instinct is sound which sees violence as the breeder of violence. A morally callous society, or even household, proliferates callousness.

Galatians 2:16, 19-21. Chronologically, v. 16 is Paul's first recorded statement on the conflict between justification (i.e., being declared not guilty because no longer guilty) by faith in Christ and by works of the law. Already the former is an axiom with him. He will later provide reasons why he holds it but no reasons are needed or compelling for an axiom. The deed of God in Jesus Christ has eliminated any element of uncertainty for Paul.

Just how Paul died to the law, *through the law*, to live for God (v. 19*a*) is unclear. His later statement that the end (*telos*) of the law is Christ is a clue of sorts (cf. Rom 10:4.) Accepting the law in a spirit of Abrahamic faith—which Paul's struggles with observant Jews of the diaspora and the Jerusalem church have led him to as his chief argument—has left him open to the grace of God made manifest in Jesus Christ (cf. Rom 3:21-26.) The fact of Christ's crucifixion probably gives an even better indication (v. 19*b*). Faith in this was for Paul the watershed. One way he argues the question is to identify the law as self-destructive because it is temporary in God's design (cf.

3:15-18.) It was at best a means to identify transgression (cf. Rom 4:15) and when transgression was removed by faith in the cross its usefulness was over. Still, how any of this came about "through the law" is a puzzle. Perhaps God had made fidelity to it during the Mosaic interim a condition of the sending of his son. The mystical death of all believers with Christ is the key, that much is clear (v. 19; cf. Rom 7:4ff.) Can it be that since the mode of this death which is a blessing for all has been described by the law as a curse (Gal 3:13; cf. Dt 21:23), death to the law has therefore come *through* the law?

Paul continues to live his "human" (*en sarki*) life but it is now a life of faith (*en pistei*, v. 20). Christ's self-abnegating love for others has made his living in Paul a reality (*ibid.*) To expect that fidelity to the law will bring justification now that Christ has died is to regard the gracious gift (*charin*) of God as pointless (*dōrean*, v. 21; Vulg. *gratis*).

Luke 7:36—8:3 (longer) or 7:36-50 (shorter). Luke seems to be accommodating a narrative he has from Mk (14:3-9; par. Mt 26:6-13), which the first two evangelists use as anticipatory of Jesus' burial, to illustrate forgiveness (v. 47), a leading Lucan *motif.* "The parable [vv. 41ff.] does not exactly fit the case. The woman does not love because she has been forgiven but vice versa" (Lampe). Lk wishes to compare her favorably, in the need for forgiveness she experiences, with Simon who is unaware of his need.

Women companions of Jesus and the Twelve are a feature of the Galilean ministry (cf. Mk 15:40f.) Their benefactions are highlighted here (8:3), as in Mary Magdalene's possessed state (note: never in the gospels her sinfulness).

TWELFTH SUNDAY OF THE YEAR (C)

(Fifth Sunday after Pentecost)

Zechariah 12:10-11. There is no indication of who the unnamed sufferer of this mysterious passage is. The "spirit of grace and petition" is a divine blessing on the Jerusalemites, bestowed somehow in connection with the victim. He has been thrust through by the very people who mourn him, an indication of a blunder or an impetuous act immediately regretted. The similarity of this verse to Is 52:13—53:12 is evident. If Hadadrimmon is a place near Megiddo, the speculation is that the grief expressed at the death of King Josiah may be intended (cf. 2 Chr 35:22-25.) Since the word is composed of two names of the Canaanite storm god, the reference may be to his annual celebration and the weeping and wailing on that occasion.

As has been mentioned before in these pages, the last six chapters of Zechariah are a collection from various hands other than the composer's of the first eight and are done in an entirely different spirit. Finding a common thread for these oracles is virtually impossible.

Were it not for the use made of v. 10 by Jn 19:37, it is doubtful any place would have been found for this reading from Zech in the lectionary. Like Jesus, the pierced victim has met his end through folly or stupidity and his true worth been discovered later.

Galatians 3:26-29. The earlier part of this chapter contains an argument intended to convince the reader of the superiority of justifying faith to the Law. The latter is likened to a monitor or guard who is a slave bringing the freeborn child to school (vv. 23ff.) With Christ came justification through faith (v. 24). This means an end to the Law's constraint (v. 23) and a new condition of sonship (v. 26). Baptism into Christ, the sign of faith, has meant "putting him on" (*enedysasthe*, v. 27), a possible reference to a white garment. The unity of all in the new condition (v. 28), as a practical reality, is something that the male, Greek freeman has had no reason to challenge since. The female response is not so enthusiastic, that of the enslaved Christian less so, and of the Jewish Christian totally inaudible. Possessing the faith of Abraham which makes one an inheritor of the ancient promise is, says Galatians, the same as being Christ's (*Christou*, v. 29).

The glorious vision of oneness in faith (*pantes . . . heis*, v. 28) and hence lack of any disability through circumcision, social condition, or sex is one that should give the modern baptized pause. One wonders if any will inherit the promise if what are described as conditions essential for all continue to go unfulfilled.

Luke 9:18-24. There is no mention of Caesarea Philippi in Lk's account of this incident, which is paralleled in Mk 8:27-30 and Mt 16:13-20). For a commentary on Mk see p. 246; for Mt see pp. 129f.

Mk 6:45—8:26 and its matching passages in Mt are not found in Lk, except for Mk 8:12*b*-15 (=Lk 11:29; 12:1). The Lucan pericope that immediately precedes this one is that of the multiplication of the loaves (the first multiplication in Mk and Mt). Lk has Jesus praying "in seclusion" (*kata monas*, v. 18) while his disciples are nearby (*synēsan autō*). He follows Mk in having Jesus speak of himself as "I," not Mt's "son of man." The inquiry is about the view of the "crowds," not "men." The response in v. 19 repeats what has been said in vv. 7f. For the rest, Lk is faithful to Mk with two exceptions; he changes "the messiah" (*ho christos*) to "the messiah of God" (v. 20) and, perhaps significantly, omits the rebuke of Peter in which the latter is described as a "satan" (cf. Mk 8:32f.) This may reflect his desire to save the reputation of the leader of the Twelve. An interest in avoiding distraction from likening the fate of the suffering disciple to that of the suffering Jesus would, however, explain the omission just as well. Mk 8:34 may contain a real invitation by Jesus to martyrdom as the cost of discipleship. If it is figurative there, Lk makes it such beyond doubt by adding "daily" (*kath' hēmeran*, v. 23) to the injunction to take up one's cross. As in Mk, only the loss of one's life for Jesus' sake (Lk omits "and the gospel's") will result in saving it (v. 24).

Jesus commands silence regarding Peter's conviction that Jesus is the messiah, precisely because he "must" (*dei*) suffer, die, and be raised (cf. vv. 21f.) This gives the concept of messiahship a meaning it has not had. Hence, presumably, continued use of the term "messiah" would cause confusion. Lk simply follows Mk 8:30f. here.

THIRTEENTH SUNDAY OF THE YEAR (C)

(Sixth Sunday after Pentecost)

1 Kings 19:16, 19-21. Elijah's succession in prophecy by Elisha is described in this passage (ca. 850 B.C.) but, more importantly, the later transition of kingship in Israel is hinted at (v. 16). Ahab continued as king in Israel until 853, when Ahaziah (cf. 1 Kgs 22:52ff.—2 Kgs 1:2-18) succeeded him for a year. Next came Ahab's other son Joram (852-41), then Jehu after his successful revolt against Ahaziah of Judah and Joram of Israel in 841 (cf. 2 Kgs 9.) The anointing of Elisha in 1 Kgs 19:16 is described at length in 2 Kgs 2:1-18, together with Elijah's departure in a flaming chariot (v. 11). The anointing of Jehu, previous to his military victory over the house of Ahab, was done prophetically by a guild prophet at Elisha's direction and is recounted in 2 Kgs 9:1-10.

Today's reading is concerned with the initial choice of Elisha. The twelve yoke of oxen with which he is plowing are surely symbolic. So, in another sense, is Elijah's throwing of his cloak over his chosen successor (cf. 2 Kgs 2:13-15.) Since Elisha's severance of his ties with his farming past could not have been more final (v. 21), Elijah's response to the younger man's request to bid his parents farewell is puzzling. What he says in Hebrew is: "Turn, for what have I done to you?" This may have been his forceful way of saying: "Leave them if you understand what I have done in naming you my successor."

Galatians 5:1, 13-18. Eleutheria (Gk., "freedom") is the name of an island in the Bahamas given to it as part of the Spanish legacy. It is surprising that the term or its Latin equivalent *libertas* does not figure more significantly in place names in the New World.

Paul has told his allegory of Sara and Hagar in support of his conviction that returning to subjection to the law (cf. 4:21) is an abjuring of the freedom that comes with being offspring of Abraham, a blessing which has been achieved for Gentiles through Christ (cf. 3:14.) He "freed us for freedom" (5:1) is a Hebraism; the point is made strongly because the yoke is not to be resumed. Paul suggests in the eleven intervening verses which do not occur in the reading that some persons other than Jewish observants are proposing circumcision to the Galatians. The latter do not seem to Paul to be sufficiently aware of the full burden of keeping the law that goes with circumcision (v. 3). He angrily proposes castration, such as the eunuchs of the cult of Cybele, goddess of fertility, engage in (v. 12; cf. Phil 3:2.) Surely his tone is ironic.

At v. 13 Paul seems to fear that the freedom he so much advocates may be mistaken for the absence of any inhibition whatever. "Flesh" (i.e., humanity left to itself) needs to be directed and the proper governor is love (*agapē*, vv. 6, 13). Without such a directing factor a terrifying number of aberrations may ensue (vv. 19ff.) Love means mutual service for Paul. It is the perfect expression of life in the spirit. Lest he be understood to teach that the law has no meaning and cannot be kept, he sums up his understanding of it in terms of Lv 19:18 (v. 14). On balance he comes out on the side of freedom from the law for those who live in the spirit (v. 18)—at least for the recipients of this letter, who seem to be preponderantly Gentiles (cf. 4:8.)

Luke 9:51-62. This pericope inaugurates "Lk's special section" which continues to 18:14. It does not depend on Mk's order. Even though there are scattered parallels with Mk throughout, those with Mt are more numerous. Material unique to Lk is found in ch. 10 through ch. 18, most of it in parables. The first five verses of this reading and vv. 60-62 are not part of any other gospel. Lk alone develops the picture of Jesus as Elijah; the others put John in this rôle.

Lk speaks of Jesus' "being taken up" (*analēmpsis*, v. 51), an echo of Elijah's mode of departure (cf. 2 Kgs 2:1, 11.) The Greek text has "when the days were fulfilled," conveying the idea of a providential plan. Samaritan resistance to pilgrims to and from Jerusalem (vv. 52f.) was a feature of the life of that time. The proposal of calling down fire is an Elijah-touch (v. 54; cf. 1 Kgs 18:24, 36ff.), probably Lk's. It receives no encouragement from Jesus (v. 55).

Verses 57-60a have their parallel in Mt 8:19-22. The second of these two sayings of Jesus (v. 60) leads to another like it (v. 62). As has been remarked in the commentary on 1 Kgs 19 above, Elisha's "looking back" seems to be so slight a matter as not to provide the model for this *logion*. It would appear that Lk possesses that of v. 62, spoken by Jesus independently of any reference to Elisha, and then provides v. 61 as an imprecise introduction to it because of vague similarity. Lk, too, may have had trouble with Elijah's meaning in v. 20!

FOURTEENTH SUNDAY OF THE YEAR (C)

(Seventh Sunday after Pentecost)

Isaiah 66:10-14. The collection of poems known as the Third-Isaiah (chs. 56-66) was compiled between the mid-6th and mid-5th centuries B.C. Little is known of the history of the community of Jewish Palestine in that period. The books of Ezra-Nehemiah suggest poverty and a certain confusion in the religious life of the people. Today's reading, beginning at v. 7, proposes salvation for Jerusalem (Zion) in terms of an instantaneous birth (vv. 7-9). Continuing the metaphor, the poet suggests that this mother-city taken for dead will once again nourish at her abundant breasts. "Salvation will come suddenly (lxvi 7-9) and will be the result of the tender care of Yahweh (lxvi 10-14)" (McKenzie).

The description of prosperity as a river has occurred in 48:18—a natural figure for life in a parched land. The gathering of the Gentiles to share in the riches of Israel after judgment is a theme of the Third-Isaiah. Their wealth (*kebhodh goyim*, v. 12) will flow like a rushing torrent. In v. 12c, the birth metaphor is returned to. The sons of the new Jerusalem will be like babes carried on the hip and fondled in the lap. YHWH as a nursing mother is a tender and uncommon biblical image. Sight of the vision will invigorate the frames (lit. "bones," v. 14a) of the onlookers, who will respond like vegetation in the presence of moisture. The array of similes is dizzying, in a collection not noted for its restraint.

All that has preceded leads up to an apocalyptic judgment in which the LORD's servants, viz., the poet and his ethically sensitive fellows, will be separated from the enemies of the LORD (v. 14*b*) by an Iranian-type conflagration (v. 15) or, in the title made famous by Henryk Sienkiewicz, "by fire and sword" (v. 16).

Galatians 6:14-18. This epistle has featured a vigorous polemic against the introduction of circumcision into a presumably Gentile Christian community by itinerant preachers who have "cast a spell" over the "senseless Galatians" (3:1). Foreskins are being made the subject of a boast (v. 13), like scalps in the days of Indian bounty-hunters. Paul deplores this pernicious rivalry to which the Galatians are falling prey. They seem to have no notion, any more than do their proselytizers, that circumcision is either the sign of the full acceptance of the Mosaic law or it means nothing. There are certain signs in our day which have been similarly uprooted from their contexts, like the motorcyclists' iron cross or the Confederate flag. None of these, however, serves as a satisfactory modern example of the binding power of covenant-circumcision evacuated of its significance. Paul finds the Galatians' folly in the realm of signification complete.

If they who have already accepted the gospel have a sign, it is the cross of Christ. For Paul this is the only legitimate subject for boasting (v. 14). In taking on its challenge he—and presumably they—have been separated from the *kosmos* and its sinfulness. Being created anew (i.e., as a *kainē ktisis*, v. 15) is all that matters. This results in adoption of the cross as one's faith-symbol. Neither circumcision, foreskin (*oute gar peritomē ti estin oute akrobystia*), nor anything else continues to be of symbolic worth.

Paul then utters a blessing on those who follow such a rule of life (*kanōn*) and in so doing designates as the "Israel of God"—the only NT occurrence of the phrase—the new race that believes in the power of the cross. He clearly means to set aside the Jewish-Gentile difference and, with it, the sign distinctive of Jewish existence. Paul does not hold circumcision in contempt. It is merely that, as a saving sign, it has been succeeded by a more effective one which transcends peoplehood. Faith in the cross creates the new Israel made up of Jews and Gentiles.

It is not clear exactly whom Paul wishes to "trouble him no longer," in v. 17. The most likely subjects are the Galatians, whose stupidity he does not wish to have brought to his attention in the future. He may be issuing a wider challenge, however, namely to any Jew who cares to fault him for the low estimate he is putting on a scar in the flesh. He can boast greater scars than circumcision which proclaim his sufferngs in the service of Jesus. These "brand marks" (*stigmata*, v. 17) are the signs of ownership in a slave's body, not the "nailprints" (*ton typon tōn hēlōn*, Jn 20:25) of the story of doubting Thomas. Paul is referring to the rigors of his mission (cf. 2 Cor 4:8-12; 6:4-10; 11:23-28), not least of them "that daily tension pressing on me, my anxiety for all the churches" (2 Cor 11:28). There is no thought here of the medieval phenomenon of the wounds of Christ reported of St. Francis of Assisi and others.

Paul concludes with his usual blessing, asking the Lord's grace or favor (*charis*, v. 18) on the quite thoroughly chastised Galatian community.

Luke 10:1-12, 17-20. The mission of Lk (vv. 1-12) is Q material, having its parallels in Mt 9:37f.; 10:16, 9, 10*a*, 11ff., 10*b*, 7f., 14f. (cf. 11th Sunday of the Year, pp. 106f., which comments on Mt 9:36—10:8.) Only Lk has the sending of the seventy, a better attested reading than NAB's seventy-two. This and other details identify the passage as a reworking of Q to describe the Gentile mission. The Jews commonly described the nations of the earth as seventy or seventy-two in number, following Gn 10 (certain ambiguities occur in vv. 24f.); Moses chooses seventy elders for judgment in Ex 24:1 and Nm 11:16. The sending "in pairs" (v. 1) will reappear in Acts in the mission of Peter and John to Samaria (Ac 8:14), of Barnabas and Saul (13:2) and Paul and Silas (15:40) to the Gentiles. Lk 10:1-12 should be compared carefully with Lk 9:1-6; there, the mission of the twelve is closer to Mt than the mission of the seventy. The later, wider appointment of disciples is set in a Samarian town (9:56) and is probably meant by Lk to typify the mission to the Gentiles which will come later, with Samaria serving as a borderland leading out to the Gentile world (cf. Ac 1:8.) For a parallel to v. 2 see Jn 4:5, likewise in a Samaritan setting.

Mt follows the injunction to carry no money and go without extra clothes and sandals with a citation of his principle of support for preachers: "The laborer is worth his keep" (Mt 10:9f.) In separating the two ideas and adding the advice not to salute anyone on the way, Lk (10:4, 7*b*; cf. 2 Kgs 4:29) changes the tenor of the saying from one of need to urgency. His advice to eat and drink what the host provides (v. 7) does not appear in Mt; it may reflect an active disregard of dietary inhibitions by preachers in Gentile lands. That the principle of their support is thought by Paul to be an ordinance of "the Lord" (the church?) is clear from 1 Cor 9:14 (cf. v. 7), despite the freedom he experiences not to accept such help.

The Greek of v. 9 is different from that of v. 11 in saying that the reign of God draws near "to you." The first declaration is in a context of healing and is consolatory; the second is judgmental.

Verses 17-20 are uniquely Lucan, his hallmark being the eschatological "joy" (*chara*) with which the seventy return. In Is 14:12 the king of Babylon is addressed as "morning star, son of the dawn" and described as having fallen from the heavens. Lk makes the Lucifer which translates Venus in the Vulgate of Is (Heb., *heilel*, "morning star") "Satan," leading to that worthy's having the name in Christian usage. The Christian denomination of Satan as Lucifer stems from the 3d c. and is influenced by the account of the war in heaven in Rev 12:7-10. It totally ignores that book's designation of Jesus as the "morning star" (22:16; not "Lucifer" in the Vulgate, however, but the *stella matutina* which is applied to Mary in the litany of Loreto). Venus is rendered by the more usual term *phôsphoros* in 2 Pet 1:19.

Jn will speak in this connection of the driving out of "the prince of this world" (12:31). The promise that the faithful Jew may tread on snakes with impunity derives from Ps 91:13. Something like it occurs in the "canonical" ending assigned to Mk (16:18), which speaks of the handling of serpents and the drinking of deadly poison as proofs of apostolicity of mission. Verse 17 of Mk 16 is probably taken from Lk 10:20. Ex 32:33 and Dn 12:1 speak of a heavenly book of record, accounting for "your names written in heaven" of v. 20.

FIFTEENTH SUNDAY OF THE YEAR (C)

(Eighth Sunday after Pentecost)

Deuteronomy 30:10-14. "This book of the law" which Dt describes as so accessible was the book of the Josian reform, whatever its content—many think chs. 12-26 and 28, perhaps as much as 4:44—30:20. The LORD's "commandments and statutes" (v. 10) are reduced to "this command" (v. 11), which is the injunction to elect life and prosperity over death and doom (v. 15), to choose between the blessing and the curse (v. 19). The passage is a favorite one of rabbis, spoken in praise of Torah and the ease with which it can be fulfilled. Christian preachers frequently apply it to love, not often to life.

The importance of today's pericope is its setting. Written as if spoken by Moses on the brink of entering Canaan (cf. 31:1), the thirtieth chapter tells the members of the scattered nation how to repent wherever they may find themselves. It does this under the guise of enjoining a fidelity in the new land which will guarantee prosperity. Since the chapter was composed long after the conquest of Canaan, it more realistically envisions a Jewish people trying to keep the law in a variety of lands and settings. The basic promise is that on condition of repentance this covenanted people can always look forward to an ingathering from dispersion which its LORD will achieve (vv. 3-5). If there is a biblical charter for the state of Israel, these verses comprise it. The orthodox rabbinate of that country, in any case, is zealous to see that Torah is kept in terms of this passage, now that the Jewish people are back in *ereṣ Israel* in numbers.

Colossians 1:15-20. These six verses have been subjected to extensive analysis of every sort. The scrutiny reveals a hymn in two strophes, vv. 15-18*a* and 18*b*-20. The hymn probably has pre-Christian origins. The first strophe makes Christ the agent of God in creation, the second his agent in the work of cosmic reconciliation. This reconciliation is possible because God has caused "absolute fullness" (*pan to plērōma*, v. 19) to reside in him. The author's main point, however, is that the Colossian church is part of that larger body over which Christ has the headship (*hē ekklēsia*, v. 18), and that its members are safely delivered from the dominion of any angelic or demonic powers that may reside in the universe (vv. 16f.) It has been conjectured that if this is a hymn, some phrase like "Praise the Lord" or "Praised be Christ" would have stood at the head (Meeks and others).

Philo, the Alexandrian Jew, spoke of the *logos* as the image and the first-born of God (cf. v. 15.) The creation of all things by God "through" and "for" Christ has a Stoic ring, in phrasing like that of 1 Cor 8:6*a* (where all things are "for" God only; in 6*b*, "through" Christ; cf. Rom 11:36.)

Christ is the first-born of all creatures (v. 16) and also of a redeemed progeny (the "first-born of the dead," v. 18). As if to challenge the pretensions of any other *plērōma* (v. 19), the epistle attributes fullness to Christ twice, specifying it in 2:9 as the fullness of deity (*tēs theotētos*) which resides in Christ bodily (*sōmatikōs*). "The church" (v. 18) was probably added to "his body" in a primitive poem which would have conceived the cosmos in that role.

It was on the cross that everything in the heavens and on earth was reconciled to God in the person of Jesus (v. 20). There, peace was made in his blood.

This hymn makes greater claims for Christ than anything in the undisputed Pauline corpus. It is true that 1 Cor 8:6 reaches a zenith in describing his intimacy with God, a passage which prepares for this one. In the Pauline letters the church is one body with Christ (cf. 1 Cor 12:12, 27; Rom 12:5) whereas here (v. 18) and in Eph 1:22 Christ is the head of the body.

He is the beginning (*archē*; cf. Rev 22:13) and the one "holding primacy" (*proteuōn*) in all things. The claim that he is "before all else" (*pro pantōn*, v. 17) may with equal force refer to place, time, or rank. While many commentators favor a temporal sense, no apodictic argument can be made that the author is claiming preexistence. The firstness of Christ with regard to the universe is total. God does not now look upon his world, whether as created or redeemed, apart from this man in glory, "his beloved son" (v. 13).

Luke 10:25-37. 2 Chronicles 28:9-15 tells an interesting story of four Ephraimite leaders and a prophet of Samaria named Oded who resisted the savagery with which certain men of Judah were slaughtered and other men and women taken captive. They opposed those who returned from the war, saying that the holding of the Judahites as slaves would make them even more guilty in the LORD's eyes. The conquered of Judah were then brought before the whole assembly, whereupon,

> The men just named [Azariah, Berechiah, Jehizkiah, and Amasa] proceeded to help the captives. All of them who were naked they clothed from the booty; they clothed them, put sandals on their feet, gave them food and drink, anointed them, and all who were weak they set on asses. They brought them to Jericho, the city of palms, to their brethren. Then they returned to Samaria (v. 15).

The wording is at least suggestive of verbal origins in Lk's narrative.

His introduction to the parable of the good Samaritan probably derives from Mk 12:28-31. If so, it is much edited. The lawyer asks how to gain everlasting life, not, which is the first commandment of all? In Mk Jesus answers. Lk has him throw the question back to the lawyer, who responds by combining Dt 6:5 with Lv 19:18 in a well-known convention of the period. Lk also has Jesus omit Dt 6:4, the phrase with which the *Sh^ema* opens: "Hear, O Israel! The LORD is our God, the LORD alone!"

The good Samaritans of 2 Chron returned the captives to Jericho, with the weak ones mounted on beasts of burden. The Samaritan in Jesus' story does the same. The tribesmen around Samaria, the old northern capital, had fallen low in Judean esteem by Jesus' day. Their chief offense was that they were losers. Conservative of their traditions, they kept worshiping at Mt. Gerizim when the victorious David decreed that the one shrine of the nation was to be in Jerusalem. By 350 B.C. or so their expulsion and ostracism at Judean hands were complete.

The parable is elicited by the lawyer's desire to "justify himself" (v. 29), although nothing in his earnest conduct up to this point has prepared us for this. The meaning of the technical biblical term "neighbor" ($r^e a^\epsilon$) was a matter in dispute in rabbinic circles and a legitimate subject of inquiry. Lk may include the story to show the superiority of the outlook of Jesus and his missionaries regarding "sinners" to that of the priests and levites of Judaism. These had a legitimate scruple with regard to proximity to corpses, a matter made explicit in the Bible regarding persons under Nazirite vow (cf. Nm 6:9-12) and extended to the general laws of ritual purity for priests.

Whatever Lk's sources or motives, he reports a rhetorically perfect tale. It lives in memory as a parable of giving help when help is needed. It redounds to the everlasting discredit of official religionists. It has also paradoxically affixed the adjective "good" to a despised people—an authentic expression of the spirit of Jesus.

SIXTEENTH SUNDAY OF THE YEAR (C)

(Ninth Sunday after Pentecost)

Genesis 18:1-10. "The terebinth of Mamre, which is at Hebron" (13:18) no longer stands but the well that watered it is easily found, off the Jerusalem-Hebron road. The well is enclosed by the massive masonry of Herod the Great. The J narrative here given seems to follow ch. 13 directly, while the P account with which ch. 17 concludes resumes at ch. 21. This pericope contains the promise to Abraham that through a son he will beget a host of nations (vv. 10, 18) which is found seven other times between chs. 12 and 21. The tale is told as an epiphany of the LORD, something which Abraham recognizes only in v. 14.

The three mysterious visitors are a favorite subject of Eastern iconography, where they are usually represented with haloes as manifestations of Father, Son, and Spirit. In the text, "the LORD appeared to Abraham" (v. 1) but the LORD does not speak until v. 13. Meanwhile, Abraham deals variously with one (vv. 3, 10) and all three (vv. 2, 4, 5, 8, 9) of his human visitors. As they go on to Sodom (v. 16; two of them? v. 22) the LORD stays on behind (vv. 17-22). The story has obviously undergone some modification at this point.

The thrust of the tale is not merely the assurance of a son that is given, but also Sarah's laugh (v. 12; cf. 17:17 for Abraham's laugh) to account for the naming of Isaac. The familiar popular etymology of the Bible derives the name *Yiṣhak* (21:3) from the form of *ṣahak* that occurs in 17:17, "he laughed"; 18:12 has another form of the verb to describe Sarah's doing the same. Sarah denies having laughed

(v. 15), in a charming vignette of who is allowed to do what around this tent.

The limitless power of the LORD is stressed in v. 14, while the divine promise of a blessing through Abraham's offspring is reiterated in v. 18. Not the least detail of the account is the warm hospitality of the nomad *sheikh* Abraham, who is described throughout as magnanimous and trusting.

Colossians 1:24-28. The present pericope tells in favor of Paul's authorship of this letter. If so, then it is probably written from prison and in conjunction with the letter to Philemon (cf. 4:7ff., 17.) Joy in suffering (v. 24) is a characteristic theme of Paul. The second part of v. 24 contains a classic puzzle. Since the writer cannot be implying to the Colossians that the sufferings of Christ were in any way insufficient (Christ's victory being described in 2:8-15 as complete), his own "filling up what is lacking in the sufferings of Christ" (*ta hysterēmata tōn thlipseōn tou Christou*) must have some other meaning. The most usual conjecture is that a divine plan for the spread of the gospel is being hinted at in which the indignities suffered by its servants like Paul are patterned on Christ's. No quota of sufferings that must be made up is necessitated by the text, however. The apostle's suffering for the sake of the body-church (v. 24; cf. v. 18) simply accompanies the preaching of a salvation that was achieved through suffering.

A divine commission (*oikonomia*) made the writer a minister (*diakonos*) in the service of this church (v. 25), he says. The *mystērion* spoken of (v. 26) is not something arcane, like the pagan mysteries that were hidden from all but the devotees of the cult-deity (cf. Rom 16:25; Eph 1:9.) Rather, the *mystērion* is God's eternal plan, only lately revealed, whereby the LORD means to live in the Gentiles through Christ. "Christ in you" is the mystery. The Colossians' present grace will be their future glory if they continue in hope: *hē elpis tēs doxēs*. There is no other Christ to proclaim but this one, the Christ now in glory, in whose image all are called to be mature (*teleios*, a term from the Greek religions for a fully initiated member).

There should be no hesitancy in seeing Col employ standard religious vocabulary in the service of what has been newly done in Christ. Protestant theologians—with Albert Schweitzer as a notable exception—tend to deny to the phrase "in Christ" or "Christ in you" any implication of mystical union. The supposition that a loss of personal individualism is entailed would account for this. More likely, however, it is because mysticism is taken as a threat to the way justifying faith functions. The Catholic is more at home with the assumption that Paul and his school are propounding a genuine Christ-mysticism, a union with him by grace which has no automatic elements and does not imperil his personhood or the believer's.

Luke 10:38-42. The parable of the good Samaritan features compassion (*to eleos*, v. 37). This next narrative features discipleship under the aspect of two forms of service. Jn knows of the tradition regarding these sisters and situates their home in Bethany (11:1). Lk has Jesus and his disciples vaguely "on their journey" (10:38), "on his way to Jerusalem" (9:53) after a rebuff at the hands of Samaritan villagers.

Martha receives a reproach from Jesus but it is not clear exactly why—whether because she is "anxious and upset" (*merimnas kai thorybazē*, v. 41; the first verb is the root of the adjective "solicitous" reprobated in Mt's sermon on the mount), or because she is not sitting and listening like Mary.

Mary, in any case, receives Jesus' praise for having chosen the "good part." *Meris* (accusative, *merida*) can mean a portion or serving, the option chosen by NAB to convey a play on kitchen words: *merimna* ("solicitude")—*merida*.

SEVENTEENTH SUNDAY OF THE YEAR(C)

(Tenth Sunday after Pentecost)

Genesis 18:20-32. The story of the Levite's concubine who was ravished unmercifully by the men of the Benjaminite city of Gibeah, after they had first beaten on the door of the pair's host and asked for the Levite himself (Jgs 19:22-26), suggests that the naming of sodomy for Sodom may be a matter of historical chance. The details of the earlier part of the Jgs narrative are so close to this narrative that it seems to be the one tale of two cities.

Ezekiel names pride, prosperity, and callousness toward the poor as the sins of Sodom (16:48-50). In Jeremiah Sodom and Gomorrah are guilty of adultery, lies, and siding with the wicked. Isaiah accuses the two Dead Sea towns of unspecified decadence (1:10; 3:9). It is very likely that their tragic end (by bituminous eruption? cf. 19:24, 28) led to the attribution of every shameful crime to these towns, given the mentality of that proto-historic past.

The LORD muses about checking on the evil reports he has heard of Sodom and Gomorrah (vv. 20f.) but does not go. He stays with Abraham while the two men/angels (lit., "messengers") proceed ahead (18:22; 19:1). The remarkable exchange of vv. 23-32, much like the haggling that goes on in an Oriental bazaar, is not only a tale of the influence of the patriarch Abraham with God. It is also a wrestling with the problem of evil. The J author wonders how much wickedness the divine trade will bear. The ten just men in the midst of a sea of iniquity are a parable of later Israel surrounded by wicked neighbors. The inexorability of catastrophe (cf. 19:13f.) is another instructive lesson.

A by-product of this bargaining session, one of the most memorable of all the biblical "strivings with God," may be the *minyan* (lit., "numbering"), the prescribed minimum of ten men for Jewish public prayer, found as early as the Dead Sea Scrolls (*San.* 1, 6 cites Nm 14: twelve tribes less Joshua and Caleb). But the main points are the candor of YHWH, who hides nothing from his trusted friend Abraham (v. 17), and the justice of him who is "judge of all the world" (v. 25).

Colossians 2:12-14. Early in this epistle there has been enunciated the motif of rescue from darkness to light in the kingdom of God's son. The forgiveness of our sins is the reality synonomous with both of these mythic conceptions (1:13f.) This same pardon reappears in v. 13 but now the antithesis is between the body of sin and flesh buried in the waters of baptism and the new life of the baptized in company with Christ (2:12f.) The baptismal symbolism has been developed by Paul in Rom 6:3-6. A difference is that there the risen life lies in the future, whereas here it is conceived as present.

The development of a spiritual understanding of circumcision was not new with Paul. Other Jewish writings had it. For the healing of uncircumcised flesh, he proposes baptism. In the graphic figure of v. 11 this rite strips away not only a piece of skin but the whole human reality insofar as it is subject to "cosmic powers other than Christ" (v. 8). The burial in water accomplishes nothing in itself, of course. It is ultimately an effective sign only if it stands for the faith of the baptized in God's forgiving power.

The bond that is nailed to the cross is a description of man's indentured status, its "claims" (v. 15) being those lodged against him when he enters into an agreement to discharge the terms of the law. The nailing of Christ to the cross was like the posting of a counterclaim. He is placarded trimphantly, and the "principalities and powers" are made fools of for all to see. They are led off in a victory train—paraded through the streets like the sorry captives of a worsted army (cf. Ps 69:19.)

Luke 11:1-13. Lk's introductory verse, which situates Jesus' instruction on how to pray in the midst of his own prayer, is peculiar to him, as is the parable of the friend at midnight (vv. 5-8). The Lord's prayer has its parallel in Mt 6:9-13; the last five verses of this pericope are paralleled in Mt 7:7-11. Both are assigned in Mt to the sermon on the mount. Only Lk has spoken of the disciples of Jn as "offering prayers" (5:33); Mk (2:18) and Mt (9:14) confine themselves to a report of fasting.

The prayer of Jesus is probably from Q material, Mt having added the phrases "Our" and "who in the heavens" (6:9), "your will be done, as in heaven so also on the earth" (v. 10), and "deliver us from the evil one" (v. 13). All are Judaic and would have a familiar ring in the ears of Mt's church. A case can be made for the elimination by Lk of such phrases, as not being usual for his Gentile readers. His retention of the very Jewish remainder, however (including the baffling *epiousios*, "daily," not found elsewhere in Greek literature), tells against the theory of an edited Lucan version of a longer Q original.

It has been pointed out that the prayer is eschatological in its entirety. It asks for the coming of God's rule (*hē basileia sou*, v. 3); for continuous bread (*ton arton hēmōn epiousin . . . to kath' hēmeran*, v. 4), which is probably bread for tomorrow given each day (*epiousa*, present participle of *epeimi*, the "coming [day]" = *mahar*, "tomorrow"); for the forgiveness of sins (*aphes*, v. 4, aorist imperative of *aphiēmi*, which yields *aphesis*, "remission"); and that the petitioners be not led to the final testing (*mē eisenegkēs . . . eis peirasmon*, v. 4). All are futurist Jewish conceptions. Some hold that the eschatological urgency of Mt is missing from Lk, who is reporting a form that is in daily Christian use and that reflects the concerns of this world. This can only be deduced from Mt's more general Jewish-eschatologizing tendency, however, not from the wording of the prayer in the two gospels. Lk retains the same types of phrases as are found in Mt and other Jewish prayers of the 1st c. and following—simply not as many of them.

The key to the parable of the shameless friend is the phrase "how much more" of v. 13 (the rabbinic *qal vahomer*, "light and heavy" = *a fortiori*). Lk makes the "good things" of Mt 7:11 read "the holy spirit," which for him is God's greatest gift to man. In line with this, two Greek MSS of the NT have in place of Lk's "hallowed be your name," "may your holy spirit come upon us and cleanse us."

Lk replaces Mt's loaf/stone example with one of his own, egg/scorpion (leaving fish/snake in place). This makes us wonder if the similarity-in-appearance principle which seems to underlie Mt's choices of objects escapes him.

The sayings about knocking and asking (vv. 9f.) are identical in Mt 7:7f., hence presumably come from Q.

EIGHTEENTH SUNDAY OF THE YEAR (C)
(Eleventh Sunday after Pentecost)

Ecclesiastes (Qoheleth) 1:2; 2:21-23. The "vanity" of these verses has nothing to do with preening (Chesterton, on a novelist who was his contemporary: "He was worse than proud. He was vain") but is equivalent to the Latin *in vanum*, "to no purpose." The Hebrew superlative of v. 2 is *hebhel hebhalim*, literally "breath of breaths" (like the construction *servus servorum* or *parthenos parthenōn*). The pope does not serve other servants; Mary is not a virgin among the rest. Both are at the top of their class. *"Utter* purposelessness" is the meaning of the biblical phrase.

Hard work is a bore. Leaving its fruits to indolent heirs is worse (v. 22). Lying awake nights thinking about the inequity of the scheme is worst of all (v. 23).

This is the Preacher's only theme and it is a profound one. The game would not be worth the candle but for the truth of 12:13f.

Colossians 3:1-5, 9-11. Verse 1 echoes 2:12 from last week's reading in its description of the life of the baptized as an already risen life. "Higher realms" (v. 1) and "things above" (v. 2) are both *ta anō*, deeds proper to the abode of Christ who is spirit, and are contrasted with "things of earth" (*ta epi tēs gēs*, vv. 2 and 5) or "nature" (*ta melē*, v. 5; lit., "members"). The latter are of the plane of earth because they can lead to vices like the five catalogued in v. 5 and those in v. 8. (Cf. the five virtues of v. 12.) The vices are to be "put to death" (v. 5).

The pre-baptismal "old self" (*ton palaion anthrōpon*, v. 9) has been replaced by the new (*ton neon*, v. 10), which is constantly refashioned according to knowledge (*eis epignōsin*; cf. 1:9, 10; 2:2, 3.) "Putting on Christ" (cf. Gal 3:27) and "the image of his son" (Rom 8:29) are the Pauline phrases which lie behind this passage, with a backward glance at "making man in our image, after our likeness" (Gn 1:26). If the Colossian error is a gnostic one, Christian life is being proposed as the true *gnōsis*. The whole "image" figure has Stoic overtones, not biblical only.

Gal 3:27ff. and Phi 15-19 have sentiments similar to those of v. 11 about the end to all social and sexual distinctions that comes with life in the Lord. "Foreigner" is literally *barbaros*, i.e., a non-Greek, while Scythians were an untutored nomad tribe from the east who by their cruelties exemplified the breed especially. Christ for the author is "everything in all of you" (*ta panta en pasin*, v. 11). Paul has used this rhetorical phrase, which does not cry out for too careful scrutiny, when speaking of God's victory at the end (1 Cor 15:28).

Luke 12:13-21. This material is found exclusively in Lk. The carefully stipulated inheritance laws in Israel have evidently been violated and the brother who asks Jesus to arbitrate is the victim. Jesus refuses the arbiter's mantle (v. 14). His comment to the crowd (v. 15) sounds like an independent logion warning against greed which Lk or his source has inserted here. As quoted, the saying stands as a reproach to both brothers, the cheated and the cheater.

The parable is self-explanatory and very much in the spirit of Eccles 2:23. One is reminded of a cartoon showing a Brink's armored car in a funeral cortège while one bystander observes to another: "He's taking it with him."

Lk, who leaves very little to the imagination, appends the saying of v. 21 as a comment on the parable. The opposition is between a man's piling up wealth "for himself (*heautō*) and "with reference to God" (*eis Theon*).

Understanding Christian life as a kind of riches that causes no loss of sleep (cf. Eccles 2:23), the homilist has a rare opportunity in these three readings to trace a unity which is really there.

NINETEENTH SUNDAY OF THE YEAR (C)

(Twelfth Sunday after Pentecost)

Wisdom 18:6-9. The theme of chapters 11-19, a midrashic homily on the exodus, is announced in 11:5: "By the things through which their foes were punished/they in their need were benefited." The children of Israel, in other words, profited by the very phenomena which, in the form of plagues, were destructive to Egypt (see 11:6, "the law of retaliation.") The theme is developed in five segments which feature contrast or opposition: 11:6-14; 11:15—16:15; 16:16-29; 17:1—18:4; 18:5—19:22. These panels are concerned successively with water from the rock, quail, manna, the pillar of fire, and, in the final instance from which today's pericope is taken, the glorification of Israel by the drowning of Pharaoh's troops. The five matching woes ("plagues") of the Egyptians were the Nile running red, the various insects and animals, the storms, the darkness, and the destruction of the first-born sons. These final nine chapters comprise a homily which may well have been delivered on the feast of Passover.

Moses was seeing the preparation of ritually slaughtered lambs for the Passover meal on the night of the tenth plague (cf. Ex 12:21-28; Wis 18:9.) In this fidelity to "the divine institution" (v. 9), Israel's chanting "the praises of the fathers" (v. 9) was mingled with the "discordant cry" and "piteous wail" (v. 10) of the despoiled enemy. "At the destruction of the first-born they [Egypt] acknowledged that the people [Israel] was God's son" (v. 13).

The antitheses pointed out in Wis, it should be noted, are by no means so clearly drawn in Ex but reflect the preacher's art.

Hebrews 11:1-2, 8-19 (longer) or 11:1-2, 8-12 (shorter). The biblical examples of faith—actually, fidelity—given in this chapter follow an exhortation to continue trusting in the mediatorial offices of Christ despite suffering (cf. 10:10-14, 29), not "sinning willfully" through apostasy (10:26). Habakkuk 2:4, which Paul employs in Rom 1:17, is used here in support of the relation between faith and justice (10:38).

The "substance of things hoped for" of former translations is *elpizomenōn hypostasis pragmatōn* (v. 11), viz., God as deliverer, one of the "things we do not see" (*ou blepoumenōn*, v. 2). A catalogue of "men approved" follows. The lectionary omits the verses that mention the creation, Abel, Enoch, and Noah, coming directly to Abraham the father of faith. His obedience in leaving Haran is mentioned first (v. 8; cf. Gn 12:1-4), then his nomad status in Canaan where, with his son-in-law and later his son, he dwelt as a foreigner. Abraham's support and stay was the conviction that a "city with foundations" (v. 10) lay in the future for him, the "sabbath rest" of 4:9. Sarah's faith is so conspicuously absent in Genesis, and the phrase *eis katabolēn spermatos* (v. 12; Vulg., *in conceptionem seminis*) so little related to a woman's part in conception (*katabolē*="deposit" or "sowing," although possibly "beginning") that "Sarah herself" (*autē Sarra*) is taken by many to be a marginal gloss or originally a dative with its iota subscripts lost in transmission.

Abraham's advanced age is exaggerated by the phrase "as good as dead." The biblical promise of a numerous progeny (cf. Gn 15:5; 22:17; 28:14; 32:12; Ex 32:13) is repeated (v. 12). The patriarch described himself to the Hittites at Hebron as a "resident alien" (*ger*) when it came time to bury Sarah (Gn 23:4). The author of Heb has extrapolated this term to all the patriarchs (vv. 13-16) in support of his argument that they looked forward to a better, i.e., a heavenly homeland (*patrida . . . epiouraniou*, vv. 14, 16). Abraham's crowning act of faith is his offering up of Isaac who is the key to the promise (v. 17). The phrasing of v. 19, "raise from the dead" (*ek nekrōn egeirein*) is almost certainly prompted by the raising up of Christ. Abraham's willingness to sacrifice and God's sparing of the boy was done *en parabolē* (v. 19), "as a symbol" or type. Cf. p. 191 on the "binding of Isaac" and on Gn 22:1-14 more generally.

Luke 12:32-48 (longer) or 12:35-40 (shorter). Verses 32, 35-38, 41, and 47-48 are uniquely Lucan; v. 33 occurs in Mt (6:19f.) in quite different form, as does v. 46. There are exact parallels in Mt to v. 34 (6:21), vv. 39f. (24:43f.), and vv. 42-45 (24:45-50).

Two different but similar parables occur in this pericope, each of which has a complicated redactional history: the Gatekeeper (12:35-38 = Mk 13:33-37) and the Servant Entrusted with Supervision (12:42-46 = Mt 24:45-50). In the first, the master has gone "abroad" in Mk, not just to a wedding, and only one man (*ho thyrōros*) watches to let him in. In Lk, "you" (*hymeis*, v. 36) must be like the men waiting, who open to him. This change has been made because of the parousial significance Lk gives it, a matter confirmed by the addition of v. 37*b*. Masters do not wait on servants in that fashion (cf. Lk 17:7f.); Christ the *Kyrios* does, as in Lk 22:27 and Jn 13:4f. In its original setting, the parable was a charge to be watchful, like the injunction of Jesus in the garden to "Be on guard" (*grēgoreite*, Mk 14:38) and to pray so as to be ready for the coming eschatological test (*peirasmos*). Whether spoken in the first instance to disciples or scribes, it has been thoroughly allegorized by the church. In Mt the parable disappears and only the injunction to watchfulness remains (24:42; cf. 25:13.) Lk makes Jesus' reward of selfless service to his own at the final banquet central (cf. 12:37*b*.)

The second parable is likewise given a parousial interpretation in Lk, whatever its earlier, simpler meaning. The slave of the Matthean telling (24:45) becomes a steward in Lk (*oikonomos*, v. 42). It has particular application to the apostles, not to all (v. 41); a special responsibility ("set over his servants," v. 42; "in charge of all his property," v. 44; "he knew his master's wishes," v. 47) falls on those to whom it is directed; they will be punished severely for failure (vv. 46*c*, 47, 48*bc*), presumably in the judgment.

J. Jeremias sees in this parable, as Jesus told it, a stern warning to the religious leaders and teachers of his time, while the early church saw in the delay ("My master is long in coming," v. 45) a reference to the *parousia*. The master was Christ who would return to judge adversely those who abused their charge.

TWENTIETH SUNDAY OF THE YEAR (C)

(Thirteenth Sunday after Pentecost)

Jeremiah 38:4-6, 8-10. The prophet's offense in the eyes of King Zedekiah's counselors is that he keeps telling the people the unpalatable truth that Babylonia is stronger than Judah and hence should be capitulated to. The four men listed in 38:1 have a "better-dead-than-Red" attitude which they keep pressing in terms of optimism and victory. Jeremiah's "disloyalty" consists in his political realism. The entire sequence resembles the rhetoric of U.S. foreign policy in Southeast Asia in the Kennedy through Nixon administrations.

The "Pashhur, son of Malchiah" of v. 1 is the emissary sent by the king to the prophet in 21:1, not the harassing chief of the temple police of the same name ("son of Immer") in 20:1. For background to today's reading, consult the commentaries on Jer 20:7-9 (p. 131), and Jer 20:10-13 (pp. 107f.)

The important thing in Jeremiah's message is that he speaks for life for his people, not death with honor (read: "the defense of political blunders at all cost") by "sword, or famine, or pestilence" (v. 2). Verse 4 is a key statement, in code language, of the doublethink of the princes.

The story is much too interesting to make stopping the public reading at v. 10 attractive. If, however, the whole chapter is read, or a passage that stops with v. 16 or v. 23, the entire homily should then be devoted to the problems raised. Not least of them is that posed by the concurrence of Jeremiah in not reporting his entire conversation with the king.

The reliance of the passion narratives of the gospels on this chapter cannot go unnoticed. In particular, the portrait of Pilate probably relies on that of the weak Zedekiah (esp. v. 5), Joseph of Arimathea on the compassionate Ethiopian eunuch ("courtier," v. 7) Ebedmelech, and above all Jesus' response to the council in Lk 22:67f. on v. 15: "If I tell you anything, you will have me killed. . . . If I counsel you, you will not listen to me!"

Hebrews 12:1-4. This "cloud of witnesses" (v. 1), a title used by Dorothy Sayers for one of her Lord Peter Wimsey detective stories, refers to the men and women of faith detailed in ch. 11. Their example should inspire Christians to lay aside all that hinders their progress (*ogkon . . . panta*, v. 1) and press on to the finish line of the contest (*trechōmen ton . . . agōna*, v. 1). Sin "which clings to us" is NAB's rendering of *euperistatos*, "entangling," the better attested reading; *euperispastos*, "distracting," is found in p[46], a Chester Beatty papyrus at Ann Arbor. The figure envisions a track man running in a robe, our "sweat-suit," rather than naked, the custom of the time (for all but Jews). The image of the footrace recalls its use by Paul (1 Cor 9:24, 26; Phil 2:16) and the author of 2 Tim (4:7f.) Jesus is spoken of as if he were starting-gun, tape, and distance in between; the begetter and completer (*archēgon* [cf. 2:10;

Ac 3:15] *kai teleiōtēn*, v. 2) of our faith. The proposing of Jesus as a model of patiently endured suffering (vv. 2*bc*, 3) is a characteristic of this letter, as it will be of the Pauline-inspired 1 Pt (1:11, 13; 4:1f., 12-19). Jesus is seated in glory at God's right hand (v. 2; cf. 1:3)—sitting in the LORD's presence being a prerogative of Davidic kings (cf. 2 Sm 7:18; Ez 44:3.)

The (Alexandrian? Roman?) Hellenist Christians to whom the treatise is addressed are reminded that, unlike Christ, their fight against sin has not yet been carried to the point of shedding blood (v. 4). This would serve to date Heb before the Neronian persecution of A.D. 64 if a Roman readership were the intended recipient.

Luke 12:49-53. Verses 49f. are peculiar to Lk while 51ff. have their Q parallel in Mt 10:35f. The images of fire and baptism (cf. Mk 10:38) are undoubtedly judgmental, with special reference to the judgment of the LORD on the priests of Ba'al when Elijah—a type of Jesus, not the Baptist, for Lk—had his God cast fire on the earth (cf. Sir 48:1-3; 1 Kgs 18:36ff.) Here Lk pictures Jesus as willing that the fire be ignited and as being under constraint (*synechomai*, v. 50) until the bath in pain of his death should be over. There may be some reference back to the baptism of John, with its imagery of judgmental fire (cf. Lk 3:16f.; Mt 3:11f.)

Lk changes Mt's "bringing" (*balein*) peace to "giving" it (*dounai*), probably to avoid repeating *balein* which he has taken from Sir, "casting fire," immediately above. He likewise makes the Semitic figure "a sword" (*machairan*, Mt 10:34) read "division" (*diamerismon*, v. 51), perhaps to avoid conveying a posture of violence for Jesus. Lk allows a sword image in 2:35 where there is no danger of misinterpretation and is alone in transmitting a mysterious sword-saying of Jesus in the garden (22:36ff.) For him this must be figurative, since in 22:49ff. Jesus counters his disciple's swordplay with an act of healing.

Verse 53 makes all the family hostilities over the person of Christ reciprocal, doubling the phrasing of Mt 18:35. The change is stylistic and not significant. Lk omits, "A man's enemies will be those of his own household" (Mt 10:36), possibly as redundant.

TWENTY-FIRST SUNDAY OF THE YEAR (C)

(Fourteenth Sunday after Pentecost)

Isaiah 66:18-21. NAB and RSV set these verses in prose but John Bright and Harold Rowley think that they are verse, with a prose gloss of nations (v. 19) and animals (v. 20) added. They represent, in any event, a culmination of the breadth of YHWH's interest in the Gentiles which was hinted at in 56:3-8; 60:3-7; and 62:2. This pericope serves as a capstone to Third-Isaiah, Second- and Third-Isaiah together, and indeed the whole book. The "sign" the LORD will choose (v. 19) is the fugitives or survivors (of the apocalyptic slaughter?) who will go forth to the peoples of Tarshish (Spain? Sardinia?), Put (Somalia? Libya?), Lud (Assyria? Lydia in Asia Minor? Egypt?) Mosoch (Meshech) and Tubal (the Ural mountains north of Assyria and southeast of the Black Sea), and Javan (=Ionia; Greece). The list is a selection taken from Gen 10:4, 6, 22, and 2, where Put is said to descend from Ham, Lud from Shem, and the remaining four from Japheth. Appearing in Trito-Isaiah it resembles a list of American Indian tribes made by a modern white who has heard the names but knows little else, and about patterns of migration nothing at all. If the scattered peoples "have never heard of my [YHWH's] fame" (v. 19), it is equally clear that his worshipers have barely heard of theirs.

Not only shall emissaries proclaim the LORD's glory to these distant lands (v. 19); their inhabitants shall come bringing "your brothers," fellow Jews, to holy Zion. They shall come on every conceivable beast and conveyance (v. 20). As the Israelites bring their offerings in clean vessels, so shall their scattered members be brought. The "some of these" (v. 21) to be chosen as priests and Levites have to be Gentiles, as a reward for their service as intermediaries and offerers. This verse would make no special sense if it referred to Jews.

Commonly the passage is taken as a gloss in its entirety but it is very much in the spirit of v. 23b, "All mankind shall worship before me, says the LORD." It is in any case "one of the most spacious views of religion and mankind which is found in the entire OT" (McKenzie).

Hebrews 12:5-7, 11-13. The quotation from Prv 3:11f. which makes up vv. 5bc and 6 reminds believers that chastisement ("discipline," "scourging") is a sure sign of sonship of the LORD. This notion is expanded in verses 7-11 which resemble certain parts of Elihu's speeches in Job. There, God chastises man on his bed of pain and brings him back from the grave so as to instruct him (33:19-33); he "saves the unfortunate through their affliction,/ and instructs them through distress" (36:15); "Sublime in his power,/ what teacher is there like him?" (36:22).

Discipline (*paideia*, vv. 5, 6, 8) is the proof of sonship, presumably because a father does not care enough about his illegitimate sons to prepare them for the short span of life. How much more will not the "Father of spirits" (cf. Nm 16:22; 27:16), whose plan it is to ready them for a share in his own holiness (*hagiotētos*, v. 10), do the same and give them thereby the "peaceable fruit of justice" (*karpon eirēnikon . . . dikaiosynēs*, v. 11)?

The last two verses, 12 and 13*a*, are echoes respectively of Is 35:3 and Prv 4:26 in the Greek. They counsel not only improving the self but the environment as well, a caution to modern moralists who want people to "shape up" without seeking any alleviation of the conditions that make it impossible.

Luke 13:22-30. This pericope is an arrangement of Q material quite different from Mt's and occurs as part of Jesus' Lucan journey toward Jerusalem (cf. v. 22) which began at 9:51 (cf. vv. 9:57; 10:38; 13:33; 17:11; 18:31.) Verses 23f. have a rough parallel in Mt 7:13f.; v. 25 faintly resembles Mt 25:10ff., the parable of the foolish virgins; v. 27 matches Mt 7:23 and vv. 28f., Mt 8:11f., where it refers to the centurion. The final saying about the first and the last (v. 30) occurs in Mt at 19:30 and 20:16.

Lk makes everything in the passage refer to the religious leaders of Israel, to confront whom Jesus is going to the holy city. They will be ejected from the messianic feast (v. 27, quoting Ps 6:9*a*) and be replaced by people from the four corners of the globe (v. 29), specifically the Gentiles of v. 30. These are Lk's candidates for the first who will be last.

TWENTY-SECOND SUNDAY OF THE YEAR (C)

(Fifteenth Sunday after Pentecost)

Sirach 3:17-18, 20, 28-29. A brief *Haustafel* or table of domestic duties in proverb form, chiefly the duties of children toward their parents, precedes today's reading. The arrogance of those who despise and anger their parents leads to advice about humbling oneself. Little needs to be said about these verses, which praise in succession humility (vv. 17-18), a sense of one's own limitations (v. 20), careful listening to epigrammatic wisdom (v. 28), and the atoning effects of almsgiving (v. 29). The higher placed one is, the more attentive should one be to thoughts of self-abnegation. Yet 10:27 serves to restore a possible imbalance:

My son, with humility have self-esteem;
    prize yourself as you deserve.

Sirach certainly numbers himself among the sages (*hakamim*) whom

v. 28 commends. His grandson tells us in the prologue that the old gentleman wrote these lines "in the nature of instruction and wisdom" so that others might profit from his counsel "in living in conformity with the divine law."

Hebrews 12:18-19, 22-24. The author proceeds from a reprobation of Esau as a fornicator and godless person—who is helpful, however, as a horrible example of irreversible choice (vv. 16f.; cf. 6:4-6)—to an evocation of the Sinai theophany. None of the awesome phenomena of old (cf. Ex 19:16, 19) accompanies the present call of Christians (vv. 22ff.) God does not now speak so fearsomely that he must be enjoined to address the people through a mediator as of old (v. 19; cf. Ex 20:19.) The contrast is between the terms of the present covenant, sealed in the "sprinkled blood" of Jesus, and those of the covenant delivered on Sinai. There, even the mediator Moses declared he was "terrified and trembling" (v. 21; cf. Dt 9:19, where he says this in another context, namely after the incident of the golden calf.) Verse 22 anticipates the final assembly in the heavenly Jerusalem, with angels and men intermingled. In v. 23 "the spirits of just men made perfect" assemble without fear before "God, the judge of all."

The "assembly of the first-born enrolled in heaven" recalls Lk 10:20, hence may refer to the entire company of Christians who have been faithful. The angels of v. 22 are less likely; slightly more so, the "just made perfect," those Hebrew saints who are inheriting the promises (cf. 6:12.)

Abel's blood cried out from the soil to be revenged (Gn 4:10) while that of Jesus "assures our entrance into the sanctuary" (Heb 10:19).

Luke 14:1, 7-14. The first fifteen verses of this chapter are special Lucan material. This is Jesus' only recorded meal as the guest of a Pharisee. After a sabbath cure of a man with dropsy (vv. 2-6) he tells a *parabolē* about the choice of places at table (vv. 7-11). It is more an instruction than a story. Jewish folk wisdom featured the notion of taking the lowest place at table, including this teaching from Prv 25:6f.:

> Claim no honor in the king's presence,
> > nor occupy the place of great men;
> For it is better that you be told, "Come up closer!"
> > than that you be humbled before the prince.

Mk 12:39 (=Lk 20:46), in which Jesus rebukes those who take the first places at banquets, has its parallel in a saying attributed to a late 1st-c. rabbi, Simeon ben Azzai. In its original form the *logion* may have been merely a reproach of selfish conduct, but Lk's appending of v. 11 about the humbled and the exalted, and the mention of the resurrection of the just in v. 14, indicate that he is using both counsels of Jesus on banquet protocol (vv. 12f. suggest inviting those who cannot repay you) to illustrate the eschatological situation.

An examination of the occurrence of the proverb, "Everyone who exalts himself shall be humbled, while he who humbles himself shall be exalted," in its various settings (Lk 14:11; 18:14; Mt 23:12) and its cognate, Mk 9:35, "If anyone wishes to rank first, he must remain the last one of all and the servant of all," is instructive. In Mt and Mk the context is the role-reversal that will mark life in the reign of God, while Lk alone uses the saying as descriptive of the way things will be at the end. The call for modest behavior at formal dinners in Lk and the proposal of a plebeian guest-list when one acts as host are thus introductions to "an 'eschatological warning,' which looks forward to the heavenly banquet, and is a call to renounce self-right-eous pretensions and to self-abasement before God" (Jeremias).

TWENTY-THIRD SUNDAY OF THE YEAR (C)

(Sixteenth Sunday after Pentecost)

Wisdom 9:13-18. This entire chapter is cast by its 1st-c. B.C. author in the form of a prayer of King Solomon. He asks that wisdom, "the attendant at your throne" (v. 4), be dispatched to him, "that she may be with me and work with me,/ that I may know what is your pleasure" (v. 10*b*). Wisdom is conceived as an attribute of God, his "holy spirit sent from on high" (v. 17*b*), which provides ethical guidance and saves those who heed her (v. 18).

The counsel of God is contrasted favorably with the uncertain deliberations of men (vv. 13f.) Even earthly matters are a puzzle to the earthbound. How much more must not matters of heavenly wisdom be (v. 16*b*)?

The body-soul contrast does not appear in the earlier Hebrew scriptures. It is not to be characterized as full-scale Greek dualism here (v. 15). Nonetheless, the vocabulary is more reminiscent of Plato than the Bible, which limits itself to observing that man's origins are in the dust of earth and his life cut off like a weaver's last thread or the taking down of a shepherd's tent (cf. Ps 103:14; Jb 4:19; Is 38:12.)

Verse 13 derives from Is 40:13; together they provide the conclusion to Paul's *diatribē* on the mystery of the election of the Gentiles at the end of Rom 11: "For 'who has known the mind of the LORD? Or who has been his counselor?' " (v. 34).

Philemon 9-10, 12-17. Paul feels that he is Philemon's partner in the gospel (*koinōnos*, v. 17) but also that the slave-owner of Colossae is indebted to him for his very life (cf. v. 19.) This indicates that he probably instructed him in the faith. He could command Philémon to take back his runaway slave Onésimus (cf. v. 8) but instead he "appeal(s) in the name of love" (v. 9). Paul is detained as a guest of the nation (v. 9)—exactly where, we cannot be sure. His imprisonment is sufficiently relaxed that it has not kept him from receiving Onesimus into the Christian community (v. 10). He now sends him back as he would his own heart (v. 12). There is no reason to omit reading v. 11 publicly since the bracketed translation of Onesimus' name as "useful" in NAB should convey the pun adequately, provided it is well read.

Paul's technique of persuasion is extremely clever. He would have kept the slave by him in the master's place except that this might be taken by Philemon as an enforced gratuity (vv. 13f.) Gratuity! The troublesome runaway has been changed into an emissary of love, like Cinderella's coach turned into a pumpkin. A better example might be Tom Sawyer's getting people to whitewash his fence for him and counting it an honor. The useless fugitive has become a beloved brother (*adelphos*, v. 16, the normal word for a person baptized). Paul proposes that the cheated Philemon snap up the chance to receive back in the Lord someone who is as good as Paul in the role of one's houseguest.

His lordly instruction to bill all charges to him (v. 18) recalls Ethel Merman's key to all hearts as a Washington hostess in *Call Me Madam*: "I'll take the check!" "If he has done you an injury, or owes you anything, charge it to me" (v. 18). One thinks of the apocryphal tale of the statue of the innkeeper on the Jericho road scanning the horizon with eyes shaded by his upraised hand, with the inscription beneath: "And if there is any further expense, I upon my return shall repay thee."

The silence of this letter on the legal fact of slavery is often remarked. The introductory remark in NAB expresses the common view: "That Onesimus the slave was 'brother' to Philemon, his legal master (v. 16), was a revolutionary idea in the context of the times."

Luke 14:25-33. Verses 25ff. have their Q parallel in Mt 10:37f. but the remainder is pure Lk. The "turning his back" (v. 26) of NAB is "hate" in Greek (*misei* = Heb. *sane*'), the usual Hebraic contrast, love-hate. "Take up one's cross" (*bastazei ton stauron*, v. 27; Mt 10:38 has *lambanei*) is widely thought to be a saying of the early church deriving from the crucifixion rather than an authentic saying of Jesus, although the latter is not impossible. This Roman form of execution was everywhere visible to the horrified Jewish eye.

The two brief parables of the builder of a tower (vv. 28ff.) and the king about to do battle (vv. 31f.) make the same point: lack of planning leads to ridicule or ruin. Lk uses the necessity of foresight in farming or war-making to underscore the point that renunciation of all one's possessions is a condition of discipleship (v. 33). The tower of v. 28 (*pyrgos*) can also mean a farm-building. Some are inclined to favor this translation because of the great money outlay; in this hypothesis, a silo rather than a shaft as a lookout for crows would be indicated. The king of Jesus' parable negotiates from weakness, in today's cold-war vocabulary (v. 32). Lk employs both stories to suggest negotiating from strength, which for him means divesting oneself of all that one has.

TWENTY-FOURTH SUNDAY OF THE YEAR (C)

(Seventeenth Sunday after Pentecost)

Exodus 32:7-11, 13-14. Jeroboam set up calves of gold in Dan and Bethel to split the people's religious allegiance and draw them away from Jerusalem (1 Kgs 12:28ff.) This act was reprehensible in the eyes of the Jerusalem-oriented author but, strangely, Jeroboam's artifacts were not. The story in 1 Kgs may be calculated to denigrate Jeroboam even further by assuming in the reader a knowledge of today's pericope. Since no mention is made of Ex there, however, some are inclined to think that things went in the other direction, namely that the molten images—not readily cast in the Sinai desert— got into Exodus after having originated in 1 Kgs. The images were not offensive in themselves being stands or bases to receive the invisible YHWH, much like the cherubim upholding the propitiatory (Ex 25:18ff.) Hosea fulminated against the "calf of Samaria" in the 8th c. (8:5f.), the earliest dependable historical reference to a view of calves as idols in themselves.

Moses pleads for his people like Abraham of old bargaining over Sodom and Gomorrah. The lawgiver reminds the LORD of his mercies in the exodus to date (v. 11) and his oath to the patriarchs to make Israel a numerous people (v. 13). The LORD's blazing wrath simmers down (v. 14), presumably lest the Egyptians say that he set his people free only to destroy them in the desert.

See Dt 9:11-21 for the same story as if told by Moses.

Aaron's part in the business is puzzling. At first his complicity in making the images is total (32:1-6) but then he is exonerated by Moses for his weakness (vv. 21-24). There is an amusing touch in his explanation, more ingenious than anything Adam put forward in his defense: "They gave it to me, and I threw it into the fire, and this calf came out" (v. 24).

One wonders how Aaron, who is usually connected with the ark of the covenant, is described here as abandoning his charismatic office and aligning himself with the enemies of YHWH. Some conjecture that his association with a golden calf in Jerusalem's later temple was originally honorific, and that it became the center of a story of idolatry only in the later apostasies of Samaria. It would be an interesting outcome of biblical criticism if this best known of tales from the desert experience should be established to have had its origins five centuries later.

1 Timothy 1:12-17. This reading is helpful in establishing the non-Pauline authorship of the epistle by the very way it goes about recalling Paul's career. It also contains the first of three "trustworthy statements" (*pistos ho logos*, v. 15; cf. also 3:1; 4:9; 2 Tim 2:11; Ti 3:8) in the epistle, which seem to be creedal, liturgical, and church-order fragments. This one, "Christ Jesus came into the world to save sinners," is probably the center around which everything else in the pericope turns. Paul's self-denunciation is so stiff that it is doubtfully his: "Of these I myself am the worst." It is true that he strongly regrets his career as a persecutor of the church (cf. Gal 1:13, 23; Phil 3:6; esp. 1 Cor 15:9, "I am the least of the apostles") but in general Paul has a very robust conscience (cf. Rom 9:1; 1 Cor 4:4; 2 Cor 1:12; 5:10) and cannot be imagined engaging in self-abnegation so strong that it sounds like a boast. Paul calling himself arrogant (v. 13) sounds more like a close observer of Paul than Paul. Praise of Christ's mercy and patience are Pauline; so is his presenting himself as a model for emulation (v. 16). But the sum is less than its parts—a Pauline anthology rather than Pauline diction.

The doxology of v. 17 mixes Hebrew and Greek elements unselfconsciously ("King of ages," "the only God," as against "immortal," "invisible") but this was not untypical of Hellenist Judaism.

Luke 15:1-32 (longer) or 1-10 (shorter). For a commentary on the first three verses of this reading and the parable of the forgiving father, see pp. 305f.

Mt 18:12f. contains the parable of the lost sheep but makes a different point of it: "It is no part of your heavenly Father's plan that a single one of these little ones shall ever come to grief." Rather than highlighting the providential care of the simple, Lk features eschatological joy over the repentance of sinners. He will do the same with the story of the recovered drachma (peculiar to him) and the longer parable which follows. The reason for the telling is withheld until v. 32 when it emerges strongly.

TWENTY-FIFTH SUNDAY OF THE YEAR (C)

(Eighteenth Sunday after Pentecost)

Amos 8:4-7. This brief, powerful oracle against oppressors of the poor echoes certain sentiments found in 2:6f. It does not seem to follow logically upon the four visions of the author (locusts, fire, plummet, fruit basket) recorded in 7:1-3, 4ff., 7ff.; 8:1ff. Amos flays dishonest tradesmen and merchants whom he accuses of oppressing the poor. They cannot wait for the religious festivals to be over so that they can return to their fixing of weights (the shekel=4 oz.; the loaded scale) and measures (the ephah=.62 bushel or 19.97 dry qt.) The feasts were calculated by the new moon, the sabbath by Friday sundown (cf. Is 1:13; Hos 2:13, NAB) and required the cessation of movement and commercial activity.

Verse 6 refers to the selling into slavery of defaulting debtors; the sale of wheat-husks is an added stroke of rapacity. YHWH is made to swear by the "pride [*gaon*: excellence, majesty] of Jacob." Since elsewhere he swears by his holiness (4:2) or by himself (6:8), we are led to conclude that this oath has the same meaning, all of Jacob's (Israel's) splendor having been derived from the LORD. YHWH means never to forget the greedy assault on the poor (v. 7). He will punish it with earthquake (v. 8), eclipse (v. 9), deprivation (v. 10), and famine (v. 11).

Amos had a deep interest in economic trends in the northern kingdom under Jeroboam II (786-46), in which the rich grew richer and the poor poorer.

1 Timothy 2:1-8. The Pauline author proposes liturgical suffrages for all (v. 1). The four types mentioned are not to be neatly distinguished. The Roman emperors (*basileōn*, v. 2) are especially to be remembered, but also all in authority (*en hyperochē*). This verse may well be a phrase taken from a liturgical prayer. It accords with a spirit of concern for the well-being of political institutions and personages found in Rom 13:1-7 and 1 Pt 2:13-17. The vote of confidence in a stable order as divinely sustained is not to be attributed to Christian self-interest. There was the genuine conviction that God's will lay behind the good sovereign or magistrate who did not despotically resist him. Nor was mere tranquillity (*hēsychion bion*, v. 2) the aim. Such stability of men and institutions was the very condition of piety and dignity (*eusebeia kai semnotēs*). Without these as a matrix, which only prayer could assure, there could be no salvation or coming to a knowledge (*epignōsis*) of the truth (v. 4).

The writer makes explicit the truth he has in mind by quoting a hymnic or creedal fragment which is probably both (v. 5). In it the uniqueness of God is strongly affirmed. Distinct from him is the one mediator between God and the human race (*heis kai mesitēs Theou kai anthrōpōn*), "man [without the article] Christ Jesus." The latter phrasing is a thrust against gnostic elements which might be denying the full manhood of the mediator. This middleman is one "giving himself as a ransom for all" (*ho dous heauton antilytron hyper pantōn*, v. 6). The word *antilytron* occurs for the only time in the NT here; more usual are *lytron anti pollōn* (Mk 10:45; Mt 20:28) and *lytrōsis* (Lk 1:68; Heb 9:12).

Paul's self-description as "herald," "apostle," and "teacher of the nations," a phrase that will recur in 2 Tim 1:11 except for mention of the Gentiles, is well-nigh unthinkable in a letter to a close associate (v. 7). Even less imaginable is his protestation that he does not lie about the gospel. The latter is obviously a modification of the phrase in Gal 1:20 where Paul strongly affirms the truthfulness of his recollection about visits to Jerusalem. Verse 7 must be taken as a declaration of the Pauline school, against all opponents, that Paul was not only the apostle and preacher he thought himself (cf. Rom 11:1; 1 Cor 1:1; 2 Cor 1:1; Gal 1:1, 9) but also a thoroughly trustworthy teacher and "apostle to the Gentiles."

Verse 8 leads into the disciplinary section on women (vv. 9-15) by citing men as the proper leaders of public prayer in the *orans* position ("hands held aloft"). Because Paul is widely thought to be a male chauvinist, the preacher should take some pains to indicate that we have in this epistle the earnest teaching of a follower of Paul, probably early 2d-c.

Luke 16:1-13 (longer) or 10-13 (shorter). The preacher who opts for the shorter reading needs to know chiefly that Lk has made a collection of four distinct money-sayings of Jesus. Each has its own power, whereas threaded together they lose force, especially when (as seems to be the case) they are being proposed as elucidations of a parable which the evangelist gives evidence of not understanding. Verse 9, also a saying delivered on another occasion, has some chance of being related to the point of Jesus' parable; the rest have none.

As Jesus told the story it probably ended at v. 8. It is a simple, forceful tale suggesting that the good should take a leaf from the book of the wicked. It carefully documents a well-known system of extortion. Various proposals have been made about the economics of entrepreneurship of the times that would result in the owner's admiration or acceptance of his wily manager's cleverness. The likeliest explanations but not the only ones are those which have the owner able to praise the middleman grudgingly because he himself has suffered no personal loss. A scheme whereby the owner knew the quotas he expected, without inquiring into those levied by his manager, would suit the facts best. In this case "owed" would have nothing to do with indebtedness but a rehearsal of the quota system which the manager had imposed on the tenants in the first place, as if the owner had set it. All he was then doing was eliminating or diminishing his profit so as to look good to them, with his own eye cocked to the future.

An explanation which sees to it that the owner suffers no loss is not essential. The owner was as deep in defrauding the laboring poor as his employee and could have appreciated a good "con" when he saw one, even though he might be its part-victim. To make Jesus' point, the wilier all around the better.

TWENTY-SIXTH SUNDAY OF THE YEAR (C)

(Nineteenth Sunday after Pentecost)

Amos 6:1, 4-7. Mention of Zion and the mount of Samaria and the complacent and overconfident leaders of a favored nation in both places immediately tells us of a warning to Judah and Israel (Ephraim), the southern and the northern kingdoms (v. 1). Normally Amos, a man of the south (1:1), does not address himself to Judah but this does not mean (as some have held) that mention of Judah's holy mountain must be a gloss. The accusation against the leaders is that by their luxurious living they are preparing for defeat—at Assyrian hands—by the very practices calculated to keep defeat farthest from their consciousness.

The denunciation in vv. 4-6 is a bill of particulars specifying why the Jews can expect no better treatment than their Syrian and Phoenician neighbors (v. 2), no deferment of the evil day of violent retribution (v. 4). The prophet does not have any difficulty in identifying Israel's infidelities as the cause of the hastening of that day. The "beds of ivory" (v. 4), like the "ivory apartments" of 3:15, describe the inlays that have been so prominent among the archaeological finds of the ancient city of Samaria (later Sebasteia).

The imputation in vv. 4, 5, and 6 is of women, song, and wine, with roasts for rich fare and body-culture thrown in besides. Joseph (i.e., the northern kingdom) is in deep political trouble because of its "fat-cat" status (v. 6b). The perpetrators of that trouble are oblivious to it.

Yet they shall all be carted off into exile (v. 7) when the day of wrath, about which verses 8-11 grow graphic, descends.

1 Timothy 6:11-16. The half-dozen verses immediately preceding, with their strong warning against the love of money as the root of all evil, especially for those deep enough in religion to make it a "means of personal gain" (v. 5), are essential to an understanding of this concluding charge. The whole epistle has been directed to workers in the service of the gospel, hence the choice of "Timothy" from the apostolic age as its recipient. An important difference is that the structures of a much later church life are evident.

Timothy is instructed to flee all harmful desires for base gain and seek everlasting life through the path of the virtues (vv. 11f.) His baptismal experience is referred to as a means to motivate him (v. 12), the noble profession of faith (*kalēn homologian*) on that occasion being likened to that of Jesus before Pilate (v. 13). He must "fight the good fight of faith." God's "command" is his charge that believers be faithful to his revelation (*epiphaneias*, v. 14) in Christ, whom he will make known in his own good time (*en kairois idiois*, v. 15). The pericope ends in a doxology which draws on phrases in praise of God found in 1:17; 2 Mc 12:15; 13:4; Rev 17:14; 19:16, all standard Hellenist-Jewish vocabulary which mixes Hebrew phrases with Greek attributes freely. No doubt it was a liturgical formula.

The normal word in the Pauline writings for Jesus' reappearance is *parousia* (cf. 2 Thes 2:8; 2 Tim 1:10; 4:1, 8; Ti 2:13.) *Epiphaneia* is used here, but without any change in meaning. The sense of the passage is that one's Christian life must be lived free from blame or reproach (v. 14) until God sees fit to reveal his son finally.

Luke 16:19-31. This perfect Lucan parable bears the stamp of a folk-tale which the evangelist, having reported, puts at the service of his continued invitation to repentance. He is equally interested in the failure of the Jews, who have every advantage, to heed "Moses and the prophets" (v. 31). Their hardened condition is such that no report of resurrection from the dead (Jesus' resurrection, i.e.) will move them. The poor beggar for Lk is the true son of Abraham. Lk will stress the theme of true sonship again, in the case of Zacchaeus (19:9), as he has done with a woman bent double for eighteen years

(13:13), and those rejected versus the accepted at the judgment (13:28f.)

Needless to say, the rich man in torment seeking comfort at the hands of Lazarus (v. 24) is an authentic touch of Jesus' teaching. His message was nothing if not a projection of the overturning of every convention and stereotype. God who sees all hearts will lay them bare at the end. His justice is not man's justice, as Isaiah said long ago.

TWENTY-SEVENTH SUNDAY OF THE YEAR (C)

(Twentieth Sunday after Pentecost)

Habakkuk 1:2-3; 2:2-4. NAB conjectures in its introduction to this book that we may have here (vv. 2f.) the first questioning of the ways of God in Israelite literature. Later the authors of Job and the Psalms will raise it to an art. ("I cry to you but you do not answer me; / you stand off and look at me, / Then you turn upon me without mercy / and with your strong hand you buffet me." [Job 30:20f.]; cf. Pss 88; 142.) The occasion is the desperate state of Judah on the brink of Nebuchadnezzar's invasion of Jerusalem in 597 B.C. The LORD says he is raising up Chaldea to do his will (vv. 5-11). There is violence and injustice everywhere, and the prophet charges God with doing nothing to alleviate it. Why must Habakkuk have to see, why must he be required to look at this clamorous discord (v. 3)? If YHWH has no intention of intervening, he could at least spare his prophet the repulsive sight of ruin.

The author then declares that he will set himself up at a guard post on a rampart to discover what response, if any, he will get from the LORD (2:1; Is 21:6-9; Ez 3:17 all use the same figure of the watchman). The answer he awaits he receives (vv. 4-20). The message is to be posted publicly (v. 2). Vindication will come soon, he is told, even if there be delay (v. 3). The programmatic opening which sets the tone for the whole oracle states that mankind is divided into two groups: the rash who trust in wealth and personal resources and the just whose integrity derives from their faith. YHWH will set about delivering his people from oppression from Chaldea and injustice from within, in accord with this analysis. Some rely on themselves; the just man relies on the LORD (*justus autem in fide sua vivet* [v. 4], Vulgate). The presence of trust (*ᵉmunah*) makes a man just or righteous, a *ṣaddik*. Its absence makes him proud and unstable (v. 4) with an insatiable appetite for destruction.

2 Timothy 1:6-8, 13-14. The second letter of Paul to Timothy is widely regarded as pseudonymous, as are 1 Tim and Ti. The reasons include weak attestation to all three pastoral epistles in early canons and papyri, the nature of their polemic against heretics, the transition from the Pauline *kērygma* to the conception of Christian faith as a *parathēkē* ("deposit," 1 Tim 6:20; 2 Tim 1:12, 14), vocabulary divergencies from Paul, the difficulty of fitting 1 and 2 Tim into his life-situation, and the un-Pauline character of the church order described in the pastorals.

St. Paul had used Hab 4:1 to press home his point that the justice and fidelity of God were displayed in his entrusting the gospel to us (Rom 1:17). Paul's disciple who writes this letter is addressing himself to some third-generation Christian (v. 5). The point the writer makes is that faith cannot be transmitted merely as a family inheritance. Neither can it be counted on to burn with the same bright flame as when a Christian received the sacraments of initiation (or was commissioned to preach, if that is the meaning of the imposition of hands; cf. v. 6.) A rekindling is constantly needed if the Christian is to continue in the spirit of power, love, and wisdom (*sōphronismos*, v. 7), which he first received. The strength God gives should help the disciple accept the hardships entailed in the gospel, as he gives testimony to "our Lord" (*to martyrion tou Kyriou hēmōn*, v. 8) and the imprisoned Paul. Paul's words delivered in faith and love (v. 13) are proposed as a model of sound teaching. This "noble deliverance" (*tēn kalēn parathēkēn*, v. 14) is to be guarded "through (*dia*) the Holy Spirit." The writer knows that the one in whom he trusts will watch over the rich treasure he has received, until the day of consummation (*eis ekeinēn tēn hēmeran*, v. 12).

Luke 17:5-10. Lk derives vv. 5f. from Q (cf. Mt 17:20) but the remaining short parable is peculiarly his. The "sycamore" of v. 6 is a *sykaminos* (sycamine, black mulberry). A mustard seed is like the faith that moves a mountain in Mt, while here it commands a tree to throw itself into the sea. Large and incommensurate effects from scarcely discernible causes are the point of this hyperbole. The grass that breaks through and breaks up concrete paving provides a modern parallel without the element of exaggeration.

Servants act like servants, says the parable. They are not waited on but do the waiting (v. 8). Such is the fixed social order of things. No verbal bouquets are handed out when this order is adhered to. The argument is *a minori ad maius*. If slaves in domestic service serve, how much more should not God's servants go beyond routine commands to do his bidding (v. 10)? Fortunately for Lk's argument, he can provide Jesus as the model for all as the one "in your midst who serves you" (22:27).

TWENTY-EIGHTH SUNDAY OF THE YEAR (C)

(Twenty-First Sunday after Pentecost)

2 Kings 5:14-17. The lectionaries recently proposed for use in the United Presbyterian Church and the United Church of Christ suggest that this reading begin at v. 9. That seems to provide the hearer with a better clue to the story than beginning at v. 14, unless it is presumed so familiar to Catholics that they need not have it reviewed in its entirety. Since the venality of Elisha's servant Gehazi will figure prominently in the tale at vv. 20-27, the refusal of Elisha to accept a gift for doing the LORD's work is of special importance. In a sense, it is a sub-plot of the story. The main plot concerns the power of the God of Elisha—a point not lost on the upright Aramean commander. An important aspect of the story is the curative power of the Jordan, which is situated in a land made holy by its association with YHWH. The mule-loads of earth are to be this land transplanted. Naaman will have to appear in the sanctuary of the god Rimmon as part of his duties as a military aide. His private holocausts, however, will be offered on the soil of Israel to Israel's God.

It would seem unwise for the preacher to make a point of Naaman's leprosy (v. 3). Victims of the disease so designated in English suffer enough already without their affliction being made symbolic of moral fault, as is commonly done. The healing power of God and the trust in him of the captive Jewish girl (v. 2) and the prophet (v. 10) are the important matters—they and the new faith of the soldier of the king of Aram (Syria).

2 Timothy 2:8-13. An impressive body of scholarly opinion situates the authorship of 1 and 2 Timothy in the early second century, as was pointed out last week, because of their similarity to documents of the sub-apostolic age. There is also the unlikeness of many phrases to those of Paul, despite the author's mammoth effort to re-create every known detail of his career. The "holding out to the end" of the christological hymn of v. 12a and the denial and unfaithfulness spoken of in 12b bring to mind the harassment of Christians which we know of from Trajan's reign (A.D. 98-117) more than they do the imprisonments of Paul (cf. Phil 1:13f.)

The author reflects a knowledge of Rom 1:3f. in v. 8 and Col 1:24 in v. 10. Leonard Bernstein's sermon of the celebrant in *Mass*, an ingenious targumic interweaving of epistle, gospel, and homily, has restored v. 9 to popular consciousness:

But you cannot imprison the word of the Lord!

Verse 11 contains one of the "dependable sayings" (*pistos ho logos*) found in 1 Tim 3:1 and 4:9. Death with Christ brings life; perseverance in suffering assures a share in his reign. (Cf.: "We are heirs of God, heirs with Christ, if only we suffer with him so as to be glorified with him," Rom 8:17.) Verse 13 features Christ's inner fidelity which is like that of YHWH—a NT *hapax* (i.e., sole occurrence).

The pericope is a sober discussion of "the choice between the faith in Christ and life itself" (Kee), with specific motivations given for perseverance and not recanting the faith under persecution. "If we deny him he will deny us" (v. 12*b*; cf. Lk 13:27.)

Luke 17:11-19. This narrative is not found elsewhere in the gospels. Luke makes the account he has from the tradition a story of the gratitude of the outsider in contrast to the ingratitude of those in the community of Jewish faith. We have come to expect this stress of his. Jesus' very appearance along the borders of Samaritan territory (v. 11) was not without risk. The lepers keep their distance (v. 12) in accordance with the requirement of Lv 13:45 that they call out their affliction. They address him as *Epistatēs*, "Master," a secular title employed by Lk six times, usually on the lips of the disciples. Jesus intimates a cure rather than referring to it specifically. His immediate response to the lepers' plea, namely that they should show themselves to the priests, does not conform to the specifications of Lv 13:9ff. or 49 where the priest acts as a quarantine officer, but comes closest to 14:3 where he declares a cure an accomplished fact. But that is not the point.

The cure of ten and the gratitude of only one who was a Samaritan, is (vv. 15ff.) This despised people had the five books of Moses in common with the Jews but their claim to their own shrine at Shechem and their heritage (cf. Josh 24) had long been rejected by the southerners of Judah. Such claims and counterclaims were not of significance to Jesus in the synoptic tradition, even though Jn has him acknowledge the rightness of Jewish faith (4:22) as a prelude to transcending both claims with a worship in "spirit and in truth." The healed Samaritan is reported as having achieved that transcendence.

TWENTY-NINTH SUNDAY OF THE YEAR (C)

(Twenty-Second Sunday after Pentecost)

Exodus 17:8-13. Joshua's name occurs for the first time in the Bible, abruptly, in v. 9. He is introduced as Moses' aide in 24:13 and appears in the narrative at 32:17. Not until Nm 13:8 does he properly get into the story. This means that the incident is out of order and ought to come much later in the book. Moreover, the Amalekites are elsewhere described (Nm 13:29; 14:25) as people of the Negev or southern Palestinian desert, not from south in the Sinai peninsula near Rephidim. This seems to be the story of a raiding party near Kadesh-barnea in the northeastern portion of Sinai, as the Israelites approach Canaan.

Moses holds up his staff (v. 9; cf. 4:17) and raises his hands as a symbolic action calculated to ensure victory, similar to the postures struck by Elijah in 1 Kgs 17:21; 18:42. Joshua is totally successful in terms of the ban (*herem = anathēma*), v. 13. Verse 16 provides a snatch of a victory song, probably sung long after. "YHWH-nissi" ("The Lord my banner") is victorious through the people Israel over the Amalekites down through the ages.

Early Christian iconography likened Moses' upraised hands, supported by Aaron and Hur, to the position of the hands of the eucharistic celebrant as *orans*. In the Exodus account it was undoubtedly more a prophetic sign than a prayer.

2 Timothy 3:14; 4:2. Verse 14 is an argument in favor of the links in a tradition, with a charge to observe fidelity included. The Scriptures (v. 15) known to the recipient from his infancy are the Hebrew law, prophets, and writings (cf. Lk 24:44.) Salvation and wisdom are available through reading them in a spirit of faith in Christ (v. 15). Only by knowing them well and interpreting them rightly can a teacher in the community be equipped for his office (v. 17). They are "inspired of God" (*theopneustos*, v. 16) and useful for instruction in faith, morals, and discipline.

The stern apostolic charge of 4:1f. to be faithful to the task of proclamation (*kēryxon ton logion*, v. 2) until the Lord returns to judge (*krinein*, v. 1) is laid upon the disciple Timothy. Jesus' appearance and his reign (*tēn epiphaneian autou kai tēn basileian*, v. 1) are realities that have in some sense already occurred. There must be an unflagging fidelity to preaching, whatever the seeming unsuitability of the occasion, until the Lord's return. It is to be done through argument, and relentlessly, but with patience (*makrothymia*) and by way of expository teaching (*didachē*).

Luke 18:1-8. Lk's corrupt judge is all his own; there are no parallels. The story resembles the parable of persistence of the householder wakened in the middle of the night (11:5-8). Lk tells this tale in response to the uncertainty of the community regarding Jesus' return. The Lord will come to do justice if he is prayed for night and day (vv. 7f.) Again, the technique is *a minori ad maius*, the Hebrew "light and heavy." If even an unjust judge must yield to a petitioner from whom he fears violence (*hypopiazē*, v. 5; lit., "strike under the eye"), how much more will not the just and generous God do for his chosen who call on him? Lk has made this a parable of prayer for the final arrival of God's reign, whatever Jesus meant in telling it originally. Sir 35:14*a*-15 tells of a widow who may well provide the model for this one.

Lk's pious conclusion (v. 8*b*) is what he makes of this tale, illustrative of persistent prayer, for the *parousia*.

THIRTIETH SUNDAY OF THE YEAR (C)

(Twenty-Third Sunday after Pentecost)

Sirach 35:15-17, 20-22. This is the passage referred to in the commentary on last week's gospel. The God of justice who knows no favorites (v. 12) is not deaf to the widow when she pours out her complaint (v. 14). Those who cause her tears to fall (v. 15) are undoubtedly the oppressor (v. 13) and the merciless and proud (v. 20) who harass the weak, the orphan, and the widow (vv. 13f.) The chief thrust of this passage is the declaration of vv. 17f., made use of by Jesus, that the prayer of the humble will be answered by God with justice and their rights restored to them. Verses 20ff. have a certain vengeful quality, reflected in the song of Mary (cf. Lk 1:51ff.), but to the Jewish mind this was simply a means of expressing God's justice. The proud and the haughty of vv. 20f. have been referred to before in 10:14-17 and 16:6-14. In the latter place the "godless" (v. 6) are overtly the rebellious Korah, the people of Sodom and Gomorrah, and others from the biblical past. Actually, a veiled polemic against the Greeks of Sirach's day is probably intended.

The incorruptibility of God, the just judge (vv. 11f.) who is as impervious to sacrifice from the possessions of the poor as to extortion, has been featured in 34:18ff. His wrath will flare up against the oppressors of widows and orphans, destroying them and leaving their women and children in the same condition, as Ex 22:21ff. had long ago promised.

2 Timothy 4:6-8, 16-18. Verses 6-8 of today's reading comprise the solemn conclusion of the hortatory material that goes to make up the bulk of the epistle. The disciple should suffer for the faith on the basis of the bond between his teacher and him (cf. 1:8, 12; 2:3-13; 3:10-12.)

The notions of "being poured out like a libation" (*spendomai*, v. 6) and of "dissolution" (*analysis*) in the sense of departure from life are reminiscent of Phil 2:17 and 1:23. Verse 7 with its three parallel clauses triumphantly reviewing the life of an apostle is a familiar part of Christian literature—almost invariably attributed to Paul. Two of the images employed come from athletic contests (cf. 1 Cor 9:24ff.; Phil 4:1.) "Keeping faith" (*pistin tērein*) was already a fixed expression meaning maintaining a trust. Professor Günther Bornkamm has cited the words attributed to Dido, "cursum peregi," from Virgil's *Aeneid* 4.653 as a parallel to *ton dromon teteleka*, "I have finished the race," where the phrase refers to the course of life which Fortuna has mapped out for her.

A crown of righteousness awaits (*apokeitai*, v. 8) the apostle, a verb which occurs both in imperial edicts of commendation and later in accounts of martyrdom (*Mart. Polycarp.* 17.1, 19.2). "On that day" (*en ekeinę tę hēmerą*) is taken by NAB to mean "that Day" [i.e., of the Lord], an interpretation influenced by 2 Tim's reference to the Lord's "appearing" (*epiphaneia*) in the role of just judge after much loving and eager longing (*ēgapēkosi*). It is the Lord who will award the faithful apostle his *stephanos*, the laurel-wreath of the successful athlete.

The immediate context of vv. 17f. is v. 16, with its mention of "my [i.e., Paul's] first hearing." An early interpretation of this passage is found in Eusebius, *History of the Church* 2.2, where the 4th-c. author follows a tradition that Paul was released from his two years of captivity at Rome, with which Acts concludes, and that he set out on a further ministry of preaching and was apprehended a second and last time. It was during this second Roman captivity that he is said by Eusebius to have written 2 Tim. On such a hypothesis, his earlier release would have constituted his deliverance "from the lion's jaws" (v. 17), the lion being imperial power. Against this theory is the fact that the pastoral epistles know of only one imprisonment of Paul. His first hearing in court (*apologia*), therefore, is meant to be an episode in his sole Roman trial. Alternatively, on the supposition that the epistle was written from a Caesarean imprisonment, he is portrayed as reporting on the events of Ac 23:1ff., with the Lord appearing at Paul's side (as in v. 11).

The reading at Mass need not be freighted with these complex historical considerations. It is a straightforward declaration of what the faithful messenger of the gospel may look forward to. There is no moral problem attaching to pseudonymous authorship, even to simulated farewells and personal messages. It was a convention of the times and is totally unrelated to our modern concept of literary forgery.

Luke 18:9-14. This two-character story of Jesus conveys two general attitudes, one of self-congratulation with "nothing to declare," the other of awareness of sin and an implicit plea for the restoration of justice. The characterization of the Pharisee is so devastating that that unfortunate class of men has been type-cast in the Christian mind ever since. Jacob Neusner has pointed out that we do not have enough data on the Pharisees from Jewish sources dating to Jesus' time to generalize on them or even to distinguish among different types. Christians, meanwhile, have generalized adversely from the synoptic data. The basic and unresolved question is, what is the relation of *hoi pharisaioi* of the gospels to *ha perushim* of talmudic literature? The latter may be the "separated," but from what or whom we cannot be sure. They may also be the "distinguishers" or the "precisionists." The gospels are interested in one type of Pharisee only, the proud one who is separated not only from all that might defile him ritually, but in a contemptuous way from the "people of the land." The more righteous seekers of wisdom in Pharisee ranks are largely disregarded, their very existence being hinted at only briefly. Both the Babylonian and Palestinian Talmuds classify the *perushim* into seven types, five of which are held up to ridicule (e.g., the knee-knocking *perushim*, those who rub themselves against the wall to draw blood, the one bent over like a pestle in a mortar), while two are praised (for fearing like Job, for loving like Abraham). The Pharisee of the Lucan parable is in neither of the latter two categories.

The Pharisee's prayer is no prayer at all. The tax-gatherer's self-accusation may very well have been true and not merely the expression of a sense of unworthiness. These *telōnai*, after all, had as their way of life a collaboration with the Romans against fellow Jews. In saying he is unworthy he may really be unworthy. This would mean that he goes home from the temple justified because he intends to amend his unjust ways. That refinement is not the point, however, so much as the attitudes of the two men in the one activity, prayer.

Lk repeats his summary conclusion on the exalted and the humbled (v. 14*b*) from his parable of places at a feast (14:11), which in turn is based on the phrase in the *Magnificat* which says that God has deposed the mighty and raised the lowly to high places (1:52).

THIRTY-FIRST SUNDAY OF THE YEAR (C)

(Twenty-Fourth Sunday after Pentecost)

Wisdom 11:23—12:2. It is possible to say in commenting on this passage that it features God's mercy (v. 23), his love (v. 24), his creation and sustenance of all things (v. 25), and the gradual character of his punishments which are primarily remedial. Yet the chief thing that leaps up from the page is none of these but the unmistakably Hellenist character of the pericope. It bristles with Greek-oriented statements about God which would never have occurred to any biblical writer of a pre-Alexandrian age. Among them are: "You can do all things," "You love all things that are," "You loathe nothing you have made," "How could a thing remain, unless you willed it?" "You spare all things because they are yours," "Your imperishable spirit is in all things." An Hebraic equivalent of some of the above might be worked out but that is not the point. The point is that the Greek world in which the author of Wisdom had his being had ontological problems (and a vocabulary to cope with them) which his Jewish forebears did not have and felt none the poorer without.

These verses are part of a digression on the subject of God's mercy (11:17—12:22) from the second of five pairs of opposites taken from the Exodus narrative. The segment on the providence of God during the exodus runs from 11:2 through 19:22, the end of the book. The present pairing sets in contrast the Egyptian worship of dumb creatures (11:15f.; 12:23-27; 15:18—16:4)—for which they were struck with plagues of small animals and serpents—and the quail which, contrariwise, benefited the Israelites. The lengthy digression (11:17—12:22), of which today's reading is a part, is triggered by mention of the punishment of sin in 11:16. God's universal love for creatures is elaborated at length in the language of Greek metaphysics.

2 Thessalonians 1:11—2:2. Verses 11f. are obviously a prayer for the recipients of the epistle that they may be strengthened against the persecution and trial which will be a necessary preliminary to the Lord's coming in glory (vv. 3-10). If they fulfill God's call in faith, that day will be one of mutual glorification for the Lord Jesus Christ and them.

In vv. 1f. of ch. 2 the author—Paul or some other—attempts to allay the anxieties which 1 Thes 4:16f. could have created. Although the latter verses end with a charge to "console one another with this message," the graphic account of the day of the Lord's coming might well have agitated or terrified Macedonian populations not accustomed to Jewish apocalyptic language. The problems of the dating and authorship of this letter stem from ch. 2 as it proceeds from here. Either Paul became aware of the fears he had aroused by his first letter and penned a second one fairly soon, naming signs and conditions that would have to be realized before the Lord could be expected back, or else some other Christian long after Paul, with 1 Thes before him, supplied reasons for the delay of the *parousia*, using a quite different set of eschatological images.

Luke 19:1-10. This is another narrative peculiar to Lk. Feeling runs high against Zacchaeus in the Jericho community (vv. 2, 7). His wealth and his reputation as a sinner are closely related details. Despite Zacchaeus's protestation of innocence (v. 8), the story ends with Jesus' declaration that he (the "son of man," for Lk) has come to search out and save the "lost"—no proper description of an innocent man. The proverb speaks of time for repentance between the stirrup and the ground. Some change of heart must have overtaken Zacchaeus while Jesus spoke, equating salvation and sonship of Abraham, or between verses 9 and 10. Verse 10 is otherwise meaningless. On the supposition that the diminutive tax-gouger repented, we have a story from life which makes the same point as the parables of ch. 15.

THIRTY-SECOND SUNDAY OF THE YEAR (C)
(Twenty-Fifth Sunday after Pentecost)

2 Maccabees 7:1-2, 9-14. Today's reading recounts the torture and death of the first, third, and fourth of seven sons of an anonymous Jewish mother (7:1), together with the edifying speeches made to their Seleucid Greek captors. The tale of the second brother (vv. 3-8) has doubtless been omitted from public reading because of its grisly details.

This book of Scripture was written in Greek by members of the Maccabean (priestly) party. The canon-makers of Iavneh did not include it late in the first century for reasons of its Greek language and their own Pharisee—hence anti-priestly—inclinations. Other collections of the Jewish Scriptures contain it. The mood of the book is pious. It proposes a theological interpretation of certain events between 180 and 161 B.C. and describes itself as a condensation of a work in five books by Jason of Cyrene (2:19-23), which is not extant. 2 Mc contains much interesting history told from the standpoint of the murdered high priest Onias (Honi; 4:30-34) and Judah the Maccabee (8:1-33), to the discredit of Jewish collaborators like Jason,

Simon, and Menelaus and the Greek general of Antiochus IV, Nicanor. Today's pericope is from one of two pious interludes which in effect are martyrologies, chs. 6-7 and the death of the Jewish elder Razis (14:37-46), the only suicide which the biblical literature praises. Elsewhere, throughout, there are prayers and soliloquies, including one by the dying Antiochus in Persia (9:12), his doubtful vow to become a Jew (v. 17), and a letter to the Jews that there is no reason to think inauthentic, which describes his turning of power over to his son Antiochus V (9:19-27).

The denial of Jewishness by breaking the food laws (cf. Dt 14:3-21) is given as the cause of the murder of the seven sons and their mother (7:1, 30). The "king" (7:3), improbably, carries out the execution. A strong theme of their resistance speeches is faith in a risen life in the body (vv. 9f., 14, 23, 29, 36) which was developed strongly through the experience of the revolt. The murdered Onias and the prophet Jeremiah appear in vision to present a sword of victory to Judas (15:12-16). A second theme of the resistance speeches is a theology of Jewish guilt which has brought God's righteous wrath on the people (7:18, 32f.) A statement of the seventh brother, "We, indeed, are suffering because of our sins" (7:32) seems to have supplied the words of admission of guilt by the so-called good thief (cf. Lk 22:41.)

Interestingly, the fourth brother denies resurrection to the wicked (7:14) whereas Dn in this same period affirms it (12:2). 2 Mc specifies that, "for you, there will be no resurrection to life." Dn promises "everlasting horror and disgrace" for the "others" than those just who shall live forever.

2 Thessalonians 2:16—3:5. Verse 15 is a charge to tenacity of Christian traditions (*paradoseis*) already received, notably by letter (viz., 1 Thes); vv. 16f. a prayer. Christ and God are jointly invoked as consolers and strengtheners in advancing the spread of the gospel (*en panti ergǭ kai logǭ agathǭ*, v. 17). Further injunction to the Thessalonians to prayer (3:1-4) concludes with an invocation of the Lord to rule their hearts (v. 5). All of this rhetoric of gratitude (2:13), encouragement (v. 15), consolation (vv. 16f.) and prayer (3:1-5) follows the grim picture of those who, in an entirely different spirit from the Thessalonians, will follow the mysterious adversary (2:4), the man (vv. 3, 8, 9) and force (v. 7) of lawlessness who seduces to apostasy and ruin (vv. 3, 10).

Observe the play on words between "faith" in 3:2b (lit., "The faith is not of all") and "faith" in v. 3 (lit., "Faithful [*pistos*] is the Lord"). The writer of 2 Thes is persuaded or convinced (*pepoithamen* from *peithō*, v. 4) that his apostolic commands are being carried out ("whatever we enjoin," *ha paraggellomen*), another instance of the expected fidelity to tradition that runs throughout the letter and contributes to the view that this is a later composition than Paul's.

Luke 20:27-38. All three synoptics have this pericope (cf. Mk 12:18-27; Mt 22:23-33.) Lk has largely been following the Marcan order and wording since 19:28, which is parallel to the beginning of Mk's ch. 11, with the exception of omitting the parable-in-act of the withered fig tree.

Lk departs from Mk's original in this account of Sadducee disbelief in bodily resurrection (apart from small verbal changes) only by omitting Jesus' charge that his challengers know neither the scriptures nor the power of God (cf. Mk 12:24; Mt 22:29.) He adds the phrase "sons of the resurrection" (v. 36*b*) and the explicitation of the mystifying argument that there will be a bodily resurrection from the fact that YHWH is God of the patriarchs, "for all live to him" (v. 38*b*). Lk (vv. 39f.), like Mt (22:33), finishes off the account with a summary indication of response, whereas Mk terminates the exchange abruptly.

Our information on Sadducee beliefs ("Sadducee" after Zadok, 1 Sm 8:17; 1 Chron 12:29) are slight, although Josephus says that they deny rewards and punishments and the persistence of the soul after death (*War* 2, 8, 14 [165]; cf. Ac 23:8.) Josephus also writes: "Sadducee doctrine is that souls perish with bodies" (*Ant.* 18, 1, 4[16]), an attempt to explain the position of this group to the Greek world in terms they themselves would never have used. The silence of the Pentateuch on survival after death—the Mosaic books being the only scriptures for this conservative party—would account for their belief. The Maccabean theology which was priestly (see commentary on the first reading above) seems to have dislodged this traditional agnosticism somewhat.

We are left to conclude that the citation of Ex 3:6 ("the passage 'at the bush,' " v. 37) means either that God is the contemporary of every age or that he is the God of the long-dead patriarchs *now*. Lk chooses the latter meaning (v. 38).

Mk (12:25) and Mt (22:30) are clear that neither marrying nor giving in marriage is a characteristic of the resurrected state. Lk's peculiar elaboration of this Marcan verse in vv. 34f. has been influential in the history of celibate life in the West. Those who marry and give in marriage, for him, are the "sons of this age" (*aiōn*=Heb. *'olam*, v. 34); those "accounted worthy (*hoi kataxiōthentes*, v. 35, 1st passive participle) of experiencing that age (*tou aiōnos ekeinou tychein*)" neither marry, give in marriage (v. 35), nor die (v. 36). Lk contrasts them as equal to angels (*isaggeloi*, v. 36) and sons of the resurrection with sons of this eon. The Vulgate translated *kataxiōthentes*, a gnomic or atemporal aorist, by *illi vero, qui digni habebuntur saeculo illo . . . neque nubent neque ducent uxores.* This translation, "those to be accounted worthy of that age . . . neither marry nor give in marriage" was pressed by the Latin fathers to mean that celibate men (*illi=hoi*) have heaven in prospect. Lk abstains from any time sequence in relating worthiness of the coming age to abstention from marriage. NAB retains his atemporal phrase by its rendition "those judged worthy . . . do not [marry or give in marriage]." The history of interpretation of this text, however, has Lk favoring abstention from marriage in this life in a way Mk and Mt do not.

THIRTY-THIRD SUNDAY OF THE YEAR (C)

(Twenty-Sixth Sunday after Pentecost)

Malachi 4:1-2 (NAB, 3:19-20). The Roman Lectionary follows the Vulgate verse enumeration, which is also that of LXX. Amos has foretold that the "day of the Lord" will be darkness and gloom, not the brightness and light expected by those who see in it only triumph for Israel (5:18ff.) The anonymous 6th—5th-c. prophet whose thoughts are recorded in this book (*Malachi*="my messenger") paints a picture of destruction for "all the proud and all evildoers" (v. 19=4:1). He uses the language of Zoroastrian hymns which portray a final conflagration. In his oracle the arrogant in Israel will be destroyed like stubble thrown into a field-oven at harvest time. The preaching of John the Baptizer called upon similar imagery (cf. Mt 3:12=Lk 3:17.)

The sun, worshiped as a god of healing in various ancient religions, is depicted in Ps 19:5ff. as a groom emerging from his bridal chamber, a joyful giant traversing the sky and touching everything with his heat. Here the prophet says that the LORD will send not only destructive heat but healing warmth as well, the rays of a "sun of justice" for those who fear his name (v. 20a=4:2a). It is the same sun the rising and setting of which mark a day-long "pure offering" among the Gentiles (1:11) while Israel presents the LORD with polluted sacrifice (v. 12). The paradox of the future is that YHWH's sun, which looks upon acceptable behavior by the nations, will heal and purify all present Israelite impurities (in temple sacrifice, 1:7f.; 2:11; in divorce, 2:14ff.; in sorcery, perjury, and the defrauding of laborers, 3:5; in the neglect of his statutes, 3:7 and holding back from him tithes and offerings, 3:8ff.)

2 Thessalonians 3:7-12. Paul's own conduct while among the Thessalonians, namely of working for his livelihood, is put forward as the "tradition" they received from him (v. 6). The word *paradosis* puts it on a par with the deliverances of the creed handed on by the apostle (cf. 1 Cor 15:3-11.) Imitation of Paul (v. 7) is a theme found in 1 Cor 4:16; 11:1; Phil 3:17; "lives of disorder" are actually those lived in laziness or idleness. His independence of the Thessalonians by self-support was a conscious choice (v. 8) for he knew he had a claim on them in justice as their teacher (v. 9; cf. 1 Cor 9:12, 18.) He was trying to set an example of industriousness for them to follow (cf. 1 Thes 2:9) which they have not done. Some are gadding about in idleness, according to report (v. 11); "not busy but . . . busybodies" —today's sidewalk superintendents—renders the Greek pun *mēden ergazomenous alla periergazomenous.*

Verse 10 was probably a proverb in current use: v. 12 repeats it. The emphasis is on not being willing (*ou thelei*) to work. This passage is the charter of the Christian work-ethic, understood as a contribution necessary for survival in the community and not as industriousness to achieve calculated temporal benefits.

Nowhere does the passage speak of the omission of contributory services as arising from expectation of an imminent appearance of the Lord. Almost all commentators infer this but 2 Thes speaks only of an idle and "kibbitzing" spirit that is abroad in the community.

Luke 21:5-19. Lk follows Mk (13:1-13) fairly faithfully here, Mt 24:1-21 staying even closer in words but departing in order (9*b* and 13 are a dismembered Marcan v. 13, with other special Matthean material inserted). Lk's contributions to this discourse about the end are to eliminate the Mount of Olives as the locus and a query put by four disciples—listed in the interesting order Peter, James, John, and Andrew (cf. Mk 13:3); to add "pestilences, terrors, and great signs" (Lk 21:11 cf. v. 25); to omit mention of the necessity of preaching the gospel to all creatures (Mk 13:10) and the Holy Spirit as speaker before tribunals (Mk 13:11, cf. Lk 12:12; Lk substitutes "a mouth and wisdom" which Jesus will supply, thereby pressing his prophetism motif); to add the phrase "not a hair of your head will be harmed" (v. 18). Lk is sure of the destruction of the temple (v. 6) but also that false claimants coming in Jesus' name ("I am he") must precede it (v. 8). Lk is alone in adding, "The time is at hand" (v. 8) as another false statement as part of his general concern with a deferred *parousia.* The same is no doubt true of his changing "but the end is not yet" (*outō*, Mk 13:7) to "does not follow immediately" (*eutheōs*, Lk 21:9). He probably knows of the destruction of Jerusalem but it does not modify his traditional apocalyptic prose.

Is 19:2 provides the model for v. 10:

> I will rouse Egypt against Egypt;
>   brother will war against brother.
> Neighbor against neighbor,
>   city against city, kingdom against kingdom.

Verses 12-19 are concerned with the conduct of the disciples in their time of trial. A case can be made for Lk's modification of Mk in small matters but not in overall emphasis. The traditional dating of Mk just before the siege of Jerusalem and Lk after, on the basis of what the former did not need to know beforehand in order to write his ch. 13, is fairly tenuous. Lk does not appear to write from hindsight any more than Mk does from foresight. Lk 21:20 does substitute "*Hotan de idete*," "When you shall have seen Jerusalem encircled by soldiers," for Mk's "awful horror" (*to bdelygma tēs erēmōseōs*, 13:14), thus providing the only solid clue that he is introducing the siege of the city into his otherwise anhistorical account of disaster. His report of the testimony of disciples (vv. 12-17) may be viewed as historical.

FEAST OF CHRIST THE KING (C)

(Last Sunday after Pentecost)

2 Samuel 5:1-3. David filled the vacuum caused by the death of Saul and his sons at the hands of the Philistines on Mount Gilboa (cf. 1 Sm 31) and was anointed king by the Judahites at Hebron (2 Sm 2:1-4). Saul's general Abner set up the son of Saul Ishbaal, briefly, as king over a variety of northerners—Jews and others—plus Benjaminites (vv. 8f.) The reign of David at Hebron was confined to the people of Judah for seven years. The forces of Ishbaal under Abner and those of David under Joab and his brother, meanwhile, continued their fighting (2 Sm 3). When Abner, offended by Ishbaal's charge of intimacy with his dead father's concubine (probably a defensive move stemming from fear of Abner's growing strength), that warrior began conversations with David that could lead to his turning all of Israel, the north, over to David peacefully (3:19ff.) When Joab heard of Abner's recent presence in Hebron he pursued and killed him to avenge the death of his brother Asahel (vv. 26ff.) David is reported as having had no part in it and mourning the death of the great warrior Abner publicly (vv. 28-39). As always in the case of David's motivations as he fought his way to the throne, it is impossible to know how much of his grief was genuine and how much his protestations of innocence meant "Gibeah papers please copy." As to David's admiration for the military feats of Abner, however, and Abner's wisdom in being ready to desert Ishbaal's cause, there can be no reasonable doubt.

Two treacherous military leaders in Ishbaal's forces dispatched him in his sleep (4:1-7) for the alleged reason that he gave up all resistance when he heard of Abner's death (v. 1). In a spirit of lively hope, they brought the king's severed head to David, who reminded them wrathfully of the short shrift he had given informers on Saul in Ziklag (v. 10). He ordered them killed for their treasonous act supposedly done on his behalf, and had Ishbaal buried decently in Hebron next to Abner (vv. 11f.) Thus David continued to have the best of several worlds, which was the story of his life.

All this leads to today's pericope describing the enthronement of the shepherd king over Israel as well as his native Judah. The elders of Israel simply repeat the fealty to David that Abner had sensed was theirs (v. 3; cf. 3:17ff.) It needs to be borne in mind that the unification of the north and the south was a settlement achieved at the top. The alignment of the tribe of Benjamin with David (v. 19) was a natural geographic one; with "Jezreel, Ephraim . . . and the rest of Israel" (2:9) it was a case of the ruling elements siding with a winner against Ishbaal, a loser. That is why the pulling apart of the two kingdoms in Jeroboam's secession from Roboam, son of Solomon, comes as no surprise. The twelve tribes were never very unified in the first place, any more than were the states of Europe in Napoleon's day. Like the little corporal, it was David who made the difference.

The parallel account to this one of David's anointing as king over Israel, quite close in detail but with "the word of the LORD as revealed through Samuel" given as the justification, is 1 Chron 11:1-3. This pious reason is not surprising in the 5th-c. retelling of Israel's history. The Chronicler saw everything from the standpoint of present temple cult and priestly dominance rather than past glories.

Colossians 1:12-20. Epaphras is Paul's co-worker at Colossae (1:7f.) who evidently is staying on with the imprisoned Paul (4:12, 18). It may be he who has brought Paul news of the "Colossian error" (2:16-23) although he is described as having reported only "your love in the Spirit" (1:8). The aberrations in the community that Paul is worried about relate to teachings about diet and feasts as having a saving quality, the worship of angels, and bodily austerities which, in effect, "indulge men's pride" (2:23).

The Pauline authorship of this epistle in its entirety is questioned because no authentic writing of Paul contains a description of Christ like that of the hymn of 1:15-20. Solutions to the problem tend to look on it as an insertion or else credit the entire forward portion of the epistle, with a variety of cut-off points suggested, to another hand.

Ephesus, Caesarea, and Rome are all claimants to the title of place of origin of this captivity epistle. One thing about it that is sure is its common provenance with Philemon (cf. 4:3, 18; Phm 9, 13.) Colossae (modern Honaz) makes a triangle with Laodicaea, a ruin, and Hierapolis, a modern resort place with numerous salt baths and motels, in the Lycus valley. Paul writes in 2:1 as if he had not met the recipients, knowing of their faith only from Epaphras and others.

The light-darkness figure of vv. 12f. is an accommodation of the theme of deliverance from Egypt and occurs in 1 Thes 5:4-9; Rom 13:11-14 (cf. also its use in Ac 26:18 and by a follower in Eph 5:8.) Paul does not refer to the reign of God extensively, only in 1 Cor 4:20; 6:9f.; Rom 14:17f. He never speaks of the kingdom of God's son as here, coming closest to it with a mention of serving Christ in God's reign (Rom 14:18).

The exalted christology of vv. 15-20 is worthy of Paul but in no sense typical of him. Not only is Christ the redeemer and agent of forgiveness (v. 14); he is the one through and for whom all things including the celestial powers, are created (v. 16). The Talmud tells of a rabbi so holy that God made all things for him but this usage in Col is another conception more consciously cosmic. The fullness (*plērōma*) of God dwells in Christ (v. 19), bodily (2:9). In other Pauline letters, Christ is "the body" (cf. 1 Cor 10:16f.; 12:12, 27.) Here, as in Eph (1:22f.), he is the head of the body-church. He not only has divine fullness among creatures but also a primacy (*archē prōtotokos ek tōn nekrōn*, v. 18). This first-born of the dead is above all a reconciler (v. 20). The blood of his cross has made peace for all discordant elements on earth and in the heavens.

Clearly Jesus is being spoken of here as a man so closely associated with God in the work of creation (v. 16) that there is some sense in which he is not a part of it. He who has the totality of deity resident in him (v. 19) is above all the cosmic powers (v. 16). One who has faith in this Jesus who has died in fulfilling the reconciling office (v. 22) has by that fact died to the cosmic forces (2:20). The alienation of the Colossians from Christ before they knew him is over (v. 21). They may not release their grasp on the faith and hope that came to them with the gospel (v. 23).

Luke 23:35-43. Lk is remarkably close to Mk's order and selection of incidents in the passion narrative yet he adds enough material of his own (the formal charge before Pilate, 23:2; the hearing before Herod, 23:6-12; the road to Golgotha, 23:27-32; the verbal exchange of the criminals on their crosses, 23:39-43) to make some like Taylor, Catchpole, and the present writer hypothecate a Lucan passion source. Verse 35 parallels Mk 15:31f., with some changes by Lk ("rulers" for "chief priests" and "scribes" as scoffers; "the messiah of God, the chosen one" for "the messiah, the king of Israel"); v. 36 parallels Mk 15:36 (the sour wine); v. 37. Mk 15:30 ("save yourself"); v. 38, Mk 15:26 (the title on the cross).

In Mk/Mt the two insurrectionists (*lēstai*) who flank Jesus "taunt him in the same way" as the onlookers. Lk makes this explicit (v. 39) by reworking the phrases attributed to the rulers in v. 35. The possible dependence of v. 41a on 2 Mc 7:32 was reported in the commentary on an earlier portion of that chapter. Jesus is asked by one of the criminals for remembrance when he comes into his *basileia* (v. 42). He responds by promising that the man will be with him "this day (*sēmeron*) . . . in paradise"—the abode of the just. Paradise is a Hebrew loan-word from the Avestan meaning enclosure or pleasure-park.

The crucifixion narrative (Lk 23:27-48) of Lk's source need not be viewed as a Marcan composition that has been modified. It can equally be seen as an independent and cohesive account to which Marcan touches have been added (vv. 34b, 38, 44f., 49).

FEASTS OF JESUS, MARY, AND THE SAINTS

IMMACULATE CONCEPTION
(December 8)

Genesis 3:9-15, 20. The description of the sin of the man (*ha 'adham*) and the woman (*ha 'ishshah*) in today's first reading is part of the Yahwist narrative which runs from 2:4*b* to 4:25. Man is, for this author, "but flesh" (6:3) "with all of its possibilities of knowledge, desire, and choice, and also its possibilities of failure and error" (Hooke). The man gives names to all the beasts and birds (2:20), for the Yahwist a sign of his power; he is at the same time incomplete in his solitude, hence woman (*ishshah*) is taken out of "her man" (*ishah*, v. 23; the Massoretic text has *ish*). The passage under consideration here tells of disobedience and the consequent disruption of God's design. It will end in 3:20 with the man's naming his wife Eve (*hawwah*) because she is the mother of "all the living" (*Kol-hai*). In other words, she is a sign of hope, not merely the man's fellow-culprit in an act of weakness.

The pair is in hiding among the trees when the story begins (v. 8), clothed because "the eyes of both of them were opened" at the eating of the fruit (v. 7). The man has hidden himself because of nakedness and fear (v. 10). The LORD God connects this self-consciousness with transgression of the command not to eat (v. 11). A sexual motif may underlie the entire tale, in which case a knowledge of "what is good and what is bad" (v. 5) would be the godlike power of immortality through the power of begetting. This interpretation is not certain. What is certain is that moral autonomy of some sort is being sought through gaining knowledge proper to God alone (cf. Dt 29:29.) The serpent in the Gilgamesh myth, which the Yahwist may be using, is cunning enough to steal from Gilgamesh the magic herb which renews life. Serpents are also a symbol of fertility in various Canaanite cults. The one in the Yahwist's story is not the devil (that identification will come much later; cf. Wis 2:24) but a deceiver (vv. 4, 13) whose counsel brings not likeness to gods (v. 5) but the necessity of death (v. 19*bc*). The story is etiological throughout, i.e., concerned with the causes of things. Like other, familiar ancient fables, it explains why snakes crawl on the ground (v. 14), why snakes are the enemies of humans (v. 15), why men are the pain and the joy of women (vv. 16), and why man's hard life ends in death (v. 19).

The temptation of the man by the woman is not an especially significant detail despite what subsequent generations have made of it. It is simply a requirement of the narrative technique's three stages. There is no doubt, of course, that the woman is a companion of the man in his sin. This makes her new name, Life (3:20), all the more telling.

Verse 15 has prompted whole libraries of Christian theological argument, much of it having little to do with the Yahwist's intent. The common older tradition was that the passage had messianic significance but later scholars (Skinner, von Rad, Westermann) concluded that it is without it, and even that man's warfare with snakes is all that is intended. The theological arguments of a former age were as much related to Mary as to text and context, the Vulgate having *ipsa* ("she") for the weakly attested *hi* rather than the likelier *hu* ("he").

The seed of the woman is probably collective humankind, the seed of the serpent the forces opposed to Yahweh in every age. Yet if David was the Yahwist's model for Adam, a royal defeat of enemies under the conqueror's foot (on the Egyptian model) may be intended. On any reading, this is an oracle of ultimate victory for the forces of life over threatening death.

Ephesians 1:3-6, 11-12. As the introduction to Ephesians in NAB says, this doxology (1:3-14) is "of the greatest importance for the cosmic significance it attaches to Christ." God's choice of those who would believe in him through the mystery of the son was made "in him" (v. 11), "our Lord Jesus Christ" (v. 3). The election preceded the history of the cosmos (v. 4). It was a matter of God's "will and pleasure" (*kata tēn eudokian tou thelēmatos autou*, v. 5); it was the result of a "decree" (*kata prothesin*) of his "will and counsel" (*kata tēn boulēn tou thelēmatos autou*, v. 11). We were therefore "predestined" (*prooristhentes*, v. 11) to praise God's glory by being the first to hope (*proēlpikotas*, v. 12) in Christ. The predestination to adoptive sonship (*huiothesian*) had as its ultimate purpose praise of the glorious favor (*doxēs tēs charitos*) he has bestowed on us in Christ, "his beloved" (v. 6). The entire cosmic plan is designed to show forth God's glory—*doxa* being the LXX word for *kabhodh*, a means of expressing what we would call his godliness or divine nature. In origin, this eulogy of believers may be a baptismal hymn about those who have been sealed in the holy spirit after accepting the word of the gospel (v. 1).

The letter is perhaps an encyclical one. Only doubtfully was it addressed, in its lack of particularity, to a community in which Paul had spent three years. This is further attested to by the omission of "at Ephesus" (1:1) from Sinaiticus, Vaticanus, Origen, and other textual witnesses. Arguments advanced which claim for it authorship by Paul or a disciple of his (generally known as "the Ephesian continuator") depend on whether Paul could have been the author of this kind of writing, so uncharacteristic of him otherwise.

The doxology resembles Col 1:9ff. in its claim for a way of life superior to anything available through *gnōsis* or the mediation of heavenly powers. In its stress on the eternal character of election it answers the objection that the church cannot be of God since it has appeared only recently. The "we" who are "the first to hope in Christ" (v. 12) are probably the members of the universal church, the "you" of v. 12, the recipients of the letter, perhaps newly aggregated to it.

Luke 1:26-38. Luke has completed the first panel of his diptych which features the mysterious circumstances surrounding the conception of John, son of Zechariah. He turns now to the second panel. The archangel Gabriel had come bearing revelations in Daniel 8, 9, and 10 (where he reduced Daniel to silence, 10:15; cf. Ez 3:26.) His identification of himself to Zechariah in Lk 1:19 resembles that of Raphael in the book of Tobit (12:15).

Luke's account of Jesus' conception has as its purpose stressing his election, indeed his divine origins. Joseph is identified as Davidic, hence royal (v. 27). Elizabeth, Aaronic and therefore priestly (v. 5), is described as Mary's kinswoman (v. 36). These details heighten the claim that Jesus is Messiah in both a royal and a priestly sense. (Cf. IQS 9:10, *The Community Rule:* "until there shall come the Prophet and the Messiahs of Aaron and Israel.")

Nazareth (v. 26) is the traditional town of Jesus' beginnings in later gospel material. *Parthenos*, v. 27, may be the ordinary word for "girl" as NEB has it, but Lk's intent is clear, as is acknowledged by that translation's rendering of *andra ou ginōskō* (literally, "I do not know man") by "I am still a virgin" (v. 34). This is the story of one who is "Son of the Most High" (v. 32), constituted as such by the latter's power which is the same as the coming upon Mary (*epeleusetai*, v. 35) of holy spirit. Gabriel's greeting, *Chaire*, makes possible the word-play of *kecharitōmenē*, "most highly favored daughter" (v. 28). The wording of the angel's message is that of messianic rule (vv. 32f.). To this announcement of her election Mary answers, with a faith like Abraham's: *Genoito*, "Let it be done" (v. 38).

PRESENTATION OF THE LORD

(February 2)

Malachi 3:1-4. It is from v. 1 that the name of this book is taken, "my messenger" (*malachi*). In 2:7 the priest is the messenger of the LORD of hosts in a chapter that charges him generically with failure in the conduct of his office (2:8f.), even though the charge against him is laid hypothetically (2:1-6): "If you do not listen, and if you do not lay it to heart . . ." (vv. 1f.) The coming messenger of the covenant of 3:1 seems to be some personification of a purified priesthood. The covenant of Levi, made void by contemptible priestly behavior (2:4, 8), will be restored and renewed through a particular messenger who will "purify the sons of Levi" (3:3). It is hard to know if he is a promised individual or the LORD himself as reformer of the institution of priesthood.

Judgment will take place at the temple, the holiest place in the nation (3:1*b*). As metal is refined in fire or cloth cleansed by lye (vv. 2*b*-3*a*), so will the sacrificing priesthood be purified (v. 3*b*). Then will it be repristinated (v. 4) and sacrifice will be offered by a class fit to do so. Judgment will be leveled against those who practice a variety of social evils (v. 5), all of them reprobated in the law: sorcery (cf. Ex 22:18), adultery (Ex 20:14), false swearing (Lv 19:12), defrauding laborers (Dt 24:14), widows, and orphans (Dt 24:17), and turning aside the stranger (*ger* = resident alien): in general, those "who do not fear me, [says the LORD of hosts]" (v. 5*bc*).

Hebrews 2:14-18. A re-reading of the commentary on Heb 2:9-11 (cf. p. 251) might be a good preparation for today's pericope, as would be those on the selections from that epistle throughout that month and November of that year (B); also, on the obedient sacrifice of Christ described in Heb 5:7-9 (p. 199), likewise Year B.

Jesus is made as if the speaker in v. 12, quoting Ps 22:23, as he announces the praise of God to his brothers in the assembly. He is represented (v. 13) as trusting in God in the manner of David in 2 Sm 22:3 and presenting himself as a sign and portent like Isaiah and his sons in the story of the document drawn up about the younger of the two, Maher-shalal-hash-baz (the Immanuel of the prophecy?) The "children" of Isaiah for the author of Hebrews are Jesus and all others of flesh and blood (v. 14) with this difference, that his tasting death was for the sake of all (v. 9). God made Jesus, who was their pioneer (*archēgos*, v. 10) in the work of salvation, perfect through suffering. This perfection was not a good of Jesus only. It robbed the prince of death of his power and freed humanity of its lifelong fear of death (vv. 14f.) The other children of Abraham were Jesus' beneficiaries, a thing that would have been impossible had he not "become like his brothers in every way" (*kata panta tois adelphois homoiōthenai*, v. 17). His status as a merciful and faithful high priest before God required it.

Verse 18 is crucial to NT christology and soteriology since it leaves in no doubt the weakness and limitations essential to a man if he is to be believed in as "true man," the affirmation about Jesus of all the Catholic creeds. It is "in the fact that" (*en hǭ*, the "since" of v. 18) he himself suffered (*peponthen*) and was subjected to trial (*peirastheis*) that he can be of help to others similarly tested (*tois peirazomenois*). This phrase cannot be confined to physical suffering, which is the least of human suffering. The second verb, occurring in the aorist passive participle and present passive participle, is the normal biblical word for eschatological testing. Jesus has been with his brothers in their extremity, says Hebrews. He could not go any lower in experiencing the anguish of the human situation. His common lot with us in our temptation, our desolation, our alienation is complete. That is why we dare to hail him as the conqueror of the fear of death and the brother who saved us.

Luke 2:32. In this shortest reading in the Roman lectionary, Lk does not reproduce any biblical place exactly. Is 42:6 and 49:6 content themselves with describing Israel as a "light to the nations" (LXX, *phōs ethnōn*). Verse 32*b* echoes Is 40:5 and 46:13 but does not literally reproduce either. The parallelism of the Lucan verse shows the manifestation of God to all in Christ:

> *light* revealed (*eis apokalypsin*) to the Gentiles,
> *glory* to your people Israel.

PETER AND PAUL, APOSTLES
(June 29)

Acts 12:1-11. The "period" of the opening phrase is the reign of the emperor Claudius (A.D. 41-54). The harassment of the church by King Herod Agrippa I (37-44), son of Aristobolus and brother of Herodias, was probably on civil charges, as the form of execution indicates. Beheading was reserved by the much later legislation of the Mishnah (*Sanhedrin* 9:1) for murderers and members of an apostate city. The book of Acts has up to this point portrayed the Jewish religious authorities as unfriendly to Christians. The text does not suggest, however, any initiation of charges by the Sanhedrin or the high priest. The historian Josephus says that Agrippa wished to be thought of as a loyal Jew. Hence, if the charges against James and Peter were religious, Agrippa would have permitted a Sanhedrin trial. This entailed the capital punishment of stoning if the finding was one of guilt. While the king might have acted arbitrarily and simply eliminated James as *persona non grata*, it is much more likely that he had him and Peter arraigned on charges of threatening the political stability of Palestinian Jewry. Since John the Baptist and Jesus had both been thought guilty of the same offense, the latter having forfeited his life on a civil charge in the area of political stability, it is not surprising that a verdict of guilty was secured on some such charge as that the apostles were proclaiming "another king," Jesus.

Acts suggests that Agrippa executed James simply to gratify public opinion (v. 3). While the capital sentence may have had that effect in certain Jewish circles, it is not to be supposed that Agrippa acted on that basis only. The author of Acts suppresses the actual charge, if he happens to know it. A distinct possibility is that James, one of the "sons of thunder" (Mk 3:17), offended the royal sensibilities with a public utterance like that of John the Baptizer before him about the conduct of the royal family.

That Peter was also being detained on a capital charge is probable since his guards were executed for letting him escape (v. 19). Great should be their reward if the "angel of the Lord" (v. 7) was a heavenly being and not an enterprising Christian adept at picking locks! In any case, the two companions of Jesus were no doubt apprehended as lingering threats to the stability of the Roman-Herodian settlement, even though more than a dozen years had passed since Jesus' death. The whole sequence would be the more comprehensible if the pair had borne the burden of association with the Zealot movement all that time, going back to the days before Jesus called him.

Eusebius in his *History of the Church* (2.9) quotes an edifying tale from the Pseudo-Clementine *Outlines*, Book VII, to the effect that the delator of James, himself a Christian, was so moved by the apostle's testimony in court that he asked for forgiveness, received it, and was beheaded along with him.

We know that Herod Agrippa's death (reported in Ac 12:20-23) occurred in spring of 44. Hence the death of James is to be dated anywhere between the accession of Claudius and the violent demise of the king.

Acts 12:11 reverts in its account of Peter's rescue to its theme of Jewish antipathy to the Christian movement.

2 Timothy 4:6-8, 17-18. The second letter of Paul to Timothy is widely regarded as pseudonymous, as are 1 Tim and Ti. The reasons include weak attestation to all three pastoral epistles in early canons and papyri, the nature of their polemic against heretics, the transition from the Pauline *kērygma* to Christian faith as a *parathēkē* ("desposit," 1 Tim 6:20; 2 Tim 1:12, 14), vocabulary divergencies from Paul, the difficulty of fitting 1 and 2 Tim into his life-situation, and the un-Pauline character of the church order described in the pastorals. For the remainder of the commentary, see pp. 378f.

Matthew 16:13-19. See pp. 129f.

TRANSFIGURATION

(August 6)

Daniel 7:9-10, 13-14. The visions of chapter 7, like the king's dream and Daniel's vision of chapter 2, are concerned with the unity and finality of history. In the apocalyptic genre, however, history is not important in itself since it is fated to disappear with the coming of the reign of God.

The four beasts referred to earlier in the chapter (lion, bear, leopard, and ten-horned horrible) are, in the first three cases, conventional motifs from the period portraying Babylon, Media, and Persia, and in the fourth, Alexander's empire (cf. the gold, silver, bronze, and iron-tile images of chapter 2.) The ten horns are the kings of the Seleucid dynasty descended from Alexander's general Seleukos—the conqueror having died without an heir (cf. the "divided kingdom" of 2:4)—while the "little horn" is Antiochus IV Epiphanes (175-63 B.C.), the most troublesome ruler of all for the author of Daniel.

The picture of Israel's deliverer as "one like a son of man" (v. 13*a*) reflects the transcendent character of the eschatological savior whose image was developed in the late Hellenistic, pre-Christian period. History is not his milieu, as had been the case with a kingly or prophetic person in all previous Jewish expectation of the future. "New attributes originating in a world other than ours are used to depict his sovereignty" (Tödt). The eschatological event which the vision of Daniel 7 describes is cosmic and universal, not historical and national. Some of the details of the vision are derived from the description in Ezekiel 1 of "the likeness of the glory of the LORD" (v. 28), among them the clouds (vv. 4, 28), the flashing fire (vv. 4, 27), and "one who had the appearance of a man" seated on "something like a throne" (v. 26). Cf. also Dt 33:2 and Is 6 for descriptions of appearances of God in his heavenly court attended by thousands of ministering spirits. Fire as the sign of judgment (vv. 9c, 10a) betrays an Iranian source, a theory borne out by the more detailed presentation of the "son of man" in IV Ezra 13 and the Similitudes of Enoch. The Ancient One with wool-white hair (9a, b) is probably so depicted to contrast the venerability of the divine Judge with the upstart kings recently—relative to him, at least—come to power.

The one "like a son of man" (q*e*bar enash) of 13a is to be distinguished from the four beasts preceding (vv. 3-8). "Son of man" is the ordinary designation of an individual, "man" being generic: "mankind." (Modern Hebrew continues to render "people" by "b*e*nei ha 'adham," "sons of man.") Unlike the beasts, who arise from earth and sea, this man-like figure comes on the clouds. He is not spoken of as a man but "like a man," a term which describes the various appearances of what are otherwise called "angels" (cf. Dn 8:15; 10:5, 6, 18 and the "man of God" of Jgs 13:6.) It is he who receives "dominion, glory, and kingship" (v. 14) which are accorded to the "holy ones of the Most High" in vv. 18 and 27; hence he is somehow their representative.

They seem at first to be faithful Israel, victorious under God over the four evil kingdoms (vv. 17f.), but the fact that the one who comes "on the clouds of heaven" (v. 13) rejoins them makes it plausible that these "holy ones" are the angelic host. They stand for a dominion of God that is to be ultimate and everlasting (vv. 14c, 27d), hence by definition eschatological or metahistorical. Further complications are the address by the "manlike figure" (geber, v. 15) or Gabriel (v. 16) to Daniel himself as "son of man" (ben 'adam, v. 18), and the designation of Israel's king by the same term in Ps 80:18b (and in Ps 146:3?).

Is something messianic thereby indicated by Dn's use of the term "like a son of man"? This is not clear. "The main point is that from now onwards the kingdom of God and his ruler will dominate in the place of the demonic world-wide kingdoms to the glory of God and for the benefit of the kingdom of God" (Volz).

There is a puzzle in the absence of a dependence in the NT of the Son of Man sayings in Q on Dn 7.

2 Peter 1:16-19. These four verses contain the main contention of this latest of the NT authors to write. His teaching is apostolic (note the shift to "we" in vv. 16, 17 from the "I" of previous verses); it is based on a historical revelation (vv. 17f.) which comes as the fulfillment of prophecy (v. 19); and it is not to be confused with the "cleverly concocted myths" (v. 16) which other false teachers are purveying (cf. 2:1, 3)—men whose lives are as morally disordered as their doctrine is false (2:10-22). Christ's "coming in power" (*dynamin kai parousian*) is the truth the author is at pains to stress; he will return to the problem of skepticism concerning it in 3:3-7. He may be defending the reality of this hoped-for event against the charge that it is a *mythos sesophismenos* more than castigating the teachings of opponents as being such, although the participle chosen (with *sophia* as its root) indicates that the opposition may be Gnostic-inclined. The claim to eyewitness status (*epoptai*, a word which also means higher-grade initiates) of Christ's majesty (*megaleiotētos*) in the transfiguration, v. 16, is put forward as evidence that he will return in glory.

The second coming of Christ, his *parousia*, is literally his "presence." The term comes from Greek religion and from the mystery cults and is used as a designation of the manifestation of a god. Josephus employs it to describe an epiphany of God, while the Testament of Judah contains the very phrase of 2 Pt 1:16, "power and presence," to make the same point. Christ's *dynamis* in this case is his godlike might as risen Lord, his present power and future coming being the chief affirmations of this epistle. The author probably got his account of the transfiguration from traditional material, not from any of the gospels, although he comes close to Mt's version. The locus of the event has become, by the time of the writing, the "holy mountain" (v. 18).

The "prophetic message" of v. 19 was a phrase current in Jewish usage to describe the entire Bible, not the books of the prophets only. As a whole, Scripture testified to Christ for Christian preachers. The "dark place" is the sinful world and the day which the dawn inaugurates is the "day" (Rom 13:12) of Christ's coming. *Phōsphoros* is Venus, the morning star, here Christ dissipating doubts and fears in the hearts of Christians. Cf. Lk 1:78 and Rev 22:16 for other uses of the dawn-figure, even if not in the same terminology. Traditional belief in the transformation of the cosmos at the end is retained by the Jewish-oriented author of 2 Pt but his eschatology has, for the first time, a personal orientation. The individual believer will be altered in his heart at the coming of Christ, a notion which traditional eschatological material does not contain.

Matthew 17:1-9. See pp. 44f.

ASSUMPTION OF THE BLESSED VIRGIN MARY

(August 15)

Revelation 11:19; 12:1-6, 10. The ark of the covenant had been lost with the destruction of the first temple. Jewish tradition held that it would reappear in the messianic age. Its visibility (v. 19a) indicates that God through his Anointed One has resumed his great power and begun his reign (v. 17). Those who laid the earth waste have been destroyed. It is time now to judge the dead and to reward the prophets and the saints (v. 18).

The portent that follows (*sēmeion mega*, v. 1) depicts the conflict of good and evil as a cosmic one, not one originating on earth. The Apocalyptist seems to have availed himself of one form of an ancient myth transmitted in Greek, Persian, and Egyptian circles —he comes closest to the Greek tale—which described the escape of a divine infant from a superhuman enemy at birth. Here at the beginning of chapter 12 we encounter the first appearance of a female figure in the book of Revelation.

The "woman" of Rev 12 had been variously Leto, Ormazd, and Isis in other mythologies. She may have been a sun goddess in the original myth employed, with the twelve signs of the zodiac as the stars in her crown and the moon at her feet. Since the cult of Cybele was widespread in Asia Minor, it is to be expected that the author of Revelation would be influenced by it. The statue of Cybele in the Museum of Berlin shows the moon at her left and the sun at her right; at other times the sun is a cloud that envelops her; in still another statue the twelve stars form her crown. Austin Farrer thinks that the author intends a veiled reference to Rachel, whose son Joseph (Gn 30:23f.; 37:9f.) in his second adolescent dream saw his parents as the sun and the moon and he and his brothers as twelve stars (of the zodiac?) A further possible reference is Eve, cursed in the pain of her childbearing (Gn 3:16) and blessed in the hope of her offspring who will strike at the serpent's head (v. 15c). While the biblical imagery cannot be discounted entirely, none of it is as close in detail as are several non-Hebrew myths. Leto, with child by Zeus, was pursued by the dragon Python. Poseidon gave her refuge on an island where she safely delivered herself of the god Apollo.

One biblical source reveals the begetting by mother Zion of a male child who is the people Israel (Is 66:7-9). Elsewhere the people is a woman, the bride of Yahweh, who wears on her head a glorious diadem (Ez 16:12). The woman's wailing in pain as she labors to give birth (Rev 12:2) is unlike the Isaian picture of a woman who gives birth before she comes to labor (Is 66:7, 8d). Micah is closer to the Apocalyptist's imagery: "Writhe in pain, grow faint, / O daughter

Zion, like a woman in travail; / For now shall you go forth from the city and dwell in the fields (4:10*ab*). The Hymns of Qumrân provide a close parallel: "She labors in her pains who bears the man. / For amid the pains of hell / there shall spring from her child-bearing crucible / a marvellous mighty counsellor; / and the man shall be delivered from out of the throes" (*Hodayoth*, III).

The huge, fiery red (*pyrros*) dragon with seven heads and ten horns has been variously interpreted as the constellation Hydra, which extends one third of the length of the zodiac, attacking Virgo; as a symbol of the imperial purple driving the Christian community off to Pella; and as Dn's fourth beast (7:7). The latter had been Alexander's empire whereas in Rev. 13:1 the beast is Rome. In any case, the dragon's quarrel is not immediately with the woman but with her child. Jewish Christians are probably intended by "her child when it should be born"—the place of "the devil, or Satan, the seducer of the whole world" (v. 9) being filled by any worldly power inimical to Christians.

The passage was probably originally Jewish, as can be deduced from its reference to final victory by Michael and his angels. If a Christian hand had framed it, the victor probably would have been Christ. A Christian hymn has been inserted at v. 10. "The accuser of our brothers" may be a veiled reference to the *delatores* who abounded in Domitian's time (81-96), busy with their attacks on Asian Christians. Satan's overthrow is achieved (v. 9) but not before the son of the woman has been identified in terms of messianic Psalm 2 which speaks (vv. 8f.) of the king's ruling all the nations with an iron rod—cf. Rev 12:5.

1 Corinthians 15:20-26. It is understandable why the church should employ this passage on the feast of Mary's Assumption since her glorification in the body, anticipatory of the resurrection of all, comes as the result of her Son's resurrection from the dead. St. Paul describes him as the first to rise under the agricultural figure "first fruits" (*aparchē*, v. 20), in which a sheaf was brought to the priest on "the day after the sabbath" following the Passover celebration (Lv 23:11), to be waved as an offering before the LORD. This had to be done along with the offering of a yearling lamb before any grain of the harvest could be eaten. In somewhat the same way, the raising of Christ by God anticipates the resurrection of all who belong to him (cf. 2 Cor 1:22; Rom 8:23; Col 1:15-23.)

Paul uses Adam as his second type of Christ, just as he will do later, more explicitly, in Rom 5:12-14. Men are of two kinds for Paul, those who are "in Adam," who will surely die as a consequence of sin, and those who are "in Christ," who will share in his victory over death (vv. 21f.) The apostle spells out his death-life antithesis with respect to sin and to justice in terms of slavery and freedom in Rom 6:20-23.

The resurrection will not occur in random fashion but in orderly stages. At Christ's coming (*parousia*, v. 23) each will rise in proper order (*en tǭ idiǭ tagmati*), those who belong to Christ following him who is first fruits. Paul refers to the consummation of all as "the end" (*to telos*, v. 24, translating the Hebrew *ha qetz*). He assumes that a variety of demonic powers must first be crushed before Christ's dominion can be complete. (Cf. 1 Cor 2:6, 8; Rom 8:20f. for Paul's idea of this world's slavery to corruption and the "rulers of the present age," a working together of evil and death, perhaps personified as Satan.) Paul may be distinguishing here, as some rabbis did in his time, between the age to come and the age of the messiah. The hostile powers have been vanquished, in part, with Christ's resurrection but their complete destruction will not be achieved until his second coming.

Meanwhile, the church's faith in the mystery of the Assumption is that Mary has won the victory over death, being the first in rank of those who are "in Christ."

Luke 1:39-56. In Lk's theology, Jesus is "Lord" from before his birth (1:43). The infancy and boyhood narratives of the first two chapters indicate what Jesus will become through what he already is. When he passes through death to glory and is made Lord and Messiah he will be no other than he was proclaimed to be at the beginning.

The story of the meeting of Mary and Elizabeth is part of Lk's John-Jesus diptych, the Baptist being identified as a prophet and witness to Jesus from before his birth. Lk may have in mind the oracle of Gn 25:23 in which the elder twin in Rebekah's womb, Esau, is fated to serve Jacob, the younger.

The "hill country" (*oreinē*) of Judah is indeterminate (v. 39). Ain Karem is a centuries-later attribution of no special merit except for its natural beauty. The baby's leaping in Elizabeth's womb may derive from the call of Jeremiah: "Before I called you in the womb I knew you, / before you were born I dedicated you, / a prophet to the nations I appointed you" (Jer 1:5). The spirit of prophecy, the holy spirit, is active throughout the Lucan account. Elizabeth acts the prophetess in praising the faith of Mary, her younger kinswoman (v. 45).

Mary's canticle as a whole is patterned on Hannah's song in 1 Sm 2:1-10 at the birth of her prophet-priest son Samuel. It is a tissue of OT allusions. Thus v. 48*b* recalls Leah's exclamation at the birth of Asher (Gn 30:13), v. 50 evokes Ps 103:17 on the kindness of the LORD from eternity (cf. Pss Sol 10:4), v. 51 recalls Ps 89:11*b*, v. 54 Is 41:8, and v. 55 Mi 7:20: "You will show faithfulness to Jacob, and grace to Abraham, / As you have sworn to our fathers from days of old." Verse 55 with its recall of the covenant made with Abraham (Gn 12:2f.; 15:1; 22:17f.; 24:7) links messianic hope with earliest promise.

A few NT MSS—some in Old Latin, and Greek ones known to Origen and Irenaeus—attribute the hymn to Elizabeth at v. 46 (in which case her "lowliness" would be the reproach of her childless condition). The manuscript tradition is not strong enough to be credited, however. Besides, such attribution would upset Lk's chiastic (i.e., X-like) balance which requires attention to the two births in the form John (1:5-25), Jesus (26-38); Jesus (39-56), John (57-80). The *Magnificat* remains a monument to God's unbounded mercy, which delights in the paradox of deposing the mighty and exalting the lowly. As messianic fruition comes closer, the mother of the messiah is fittingly declared blessed for ages to come.

Verse 56 tells us nothing about whether Mary was present for the birth of John. Luke's narrative technique requires that she be off the scene, though not necessarily literally, before he proceeds to his next frame.

ALL SAINTS

(November 1)

Revelation 7:2-4, 9-14. Six seals on a scroll which had been handed to the Lamb by the One who sat on the throne (cf. Rev 5:7) were opened in ch. 6. At the beginning of ch. 8 (v. 1), the Lamb opens the seventh seal. Hence the present chapter, 7, represents an interruption like the interruption between the sixth and seventh trumpet-blasts of 9:13 and 11:15. The four angels restraining the earth's winds (v. 1) at its four corners (*gōnias*) are from Ez 7:2 and 37:9. The corners, not the compass-points, are normally sources of destruction as in 7:2 rather than of life (to dry bones) as in 37:9. The underlying concept is the apocalyptic Jewish one of spirits charged with control of the elements. In v. 1 they achieve a calm on the earth.

This calm sets the stage for imprinting the seal (*sphragis*) of the living God on the foreheads of his servants (vv. 2-4), once the land and sea and trees have been forcibly stilled. God's enemies, represented by locusts (9:4), will be commanded to spare those thus sealed, just as the Israelites who bore the bloodmark on their houses were rendered immune from being struck down in Egypt (cf. Ex 12:13.) Ezekiel 9:4 with its symbolism of the Hebrew letter Taw on the brows of mourners—rendered in NAB by the more familiar English "X"—is probably the source of this saving sign. The "seal" of this chapter will be specified as the name of the Lamb and of his Father in 14:1 (if the reference there is to the same group) and 22:4. The word *sphragis* emerges in the mid-second century as a term for baptism, a sealing of the faith begun in repentance, according to the researches of F. J. Dölger (*Sphragis*, 1911).

The completion of God's people is represented by the squaring of twelve, the number of the tribes, and multiplication by a thousand (v. 4). In their own minds believers in Christ were the authentic Israel. The omission of the tribe of Dan is a puzzle, as is the listing of Manasseh where we should have expected his father Joseph (cf. Gn 48:1, 13, 14; 49:16f., 22f.) Yet Hebrew literature, including the Bible, lists the twelve tribes in a variety of namings and sequences. Judah no doubt comes first (v. 5) because Jesus descends from him. It is not certain that the celibates (*parthenoi*) of 14:4, probably a figure for martyrs, are identical with the believers of ch. 7, although the number is the same.

The 144,000 are the "huge crowd" assembled from every "nation and race, people and tongue" (v. 9). The vision of vv. 9-17 is undoubtedly meant to strengthen fearful Christians against their own "great trial" (v. 14), an anticipation of the final apocalyptic engagement. The martyrs have survived in the sense that they have kept their faith and their honor. The white robes and palm branches are signs of a victory already achieved. Joining angels and others around the throne, the victors sing the praises of God (v. 12) in a phrase reminiscent of Ps 3:9 which says, "Salvation is the LORD's!"

The entire vision could very well be Jewish, with "the Lamb" substituted for "God" in vv. 9, 10, and 14, martyrdom being signified by the phrase, "made white [i.e., resplendent, glorious] in blood."

1 John 3:1-3. Verse 1 is an utterance of joyous amazement that God should have made those who receive the Son to be his children (cf. Jn 1:12.) The Johannine "world" can no more recognize this sonship in us than it did in him (v. 1). Spiritual likeness to God, which is the present reality, is perhaps being identified as the cause of an even greater likeness when full light and the vision of the son reveal him as he is. The son is "pure" (*hagnos*, v. 3), he is sinless (cf. vv. 5, 7, 8.) That is why our hope is based on him (v. 3).

While it is certain that such claims of sinlessness are being made for Christ, it is doubtful that 6a means to reprobate a heretical position adhered to by some who are "in him." It is even less likely that the statement, "The man who remains in him does not sin," is itself heretical. What cannot be denied, however, is that the Johannine literature is sectarian in the sense that it reflects the convictions of a particular group distinguished from others which do not have its peculiar faith in Jesus as the Christ.

Matthew 5:1-12. See pp. 33f.

NEW TESTAMENT